Public Law
Cases, Materials, and Commentary
Second Edition

GENERAL EDITORS

Neil Craik
Faculty of Law
University of New Brunswick

Craig Forcese
Faculty of Law
University of Ottawa

CONTRIBUTING EDITORS

Philip Bryden
Faculty of Law
University of New Brunswick

Peter Carver
Faculty of Law
University of Alberta

Richard Haigh
Faculty of Law
Osgoode Hall Law School

Ed Ratushny
Faculty of Law
University of Ottawa

Ruth Sullivan
Faculty of Law
University of Ottawa

2011
Emond Montgomery Publications
Toronto, Canada

Emond Montgomery Publications Limited
60 Shaftesbury Avenue
Toronto, ON M4T 1A3
http://www.emp.ca/lawschool

Printed in Canada.
Reprinted April 2013

We acknowledge the financial support of the Government of Canada through the Canada Book Fund for our publishing activities.

Acquisitions editor: Bernard Sandler

Marketing manager: Christine Davidson

Supervising editor: Jim Lyons

Production and copy editor: Cindy Fujimoto

Permissions editor and proofreader: Debbie Gervais

Library and Archives Canada Cataloguing in Publication

Public law : cases, materials and commentary / general editors, Neil Craik, Craig Forcese; contributing editors, Philip Bryden ... [et al.]. — 2nd ed.

ISBN 978-1-55239-465-6

1. Public law — Canada — Textbooks.   2. Public law — Canada — Cases.
I. Craik, Neil, 1965-   II. Forcese, Craig   III. Bryden, Philip, 1953-

KE4120.P83 2011   342.71   C2011-903280-5
KF4482.P83 2011

Acknowledgments

This book, like others of its nature, contains extracts from published materials. We have attempted to request permission from and to acknowledge in the text all sources of such material. We wish to make specific reference here to the authors, publishers, journals, and institutions that have been generous in giving their permission to reproduce works in this text. If we have inadvertently overlooked any acknowledgment, we offer our sincere apologies and undertake to rectify the omission in any further editions.

Canadian Judicial Council, *About the CJC* (Ottawa: Office of the Commissioner for Federal Judicial Affairs, 2006), www.fja.gc.ca. Reproduced with the permission of the Canadian Judicial Council.

Canadian Judicial Council, *Report of the Canadian Judicial Council to the Minister of Justice Under Section 63(1) of the Judges Act Concerning the Conduct of Mr. Justice Jean Bienvenue of the Superior Court of Quebec in R v. T. Théberge* (Ottawa: Office of the Commissioner for Federal Judicial Affairs, 1996), www.fja.gc.ca. Reproduced with the permission of the Canadian Judicial Council.

Department of Justice Canada, 2005. *Canada's Court System: Figure: Outline of Canada's Court System and accompanying text pages 2 to 9*. Reproduced with the permission of the Minister of Public Works and Government Services 2011.

Department of Justice Canada, April 2005. *Proposal To Reform the Supreme Court of Canada Appointments Process* (Ottawa: Department of Justice, 2005), www.justice.gc.ca/eng/dept-min/pub/scc-csc/index.html. Reproduced with the permission of the Minister of Public Works and Government Services Canada 2011.

Elections Canada, *Canada's Electoral System* (Ottawa: Chief Electoral Officer of Canada, 2001). Reproduced with the permission of Elections Canada.

House of Commons, "Conflict of Interest Code for Members of the House of Commons," in *Standing Orders*, appendix 2 (Ottawa: House of Commons, 2004). Reprinted by permission of the House of Commons.

House of Commons, *Précis of Procedure* (Ottawa: House of Commons, 2003). Reprinted by permission of the House of Commons.

Law Commission of Canada, *Crossing Borders: Law in a Globalized World* (Ottawa: Government of Canada, 2006), http://www.lcc.gc.ca/research_project/gr/gbb/dp/crossing_borders_ dp-en.asp. Reproduced with the permission of the Minister of Public Works and Government Services 2011.

Law Reform Commission of Canada, "Independent Administrative Agencies," Working Paper 25 (Ottawa: Law Reform Commission of Canada, 1980). Department of Justice Canada. Reproduced with the permission of the Minister of Public Works and Government Services Canada 2011.

Office of the Commissioner for Federal Judicial Affairs, *Process for an Application for Appointments* (Ottawa: Office of the Commissioner for Federal Judicial Affairs, 2009), http://www.fja.gc.ca/appointments-nominations/process-regime-eng.html. Reproduced with the permission of the Office of the Commissioner for Federal Judicial Affairs.

Remarks of the Right Honourable Beverley McLachlin, PC, Respecting Democratic Roles (Ottawa: Supreme Court of Canada, 2011), http://www.scc-csc.gc.ca/court-cour/ju/spe-dis/bm04-11-12-eng.asp. Reproduced with the permission of the Supreme Court of Canada, 2011.

Special Committee on the Reform of the House of Commons, *Report* (Ottawa: Canadian government Publishing Centre, Supply and Services Canada, June 1985). Reprinted by permission of the House of Commons.

Ruth Sullivan, *Sullivan on the Construction of Statutes*, 5th edition (Markham, ON: Butterworths, 2008), pp. 1-3 and 4-7. Reproduced with the permission of the publisher LexisNexis Canada Inc.

Margaret Young, *Conflict-of-Interest Rules for Federal Legislators*, Law and Government Division, Parliamentary Research Branch (Ottawa: Library of Parliament, December 2003). Reproduced with the permission of the Library of Parliament, 2011.

Preface to the Second Edition

Almost every law school in Canada, as part of its first-year curriculum, offers a course that focuses on legal processes and legal institutions. Common to these courses is the view that students beginning a career in law need to understand how the law is made, as well as the nature of and relationships between those institutions that create and apply legal rules and principles. Certainly, students and law professors might address many of these issues in the conventional substantive courses of the first-year curriculum; however, introductory public law courses proceed from the premise that these issues are sufficiently foundational to merit separate and in-depth examination. That said, it is also clear that law schools incorporate the study of legal processes and institutions in a wide variety of ways. Some law schools focus on the theoretical aspects of defining law and the law's relationship to social ordering; others may integrate this material more closely with constitutional or procedural questions.

With these observations in mind, our principal objective in assembling these materials was to provide a volume covering essential issues common to the majority of courses addressing legal process and institutional issues. We hope that this book will form the core materials of such courses. We decided that it was better to include less material (and allow individual professors to supplement the volume to best fit their courses) than to risk including material that might be superfluous to some course designs. For the same reason, we have opted not to include sets of notes and questions following sections of the text. In other words, we have sought to prepare a succinct volume that can be easily integrated into the variable introductory public law courses offered across the country.

The second edition incorporates major changes in Canadian public law since the publication of the first edition in 2006, including the Supreme Court of Canada's reconsideration of the approach to judicial review of administrative action in *Dunsmuir v. New Brunswick*, 2008 SCC 9. We were also able to incorporate some recent policy developments, such as a new Supreme Court of Canada judicial appointment process and the controversial use of prorogation powers by the prime minister. In revising the chapters for the second edition, we have been very fortunate to receive comments from colleagues who used the first edition, which were very helpful in our preparations, and for which we are extremely grateful. We would also like to thank the editorial team at Emond Montgomery for coordinating our efforts and for their editorial and production support.

Neil Craik
Craig Forcese
June 2011

Table of Contents

PART III   INTERPLAY BETWEEN THE COURTS AND THE POLITICAL BRANCHES OF GOVERNMENT

Detailed Table of Contents

PART III INTERPLAY BETWEEN THE COURTS AND THE POLITICAL BRANCHES OF GOVERNMENT

Table of Cases

A page number in bold-face type indicates that the text of the case or a portion thereof is reproduced. A page number in light-face type indicates that the case is quoted briefly, referred to, or mentioned.

CHAPTER ONE

Introduction

This book is about the building blocks of Canadian public law. Public law is intended, in the context of this volume, to refer to those legal institutions and legal arrangements that structure the relationships between the individual and the state and between the constituent parts of the state itself. These relationships are foundational to our understanding of the Canadian legal system as a whole because it is through these institutions that legal relations, whether of a public or private nature, are generated and sustained.

Within the Canadian legal and political tradition it is common to draw a distinction between public law and private law, the former being concerned with the relations between individuals and the state and the latter being concerned with mediating relations between individuals. This distinction is largely a functional one, in the sense that classifying an area of law as being private or public serves as a useful indicator of the activities, participants, and principal concerns that are subject to the rules of that area. So, for example, in common law countries we tend to classify constitutional, administrative, criminal, and other areas of regulatory law (such as environmental law and tax law) as being areas of public law, because these areas of law contain rules that define the scope of governmental authority and the manner of its exercise. Similarly, areas such as tort law, contract law, and property law are considered areas of private law because they are principally concerned with the correlative rights and duties between individuals.

The distinction between public law and private law should not, however, be viewed as creating two autonomous disciplines. There are many examples of private law doctrines bringing broader public concerns to bear on disputes between individuals, as illustrated by the rule discussed in *Re Drummond Wren*, excerpted in chapter 2, declaring a contractual provision void where the provision is contrary to public policy. Likewise, there are occasions where governmental authorities are subject to private law rules where, for example, a governmental authority breaches a contract or acts negligently. On a more fundamental level, it must also be understood that governmental institutions, such as legislatures and courts, will have a profound impact on areas of private law. Statutes may define the substantive rights and duties that individuals owe one another; courts will be responsible for determining those rights; and the executive branch may be called upon to enforce private rights by coercive means. The simple point being that the subject of this book—governmental authority—is fundamental to both private law and public law.

Because we are principally concerned with the origins and exercise of governmental authority, "power" is a recurrent theme throughout this book. Of course, our interest lies chiefly in relation to a certain kind of power; that which is legitimized through the creation of legal institutions and whose legitimacy is sustained by adherence to the rules governing its exercise. In this regard, the materials that follow introduce you to the sources of government-al authority in Canada; the distribution of powers between the federal government and the provincial governments; the separation of powers among the legislative, the executive, and the judicial branches of the government; and the constraints on the power of the state over its citizens. This last area points to a second theme that animates these materials—that of accountability. In this regard, many of the materials are intended to demonstrate how governmental authority is qualified by legal rules, and how the different legal institutions that are created are made accountable to one another and to the citizenry itself.

Our purpose here is to trace the interplay between these manifestations of power and accountability and to portray the Canadian legal system in a fashion that will provide a context for what you learn in other private and public law courses. Whereas many of your other courses are about the "trees" that comprise the legal "forest," this book seeks to provide a bird's-eye view of that "forest," allowing you to understand its size and scope, its shape and contours.

We have divided the book into three parts, each with several chapters. Part I sets the stage for our more detailed discussion of public law themes. It does this in two ways. First, in chapter 2, we step back and examine questions of legal theory and legal history that inform the Canadian legal system. Here we introduce you to a number of different approaches to understanding the nature of legal authority that have influenced legal outcomes in Canada. This chapter also examines the origins and nature of the common and civil law traditions in Canada. In addition, this chapter discusses the relationship between law and aboriginal peoples as a distinct influence on the development of Canadian law. In a similar vein, we briefly outline the concept of public international law, which is itself becoming an important source of legal rights and obligations in Canada. Finally, we introduce you to a key source of law in these materials—statutory law.

Chapter 3 presents many constitutional themes that animate Canadian public law. We discuss constitutionalism and the rule of law and then provide an overview of the exercise of public power in Canada, focusing on the separation of powers among the legislative, executive, and judicial branches of government. In this chapter, we also explore how Canada's Constitution is amended.

In part II of this book, we explore in greater detail the key "actors" in public law. In chapter 4, we focus on the federal Parliament, discussing its various components and its operations, including such things as parliamentary privilege and the parliamentary law-making function.

Chapter 5 examines the executive branch and the exercise of executive authority. It discusses the composition of the executive branch and the sources of executive power in our system of parliamentary democracy. It pays particular attention to the executive law-making function through regulations.

Chapter 6 turns to the judiciary, providing an overview of the structure of the Canadian court system and exploring in detail the means by which judges are appointed to Canadian courts. It then focuses on the vital concept of "judicial independence," exploring the concepts of security of tenure, financial independence, and administrative independence.

In part III we turn to a closer examination of the interrelation between the courts and the political branches of government—the executive and the legislature. In chapter 7, we consider the role of the courts in applying the statutory law determined by the legislative branch. Here we discuss the doctrines of statutory interpretation, which are designed to inform judicial interpretation of legislative language.

In chapter 8, we conclude this book with an examination of the judicial role in policing the political branches on both constitutional grounds (in the case of both the legislature and executive) and administrative law grounds (in the case of the executive). Here we pose important questions about the appropriate role of courts in a democratic system.

Given the breadth of these materials, we have tried to tie the chapters together by using, where appropriate, the federal human rights regime as a common example. As a result, throughout the book, we make reference to cases and legislative material that relate to this scheme. Our intention is not so much to provide students with a comprehensive understanding of this complex area of law, but rather to add a further measure of coherence to this book by showing how the different legal institutions, processes, and rules operate in a common context.

Taken together, these materials provide an essential foundation to a fuller understanding of both Canadian law and Canadian government.

PART I

Setting the Stage

CHAPTER TWO

Nature, Divisions, and Sources of Law

In order to provide some theoretical context for the chapters that follow, this chapter considers the nature, divisions, and sources of Canadian law, writ large. Section I provides an overview of several schools of legal theory—positivism, natural law, feminism, critical legal studies, and law and economics—with the intent of showing how competing approaches to understanding the nature of law and its relationship to social and political factors can affect judicial decision making. Section II traces the origins of Canadian law, focusing on historical sources of law—namely, aboriginal, common law, and civil law traditions; then examines the increasingly influential role of international law in defining domestic legal rights and obligations; and finally discusses statutory law, juxtaposing it with the common law.

I. LEGAL THEORY IN RELATION TO PUBLIC LAW

A. Introduction

Throughout history, those who have thought and written about law have developed a number of—sometimes very diverse—theories related to law. At their heart, legal theories have tended to focus on several related questions. First, what is the relationship between law and morality? Is law necessarily derived from universal moral truths? Are morally repugnant laws nevertheless binding? Second, what is the relationship between law and power? Is law simply rules backed by force? To what degree does law primarily reflect the preferences of powerful societal actors or dominant cultural forces? The answers to these questions not only allow us to differentiate law from non-law, but also shed light on the nature of the multiple sources of law within a society, and the relationship between laws among groups of societies. In considering these questions, we recognize that law is not a discrete set of principles without a context. Legal systems are built around ideas that are historically and culturally specific. Our Anglo-Canadian system of law, based largely on the English common law system, reflects our Canadian values. So too does the Quebec civil law.

In order to situate Canadian public law in relation to some broader social debates, this section looks at public law through the lens of several prominent approaches to legal scholarship—positivism and natural law, feminism, critical legal studies, and law and economics. Of course, this section is not intended to be a comprehensive survey of jurisprudence, but rather seeks to illustrate how differing conceptualizations of law affect legal outcomes.

B. Positivism and Natural Law

A principal inquiry in legal theory is the extent to which law should be identified with moral-ity. Positivism and natural law theories, at least in their classical form, treat this fundamental notion very differently. Legal positivism reflects the belief that law is nothing more than the rules and principles that actually govern or regulate a society. Positivism insists on the sepa-ration of law and morality, and, as a result, focuses on describing laws without reference to justness or legitimacy. Natural law theory, on the other hand, is aspirational in the sense that laws, properly called, are not simply all those official rules and principles that govern us, but only those that adhere to certain moral truths, most often of a universal and immutable nature.

The basic contours of legal positivism were set out by John Austin in the 18th century. He proposed three basic theories about law:

1. that law is a command issued by the "uncommanded commander"—the sovereign;
2. that such commands are backed by threats; and
3. a sovereign is one who is habitually obeyed.

While his theory has undergone refinements over the years, the basic idea remains, that law is created by humans. Natural law, developed through such writers as Aristotle and St. Thomas Aquinas, is based on the theory that law arises from "nature" or by beliefs accepted by people; it found some of its greatest proponents within the Catholic church. In the natural law tradition, for a law to be a true law, it must comport with the values accepted by society.

There is little doubt that, at one level, law and morality are linked. Many of our most basic criminal laws, for example, are based on traditional Judeo-Christian conceptions of morality. But law and morality can also part ways: many contract laws, for example, exist to facilitate commercial transactions and do not immediately seem connected to any conception of morality. Moreover, law must address specific and detailed problems and objects, whereas morality is usually framed in general and open-ended concepts. For example, laws related to licensing automobile drivers must spell out specific information on different categories of licence and the age restrictions that might apply. Law is also generally thought to be deter-minate and certain, while morality can be contingent and relative. Moral disagreements and controversies are issues of great moment that have been debated and argued by philoso-phers for centuries. Legal disputes and controversies should be capable of resolution by lawyers and judges. In this regard, natural law does not deny the necessity of positive law, but where positive law contravenes natural law, the contravening positive law rules are held by natural law theorists not to be "true" law in the sense that a citizen (or a judge) owes no allegiance to them. Positivists, on the other hand, are not unconcerned with questions of justice, but rather maintain that the issue of what law is, is necessarily separate and distinct from the question of what law ought to be.

The two cases that follow, *Re Drummond Wren* and *Re Noble and Wolf*, arguably represent a natural law and positivist view, respectively, of legal theory. Note how the judge in *Drum-mond Wren* attempts to appeal to our moral conscience, while the judge in *Noble and Wolf* relies on the supposed certainty of positive law. As an exercise in legal reasoning, however, try to analyze *each* decision on the basis of a natural *and* a positive understanding of law.

Re Drummond Wren
[1945] OR 778 (HC)

[The Worker's Educational Association (WEA) had purchased a lot in East York (now part of Toronto), intending to build a house on it and then raffle it off for fund-raising purposes. The land was restricted by a covenant pronouncing that it was "not to be sold to Jews or persons of objectionable nationality." The WEA applied to have the covenant declared invalid. One of the grounds argued was that the racially restrictive covenant was void as against public policy; another was that it contravened the provisions of the *Racial Discrimination Act*, SO 1944, c. 51 passed by the Ontario legislature in 1944. This statute was designed to combat the once prevalent "Whites Only" and "No Jews Allowed" signs that were displayed in store windows, at beaches, and at other public places. Section 1 prohibited the publication or display of representations indicating an intent to discriminate on the basis of race or creed (the contemporary version is s. 13 of the Ontario *Human Rights Code*, RSO 1990, c. H.19).]

MACKAY J: … The applicant's argument is founded on the legal principle, briefly stated in 7 Hals. (2nd ed.), pp. 153-4, that: "Any agreement which tends to be injurious to the public or against the public good is void as being contrary to public policy." Public policy, in the words of Halsbury, "varies from time to time."

In "The Growth of Law," Mr. Justice Cardozo says:

> Existing rules and principles can give us our present location, our bearings, our latitude and longitude. The inn that shelters for the night is not the journey's end. The law, like the traveller, must be ready for the morrow. It must have a principle of growth.

And Mr. Justice Oliver Wendell Holmes, in "The Common Law" says:

> The very considerations which judges most rarely mention and always with an apology are the secret root from which the law draws all the juices of life. I mean, of course, what is expedient for the community concerned.

The matter of not creating new heads of public policy has been discussed at some length by Mr. Justice McCardie in *Naylor, Benzon & Co. v. Krainische Industrie Gesellschaft*, [1918] 1 KB 331, later affirmed by the Court of Appeal, [1918] 2 KB 486.

There he points out [at 342-43] that "the Courts have not hesitated in the past to apply the doctrine (of public policy) whenever the facts demanded its application." "The truth of the matter," he says, seems to be that public policy is a variable thing. It must fluctuate with the circumstances of the time. This view is exemplified by the decisions which were discussed by the House of Lords in *Nordenfelt v. Maxim Nordenfelt Guns and Ammunition Co.*, [1894] AC 535. … The principles of public policy remain the same, though the application of them may be applied in novel ways. The ground does not vary. As it was put by Tindal CJ in *Horner v. Graves* (1831), 7 Bing. 735, 743 [131 ER 284]: "Whatever is injurious to the interests of the public is void, on the ground of public policy."

It is a well-recognized rule that Courts may look at various Dominion and Provincial Acts and public law as an aid in determining principles relative to public policy: See *Walkerville Brewing Co. v. Mayrand*, [1929] 2 DLR 945.

First and of profound significance is the recent San Francisco Charter, to which Canada was a signatory, and which the Dominion Parliament has now ratified. The preamble to this Charter reads in part as follows:

> We the peoples of the United Nations determined to save succeeding generations from the scourge of war, which twice in our lifetime has brought untold sorrow to mankind, and to re-affirm faith in fundamental human rights, in the dignity and worth of the human person, in the equal rights of men and women and of nations large and small … and for these ends to practice tolerance and live together in peace with one another as good neighbours. …

Under Articles 1 and 55 of this Charter, Canada is pledged to promote "universal respect for, and observance of, human rights and fundamental freedoms for all without distinction as to race, sex, language, or religion."

In the Atlantic Charter to which Canada has subscribed, the principles of freedom from fear and freedom of worship are recognized.

Section 1 of the *Racial Discrimination Act* provides:

> 1. No person shall, —
>   (a) publish or display or cause to be published or displayed; or
>   (b) permit to be published or displayed on lands or premises or in a newspaper, through a radio broadcasting station or by means of any other medium which he owns or controls, any notice, sign, symbol, emblem or other representation indicating discrimination or an intention to discriminate against any person or any class of persons for any purpose because of the race or creed of such person or class of persons.

· · ·

Proceeding from the general to the particular, the argument of the applicant is that the impugned covenant is void because it is injurious to the public good. This deduction is grounded on the fact that the covenant against sale to Jews or to persons of objectionable nationality prevents the particular piece of land from ever being acquired by the persons against whom the covenant is aimed, and that this prohibition is without regard to whether the land is put to residential, commercial, industrial or other use. How far this is obnoxious to public policy can only be ascertained by projecting the coverage of the covenant with respect both to the classes of persons whom it may adversely affect, and to the lots or sub-divisions of land to which it may be attached. So considered, the consequences of judicial approbation of such a covenant are portentous. If sale of a piece of land can be prohibited to Jews, it can equally be prohibited to Protestants, Catholics or other groups or denomina-tions. If the sale of one piece of land can be so prohibited, the sale of other pieces of land can likewise be prohibited. In my opinion, nothing could be more calculated to create or deepen divisions between existing religious and ethnic groups in this Province, or in this country, than the sanction of a method of land transfer which would permit the segregation and confinement of particular groups to particular business or residential areas, or conversely, would exclude particular groups from particular business or residential areas. The unlikeli-hood of such a policy as a legislative measure is evident from the contrary intention of the recently enacted *Racial Discrimination Act*, and the judicial branch of government must take full cognizance of such factors.

Ontario, and Canada too, may well be termed a Province, and a country, of minorities in regard to the religious and ethnic groups which live therein. It appears to me to be a moral duty, at least, to lend aid to all forces of cohesion, and similarly to repel all fissiparous tendencies which would imperil national unity. The common law Courts have, by their actions over the years, obviated the need for rigid constitutional guarantees in our polity by their wise use of the doctrine of public policy as an active agent in the promotion of the public weal. While Courts and eminent Judges have, in view of the powers of our Legislatures, warned against inventing new heads of public policy, I do not conceive that I would be breaking new ground were I to hold the restrictive covenant impugned in this proceeding to be void as against public policy. Rather would I be applying well-recognized principles of public policy to a set of facts requiring their invocation in the interest of the public good.

That the restrictive covenant in this case is directed in the first place against Jews lends poignancy to the matter when one considers that anti-Semitism has been a weapon in the hands of our recently-defeated enemies and the scourge of the world. But this feature of the case does not require innovation in legal principle to strike down the covenant; it merely makes it more appropriate to apply existing principles. If the common law of treason encompasses the stirring up of hatred between different classes of His Majesty's subjects, the common law of public policy is surely adequate to void the restrictive covenant which is here attacked.

My conclusion therefore is that the covenant is void because [it is] offensive to the public policy of this jurisdiction. This conclusion is reinforced, if reinforcement is necessary, by the wide official acceptance of international policies and declarations frowning on the type of discrimination which the covenant would seem to perpetuate.

It may not be inexpedient or improper to refer to a few declarations made by outstanding leaders under circumstances that arrest the attention and demand consideration of mankind. I first quote the late President Roosevelt:

> Citizens, regardless of religious allegiance, will share in the sorrow of our Jewish fellow-citizens over the savagery of the Nazis against their helpless victims. The Nazis will not succeed in exterminating their victims any more than they will succeed in enslaving mankind. The American people not only sympathize with all victims of Nazi crimes but will hold the perpetrators of these crimes to strict accountability in a day of reckoning which will surely come.
>
> I express the confident hope that the Atlantic Charter and the just World Order to be made possible by the triumph of the United Nations will bring the Jews and oppressed people in all lands the four freedoms which Christian and Jewish teachings have largely inspired.

And of the Right Honourable Winston Churchill:

> In the day of victory the Jew's sufferings and his part in the struggle will not be forgotten. Once again, at the appointed time, he will see vindicated those principles of righteousness which it was the glory of his fathers to proclaim to the world. Once again it will be shown that, though the mills of God grind slowly, yet they grind exceeding small.

And of General Charles de Gaulle:

> Be assured that since we have repudiated everything that has falsely been done in the name of France after June 23rd, the cruel decrees directed against French Jews can and will have no

validity in Free France. These measures are not less a blow against the honour of France than they are an injustice against her Jewish citizens.

When we shall have achieved victory, not only will the wrongs done in France itself be righted, but France will once again resume her traditional place as a protagonist of freedom and justice for all men, irrespective of race or religion, in a new Europe.

. . .

I do not deem it necessary for the purpose of this case to deal with [the argument that the covenant violates s. 1 of the *Racial Discrimination Act*], except to say that it appears to me to have considerable merit. My opinion as to the public policy applicable to this case in no way depends on the terms of the *Racial Discrimination Act*, save to the extent that such Act constitutes a legislative recognition of the policy which I have applied. ...

An order will therefore go declaring that the restrictive covenant attacked by the applicant is void and of no effect.

Re Noble and Wolf
[1948] OR 579 (HC)

[Individual cottage lots in the Beach O' Pines subdivision on the shores of Lake Huron contained a covenant that the lands shall not be sold or transferred to any person of the "Jewish, Hebrew, Semitic, Negro or coloured race or blood." Relying on the precedent established in *Re Drummond Wren* three years earlier, Bernard Wolf, an interested purchaser of a cottage lot, applied to have the covenant rendered invalid on grounds of public policy. This time, however, other property owners defended the covenant. The Beach O' Pines Protective Association argued that there was a congenial summer community among its members and cottage value would be lost if any change to its character occurred.]

SCHROEDER J: ... Counsel for the vendor cites and relies upon the very able judgment of Mackay J in *Re Drummond Wren*, [1945] 4 DLR 674, rendered on a motion for a declaration that a restrictive covenant that the land was "not to be sold to Jews or persons of objectionable nationality" was void and of no effect. In a carefully considered judgment, Mackay J reached the conclusion, as summarized in the headnote in the Ontario Reports, that the particular covenant was contrary to public policy in that it "tends to create or deepen divisions between religious and ethnic groups, and is in conflict with prevailing public opinion, as exemplified in the *Racial Discrimination Act, 1944*, and other statutes and public documents."

The case cited is a decision of a Court of co-ordinate jurisdiction and I am not necessarily bound by it. Under s. 31 of the *Judicature Act*, RSO 1937, c. 100, I may, if I deem the decision to be wrong and of sufficient importance to be considered in a higher Court, refer this case to the Court of Appeal, but I do not propose to adopt that course. I have given careful consideration and study to the learned judgment of my brother Mackay and regret that I find myself in disagreement with it. It is with the utmost respect that I proceed to state the reasons which have led me to an opposite conclusion.

It may be observed at the outset that Mackay J did not have the benefit of opposing argument on the motion before him. In the case at bar I would have been left in the same position but for the intervention of the persons on whom notice of motion was served pursuant
to the order of Mackay J hereinbefore mentioned, because both the vendor and the purchaser were ad idem in their attack upon the validity of the covenant in question. Let it also
be stated that in the case before my brother Mackay he was not concerned with a summer
colony as in the case under consideration, but with a residential subdivision on O'Connor
Drive in the City of Toronto, where the residents sought shelter rather than recreation. Also,
the restriction in that case was unlimited in point of duration.

[After describing the sources relied upon by Mackay J, Schroeder J continued:]

Mackay J would seem to have evolved what I regard as an entirely novel head of public
policy.

In approaching this aspect of the problem the Court must bear in mind the frequent
injunctions of higher tribunals as to the danger of allowing judicial tribunals "to roam un-
checked in the field occupied by that unruly horse, public policy." No more enlightening
pronouncement can be found, in my opinion, than in the judgment of Lord Atkin in *Fender
v. St. John-Mildmay*, [1938] AC 1 at pp. 10-12, from which I quote:

> I propose in the first instance to say something upon the doctrine of public policy generally. My
> Lords, from time to time judges of the highest reputation have uttered warning notes as to the
> danger of permitting judicial tribunals to roam unchecked in this field. The "unruly horse" of
> Hobart CJ is commonplace. I will content myself with two passages both of which have the
> authority of the approval of Lord Halsbury. In *Jason v. Driefontein Consolidated Mines*, [1902]
> AC 484, 491, he cites this passage from Marshall on Marine Insurance:
>
> > To avow or insinuate that it might, in any case, be proper for a judge to prevent a party
> > from availing himself of an indisputable principle of law, in a Court of justice, upon the
> > ground of some notion of fancied policy or expedience, is a new doctrine in Westmin-
> > ster Hall, and has a direct tendency to render all law vague and uncertain.

"Public policy," said Parke B in *Egerton v. Brownlow*, 4 HLC 1, 123, [10 ER 359], "is a
vague and unsatisfactory term, and calculated to lead to uncertainty and error, when applied to the decision of legal rights; it is capable of being understood in different senses; it
may, and does, in its ordinary sense, mean 'political expedience,' or that which is best for the
common good of the community; and in that sense there may be every variety of opinion,
according to education, habits, talents, and dispositions of each person, who is to decide
whether an act is against public policy or not. To allow this to be a ground of judicial decision, would lead to the greatest uncertainty and confusion. It is the province of the states-
man, and not the lawyer, to discuss, and of the Legislature to determine, what is best for the
public good, and to provide for it by proper enactments. It is the province of the judge to
expound the law only; the written from the statutes; the unwritten or common law from the
decisions of our predecessors and of our existing Courts, from text writers of acknowledged
authority, and upon the principles to be clearly deduced from them by sound reason and
just inference; not to speculate upon what is the best, in his opinion, for the advantage of the

community. Some of these decisions may have no doubt been founded upon the prevailing and just opinions of the public good; for instance, the illegality of covenants in restraint of marriage or trade. They have become a part of the recognized law, and we are therefore bound by them, but we are not thereby authorized to establish as law everything which we may think for the public good, and prohibit everything which we think otherwise." ...

· · ·

To hold on the basis of Canadian treaty obligations and on the basis of the provincial legislation and regulations and other public documents, referred to in the judgment of Mackay J, that there is a public policy in Ontario which prohibits the use of and renders void any covenant such as the one under review, seems to me to involve an arbitrary extension of the rules which say that a given contract is void as being opposed to public policy. It is trite law that common law rights are not to be deemed to be abrogated by statute unless the legislative intent to do so is expressed in very clear language. It follows logically, it seems to me, that for a Court to invent new heads of public policy and found thereon nullification of established rights or obligations—in a sense embarking upon a course of judicial legislation— is a mode of procedure not to be encouraged or approved.

While it may fairly be assumed that the public policy of this country is opposed to the taking of affirmative action by any competent legislative authority which would be inconsistent with the sentiments or ideals expressed in these treaties or enactments, it would, in my view, constitute a radical departure from established principle to deduce therefrom any policy of the law which may be claimed to transcend the paramount public policy that one is not lightly to interfere with the freedom of contract. It is no doubt desirable that freedom of contract should be reconciled with other public interests which are regarded as of not less importance—something which cannot always be accomplished without difficulty; nevertheless, if there is any doubt as to the prevailing public policy or its effect, I should deem it to be the duty of the Court to extend the benefit of the doubt to the contract which the supposed public policy is claimed to supersede. The notion of any danger to public interests involved in the use of restrictive covenants such as the one in question seems to me fanciful and unreal. Whatever view I may entertain, based upon my conception of justice, morality or convenience, I must always have present to my mind the proper conception of the judicial function, namely, to expound and interpret the law and not to create the law based on my individual notion or opinion of what the law ought to be. I cannot conceive of any established principle of law or any principles recognized in the Courts or by the State as part of our public law which enables me to conclude that the covenant under review should be struck down as offending against the policy of the law. Lord Roche, who was one of the dissentient Lords in the case of *Fender v. St. John-Mildmay*, but who did not differ from the majority of the House in the views expressed by them as to the function of the Courts in relation to the matter of public policy, stated at pp. 54-5 ([1938] AC):

> Now to evolve new heads of public policy or to subtract from existing and recognized heads of public policy if permissible to the Courts at all, which is debatable, would in my judgment certainly only be permissible upon some occasion as to which the legislature was for some reason unable to speak and where there was substantial agreement within the judiciary and where circumstances had fundamentally changed.

In my view it is within the province of the competent legislative bodies to discuss and determine what is best for the public good and to provide for it by the proper enactments. Such matters can with greater propriety and safety be left to the duly elected representatives of the people assembled in Parliament or in the Legislature.

For the reasons set forth, I hold that the said covenant is valid and enforceable and that the vendor has not satisfactorily answered the purchaser's objection thereto.

The motion will, therefore, be dismissed. The vendor shall pay the costs of the third parties who intervened after being served with notice of these proceedings but no costs are awarded to the purchaser who supported the vendor's motion.

An appeal by Wolf to the Ontario Court of Appeal was dismissed—*Re Noble and Wolf*, [1949] OR 503 (CA). On further appeal to the Supreme Court of Canada, the appeal was allowed and the racially restrictive covenant struck down, but on technical grounds resulting from the application of well-established common law rules—*Noble and Wolf v. Alley*, [1951] SCR 64. There was no discussion on the public policy implications of restrictive covenants.

From the vantage point of 2006, discriminatory covenants are obviously unforgivable, and the *Re Noble and Wolf* decision unsatisfactory. But consider this point: after the Ontario Court of Appeal decision in *Re Noble and Wolf*, and before its hearing at the Supreme Court of Canada, the Ontario legislature passed the following provision (now s. 22 of the *Conveyancing and Law of Property Act*, RSO 1990, c. C.34):

> Every covenant made after the 24th day of March, 1950, that but for this section would be annexed to and run with land and that restricts the sale, ownership, occupation or use of land because of the race, creed, colour, nationality, ancestry or place of origin of any person is void and of no effect.

Similar provisions have been enacted in other provinces in Canada. The legislatures, in other words, acted to correct a deficiency that at least some judges (applying the common law) were unprepared to correct. In our democratic system, how assertive should judges be in applying "public policy" or other grounds to graft new moral positions onto the law? Is that their proper role? Should it matter whether the law in question being applied by the court is a piece of legislation or a common law principle?

As is discussed later in these materials, debates on the proper role of judges in our democratic system are commonplace in Canada, especially following the enactment of the *Canadian Charter of Rights and Freedoms*. It is commonly agreed that, absent a constitutional justification, courts apply (rather than strike down or question) legislation. In so doing, they respond to the "supremacy" of Parliament (or the provincial legislatures) in law making. But what if the law in question is not a statute, but is instead a common law doctrine—judge-made law. Why should contemporary judges with contemporary moral beliefs defer to the (sometimes quite dated) morality of prior judges? Keep this question in mind when reviewing the next section, dealing with the evolution of law's treatment of women.

Both positivism and natural law are descriptive theories in that they are principally concerned with identifying what law is, as opposed to what law ought to be. (Natural law approaches, while they identify law with reference to normative criteria, are nevertheless engaged in describing law as it exists.) The remaining approaches in this section are normative theories in that they seek to describe how existing laws fail to achieve an external objective, be it gender or class equality or the efficient distribution of scarce societal resources. Feminism, critical legal studies, and law and economics approaches are often critical in their posture and oriented toward reform.

C. Feminist Perspectives on Law

1. Introduction

Feminist perspectives on law look at the extent to which women are disadvantaged by legal rules and institutions that arise in societies that are patriarchal and as such subordinate the interests of women and fail to account for the experiences of women in the creation of legal rules. The earliest feminist movements in law, beginning in the late 19th century, centred on gaining the voting franchise for women and the reform of marriage laws. These were largely successful. Once that occurred, the next stage of feminism involved attacks on discriminatory employment practices and criminal laws. It was not until the 1960s, however, that feminism matured into a defined movement and developed more widespread currency.

Much of feminist legal philosophy reflects a critique (and oftentimes a rejection) of liberalism as a political ideology. Laws that existed from the 17th century, even those based on liberal ideals such as individualism and liberty, did not typically respond to the needs of women and more often than not aided in their oppression. So-called liberal laws often contributed to the gross inequality between genders. Despite the ideals of liberalism, many of these laws had existed for centuries (and in some cases still do).

2. Early Formalist Feminism

In its early manifestations, feminism was largely concerned with seeking women's formal equality with men. This required an examination of laws to determine whether there was any express bias against women. The goal was to replace laws that favoured men with more neutral laws. The suffrage movement in the early part of the 20th century (focusing on the vote) followed such an approach.

Throughout Canada, prior to 1916, laws related to elections did not allow women to vote. In that year, women in Manitoba, Saskatchewan, and Alberta became enfranchised through political struggle. Laws in those provinces were revised to allow women to vote. Other provinces soon followed suit. In 1918, Parliament passed the *Women's Suffrage Act*, SC 1918, c. 20, which gave every female British subject over age 21 the right to vote, as long as she possessed the same qualifications required for men under the provincial franchise.

Despite these political advancements, women remained barred from holding a Senate seat as successive federal governments refused to extend women's rights that far. All relied on s. 24 of the *British North America Act* of 1867 (now the *Constitution Act, 1867*, 30 & 31 Vict., c. 3), which stated that only "qualified Persons" were eligible to be appointed to the Senate.

Governments argued that women would not have been considered to be "qualified persons" at the time the 1867 Act was passed. By 1926, frustrated at continued government inaction, five women—Judge Emily Murphy, Nellie McClung, Louise McKinney, Irene Parlby, and Henrietta Muir Edwards—petitioned to have the government direct the Supreme Court to rule on the constitutional question whether, based on s. 24, women could be considered candidates for the Senate. The Supreme Court of Canada found that "qualified persons" did not include women, basing its judgment on a formulaic and traditional interpretation. An appeal was launched to the Judicial Committee of the Privy Council. The decision, known as the *"Persons"* case, is excerpted below. The approach the Privy Council took to interpreting the Canadian Constitution, which understood constitutions as evolving documents that could respond to changes in society over time, remains an important guide to constitutional interpretation today.

Edwards v. AG Canada
[1930] AC 124, 1 DLR 98 (PC) (footnotes omitted)

LORD SANKEY LC: By s. 24 of the *BNA Act, 1867*, it is provided that, "The Governor General shall from Time to Time, in the Queen's Name, by Instrument under the Great Seal of Canada, summon qualified Persons to the Senate; and, subject to the Provisions of this Act, every Person so summoned shall become and be a Member of the Senate and a Senator."

The question at issue in this appeal is whether the words "qualified persons" in that section include a woman, and consequently whether women are eligible to be summoned to and become members of the Senate of Canada.

Of the appellants, Henrietta Muir Edwards is the Vice-President for the Province of Alberta of the National Council of Women for Canada; Nellie L. McClung and Louise C. McKinney were for several years members of the Legislative Assembly of the said province; Emily F. Murphy is a police magistrate in and for the said province; and Irene Parlby is a member of the Legislative Assembly of the said province and a member of the Executive Council thereof.

[An account of the judgments of the Supreme Court of Canada is omitted.]

Their Lordships are of the opinion that the word "persons" in s. 24 does include women, and that women are eligible to be summoned to and become members of the Senate of Canada.

In coming to a determination as to the meaning of a particular word in a particular Act of Parliament it is permissible to consider two points—namely: (i) The external evidence derived from extraneous circumstances such as previous legislation and decided cases. (ii) The internal evidence derived from the Act itself. As the counsel on both sides have made great researches and invited their Lordships to consider the legal position of women from the earliest times, in justice to their argument they propose to do so and accordingly turn to the first of the above points—namely: (i) The external evidence derived from extraneous circumstances.

The exclusion of women from all public offices is a relic of days more barbarous than ours, but it must be remembered that the necessity of the times often forced on man customs which in later years were not necessary. Such exclusion is probably due to the fact that the deliberative assemblies of the early tribes were attended by men under arms, and women did not bear arms. "Nihil autem neque publicae neque privatae rei, nisi armati, agunt": Tac.

Germ., c. 13. Yet the tribes did not despise the advice of women. "Inesse quin etiam sanctum et providum putant, nec aut consilia earum aspernantur aut responsa neglegunt": Germ., c. 8. The likelihood of attack rendered such a proceeding unavoidable, and after all what is necessary at any period is a question for the times upon which opinion grounded on experience may move one way or another in different circumstances. This exclusion of women found its way into the opinions of the Roman jurists, Ulpian (AD 211) laying it down. "Feminae ab omnibus officiis civilibus vel publicis remotae sunt": Dig. 1.16.195. The barbarian tribes who settled in the Roman Empire, and were exposed to constant dangers, naturally preserved and continued the tradition.

In England no woman under the degree of a Queen or a Regent, married or unmarried, could take part in the government of the State. A woman was under a legal incapacity to be elected to serve in Parliament and even if a peeress in her own right she was not, nor is, entitled as an incident of peerage to receive a writ of summons to the House of Lords.

Various authorities are cited in the recent case of Viscountess Rhondda's Claim, where it was held that a woman was not entitled to sit in the House of Lords. Women were, moreover, subject to a legal incapacity to vote at the election of members of Parliament: Coke, 4 Inst., p. 5; *Chorlton v. Lings*; or of town councillor: *Reg. v. Harrald*; or to be elected members of a County Council: *Beresford-Hope v. Sandhurst*. They were excluded by the common law from taking part in the administration of justice either as judges or as jurors, with the single exception of inquiries by a jury of matrons upon a suggestion of pregnancy: Coke, 2 Inst. 119, 3 Bl. Comm. 362. Other instances are referred to in the learned judgment of Willes J in *Chorlton v. Lings*.

No doubt in any code where women were expressly excluded from public office the problem would present no difficulty, but where instead of such exclusion those entitled to be summoned to or placed in public office are described under the word "person" different considerations arise.

The word is ambiguous and in its original meaning would undoubtedly embrace members of either sex. On the other hand, supposing in an Act of Parliament several centuries ago it had been enacted that any person should be entitled to be elected to a particular office it would have been understood that the word only referred to males, but the cause of this was not because the word "person" could not include females but because at Common Law a woman was incapable of serving a public office. The fact that no woman had served or has claimed to serve such an office is not of great weight when it is remembered that custom would have prevented the claim being made, or the point being contested.

Customs are apt to develop into traditions which are stronger than law and remain unchallenged long after the reason for them has disappeared.

The appeal to history therefore in this particular matter is not conclusive.

· · ·

Over and above that, their Lordships do not think it right to apply rigidly to Canada of to-day the decisions and the reasonings therefor which commended themselves, probably rightly, to those who had to apply the law in different circumstances, in different centuries to countries in different stages of development. Referring therefore to the judgment of the Chief Justice and those who agreed with him, their Lordships think that the appeal to Roman Law and to early English decisions is not of itself a secure foundation on which to build the interpretation of the *BNA Act, 1867*. ...

Their Lordships now turn to the second point—namely, (ii) the internal evidence derived from the Act itself.

Before discussing the various sections they think it necessary to refer to the circumstances which led up to the passing of the Act.

The communities included within the Britannic system embrace countries and peoples in every stage of social, political and economic development and undergoing a continuous process of evolution. His Majesty the King in Council is the final Court of Appeal from all these communities and this Board must take great care therefore not to interpret legislation meant to apply to one community by a rigid adherence to the customs and traditions of another. ...

The *BNA Act* planted in Canada a living tree capable of growth and expansion within its natural limits. The object of the Act was to grant a Constitution to Canada. "Like all written constitutions it has been subject to development through usage and convention": Canadian Constitutional Studies, Sir Robert Borden, (1922), p. 55.

Their Lordships do not conceive it to be the duty of this Board and it is certainly not their desire—to cut down the provisions of the Act by a narrow and technical construction, but rather to give it a large and liberal interpretation so that the Dominion to a great extent, but within certain fixed limits, may be mistress in her own house, as the provinces to a great extent, but within certain fixed limits, are mistresses in theirs. "The Privy Council, indeed, has laid down that Courts of law must treat the provisions of the *British North America Act* by the same methods of construction and exposition which they apply to other statutes. But there are statutes and statutes; and the strict construction deemed proper in the case, for example, of a penal or taxing statute or one passed to regulate the affairs of an English parish, would be often subversive of parliament's real intent if applied to an Act passed to ensure the peace, order and good government of a British colony": Clement's Canadian Constitution, 3rd ed., p. 347.

· · ·

It must be remembered, too, that their Lordships are not here considering the question of the legislative competence either of the Dominion or its provinces which arises under ss. 91 and 92 of the Act providing for the distribution of legislative powers and assigning to the Dominion and its provinces their respective spheres of Government. Their Lordships are concerned with the interpretation of an Imperial Act, but an Imperial Act which creates a constitution for a new country. Nor are their Lordships deciding any question as to the rights of women but only a question as to their eligibility for a particular position. No one either male or female has a right to be summoned to the Senate. ...

Such being the general analysis of the Act, their Lordships turn to the special sections dealing with the Senate. [A close textual review of various provisions of the *BNA Act* is omitted.]

· · ·

If Parliament had intended to limit the word "persons" in s. 24 to male persons it would surely have manifested such intention by an express limitation as it has done in ss. 41 and 84. The fact that certain qualifications are set out in s. 23 is not an argument in favour of further limiting the class, but is an argument to the contrary because it must be presumed that Parliament has set out in s. 23 all the qualifications deemed necessary for a Senator and it does not state that one of the qualifications is that he must be a member of the male sex. ...

A heavy burden lies on an appellant who seeks to set aside a unanimous judgment of the Supreme Court, and this Board will only set aside such a decision after convincing argument and anxious consideration, but having regard: (1) To the object of the Act—namely, to provide a constitution for Canada, a responsible and developing State; (2) That the word "person" is ambiguous and may include members of either sex; (3) That there are sections in the Act above referred to which show that in some cases the word "person" must include females; (4) That in some sections the words "male persons" is expressly used when it is desired to confine the matter in issue to males, and (5) To the provisions of the *Interpretation Act*; their Lordships have come to the conclusion that the word "persons" in s. 24 includes members both of the male and female sex and that, therefore, the question propounded by the Governor-General must be answered in the affirmative and that women are eligible to be summoned to and become members of the Senate of Canada, and they will humbly advise His Majesty accordingly.

Appeal allowed.

3. Contemporary Feminism

As feminist analysis became more sophisticated through the 20th century, feminism and feminist legal theory evolved. More theoretical frameworks and disciplines were scrutinized. It examined areas of law previously thought to be immune to gender discrimination. It applied the disciplines of sociology and criminology to study issues such as violence against women. It also became more fractured as a movement. Some strands became radicalized. Others remained more conservative: see Patricia Smith, ed., *Feminist Jurisprudence* (New York: Oxford University Press, 1993).

Today, it is seen as simplistic to argue that there is a monolithic group of "feminist scholars"—like any well-developed philosophy, feminism is now filled with complexity and richness. There are "liberal feminists" who argue that it is possible to have gender equality within a liberal conceptual framework: see Margaret Davies, *Asking the Law Question* (Sydney: Law Book Company Limited, 1994), at 179-90. Other, more radical feminists are not so sure, as divisions between men and women are seen as fundamental and attributable to the very notion of liberal society: see Kate Millet, *Sexual Politics* (New York: Simon & Schuster, 1990). Some would argue that Western law is partial: law's rules and structure are premised on a belief system that prefers men and their view of the world. The legal system is thus paternalistic and male-centred: for example, the idea of "rights" can be seen as a masculine concept. Rights-based cultures create a society where many people care only about their own rights and feel threatened by others who are equally self-absorbed. A male focus on the rights of disconnected individuals ignores the human element of law: see Ngaire Naffine, *Law and the Sexes: Explorations in Feminist Jurisprudence* (Sydney: Allen & Unwin, 1990). Others view law as fostering social practices that are combative and litigation oriented—where the idea of a dispassionate judge handing down decisions is also cast as male-centric. Vague notions of "policy," "common sense," or "human nature" have also found their way into law, and been used by judges to preserve male privilege: see Catherine McKinnon, "Feminist Discourse, Moral Values and the Law" (1985), 34 *Buff. L Rev.* 21.

Regardless of whether one subscribes to a liberal or radical vision of feminism, implicit in many of feminism's central themes is that women, given the ability to re-construct society, could do better. The subject of abortion provides a good forum to examine how feminist theory may translate this into practice.

Over the last 30 or so years, rights surrounding abortion have been one of the most contentious areas of public debate. Prior to that time, many countries had criminalized or restricted most, if not all, forms of abortion. Canada was no different. In 1988, in the case of *R v. Morgentaler*, the Supreme Court was asked to determine whether s. 251 of the *Criminal Code*—criminalizing the procurement of an abortion unless properly authorized by a physician—was contrary to s. 7 of the *Canadian Charter of Rights and Freedoms*.

The facts are straightforward. Three doctors, Henry Morgentaler, Leslie Frank Smoling, and Robert Scott, were charged with the offence of procuring a miscarriage contrary to s. 251(1). The majority of the court found the provision to offend the Charter. Justice Bertha Wilson, who agreed with the majority in the end result, rendered a separate opinion. Her decision is an example of a modern feminist approach to a public law concern—note how her opinion takes a woman's point of view, in finding that a woman should not be required to carry a baby to term if she does not wish to.

R v. Morgentaler
[1988] 1 SCR 30, 44 DLR (4th) 385, 62 CR (3d) 1

[Drs. Morgentaler, Smoling, and Scott were each charged with conspiracy to procure a miscarriage contrary to ss. 251(1) and 423(1)(d) of the *Criminal Code*. They were acquitted at trial, but a Crown appeal against that acquittal was allowed and a new trial ordered. On appeal by the accused to the Supreme Court of Canada it was argued that s. 251 of the *Criminal Code* was unconstitutional on the basis that it offended the guarantee to life, liberty, and security of the person found in s. 7 of the *Canadian Charter of Rights and Freedoms*. Section 251(1) of the *Criminal Code* prohibits abortions except in circumstances described in s. 251(4)—in effect, subs. (4) requires a woman to obtain a certificate from a therapeutic abortion committee and then requires that the abortion be carried out by a physician other than the member of the committee in an accredited or approved hospital. There must be at least three physicians on the committee. Evidence was led at trial as to delays encountered by women attempting to comply with the committee procedure and concerning access to abortion services in many parts of Canada.]

WILSON J: At the heart of this appeal is the question whether a pregnant woman can, as a constitutional matter, be compelled by law to carry the foetus to term. The legislature has proceeded on the basis that she can be so compelled and, indeed, has made it a criminal offence punishable by imprisonment under s. 251 of the Criminal Code, RSC 1970, c. C-34, for her or her physician to terminate the pregnancy unless the procedural requirements of the section are complied with.

My colleagues, the Chief Justice and Justice Beetz, have attacked those requirements in reasons which I have had the privilege of reading. They have found that the requirements do not comport with the principles of fundamental justice in the procedural sense and have concluded that, since they cannot be severed from the provisions creating the substantive offence, the whole of s. 251 must fall.

With all due respect, I think that the Court must tackle the primary issue first. A consideration as to whether or not the procedural requirements for obtaining or performing an abortion comport with fundamental justice is purely academic if such requirements cannot as a constitutional matter be imposed at all. If a pregnant woman cannot, as a constitutional matter, be compelled by law to carry the foetus to term against her will, a review of the procedural requirements by which she may be compelled to do so seems pointless. Moreover, it would, in my opinion, be an exercise in futility for the legislature to expend its time and energy in attempting to remedy the defects in the procedural requirements unless it has some assurance that this process will, at the end of the day, result in the creation of a valid criminal offence. I turn, therefore, to what I believe is the central issue that must be addressed.

1. The Right of Access to Abortion

. . .

I agree with the Chief Justice that we are not called upon in this case to delineate the full content of the right to life, liberty and security of the person. This would be an impossible task because we cannot envisage all the contexts in which such a right might be asserted. What we are asked to do, I believe, is define the content of the right in the context of the legislation under attack. Does section 251 of the Criminal Code which limits the pregnant woman's access to abortion violate her right to life, liberty and security of the person within the meaning of s. 7?

. . .

The idea of human dignity finds expression in almost every right and freedom guaranteed in the Charter. Individuals are afforded the right to choose their own religion and their own philosophy of life, the right to choose with whom they will associate and how they will express themselves, the right to choose where they will live and what occupation they will pursue. These are all examples of the basic theory underlying the Charter, namely that the state will respect choices made by individuals and, to the greatest extent possible, will avoid subordinating these choices to any one conception of the good life.

Thus, an aspect of the respect for human dignity on which the Charter is founded is the right to make fundamental personal decisions without interference from the state. This right is a critical component of the right to liberty. Liberty … is a phrase capable of a broad range of meaning. In my view, this right, properly construed, grants the individual a degree of autonomy in making decisions of fundamental personal importance.

This view is consistent with the position I took in the case of *R v. Jones*, [1986] 2 SCR 284. One issue raised in that case was whether the right to liberty in s. 7 of the Charter included a parent's right to bring up his children in accordance with his conscientious beliefs. In concluding that it did I stated at pp. 318-19:

> I believe that the framers of the Constitution in guaranteeing "liberty" as a fundamental value in a free and democratic society had in mind the freedom of the individual to develop and realize his potential to the full, to plan his own life to suit his own character, to make his own choices for good or ill, to be non-conformist, idiosyncratic and even eccentric—to be, in today's

parlance, "his own person" and accountable as such. John Stuart Mill described it as "pursuing our own good in our own way." This, he believed, we should be free to do "so long as we do not attempt to deprive others of theirs or impede their efforts to obtain it."

• • •

The question then becomes whether the decision of a woman to terminate her pregnancy falls within this class of protected decisions. I have no doubt that it does. This decision is one that will have profound psychological, economic and social consequences for the pregnant woman. The circumstances giving rise to it can be complex and varied and there may be, and usually are, powerful considerations militating in opposite directions. It is a decision that deeply reflects the way the woman thinks about herself and her relationship to others and to society at large. It is not just a medical decision; it is a profound social and ethical one as well. Her response to it will be the response of the whole person.

It is probably impossible for a man to respond, even imaginatively, to such a dilemma not just because it is outside the realm of his personal experience (although this is, of course, the case) but because he can relate to it only by objectifying it, thereby eliminating the subjective elements of the female psyche which are at the heart of the dilemma. As Noreen Burrows, Lecturer in European Law at the University of Glasgow, has pointed out in her essay on "International Law and Human Rights: The Case of Women's Rights," in *Human Rights: From Rhetoric to Reality* (1986), the history of the struggle for human rights from the eighteenth century on has been the history of men struggling to assert their dignity and common humanity against an overbearing state apparatus. The more recent struggle for women's rights has been a struggle to eliminate discrimination, to achieve a place for women in a man's world, to develop a set of legislative reforms in order to place women in the same position as men. It has not been a struggle to define the rights of women in relation to their special place in the societal structure and in relation to the biological distinction between the two sexes. Thus, women's needs and aspirations are only now being translated into protected rights. The right to reproduce or not to reproduce which is in issue in this case is one such right and is properly perceived as an integral part of modern woman's struggle to assert her dignity and worth as a human being.

Given then that the right to liberty guaranteed by s. 7 of the Charter gives a woman the right to decide for herself whether or not to terminate her pregnancy, does s. 251 of the Criminal Code violate this right? Clearly it does. The purpose of the section is to take the decision away from the woman and give it to a committee. Furthermore, as the Chief Justice correctly points out … the committee bases its decision on "criteria entirely unrelated to [the pregnant woman's] priorities and aspirations." The fact that the decision whether a woman will be allowed to terminate her pregnancy is in the hands of a committee is just as great a violation of the woman's right to personal autonomy in decisions of an intimate and private nature as it would be if a committee were established to decide whether a woman should be allowed to continue her pregnancy. Both these arrangements violate the woman's right to liberty by deciding for her something that she has the right to decide for herself.

• • •

[T]he present legislative scheme for the obtaining of an abortion clearly subjects pregnant women to considerable emotional stress as well as to unnecessary physical risk. I believe, however, that the flaw in the present legislative scheme goes much deeper than that. In essence, what it does is assert that the woman's capacity to reproduce is not to be subject to her own control. It is to be subject to the control of the state. She may not choose whether to exercise her existing capacity or not to exercise it. This is not, in my view, just a matter of interfering with her right to liberty in the sense (already discussed) of her right to personal autonomy in decision-making, it is a direct interference with her physical "person" as well. She is truly being treated as a means—a means to an end which she does not desire but over which she has no control. She is the passive recipient of a decision made by others as to whether her body is to be used to nurture a new life. Can there be anything that comports less with human dignity and self-respect? How can a woman in this position have any sense of security with respect to her person? I believe that s. 251 of the Criminal Code deprives the pregnant woman of her right to security of the person as well as her right to liberty.

· · ·

I believe, therefore, that a deprivation of the s. 7 right which has the effect of infringing a right guaranteed elsewhere in the Charter cannot be in accordance with the principles of fundamental justice.

[Wilson J next went on to determine that the *Criminal Code* provisions also offend a woman's freedom of conscience and religion under s. 2(a) of the Charter (regardless of whether such conscientiously held beliefs are grounded in religion or a secular morality).]

· · ·

Section 251 of the Criminal Code takes the decision away from the woman at all stages of her pregnancy. It is a complete denial of the woman's constitutionally protected right under s. 7, not merely a limitation on it. It cannot, in my opinion, meet the proportionality test in *Oakes*. It is not sufficiently tailored to the legislative objective and does not impair the woman's right "as little as possible." It cannot be saved under s. 1. Accordingly, even if the section were to be amended to remedy the purely procedural defects in the legislative scheme referred to by the Chief Justice and Beetz J it would, in my opinion, still not be constitutionally valid.

One final word. I wish to emphasize that in these reasons I have dealt with the existence of the developing foetus merely as a factor to be considered in assessing the importance of the legislative objective under s. 1 of the Charter. I have not dealt with the entirely separate question whether a foetus is covered by the word "everyone" in s. 7 so as to have an independent right to life under that section. The Crown did not argue it and it is not necessary to decide it in order to dispose of the issues on this appeal.

Compared with the other justices in the *Morgentaler* decision, Wilson J looks at the very heart of the matter—whether a pregnant woman can be compelled by law to carry a foetus to term. The judgment is in keeping with her philosophy. Madam Justice Wilson was a Supreme Court of Canada judge during the formative years of the Charter, from 1982 to 1991. She was the first woman appointed to the Supreme Court and participated in many groundbreaking Charter decisions. Feminists, for the most part, heralded her judgments as showing, for the first time, a true understanding of the plight of women in Canadian law. Critics saw her as using the Charter to expand the role of a judge beyond principles established by liberal democratic theory and constitutional adjudication. She has been said to be as much a legislator for women's rights as a judge: see Robert E. Hawkins and Robert Martin, "Democracy, Judging and Bertha Wilson" (1995), 41 *McGill LJ* 1.

D. Critical Legal Studies

1. Introduction

Like some forms of feminism, critical legal studies (CLS)—a school of legal theory developed largely during the 1980s in the United States—is a radical alternative to established legal theories. CLS adherents reject that there is any kind of "natural legal order" discoverable by objective means. As described by A. Thomson:

> While traditional jurisprudence claims to be able to reveal through pure reason a picture of an unchanging and universal unity beneath the manifest changeability and historical variability of laws, legal institutions and practices, and thus to establish a foundation in reason for actual legal systems, critical legal theory not only denies the possibility of discovering a universal foundation for law through pure reason, but sees the whole enterprise of jurisprudence … as operating to confer a spurious legitimacy on law and legal systems.

A. Thomson, "Critical Approaches to Law: Who Needs Legal Theory?" in I. Grigg-Spall and P. Ireland, eds., *The Critical Lawyers' Handbook* (London: Pluto Press, 1992), at 2.

CLS is a direct descendent of Legal Realism, an approach that rose to prominence in the 1920s and lasted until the 1940s. Legal Realism attacked two fundamental axioms of the traditional, formalist understanding of the common law: that common law legal rules were neutral and objective, and that the rules themselves could be determined with sufficient certainty. Realists maintained that all legal rules were indeterminate in the sense that any articulation of a rule was subject to multiple interpretations. As a consequence, when judges decided cases they were not involved in an objective exercise of discovering the meaning of some pre-existing rule or mechanistically applying a rule to a set of facts (since the indeterminate nature of legal rules conferred discretion on judges to choose from a variety of alternative interpretations), but rather the result would reflect the unstated public policy preferences of the judge. The inconsistent results in the contrasting cases of *Re Drummond Wren* and *Re Noble and Wolf* provide an example of the way in which a judge's predisposition may affect legal outcomes. In essence, Legal Realism called into question the autonomy of law from broader social and political considerations.

Legal Realists also believed in the importance of interdisciplinary approaches to law (given their understanding of law's contingency on social, economic, and political conditions), a view that became even more important to CLS scholars. Because of law's subjectivity, and its connection to other disciplines, the Realists sought to use the law as a tool to change society.

CLS takes this approach further. It is a direct attack on traditional legal theory, scholarship, and education. According to its main precepts, law, far from attempting to symbolize justice, institutionalizes and legitimates the authority and power of particular social groups or classes. The rule of law is not a rational, quasi-scientific ordering of society's norms, but is indeterminate, full of subjective interpretation and a large degree of incoherency.

Much of CLS theory is post-Marxist and usually associated with the left. Three key stages (posited by Trubek) govern the application of CLS ideas to legal thought: "hegemonic consciousness" (a concept derived from the Italian Marxist scholar Antonio Gramsci); "reification" (a Marxist term meaning to convert into something material); and "denial" (the psychoanalytical term as used by Freud). At the first stage, its proponents argue that many, if not most, Western laws are maintained by a system of beliefs that have their foundation in a liberal, market-driven economy. While many see these laws as natural and commonsensical, in fact, they reflect only the transitory, arbitrary interests of a dominant class: see David Trubek, "Where the Action Is: Critical Legal Studies and Empiricism" (1984), 36 *Stan. L Rev.* 575.

In the second stage, these beliefs are reified into a material thing: they are presented as essential, necessary, and objective. The laws that prop up this belief system necessarily follow suit, becoming equally incontrovertible.

In the final phase, laws and legal thinking aid in the denial of real truths: they assist in our coping with a vast storehouse of contradictions that would be too painful for us to hold in our consciousness. In other words, for a CLS scholar, the denial occurs between the promise of a certain state of law—such as equality—and the reality—such as the vast amounts of discrimination or racism that can be found so readily in society if only we look.

The liberal belief that law should be certain and neutral is, for CLS scholars, illusory. Law reproduces the oppressive characteristic of contemporary Western societies. Moreover, law is not independent or instrumental—it is simply another form of politics. Lawyers and the legal profession are part of this pretense. But there is nothing special about legal reasoning to distinguish it from other forms of reasoning—nothing about lawyers that should give them a monopoly on reason or justice. In other words, they are neither exceptional nor should they be privileged.

Finally, CLS questions another of law's central assumptions, that the individual is an autonomous agent. While the law assumes that individuals can make decisions based on reason that is detached from political, social, or economic constraints, CLS holds that individuals are tied to, and part of, such things as their communities, socio-economic class, gender, and race to the extent that they are not autonomous actors. Rather, their circumstances determine and therefore limit the choices presented to them.

2. Judging with CLS: A Case Study

The CLS movement can be very theory-driven and densely philosophical. Along with its post-modernist offshoots, it is still considered radical, avant-garde, and outside most mainstream legal thought. Because of this, the movement was never likely to garner wholesale acceptance outside academia. However, it would be naïve to think that some lawyers and judges who attended law school during the 1970s and 1980s were not influenced by it. In the following excerpt from *R v. R.D.S.*, compare the judges' approach to questions of race and equality with that of the judges in *Re Drummond Wren* and *Re Noble and Wolf* excerpted above. Consider whether the differing opinions of the judges in *R v. R.D.S.* arise from different conceptions of the practice of judging itself. Also, examine the differences in approach of the two majority decisions with the approach of the dissent. Which, if any, reflects the insights of CLS scholarship regarding the impossibility of objectivity and the law's lack of autonomy from the social and political context in which law operates?

R v. R.D.S.
[1997] 3 SCR 484, 151 DLR (4th) 193, 10 CR (5th) 1

[A white police officer arrested a black 15-year-old who had allegedly interfered with the arrest of another youth. The accused was charged with three offences dealing with unlawfully assaulting and unlawfully resisting a police officer. The police officer and the accused were the only witnesses and their accounts of the relevant events differed widely. The Youth Court judge weighed the evidence and determined that the accused should be acquitted. While delivering her oral reasons, the judge remarked in response to a rhetorical question by the Crown, that police officers had been known to mislead the court in the past, that they had been known to overreact particularly with non-white groups, and that that would indicate a questionable state of mind. She also stated that her comments were not tied to the police officer testifying before the court. The Crown challenged these comments as raising a reasonable apprehension of bias. The Crown appealed to the Nova Scotia Supreme Court (Trial Division); the appeal was allowed and a new trial was ordered on the basis that the judge's remarks gave rise to a reasonable apprehension of bias. This judgment was upheld by a majority of the Nova Scotia Court of Appeal, and this decision was appealed, in turn, to the Supreme Court of Canada.]

CORY J: In this appeal, it must be determined whether a reasonable apprehension of bias arises from comments made by the trial judge in providing her reasons for acquitting the accused. ...

B. Ascertaining the Existence of a Reasonable Apprehension of Bias

(i) Fair Trial and the Right to an Unbiased Adjudicator

A system of justice, if it is to have the respect and confidence of its society, must ensure that trials are fair and that they appear to be fair to the informed and reasonable observer. This is a fundamental goal of the justice system in any free and democratic society.

· · ·

Canada is not an insular, homogeneous society. It is enriched by the presence and contributions of citizens of many different races, nationalities and ethnic origins. The multicultural nature of Canadian society has been recognized in s. 27 of the Charter. Section 27 provides that the Charter itself is to be interpreted in a manner that is consistent with the preservation and enhancement of the multicultural heritage of Canadians. Yet our judges must be particularly sensitive to the need not only to be fair but also to appear to all reasonable observers to be fair to all Canadians of every race, religion, nationality and ethnic origin. This is a far more difficult task in Canada than it would be in a homogeneous society. Remarks which would pass unnoticed in other societies could well raise a reasonable apprehension of bias in Canada.

· · ·

The question which must be answered in this appeal is whether the comments made by Judge Sparks in her reasons give rise to a reasonable apprehension that she was not impartial as between the Crown and the accused. The Crown's position, in essence, is that Judge Sparks did not give the essential and requisite appearance of impartiality because her comments indicated that she prejudged an issue in the case, or to put it another way, she reached her determination on the basis of factors which were not in evidence.

· · ·

(iii) What Is Bias?

It may be helpful to begin by articulating what is meant by impartiality. In deciding whether bias arises in a particular case, it is relatively rare for courts to explore the definition of bias. In this appeal, however, this task is essential, if the Crown's allegation against Judge Sparks is to be properly understood and addressed. See Prof. Richard F. Devlin, "We Can't Go On Together with Suspicious Minds: Judicial Bias and Racialized Perspective in R v. R.D.S." (1995), 18 Dalhousie LJ 408, at pp. 438-39.

· · ·

[I]n the context of the current appeal, it is vital to bear in mind that the test for reasonable apprehension of bias applies equally to all judges, regardless of their background, gender, race, ethnic origin, or any other characteristic. A judge who happens to be black is no more likely to be biased in dealing with black litigants, than a white judge is likely to be biased in favour of white litigants. All judges of every race, colour, religion, or national background are entitled to the same presumption of judicial integrity and the same high threshold for a finding of bias. Similarly, all judges are subject to the same fundamental duties to be and to appear to be impartial.

(v) Judicial Integrity and the Importance of Judicial Impartiality

Often the most significant occasion in the career of a judge is the swearing of the oath of office. It is a moment of pride and joy coupled with a realization of the onerous responsibility that goes with the office. The taking of the oath is solemn and a defining moment etched forever in the memory of the judge. The oath requires a judge to render justice impartially. To take that oath is the fulfilment of a life's dreams. It is never taken lightly. Throughout their careers, Canadian judges strive to overcome the personal biases that are common to all humanity in order to provide and clearly appear to provide a fair trial for all who come before them. Their rate of success in this difficult endeavour is high.

· · ·

It is right and proper that judges be held to the highest standards of impartiality since they will have to determine the most fundamentally important rights of the parties appearing before them. This is true whether the legal dispute arises between citizen and citizen or between the citizen and the state. Every comment that a judge makes from the bench is weighed and evaluated by the community as well as the parties. Judges must be conscious of this constant weighing and make every effort to achieve neutrality and fairness in carrying out their duties. This must be a cardinal rule of judicial conduct.

The requirement for neutrality does not require judges to discount the very life experiences that may so well qualify them to preside over disputes. It has been observed that the duty to be impartial

> does not mean that a judge does not, or cannot bring to the bench many existing sympathies, antipathies or attitudes. There is no human being who is not the product of every social experi-

ence, every process of education, and every human contact with those with whom we share the planet. Indeed, even if it were possible, a judge free of this heritage of past experience would probably lack the very qualities of humanity required of a judge. Rather, the wisdom required of a judge is to recognize, consciously allow for, and perhaps to question, all the baggage of past attitudes and sympathies that fellow citizens are free to carry, untested, to the grave.

True impartiality does not require that the judge have no sympathies or opinions; it requires that the judge nevertheless be free to entertain and act upon different points of view with an open mind. (Canadian Judicial Council, Commentaries on Judicial Conduct (1991), at p. 12.)

It is obvious that good judges will have a wealth of personal and professional experience, that they will apply with sensitivity and compassion to the cases that they must hear. The sound belief behind the encouragement of greater diversity in judicial appointments was that women and visible minorities would bring an important perspective to the difficult task of judging. See for example the discussion by the Honourable Maryka Omatsu, "The Fiction of Judicial Impartiality" (1997), 9 CJWL 1. See also *Devlin, supra*, at pp. 408-9.

Regardless of their background, gender, ethnic origin or race, all judges owe a fundamental duty to the community to render impartial decisions and to appear impartial. It follows that judges must strive to ensure that no word or action during the course of the trial or in delivering judgment might leave the reasonable, informed person with the impression that an issue was predetermined or that a question was decided on the basis of stereotypical assumptions or generalizations.

(vi) Should Judges Refer to Aspects of Social Context in Making Decisions?

It is the submission of the appellant and interveners that judges should be able to refer to social context in making their judgments. It is argued that they should be able to refer to power imbalances between the sexes or between races, as well as to other aspects of social reality. The response to that submission is that each case must be assessed in light of its particular facts and circumstances. Whether or not the use of references to social context is appropriate in the circumstances and whether a reasonable apprehension of bias arises from particular statements will depend on the facts of the case.

. . .

Certainly judges may, on the basis of expert evidence adduced, refer to relevant social conditions in reasons for judgment. In some circumstances, those references are necessary, so that the law may evolve in a manner which reflects social reality. ...

(vii) Use of Social Context in Assessing Credibility

. . .

[I]t is ... the individualistic nature of a determination of credibility that requires the judge, as trier of fact, to be particularly careful to be and to appear to be neutral. This obligation requires the judge to walk a delicate line. On one hand, the judge is obviously permitted to use common sense and wisdom gained from personal experience in observing and judging the trustworthiness of a particular witness on the basis of factors such as testimony and demeanour. On the other hand, the judge must avoid judging the credibility of the witness on the basis of generalizations or upon matters that were not in evidence.

At the commencement of their testimony all witnesses should be treated equally without regard to their race, religion, nationality, gender, occupation or other characteristics. It is only after an individual witness has been tested and assessed that findings of credibility can be made. Obviously the evidence of a policeman, or any other category of witness, cannot be automatically preferred to that of accused persons, any more than the testimony of blue eyed witnesses can be preferred to those with gray eyes. That must be the general rule. In particular, any judicial indication that police evidence is always to be preferred to that of a black accused person would lead the reasonable and knowledgeable observer to conclude that there was a reasonable apprehension of bias.

In some circumstances it may be acceptable for a judge to acknowledge that racism in society might be, for example, the motive for the overreaction of a police officer. This may be necessary in order to refute a submission that invites the judge as trier of fact to presume truthfulness or untruthfulness of a category of witnesses, or to adopt some other form of stereotypical thinking. Yet it would not be acceptable for a judge to go further and suggest that all police officers should therefore not be believed or should be viewed with suspicion where they are dealing with accused persons who are members of a different race. Similarly, it is dangerous for a judge to suggest that a particular person overreacted because of racism unless there is evidence adduced to sustain this finding. It would be equally inappropriate to suggest that female complainants, in sexual assault cases, ought to be believed more readily than male accused persons solely because of the history of sexual violence by men against women.

If there is no evidence linking the generalization to the particular witness, these situations might leave the judge open to allegations of bias on the basis that the credibility of the individual witness was prejudged according to stereotypical generalizations. This does not mean that the particular generalization—that police officers have historically discriminated against visible minorities or that women have historically been abused by men—is not true, or is without foundation. The difficulty is that reasonable and informed people may perceive that the judge has used this information as a basis for assessing credibility instead of making a genuine evaluation of the evidence of the particular witness' credibility. As a general rule, judges should avoid placing themselves in this position.

To state the general proposition that judges should avoid making comments based on generalizations when assessing the credibility of individual witnesses does not lead automatically to a conclusion that when a judge does so, a reasonable apprehension of bias arises. In some limited circumstances, the comments may be appropriate. Furthermore, no matter how unfortunate individual comments appear in isolation, the comments must be examined in context, through the eyes of the reasonable and informed person who is taken to know all the relevant circumstances of the case, including the presumption of judicial integrity, and the underlying social context.

· · ·

C. *Application of These Principles to the Facts*

Did Judge Sparks' comments give rise to a reasonable apprehension of bias? In order to answer that question, the nature of the Crown's allegation against Judge Sparks must be clearly understood. At the outset, it must be emphasized that it is obviously not appropriate to allege bias against Judge Sparks simply because she is black and raised the prospect of racial discrimination. Further, exactly the same high threshold for demonstrating reasonable apprehension of bias must be applied to Judge Sparks in the same manner it would be to all judges. She benefits from the presumption of judicial integrity that is accorded to all who swear the judicial oath of office. The Crown bears the onus of displacing this presumption with "cogent evidence."

. . .

The history of anti-black racism in Nova Scotia was documented recently by the *Royal Commission on the Donald Marshall Jr. Prosecution* (1989). It suggests that there is a realistic possibility that the actions taken by the police in their relations with visible minorities demonstrate both prejudice and discrimination. I do not propose to review and comment upon the vast body of sociological literature referred to by the parties. It was not in evidence at trial. In the circumstances it will suffice to say that they indicate that racial tension exists at least to some degree between police officers and visible minorities. Further, in some cases, racism may have been exhibited by police officers in arresting young black males. …

. . .

V. Conclusion

In the result the judgments of the Court of Appeal and of Glube CJSC are set aside and the decision of Judge Sparks dismissing the charges against R.D.S. is restored. I must add that since writing these reasons I have had the opportunity of reading those of Major J. It is readily apparent that we are in agreement as to the nature of bias and the test to be applied in order to determine whether the words or actions of a trial judge raise a reasonable apprehension of bias. The differences in our reasons lies in the application of the principles and test we both rely upon to the words of the trial judge in this case. The principles and the test we have both put forward and relied upon are different from and incompatible with those set out by Justices L' ux-Dubé and McLachlin.

L'HEUREUX-DUBÉ AND McLACHLIN JJ:

I. Introduction

We have read the reasons of our colleague, Justice Cory, and while we agree that this appeal must be allowed, we differ substantially from him in how we reach that outcome. As a result, we find it necessary to write brief concurring reasons.

We endorse Cory J's comments on judging in a multicultural society, the importance of perspective and social context in judicial decision-making, and the presumption of judicial integrity. However, we approach the test for reasonable apprehension of bias and its application to the case at bar somewhat differently from our colleague.

In our view, the test for reasonable apprehension of bias established in the jurisprudence is reflective of the reality that while judges can never be neutral, in the sense of purely objective, they can and must strive for impartiality. It therefore recognizes as inevitable and appropriate that the differing experiences of judges assist them in their decision-making process and will be reflected in their judgments, so long as those experiences are relevant to the cases, are not based on inappropriate stereotypes, and do not prevent a fair and just determination of the cases based on the facts in evidence.

We find that on the basis of these principles, there is no reasonable apprehension of bias in the case at bar. Like Cory J we would, therefore, overturn the findings by the Nova Scotia Supreme Court (Trial Division) and the majority of the Nova Scotia Court of Appeal that a reasonable apprehension of bias arises in this case, and restore the acquittal of R.D.S. This said, we disagree with Cory J's position that the comments of Judge Sparks were unfortunate, unnecessary, or close to the line. Rather, we find them to reflect an entirely appropriate recognition of the facts in evidence in this case and of the context within which this case arose—a context known to Judge Sparks and to any well-informed member of the community.

II. The Test for Reasonable Apprehension of Bias

. . .

A. The Nature of Judging

As discussed above, judges in a bilingual, multiracial and multicultural society will undoubtedly approach the task of judging from their varied perspectives. They will certainly have been shaped by, and have gained insight from, their different experiences, and cannot be expected to divorce themselves from these experiences on the occasion of their appointment to the bench. In fact, such a transformation would deny society the benefit of the valuable knowledge gained by the judiciary while they were members of the Bar. As well, it would preclude the achievement of a diversity of backgrounds in the judiciary. The reasonable person does not expect that judges will function as neutral ciphers; however, the reasonable person does demand that judges achieve impartiality in their judging.

It is apparent, and a reasonable person would expect, that triers of fact will be properly influenced in their deliberations by their individual perspectives on the world in which the events in dispute in the courtroom took place. Indeed, judges must rely on their background knowledge in fulfilling their adjudicative function. …

At the same time, where the matter is one of identifying and applying the law to the findings of fact, it must be the law that governs and not a judge's individual beliefs that may conflict with the law. Further, notwithstanding that their own insights into human nature will properly play a role in making findings of credibility or factual determinations, judges must make those determinations only after being equally open to, and considering the views of, all parties before them. The reasonable person, through whose eyes the apprehension of bias is assessed, expects judges to undertake an open-minded, carefully considered, and dispassionately deliberate investigation of the complicated reality of each case before them.

It is axiomatic that all cases litigated before judges are, to a greater or lesser degree, complex. There is more to a case than who did what to whom, and the questions of fact and law to be determined in any given case do not arise in a vacuum. Rather, they are the consequence of numerous factors, influenced by the innumerable forces which impact on them in a particular context. Judges, acting as finders of fact, must inquire into those forces. In short, they must be aware of the context in which the alleged crime occurred.

Judicial inquiry into the factual, social and psychological context within which litigation arises is not unusual. Rather, a conscious, contextual inquiry has become an accepted step towards judicial impartiality. In that regard, Professor Jennifer Nedelsky's "Embodied Diversity and the Challenges to Law" (1997), 42 *McGill LJ* 91, at p. 107, offers the following comment:

> What makes it possible for us to genuinely judge, to move beyond our private idiosyncrasies and preferences, is our capacity to achieve an "enlargement of mind." We do this by taking different perspectives into account. This is the path out of the blindness of our subjective private conditions. The more views we are able to take into account, the less likely we are to be locked into one perspective … . It is the capacity for "enlargement of mind" that makes autonomous, impartial judgment possible. …

. . .

IV. *Application of the Test to the Facts*

. . .

While it seems clear that Judge Sparks did not in fact relate the officer's probable overreaction to the race of the appellant R.D.S., it should be noted that if Judge Sparks had chosen to attribute the behaviour of Constable Stienburg to the racial dynamics of the situation, she would not necessarily have erred. As a member of the community, it was open to her to take into account the well-known presence of racism in that community and to evaluate the evidence as to what occurred against that background.

That Judge Sparks recognized that police officers sometimes overreact when dealing with non-white groups simply demonstrates that in making her determination in this case, she was alive to the well-known racial dynamics that may exist in interactions between police officers and visible minorities. …

V. *Conclusion*

In the result, we agree with Cory J as to the disposition of this case. We would allow the appeal, overturn the findings of the Nova Scotia Supreme Court (Trial Division) and the majority of the Nova Scotia Court of Appeal, and restore the acquittal of the appellant R.D.S.

MAJOR J (dissenting): I have read the reasons of Justices L'Heureux-Dubé and McLachlin and those of Justice Cory and respectfully disagree with the conclusion they reach.

… This appeal should not be decided on questions of racism but instead on how courts should decide cases. In spite of the submissions of the appellant and interveners on his behalf, the case is primarily about the conduct of the trial. A fair trial is one that is based on the law, the outcome of which is determined by the evidence, free of bias, real or apprehended. Did the trial judge here reach her decision on the evidence presented at the trial or did she rely on something else?

In view of the manner in which this appeal was argued, it is necessary to consider two points. First, we should consider whether the trial judge in her reasons, properly instructed herself on the evidence or was an error of law committed by her. The second, and somewhat intertwined question, is whether her comments above could cause a reasonable observer to apprehend bias. The offending comments in the statement are:

> "police officers have been known to [mislead the court] in the past"; (ii) "police officers do over-react, particularly when they are dealing with non-white groups"; (iii) "[t]hat to me indicates a state of mind right there that is questionable"; (iv) "[i]t seems to be in keeping with the preva-lent attitude of the day"; and, (v) "based upon my comments and based upon all the evidence before the court I have no other choice but to acquit."

The trial judge stated that "police officers have been known to [mislead the court] in the past" and that "police officers do overreact, particularly when they are dealing with non-white groups" and went on to say "[t]hat to me indicates a state of mind right there that is questionable." She in effect was saying, "sometimes police lie and overreact in dealing with non-whites, therefore I have a suspicion that this police officer may have lied and over-reacted in dealing with this non-white accused." This was stereotyping all police officers as liars and racists, and applied this stereotype to the police officer in the present case. The trial judge might be perceived as assigning less weight to the police officer's evidence because he is testifying in the prosecution of an accused who is of a different race. Whether racism exists in our society is not the issue. The issue is whether there was evidence before the court upon which to base a finding that this particular police officer's actions were motivated by racism. There was no evidence of this presented at the trial.

Our jurisprudence has repeatedly prohibited the introduction of evidence to show pro-pensity. In the present case had the police officer been charged with assault the trial judge could not have reasoned that as police officers have been known to mislead the Court in the past that based on that evidence she rejected this police officer's credibility and found him guilty beyond reasonable doubt.

In the same vein, statistics show that young male adults under the age of 25 are respon-sible for more accidents than older drivers. It would be unacceptable for a court to accept evidence of that fact to find a defendant liable in negligence yet that is the consequence of the trial judge's reasoning in this appeal.

It is possible to read the trial judge's reference to the "prevalent attitude of the day" as meaning her view of the prevalent attitude in society today. If the trial judge used the "prevalent attitude of society" towards non-whites as evidence upon which to draw an infer-ence in this case, she erred, as there were no facts in evidence from which to draw that infer-ence. It would be stereotypical reasoning to conclude that, since society is racist, and, in effect, tells minorities to "shut up," we should infer that this police officer told this appellant minority youth to "shut up." This reasoning is flawed.

Trial judges have to base their findings on the evidence before them. It was open to the appellant to introduce evidence that this police officer was racist and that racism motivated his actions or that he lied. This was not done. For the trial judge to infer that based on her general view of the police or society is an error of law. For this reason there should be a new trial.

. . .

The life experience of this trial judge, as with all trial judges, is an important ingredient in the ability to understand human behaviour, to weigh the evidence, and to determine credibility. It helps in making a myriad of decisions arising during the course of most trials. It is of no value, however, in reaching conclusions for which there is no evidence. The fact that on some other occasions police officers have lied or overreacted is irrelevant. Life experience is not a substitute for evidence. There was no evidence before the trial judge to support the conclusions she reached.

The trial judge could not decide this case based on what some police officers did in the past without deciding that all police officers are the same. As stated, the appellant was entitled to call evidence of the police officer's conduct to show that there was in fact evidence to support either his bias or racism. No such evidence was called. The trial judge presumably called upon her life experience to decide the issue. This she was not entitled to do.

The bedrock of our jurisprudence is the adversary system. Criminal prosecutions are less adversarial because of the Crown's duty to present all the evidence fairly. The system depends on each side's producing facts by way of evidence from which the court decides the issues. Our system, unlike some others, does not permit a judge to become an independent investigator to seek out the facts.

Canadian courts have, in recent years, criticized the stereotyping of people into what is said to be predictable behaviour patterns. If a judge in a sexual assault case instructed the jury or him- or herself that because the complainant was a prostitute he or she probably consented, or that prostitutes are likely to lie about such things as sexual assault, that decision would be reversed. Such presumptions have no place in a system of justice that treats all witnesses equally. Our jurisprudence prohibits tying credibility to something as irrelevant as gender, occupation or perceived group predisposition.

It can hardly be seen as progress to stereotype police officer witnesses as likely to lie when dealing with non-whites. This would return us to a time in the history of the Canadian justice system that many thought had past. This reasoning, with respect to police officers, is no more legitimate than the stereotyping of women, children or minorities.

In my opinion the comments of the trial judge fall into stereotyping the police officer. She said, among other things, that police officers have been known to mislead the courts, and that police officers overreact when dealing with non-white groups. She then held, in her evaluation of this particular police officer's evidence, that these factors led her to "a state of mind right there that is questionable." The trial judge erred in law by failing to base her conclusions on evidence.

· · ·

I agree with the approach taken by Cory J with respect to the nature of bias and the test to be used to determine if the words or actions of a judge give rise to apprehension of bias. However, I come to a different conclusion in the application of the test to the words of the trial judge in this case. It follows that I disagree with the approach to reasonable apprehension of bias put forward by Justices L'Heureux-Dubé and McLachlin.

The error of law that I attribute to the trial judge's assessment of the evidence or lack of evidence is sufficiently serious that a new trial is ordered.

In the result, I would uphold the disposition of Flinn JA in the Court of Appeal (1995), 145 NSR (2d) 284, and dismiss the appeal.

E. Law and Economics

1. Introduction

Both positivism and natural law are concerned with concepts of law and justice, even if they diverge as to how the two relate to one another. Both are also based largely on Western, liberal ideas about law and society. In contrast, feminism and critical studies take issue with the liberal basis of law and its relationship to justice; both attempt to establish alternate visions of what justice might be. Law and economics theories look at law from another perspective, grounded less in moral theory and more in ideas about efficiency. As with the other theories, however, law and economics seeks to explain law in operation.

Law and economics scholars have applied economic analysis to explain contract law, crime, torts, family law, property, legislation, abortion, and more: see generally, Ronald Coase, "Economics and Contiguous Disciplines" (1978), *J Legal Stud*. 201 and Richard Posner, *The Economic Analysis of Law*, 6th ed. (New York: Aspen Publishers, 2003). As in other perspectives on law, there is no single approach to linking law and economics. However, most of the work in this area originated out of the "Chicago School" in the 1970s, which had a strong free-market, neo-liberal philosophical base.

A traditional law and economics approach applies economics methodology to legal rules in order to assess whether the rules will result in outcomes that are efficient. Efficiency tends to be defined in terms of an ideal where the welfare of each of the relevant parties can no longer be maximized except at the expense of other parties, referred to as a state of "Pareto optimality." In this regard, law and economics is sometimes criticized as ignoring questions respecting distributive justice. Central to all economic analysis is the assumption that human beings are rational actors. Individuals have preferences and act in order to achieve those preferences; they act as if they were rational maximizers of their welfare. This form of analysis was first applied on common law rules developed in private law areas such as torts and contracts.

2. Public Law and Economic Theory

a. Overview

Like law and justice, however, justice and efficiency are also interrelated. For one, governments have to consider the costs of providing and maintaining the institutions of justice. But more broadly, to the extent that justice involves considerations of utility, efficiency, it has been argued, can be seen as a concept concerned with maximizing justice.

An economic approach similar to that employed for private law can therefore be used to understand policy goals in the public realm. The economic theory of regulation, or public choice theory, applies basic economic theory in an attempt to understand public policy. It attempts to explain government intervention as a "corrective" to market failure. The theory seeks to understand why some government programs seem to run counter to the public good, or at least do not maximize the public good. In its pure form the economic theory of public law begins at the same place as the economic theory of private law: policy makers are assumed to act in order to maximize political support. They are not necessarily attempting to maximize social welfare, therefore, but are motivated largely by self-interest: see J. Buchanan and R. Tollison, eds., *The Theory of Public Choice—II* (Ann Arbor, MI: University of Michigan Press, 1984) and Arthur Pigou, *The Economics of Welfare*, 4th ed. (London: Macmillan, 1932).

A basic proposition of public choice theory is that diffuse and fragmented groups are less effective than more focused and concentrated groups in achieving success in the political arena and in influencing legislators and regulators: see I. McLean, *Public Choice: An Introduction*, 2nd ed. (Oxford: Blackwell, 1996) and D. Mueller, ed., *Perspectives on Public Choice* (Cambridge: Cambridge University Press, 1997).

If both these expectations are true, one might expect legislation to favour the self-interest of legislators and/or the interests of powerful social groups. There is an echo, therefore, in the public choice critique of the complaints voiced by the CLS and feminist scholars. Ask yourself, as you progress through these materials, whether Canadian public law sufficiently guards against these predicted outcomes.

b. Examples

One of the themes in public law is to show how common law has been displaced by policy formulation (in the form of legislation) as the primary means of social regulation: see E. Rubin, "Law and Legislation in the Administrative State" (1989), 89 *Colum. L Rev.* 369. A number of important questions, therefore, lie at the heart of this analysis: What, in economic terms, is the problem that a legal rule or structure is attempting to resolve? What effect does this rule have on society? Why do we have the laws that we have? Should we have different laws?

Consider how the Supreme Court of Canada relies on some basic economic theory about the value of money and its relationship to contractual breaches in the following decision.

Bank of America Canada v. Mutual Trust Co.
[2002] 2 SCR 601

[The appellant, Bank of America Canada, had advanced money to a developer, and the respondent, Mutual Trust, had undertaken to advance money to the purchaser of houses being built by the developer in a device called a "Takeout Mortgage Commitment" (TOC). The developer assigned its rights against Mutual Trust to Bank of America Canada. The funds advanced by Mutual Trust under the TOC would have discharged the loan made by Bank of America Canada to the developer. Mutual Trust backed out of the deal when the real estate market collapsed in the early 1990s. The amount of Bank of America Canada's loss was about $10 million—the difference between what it was owed and what it recovered when it sold the development after Mutual Trust's default.

The trial judge awarded interest on this amount at a compound rate that reflected the interest rate charged in the agreement between the parties. The Ontario Court of Appeal allowed Mutual Trust's appeal, relying on s. 128 of the *Courts of Justice Act* in substituting a simple interest rate for the compound rate allowed by the trial judge. The difference between the two amounts was in the order of $5 million. Bank of America Canada appealed.]

MAJOR J:

VI. Analysis

A. Jurisdiction

(1) The Time-Value of Money

[21] The value of money decreases with the passage of time. A dollar today is worth more than the same dollar tomorrow. Three factors account for the depreciation of the value of money: (i) opportunity cost (ii) risk, and (iii) inflation.

[22] The first factor, opportunity cost, reflects the uses of the dollar which are foregone while waiting for it. The value of the dollar is reduced because the opportunity to use it is absent. The second factor, risk, reflects the uncertainty inherent in delaying possession. Possession of a dollar today is certain but the expectation of the same dollar in the future involves uncertainty. Perhaps the future dollar will never be paid. The third factor, inflation, reflects the fluctuation in price levels. With inflation, a dollar will not buy as much goods or services tomorrow as it does today (G. H. Sorter, M.J. Ingberman and H.M. Maximon, *Financial Accounting: An Events and Cash Flow Approach* (1990), at p. 14). The time-value of money is common knowledge and is one of the cornerstones of all banking and financial systems.

[23] Simple interest and compound interest each measure the time value of the initial sum of money, the principal. The difference is that compound interest reflects the time-value component to interest payments while simple interest does not. Interest owed today but paid in the future will have decreased in value in the interim just as the dollar example described in paras. 21-22. Compound interest compensates a lender for the decrease in value of all money which is due but as yet unpaid because unpaid interest is treated as unpaid principal.

[24] Simple interest makes an artificial distinction between money owed as principal and money owed as interest. Compound interest treats a dollar as a dollar and is therefore a more precise measure of the value of possessing money for a period of time. Compound interest is the norm in the banking and financial systems in Canada and the western world and is the standard practice of both the appellant and respondent.

(2) Contract Damages

. . .

(b) Restitution Damages

[30] The other side of the coin is to examine the effect of the breach on the defendant. In contract, restitution damages can be invoked when a defendant has, as a result of his or her own breach, profited in excess of his or her expected profit had the contract been performed but the plaintiff's loss is less than the defendant's gain. So the plaintiff can be fully paid his damages with a surplus left in the hands of the defendant. This occurs with what has been described as an efficient breach of contract. In some but not all cases, the defendant may be required to pay such profits to the plaintiff as restitution damages (Waddams, [*The Law of Damages*, 3rd ed. (Aurora, ON: Canada Law Book, 1997)], at p. 474).

[31] Courts generally avoid this measure of damages so as not to discourage efficient breach (i.e., where the plaintiff is fully compensated and the defendant is better off than if he or she had performed the contract) (Waddams, *supra*, at p. 473). Efficient breach is what economists describe as a Pareto optimal outcome where one party may be better off but no one is worse off, or expressed differently, nobody loses. Efficient breach should not be discouraged by the courts. This lack of disapproval emphasizes that a court will usually award money damages for breach of contract equal to the value of the bargain to the plaintiff.

II. CANADIAN LEGAL INHERITANCES

A. Law from History, Custom, and Tradition

The system, structure, and organization of laws and government in Canada were not created in a vacuum. Much of our current legal regime depends on the common law and a series of British imperial statutes, which were received into Canada upon its acquisition as a territorial possession of the British Crown. Quebec, given its French history and civil law origins, is different. Quebec remains a civil law jurisdiction, albeit one heavily influenced by the common law tradition. At the same time, it is important for a legal system to recognize that Canada was populated by aboriginal First Nations prior to its colonization by the European empires. Belatedly, aboriginal interests and concepts have emerged as a source of law in Canada.

In Canada, the transition between colonial law and full legal independence took place over a period of almost 200 years. A very brief review of that history will place this section in context.

After the British conquered New France on the Plains of Abraham (the Battle of Quebec), France ceded the land to Great Britain under the *Treaty of Paris, 1763*. The *Royal Proclamation of 1763* provided for the imposition of English law on the new colony, which altered the common law rule that in the case of conquest, the laws of the conquered state would prevail (see section II.A.2 below):

> Whereas We have taken into Our Royal Consideration the extensive and valuable Acquisitions in America, secured to our Crown by the late Definitive Treaty of Peace, concluded at Paris. the 10th Day of February last; and being desirous that all Our loving Subjects, as well of our Kingdom as of our Colonies in America, may avail themselves with all convenient Speed, of the great Benefits and Advantages which must accrue therefrom to their Commerce, Manufactures, and Navigation, We have thought fit, with the Advice of our Privy Council to issue this our Royal Proclamation, hereby to publish and declare to all our loving Subjects, that we have, with the Advice of our Said Privy Council, granted our Letters Patent, under our Great Seal of Great Britain, to erect, within the Countries and Islands ceded and confirmed to Us by the said Treaty, Four distinct and separate Governments, styled and called by the names of Quebec, East Florida, West Florida and Grenada, and limited and bounded as follows … .
>
> … And We have also given Power to the said Governors, with the consent of our Said Councils, and the Representatives of the People so to be summoned as aforesaid, to make, constitute, and ordain Laws, Statutes, and Ordinances for the Public Peace, Welfare, and good Government of our said Colonies, and of the People and Inhabitants thereof, as near as may be agreeable to the Laws of England, and under such Regulations and Restrictions as are used in other Colonies;

and in the mean Time, and until such Assemblies can be called as aforesaid, all Persons Inhabiting in or resorting to our Said Colonies may confide in our Royal Protection for the Enjoyment of the Benefit of the Laws of our Realm of England; … .

Just over ten years later, the British government recognized that they needed to address growing unrest over the imposition of British rule and laws. In 1774, therefore, the British Parliament enacted, as an imperial statute, the *Quebec Act, 1774*, 14 Geo. III, c. 83 (UK), which, among other provisions, restored civil law as the law of Quebec (a wide territory that included much of what is now Ontario), except for the English criminal law, which was retained.

Imperial statutes were statutes that applied in British colonies by virtue of their own force. They could only be amended by British Parliament. The position of imperial statutes was further clarified by the *Colonial Laws Validity Act, 1865*, 28 & 29 Vict. c. 63. It set forth that an imperial statute, defined as an act of the British Parliament, was deemed to extend and be made applicable to colonies only if the statute expressly or by necessary implication made that clear. The Act was intended to extend the powers of colonial legislatures by clarifying that only laws "repugnant" to an imperial statute would be void—all others would be allowed to stand. It also, however, left colonial legislatures unable to alter imperial statutes that applied.

In 1867, the colonies of British North America were joined in confederation and Canada became a self-ruling Dominion. The *British North America Act*, another imperial statute, created many of the systems of government that exist today (and is still one of Canada's main constitutional documents, now called the *Constitution Act, 1867*). However, some vestiges of the colonial past remained: in particular, the nature of the *Constitution Act, 1867* as an imperial statute meant that Canada could not amend its own constituting document, because s. 129 of the *Constitution Act, 1867* maintained the requirement from the *Colonial Laws Validity Act* that imperial statutes could only be altered by Parliament in Westminster. This requirement was subsequently lessened through the adoption of the *Statute of Westminster, 1931*, 22 & 23 Geo. V c. 4, which stated that no law made by the Parliament of the United Kingdom would apply to any of its dominions unless specifically requested and consented to by a dominion. It also repealed the *Colonial Laws Validity Act*, and granted to each dominion the power to repeal or amend imperial statutes. One anomaly remained—the *Constitution Act, 1867* was exempt from this provision, mainly in order to ensure that the nature of Canada as a federal system, with equal powers granted to the federal Parliament and the provincial legislatures, remained intact. Finally, in 1982, with the patriation of the Constitution, through the *Canada Act 1982* (UK), 1982, c. 11 and the *Constitution Act, 1982*, Canada's independence became complete.

(It is also worth noting that until 1949, Canadian judgments could be appealed to the Privy Council, which meant that for many years Canadian judges had to be especially cognizant of Privy Council and House of Lords decisions. This practice was abolished in 1949 with an amendment to the *Court Act*, 13 Geo. VI, 1949, 2nd Sess., c. 37, s. 2.)

With that background, the next section discusses law and aboriginal peoples before we turn to some basic concepts of civil and common law.

1. Law and Aboriginal Peoples

The term "aboriginal peoples" is used to refer to three major groups of indigenous people in Canada: the Indians, Inuit, and Métis. Aboriginal peoples are the descendants of the pre-European inhabitants of North America, believed to have ventured into the New World via the Bering Strait during the last ice age (with new evidence pointing to even earlier origins). Consequently, aboriginal people were inhabitants of what is today Canada long before the French and English colonizers.

At least some early Canadian cases recognized that the assumption of control by the British Crown during the colonial period did not automatically erase aboriginal legal systems. Thus, in *Connolly v. Woolrich* (1867), 17 RJRQ 75, Monk J upheld the validity of an 1803 marriage under Indian custom between an European and Indian, writing that the assertion of English sovereignty did not annul "the territorial rights, political organization, such as it was, or the laws and usages of the Indian tribes."

However, this approach did not prevail in subsequent Canadian case law, and being the original inhabitants of Canada has not conferred upon aboriginal peoples a legal status sufficient to protect their cultural, political, and economic rights throughout much of their history after colonization. The following excerpt from a UN report is apposite:

> Much of [aboriginal peoples'] land has been taken away and whatever land is left to them is subject to constant encroachment. Their culture and their social and legal institutions and systems have been constantly under attack at all levels, through the media, the law and the public education systems. It is only natural, therefore, that there should be resistance to further loss of their land and rejection of the distortion or denial of their history and culture and defensive/offensive reaction to the continual linguistic and cultural aggressions and attacks on their way of life, their social and cultural integrity and their very physical existence. They have a right to continue to exist, to defend their lands, to keep and to transmit their culture, their language, their social and legal institutions and systems and their ways of life, which have been illegally and unjustifiably attacked.

Martinez Cobo, United Nations Special Rapporteur, *Problems of Discrimination Against Indigenous Peoples*, UN Doc. E/CN.4/Sub.2/1983/21/add.8 at 49.

For years, there has been little or no place in our legal system for the original inhabitants. As explored below in greater detail, our laws, legal institutions, and constitutional arrangements, as commonly understood, come from Europe. This arises out of a debate as to what constitutes "law" and whether indigenous peoples in Canada practised law prior to European arrival. Some maintain that indigenous peoples in North America were "pre-legal." They believe that societies only possess laws if they are declared by some recognized power that is capable of enforcing such a proclamation (recall John Austin's legal positivism in I.B above). In this view, indigenous legal tradition is thus related to customary law, but not clothed with true legality. Even though indigenous peoples occupied the land first, the arguments as to their legal system often took the form that their laws and customs were too unfamiliar or too primitive to justify compelling European settlers to obey them. As Brian Slattery noted, over 25 years ago: "[All our] law-making bodies ultimately owe their authority to the British Parliament or British Crown. There are ... no indigenous laws, rights, legislatures or courts in Canada": see Brian Slattery, "The Hidden Constitution: Aboriginal Rights in Canada" (1984), 32 *Am.*

J Comp. Law 361. Now this is seen as a wilfully impoverished view of indigenous law; slowly, changes are occurring in conceptions of Canadian law.

For contemporary aboriginal law scholars, indigenous law is as diverse as any other: customary, positivistic, deliberative, and naturalistic (see John Borrows, *Canada's Indigenous Constitution* (Toronto: University of Toronto Press, 2010), at 13—the following account draws heavily from this work). The doctrine of reception (by which colonial laws are "received" into new territory—discussed in more detail at part II.A.2.a below) does not incorporate indigenous peoples' wisdom and learning. In formulating a colonial legal system, reception, as practised in the 18th and 19th centuries, negated most of the original inhabitants' laws and meanings. It is only very recently, in jurisprudence and in scholarly writings, where these wrongs have begun to be righted. As the Supreme Court stated in 1996 in *R v. Van der Peet*, [1996] 2 SCR 507, at para. 263:

> The history of the interface of Europeans and the common law with aboriginal peoples is a long one. As might be expected of such a long history, the principles by which the interface has been governed have not always been consistently applied. Yet running through this history, from its earliest beginnings to the present time is a golden thread—the recognition by the common law of the ancestral laws and customs of the aboriginal peoples who occupied the land prior to European settlement.

The Court has learned from recent scholarship; John Borrows is one of Canada's leading aboriginal scholars. He argues for a re-imagining of aboriginal law. For him, "Canada cannot presently, historically, legally, or morally claim to be built upon European-derived law alone. … If Indigenous laws are not recognized, we potentially construct Canadian law on a faulty premise that places Indigenous peoples lower on a 'scale of civilization' because of their non-European organization" (Borrows, *supra*, at 16).

The colonists did not discover Canada. Therefore, the Crown's laws should not entirely displace indigenous law. Reception was a legal fiction necessary to colonialism. This simple fact has been judicially recognized, but only relatively recently. The Supreme Court made note of it in 1973 in *Calder v. Attorney General (B.C.)*, [1973] SCR 313 at 328: "the fact is that when the settlers came, the Indians were there, organized in societies and occupying the land as their forefathers had done for centuries. This is what Indian title means and it does not help one in the solution of this problem to call it a 'personal or usufructuary right.'" The Court stated it much more bluntly in *Haida Nation v. British Columbia (Minister of Forests)*, [2004] 3 SCR 511, at para. 25: "[p]ut simply, Canada's Aboriginal peoples were here when Europeans came, and were never conquered."

Nevertheless, despite their potential to assist in providing ways of resolving pressing issues, indigenous laws have an uncertain status in Canada's formal legal system. In Canada, by virtue of s. 91(24) of the *Constitution Act, 1867*, the federal Parliament has power over "Indians" and "lands reserved for the Indians." Although it was originally conceived of as an important power to enable the federal government to protect "Indians" from exploitation by local settlers, the history of federal power, as contained in the *Indian Act*, RSC 1985, c. I-5, and elsewhere, is a history filled with missteps and wrong choices. For a good overview, see D. Jenness, *The Indians of Canada*, 6th ed. (Toronto: University of Toronto Press, 1963).

In 1982, with the patriation of the Constitution, aboriginal rights were constitutionally entrenched in s. 35 of the *Constitution Act, 1982*. The provision protects "existing aboriginal and treaty rights of the aboriginal peoples of Canada." Although the extent of these rights remains unsettled, the recognition and acknowledgement of aboriginal law and rights has come to the forefront of legal debate in Canada since this time.

A significant amount of jurisprudence in Canada expanding on aboriginal rights since 1982 has contributed to this debate. Although many economic, social, and health indicators continue to show that Canada's aboriginal peoples are much worse off than other Canadians, and the paternalistic nature of the *Indian Act* continues to control many aspects of their lives, the constitutionalization of aboriginal rights has restored at least some recognition of the aboriginal interests in Canadian law. Consider the following discussion in *Mitchell*.

Mitchell v. MNR
[2001] 1 SCR 911, 199 DLR (4th) 385, 83 CRR (2d) 1

McLACHLIN CJ: ...

What Is the Nature of Aboriginal Rights?

[9] Long before Europeans explored and settled North America, aboriginal peoples were occupying and using most of this vast expanse of land in organized, distinctive societies with their own social and political structures. The part of North America we now call Canada was first settled by the French and the British who, from the first days of exploration, claimed sovereignty over the land on behalf of their nations. English law, which ultimately came to govern aboriginal rights, accepted that the aboriginal peoples possessed pre-existing laws and interests, and recognized their continuance in the absence of extinguishment, by cession, conquest, or legislation. ... At the same time, however, the Crown asserted that sovereignty over the land, and ownership of its underlying title, vested in the Crown .... With this assertion arose an obligation to treat aboriginal peoples fairly and honourably, and to protect them from exploitation, a duty characterized as "fiduciary" in *Guerin v. The Queen*, [1984] 2 SCR 335.

[10] Accordingly, European settlement did not terminate the interests of aboriginal peoples arising from their historical occupation and use of the land. To the contrary, aboriginal interests and customary laws were presumed to survive the assertion of sovereignty, and were absorbed into the common law as rights, unless (1) they were incompatible with the Crown's assertion of sovereignty, (2) they were surrendered voluntarily via the treaty process, or (3) the government extinguished them: see B. Slattery, "Understanding Aboriginal Rights" (1987), 66 Can. Bar Rev. 727. Barring one of these exceptions, the practices, customs and traditions that defined the various aboriginal societies as distinctive cultures continued as part of the law of Canada. ...

[11] The common law status of aboriginal rights rendered them vulnerable to unilateral extinguishment, and thus they were "dependent upon the good will of the Sovereign." ... This situation changed in 1982, when Canada's constitution was amended to entrench existing aboriginal and treaty rights: *Constitution Act, 1982*, s. 35(1). The enactment of s. 35(1) elevated existing common law aboriginal rights to constitutional status (although, it is important to note, the protection offered by s. 35(1) also extends beyond the aboriginal rights

recognized at common law: *Delgamuukw v. British Columbia*, [1997] 3 SCR 1010, at para. 136). Henceforward, aboriginal rights falling within the constitutional protection of s. 35(1) could not be unilaterally abrogated by the government. However, the government retained the jurisdiction to limit aboriginal rights for justifiable reasons, in the pursuit of substantial and compelling public objectives.

The following excerpt from *Delgamuukw v. British Columbia* provides an overview of recent developments in the area of aboriginal rights in the context of aboriginal title to land.

Delgamuukw v. British Columbia
[1997] 3 SCR 1010, 153 DLR (4th) 193, 66 BCLR (3d) 285

LAMER CJ (Cory and Major JJ concurring):

I. Introduction

[1] This appeal is the latest in a series of cases in which it has fallen to this Court to interpret and apply the guarantee of existing aboriginal rights found in s. 35(1) of the *Constitution Act, 1982*. ... [T]his appeal raises a set of interrelated and novel questions which revolve around a single issue—the nature and scope of the constitutional protection afforded by s. 35(1) to common law aboriginal title. ...

II. Facts

[Lamer CJ reviewed the complicated facts giving rise to the dispute. In essence, the appellants, chiefs of the Gitksan or Wet'suwet'en tribes, claimed aboriginal title—that is, an interest in land that arises by virtue of an aboriginal group's historic association with those lands—over separate portions of 58,000 square kilometres in British Columbia. The province of British Columbia counterclaimed for a declaration that the appellants have no right or interest in the territory or, alternatively, that the appellants' cause of action ought to be for compensation from the government of Canada. He went on to discuss the decisions at trial and at the BC Court of Appeal and matters related to factual findings at trial.]

• • •

C. What Is the Content of Aboriginal Title, How Is It Protected by s. 35(1), and What Is Required for Its Proof?

• • •

(b) The Content of Aboriginal Title

• • •

[117] ... I have arrived at the conclusion that the content of aboriginal title can be summarized by two propositions: first, that aboriginal title encompasses the right to exclusive use and occupation of the land held pursuant to that title for a variety of purposes, which

need not be aspects of those aboriginal practices, customs and traditions which are integral to distinctive aboriginal cultures; and second, that those protected uses must not be irreconcilable with the nature of the group's attachment to that land. For the sake of clarity, I will discuss each of these propositions separately.

. . .

[124] ... [T]he content of aboriginal title is not restricted to those uses which are elements of a practice, custom or tradition integral to the distinctive culture of the aboriginal group claiming the right. However, nor does aboriginal title amount to a form of inalienable fee simple, as I will now explain.

(c) Inherent Limit: Lands Held Pursuant to Aboriginal Title Cannot Be Used in a Manner That Is Irreconcilable with the Nature of the Attachment to the Land Which Forms the Basis of the Group's Claim to Aboriginal Title

[125] The content of aboriginal title contains an inherent limit that lands held pursuant to title cannot be used in a manner that is irreconcilable with the nature of the claimants' attachment to those lands. This limit on the content of aboriginal title is a manifestation of the principle that underlies the various dimensions of that special interest in land—it is a *sui generis* interest that is distinct from "normal" proprietary interests, most notably fee simple.

[126] I arrive at this conclusion by reference to the other dimensions of aboriginal title which are *sui generis* as well. I first consider the source of aboriginal title. As I discussed earlier, aboriginal title arises from the prior occupation of Canada by aboriginal peoples. That prior occupation is relevant in two different ways: first, because of the physical fact of occupation, and second, because aboriginal title originates in part from pre-existing systems of aboriginal law. However, the law of aboriginal title does not only seek to determine the historic rights of aboriginal peoples to land; it also seeks to afford legal protection to prior occupation in the present-day. Implicit in the protection of historic patterns of occupation is a recognition of the importance of the continuity of the relationship of an aboriginal community to its land over time.

[127] I develop this point below with respect to the test for aboriginal title. The relevance of the continuity of the relationship of an aboriginal community with its land here is that it applies not only to the past, but to the future as well. That relationship should not be prevented from continuing into the future. As a result, uses of the lands that would threaten that future relationship are, by their very nature, excluded from the content of aboriginal title.

[128] Accordingly, in my view, lands subject to aboriginal title cannot be put to such uses as may be irreconcilable with the nature of the occupation of that land and the relationship that the particular group has had with the land which together have given rise to aboriginal title in the first place. As discussed below, one of the critical elements in the determination of whether a particular aboriginal group has aboriginal title to certain lands is the matter of the occupancy of those lands. Occupancy is determined by reference to the activities that have taken place on the land and the uses to which the land has been put by the particular group. If lands are so occupied, there will exist a special bond between the group and the land in question such that the land will be part of the definition of the group's

distinctive culture. It seems to me that these elements of aboriginal title create an inherent limitation on the uses to which the land, over which such title exists, may be put. For example, if occupation is established with reference to the use of the land as a hunting ground, then the group that successfully claims aboriginal title to that land may not use it in such a fashion as to destroy its value for such a use (e.g., by strip-mining it). Similarly, if a group claims a special bond with the land because of its ceremonial or cultural significance, it may not use the land in such a way as to destroy that relationship (e.g., by developing it in such a way that the bond is destroyed, perhaps by turning it into a parking lot).

[129] It is for this reason also that lands held by virtue of aboriginal title may not be alienated. Alienation would bring to an end the entitlement of the aboriginal people to occupy the land and would terminate their relationship with it. I have suggested above that the inalienability of aboriginal lands is, at least in part, a function of the common law principle that settlers in colonies must derive their title from Crown grant and, therefore, cannot acquire title through purchase from aboriginal inhabitants. It is also, again only in part, a function of a general policy "to ensure that Indians are not dispossessed of their entitlements": see *Mitchell v. Peguis Indian Band*, [1990] 2 SCR 85 at p. 133, 71 DLR (4th) 193. What the inalienability of lands held pursuant to aboriginal title suggests is that those lands are more than just a fungible commodity. The relationship between an aboriginal community and the lands over which it has aboriginal title has an important non-economic component. The land has an inherent and unique value in itself, which is enjoyed by the community with aboriginal title to it. The community cannot put the land to uses which would destroy that value.

· · ·

[131] Finally, what I have just said regarding the importance of the continuity of the relationship between an aboriginal community and its land, and the non-economic or inherent value of that land, should not be taken to detract from the possibility of surrender to the Crown in exchange for valuable consideration. On the contrary, the idea of surrender reinforces the conclusion that aboriginal title is limited in the way I have described. If aboriginal peoples wish to use their lands in a way that aboriginal title does not permit, then they must surrender those lands and convert them into non-title lands to do so.

[132] The foregoing amounts to a general limitation on the use of lands held by virtue of aboriginal title. It arises from the particular physical and cultural relationship that a group may have with the land and is defined by the source of aboriginal title over it. This is not, I must emphasize, a limitation that restricts the use of the land to those activities that have traditionally been carried out on it. That would amount to a legal strait-jacket on aboriginal peoples who have a legitimate legal claim to the land. The approach I have outlined above allows for a full range of uses of the land, subject only to an overarching limit, defined by the special nature of the aboriginal title in that land.

(d) Aboriginal Title Under s. 35(1) of the Constitution Act, 1982

[133] Aboriginal title at common law is protected in its full form by s. 35(1). This conclusion flows from the express language of s. 35(1) itself, which states in full: "[t]he *existing* aboriginal and treaty rights of the aboriginal peoples of Canada are hereby recognized and affirmed" (emphasis added). On a plain reading of the provision, s. 35(1) did not create

aboriginal rights; rather, it accorded constitutional status to those rights which were "exist-ing" in 1982. The provision, at the very least, constitutionalized those rights which aborigi-nal peoples possessed at common law, since those rights existed at the time s. 35(1) came into force. Since aboriginal title was a common law right whose existence was recognized well before 1982 (e.g., *Calder* [*v. Attorney-General of British Columbia*, [1973] SCR 313]), s. 35(1) has constitutionalized it in its full form.

. . .

(ii) The Test for the Proof of Aboriginal Title

[143] In order to make out a claim for aboriginal title, the aboriginal group asserting title must satisfy the following criteria: (i) the land must have been occupied prior to sover-eignty, (ii) if present occupation is relied on as proof of occupation pre-sovereignty, there must be a continuity between present and pre-sovereignty occupation, and (iii) at sover-eignty, that occupation must have been exclusive.

[La Forest J (L'Heureux-Dubé J concurring) and McLachlin J both rendered decisions con-curring with the basic reasoning of Lamer CJ.]

Canada is a legally pluralistic state: civil law, common law, and indigenous law each define ways of resolving disputes and organizing society. To John Borrows, this plurality does not arise from colonial rules of reception: "The validity of each legal tradition does not rest solely on its historic acceptance or how it is received by other traditions. The strength of a tradition [depends] on how well it develops and remains relevant under changing circumstances" (Borrows, at 8). The solution to the complexity of overlapping, pluralist legal systems that do not always align is, in Borrows' view, not to "abandon law," but to work toward changing our "interpretation" of law (at 20). The solution lies in working out the broad implications of treat-ies between indigenous peoples and the Crown where the impasse between competing legal theories can be overborne. As Borrows states at 20-21:

> Since First Nations legal traditions were the first laws of our countries and were not extinguished
> through discovery, occupation, prescription, or conquest, they could be viewed as retaining their
> force. Furthermore, when treaties are made they can be seen as creating an inter-societal frame-
> work in which first laws intermingle with Imperial laws to foster peace and order across
> communities.

It is in this kind of broad understanding regarding the nature and application of treaties where peaceful reception and intermingling of common law and civil law traditions within Canada could occur. We have, in a sense, all benefited from each other: European laws were (and will be) modified as much by indigenous laws through treaties as they were by the fact of transplantation to another continent. Treaties can be interpreted as a way to recognize indigenous traditions alongside European ones (see Borrows, at 21).

2. Canada's Common and Civil Law Traditions

a. Reception of European Law

Despite renewed recognition of indigenous interests in Canadian law, and calls for even further recognition by authors such as Borrows, it is still a fact that much of Canadian law stems from its European inheritance. Indeed, note how in the discussion on aboriginal rights above, the recent revival of aboriginal rights in modern Canada is characterized as a "common law" creation, or a product of constitutional changes by Canada's political bodies.

This observation raises a question: how were Canada's dominant common (and in Quebec, civil) law traditions "received" from their European origins? Not surprisingly, given the ultimate success of Britain in claiming suzerainty over northern North America, British concepts of "reception" determine the response to this question.

William Blackstone, in his *Commentaries on the Laws of England*, best summarized how colonial laws were to apply in the New World. The laws in force depended on whether colonies were simply settled, or were conquered or ceded by indigenous peoples. In the latter case, pre-existing laws of the indigenous sovereign remained in force, subject to modification or replacement by the Crown or Parliament where necessary to operate government. The English common law was to have little or no authority. In the case of settlement, by comparison, a legal vacuum existed that must be filled; some form of law was required to govern new colonies. In the case of British settlements, this was a mixture of common and statutory law: see "Introduction," sec. IV, in *Blackstone's Commentaries*, vol. 1 (London: Cavendish, 2001).

The Privy Council decision in *Cooper v. Stuart* highlights the basic principles surrounding the rules of reception. Lord Watson provides a general overview of how British colonies adopted English law. The case focused on the application of the common law "rule against perpetuities" (a property law rule designed to limit the duration of a condition imposed as part of the transfer of land) in New South Wales colony, now part of Australia.

Cooper v. Stuart
(1889), 14 App. Cas. 286 (PC)

LORD WATSON: In support of the second objection, it was maintained for the appellant, in the first place, that the English rule against perpetuities, as now settled, applied in all its entirety to the Colony of New South Wales in the year 1823; and, in the second place, that the rule, as established in the law of England, applies to reservations made by the Crown in the interests of the public.

. . .

It does not appear to their Lordships to be necessary, for the purposes of the present case, to decide whether the Crown, in attaching such reservations to grants of land in England, would be affected by the rule against perpetuities. In order to succeed in this appeal, it is not enough for the appellant to establish that the Crown would be within the rule here; he must also shew that the rule, in so far as it affects the Crown, was operative in the Colony of New

South Wales at the time when his land was originally granted to William Hutchinson; and that, in the opinion of their Lordships, he has failed to do.

The extent to which English law is introduced into a British Colony, and the manner of its introduction, must necessarily vary according to circumstances. There is a great difference between the case of a Colony acquired by conquest or cession, in which there is an established system of law, and that of a Colony which consisted of a tract of territory practically unoccupied, without settled inhabitants or settled law, at the time when it was peacefully annexed to the British dominions. The Colony of New South Wales belongs to the latter class. In the case of such a Colony the Crown may by ordinance, and the Imperial Parliament, or its own legislature when it comes to possess one, may by statute declare what parts of the common and statute law of England shall have effect within its limits. But, when that is not done, the law of England must (subject to well-established exceptions) become from the outset the law of the Colony, and be administered by its tribunals. In so far as it is reasonably applicable to the circumstances of the Colony, the law of England must prevail, until it is abrogated or modified, either by ordinance or statute. The often-quoted observations of Sir William Blackstone (1 Comm. 107) appear to their Lordships to have a direct bearing upon the present case. …

Blackstone, in that passage, was setting right an opinion attributed to Lord Holt, that all laws in force in England must apply to an infant Colony of that kind. If the learned author had written at a later date he would probably have added that, as the population, wealth, and commerce of the Colony increase, many rules and principles of English law, which were unsuitable to its infancy, will gradually be attracted to it; and that the power of remodelling its laws belongs also to the colonial legislature.

Their Lordships have not been referred to any Act or Ordinance declaring that the laws of England, or any portion of them, are applicable to New South Wales. There was no land law or tenure existing in the Colony at the time of its annexation to the Crown; and, in that condition of matters, the conclusion appears to their Lordships to be inevitable that, as soon as colonial land became the subject of settlement and commerce, all transactions in relation to it were governed by English law, in so far as that law could be justly and conveniently applied to them. …

Their Lordships have recently had occasion to consider, in *Jex v. McKinney and Others*, the authorities bearing upon the question of the suitability of English law to colonial circumstances. That case differed from the present in this respect, that there the law of England was introduced into the Colony by statute, and not by the silent operation of constitutional principles; but its introduction was qualified by words which excluded the application of laws prevailing here which were unsuitable in their nature to the needs of the Colony.

The rule against perpetuities, as applied to persons and gifts of a private character, though not finally settled in all its details, until a comparatively recent date, is, in its principle, an important feature of the common law of England. To that extent it appears to be founded upon plain considerations of policy, and, in some shape or other, finds a place in most, if not in all, complete systems of jurisprudence. Their Lordships see no reason to suppose that the rule, so limited, is not required in New South Wales by the same considerations which have led to its introduction here, or that its operation in that colony would be less beneficial than in England. The learned judges of the Supreme Court of the colony, in deciding this case, proceeded on the assumption that the rule applies there as between subject and subject; and their Lordships are of opinion that the assumption is well founded.

Assuming next (but for the purposes of this argument only) that the rule has, in England, been extended to the Crown, its suitability, when so applied, to the necessities of a young Colony raises a very different question. The object of the Government, in giving off public lands to settlers, is not so much to dispose of the land to pecuniary profit as to attract other colonists. It is simply impossible to foresee what land will be required for public uses before the immigrants arrive who are to constitute the public. Their prospective wants can only be provided for in two ways, either by reserving from settlement portions of land, which may prove to be useless for the purpose for which they are reserved, or by making grants of land in settlement, retaining the right to resume such parts as may be found necessary for the uses of an increased population. To adopt the first of these methods might tend to defeat the very objects which it is the duty of a colonial governor to promote; and a rule which rests on considerations of public policy cannot be said to be reasonably applied when its application may probably lead to that result.

Their Lordships have, accordingly, come to the conclusion that, assuming the Crown to be affected by the rule against perpetuities in England, it was nevertheless inapplicable, in the year 1823, to Crown grants of land in the Colony of New South Wales, or to reservations or defeasances in such grants to take effect on some contingency more or less remote, and only when necessary for the public good.

As this discussion and case suggest, the applicable rules of reception varied between conquered and "settled" colonies. In North America, the problem of determining which of these rules of reception would apply was compounded by two facts: (1) aboriginal peoples were already present, so true "settlement" in Blackstone's definition could not apply; and (2) France also had an interest in much of British North America, and claimed much of its territory. Indeed, much of modern day Ontario and Quebec were originally part of New France, which was then conquered by the English in 1759 and ceded by France in the *Treaty of Paris, 1763*.

In practice, the rule of conquest was applied to central Canada, and the rule on settlement everywhere else. Although this did not immediately occur—English law was initially imposed on the new colony of Quebec—the *Quebec Act, 1774* (14 Geo III, c. 83 (UK)) correctly restored the pre-conquest French civil law as the law of Quebec. Subsequently, the *Constitutional Act, 1791* (31 Geo. III, c. 31) divided Quebec into two provinces: English-speaking Upper Canada and French-speaking Lower Canada. After a short time, Upper Canada enacted legislation receiving the common law of England as the applicable legal code. In Lower Canada, except for criminal matters, the "Laws of Canada" applied in relation to "Property and Civil Rights"—that is, private law matters. The "Laws of Canada" meant the civil law of New France, which consisted mainly of the *Coutume de Paris* supplemented by Roman law, legislation, and canon laws. These various sources were codified in 1866 by the *Civil Code of Lower Canada*.

Meanwhile, the Maritimes and (when established) the western provinces were largely governed by the British common law. These regions were regarded as "settled" (as opposed to conquered) territories (an approach that ignored the aboriginal presence). As Peter Hogg notes:

> The settled classification entailed the automatic reception of English, not French law, a result that was congenial to the English population. In the case of the three maritime provinces, which as a matter of historical fact were acquired by cession from France, the possibility of the survival of French law seems never to have been seriously considered. The reception of English law into these provinces has often been explained on the patently false belief that they were "settled" colonies.

Constitutional Law of Canada (student ed.) (Toronto: Carswell, 2004), sec. 2.1, at 30-31.

The rules of reception dictated that the entire body of English law, both statutory and common, was imported into the settled colony. Local exceptions and variances were allowed where the received laws would be unsuitable to the circumstances of the colony. In the case of statute law, the date of reception was important because it was used to determine which English statutory law applied: all statutes passed prior to such date were automatically "received" (unless clearly unsuitable) and remained in force. Those passed after such date did not apply unless, expressly or by clear implication, they were intended to apply. Even a statute that was repealed in England after the reception date would still be in force in the colonies unless it was clearly intended to be repealed in a colony.

In Canada, the dates of reception of some provinces are not clearly marked because there was no obvious statutory source providing for the administration of a province or colony. For example, Ontario, British Columbia, and Alberta received the common law on September 17, 1792, November 19, 1858, and July 15, 1870, respectively, whereas Manitoba "received" the common law through the grant of "Rupert's Land" to the Hudson Bay Company on May 2, 1670, but subsequently adopted a statute fixing July 15, 1870 as the date of reception (see Bora Laskin, *The British Tradition in Canadian Law* (London: Stevens & Sons, 1969), at 7-8). (Compare also to Australia, where the British Parliament passed *An Act To Provide for the Administration of Justice in New South Wales and Van Diemen's Land* in 1828, which indicated July 28, 1828 as the cut-off date for New South Wales and Tasmania, and thus allowed starting points for the application of English law to Victoria, Queensland, Western Australia, and South Australia: see A. Castles, "The Reception and Status of English Law in Australia" (1963), 2 *Adel. LR* 1.) Thus, the courts became the arbiters of settlement dates for some provinces, and determined the date of statutory reception to be "the date of the institution of a local legislature in a colony": *Young v. Blaikie* (1822), 1 Nfld. LR 277, 283 (SC).

The date of reception for the common law was much less important. As discussed further below, common law decisions simply declared what had always been the law from time immemorial. Therefore, common law decisions operated retrospectively and applied to all colonies equally. Common law, as Blackstone also noted, is a universal, uniform set of principles and precepts. That the Judicial Committee of the Privy Council was the final court of appeal throughout the British Empire, and could ensure some measure of uniformity over the common law, aided this notion. Once a decision was made by either the Privy Council or the House of Lords on a common law principle, all common law jurisdictions, at least in the formative years, would accept that decision as binding.

b. *Nature of the Common and Civil Law*

As this discussion implies, the common law is an English invention. It is judge-made law, developed through the common law courts (as opposed to the Court of Chancery—see below). In its beginning, the common law did not consist of any written "laws" as we would understand them today, but was simply a collection of court decisions, not always written down. Two fundamental ideas permeate common law theory: (1) judges do not make the law but merely declare it; and (2) all relevant past decisions are considered as evidence of the law, and judges infer from these precedents what is the true law in a given instance. In strict terms, therefore, the common law is the law constructed out of a series of cases. Blackstone described it in this way:

> [I]t is an established rule to abide by former precedents, where the same points come again in litigation: as well to keep the scale of justice even and steady, and not liable to waver with every new judge's opinion; as also because the law in that case being solemnly declared and determined, what before was uncertain, and perhaps indifferent, is now become a permanent rule, which it is not in the breast of any subsequent judge to alter or vary from, according to his private sentiments: he being sworn to determine, not according to his private judgment, but according to the known laws and customs of the land; not delegated to pronounce a new law, but to maintain and expound the old one.

Blackstone, "Introduction," sec. III, in *Commentaries on the Laws of England*, vol. 1 (London: Cavendish, 2001), at 51.

Under this 18th century view, the common law is perceived as a set of fixed rules, unearthed by judges from cases through deductive legal reasoning, analogy, and application of precedent. Case law is then reported in volumes, approved and vetted by judges, which contain, in theory, all the given law up to that date.

Contemporary understanding of the common law has changed (as was shown in some of the legal theories discussed in section I). But some of the elegance and simplicity of it has remained. Although common law jurisdictions such as Canada no longer rely exclusively on case law—as this book makes plain in later chapters, statutory sources of law are ubiquitous in all provinces—it is largely true that cases remain a key source of law, while statutes are (at least traditionally) seen as incursions into the common law. This underlying methodology has shaped and continues to shape the thinking of common law lawyers and jurists.

On the other hand, Quebec inherited the vastly different legal tradition of the civil law. This following discussion on the "civilian" tradition is necessarily brief. For a more elaborate discussion on the civilian system in Quebec (and one on which the present discussion relies), see Julie Bedard, "Transsystemic Teaching of Law at McGill: Radical Changes, Old and New Hats" (2001), 27 *Queen's LJ* 237.

France, before the Revolution, was divided into provinces, each of which had its lawmaking parliament. Provinces of northern and central France were governed by customary laws, while the south of France was governed by written law, derived from the laws of old Rome.

From 1608 to 1664, the first colonists of New France followed the customary law that was in effect from their own province of origin in France. In 1664, the King of France decreed that the colony would be subject to the customary law of Paris, which ended the existing patchwork of laws. "Paris Custom" would serve as the main source of law throughout New France.

Later, authorities went on to add French law to the customary law, which included royal decrees and ordinances, canon law relating to marriages, and Roman law relating to obligations.

Despite its origin as customary law, the Custom of Paris was a codified system of law. It was first enacted in 1510, and revised in 1580. In its revised form, as first adopted in Quebec, it was divided into twelve titles, comprising nearly 300 sections. These existed in Quebec until the defeat of the French in 1759; when the British passed the *Quebec Act, 1774*, the provisions were reintroduced.

In 1866 the laws were codified into the *Civil Code of Lower Canada*. The Code's provisions were derived primarily from the judicial interpretations of the law that had been in force to that date in Lower Canada, although it was also inspired by some of the modernizations found in the 1804 Napoleonic code and the Louisiana Civil Code. At Confederation, the *Civil Code of Lower Canada* replaced most of the laws inherited from the Custom of Paris, but incorporated some elements of English law as it had been applied in Lower Canada, such as the English law of trusts.

What makes a civilian law different from a common law system? Unlike the English common law, civil law arises out of the Roman law of Justinian's *Corpus Juris Civilis*. The civil law is based not on cases but established laws, generally written as broad legal principles. It also includes doctrinal writings and interpretations written by learned scholars. This contrasts with the common law's judge-centred application of facts to uncovered legal rules.

Many civilian jurisdictions rely on civil codes; however, the difference between civil and common law lies more in their different methodological approaches as opposed to codification per se. In civil law countries, legislation is seen as the primary source of law. Judgments normally rely on the provisions of codes and statutes, from which solutions in particular cases are derived. Judicial reasoning is based extensively on the general principles of the rule or code. On the other hand, common law methodology, even where statutory sources of law are present, employs analogical reasoning from statutory provisions to fill gaps.

This "bijuralism" remains largely intact today. As a result, Canada is a mixed-law jurisdiction. This means that the British common law is the basis of private law in all provinces except Quebec. Canadian federal law, which applies in all provinces, also derives from the common law. Private law in Quebec, on the other hand, is based on the French civil law tradition. But due to the overwhelming influence of the common law, the Quebec legal system has many aspects of a common law jurisdiction.

Quebec's private law derives from its current manifestation of the *Civil Code*, its provincial statutes, and from federal private law. The *Civil Code of Quebec* reflects the bijural nature of Canada's legal systems: it relies on civil law jurisdictions such as France and Germany to preserve its civilian integrity, but marries that with common law rules to ensure better harmonization with the rest of Canada and the United States. Civilian law methodology therefore evolves within a larger common law institutional framework.

As examples, Quebec's legislative, judicial, executive, and administrative institutions and processes belong to the English tradition, while the content of many of its private laws are civilian based. The Quebec National Assembly is a law-making body that follows closely the parliamentary style of the English system. Quebec judges are not graduates of a school for the judiciary, as are their counterparts in most civilian jurisdictions, but are drawn from among practising lawyers as common law judges are. Quebec Superior Courts

are responsible for the administration of all laws, provincial and federal, whereas most civilian court systems are separated jurisdictionally into public and private disputes. Judges behave and perform in a common law style, as Bedard notes:

> Judicial decisions in Quebec are reported in the English rather than the French mode. Judges
> give individual opinions, and dissenting opinions are not only permitted but frequent. This is
> inconsistent with the civil law theory that there can only be one answer to a legal question as the
> logical outcome of deductive reasoning. The style of judgments is also much closer to that of
> English or American cases than of French cases. Although *stare decisis* is not part of Quebec law,
> court decisions are given considerable weight in judicial analysis.

Bedard, above, at 246.

All of this occurs within a context of an adversarial regime and procedural rules that
would be familiar to any common law lawyer in the rest of Canada. For a brief history of Canada and its dual legal systems, see G.P. Browne, ed., *Documents on the Confederation of British
North America* (Toronto: McClelland & Stewart, 1969) and Peter Hogg, *Constitutional Law of
Canada*, above.

c. The Operation of Common Law and Precedent

How does the common law work in practice? The law must have some stability and certainty.
The genius of the common law is that it makes adherence to legal principles established on
past cases a foundational principle that inevitably leads to a more or less stable and certain
legal structure. Reliance on past cases is called the principle of *stare decisis* (let the decision
stand) and is related to the doctrine of precedent. In common law systems, precedents are
usually made up of principles from previous cases; the principles, however, may arise from
the interpretation of a statute or constitutional provision, or through the common law reasoning employed by a previous judge or judges. *Stare decisis* is the formal term to describe
how the common law relies on precedent. The value of a precedent is connected to the level
of court from which it originates.

In common law systems, lawyers must pay careful attention to the rank of a court in the
judicial hierarchy for two reasons: first, because a higher ranking court is not bound to follow
the decision of a lower court and second, because some courts do not apply the rule of *stare
decisis* with respect to their own prior decisions.

The outward simplicity of the question of a court's ranking is made more complicated
because the hierarchy and the attitude of various courts have changed from time to time. For
example, as previously mentioned, appeals from Canadian courts to the Privy Council were
abolished in stages, starting with criminal appeals in 1933, and ending with all appeals in
1949. This means that decisions of the Privy Council during this period are binding on Canadian courts, but not after. In Ontario, from 1895 to 1931 there was a section of the *Judicature
Act* obliging a judge of the High Court not "to disregard or depart from a prior known decision of any other judge of co-ordinate authority on any question of law or practice without
his concurrence" (see, for example, RSO 1927, c. 88, s. 31(2)). Moreover, the Supreme Court of
Canada is now not bound by its own decisions or those of the Privy Council, although it was
in the past (see *Reference re Agricultural Products Marketing Act*, [1978] 2 SCR 1198 at 1257). In
sum, the current position for most courts in Canada is as follows:

- All Canadian courts, except the Supreme Court of Canada, are bound to follow a precedent of the Supreme Court of Canada and any pre-1949 decision of the Privy Council that has not been overruled by the Supreme Court of Canada. A minority opinion of the Supreme Court of Canada is, however, not binding.
- Provincial courts of appeal are not bound to follow a decision of the appellate court of another province.
- Provincial courts of appeal will generally be bound by their own prior decisions (in Ontario, if the liberty of the subject is involved or the prior decision was given *per incuriam*—inadvertently, without consideration of an applicable authority or statutory provision—then this rule may be relaxed: see *R v. Godedarov* (1974), 3 OR (2d) 23 (CA); appellate courts in certain other provinces, however, have allowed themselves greater freedom in overruling their own prior decisions (see Gerald L. Gall, *The Canadian Legal System*, 2nd ed. (Toronto: Carswell Legal Publications, 1983), at 220 and 226, and authorities cited therein).
- Provincial courts lower than the highest appellate court are bound to follow a decision of that province's appellate court.
- Provincial courts at any level are not bound by the decisions of the appellate courts of other provinces or by decisions of the Federal Court of Appeal.
- A decision of a court of coordinate jurisdiction is not binding; however, it is highly persuasive. This is because Canada's court system is unified under the Supreme Court of Canada and the presence of judicial comity, which is the respect that one court holds for the decisions of another.

(Adapted from Paul Perell, "Stare decisis and techniques of legal reasoning and legal argument" on *Best Guide to Canadian Legal Research*, http://legalresearch.org/docs/perell.html; accessed April 11, 2011.)

Precedent in law helps in categorization. Precedent economizes on information and minimizes idiosyncratic conclusions. It thus serves a variety of purposes: it aids in the stability and coherence of the law, making it more predictable; it provides fairness in decision making; it promotes efficiency and eliminates sources of error, such as judicial bias; and it fulfills a symbolic role by recognizing the relationship between courts and the legislature. It therefore has independent value.

The difficulty for lawyers is often determining which parts of a precedent are binding in subsequent cases. As Stephen Waddams notes:

> Not everything a judge says in the course of deciding a case can be binding on her successors, or the common law would have perished long before now from a surfeit of precedents. What is said to be binding is the "decision," but this is an ambiguous concept. The actual facts of the case never arise again in identical form. … A general rule is given that explains the result in the instant case and will apply to at least some other cases. It is this rule, called the *ratio decidendi* (reason of deciding) that is said to constitute the binding rule for purposes of precedent. Everything else that is said by the judge is called *obiter dicta* (things said by the way). In theory the *ratio decidendi* is binding on lower courts, but the *obiter dicta* are not.

Stephen Waddams, *Introduction to the Study of Law*, 5th ed. (Scarborough, ON: Carswell, 1997), at 75.

As Waddams further states (at 77):

> [T]here is no "true" *ratio decidendi* of a decision. The *ratio decidendi* of a case is only as wide as a subsequent court will concede it to be. This is not to say that the doctrine of *stare decisis* is meaningless. Sometimes a judge will find herself unable to distinguish a former case on any rationally acceptable ground. But the doctrine is a good deal less rigid than it might at first appear.

Every case has to be looked at from two points of view: (1) that of the narrowest rule that a subsequent unkind court will concede has been laid down, and (2) the widest rule that a later friendly court could use to support a more novel position: see Karl Llewellyn, *The Bramble Bush: On Our Law and Its Study* (Dobbs Ferry, NY: Oceana Publications, 1960), at 68.

An example illustrates these issues. In the Supreme Court of Canada case of *Seneca College v. Bhadauria*, [1981] 2 SCR 181 (a case concerned with whether the human rights regime set out in the Ontario *Human Rights Code* covers the entire field of anti-discrimination law, including common law actions for damages arising from discriminatory behaviour), Laskin CJ stated:

> For the foregoing reasons, I would hold that not only does the Code foreclose any civil action based directly upon a breach thereof but it also excludes any common law action based on an invocation of the public policy expressed in the [Ontario *Human Rights Code*]. The Code itself has laid out the procedures for vindication of that public policy, procedures which the plaintiff respondent did not see fit to use.

On a wide reading of Laskin CJ's reasoning, no claim based on a breach of the Ontario *Human Rights Code*, or the public policy found within it, is available to any future litigant (unless the Supreme Court of Canada decides to overrule itself). Consider the following excerpt from *Canada Trust Co. v. Ontario Human Rights Commission*. In it, Tarnopolsky JA takes a much narrower reading of *Bhadauria*—"distinguishing" that case and constraining it to its facts—in order to allow the claim for discrimination in the context of a trust claim. Do you find his reasoning satisfactory?

Canada Trust Co. v. Ontario Human Rights Commission
(1990), 74 OR (2d) 481 (CA)

[This case was concerned with whether the terms of a scholarship trust established in 1923 are contrary to public policy. If they are, the question then is whether the cy-près doctrine can be applied to preserve the trust. The terms of the trust restricted the scholarship funds to white Christians of British Nationality or British parentage.]

TARNOPOLSKY JA (concurring in result): … All these submissions can be summarized into three main issues:

1. Did McKeown J have jurisdiction to determine this matter or should he have deferred to the jurisdiction of the Ontario Human Rights Commission?

· · ·

Since 1971, the Ontario Human Rights Commission and its equivalents in the Provinces of Alberta and British Columbia, together with other bodies, have expressed concerns over conditions of eligibility to officials of the trustee. There are universities which, in the last ten years, have also complained or expressed concern to officers of the Foundation regarding eligibility requirements. Notwithstanding instances of this kind, the Foundation receives approximately 230 new and renewal applications annually.

Evidence was submitted to McKeown J to show that there exist in Ontario and elsewhere in Canada numerous educational scholarships which contain eligibility restrictions based on race, ancestry, place of origin, ethnic origin, citizenship, creed, sex, age, marital status, family status and handicap.

III. The Jurisprudence

(1) Jurisdiction—Human Rights Commission or Court?

The Ontario Human Rights Commission submitted that McKeown J should have deferred to the Commission to exercise its jurisdiction under the Human Rights Code, 1981 with respect to the complaint against the trustee that the Leonard Trust contravenes the Code. In considering this submission one must start with the following fundamental proposition offered by Dubin ACJO in *Blainey v. Ontario Hockey Assn.* (1986), 54 OR (2d) 513, at pp. 532-33:

> … [T]he Human Rights Code provides a comprehensive scheme for the investigation and ad-judication of complaints of discrimination. There is a very broad right of appeal to the Court from the ultimate determination of a board of inquiry constituted under the Human Rights Code. The procedure provided for in the Human Rights Code must first be pursued before resort can be made to the Court. This was so held in *Board of Governors of Seneca College v. Bhadauria*, [1981] 2 SCR 181, 124 DLR (3d) 193. … Chief Justice Laskin, speaking for the Court, stated at p. 183 SCR, pp. 194-5 DLR:
>
> > In my opinion, the attempt of the respondent to hold the judgment in her favour on the ground that a right of action springs directly from a breach of The Ontario Human Rights Code cannot succeed. The reason lies in the comprehensiveness of the Code in its administrative and adjudicative features, the latter including a wide right of appeal to the Courts on both fact and law.
>
> And at pp. 194-5 SCR, p. 203 DLR:
>
> > The view taken by the Ontario Court of Appeal is a bold one and may be commended as an attempt to advance the common law. In my opinion, however, this is foreclosed by the legislative initiative which overtook the existing common law in Ontario and established a different regime which does not exclude the courts but rather makes them part of the enforcement machinery under the Code.
> >
> > For the foregoing reasons, I would hold that not only does the Code foreclose any civil action based directly upon a breach thereof but it also excludes any common law action based on an invocation of the public policy expressed in the Code. The Code itself has laid out the procedures for vindication of that public policy, procedures which the plaintiff respondent did not see fit to use.

Nevertheless, although this may be taken as a starting proposition, I agree with McKeown J that in this case several factors militate towards the High Court, as the superior court of inherent jurisdiction in this province, assuming jurisdiction despite a complaint being filed with the Human Rights Commission with respect to the same subject-matter.

In the first place, the state of the law dealt with by this court and the Supreme Court of Canada in *Seneca College of Applied Arts and Technology v. Bhadauria*, [1981] 2 SCR 181 is in contrast with the situation in this case. In *Bhadauria* this court had attempted "to advance the common law" in filling a void by creating a new tort of discrimination. The Supreme Court held that not to be necessary because of the comprehensive scheme of the Ontario Human Rights Code, RSO 1970, c. 318 [later RSO 1980, c. 340]. Here, however, we are concerned with the administration of a trust, over which superior courts have had inherent jurisdiction for centuries and, in particular, with respect to charitable or public trusts. As noted at the beginning of this judgment, the trustee in this case applied to the High Court for advice and direction pursuant to the trust instrument itself as well as s. 60 of the *Trustee Act*.

Second, we are not concerned here with a typical proceeding under the Human Rights Code, 1981 in which an allegation of discrimination is brought against a respondent. The Commission's first mandate is to effect a settlement. However, the trustee has no authority, absent authorization of the trust deed or legislation or a court order, to enter into a settlement which would be contrary to the terms of the trust. Even if no settlement could be effected and a board of inquiry were to be appointed, there is serious question as to whether the board could grant an adequate remedy. Its remedial authority is governed by s. 40(1) of the Code. If a Code infringement is found, the board may, by order,

(a)   direct the party to do anything that, in the opinion of the board, the party ought to do to achieve compliance with this Act, both in respect of the complaint and in respect of future practices; and

(b)   direct the party to make restitution, including monetary compensation, for loss arising out of the infringement, and, where the infringement has been engaged in wilfully or recklessly, monetary compensation may include an award, not exceeding $10,000, for mental anguish.

These remedial powers do not appear to give the board of inquiry the power to alter the terms of the trust or declare it void. In any case, resort to a court would have to be made to determine authoritatively whether such power exists.

Finally, I agree with McKeown J that this is not a case where the fact-finding role of the Commission and a board of inquiry would be required. Even in *Bell v. Ontario Human Rights Commission*, [1971] SCR 756, 18 DLR (3d) 1, where some further fact-finding and, particularly, fact-verification might have been useful, Martland J, on behalf of the majority on the Supreme Court of Canada, quoted Lord Goddard in *R v. Tottenham and District Rent Tribunal; Ex parte Northfield (Highgate) Ltd.*, [1957] 1 QB 103, at p. 108, to the effect that:

... [W]here there is a clear question of law not depending upon particular facts—because there is no fact in dispute in this case—there is no reason why the applicants should not come direct to this court for prohibition. ...

Similarly, here, I agree with McKeown J that we are concerned with a question of law; there are no facts in dispute. The trustee is entitled to come to the superior court pursuant to s. 60 of the *Trustee Act* to seek advice and direction.

[Tarnopolsky JA invoked the cy-près doctrine to bring the trust into accord with public policy by removing all offensive restrictions, thus permitting it to remain a scholarship.]

d. Common Law and Equity

We have already examined our legal inheritances such as the British common law, the French civil law, and aboriginal systems of law. The term "common law" in those discussions was used in the wide sense to distinguish it from the civilian law systems. It was used to mean a system of law based primarily on judicial decisions. But "common law" has a variety of other "internal" meanings according to context. For instance, common law must sometimes be distinguished from the body of law produced from the Chancery court and known as equity.

Equity is formally defined as the body of law developed by the Court of Chancery prior to that court's dismantling—in most common law countries this was shortly after 1873. Courts of Chancery were originally separate from the common law courts. Thus, equity developed in tandem with the common law. Its original function was to provide a corrective to the perceived harshness of the common law. The equitable jurisdiction began as a fluid, pragmatic, conscience-based system of law, profoundly anti-formal and anti-establishment. Cases were decided according to the rules of equity and good conscience; there was no abstract, formal methodology and no strict doctrine of precedent.

This is not as strange an idea as it might seem. Some form of equity is probably necessary in any modern legal system. Law as a body of rules and principles is by its nature concerned with generalities—groups or classes of persons and events, rather than individuals and discrete happenings. Because of this, law sometimes fails to achieve adequate justice in the particular case. Equity is a supplementary system that allows for the exigencies of the special case. In its ideal form, its principles are more clearly tied to considerations of conscience, morality, and the conduct of particular persons than those of the law.

In Canada, equity has provided some of the more progressive decisions in the area of private law. Typically, matters falling within the equitable jurisdiction of Chancery courts included disputes relating to:

- property (trusts; married women's property; equitable rules related to transfer);
- contracts (remedies such as specific performance and injunctions; undue influence, mistake, and misrepresentation);
- procedure (set-off and account);
- guardianship; and
- commercial matters (fiduciary duties; subrogation and contribution).

In 1873, the administration of the equitable and common law systems was fused through the adoption of the judicature acts (copied shortly thereafter in Canadian jurisdictions). These acts ended the existence of the separate Chancery Court. Since then, equitable principles have continued to develop alongside common law principles: the rules of common law and equity are now applied concurrently in all superior courts, with equity prevailing in cases of conflict.

The modern view of the equitable jurisdiction is that of a body of rules, principles, maxims, and doctrines that originated in the Court of Chancery but that has continued to evolve and develop since its abolition. It is now simply part of our law. Equitable doctrines continue to exist, but they are referred to as equitable only because of historical accident, not because they are substantially different from common law doctrines. Nevertheless, these doctrines are important components of Canadian law in the 21st century, and reflect a continuing commitment to conscience and moral-based decision making. Furthermore, despite the fact that the bulk of equity jurisprudence arose in the private law realm, equitable principles are slowly making inroads into public law.

Re DeLaurier is an early example of a case in which the equitable doctrine of fiduciary was invoked to protect the religious upbringing of a child. Note how the court relies on equitable principles to interpret a statutory provision.

Re DeLaurier
[1934] SCR 149, 1 DLR 790

[Appellants applied in the Supreme Court of Ontario for the custody of their infant child Thelma, who, for about 10 years from early infancy, had been in the care of the respondents. The appellants were Roman Catholics and the respondents were Protestants and the child had become identified with the respondents' church. The application was dismissed, an appeal to the Court of Appeal for Ontario was dismissed, and an appeal was brought to the Supreme Court of Canada.]

HUGHES J: … The appellants rely strongly on section 24 of the *Infants Act*, RSO, 1927, chapter 186, which reads as follows:

> Nothing in this Act shall change the law as to the authority of the father in respect of the religious faith in which his child is to be educated.

Section 21 of the *Judicature Act*, RSO, 1927, chapter 88, provides as follows:

> In questions relating to the custody and education of infants, and generally in all matters in which there is any conflict or variance between the rules of equity and the rules of the common law with reference to the same matter, the rules of equity shall prevail.

In equity a principle was early established that the court might control or ignore the parental right but in so doing it should act cautiously, and should act in opposition to the parent only when judicially satisfied that the welfare of the child required that the parental right should be suspended or superseded.

In the present case, Mr. Justice Kerwin interviewed the infant and then dismissed the application of the appellants, and Mr. Justice McEvoy had some time before [he] dismissed a similar application after seeing the parties and hearing their evidence. The Court of Appeal affirmed these dismissals, and, as the orders of dismissal were in the nature of discretionary orders, I do not know on what principle this Court can now interfere. The appeal, therefore, should be dismissed with costs, against which should be set off the costs of the motion to quash the appeal fixed at $75.

CROCKET J: … One thing the evidence clearly shews—that Thelma has been completely out of touch with her natural parents for a period of now over ten years and that her mother has had no contact with her since a few weeks or at most a few months after her birth.

After a careful examination of the evidence and the learned trial judge's (Kerwin J) conclusion thereupon and the reasons he gives for his decision, we are satisfied that he in no manner disregarded the provisions of s. 24 of the Ontario *Infants Act*, upon which the appellants much rely. The effect of this section, no doubt, is that none of the provisions of that statute shall be deemed to alter whatever authority the father may otherwise by law possess as to the religious faith in which his child is to be educated. This authority, however wide it may have been at common law, must now be measured by the rules of equity, which in virtue of the express provisions of the *Judicature Act* prevail in Ontario as they do in England, and, in cases of this kind, recognize the welfare of the child as the predominant consideration. If the general welfare of the child requires that the father's rights in respect of the religious faith in which his offspring is to be reared, should be suspended or superseded, the courts in the exercise of their equitable jurisdiction have undoubted power to override them, as they have power to override all other parental rights, though in doing so they must act cautiously. …

Due consideration is, of course, to be given in all cases to the father's wishes but if the court is satisfied in any case upon a consideration of all the facts and circumstances, as shewn by the evidence, that the father's wishes conflict with the child's own best interests, viewed from all angles—material, physical, moral, emotional and intellectual as well as religious—then the father's wishes must yield to the welfare of the child.

In recent years, equitable principles have been adapted to public law circumstances. The equitable fiduciary obligation, long thought to apply only to private matters, has evolved into the public realm. In certain circumstances, as the next two excerpts show, the Crown may be under a fiduciary obligation to particular individuals or groups.

Guerin v. Canada
[1984] 2 SCR 335, 13 DLR (4th) 321, 59 BCLR 301

DICKSON J (Beetz, Chouinard, and Lamer JJ concurring): The question is whether the appellants, the Chief and Councillors of the Musqueam Indian Band, suing on their own behalf and on behalf of all other members of the Band, are entitled to recover damages from the federal Crown in respect of the leasing to a golf club of land on the Musqueam Indian Reserve. Collier J of the Trial Division of the Federal Court declared that the Crown was in breach of trust. He assessed damages at $10,000,000. The Federal Court of Appeal allowed a Crown appeal, set aside the judgment of the Trial Division and dismissed the action.

Before adverting to the facts, reference should be made to several of the relevant sections of the *Indian Act*, RSC 1952, c. 149, as amended. Section 18(1) provides in part that reserves shall be held by Her Majesty for the use of the respective Indian Bands for which they were set apart. Generally, lands in a reserve shall not be sold, alienated, leased or otherwise disposed of until they have been surrendered to Her Majesty by the Band for whose use and benefit in common the reserve was set apart (s. 37). A surrender may be absolute or qualified, conditional or unconditional (s. 38(2)). To be valid, a surrender must be made to Her Majesty, assented to by a majority of the electors of the Band, and accepted by the Governor in Council (s. 39(1)).

. . .

IV. Fiduciary Relationship

The issue of the Crown's liability was dealt with in the courts below on the basis of the existence or non-existence of a trust. In dealing with the different consequences of a "true" trust, as opposed to a "political" trust, Le Dain J noted that the Crown could be liable only if it were subject to an "equitable obligation enforceable in a court of law." I have some doubt as to the cogency of the terminology of "higher" and "lower" trusts, but I do agree that the existence of an equitable obligation is the *sine qua non* for liability. Such an obligation is not, however, limited to relationships which can be strictly defined as "trusts." As will presently appear, it is my view that the Crown's obligations vis-à-vis the Indians cannot be defined as a trust. That does not, however, mean that the Crown owes no enforceable duty to the Indians in the way in which it deals with Indian land.

In my view, the nature of Indian title and the framework of the statutory scheme established for disposing of Indian land places upon the Crown an equitable obligation, enforceable by the courts, to deal with the land for the benefit of the Indians. This obligation does not amount to a trust in the private law sense. It is rather a fiduciary duty. If however, the Crown breaches this fiduciary duty it will be liable to the Indians in the same way and to the same extent as if such a trust were in effect.

The fiduciary relationship between the Crown and the Indians has its roots in the concept of aboriginal, native or Indian title. The fact that Indian Bands have a certain interest in lands does not, however, in itself give rise to a fiduciary relationship between the Indians and the Crown. The conclusion that the Crown is a fiduciary depends upon the further proposition that the Indian interest in the land is inalienable except upon surrender to the Crown.

An Indian Band is prohibited from directly transferring its interest to a third party. Any sale or lease of land can only be carried out after a surrender has taken place, with the Crown then acting on the Band's behalf. The Crown first took this responsibility upon itself in the Royal Proclamation of 1763. It is still recognized in the surrender provisions of the *Indian Act*. The surrender requirement, and the responsibility it entails, are the source of a distinct fiduciary obligation owed by the Crown to the Indians. In order to explore the character of this obligation, however, it is first necessary to consider the basis of aboriginal title and the nature of the interest in land which it represents.

. . .

In [the political trust cases] the party claiming to be beneficiary under a trust depended entirely on statute, ordinance or treaty as the basis for its claim to an interest in the funds in question. The situation of the Indians is entirely different. Their interest in their lands is a pre-existing legal right not created by Royal Proclamation, by s. 18(1) of the *Indian Act*, or by any other executive order or legislative provision.

· · ·

Indians have a legal right to occupy and possess certain lands, the ultimate title to which is in the Crown. While their interest does not, strictly speaking, amount to beneficial ownership, neither is its nature completely exhausted by the concept of a personal right. It is true that the *sui generis* interest which the Indians have in the land is personal in the sense that it cannot be transferred to a grantee, but it is also true, as will presently appear, that the interest gives rise upon surrender to a distinctive fiduciary obligation on the part of the Crown to deal with the land for the benefit of the surrendering Indians. These two aspects of Indian title go together, since the Crown's original purpose in declaring the Indians' interest to be inalienable otherwise than to the Crown was to facilitate the Crown's ability to represent the Indians in dealings with third parties. The nature of the Indians' interest is therefore best characterized by its general inalienability, coupled with the fact that the Crown is under an obligation to deal with the land on the Indians' behalf when the interest is surrendered. Any description of Indian title which goes beyond these two features is both unnecessary and potentially misleading.

(c) The Crown's Fiduciary Obligation

The concept of fiduciary obligation originated long ago in the notion of breach of confidence, one of the original heads of jurisdiction in Chancery. In the present appeal its relevance is based on the requirement of a "surrender" before Indian land can be alienated.

The Royal Proclamation of 1763 provided that no private person could purchase from the Indians any lands that the Proclamation had reserved to them, and provided further that all purchases had to be by and in the name of the Crown, in a public assembly of the Indians held by the governor or commander-in-chief of the colony in which the lands in question lay. As Lord Watson pointed out in *St. Catherine's Milling [and Lumber Co. v. The Queen* (1888), 14 App. Cas. 46], at p. 54, this policy with respect to the sale or transfer of the Indians' interest in land has been continuously maintained by the British Crown, by the governments of the colonies when they became responsible for the administration of Indian affairs, and, after 1867, by the federal government of Canada. Successive federal statutes, predecessors to the present *Indian Act*, have all provided for the general inalienability of Indian reserve land except upon surrender to the Crown, the relevant provisions in the present Act being ss. 37-41.

The purpose of this surrender requirement is clearly to interpose the Crown between the Indians and prospective purchasers or lessees of their land, so as to prevent the Indians from being exploited. This is made clear in the Royal Proclamation itself, which prefaces the provision making the Crown an intermediary with a declaration that "great Frauds and Abuses have been committed in purchasing Lands of the Indians, to the great Prejudice of our Interests, and to the great Dissatisfaction of the said Indians … ." Through the confirmation in the *Indian Act* of the historic responsibility which the Crown has undertaken, to act on behalf of the Indians so as to protect their interests in transactions with third parties, Parliament has conferred upon the Crown a discretion to decide for itself where the Indians' best interests really lie. This is the effect of s. 18(1) of the Act.

This discretion on the part of the Crown, far from ousting, as the Crown contends, the jurisdiction of the courts to regulate the relationship between the Crown and the Indians, has the effect of transforming the Crown's obligation into a fiduciary one. Professor Ernest Weinrib maintains in his article "The Fiduciary Obligation" (1975), 25 UTLJ 1, at p. 7, that "the hallmark of a fiduciary relation is that the relative legal positions are such that one party is at the mercy of the other's discretion." ...

... [W]here by statute, agreement, or perhaps by unilateral undertaking, one party has an obligation to act for the benefit of another, and that obligation carries with it a discretionary power, the party thus empowered becomes a fiduciary. Equity will then supervise the relationship by holding him to the fiduciary's strict standard of conduct.

It is sometimes said that the nature of fiduciary relationships is both established and exhausted by the standard categories of agent, trustee, partner, director, and the like. I do not agree. It is the nature of the relationship, not the specific category of actor involved that gives rise to the fiduciary duty. The categories of fiduciary, like those of negligence, should not be considered closed. See, e.g. *Laskin v. Bache & Co. Inc.* (1971), 23 DLR (3d) 385 (Ont. CA), at p. 392; *Goldex Mines Ltd. v. Revill* (1974), 7 OR 216 (Ont. CA), at p. 224.

It should be noted that fiduciary duties generally arise only with regard to obligations originating in a private law context. Public law duties, the performance of which requires the exercise of discretion, do not typically give rise to a fiduciary relationship. As the "political trust" cases indicate, the Crown is not normally viewed as a fiduciary in the exercise of its legislative or administrative function. The mere fact, however, that it is the Crown which is obligated to act on the Indians' behalf does not of itself remove the Crown's obligation from the scope of the fiduciary principle. As was pointed out earlier, the Indians' interest in land is an independent legal interest. It is not a creation of either the legislative or executive branches of government. The Crown's obligation to the Indians with respect to that interest is therefore not a public law duty. While it is not a private law duty in the strict sense either, it is nonetheless in the nature of a private law duty. Therefore, in this *sui generis* relationship, it is not improper to regard the Crown as a fiduciary.

K.L.B. v. British Columbia
[2003] 2 SCR 403, 230 DLR (4th) 513, 18 BCLR (4th) 1

[The appellants suffered abuse in two successive foster homes. In the second home the appellants were also exposed to inappropriate sexual behaviour by the older adopted sons. On one occasion, K. was sexually assaulted by one of these young men. The trial judge found that the government had failed to exercise reasonable care in arranging suitable placements for the children and in monitoring and supervising these placements. She also found that the children had suffered lasting damage as a result of their stays in the two homes. She rejected the defence that the tort actions were barred by the BC *Limitation Act*. The Court of Appeal allowed the Crown's appeal. All three judges found that the appellants' claims were statute-barred, with the exception of K.'s claim for sexual assault. In addition, all three judges overturned the ruling that the government had breached its fiduciary duty to the children. The majority, however, upheld the trial judge's conclusion that the government was vicariously liable and in breach of a non-delegable duty of care in the placement and supervision of the children. The appellants appealed to the Supreme Court of Canada.]

McLACHLIN CJ: [1] This appeal raises the question of whether, and on what grounds, the government can be held liable for the tortious conduct of foster parents toward children whom the government has placed under their care. The appeal was heard together with *M.B. v. British Columbia*, [2003] 2 SCR 477, 2003 SCC 53, and *E.D.G. v. Hammer*, [2003] 2 SCR 459, 2003 SCC 52, which raise many of the same issues.

· · ·

III. Analysis

A. Is There Any Legal Basis on Which the Government Could Be Held Liable for the Harm That the Appellants Suffered in Foster Care?

[11] Three grounds of government liability were canvassed by the trial judge, and a fourth added by the Court of Appeal: (1) direct negligence by the government; (2) vicarious liability of the government for the tortious conduct of the foster parents; (3) breach of non-delegable duty by the government; and (4) breach of fiduciary duty by the government.

· · ·

4. Liability for Breach of Fiduciary Duty

[38] The parties to this case do not dispute that the relationship between the government and foster children is fiduciary in nature. This Court has held that parents owe a fiduciary duty to children in their care: *M. (K.) v. M. (H.)*, [1992] 3 SCR 6. Similarly, the British Columbia Court of Appeal has held that guardians owe a fiduciary duty to their wards: *B. (P.A.) v. Curry* (1997), 30 BCLR (3d) 1. The government, through the Superintendent of Child Welfare, is the legal guardian of children in foster care, with power to direct and supervise their placement. The children are doubly vulnerable, first as children and second because of their difficult pasts and the trauma of being removed from their birth families. The parties agree that, standing in the parents' stead, the Superintendent has considerable power over vulnerable children, and that his placement decisions and monitoring may affect their lives and well-being in fundamental ways.

[39] Where the parties disagree is over the content of the duty that this fiduciary relationship imposes on the government—over what actions and inactions amount to a breach of this duty. The appellants argue that the duty is simply to act in the best interests of foster children. The government, on the other hand, argues for a more narrowly defined duty—a duty to avoid certain harmful actions that constitute a betrayal of trust, of loyalty and of disinterest. For the reasons that follow, I conclude that the government's view must prevail.

[40] First a procedural point. Fiduciary duties arise in a number of different contexts, including express trusts, relationships marked by discretionary power and trust, and the special responsibilities of the Crown in dealing with aboriginal interests. Although the parties' view seemed to be that the Superintendent's fiduciary duty was a private law duty arising from the relationship between the Superintendent and the children, they also suggested

at times that it arose from the public law responsibilities imposed on the Superintendent by the *Protection of Children Act*. On the latter view, the Superintendent's fiduciary obligations would be closer to the fiduciary obligations of the Crown toward aboriginal peoples, which have been held to include a requirement of using due diligence in advancing particular interests of aboriginal peoples: *Wewaykum Indian Band v. Canada*, [2002] 4 SCR 245, 2002 SCC 79; *Blueberry River Indian Band v. Canada (Department of Indian Affairs and Northern Development)*, [1995] 4 SCR 344; *Guerin v. The Queen*, [1984] 2 SCR 335. In my opinion, this latter view of the Superintendent's fiduciary obligation cannot succeed. A fiduciary obligation to promote the best interests of foster children while in foster care cannot be implied from the statute, because the statute evinces a clear intent that these children be nurtured in a private home environment; and, as discussed above, this effectively eliminates the government's capacity to exercise close supervision in relation to the foster parents' day-to-day conduct. The statute could not, therefore, consistently imply that the Superintendent stands under a fiduciary duty to exercise due diligence in ensuring on a day-to-day basis that the foster children's best interests are promoted.

[41]   What, however, might the content of the fiduciary duty be if it is understood, instead, as a private law duty arising simply from the relationship of discretionary power and trust between the Superintendent and the foster children? In *Lac Minerals Ltd. v. International Corona Resources Ltd.*, [1989] 2 SCR 574, at pp. 646-47, La Forest J noted that there are certain common threads running through fiduciary duties that arise from relationships marked by discretionary power and trust, such as loyalty and "the avoidance of a conflict of duty and interest and a duty not to profit at the expense of the beneficiary." However, he also noted that "[t]he obligation imposed may vary in its specific substance depending on the relationship" (p. 646). Because such obligations will vary in their content depending on the nature of the relationship involved, we should determine the content of the obligation owed by the government to foster children by focussing on analogous cases. This suggests that in determining the content of the fiduciary obligation here at issue, we should focus generally on cases dealing with the relationship of children to caregivers, and more particularly on the relationship between parents (in whose stead the Superintendent stands) and their children.

· · ·

[50]   Returning to the facts of this case, there is no evidence that the government put its own interests ahead of those of the children or committed acts that harmed the children in a way that amounted to betrayal of trust or disloyalty. The worst that can be said of the Superintendent is that he, along with the social workers, failed properly to assess whether the children's needs and problems could be met in the designated foster homes; failed to discuss the limits of acceptable discipline with the foster parents; and failed to conduct frequent visits to the homes given that they were overplaced and had a documented history of risk (trial judgment, at para. 74). The essence of the Superintendent's misconduct was negligence, not disloyalty or breach of trust. There is no suggestion that he was serving anyone's interest but that of the children. His fault was not disloyalty, but failure to take sufficient care.

[51]   I would therefore uphold the Court of Appeal's conclusion that the government did not breach its fiduciary duty to the appellants.

Subsequent cases involving the Crown's treatment toward aboriginal peoples have cemented the finding of a fiduciary relationship outlined in *Guerin*. In other areas, there is still some uncertainty and the outer limits of Crown fiduciary responsibility remain untested. See, for example, *Authorson v. Canada (Attorney General)*, [2003] 2 SCR 40.

B. International Law

Discussions of Canadian law often ignore international law. This is an unfortunate oversight, given the increasing importance of international law in shaping Canadian domestic law. Consider the Law Commission's brief overview below of international law and its reception into Canadian domestic law.

Law Commission of Canada, *Crossing Borders: Law in a Globalized World*
(Ottawa: Government of Canada, 2006)

I. The Separate Species of Law

In the modern legal system, two different (and at times separate) species of law exist: international and domestic.

A. Domestic Law

Domestic law is the body of principle most people encounter most of the time. In Canada, domestic law exists as legislation enacted by the legislatures or made as regulations by the executives. Outside Québec, domestic law also comes in the form of the common law, an amorphous body of principle developed by common law courts through the application of precedent, and persisting most vigorously in the private law areas of torts, contracts and property. At the pinnacle of domestic law is constitutional law. In Canada, constitutional law comes in both written and unwritten forms. Written constitutional law is essentially entrenched legislation, incapable of amendment without special procedures, and given pre-eminence over conflicting statutory law. Unwritten constitutional law also has this primacy, but is the product of judicial decision-making.

B. International Law

International law also comes in different flavours. The two most significant sources of international law are treaties and "customary international law." Put simply, treaties are law-making contracts between states. When the treaty binds two states, it is known as a "bilateral" treaty. When it binds a larger number of states, it is called a "multilateral" treaty. There is no magic to the term "treaty." Treaties go by a variety of alternate names, including treaty, convention, covenant, protocol, agreement, charter, and statute. While there are historical reasons for the use of these terms, the international legal effect of a treaty does not vary according to the word used to describe it.

There are literally thousands of treaties, webbing the world together in a complicated pattern of bilateral and multilateral international legal obligations. Some constitute an exchange of promises between states as to how they will act on the international plane. They affect a state's foreign policy without necessitating changes to domestic law. Others require states to change their internal policies, practices and often laws in order to meet obligations set out in the treaty.

Customary international law is a very different concept. Treaties are binding on the states that are parties to them, and generally on no others. Customary international law binds all states, excepting only those that have been sufficiently persistent in rejecting it prior to its emergence as a binding norm. The content of a treaty is discerned from its text. Customary international law is much more amorphous. It is formed by general and universal state practice, undertaken by states with a sense of legal obligation (called *opinio juris*). When these two ingredients—state practice and the *opinio juris*—become sufficiently widespread among the states of the world (a threshold not clearly defined by international law), the practice in question is said to become legally binding as customary international law.

A commonly cited example is the *Universal Declaration of Human Rights*. Originally introduced as a resolution of the UN General Assembly in 1948, the Declaration was intended as a purely aspirational document, without legal force. It was, in other words, "soft" law, a concept discussed in greater detail below. Over time, however, a combination of state practice and an emerging view on the legally obligatory nature of the rights found in the document have prompted many to consider the Declaration customary international law, in whole or at least in part. In 1995, a Canadian minister reported that: "Canada regards the principles of the Universal Declaration of Human Rights as entrenched in customary international law binding on all governments." [Government of Canada, "Notes for an Address by the Honourable Christine Stewart, Secretary of State (Latin America and Africa) at the 10th Annual Consultation Between Non-Governmental Organizations and the Department of Foreign Affairs and International Trade," Ottawa, January 17, 1995.]

. . .

III. International Law as Part of Canadian Law

[F]or the most part, the executive branch of the federal government negotiates treaties and other international instruments on behalf of Canada. Once a treaty is signed and ratified, Canada is bound and must comply with it or risk being found in contravention. The government must ensure that domestic law does not run counter to international law. How does international law interact with domestic law? The answer depends on the source of the international law: does it come from treaties or from customary law?

A. Receiving Treaties into Domestic Law and Questions of Legitimacy

1. "Dualism" and the Separate Solitudes of Domestic and International Law

Canada traditionally considers domestic law and treaty law as two distinct universes. By approaching these two spheres of law as separate solitudes, Canada is a "dualist" jurisdiction. An international treaty may require Canada, as a matter of international law, to change its domestic law. But in the dualist tradition, that treaty has no direct effect in domestic law until domestic legislation is passed to "transform" or "implement" it into Canadian law.

2. Dualism as a Rational Reaction to Democratic Legitimacy Questions in International Law-Making

At one level, dualism is a sensible philosophy. It seems a necessary response to the Canadian system, where Parliament and the provincial legislatures are supposed to make laws but where the federal executive branch dominates treaty-making. If treaties entered into by the federal executive had immediate and direct effect as the laws of Canada, the government's treaty-making power could enable the executive to do an end-run around Parliament's federal law-making monopoly. By concluding an international treaty requiring, for instance, extended patent protection, the executive would essentially legislate a matter otherwise governed by an Act of Parliament, in this case the *Patent Act*. In this way, the executive would short-circuit Parliament's supremacy in law-making.

Moreover, if treaties had immediate effect as laws, the federal executive could also dance around the division of powers in the *Constitution Act, 1867* by employing its treaty-signing powers to legislate in provincial areas.

To avoid these problems, Canadian law insists that treaties be transformed into domestic federal law by an Act of Parliament. In constitutional law, when a treaty deals with provincial matters, it is the provincial legislatures who must legislate the treaty into domestic law. Put another way, dualism responds to concerns about the democratic legitimacy of the treaty-making process by factoring elected legislatures back into the equation.

3. The Dualist Dilemma

Dualism may be driven by legitimate concerns. It does, however, create real problems. When Parliament fails to implement treaty law into domestic law the result is an unfortunate legal quandary: Canada is bound by the treaty as a matter of international law, and yet its policy-makers need not abide by the treaty under the terms of domestic law. This problem is remedied if the federal government delays ratification until Parliament and the provincial legislatures revise laws to bring them into compliance with the anticipated international obligation. There are, however, instances where Canada's domestic laws remain unmodified, even as new treaties are ratified.

Subsequently, when legislators become sensitive to allegations of non-compliance with Canada's international obligations, they will enact legislation transforming treaty obligations into domestic law. But in so doing, federal and provincial legislators must curb their discretion and implement an agreement ratified only by the federal executive branch. Little practical room remains for a legislator intent on observing Canada's international obligations to query, amend or reject a bill implementing an international obligation.

In summary, when the federal government exercises its power to conclude an international treaty, Parliament and provincial legislatures may face a dilemma in cases where the law is not consistent with the treaty. They may choose to disregard that international obligation, preserving their supreme law-making role in Canadian democracy at the potential cost of Canada's adherence to an international rule of law. Alternatively, they may implement these international requirements into domestic law, but with their role limited to stamping "approved" onto a treaty concluded exclusively by the federal executive branch. As globalization increases, this dilemma will become progressively more acute.

· · ·

B. Customary International Law Reception and Legitimacy

1. The Incorporation of Customary International Law

Canada's approach to customary international law is very different from its "dualist" treaty reception doctrines. Once a rule becomes recognized as customary law, it is *automatically* part of the Canadian common law. With customary international law, in other words, Canada is a "monist" rather than a "dualist" jurisdiction.

But, like the rest of the common law, directly-incorporated customary international law can always be displaced or overturned by a statute that is inconsistent with it. The Ontario Court of Appeal recently summarized the rule this way: "customary rules of international law are directly incorporated into Canadian domestic law unless explicitly ousted by contrary legislation. So far as possible, domestic legislation should be interpreted consistently with those obligations." [*Bouzari v. Iran* (2004), 71 OR (3d) 675, at paras. 65-66 (CA). See also *Jose Pereira E Hijos S.A. v. Canada (Attorney General)*, [1997] 2 FC 84, at para. 20 (TD).]

2. Issues Raised by the Incorporation of Customary International Law

Several obvious issues are raised by this approach. First, when a legislature *does* legislate in a manner that displaces customary international law, Canada may be subsequently in violation of its international obligations.

Second, if customary international law is part of the *common law* of Canada, its existence as domestic law is a matter determined by the courts exclusively. This customary international law is itself created by the international system in an organic rather than negotiated fashion. If customary international law is subsequently incorporated directly into Canadian law by the courts, there may never be any clear and direct input by political branches of government into the rules by which law in Canada is made binding.

On a third, related point, since the content of customary international law is sometimes uncertain (and disputed), courts asked to apply it as the domestic law of Canada rely on expert testimony (often competing) from international lawyers and academics, raising further questions of legitimacy.

But how offensive these last two phenomena are to Canada's democratic order may be debated. Certainly, the common law tradition in Canada accepts that courts should have a law-making role, applying a domestic law developed by judges and not legislators. Is this tradition suddenly illegitimate when judges rely on outside experts to guide their deliberations?

C. Statutory Law

1. Introduction

As noted in previous sections, much of early English law developed through the accumulation of case law and the interpretation of judges, as opposed to being set out in legislation. In essence, this is the definition of the common law. Whole areas of law, particularly those studied in the first year of law school, such as contracts, torts, and property, have developed largely from common law rules. There has been little in the way of statutory law to effect changes in these areas.

Parliament and provincial legislatures are free, however, to enact new statutes to displace the common law. They are also free to develop policy in entirely new directions, not by replacing or modifying the common law, but by enacting statutes in undeveloped areas. In modern states, many areas of law are almost wholly controlled by statutory enactments. Later chapters of this book focus on statutes and the rules that govern them. In this introduction, we simply make a few key points about the relationship between statutes and the common law.

2. Statutes and the Common Law: A Complex Mix

One basic principle of common law interpretation is that a statutory rule will supersede a judge-made rule. This is relatively easy to apply in many situations. For example, where a court interprets a rule banning "vehicles" from a public park so as not to include baby carriages, and a legislature then passes a new provision defining "vehicles" expressly to include baby carriages, the prior court decision is no longer valid. But the theory may be more difficult to apply where the statutory scheme does not expressly overturn a common law rule, or where the common law ventures into new territories.

The interplay among common law, statutory law, and constitutional law can be complex. Consider the issue of same-sex marriage, a subject of contemporary debate around the world. As a result of the decision by the Supreme Court of Canada in the *Reference re Same-Sex Marriage Act*, [2004] 3 SCR 698, and the ensuing legislation, the *Civil Marriage Act*, SC 2005, c. 33, it is now legal everywhere in Canada for persons to marry someone of the same sex.

This recent shift in policy overcomes a century or more of common and civil law tradition—the definition of marriage as the union of one man and one woman was a common law rule that applied in all the common law provinces; in Quebec, the heterosexual definition was implicit in the 1866 *Civil Code of Lower Canada* and became explicit when new civil code provisions were confirmed by federal legislation as recently as 2001.

The impetus for the modern changes allowing same-sex marriage arose piecemeal, through a series of constitutional cases that began by establishing equal benefits for homosexual couples. See, for example *M. v. H.*, [1999] 2 SCR 3 and *Egan v. Canada*, [1995] 2 SCR 513. Then, in the early part of the 2000s, a trilogy of cases in British Columbia, Ontario, and Quebec challenged the heterosexual definition of marriage itself as a breach of the *Canadian Charter of Rights and Freedoms*: *EGALE Canada Inc. v. Canada*, [2001] 95 BCLR; *Halpern v. Canada (Attorney General)* (2003), 65 OR (3d) 161; *Hendricks v. Quebec* (2004), 238 DLR (4th) 577 (QCCA); aff'g. [2002] RDF 1022 (QCSC). The following excerpt from *Halpern v. Canada (Attorney General)* gives a brief glimpse into the intricate relationship between custom, common law, civil law, and constitutional law that exists in contemporary Canada.

Halpern v. Canada (Attorney General)
(2003), 65 OR (3d) 161, 172 OAC 276, 225 DLR (4th) 529 (CA)

BY THE COURT (McMurtry CJO, MacPherson and Gillese JJA):

A. Introduction

[1] The definition of marriage in Canada, for all of the nation's 136 years, has been based on the classic formulation of Lord Penzance in *Hyde v. Hyde and Woodmansee* (1866), LR 1 P & D 130, [1861-73] All ER Rep. 175 at p. 177 All ER, p. 133 P & D: "I conceive that marriage, as understood in Christendom, may for this purpose be defined as the voluntary union for life of one man and one woman, to the exclusion of all others." The central question in this appeal is whether the exclusion of same-sex couples from this common law definition of marriage breaches ss. 2(a) or 15(1) of the *Canadian Charter of Rights and Freedoms* (the "Charter") in a manner that is not justified in a free and democratic society under s. 1 of the Charter.

[2] This appeal raises significant constitutional issues that require serious legal analysis. That said, this case is ultimately about the recognition and protection of human dignity and equality in the context of the social structures available to conjugal couples in Canada.

[3] In *Law v. Canada (Minister of Employment and Immigration)*, [1999] 1 SCR 497, 170 DLR (4th) 1, at p. 530 SCR, Iacobucci J, writing for a unanimous court, described the importance of human dignity:

> Human dignity means that an individual or group feels self-respect and self-worth. It is concerned with physical and psychological integrity and empowerment. Human dignity is harmed by unfair treatment premised upon personal traits or circumstances which do not relate to individual needs, capacities, or merits. It is enhanced by laws which are sensitive to the needs, capacities, and merits of different individuals, taking into account the context underlying their differences. Human dignity is harmed when individuals and groups are marginalized, ignored, or devalued, and is enhanced when laws recognize the full place of all individuals and groups within Canadian society.

[4] The *Ontario Human Rights Code*, RSO 1990, c. H.19, also recognizes the importance of protecting the dignity of all persons. The preamble affirms that "the inherent dignity and the equal and inalienable rights of all members of the human family is the foundation of freedom, justice and peace in the world." It states:

> [I]t is public policy in Ontario to recognize the dignity and worth of every person and to provide for equal rights and opportunities without discrimination that is contrary to law, and having as its aim the creation of a climate of understanding and mutual respect for the dignity and worth of each person so that each person feels a part of the community and able to contribute fully to the development and well-being of the community and the Province[.]

[5] Marriage is, without dispute, one of the most significant forms of personal relationships. For centuries, marriage has been a basic element of social organization in societies around the world. Through the institution of marriage, individuals can publicly express their love and commitment to each other. Through this institution, society publicly recognizes expressions of love and commitment between individuals, granting them respect and

legitimacy as a couple. This public recognition and sanction of marital relationships reflect society's approbation of the personal hopes, desires and aspirations that underlie loving, committed conjugal relationships. This can only enhance an individual's sense of self-worth and dignity.

[6] The ability to marry, and to thereby participate in this fundamental societal institution, is something that most Canadians take for granted. Same-sex couples do not; they are denied access to this institution simply on the basis of their sexual orientation.

[7] Sexual orientation is an analogous ground that comes under the umbrella of protection in s. 15(1) of the Charter: see *Egan v. Canada*, [1995] 2 SCR 513, 124 DLR (4th) 609, and *M. v. H.*, [1999] 2 SCR 3, 171 DLR (4th) 577. As explained by Cory J in *M. v. H.* at pp. 52-53 SCR:

> In *Egan* ... this Court unanimously affirmed that sexual orientation is an analogous ground to those enumerated in s. 15(1). Sexual orientation is "a deeply personal characteristic that is either unchangeable or changeable only at unacceptable personal costs" (para. 5). In addition, a majority of this Court explicitly recognized that gays, lesbians and bisexuals, "whether as individuals or couples, form an identifiable minority who have suffered and continue to suffer serious social, political and economic disadvantage" (para. 175, per Cory J; see also para. 89, per L'Heureux-Dubé J).

[8] Historically, same-sex equality litigation has focused on achieving equality in some of the most basic elements of civic life, such as bereavement leave, health care benefits, pensions benefits, spousal support, name changes and adoption. The question at the heart of this appeal is whether excluding same-sex couples from another of the most basic elements of civic life—marriage—infringes human dignity and violates the Canadian Constitution.

B. Facts

(1) The Parties and the Events

[9] Seven gay and lesbian couples (the "Couples") want to celebrate their love and commitment to each other by getting married in civil ceremonies. In this respect, they share the same goal as countless other Canadian couples. Their reasons for wanting to engage in a formal civil ceremony of marriage are the same as the reasons of heterosexual couples. By way of illustration, we cite the affidavits of three of the persons who seek to be married:

[Affidavits omitted.]

[10] The Couples applied for civil marriage licences from the Clerk of the City of Toronto. The Clerk did not deny the licences but, instead, indicated that she would apply to the court for directions, and hold the licences in abeyance in the interim. The Couples commenced their own application. By order dated August 22, 2000, Lang J transferred the Couples' application to the Divisional Court. The Clerk's application was stayed on consent.

[11] In roughly the same time frame, the Metropolitan Community Church of Toronto ("MCCT"), a Christian church that solemnizes marriages for its heterosexual congregants, decided to conduct marriages for its homosexual members. Previously, MCCT had felt

constrained from performing marriages for same-sex couples because it understood that the municipal authorities in Toronto would not issue a marriage licence to same-sex couples. However, MCCT learned that the ancient Christian tradition of publishing the banns of marriage was a lawful alternative under the laws of Ontario to a marriage licence issued by municipal authorities: see *Marriage Act*, RSO 1990, c. M.3, s. 5(1).

· · ·

[14] In compliance with the laws of Ontario, MCCT submitted the requisite documentation for the two marriages to the Office of the Registrar General: see *Vital Statistics Act*, RSO 1990, c. V.4, s. 19(1) and the Regulations under the *Marriage Act*, RRO 1990, Reg. 738, s. 2(3). The Registrar refused to accept the documents for registration, citing an alleged federal prohibition against same-sex marriages. As a result, MCCT launched its application to the Divisional Court.

· · ·

C. Issues

[25] We frame the issues as follows:

(1) What is the common law definition of marriage? Does it prohibit same-sex marriages? (2) Is a constitutional amendment required to change the common law definition of marriage, or can a reformulation be accomplished by Parliament or the courts? (3) Does the common law definition of marriage infringe MCCT's rights under ss. 2(a) and 15(1) of the Charter? (4) Does the common law definition of marriage infringe the Couples' equality rights under s. 15(1) of the Charter? (5) If the answer to question 3 or 4 is "Yes," is the infringement saved by s. 1 of the Charter? (6) If the common law definition of marriage is unconstitutional, what is the appropriate remedy and should it be suspended for any period of time?

D. Analysis

[26] Before turning to the issues raised by the appeal, we make four preliminary observations.

[27] First, the definition of marriage is found at common law. The only statutory reference to a definition of marriage is found in s. 1.1 of the *Modernization of Benefits and Obligations Act*, SC 2000, c. 12, which provides:

1.1 For greater certainty, the amendments made by this Act do not affect the meaning of the word "marriage," that is, the lawful union of one man and one woman to the exclusion of all others.

[28] The *Modernization of Benefits and Obligations Act* is the federal government's response to the Supreme Court of Canada's decision in *M. v. H.* The Act extends federal benefits and obligations to all unmarried couples that have cohabited in a conjugal relationship for at least one year, regardless of sexual orientation. As recognized by the parties, s. 1.1 does not purport to be a federal statutory definition of marriage. Rather, s. 1.1 simply affirms that the Act does not change the common law definition of marriage.

[29] Second, it is clear and all parties accept that, the common law is subject to Charter scrutiny where government action or inaction is based on a common law rule: see *British*

Columbia Government Employees' Union v. British Columbia (Attorney General), [1988] 2 SCR 214, 53 DLR (4th) 1; *R v. Swain*, [1991] 1 SCR 933, 63 CCC (3d) 481; *R v. Salituro*, [1991] 3 SCR 654, 8 CRR (2d) 173; and *Hill v. Church of Scientology of Toronto*, [1995] 2 SCR 1130, 126 DLR (4th) 129. Accordingly, there is no dispute that the AGC was the proper respondent in the applications brought by the Couples and MCCT, and that the common law definition of marriage is subject to Charter scrutiny.

• • •

(1) The Common Law Rule Regarding Marriage

[35] The preliminary argument on this appeal advanced by the Couples is that there is no common law bar to same-sex marriages. The intervener Egale Canada Inc. ("Egale") supported this argument and expanded on the Couples' submissions.

[36] As previously mentioned, the classic formulation of marriage is found in the English decision of *Hyde v. Hyde and Woodmansee*, "the voluntary union for life of one man and one woman, to the exclusion of all others." Egale argues that *Hyde and Corbett v. Corbett*, [1970] 2 All ER 33 (PDA), the other English case cited as authority for the common law restriction against same-sex marriage, have a weak jurisprudential foundation and ought not to be followed. Egale points out that *Hyde* dealt with the validity of a potentially polygamous marriage, and argues that the comments in *Hyde* about marriage being between opposite-sex persons are obiter. With respect to Corbett, Egale argues that it is based on outdated, narrow notions of sexual relationships between women and men. The Couples adopt Egale's submissions, and further argue that *M. v. H.* overruled, by implication, any common law restriction against same-sex marriages.

[37] In our view, the Divisional Court was correct in concluding that there is a common law rule that excludes same-sex marriages. This court in *Iantsis v. Papatheodorou*, [1971] 1 OR 245 at p. 248, 15 DLR (3d) 53, adopted the *Hyde* formulation of marriage as the union between a man and a woman. This understanding of the common law definition of "marriage" is reflected in s. 1.1 of the *Modernization of Benefits and Obligations Act*, which refers to the definition of "marriage" as "the lawful union of one man and one woman to the exclusion of all others." Further, there is no merit to the submission that *M. v. H.* overruled, by implication, the common law definition of "marriage." In *M. v. H.*, Iacobucci J stated, at p. 83:

> This appeal does not challenge traditional conceptions of marriage, as s. 29 of the [*Family Law Act*, RSO 1990, c. F.3] expressly applies to unmarried opposite-sex couples. That being said, I do not wish to be understood as making any comment on marriage or indeed on related issues.

(2) Constitutional Amendment

[38] The *Constitution Act, 1867* divides legislative powers relating to marriage between the federal and provincial governments. The federal government has exclusive jurisdiction over "Marriage and Divorce": s. 91(26). The provinces have exclusive jurisdiction over the solemnization of marriage: s. 92(12).

[39] The intervenor, The Association for Marriage and the Family in Ontario (the "Association"), takes the position that the word "marriage," as used in the *Constitution Act,*

1867, is a constitutionally entrenched term that refers to the legal definition of marriage that existed at Confederation. The Association argues that the legal definition of marriage at Confederation was the "union of one man and one woman." As a constitutionally entrenched term, this definition of marriage can be amended only through the formal constitutional amendment procedures. As a consequence, neither the courts nor Parliament have jurisdiction to reformulate the meaning of marriage.

• • •

[41] In our view, the Association's constitutional amendment argument is without merit for two reasons. First, whether same-sex couples can marry is a matter of capacity. There can be no issue, nor was the contrary argued before us, that Parliament has authority to make laws regarding the capacity to marry. Such authority is found in s. 91(26) of the *Constitution Act, 1867*.

[42] Second, to freeze the definition of marriage to whatever meaning it had in 1867 is contrary to this country's jurisprudence of progressive constitutional interpretation. This jurisprudence is rooted in Lord Sankey's words in *Edwards v. AG Canada*, [1930] AC 124, [1929] All ER Rep. 571 (PC) at p. 136 AC: "The *British North America Act* planted in Canada a living tree capable of growth and expansion within its natural limits." Dickson J reiterated the correctness of this approach to constitutional interpretation in *Hunter v. Southam Inc.*, [1984] 2 SCR 145, 11 DLR (4th) 641, at p. 155 SCR:

> The task of expounding a constitution is crucially different from that of construing a statute. A statute defines present rights and obligations. It is easily enacted and as easily repealed. A constitution, by contrast, is drafted with an eye to the future. Its function is to provide a continuing framework for the legitimate exercise of governmental power and, when joined by a Bill or a Charter of Rights, for the unremitting protection of individual rights and liberties. Once enacted, its provisions cannot easily be repealed or amended. It must, therefore, be capable of growth and development over time to meet new social, political and historical realities often unimagined by its framers. The judiciary is the guardian of the constitution and must, in interpreting its provisions, bear these considerations in mind.

[43] In *Constitutional Law of Canada*, looseleaf (Scarborough: Carswell, 1997) at 15-43 to 15-44, Professor Peter W. Hogg explained that Canada has changed a great deal since Confederation, and "[t]he doctrine of progressive interpretation is one of the means by which the *Constitution Act, 1867* has been able to adapt to the changes in Canadian society."

• • •

[46] In our view, "marriage" does not have a constitutionally fixed meaning. Rather, like the term "banking" in s. 91(15) and the phrase "criminal law" in s. 91(27), the term "marriage" as used in s. 91(26) of the *Constitution Act, 1867* has the constitutional flexibility necessary to meet changing realities of Canadian society without the need for recourse to constitutional amendment procedures.

[The court found that the common law definition of "marriage" infringed the claimants' rights under s. 15(1) of the Charter and this definition was not saved by s. 1 of the Charter.]

• • •

[156] To remedy the infringement of these constitutional rights, we:

(1) declare the existing common law definition of marriage to be invalid to the extent that it refers to "one man and one woman";

(2) reformulate the common law definition of marriage as "the voluntary union for life of two persons to the exclusion of all others";

(3) order the declaration of invalidity in (1) and the reformulated definition in (2) to have immediate effect;

(4) order the Clerk of the City of Toronto to issue marriage licences to the Couples; and

(5) order the Registrar General of the Province of Ontario to accept for registration the marriage certificates of Kevin Bourassa and Joe Varnell and of Elaine and Anne Vautour.

In the aftermath of *Halpern*, the federal government decided to accept the result reached by the Ontario Court of Appeal and thus did not seek leave to appeal to the Supreme Court of Canada. Two intervenors, the Association for Marriage and the Family in Ontario and the Interfaith Coalition on Marriage and the Family, tried to have the Supreme Court hear an appeal; however, their motion for leave to appeal was quashed by the court on October 10, 2003.

In July 2003 the federal government produced a draft bill that would redefine marriage. Before proceeding with the introduction of the bill in Parliament, the government decided to refer four questions regarding its validity to the Supreme Court of Canada. The court handed down its decision in *Reference re Same-Sex Marriage Act*, [2004] 3 SCR 698, upholding the bill and effectively allowing for same-sex marriages in all provinces. It is now proclaimed as the *Civil Marriage Act*, SC 2005, c. 33. The Act allows for same-sex marriage while ensuring religious freedom by allowing officials of religious groups to refuse to perform same-sex marriages if doing so would be contrary to their religious beliefs.

CHAPTER THREE

Recurring Constitutional Principles in Canadian Public Law

The animating thesis of this chapter is the idea that the best way to understand the meaning and significance of public law is to come to grips with a few foundational principles that underlie the structure of public law. These principles derive both from the text of Canada's Constitution and from the logic of its design. The useful thing about these foundational principles is that they can be consistently relied upon: once we define them and establish their boundaries in relation to each other, we can count on them to point us in the right direction to answering real world legal problems. They are the closest thing we have to touchstones in the seemingly ever-shifting world of legal interpretation and argument. In the Canadian legal system, one will not hear a court saying things such as "here we have an exception to the principle of the rule of law," or "constitutional supremacy does not apply in these circumstances." The principles apply, and they provide explanations.

Public law concerns the relationship between the state and civil society. Private persons may only create legal rights and duties between each other on the basis of consent. The state, on the other hand, may impose obligations on private persons without their individual consent. It does so as the holder of all authoritative power in society. That the state holds all legitimate power is a form of guarantee that individuals and corporate persons cannot exercise arbitrary power over one another. Nevertheless, in a society governed by the rule of law, the state itself may not act arbitrarily. To be legitimate, the state must act in accordance with law established by democratic institutions. The starting point in assessing the legitimacy of state action—and its adherence to "the rule of law"—is the constitution.

A constitution establishes a foundation for the rule of law in two ways. First, it establishes 1) *who* can make the ordinary law of the land, and also spells out any *limits* on the content of the ordinary law. In Canada, the division of powers found primarily in ss. 91 and 92 of the *Constitution Act, 1867* identifies which level of legislature is empowered to make ordinary statutory law. The *Charter of Rights and Freedoms* is an important source of constitutional limits on what statutes may prescribe. In these ways the Constitution acts as a "rule of recognition," a way of identifying what is legitimate and binding law in society.

Second, a constitution establishes the governing relationships between the institutions 2) or branches of the state that perform the functions needed to make law effective in society. It is often said that under our constitutional system the role of the legislature is to make law, the role of the judiciary is to interpret the law, and the role of the executive is to implement the law. Although generally accurate, this classic formulation oversimplifies the actual nature of these institutional relationships in Canada.

These two functions or purposes of a constitution—to act as a rule of recognition, and to establish the relationships between branches of the state—describe the overall shape of this chapter. Section I of the chapter addresses the nature of Canada's Constitution and the principles of "rule of law" and "constitutional supremacy." These are starting places for understanding constitutional law—the area of legal studies concerned with how state power is circumscribed and regulated by the Constitution.

Section II deals with how public power is exercised under the Constitution by the legislative, executive, and judicial branches of the Canadian state. The relationships between these three branches are characterized by a number of constitutional principles. While these principles form part of Canada's constitutional framework, they are also crucial to our understanding of the exercise of lawful public authority, which is the central concern of "administrative law." Constitutional and administrative law comprise the two major elements of public law.

Section III concerns the issue of how the Constitution itself can be amended. While a constitution serves its purposes by providing a stable grounding for the making, changing, and administering of ordinary law, it must also be capable of adapting to the changing nature and conditions of the society it purports to govern. As it happens, the question of how to allow for constitutional amendment has long been one of the most troubled areas of Canadian law and politics.

This chapter is presented through brief explanatory comments intended to give an overview of each of the constitutional principles being discussed, followed by excerpts drawn from leading judicial decisions. One case has pride of place in this presentation. In *Reference re Secession of Quebec*, [1998] 2 SCR 217, the Supreme Court of Canada provided a mini-treatise on the nature of Canadian constitutionalism, in the context of the most fundamental question any political community can face: whether and how it can be broken up. The *Secession Reference* touches on several of the themes discussed in this chapter. For that reason, portions of this unanimous judgment appear in different sections of the chapter.

The *Secession Reference* is known for having established the importance of "unwritten principles of the Constitution" as part of Canadian law. In its judgment, the court identified four unwritten principles—federalism, democracy, constitutionalism and the rule of law, and protection of minority rights. This chapter does not strictly track the court's discussion of those four principles. Rather, the intention is to set out and elaborate principles derived from Canada's constitutional history and structure that help to explain the shape and operation of public law in Canada. Six principles help to provide this explanation and are discussed in the course of the chapter. The six principles, along with brief definitions, are as follows:

- *Rule of law*—All exercises of legitimate public power must have a source in law, and every state official or agency is subject to constraint of the law.
- *Constitutional supremacy*—The Constitution is the supreme law of the society, and any ordinary law that is inconsistent with the Constitution is of no force or effect.
- *Separation of powers*—Public power is exercised through three institutional branches at the federal and provincial levels—the legislature, the executive, and the judiciary—and each branch carries out its functions in a distinct manner.

- *Parliamentary supremacy*—Subject to the Constitution, the legislative branch of the state is the holder of all legitimate public power and may enact any ordinary statute law and delegate any of its power as it deems fit.
- *Federalism*—Legislative sovereignty in Canada is divided between a national legislature, or Parliament, and provincial legislatures, according to a division of law-making powers or jurisdictions set out in the Constitution.
- *Judicial independence*—The judicial branch of the state must have a sufficient degree of institutional independence from the legislative and executive branches of the state in order to perform its constitutional law functions.

These recurring constitutional principles frame many of the public law issues analyzed more closely elsewhere in this volume. However, the constitutional foundations of Canadian public law are not easily grasped in isolation and are best understood as forming an integrated whole, whereby the principles work together and complement one another. Consequently, a number of the cases that follow have relevance to more than one or two of the issues referred to in the chapter and should be approached with that in mind.

I. CONSTITUTIONALISM IN CANADA

A. What Comprises the Constitution of Canada?

We commonly think of Canada as having a written constitution, embodied in two documents produced at distinct historical moments: the *Constitution Act, 1867* and the *Constitution Act, 1982*. The principal achievement of the 1867 Act is federalism: the division of legislative powers between a national Parliament and the legislatures of the provinces. The division of powers is largely effected through the listing of federal and provincial areas of jurisdiction in ss. 91 and 92, respectively, of the *Constitution Act, 1867*. The 1982 Act is primarily known for the *Canadian Charter of Rights and Freedoms* ("the Charter"), which guarantees a set of individual and minority rights. The Charter, however, is only one part of the *Constitution Act, 1982*, which also deals with aboriginal rights, equalization, and constitutional amendment.

Importantly, the *Constitution Act, 1982* provides an express definition of the Constitution and its legal status. Sections 52(1) and (2) of Act read:

> 52(1) The Constitution of Canada is the supreme law of Canada, and any law that is inconsistent with the provisions of the Constitution is, to the extent of the inconsistency, of no force or effect.
>
> (2) The Constitution of Canada includes
>> (a) the *Canada Act 1982*, including this Act;
>> (b) the Acts and orders referred to in the schedule; and
>> (c) any amendment to any Act or order referred to in paragraph (a) or (b).

By using the word "includes," s. 52(2) contemplates that the Constitution may comprise more elements than are stated in that section. In fact, the list in s. 52(2) is understood to refer only to the *text* of the Canadian Constitution—that is, its written components.

The two principal sources of unwritten constitutional norms are what are known as "constitutional conventions" and "unwritten principles of the Constitution." While these two concepts both refer to unwritten norms, they differ in important respects, including the purposes they serve, their legal status, and how they are derived or recognized. The longer-standing of these concepts, that of constitutional conventions, will be discussed first.

The British Constitution, a wholly unwritten construct, has long been understood to include certain conventions or customs that govern the workings and interaction of the branches of the state. In stating in the preamble to the *Constitution Act, 1867* that Canada was to have "a Constitution similar in Principle to that of the United Kingdom," the framers of Canada's Constitution signalled their intention to adopt those same conventions, and indeed the very concept of conventions, from British theory and practice.

The Supreme Court of Canada's clearest and most influential statement on the nature of conventions in Canada's constitutional framework is found in *Re Resolution to amend the Constitution* (the "*Patriation Reference*"), a cased decided in the midst of a constitutional crisis. In 1981, the federal government of Prime Minister Trudeau decided to pursue amendment and patriation of the Constitution on the basis of an agreement with only two of the ten provinces, Ontario and New Brunswick. The eight provinces opposed to the agreement (the "Gang of Eight") sought a court ruling that this unilateral proposal to amend the Constitution breached a convention of the Constitution. A majority of the Supreme Court agreed. In doing so, the majority made the following findings about the nature and effect of conventions of the Constitution:

1. Conventions come into existence on the basis of three factors:
   a. a practice or agreement developed by political actors;
   b. a recognition by political actors that they are bound to follow the convention; and
   c. the existence of a normative reason—that is, a purpose—for the convention. (In the *Patriation Reference* itself, the majority located a normative reason for a convention of "substantial provincial agreement" in the federal nature of Canadian democracy.)

2. Although part of the Constitution, conventions are *not* "law," and as such *cannot be enforced by the courts*. They acquire and retain their binding force by agreement, and ultimately in the realm of politics. However, courts may recognize a convention.

The Patriation Reference
[1981] 1 SCR 753

MARTLAND, RITCHIE, DICKSON, BEETZ, CHOUINARD, and LAMER JJ: The second question in the *Manitoba Reference* [(1981), 117 DLR (3d) 1] and *Newfoundland Reference* [(1981), 118 DLR (3d) 1] is the same:

> 2. Is it a constitutional convention that the House of Commons and Senate of Canada will not request Her Majesty the Queen to lay before the Parliament of the United Kingdom of Great Britain and Northern Ireland a measure to amend the Constitution of Canada affecting federal-provincial relationships or the powers, rights or privileges granted or secured by the Constitution of Canada to the provinces, their legislatures or governments without first obtaining the agreement of the provinces?

· · ·

The Nature of Constitutional Conventions

A substantial part of the rules of the Canadian constitution are written. They are contained not in a single document called a constitution but in a great variety of statutes some of which have been enacted by the Parliament at Westminster, such as the *British North America Act, 1867,* 1867 (UK), c. 3 (the *BNA Act*), or by the Parliament of Canada, such as *The Alberta Act, 1905* (Can.), c. 3, *The Saskatchewan Act, 1905* (Can.), c. 42 … .

Another part of the Constitution of Canada consists of the rules of the common law. These are rules which the courts have developed over the centuries in the discharge of their judicial duties. An important portion of these rules concerns the prerogative of the Crown. …

The common law provides that the authority of the Crown includes for instance the prerogative of mercy or clemency [*Reference as to the Effect of the Exercise of the Royal Prerogative of Mercy upon Deportation Proceedings*, [1933] SCR 269] and the power to incorporate by charter so as to confer a general capacity analogous to that of a natural person [*Bonanza Creek Gold Mining Co. v. The King*, [1916] 1 AC 566]. … It is also under the prerogative and the common law that the Crown appoints and receives ambassadors, declares war, concludes treaties and it is in the name of the Queen that passports are issued.

Those parts of the Constitution of Canada which are composed of statutory rules and common law rules are generically referred to as the law of the constitution. In cases of doubt or dispute, it is the function of the courts to declare what the law is and since the law is sometimes breached, it is generally the function of the courts to ascertain whether it has in fact been breached in specific instances and, if so, to apply such sanctions as are contemplated by the law, whether they be punitive sanctions or civil sanctions such as a declaration of nullity. Thus, when a federal or a provincial statute is found by the courts to be in excess of the legislative competence of the legislature which has enacted it, it is declared null and void and the courts refuse to give effect to it. In this sense it can be said that the law of the constitution is administered or enforced by the courts.

But many Canadians would perhaps be surprised to learn that important parts of the constitution of Canada, with which they are the most familiar because they are directly involved when they exercise their right to vote at federal and provincial elections, are nowhere to be found in the law of the constitution. For instance it is a fundamental requirement of the constitution that if the opposition obtains the majority at the polls, the government must tender its resignation forthwith. But fundamental as it is, this requirement of the constitution does not form part of the law of the constitution.

It is also a constitutional requirement that the person who is appointed prime minister or premier by the Crown and who is the effective head of the government should have the support of the elected branch of the legislature; in practice this means in most cases the leader of the political party which has won a majority of seats at a general election. Other ministers are appointed by the Crown on the advice of the prime minister or premier when he forms or reshuffles his cabinet. Ministers must continuously have the confidence of the elected branch of the legislature, individually and collectively. Should they lose it, they must either resign or ask the Crown for a dissolution of the legislature and the holding of a general election. Most of the powers of the Crown under the prerogative are exercised only upon the advice of the prime minister of the cabinet which means that they are effectively exercised by the latter, together with the innumerable statutory powers delegated to the Crown in council.

Yet none of these essential rules of the constitution can be said to be a law of the constitution. It was apparently Dicey who, in the first edition of his *Law of the Constitution*, in 1885, called them the "conventions of the constitution" (see W.S. Holdsworth, "The Conventions of the Eighteenth Century Constitution" (1932), 17 Iowa Law Rev. 161), an expression which quickly became current. What Dicey described under these terms are the principles and rules of responsible government, several of which are stated above and which regulate the relations between the Crown, the prime minister, the cabinet and the two Houses of Parliament. These rules developed in Great Britain by way of custom and precedent during the nineteenth century and were exported to such British colonies as were granted self-government.

Dicey first gave the impression that constitutional conventions are a peculiarly British and modern phenomenon. But he recognized in later editions that different conventions are found in other constitutions. As Sir William Holdsworth wrote (*supra*, at p. 162):

> In fact conventions must grow up at all times and in all places where the powers of government are vested in different persons or bodies—where in other words there is a mixed constitution. "The constituent parts of a state," said Burke [French Revolution, 28], "are obliged to hold their public faith with each other, and with all those who derive any serious interest under their engagements, as much as the whole state is bound to keep its faith with separate communities." Necessarily conventional rules spring up to regulate the working of the various parts of the constitution, their relations to one another, and to the subject.

. . .

A federal constitution provides for the distribution of powers between various legislatures and governments and may also constitute a fertile ground for the growth of constitutional conventions between those legislatures and governments. It is conceivable for instance that usage and practice might give birth to conventions in Canada relating to the holding of federal-provincial conferences, the appointment of lieutenant governors, the reservation and disallowance of provincial legislation. It was to this possibility that Duff CJ alluded when he referred to "constitutional usage or constitutional practice" in *Reference re Disallowance and Reservation of Provincial Legislation* [[1938] SCR 71], at p. 78. He had previously called them "recognized constitutional conventions" in *Wilson v. Esquimalt and Nanaimo Railway Co.* [[1922] 1 AC 202], at p. 210.

The main purpose of constitutional conventions is to ensure that the legal framework of the constitution will be operated in accordance with the prevailing constitutional values or principles of the period. For example, the constitutional value which is the pivot of the conventions stated above and relating to responsible government is the democratic principle: the powers of the state must be exercised in accordance with the wishes of the electorate; and the constitutional value or principle which anchors the conventions regulating the relationship between the members of the Commonwealth is the independence of the former British colonies.

Being based on custom and precedent, constitutional conventions are usually unwritten rules. Some of them, however, may be reduced to writing and expressed in the proceedings and documents of imperial conferences, or in the preamble of statutes such as the *Statute of Westminster, 1931*, or in the proceedings and documents of federal–provincial conferences. They are often referred to and recognized in statements made by members of governments.

The conventional rules of the constitution present one striking peculiarity. In contradistinction to the laws of the constitution, they are not enforced by the courts. One reason for this situation is that, unlike common law rules, conventions are not judge-made rules. They are not based on judicial precedents but on precedents established by the institutions of government themselves. Nor are they in the nature of statutory commands which it is the function and duty of the courts to obey and enforce. Furthermore, to enforce them would mean to administer some formal sanction when they are breached. But the legal system from which they are distinct does not contemplate formal sanctions for their breach.

Perhaps the main reason why conventional rules cannot be enforced by the courts is that they are generally in conflict with the legal rules which they postulate and the courts are bound to enforce the legal rules. The conflict is not of a type which would entail the commission of any illegality. It results from the fact that legal rules create wide powers, discretions and rights which conventions prescribe should be exercised only in a certain limited manner, if at all.

· · ·

Whether the Convention Exists

It was submitted by counsel for Canada, Ontario and New Brunswick that there is no constitutional convention, that the House of Commons and Senate of Canada will not request Her Majesty the Queen to lay before the Parliament at Westminster a measure to amend the Constitution of Canada affecting federal-provincial relationships, etc., without first obtaining the agreement of the provinces.

It was submitted by counsel for Manitoba, Newfoundland, Quebec, Nova Scotia, British Columbia, Prince Edward Island and Alberta that the convention does exist, that it requires the agreement of all the provinces and that the second question in the Manitoba and Newfoundland References should accordingly be answered in the affirmative.

Counsel for Saskatchewan agreed that the question be answered in the affirmative but on a different basis. He submitted that the convention does exist and requires a measure of provincial agreement. Counsel for Saskatchewan further submitted that the Resolution before the Court has not received a sufficient measure of provincial consent.

We wish to indicate at the outset that we find ourselves in agreement with the submissions made on this issue by counsel for Saskatchewan.

· · ·

Requirements for Establishing a Convention

The requirements for establishing a convention bear some resemblance with those which apply to customary law. Precedents and usage are necessary but do not suffice. They must be normative. We adopt the following passage of Sir W. Ivor Jennings, *The Law and the Constitution* (5th ed., 1959), at p. 136:

→3 requirements to establish a convention...

We have to ask ourselves three questions: first, what are the precedents; secondly, did the actors in the precedents believe that they were bound by a rule; and thirdly, is there a reason for the rule? A single precedent with a good reason may be enough to establish the rule. A whole string of precedents without such a reason will be of no avail, unless it is perfectly certain that the persons concerned regarded them as bound by it.

[The six justices continued on to apply the three-part test set out by Professor Jennings. On part (i), they found that in terms of precedent, in all previous 22 instances of amendments to the Canadian Constitution, there had been approval by affected provinces. The justices concluded that "no amendment changing provincial legislative powers has been made since Confederation when agreement of a province whose legislative powers would have been changed was withheld." On part (ii), the justices found that although the record is imprecise, the prime ministers and premiers on those earlier occasions of amending the Constitution appeared to have acted on the basis that provincial agreement was necessary.]

Nor can it be said that this lack of precision is such as to prevent the principle from acquiring the constitutional *status* of a conventional rule. If a consensus had emerged on the measure of provincial agreement, an amending formula would quickly have been enacted and we would no longer be in the realm of conventions. To demand as much precision as if this were the case and as if the rule were a legal one is tantamount to denying that this area of the Canadian constitution is capable of being governed by conventional rules.

Furthermore, the Government of Canada and the governments of the provinces have attempted to reach a consensus on a constitutional amending formula in the course of ten federal-provincial conferences held in 1927, 1931, 1935, 1950, 1960, 1964, 1971, 1978, 1979 and 1980 (see Gerald A. Beaudoin … , at p. 346). A major issue at these conferences was the quantification of provincial consent. No consensus was reached on this issue. But the discussion of this very issue for more than fifty years postulates a clear recognition by all the governments concerned of the principle that a substantial degree of provincial consent is required.

It would not be appropriate for the Court to devise in the abstract a specific formula which would indicate in positive terms what measure of provincial agreement is required for the convention to be complied with. Conventions by their nature develop in the political field and it will be for the political actors, not this Court, to determine the degree of provincial consent required.

It is sufficient for the Court to decide that at least a substantial measure of provincial consent is required and to decide further whether the situation before the Court meets with this requirement. The situation is one where Ontario and New Brunswick agree with the proposed amendments whereas the eight other provinces oppose it. By no conceivable standard could this situation be thought to pass muster. It clearly does not disclose a sufficient measure of provincial agreement. Nothing more should be said about this.

(iii) A Reason for the Rule

The reason for the rule is the federal principle. Canada is a federal union. The preamble of the *BNA Act* states that

> … the Provinces of Canada, Nova Scotia, and New Brunswick have expressed their Desire to be federally united … .

The federal character of the Canadian Constitution was recognized in innumerable judicial pronouncements. We will quote only one, that of Lord Watson in *Liquidators of the Maritime Bank of Canada v. Receiver-General of New Brunswick* [[1892] AC 437 (PC)], at pp. 441-42:

> The object of the Act was neither to weld the provinces into one, nor to subordinate provincial governments to a central authority, but to create a federal government in which they should all be represented, entrusted with the exclusive administration of affairs in which they had a common interest, each province retaining its independence and autonomy.

The federal principle cannot be reconciled with a state of affairs where the modification of provincial legislative powers could be obtained by the unilateral action of the federal authorities. It would indeed offend the federal principle that "a radical change to … [the] constitution [be] taken at the request of a bare majority of the members of the Canadian House of Commons and Senate" (Report of Dominion Provincial Conference, 1931, at p. 3).

This is an essential requirement of the federal principle which was clearly recognized by the Dominion-Provincial Conference of 1931. This conference had been convened to consider the proposed Statute of Westminster as well as a draft of s. 7 which dealt exclusively with the Canadian position.

At the opening of the conference, Prime Minister Bennett said:

> It should be noted that nothing in the Statute confers on the Parliament of Canada the power to alter the constitution.
>
> • • •
>
> The […] *general principle is* that the Canadian Parliament will not request an amendment directly affecting federal–provincial relationships without prior consultation and agreement with the provinces.

The purpose of this conventional rule is to protect the federal character of the Canadian Constitution and prevent the anomaly that the House of Commons and Senate could obtain by simple resolutions what they could not validly accomplish by statute.

It was contended by counsel for Canada, Ontario and New Brunswick that the proposed amendments would not offend the federal principle and that, if they became law, Canada would remain a federation. The federal principle would even be reinforced, it was said, since the provinces would as a matter of law be given an important role in the amending formula.

It is true that Canada would remain a federation if the proposed amendments became law. But it would be a different federation made different at the instance of a majority in the Houses of the federal Parliament acting alone. It is this process itself which offends the federal principle.

consent of all provinces needed, not just 2 (ON + NB)

Conclusion

We have reached the conclusion that the agreement of the provinces of Canada, no views being expressed as to its quantification, is constitutionally required for the passing of the "Proposed Resolution for a Joint Address to Her Majesty the Queen respecting the Constitution of Canada" and that the passing of this Resolution without such agreement would be unconstitutional in the conventional sense.

The decision of the Supreme Court of Canada in the *Patriation Reference* that unilateral patriation and amendment of the Constitution by the federal government would be "unconstitutional in the conventional sense" did not have the force of law. Nevertheless, it caused all eleven governments of Canada to make one further attempt to negotiate an agreement on constitutional reform, which resulted in the *Constitution Act, 1982*. Roughly sixteen years later, the Supreme Court of Canada was again called upon to make a ruling on the shape of the Constitution in the context of a national crisis.

In the *Secession Reference*, the Supreme Court of Canada based its ruling on "unwritten principles" of the Constitution, and in so doing distinguished principles from conventions. One notable distinction is that while conventions lack the force of law, the unwritten principles do have the force of law and can be enforced by the courts. For this reason alone, unwritten principles are crucial to understanding the legal constraints under which public power is exercised by the Canadian state.

This first excerpt from the *Secession Reference* contains the Supreme Court's discussion of the relationship between the unwritten principles and the text of the Constitution. The discussion in paras. 49 to 54 of the judgment has an internal momentum. The Court starts by describing unwritten constitutional principles as being part of the structure or "architecture" of the Constitution, a form of background to the text or wording of the Constitution that retains its primacy. The Court then states that the principles may be helpful to a proper interpretation of the text. In its final and most striking statement, however, the court describes unwritten principles as having the force of law and imposing substantive limits on the powers of government.

how the principles are outlined/described.

Reference re Secession of Quebec
[1998] 2 SCR 217

THE COURT:

I. Introduction

[1] This Reference requires us to consider momentous questions that go to the heart of our system of constitutional government. The observation we made more than a decade ago in *Reference re Manitoba Language Rights*, [1985] 1 SCR 721 (*Manitoba Language Rights Reference*), at p. 728, applies with equal force here: as in that case, the present one "combines

legal and constitutional questions of the utmost subtlety and complexity with political questions of great sensitivity." In our view, it is not possible to answer the questions that have been put to us without a consideration of a number of underlying principles. An exploration of the meaning and nature of these underlying principles is not merely of academic interest. On the contrary, such an exploration is of immense practical utility. Only once those underlying principles have been examined and delineated may a considered response to the questions we are required to answer emerge.

[2] The questions posed by the Governor in Council by way of Order in Council PC 1996-1497, dated September 30, 1996, read as follows:

1. Under the Constitution of Canada, can the National Assembly, legislature or government of Quebec effect the secession of Quebec from Canada unilaterally?
2. Does international law give the National Assembly, legislature or government of Quebec the right to effect the secession of Quebec from Canada unilaterally? In this regard, is there a right to self-determination under international law that would give the National Assembly, legislature or government of Quebec the right to effect the secession of Quebec from Canada unilaterally?
3. In the event of a conflict between domestic and international law on the right of the National Assembly, legislature or government of Quebec to effect the secession of Quebec from Canada unilaterally, which would take precedence in Canada?

· · ·

III. Reference Questions

· · ·

[32] As we confirmed in *Reference re Objection by Quebec to a Resolution to amend the Constitution*, [1982] 2 SCR 793, at p. 806, "The *Constitution Act, 1982* is now in force. Its legality is neither challenged nor assailable." The "Constitution of Canada" certainly includes the constitutional texts enumerated in s. 52(2) of the *Constitution Act, 1982*. Although these texts have a primary place in determining constitutional rules, they are not exhaustive. The Constitution also "embraces unwritten, as well as written rules," as we recently observed in the *Provincial Judges Reference* [*Reference re Remuneration of Judges of the Provincial Court of Prince Edward Island*, [1997] 3 SCR 3], at para. 92. Finally, as was said in the *Patriation Reference* [*Reference re Resolution To Amend the Constitution*, [1981] 1 SCR 753], at p. 874, the Constitution of Canada includes

> the global system of rules and principles which govern the exercise of constitutional authority in the whole and in every part of the Canadian state.

These supporting principles and rules, which include constitutional conventions and the workings of Parliament, are a necessary part of our Constitution because problems or situations may arise which are not expressly dealt with by the text of the Constitution. In order to endure over time, a constitution must contain a comprehensive set of rules and principles which are capable of providing an exhaustive legal framework for our system of government. Such principles and rules emerge from an understanding of the constitutional text itself, the historical context, and previous judicial interpretations of constitutional meaning. In our view, there are four fundamental and organizing principles of the Constitution which are relevant to addressing the question before us (although this enumeration is by no means exhaustive): federalism; democracy; constitutionalism and the rule of law; and respect for minorities. The foundation and substance of these principles are addressed in the following paragraphs. We will then turn to their specific application to the first reference question before us.

· · ·

[49]   What are those underlying principles? Our Constitution is primarily a written one, the product of 131 years of evolution. Behind the written word is an historical lineage stretching back through the ages, which aids in the consideration of the underlying constitutional principles. These principles inform and sustain the constitutional text: they are the vital unstated assumptions upon which the text is based. The following discussion addresses the four foundational constitutional principles that are most germane for resolution of this Reference: federalism, democracy, constitutionalism and the rule of law, and respect for minority rights. These defining principles function in symbiosis. No single principle can be defined in isolation from the others, nor does any one principle trump or exclude the operation of any other.

[50]   Our Constitution has an internal architecture, or what the majority of this Court in *OPSEU v. Ontario (Attorney General)*, [1987] 2 SCR 2, at p. 57, called a "basic constitutional structure." The individual elements of the Constitution are linked to the others, and must be interpreted by reference to the structure of the Constitution as a whole. As we recently emphasized in the *Provincial Judges Reference*, certain underlying principles infuse our Constitution and breathe life into it. Speaking of the rule of law principle in the *Manitoba Language Rights Reference, supra*, at p. 750, we held that "the principle is clearly implicit in the very nature of a Constitution." The same may be said of the other three constitutional principles we underscore today.

[51]   Although these underlying principles are not explicitly made part of the Constitution by any written provision, other than in some respects by the oblique reference in the preamble to the *Constitution Act, 1867*, it would be impossible to conceive of our constitutional structure without them. The principles dictate major elements of the architecture of the Constitution itself and are as such its lifeblood.

[52]   The principles assist in the interpretation of the text and the delineation of spheres of jurisdiction, the scope of rights and obligations, and the role of our political institutions. Equally important, observance of and respect for these principles is essential to the ongoing process of constitutional development and evolution of our Constitution as a "living tree," to invoke the famous description in *Edwards v. Attorney-General for Canada*, [1930] AC 124 (PC), at p. 136. As this Court indicated in *New Brunswick Broadcasting Co. v. Nova Scotia (Speaker of the House of Assembly)*, [1993] 1 SCR 319, Canadians have long recognized the existence and importance of unwritten constitutional principles in our system of government.

[53]   Given the existence of these underlying constitutional principles, what use may the Court make of them? In the *Provincial Judges Reference, supra*, at paras. 93 and 104, we cautioned that the recognition of these constitutional principles (the majority opinion referred to them as "organizing principles" and described one of them, judicial independence, as an "unwritten norm") could not be taken as an invitation to dispense with the written text of the Constitution. On the contrary, we confirmed that there are compelling reasons to

↳ JI = "unwritten norm"

insist upon the primacy of our written constitution. A written constitution promotes legal certainty and predictability, and it provides a foundation and a touchstone for the exercise of constitutional judicial review. However, we also observed in the *Provincial Judges Reference* that the effect of the preamble to the *Constitution Act, 1867* was to incorporate certain constitutional principles by reference, a point made earlier in *Fraser v. Public Service Staff Relations Board*, [1985] 2 SCR 455, at pp. 462-63. In the *Provincial Judges Reference*, at para. 104, we determined that the preamble "invites the courts to turn those principles into the premises of a constitutional argument that culminates in the filling of gaps in the express terms of the constitutional text."

[54] Underlying constitutional principles may in certain circumstances give rise to substantive legal obligations (have "full legal force," as we described it in the *Patriation Reference, supra*, at p. 845), which constitute substantive limitations upon government action. These principles may give rise to very abstract and general obligations, or they may be more specific and precise in nature. The principles are not merely descriptive, but are also invested with a powerful normative force, and are binding upon both courts and governments. "In other words," as this Court confirmed in the *Manitoba Language Rights Reference, supra*, at p. 752, "in the process of Constitutional adjudication, the Court may have regard to unwritten postulates which form the very foundation of the Constitution of Canada." It is to a discussion of those underlying constitutional principles that we now turn.

In the *Secession Reference*, there is little question that the Supreme Court was effectively expanding judicial authority in the constitutional sphere. The text of the Constitution is written by political representatives at the federal and provincial levels. Unwritten principles can be identified and elucidated only by courts. It is important to note, however, that in recognizing the primacy of the text of the Constitution, the court implicitly stated that unwritten principles cannot be viewed as overriding the text. Their substantive role, at least to date, has been limited to supplementing or "filling gaps" in the text.

⤷ Constitution supreme, principles merely supplement; "fill gaps"

B. The Principle of the Rule of Law

In the *Secession Reference*, the Supreme Court of Canada viewed the principles of "constitutional supremacy" and "rule of law" as closely connected, but nevertheless went on to distinguish between them (at para. 72):

> The constitutionalism principle bears considerable similarity to the rule of law, although they are not identical. The essence of constitutionalism in Canada is embodied in s. 52(1) of the *Constitution Act, 1982*, which provides that "[t]he Constitution of Canada is the supreme law of Canada, and any law that is inconsistent with the provisions of the Constitution is, to the extent of the inconsistency, of no force or effect." Simply put, the constitutionalism principle requires that all government action comply with the Constitution. The rule of law principle requires that all government action must comply with the law, including the Constitution.

In this usage, the rule of law is broader than constitutionalism, and indeed its necessary prerequisite. For like reasons, we think it helpful to separate our consideration of the principles of the rule of law and of constitutionalism, and to deal with the rule of law first.

The rule of law has a range of possible meanings. The one most familiar to common parlance is that a society should strive to operate on "the rule of law rather than the rule of men or women." This is another way of saying that even the most powerful state organs and officials are subordinate to the law. They may not act according to their simple wishes and desires, but must act in compliance with the law.

The replacing of arbitrary, unconstrained power with rule-governed authority is clearly a normative purpose of law. However, to the extent that law is made by men and women, the rule of law poses a paradox. How do you make law the governing principle in society when that law is made by human beings, and must remain sufficiently pliable to respond to their democratically expressed wishes to change it? Many contemporary societies, including Canada's, have resolved this dilemma by making their constitutions supreme over "ordinary" law. The constitution serves, as some have called it, as "a law to make law": the ground rules for law-making and governance.

In considering the concept of the rule of law, however, it is helpful to remember that the principle speaks to the supremacy of both constitutional law *and* ordinary law over the actions of state officials. This idea is embodied in the concept of statutory authority: executive government actors only have power to act in society to the degree that they have been granted that power by ordinary law, principally in the form of statutes enacted by legislatures. This has two quite practical implications. First, government actors may always be questioned about the (statutory) source of their actions—and must always have an answer; and second, the exercise of government authority is always subject to review by the judiciary with respect to whether it is consistent with its statutory grant.

The idea that all state officials are subject to the legal order, and to the same legal obligations as are individual citizens, was most strikingly affirmed by a majority of the Supreme Court in *Roncarelli v. Duplessis*. In that pre-Charter case, the director of the province's liquor commission, acting under the express direction of Premier Maurice Duplessis, revoked the licence of a Montreal restaurateur who had posted bail for several hundred Jehovah's Witnesses, a group that had attracted the particular animus of the premier. The director purported to be acting under the commission's unqualified statutory power to cancel permits "at its discretion." The court rejected the idea that any statute could delegate such untrammelled power to a government official, or that the premier could manipulate his own powers to pursue a personal vendetta. Statutory powers must be limited to the express or implied purposes for which they were granted, a principle enforceable by the judiciary.

Roncarelli v. Duplessis
[1959] SCR 121

RAND J (Judson J concurring): It is then wholly as a private citizen, an adherent of a religious group, holding a liquor licence and furnishing bail to arrested persons for no other purpose than to enable them to be released from detention pending the determination of the charges against them, and with no other relevant considerations to be taken into account, that he is involved in the issues of this controversy.

The complementary state of things is equally free from doubt. From the evidence of Mr. Duplessis and Mr. Archambault alone, it appears that the action taken by the latter as the general manager and sole member of the Commission was dictated by Mr. Duplessis as Attorney-General and Prime Minister of the province; that that step was taken as a means of bringing to a halt the activities of the Witnesses, to punish the appellant for the part he had played not only by revoking the existing licence but in declaring him barred from one "forever," and to warn others that they similarly would be stripped of provincial "privileges" if they persisted in any activity directly or indirectly related to the Witnesses and to the objectionable campaign. The respondent felt that action to be his duty, something which his conscience demanded of him; and as representing the provincial government his decision became automatically that of Mr. Archambault and the Commission. ...

In these circumstances, when the *de facto* power of the Executive over its appointees at will to such a statutory public function is exercised deliberately and intentionally to destroy the vital business interests of a citizen, is there legal redress by him against the person so acting? This calls for an examination of the statutory provisions governing the issue, re-newal and revocation of liquor licences and the scope of authority entrusted by law to the Attorney-General and the government in relation to the administration of the Act.

The liquor law is contained in RSQ 1941, c. 255, entitled *An Act Respecting Alcoholic Liquor*. A Commission is created as a corporation, the only member of which is the general manager ... . Dealing with cancellation, the section [s. 35 of the Act] provides that the "Commission may cancel any permit at its discretion." ... The provisions of the statute, which may be supplemented by detailed regulations, furnish a code for the complete administration of the sale and distribution of alcoholic liquors directed by the Commission as a public service, for all legitimate purposes of the populace. It recognizes the association of wines and liquors as embellishments of food and its ritual and as an interest of the public. As put in Macbeth, the "sauce to meat is ceremony," and so we have restaurants, cafés, hotels and other places of serving food, specifically provided for in that association. ...

The field of licensed occupations and businesses of this nature is steadily becoming of greater concern to citizens generally. It is a matter of vital importance that a public administration that can refuse to allow a person to enter or continue a calling which, in the absence of regulation, would be free and legitimate, should be conducted with complete impartiality and integrity; and that the grounds for refusing or cancelling a permit should unquestionably be such and such only as are incompatible with the purposes envisaged by the statute: the duty of a Commission is to serve those purposes and those only. A decision to deny or cancel such a privilege lies within the "discretion" of the Commission; but that means that decision is to be based upon a weighing of considerations pertinent to the object of the administration.

In public regulation of this sort there is no such thing as absolute and untrammelled "discretion," that is that action can be taken on any ground or for any reason that can be suggested to the mind of the administrator; no legislative Act can, without express language, be taken to contemplate an unlimited arbitrary power exercisable for any purpose, however capricious or irrelevant, regardless of the nature or purpose of the statute. Fraud and corruption in the Commission may not be mentioned in such statutes but they are always implied as exceptions. "Discretion" necessarily implies good faith in discharging public duty; there is always a perspective within which a statute is intended to operate; and any clear departure from its lines or objects is just as objectionable as fraud or corruption. Could an applicant be refused a permit because he had been born in another province, or because of the colour of his hair? The legislature cannot be so distorted.

To deny or revoke a permit because a citizen exercises an unchallengeable right totally irrelevant to the sale of liquor in a restaurant is equally beyond the scope of the discretion conferred. There was here not only revocation of the existing permit but a declaration of a future, definitive disqualification of the appellant to obtain one: it was to be "forever." This purports to divest his citizenship status of its incident of membership in the class of those of the public to whom such a privilege could be extended. Under the statutory language here, that is not competent to the Commission and *a fortiori* to the government or the respondent. ...

It may be difficult if not impossible in cases generally to demonstrate a breach of this public duty in the illegal purpose served; there may be no means, even if proceedings against the Commission were permitted by the Attorney-General, as here they were refused, of compelling the Commission to justify a refusal or revocation or to give reasons for its action; on these questions I make no observation; but in the case before us that difficulty is not present: the reasons are openly avowed.

The act of the respondent through the instrumentality of the Commission brought about a breach of an implied public statutory duty toward the appellant; it was a gross abuse of legal power expressly intended to punish him for an act wholly irrelevant to the statute, a punishment which inflicted on him, as it was intended to do, the destruction of his economic life as a restaurant keeper within the province. Whatever may be the immunity of the Commission or its member from an action for damages, there is none in the respondent. He was under no duty in relation to the appellant and his act was an intrusion upon the functions of a statutory body. The injury done by him was a fault engaging liability ... . That, in the presence of expanding administrative regulation of economic activities, such a step and its consequences are to be suffered by the victim without recourse or remedy, that an administration according to law is to be superseded by action dictated by and according to the arbitrary likes, dislikes and irrelevant purposes of public officers acting beyond their duty, would signalize the beginning of disintegration of the rule of law as a fundamental postulate of our constitutional structure. An administration of licences on the highest level of fair and impartial treatment to all may be forced to follow the practice of "first come, first served," which makes the strictest observance of equal responsibility to all of even greater importance; at this stage of developing government it would be a danger of high consequence to tolerate such a departure from good faith in executing the legislative purpose. ...

"Good faith" in this context, applicable both to the respondent and the general manager, means carrying out the statute according to its intent and for its purpose; it means good faith in acting with a rational appreciation of that intent and purpose and not with an improper intent and for an alien purpose; it does not mean for the purposes of punishing a person for exercising an unchallengeable right; it does not mean arbitrarily and illegally attempting to divest a citizen of an incident of his civil status.

↳ meaning of "good faith"

The Supreme Court's discussion of four principles of the Constitution in the *Secession Reference* raised the possibility of making arguments that each of these principles, and any other that might later come to be recognized, has a substantive content that directs and limits state action. With respect to the rule of law principle, this includes the idea that ordinary law must meet certain qualitative standards—including not being retrospective, or not being directed at a small class of persons—in order to be constitutional, quite apart from any limits expressly stated in the Constitution. This idea was examined in *British Columbia v. Imperial Tobacco Canada Ltd.*

In 2000, the BC legislature enacted the *Tobacco Damages and Health Care Costs Recovery Act*, SBC 2000, c. 30, creating a civil cause of action for the BC government against tobacco manufacturers with respect to health care costs incurred by the government for tobacco-related illnesses resulting from tortious or other misconduct by the manufacturers. The legislation facilitated the making of aggregate claims for expenses incurred for whole populations of affected individuals, created evidentiary presumptions in favour of the government, and expressly stated that it operated retrospectively. Pursuant to the legislation, the government commenced legal actions against several large tobacco manufacturers. The defendant companies challenged the constitutionality of the legislation. Their first argument, that the statute was beyond provincial powers due to its extraterritorial aspects, was dismissed by the Supreme Court.

The manufacturers also argued that legislation breached the unwritten constitutional principles of judicial independence and the rule of law. With respect to the latter, the defendants argued that several features of the statute—including its retrospective effect, its particularity in creating a cause of action between a single plaintiff and a small group of defendants, and the presumptions favouring the plaintiff—violated substantive norms of the rule-of-law principle. The court's unanimous decision was written by Justice Major.

British Columbia v. Imperial Tobacco Canada Ltd.
[2005] 2 SCR 473, 2005 SCC 49

➞ the "Act"

MAJOR J: [1] The *Tobacco Damages and Health Care Costs Recovery Act*, SBC 2000, c. 30 (the "Act"), authorizes an action by the government of British Columbia against a manufacturer of tobacco products for the recovery of health care expenditures incurred by the government in treating individuals exposed to those products. Liability hinges on those individuals having been exposed to tobacco products because of the manufacturer's breach of a duty owed to persons in British Columbia, and on the government of British Columbia having incurred health care expenditures in treating disease in those individuals caused by such exposure.

[2] These appeals question the constitutional validity of the Act. The appellants, each of which was sued by the government of British Columbia pursuant to the Act, challenge its constitutional validity on the basis that it violates (1) territorial limits on provincial legislative jurisdiction; (2) the principle of judicial independence; and (3) the principle of the rule of law.

. . .

I. Background

A. The Legislation

[4] The Act, in its entirety, is reproduced in the Appendix. Its essential aspects are summarized below.

[5] Section 2(1) is the keystone of the Act. It reads:

> The government has a direct and distinct action against a manufacturer to recover the cost of health care benefits caused or contributed to by a tobacco related wrong.

. . .

[7] Viewed in this light, s. 2(1) creates a cause of action by which the government of British Columbia may recover from a tobacco manufacturer money spent treating disease in British Columbians, where such disease was caused by exposure to a tobacco product (whether entirely in British Columbia or not), and such exposure was caused by that manufacturer's tort in British Columbia, or breach of a duty owed to persons in British Columbia.

[8] The cause of action created by s. 2(1), besides being "direct and distinct," is not a subrogated claim: s. 2(2). Nor is it barred by the *Limitation Act*, RSBC 1996, c. 266, s. 6(1). Crucially, it can be pursued on an aggregate basis—i.e. in respect of a population of persons for whom the government has made or can reasonably be expected to make expenditures: s. 2(4)(b).

[9] Where the government's claim is made on an aggregate basis, it may use statistical, epidemiological and sociological evidence to prove its case: s. 5(b). It need not identify, prove the cause of disease or prove the expenditures made in respect of any individual member of the population on which it bases its claim: s. 2(5)(a). Furthermore, health care records and related information in respect of individual members of that population are not compellable, except if relied upon by an expert witness: ss. 2(5)(b) and (c). However, the court is free to order the discovery of a "statistically meaningful sample" of the health care records of individual members of that population, stripped of personal identifiers: ss. 2(5) (d) and (e).

[10] Pursuant to ss. 3(1) and (2), the government enjoys a reversed burden of proof in respect of certain elements of an aggregate claim. Where the aggregate claim is, like the one brought against each of the appellants, to recover expenditures in respect of disease caused by exposure to cigarettes, the reversed burden of proof operates as follows. ...

[11] In this way, it falls on a defendant manufacturer to show that its breach of duty did not give rise to exposure, or that exposure resulting from its breach of duty did not give rise to the disease in respect of which the government claims for its expenditures. The reversed burden of proof on the manufacturer is a balance of probabilities: s. 3(4).

[12] Where the aforementioned presumptions apply, the court must determine the portion of the government's expenditures after the date of the manufacturer's breach that resulted from exposure to cigarettes: s. 3(3)(a). The manufacturer is liable for such expenditures in proportion to its share of the market for cigarettes in British Columbia, calculated over the period of time between its first breach of duty and trial: ss. 3(3)(b) and 1(6).

[13] In an action by the government, a manufacturer will be jointly and severally liable for expenditures arising from a joint breach of duty (i.e. for expenditures caused by disease,

which disease was caused by exposure, which exposure was caused by a joint breach of duty to which the manufacturer was a party): s. 4(1).

[14] Pursuant to s. 10, all provisions of the Act operate retroactively.

. . .

III. Issues

[25] McLachlin CJ stated the following constitutional questions:

(3rd con. question...)   . . .

3. Is the *Tobacco Damages and Health Care Costs Recovery Act*, SBC 2000, c. 30, constitutionally invalid, in whole or in part, as offending the rule of law?

IV. Analysis

. . .

C. Rule of Law

[57] The rule of law is "a fundamental postulate of our constitutional structure" (*Roncarelli v. Duplessis*, [1959] SCR 121, at p. 142) that lies "at the root of our system of government" (*Reference re Secession of Quebec*, [1998] 2 SCR 217, at para. 70). It is expressly acknowledged by the preamble to the *Constitution Act, 1982*, and implicitly recognized in the preamble to the *Constitution Act, 1867*: see *Reference re Manitoba Language Rights*, [1985] 1 SCR 721, at p. 750.

[58] This Court has described the rule of law as embracing three principles. The first recognizes that "the law is supreme over officials of the government as well as private individuals, and thereby preclusive of the influence of arbitrary power": *Reference re Manitoba Language Rights*, at p. 748. The second "requires the creation and maintenance of an actual order of positive laws which preserves and embodies the more general principle of normative order": *Reference re Manitoba Language Rights*, at p. 749. The third requires that "the relationship between the state and the individual ... be regulated by law": *Reference re Secession of Quebec*, at para. 71.

[59] So understood, it is difficult to conceive of how the rule of law could be used as a basis for invalidating legislation such as the Act based on its content. That is because none of the principles that the rule of law embraces speak directly to the terms of legislation. The first principle requires that legislation be applied to all those, including government officials, to whom it, by its terms, applies. The second principle means that legislation must exist. And the third principle, which overlaps somewhat with the first and second, requires that state officials' actions be legally founded. See R. Elliot, "References, Structural Argumentation and the Organizing Principles of Canada's Constitution" (2001), 80 *Can. Bar Rev.* 67, at pp. 114-15.

[60] This does not mean that the rule of law as described by this Court has no normative force. As McLachlin CJ stated in Babcock, at para. 54, "unwritten constitutional principles," including the rule of law, "are capable of limiting government actions." See also *Reference re Secession of Quebec*, at para. 54. But the government action constrained by the rule of law as understood in *Reference re Manitoba Language Rights* and *Reference re Secession of Quebec*

is, by definition, usually that of the executive and judicial branches. Actions of the legislative branch are constrained too, but only in the sense that they must comply with legislated requirements as to manner and form (i.e. the procedures by which legislation is to be enacted, amended and repealed).

[61] Nonetheless, considerable debate surrounds the question of what additional principles, if any, the rule of law might embrace, and the extent to which they might mandate the invalidation of legislation based on its content. P.W. Hogg and C.F. Zwibel write in "The Rule of Law in the Supreme Court of Canada" (2005), 55 UTLJ 715, at pp. 717-18:

> Many authors have tried to define the rule of law and explain its significance, or lack thereof. Their views spread across a wide spectrum. ... T.R.S. Allan, for example, claims that laws that fail to respect the equality and human dignity of individuals are contrary to the rule of law. Luc Tremblay asserts that the rule of law includes the liberal principle, the democratic principle, the constitutional principle, and the federal principle. For Allan and Tremblay, the rule of law demands not merely that positive law be obeyed but that it embody a particular vision of social justice. Another strong version comes from David Beatty, who argues that the "ultimate rule of law" is a principle of "proportionality" to which all laws must conform on pain of invalidity (enforced by judicial review). In the middle of the spectrum are those who, like Joseph Raz, accept that the rule of law is an ideal of constitutional legality, involving open, stable, clear, and general rules, even-handed enforcement of those laws, the independence of the judiciary, and judicial review of administrative action. Raz acknowledges that conformity to the rule of law is often a matter of degree, and that breaches of the rule of law do not lead to invalidity.

See also W.J. Newman, "The Principles of the Rule of Law and Parliamentary Sovereignty in Constitutional Theory and Litigation" (2005), 16 NJCL 175, at pp. 177-80.

[62] This debate underlies Strayer JA's apt observation in *Singh v. Canada (Attorney General)*, [2000] 3 FC 185 (CA), at para. 33, that "[a]dvocates tend to read into the principle of the rule of law anything which supports their particular view of what the law should be."

only #1 and #2 covered

[63] The appellants' conceptions of the rule of law can fairly be said to fall at one extreme of the spectrum of possible conceptions and to support Strayer JA's thesis. They submit that the rule of law requires that legislation (1) be prospective; (2) be general in character; (3) not confer special privileges on the government, except where necessary for effective governance; and (4) ensure a fair civil trial. And they argue that the Act breaches each of these requirements, rendering it invalid.

[64] A brief review of this Court's jurisprudence will reveal that none of these requirements enjoy constitutional protection in Canada. But before embarking on that review, it should be said that acknowledging the constitutional force of anything resembling the appellants' conceptions of the rule of law would seriously undermine the legitimacy of judicial review of legislation for constitutionality. That is so for two separate but interrelated reasons.

[65] First, many of the requirements of the rule of law proposed by the appellants are simply broader versions of rights contained in the Charter. For example, the appellants' proposed fair trial requirement is essentially a broader version of s. 11(d) of the Charter, which provides that "[a]ny person charged with an offence has the right ... to ... a fair and public hearing." But the framers of the Charter enshrined that fair trial right only for those "charged with an offence." If the rule of law constitutionally required that all legislation

provide for a fair trial, s. 11(d) and its relatively limited scope (not to mention its qualification by s. 1) would be largely irrelevant because everyone would have the unwritten, but constitutional, right to a "fair ... hearing." (Though, as explained in para. 76, infra, the Act provides for a fair trial in any event.) Thus, the appellants' conception of the unwritten constitutional principle of the rule of law would render many of our written constitutional rights redundant and, in doing so, undermine the delimitation of those rights chosen by our constitutional framers. That is specifically what this Court cautioned against in *Reference re Secession of Quebec*, at para. 53:

> Given the existence of these underlying constitutional principles, what use may the Court make of them? In [*Reference re Remuneration of Judges of the Provincial Court of Prince Edward Island*], at paras. 93 and 104, we cautioned that *the recognition of these constitutional principles ... could not be taken as an invitation to dispense with the written text of the Constitution. On the contrary, we confirmed that there are compelling reasons to insist upon the primacy of our written constitution.* A written constitution promotes legal certainty and predictability, and it provides a foundation and a touchstone for the exercise of constitutional judicial review. [Emphasis added.]

[66] Second, the appellants' arguments overlook the fact that several constitutional principles other than the rule of law that have been recognized by this Court—most notably democracy and constitutionalism—very strongly favour upholding the validity of legislation that conforms to the express terms of the Constitution (and to the requirements, such as judicial independence, that flow by necessary implication from those terms). Put differently, the appellants' arguments fail to recognize that in a constitutional democracy such as ours, protection from legislation that some might view as unjust or unfair properly lies not in the amorphous underlying principles of our Constitution, but in its text and the ballot box. See *Bacon v. Saskatchewan Crop Insurance Corp.* (1999), 180 Sask. R 20 (CA), at para. 30, Elliot, at pp. 141-42, Hogg and Zwibel, at p. 718, and Newman, at p. 187.

[67] The rule of law is not an invitation to trivialize or supplant the Constitution's written terms. Nor is it a tool by which to avoid legislative initiatives of which one is not in favour. On the contrary, it requires that courts give effect to the Constitution's text, and apply, by whatever its terms, legislation that conforms to that text.

[68] A review of the cases showing that each of the appellants' proposed requirements of the rule of law has, as a matter of precedent and policy, no constitutional protection is conclusive of the appellants' rule of law arguments.

(1) Prospectivity in the Law

[69] Except for criminal law, the retrospectivity and retroactivity of which is limited by s. 11(g) of the Charter, there is no requirement of legislative prospectivity embodied in the rule of law or in any provision of our Constitution. Professor P.W. Hogg sets out the state of the law accurately (in *Constitutional Law of Canada* (loose-leaf ed.), vol. 1, at p. 48-29):

> Apart from s. 11(g), Canadian constitutional law contains no prohibition of retroactive (or ex post facto laws). There is a presumption of statutory interpretation that a statute should not be given retroactive effect, but, if the retroactive effect is clearly expressed, then there is no room

for interpretation and the statute is effective according to its terms. Retroactive statutes are in fact common.

[70] Hence, in *Air Canada v. British Columbia*, [1989] 1 SCR 1161, at p. 1192, La Forest J, writing for a majority of this Court, characterized a retroactive tax as "not constitutionally barred." And in *Cusson v. Robidoux*, [1977] 1 SCR 650, at p. 655, Pigeon J, for a unanimous Court, said that it would be "untenable" to suggest that legislation reviving actions earlier held by this Court (in *Notre-Dame Hospital v. Patry*, [1975] 2 SCR 388) to be time-barred was unconstitutional.

[71] The absence of a general requirement of legislative prospectivity exists despite the fact that retrospective and retroactive legislation can overturn settled expectations and is sometimes perceived as unjust: see E. Edinger, "Retrospectivity in Law" (1995), 29 UBC L Rev. 5, at p. 13. Those who perceive it as such can perhaps take comfort in the rules of statutory interpretation that require the legislature to indicate clearly any desired retroactive or retrospective effects. Such rules ensure that the legislature has turned its mind to such effects and "determined that the benefits of retroactivity [or retrospectivity] outweigh the potential for disruption or unfairness": *Landgraf v. USI Film Products*, 511 US 244 (1994), at p. 268.

[72] It might also be observed that developments in the common law have always had retroactive and retrospective effect. Lord Nicholls of Birkenhead recently explained this point in *In re Spectrum Plus Ltd.*, [2005] 3 WLR 58, [2005] UKHL 41, at para. 7:

> A court ruling which changes the law from what it was previously thought to be operates retrospectively as well as prospectively. The ruling will have a retrospective effect so far as the parties to the particular dispute are concerned, as occurred with the manufacturer of the ginger beer in *Donoghue v. Stevenson*, [1932] AC 562. When Mr Stevenson manufactured and bottled and sold his ginger beer the law on manufacturers' liability as generally understood may have been as stated by the majority of the Second Division of the Court of Session and the minority of their Lordships in that case. But in the claim Mrs Donoghue brought against Mr Stevenson his legal obligations fell to be decided in accordance with Lord Atkin's famous statements. Further, because of the doctrine of precedent the same would be true of everyone else whose case thereafter came before a court. Their rights and obligations would be decided according to the law as enunciated by the majority of the House of Lords in that case even though the relevant events occurred before that decision was given.

This observation adds further weight, if needed, to the view that retrospectivity and retroactivity do not generally engage constitutional concerns.

#2

(2) Generality in the Law, Ordinary Law for the Government, and Fair Civil Trials

[73] Two decisions of this Court defeat the appellants' submission that the Constitution, through the rule of law, requires that legislation be general in character and devoid of special advantages for the government (except where necessary for effective governance), as well as that it ensure a fair civil trial.

[74] The first is *Air Canada*. In it, a majority of this Court affirmed the constitutionality of 1981 amendments to the *Gasoline Tax Act, 1948*, RSBC 1960, c. 162, that retroactively taxed certain companies in the airline industry. The amendments were meant strictly to

defeat three companies' claims, brought in 1980, for reimbursement of gasoline taxes paid between 1974 and 1976, the collection of which was *ultra vires* the legislature of British Columbia. The legislative amendments, in addition to being retroactive, were for the benefit of the Crown, aimed at a particular industry with readily identifiable members and totally destructive of that industry's ability to pursue successfully their claims filed a year earlier. Nonetheless, the constitutionality of those amendments was affirmed by a majority of this Court.

[75] The second is *Authorson v. Canada (Attorney General)*, [2003] 2 SCR 40, 2003 SCC 39, in which this Court unanimously upheld a provision of the *Department of Veterans Affairs Act*, RSC 1985, c. V-1, aimed specifically at defeating certain disabled veterans' claims, the merits of which were undisputed, against the federal government. The claims concerned interest owed by the government on the veterans' benefit accounts administered by it, which interest it had not properly credited for decades. Though the appeal was pursued on the basis of the *Canadian Bill of Rights*, SC 1960, c. 44, the decision confirmed that it was well within Parliament's power to enact the provision at issue—despite the fact that it was directed at a known class of vulnerable veterans, conferred benefits on the Crown for "undisclosed reasons" (para. 62) and routed those veterans' ability to have any trial—fair or unfair—of their claims. See para. 15:

> The *Department of Veterans Affairs Act*, s. 5.1(4) takes a property claim from a vulnerable group, in disregard of the Crown's fiduciary duty to disabled veterans. However, that taking is within the power of Parliament. The appeal has to be allowed.

[76] Additionally, the appellants' conception of a "fair" civil trial seems in part to be of one governed by customary rules of civil procedure and evidence. As should be evident from the analysis concerning judicial independence, there is no constitutional right to have one's civil trial governed by such rules. Moreover, new rules are not necessarily unfair. Indeed, tobacco manufacturers sued pursuant to the Act will receive a fair civil trial, in the sense that the concept is traditionally understood: they are entitled to a public hearing, before an independent and impartial court, in which they may contest the claims of the plaintiff and adduce evidence in their defence. The court will determine their liability only following that hearing, based solely on its understanding of the law as applied to its findings of fact. The fact that defendants might regard that law (i.e. the Act) as unjust, or the procedural rules it prescribes as unprecedented, does not render their trial unfair.

[77] The Act does not implicate the rule of law in the sense that the Constitution comprehends that term. It follows that the Act is not unconstitutional by reason of interference with it.

The Supreme Court of Canada had further opportunity to consider an argument going to substantive content of the rule of law principle in *British Columbia (Attorney General) v. Christie*. There, the court rejected the idea that the rule of law incorporates a right of access to legal counsel in all judicial proceedings, a right which the plaintiff claimed was violated by a provincial tax on lawyer's services.

British Columbia (Attorney General) v. Christie
[2007] 1 SCR 873

THE COURT: [1] In 1993, British Columbia enacted the *Social Service Tax Amendment Act (No. 2)*, 1993, SBC 1993, c. 24, imposing a 7 percent tax on the purchase price of legal services. The purpose of the tax was said to be to fund legal aid in the province. However, the tax collected is put into general revenue, and it is difficult to ascertain how much (if any) of the tax collected is put towards legal aid, or other initiatives aimed at increasing access to justice. The legal profession is the only profession in British Columbia whose services are taxed in this way.

[2] This case is the latest in a series of challenges to the tax and its predecessor, the *Social Service Tax Amendment Act, 1992*, SBC 1992, c. 22. It was brought by Mr. Dugald Christie, a litigation lawyer who worked with poor and low income people in Vancouver. Mr. Christie was consumed by a passion to provide legal services to those at the margins of society. It was a passion that ultimately took his life; last year, on a cross-Canada bicycle trip to raise funds for the cause, he was struck and killed on a stretch of highway near Sault Ste. Marie, Ontario.

[3] Mr. Christie's action to have the legal services tax declared unconstitutional was rooted in his experience of the effects of the tax on his practice. Mr. Christie charged low fees. His net income in the years 1991 to 1999 did not exceed $30,000 per year. Often his clients were not able to pay the bills he rendered for legal services, either on time or at all. Yet the Act required him to submit the tax to government even though the fees on which it had been levied had not been paid. Mr. Christie's small income made this difficult. On March 10, 1997, the government sent Mr. Christie a demand notice. A few days later, without ascertaining the reason for non-payment or attempting to work out a payment schedule, the province seized $972.11 from Mr. Christie's bank account. It seized a further $5,349.64 in December 1997. Mr. Christie stopped practising law and did not resume the practice until July 2000.

. . .

II. Analysis

[10] The respondent's claim is for effective access to the courts which, he states, necessitates legal services. This is asserted not on a case-by-case basis, but as a general right. What is sought is the constitutionalization of *a particular type of access* to justice—access aided by a lawyer where rights and obligations are at stake before a court or tribunal. In order to succeed, the respondent must show that the Canadian Constitution mandates this particular form or quality of access. The question is whether he has done so. In our view, he has not.

[11] We take as our starting point the definition of the alleged constitutional principle offered by the majority of the Court of Appeal ... —the right to be represented by a lawyer in court or tribunal proceedings where a person's legal rights and obligations are at stake, in order to have effective access to the courts or tribunal proceedings.

[12] We will first discuss what the proposed right entails. We will then ask whether the right, thus described, is prescribed by the Constitution.

[13] This general right to be represented by a lawyer in a court or tribunal proceedings where legal rights or obligations are at stake is a broad right. It would cover almost all—if not all—cases that come before courts or tribunals where individuals are involved. Arguably, corporate rights and obligations would be included since corporations function as vehicles for individual interests. Moreover, it would cover not only actual court proceedings, but also related legal advice, services and disbursements. Although the respondent attempted to argue otherwise, the logical result would be a constitutionally mandated legal aid scheme for virtually all legal proceedings, except where the state could show this is not necessary for effective access to justice.

· · ·

[18] A second argument is that the right to have a lawyer in cases before courts and tribunals dealing with rights and obligations is constitutionally protected, either as an aspect of the rule of law, or a precondition to it.   ↗ repeated from p. 97, para 57

[19] The rule of law is a foundational principle. This Court has described it as "a fundamental postulate of our constitutional structure" (*Roncarelli v. Duplessis*, [1959] SCR 121, at p. 142) that "lie[s] at the root of our system of government" (*Reference re Secession of Quebec*, [1998] 2 SCR 217, at para. 70). It is explicitly recognized in the preamble to the *Constitution Act, 1982*, and implicitly recognized in s. 1 of the Charter, which provides that the rights and freedoms set out in the Charter are "subject only to such reasonable limits *prescribed by law* as can be demonstrably justified in a free and democratic society." And, as this Court recognized in *Reference re Manitoba Language Rights*, [1985] 1 SCR 721, at p. 750, it is implicit in the very concept of a constitution.

[20] The rule of law embraces at least three principles. The first principle is that the "law is supreme over officials of the government as well as private individuals, and thereby preclusive of the influence of arbitrary power": *Reference re Manitoba Language Rights*, at p. 748. The second principle "requires the creation and maintenance of an actual order of positive laws which preserves and embodies the more general principle of normative order": ibid., at p. 749. The third principle requires that "the relationship between the state and the individual ... be regulated by law" ... .

[21] It is clear from a review of these principles that general access to legal services is not a currently recognized aspect of the rule of law. However, in *Imperial Tobacco,* this Court left open the possibility that the rule of law may include additional principles. It is therefore necessary to determine whether general access to legal services in relation to court and tribunal proceedings dealing with rights and obligations is a fundamental aspect of the rule of law.

[22] Before examining this question, it is important to note that this Court has repeatedly emphasized the important role that lawyers play in ensuring access to justice and upholding the rule of law: *Andrews v. Law Society of British Columbia*, [1989] 1 SCR 143, at p. 187; *MacDonald Estate v. Martin*, [1990] 3 SCR 1235, at p. 1265; *Fortin v. Chrétien*, [2001] 2 SCR 500, 2001 SCC 45, at para. 49; *Law Society of British Columbia v. Mangat*, [2001] 3 SCR 113, 2001 SCC 67, at para. 43; *Lavallee, Rackel & Heintz v. Canada (Attorney General)*, [2002] 3 SCR 209, 2002 SCC 61, at paras. 64-68, per LeBel J (dissenting in part but not on this point). This is only fitting. Lawyers are a vital conduit through which citizens access the courts, and the law. They help maintain the rule of law by working to ensure that unlawful private and unlawful state action in particular do not go unaddressed. The role that lawyers

play in this regard is so important that the right to counsel in some situations has been given constitutional status.

[23] The issue, however, is whether *general* access to legal services in relation to court and tribunal proceedings dealing with rights and obligations is a fundamental aspect of the rule of law. In our view, it is not. Access to legal services is fundamentally important in any free and democratic society. In some cases, it has been found essential to due process and a fair trial. But a review of the constitutional text, the jurisprudence and the history of the concept does not support the respondent's contention that there is a broad general right to legal counsel as an aspect of, or precondition to, the rule of law.

[24] The text of the Charter negates the postulate of the general constitutional right to legal assistance contended for here. It provides for a right to legal services in one specific situation. Section 10(b) of the Charter provides that everyone has the right to retain and instruct counsel, and to be informed of that right "on arrest or detention." If the reference to the rule of law implied the right to counsel in relation to all proceedings where rights and obligations are at stake, s. 10(b) would be redundant.

[25] Section 10(b) does not exclude a finding of a constitutional right to legal assistance in other situations. Section 7 of the Charter, for example, has been held to imply a right to counsel as an aspect of procedural fairness where life, liberty and security of the person are affected: see *Dehghani v. Canada (Minister of Employment and Immigration)*, [1993] 1 SCR 1053, at p. 1077; *New Brunswick (Minister of Health and Community Services) v. G. (J.)*, [1999] 3 SCR 46. But this does not support a general right to legal assistance whenever a matter of rights and obligations is before a court or tribunal. Thus in *New Brunswick*, the Court was at pains to state that the right to counsel outside of the s. 10(b) context is a case-specific multi-factored enquiry (see para. 86).

[26] Nor has the rule of law historically been understood to encompass a general right to have a lawyer in court or tribunal proceedings affecting rights and obligations. The right to counsel was historically understood to be a limited right that extended only, if at all, to representation in the criminal context: M. Finkelstein, *The Right to Counsel* (1988), at pp. 1-4 to 1-6; W. S. Tarnopolsky, "The Lacuna in North American Civil Liberties—The Right to Counsel in Canada" (1967), 17 *Buff. L Rev.* 145; Comment, "An Historical Argument for the Right to Counsel During Police Interrogation" (1964), 73 *Yale LJ* 1000, at p. 1018.

[27] We conclude that the text of the Constitution, the jurisprudence and the historical understanding of the rule of law do not foreclose the possibility that a right to counsel may be recognized in specific and varied situations. But at the same time, they do not support the conclusion that there is a general constitutional right to counsel in proceedings before courts and tribunals dealing with rights and obligations.

C. The Principle of Constitutional Supremacy

In the *Secession Reference*, the Supreme Court confirmed that with s. 52(1) of the *Constitution Act, 1982* the Canadian system of government operates under a principle of constitutional supremacy. In the sense that the judiciary had always been prepared to rule laws invalid pursuant to the division of powers between the federal and provincial levels of government, this was nothing new. Nevertheless, the court described the 1982 constitutional arrangements as completing a transformation over time from a system based "largely" on the principle of parliamentary supremacy (or sovereignty) to one of constitutional supremacy. This relates closely to the arrival in 1982 of the *Canadian Charter of Rights and Freedoms*—written constitutional rights that enhanced limits on the substantive laws that could be enacted by Canada's sovereign legislatures.

In the *Secession Reference*, the Supreme Court set out its understanding of the principle of "constitutionalism," or "constitutional supremacy." As we have already noted, the court linked this concept to the rule-of-law principle.

Reference re Secession of Quebec
[1998] 2 SCR 217

Constitutionalism and the Rule of Law

[70] The principles of constitutionalism and the rule of law lie at the root of our system of government. The rule of law, as observed in *Roncarelli v. Duplessis*, [1959] SCR 121, at p. 142, is "a fundamental postulate of our constitutional structure." As we noted in the *Patriation Reference* ... , at pp. 805-6, "[t]he 'rule of law' is a highly textured expression, importing many things which are beyond the need of these reasons to explore but conveying, for example, a sense of orderliness, of subjection to known legal rules and of executive accountability to legal authority." At its most basic level, the rule of law vouchsafes to the citizens and residents of the country a stable, predictable and ordered society in which to conduct their affairs. It provides a shield for individuals from arbitrary state action.

[71] In the *Manitoba Language Rights Reference* ... , at pp. 747-52, this Court outlined the elements of the rule of law. We emphasized, first, that the rule of law provides that the law is supreme over the acts of both government and private persons. There is, in short, one law for all. Second, we explained, at p. 749, that "the rule of law requires the creation and maintenance of an actual order of positive laws which preserves and embodies the more general principle of normative order." It was this second aspect of the rule of law that was primarily at issue in the *Manitoba Language Rights Reference* itself. A third aspect of the rule of law is, as recently confirmed in the *Provincial Judges Reference* ... , at para. 10, that "the exercise of all public power must find its ultimate source in a legal rule." Put another way, the relationship between the state and the individual must be regulated by law. Taken together, these three considerations make up a principle of profound constitutional and political significance.

[72] The constitutionalism principle bears considerable similarity to the rule of law, although they are not identical. The essence of constitutionalism in Canada is embodied in s. 52(1) of the *Constitution Act, 1982*, which provides that "[t]he Constitution of Canada is the supreme law of Canada, and any law that is inconsistent with the provisions of the Constitution is, to the extent of the inconsistency, of no force or effect." Simply put, the constitutionalism principle requires that all government action comply with the Constitution. The rule of law principle requires that all government action must comply with the law, including the Constitution. This Court has noted on several occasions that with the adoption of the Charter, the Canadian system of government was transformed to a significant extent

↗ due to Charter

from a system of Parliamentary supremacy to one of constitutional supremacy. The Constitution binds all governments, both federal and provincial, including the executive branch (*Operation Dismantle Inc. v. The Queen*, [1985] 1 SCR 441, at p. 455). They may not transgress its provisions: indeed, their sole claim to exercise lawful authority rests in the powers allocated to them under the Constitution, and can come from no other source.

[73] An understanding of the scope and importance of the principles of the rule of law and constitutionalism is aided by acknowledging explicitly why a constitution is entrenched beyond the reach of simple majority rule. There are three overlapping reasons.

[74] First, a constitution may provide an added safeguard for fundamental human rights and individual freedoms which might otherwise be susceptible to government interference. Although democratic government is generally solicitous of those rights, there are occasions when the majority will be tempted to ignore fundamental rights in order to accomplish collective goals more easily or effectively. Constitutional entrenchment ensures that those rights will be given due regard and protection. Second, a constitution may seek to ensure that vulnerable minority groups are endowed with the institutions and rights necessary to maintain and promote their identities against the assimilative pressures of the majority. And third, a constitution may provide for a division of political power that allocates political power amongst different levels of government. That purpose would be defeated if one of those democratically elected levels of government could usurp the powers of the other simply by exercising its legislative power to allocate additional political power to itself unilaterally.

[75] The argument that the Constitution may be legitimately circumvented by resort to a majority vote in a province-wide referendum is superficially persuasive, in large measure because it seems to appeal to some of the same principles that underlie the legitimacy of the Constitution itself, namely, democracy and self-government. In short, it is suggested that as the notion of popular sovereignty underlies the legitimacy of our existing constitutional arrangements, so the same popular sovereignty that originally led to the present Constitution must (it is argued) also permit "the people" in their exercise of popular sovereignty to secede by majority vote alone. However, closer analysis reveals that this argument is unsound, because it misunderstands the meaning of popular sovereignty and the essence of a constitutional democracy.

[76] Canadians have never accepted that ours is a system of simple majority rule. Our principle of democracy, taken in conjunction with the other constitutional principles discussed here, is richer. Constitutional government is necessarily predicated on the idea that the political representatives of the people of a province have the capacity and the power to commit the province to be bound into the future by the constitutional rules being adopted. These rules are "binding" not in the sense of frustrating the will of a majority of a province, but as defining the majority which must be consulted in order to alter the fundamental balances of political power (including the spheres of autonomy guaranteed by the principle of federalism), individual rights, and minority rights in our society. Of course, those constitutional rules are themselves amenable to amendment, but only through a process of negotiation which ensures that there is an opportunity for the constitutionally defined rights of all the parties to be respected and reconciled.

[77] In this way, our belief in democracy may be harmonized with our belief in constitutionalism. Constitutional amendment often requires some form of substantial consensus

precisely because the content of the underlying principles of our Constitution demand it. By requiring broad support in the form of an "enhanced majority" to achieve constitutional change, the Constitution ensures that minority interests must be addressed before proposed changes which would affect them may be enacted.

[78] It might be objected, then, that constitutionalism is therefore incompatible with democratic government. This would be an erroneous view. Constitutionalism facilitates—indeed, makes possible—a democratic political system by creating an orderly framework within which people may make political decisions. Viewed correctly, constitutionalism and the rule of law are not in conflict with democracy; rather, they are essential to it. Without that relationship, the political will upon which democratic decisions are taken would itself be undermined.

The doctrine of constitutional supremacy carries with it certain necessary implications that speak to other aspects of public law. The following are worth noting.

1. Hierarchy of Law

To state that the Constitution is Canada's "supreme law" implies a hierarchy of law. Specifically, it implies a distinction between constitutional law and non-constitutional law, or "ordinary law." In the Canadian legal tradition, "ordinary law" contains its own hierarchy between statute law (written laws enacted by legislators) and common law (private law principles developed over time by judicial precedent). The doctrine of parliamentary supremacy stands for the proposition that a rule of the common law can be overridden or amended by express statement of the legislature in the form of a statute.

The relationship between the Constitution and common law in the Charter era has been fraught with more difficulty. The Supreme Court of Canada made early statements that implied limits on the degree to which the common law could be measured against the Charter—see *RWDSU v. Dolphin Delivery*, [1986] 2 SCR 573. More recent statements have expanded the reach of Charter law to influence the development of common law rules. See, for example, *Pepsi-Cola Canada Beverages (West) Ltd. v. Retail, Wholesale and Department Stores Union, Local 558*, [2002] SCR 156 and *Reference re Same-Sex Marriage*, [2004] 3 SCR 698.

For its part, statute law is binding to the extent that it is not inconsistent with the Constitution.

2. Adjudication

To effect constitutional supremacy requires a mechanism for adjudicating alleged inconsistencies between the Constitution and ordinary law, including the power to declare (and enforce) the invalidity of inconsistent ordinary law. Constitutions can never be so detailed and specific as to allow for the possibility of a "self-enforcing" Constitution whose meanings are so evident that everyone can agree on its strictures. The Constitution must be interpreted in order to be applied to the complex and ever-variable conditions within Canadian society.

Our system accepts that constitutional interpretation cannot be performed definitively by the same body that enacts the ordinary law subject to constitutional scrutiny—that is, the *judicial independence.*

legislature. This does not mean that legislatures cannot play a significant role in developing understandings of constitutional text, or making persuasive arguments about why particular legislation is consistent with that text. However, it does mean that the legislature cannot maintain the authoritative voice on the Constitution's interpretation.

This means that in the ordinary course, our system requires that the legislature will be checked by a judiciary with the authority to interpret and apply the Constitution. This judicial function speaks to the need for a robust principle of judicial independence, preserving the interpreters of the Constitution from political interference in their decision making.

The logic of constitutional supremacy does not define the name or particular composition of the body playing this adjudicative function. In the United States, the US Supreme Court expressly confirmed this role for itself in a famous decision by Chief Justice John Marshall, *Marbury v. Madison*, 5 US (Cranch 1) 137 (1803), excerpted in chapter 8, below. Canada's courts and the Judicial Committee of the Privy Council assumed this jurisdiction with respect to the division of powers from the earliest days of Confederation, without feeling the need to discuss the source of their authority to do so; s. 52 of the *Constitution Act, 1982* now provides that source. In Canada, the role has been assigned to the same courts and judges that decide all legal disputes in this society. Other countries have developed special adjudicative bodies or constitutional courts whose sole jurisdiction lies in that domain. In South Africa, membership on the Constitutional Court is not limited to lawyers, as is the case in Canada. The point is that a system of constitutional supremacy requires an independent body with interpretive power.

In Canada, a recent debate has centred on whether administrative tribunals—that is, adjudicative bodies established by the legislature as part of the executive branch of government—should be entitled to interpret and apply the Charter to invalidate legislation. In his reasons for judgment concurring in the result in *Cooper v. Canada (Human Rights Commission)*, [1996] 3 SCR 854, Chief Justice Lamer stated (at para. 2):

> Although judicial review is necessary to preserve important constitutional values, in a democracy like Canada it is inherently controversial, because it confers on unelected officials the power to question decisions which are arrived at through the democratic process. For this reason, in my view, *as a matter of constitutional principle* that power must be reserved to the courts and should not be given over to bodies that are mere creatures of the legislature, whose members are usually vulnerable to removal with every change of government, and whose decisions in some circumstances are made within the parameters of guidelines established by the executive branch of government. [Emphasis in original.]

Chief Justice Lamer's views on this subject ran contrary to the dominant strand of Supreme Court of Canada jurisprudence at the time, and they were expressly rejected by the court in *Nova Scotia (Workers' Compensation Board) v. Martin*, [2003] 2 SCR 504 (at para. 47). Writing for the court, Mr. Justice Gonthier observed (at para. 34) that the relevant question is "whether the tribunal's mandate includes jurisdiction to rule on the constitutionality of the challenged provision. ... This question is answered by applying a presumption, based on the principle of constitutional supremacy ... that all legal decisions will take into account the supreme law of the land. Thus, as a rule, 'an administrative tribunal which has been conferred the power to interpret law holds a concomitant power to determine whether that law is constitutionally valid.'" See also *Tranchemontagne v. Ontario (Director, Disability Support Pro-*

gram), [2006] 1 SCR 513, a case dealing with the constitutional jurisdiction of Ontario's Social Benefits Tribunal.

At first blush, the notion that administrative tribunals (that is, potentially non-independent, executive bodies) may be empowered to apply the Charter seems inconsistent with the notion of constitutional interpretation by an independent body. Still, as we discuss in chapter 8, there will inevitably be a court competent to "judicially review" a tribunal decision. Ultimately, therefore, independent courts have the final adjudicative word.

3. Counter-Majoritarianism

To a greater or lesser degree depending on the nature and quality of a particular electoral system, legislatures express majority preferences. These may change over time, even very short times, and at any one time there may be a great many "majorities" represented in Parliament going to a whole host of different policy issues.

Constitutional supremacy represents a check on majoritarian democracy. It places limits on, or obstacles in the way of, majority preferences. The limits may favour individuals, minority groups, or regional populations. The point is that there is no need for a supreme Constitution other than to place checks on legislative majorities. The adjudicative body that interprets and enforces the Constitution must therefore be recognized as having the legitimate function of ruling against majority preferences. This is not to say that judicial rulings on constitutional issues must always or necessarily run counter to majority views as expressed by legislatures, or that legislatures always accurately express views of a majority. It is to say that in a system of constitutional supremacy, the power to interpret and enforce the Constitution against majority preferences must be present.

The particular checks on majoritarianism embodied in a constitution have a historical dimension. That is, the framers of a constitution anticipate for the future what values deserve protection from majority preferences. Present majorities may well find themselves subject to constitutional limits created by people with very different views, in a very different society. For this reason, the need for ways to amend a constitution are recognized in all known political communities. ⤷ *needs to be able to change! Adapt!.*

4. Amendment by Super-Majority

Constitutional supremacy implies that a constitution cannot be amended in the same way that ordinary legislation is enacted. If the same Parliament that passes ordinary legislation is also able to amend the Constitution itself, it is not bound by the Constitution. It can merely alter its terms whenever it encounters a constitutional difficulty. The process for amending a constitution must involve a "super-majority," which brings in more or other elements of society than comprise a legislative majority. The particular super-majority required will speak to a nation's understanding of itself and what is most important to its ongoing existence. The amending formula adopted in part V of the *Constitution Act, 1982* (discussed further below) turns largely on federalism. It requires majorities of federal and provincial legislatures to agree on proposed changes.

II. THE EXERCISE OF PUBLIC POWER IN CANADA

A. The Principle of the Separation of Powers

The separation-of-powers doctrine refers to the division of governmental functions between the legislative, executive, and judicial branches of the state. Each branch is defined by its relationship to law: the making of law (legislature), the implementing of law (executive), and the interpreting and applying of law (judiciary). The framers of the American Constitution adopted a model of strict separation between the three branches for the purpose of balancing them against each other and reducing the possibility of concentrating public power in any one person or institution.

The parliamentary tradition adopted by Canada's founders does not rely on a similarly strict separation of legislative, executive, and judicial powers. It gives pre-eminence to the legislative branch, to which the executive is made subordinate. Furthermore, the parliamentary system contemplates an overlapping of personnel between the legislature and the executive. The prime minister and members of his or her Cabinet, who comprise the executive council "advising" the head of state, are elected members of the legislature. This is not the case in the United States. There, the president as chief executive has constitutional powers independent of Congress, is elected separately from Congress, and appoints Cabinet members from outside Congress.

The absence of a strict separation-of-powers doctrine has led some to question the utility of the concept for Canadian constitutional law. Take, for example, Dickson CJ's comments in *Re Residential Tenancies Act*, [1981] 1 SCR 714:

> [T]here is no general "separation of powers" in the *British North America Act, 1867*. Our Constitution does not separate the legislative, executive, and judicial functions and insist that each branch of government exercise only its own function.

Nevertheless, the distinction between the legislature, executive, and judiciary is important to Canadian public law. It serves two principal purposes: (1) a functional purpose of identifying the institutional homes of each of the three major forms of public power, and (2) a normative purpose of providing general boundaries for the operation of each institution.

On the functional side, the *Constitution Act, 1867* itself divides public power into the three branches. Part III of the Act describes "executive power" at the federal level (ss. 9 to 16); part IV, federal "legislative power" (ss. 17 to 57); and part V, provincial "executive power" (ss. 58 to 68) and provincial "legislative power" (ss. 69 to 90). Part VII deals with the "judicature" (ss. 96 to 101).

More important, however, is the recognition that each of these powers represents a unique form of authoritative decision making. Legislative decision making is prospective (oriented to the future), broad in impact (oriented to the public interest, or the interests of large groups), and open-ended in range of outcomes; judicial decision making is retrospective (oriented to past events), localized in impact (oriented to individual disputes), and narrow in outcome (oriented to the application of principles to facts to produce the "right" outcome). Executive or administrative decision making shares features of both legislative and judicial decision making, and is the most difficult to define.

That the separation of powers has assumed the aspect of a principle that limits the ability of one branch of the state to intrude on the activity of another has been illustrated most clearly in recent Supreme Court judgments dealing with the power of the judiciary to order remedies for breaches of Charter rights under s. 24(1) of the *Charter of Rights and Freedoms*, which reads:

> 24(1) Anyone whose rights or freedoms, as guaranteed by this Charter, have been infringed or denied may apply to a court of competent jurisdiction to obtain such remedy as the court considers appropriate and just in the circumstances.

In *Doucet-Boudreau v. Nova Scotia (Minister of Education)*, [2003] 3 SCR 3, the court dealt with a challenge by the provincial government to the constitutionality of a s. 24(1) order by a superior court judge that not only obliged the Ministry of Education to complete construction of new schools for minority French language instruction, but also required it to report periodically to the judge on its compliance with the order. The province argued that a "structural injunction" of this kind improperly placed the court in the role of an administrator and usurped the functions of executive government. Justices LeBel and Deschamps, in dissent, agreed with Nova Scotia. The Court majority upheld the trial judge's order, but made the following comments (at paras. 33 and 34) about the need to maintain a boundary between judicial and executive functions in the remedial area (see chapter 8 for a longer excerpt):

> This tradition of compliance [with court orders] takes on a particular significance in the constitutional law context, where courts must ensure that government behaviour conforms with constitutional norms but in doing so must also be sensitive to the separation of function among the legislative, judicial and executive branches. While our Constitution does not expressly provide for the separation of powers ... , the functional separation among the executive, legislative and judicial branches of governance has frequently been noted. ... In *New Brunswick Broadcasting Co. v. Nova Scotia (Speaker of the House of Assembly)*, [1993] 1 SCR 319, McLachlin J (as she then was) stated, at p. 389:
>
> > Our democratic government consists of several branches: the Crown, as represented by the Governor General and the provincial counterparts of that office; the legislative body; the executive; and the courts. It is fundamental to the working of government as a whole that all these parts play their proper role. It is equally fundamental that no one of them overstep its bounds, that each show proper deference for the legitimate sphere of activity of the other.
>
> In other words, in the context of constitutional remedies, courts must be sensitive to their role as judicial arbiters and not fashion remedies which usurp the role of the other branches of governance by taking on tasks to which other persons or bodies are better suited. Concern for the limits of the judicial role is interwoven throughout the law. The development of the doctrines of justiciability, and to a great extent mootness, standing, and ripeness resulted from concerns about the courts overstepping the bounds of the judicial function and their role vis-à-vis other branches of government.

In *Canada (Prime Minister) v. Khadr*, the court declined to make an order under s. 24(1) that the federal government make a formal request to the US government for the repatriation of Omar Khadr from Guantanamo Bay to remedy the breach of Mr. Khadr's Charter s. 7 rights caused by the participation of Canadian government officials in his illegal interrogation, viewing such an order as an intrusion on the executive's prerogative power to conduct diplomacy with foreign countries as it sees fit.

Canada (Prime Minister) v. Khadr
[2010] 1 SCR 44

THE COURT: [33] Second, is the remedy sought precluded by the fact that it touches on the Crown prerogative over foreign affairs? A connection between the remedy and the breach is not the only consideration. As stated in *Doucet-Boudreau*, an appropriate and just remedy is also one that "must employ means that are legitimate within the framework of our constitutional democracy" (para. 56) and must be a "judicial one which vindicates the right while invoking the function and powers of a court" (para. 57). The government argues that courts have no power under the Constitution of Canada to require the executive branch of government to do anything in the area of foreign policy. It submits that the decision not to request the repatriation of Mr. Khadr falls directly within the prerogative powers of the Crown to conduct foreign relations, including the right to speak freely with a foreign state on all such matters: P.W. Hogg, *Constitutional Law of Canada* (5th ed. Supp.), at p. 1-19.

[34] The prerogative power is the "residue of discretionary or arbitrary authority, which at any given time is legally left in the hands of the Crown": *Reference as to the Effect of the Exercise of Royal Prerogative of Mercy Upon Deportation Proceedings*, [1933] SCR 269, at p. 272, per Duff CJ, quoting A.V. Dicey, *Introduction to the Study of the Law of the Constitution* (8th ed. 1915), at p. 420. It is a limited source of non-statutory administrative power accorded by the common law to the Crown: Hogg, at p. 1-17.

[35] The prerogative power over foreign affairs has not been displaced by s. 10 of the *Department of Foreign Affairs and International Trade Act*, RSC 1985, c. E-22, and continues to be exercised by the federal government. The Crown prerogative in foreign affairs includes the making of representations to a foreign government: *Black v. Canada (Prime Minister)* (2001), 199 DLR (4th) 228 (Ont. CA). We therefore agree with O'Reilly J's implicit finding (paras. 39, 40 and 49) that the decision not to request Mr. Khadr's repatriation was made in the exercise of the prerogative over foreign relations.

[36] In exercising its common law powers under the royal prerogative, the executive is not exempt from constitutional scrutiny: *Operation Dismantle v. The Queen*, [1985] 1 SCR 441. It is for the executive and not the courts to decide whether and how to exercise its powers, but the courts clearly have the jurisdiction and the duty to determine whether a prerogative power asserted by the Crown does in fact exist and, if so, whether its exercise infringes the Charter (*Operation Dismantle*) or other constitutional norms (*Air Canada v. British Columbia (Attorney General)*, [1986] 2 SCR 539).

[37] The limited power of the courts to review exercises of the prerogative power for constitutionality reflects the fact that in a constitutional democracy, all government power must be exercised in accordance with the Constitution. This said, judicial review of the exercise of the prerogative power for constitutionality remains sensitive to the fact that the executive branch of government is responsible for decisions under this power, and that the executive is better placed to make such decisions within a range of constitutional options.

The government must have flexibility in deciding how its duties under the power are to be discharged: see, e.g., *Reference re Secession of Quebec*, [1998] 2 SCR 217, at paras. 101-2. But it is for the courts to determine the legal and constitutional limits within which such decisions are to be taken. It follows that in the case of refusal by a government to abide by constitutional constraints, courts are empowered to make orders ensuring that the government's foreign affairs prerogative is exercised in accordance with the constitution: *United States v. Burns*, 2001 SCC 7, [2001] 1 SCR 283.

[38] Having concluded that the courts possess a narrow power to review and intervene on matters of foreign affairs to ensure the constitutionality of executive action, the final question is whether O'Reilly J misdirected himself in exercising that power in the circumstances of this case (*R v. Bjelland*, 2009 SCC 38, [2009] 2 SCR 651, at para. 15; *R v. Regan*, 2002 SCC 12, [2002] 1 SCR 297, at paras. 117-18). (In fairness to the trial judge, we note that the government proposed no alternative (trial judge's reasons, at para. 78).) If the record and legal principle support his decision, deference requires we not interfere. However, in our view that is not the case.

[39] Our first concern is that the remedy ordered below gives too little weight to the constitutional responsibility of the executive to make decisions on matters of foreign affairs in the context of complex and ever-changing circumstances, taking into account Canada's broader national interests. For the following reasons, we conclude that the appropriate remedy is to declare that, on the record before the Court, Canada infringed Mr. Khadr's s. 7 rights, and to leave it to the government to decide how best to respond to this judgment in light of current information, its responsibility for foreign affairs, and in conformity with the *Charter*.

[40] As discussed, the conduct of foreign affairs lies with the executive branch of government. The courts, however, are charged with adjudicating the claims of individuals who claim that their Charter rights have been or will be violated by the exercise of the government's discretionary powers: *Operation Dismantle*.

[41] In some situations, courts may give specific directions to the executive branch of the government on matters touching foreign policy. For example, in *Burns*, the Court held that it would offend s. 7 to extradite a fugitive from Canada without seeking and obtaining assurances from the requesting state that the death penalty would not be imposed. The Court gave due weight to the fact that seeking and obtaining those assurances were matters of Canadian foreign relations. Nevertheless, it ordered that the government seek them.

[42] The specific facts in *Burns* justified a more specific remedy. The fugitives were under the control of Canadian officials. It was clear that assurances would provide effective protection against the prospective *Charter* breaches: it was entirely within Canada's power to protect the fugitives against possible execution. Moreover, the Court noted that no public purpose would be served by extradition without assurances that would not be substantially ·served by extradition with assurances, and that there was nothing to suggest that seeking such assurances would undermine Canada's good relations with other states: *Burns*, at paras. 125 and 136.

[43] The present case differs from *Burns*. Mr. Khadr is not under the control of the Canadian government; the likelihood that the proposed remedy will be effective is unclear; and the impact on Canadian foreign relations of a repatriation request cannot be properly assessed by the Court.

B. Legislative Power

In Canada, the legislative branch of the state is divided between the federal legislature, or Parliament, comprising the elected House of Commons and an appointed Senate, and the elected legislatures in each province. Both levels of legislature derive their powers to make laws from Canada's Constitution. The division of authority between the two legislative levels is a feature of federalism. Other law-making bodies in Canada, including elected municipal councils and school boards, receive their powers by delegation from the legislatures and do not otherwise have sovereign status under the Constitution.

1. The Principle of Parliamentary Supremacy

In the *Secession Reference*, the Supreme Court stated the following at paragraph 73:

> This Court has noted on several occasions that with the adoption of the Charter, the Canadian system of government was transformed to a significant extent from a system of Parliamentary supremacy to one of constitutional supremacy.

What does "parliamentary supremacy" (or "sovereignty") mean? How does it relate to "constitutional supremacy"? If the Canadian system of government has been "transformed to a significant extent" from one to the other, what remains of parliamentary supremacy and how important is it to our public law?

The principle of parliamentary supremacy is and was the basic constitutional rule of British constitutional law that Canada's founders adopted. That they intended to do so is made clear in the preamble to the *Constitution Act, 1867*, which states that it is the desire of the three federating provinces to adopt "a Constitution similar in Principle to the United Kingdom."

British constitutional history is the story of a long and often bloody struggle to bring the monarchy and executive government under the authority of Parliament as the body representing the people of the country. The evolution of Parliament into a representative body elected by universal adult franchise is itself a dramatic and somewhat later developing story, not yet finished if we consider the continued role of the unelected House of Lords in the United Kingdom and Senate in Canada. Nevertheless, to the degree elected legislatures embody democratic values, the reposing of all legitimate state power in the legislature is profoundly democratic.

The simplicity of parliamentary supremacy as a constitutional principle explains why it does not require a written embodiment. Indeed, the British Constitution is famously unwritten. If the framers of Canada's Constitution truly wished to adopt the British principle, why did they do so in a written document, the *Constitution Act, 1867*? The short answer is federalism. Canada was founded on the basis of dividing legislative power between a national legislature, Parliament, and regional or provincial legislatures. As with any contract of any complexity intended to bind wary parties not sure how far each can be trusted, this could only be done in writing. The division of powers between the federal and provincial legislatures became the distinctive Canadian answer to the question of "who" has law-making authority.

If the existence of a written Constitution that placed limits on which jurisdiction could pass what laws is all that is required to have "constitutional supremacy," then Canada has operated on this basis since 1867. That is not, however, how the Canadian system was understood. Rather, the principle of parliamentary supremacy remained predominant, qualified only by federalism. That is, Canada's federal and provincial legislatures were understood to be the sole sovereign holders of state authority, subject to authority being divided between them along the lines largely set out in ss. 91 and 92 of the *Constitution Act, 1867*. With the limited exception of denominational school rights in s. 93 and official language protections in s. 133, Canada's legislatures remained able between them to enact any law they so chose. The doctrine of exhaustion of state power meant that if one level of legislature was unable to enact a law for jurisdictional reasons, then the law could be passed by the other level.

With the *Constitution Act, 1982*, Canada adopted both a *Charter of Rights and Freedoms* and an express declaration of constitutional supremacy. These two developments were hardly coincidental. The Charter imposed significant new limits on the substantive laws that could be passed by either level of legislature—that is, it provided a new and significantly different answer to the question of "what" laws can be enacted. With these limits, the concept of parliamentary supremacy was modified beyond the point at which it could reasonably be used to describe the constitutional system. The limits placed on substantive law making by the Charter, together with the existing limits on who can pass which laws set out in ss. 91 and 92 of the 1867 Act, virtually required a recognition of the written Constitution as being the supreme source of law-making authority in Canada.

The framers of the *Canadian Charter of Rights and Freedoms* were, not surprisingly, sensitive to the impact that entrenched individual rights would have on the principle of parliamentary sovereignty. Certain provincial governments strenuously defended this principle. They reached a compromise with the federal government and the other provinces by agreeing to include an override provision, s. 33, in the Charter. The override allows either Parliament or a provincial legislature to enact legislation in contravention of certain Charter rights if the legislation contains an explicit declaration pursuant to s. 33. The effect of s. 33, colloquially referred to as the "notwithstanding clause" of the Charter, was to reassert parliamentary sovereignty, albeit in an attenuated form.

For this and other reasons, parliamentary sovereignty retains considerable utility and explanatory power with respect to Canadian law. In particular, it remains of great importance with respect to explaining the relationship between legislative and executive power in Canada. While the Constitution has been made supreme over Parliament and the provincial legislatures, the latter remain supreme vis-à-vis the executive branch. Most of the executive's authority derives from delegation under statutes enacted by the legislature. To the extent that the executive is brought under the Constitution, as the court stated in the *Secession Reference*, this is largely accomplished indirectly, or at one remove: executive action must comply with the provisions of the Constitution because it can be authorized only by statutes that themselves are consistent with the Constitution.

Babcock v. Canada, [2002] 3 SCR 3 provides an example of how the court has approached parliamentary sovereignty as a principle in Canadian constitutional law. In *Babcock*, the government of Canada sought to rely on a statutory right of non-disclosure of Cabinet documents, despite the documents having already been disclosed in the course of litigation. The applicants sought to invoke unwritten principles such as the rule of law to support an argument that disclosure should be required despite the clear statutory statement to the contrary. The court found that parliamentary sovereignty decided the issue.

Babcock v. Canada (Attorney General)
[2002] 3 SCR 3

McLACHLIN CJ (Gonthier, Iacobucci, Major, Bastarache, Binnie, Arbour, and LeBel JJ concurring): [1] This case raises the issue of when, if ever, Cabinet confidences must be disclosed in litigation between the government and private citizens.

[2] On June 6, 1990, the Treasury Board of Canada set the pay of Department of Justice
lawyers working in the Toronto Regional Office at a higher rate than that of lawyers working
elsewhere. Vancouver staff lawyers brought an action in the Supreme Court of British Columbia, contending that by failing to pay them the same salaries as Toronto lawyers the government breached their contracts of employment and the fiduciary duty toward them.

[3] The action proceeded, and the parties exchanged lists of relevant documents in December 1996, as required by the BC Supreme Court Rules. A supplemental list of documents was delivered by the government in June 1997. The government listed a number of
documents as producible.

. . .

[5] … The government, nearly two years after it delivered the first list of documents,
changed its position on disclosure of documents. It delivered a certificate of the Clerk of the
Privy Council pursuant to s. 39(1) of the *Canada Evidence Act*, RSC 1985, c. C-5, objecting
to the disclosure of 51 documents and any examination thereon, on the ground that they
contain "information constituting confidences of the Queen's Privy Council for Canada."
The certificate claimed protection for 12 government documents previously listed as producible (some of which had already been disclosed), for five documents in the control or
possession of the plaintiffs, and for 34 government documents and information previously
listed as not producible.

[6] The plaintiffs (respondents) brought an application to compel production of the
documents for which the government claimed protection. The chambers judge, Edwards J,
ruled against them, holding that s. 39 of the *Canada Evidence Act* was constitutional and
clear. If the Clerk of the Privy Council filed a certificate, that was the end of the matter, and
the courts had no power to set the certificate aside. A majority of the Court of Appeal reversed this decision and ordered production of the documents on the ground that the government had waived its right to claim confidentiality by listing some of the documents as
producible and by disclosing selective information in the McCoy affidavit. The government
appeals this decision to this Court.

. . .

III. Issues

[14] 1. What is the nature of Cabinet confidentiality and the processes by which it may
be claimed and relinquished? 2. Is s. 39 of the *Canada Evidence Act* constitutional?

IV. Discussion

A. The Principles

[15] Cabinet confidentiality is essential to good government. The right to pursue justice
in the courts is also of primary importance in our society, as is the rule of law, accountability

of the executive, and the principle that official actions must flow from statutory authority clearly granted and properly exercised. Yet sometimes these fundamental principles conflict. How are such conflicts to be resolved? That is the question posed by this appeal.

. . .

[21] Section 39 of the *Canada Evidence Act* is Canada's response to the need to provide a mechanism for the responsible exercise of the power to claim Cabinet confidentiality in the context of judicial and quasi-judicial proceedings. It sets up a process for bringing information within the protection of the Act. Certification by the Clerk of the Privy Council or by a minister of the Crown, is the trigger by which information becomes protected. The Clerk must certify that the "information constitutes a confidence of the Queen's Privy Council for Canada." For more particularity, s. 39(2) sets out categories of information that falls within its scope.

[22] Section 39(1) permits the Clerk to certify information as confidential. It does not restrain voluntary disclosure of confidential information. …

[23] If the Clerk or minister *chooses* to certify a confidence, it gains the protection of s. 39. Once certified, information gains greater protection than at common law. If s. 39 is engaged, the "court, person or body with jurisdiction" hearing the matter *must* refuse disclosure; "disclosure of the information shall be refused." Moreover, this must be done "without examination or hearing of the information by the court, person or body." This absolute language goes beyond the common law approach of balancing the public interest in protecting confidentiality and disclosure on judicial review. Once information has been validly certified, the common law no longer applies to that information.

. . .

C. The Constitutionality of Section 39

[53] Because s. 39 applies to the undisclosed documents, it is necessary to consider the constitutional questions in this case. The respondents argue that s. 39 of the *Canada Evidence Act* is of no force or effect by reason of one or both of the preamble to the *Constitution Act, 1867* and s. 96 of the *Constitution Act, 1867*.

(1) The Preamble to the Constitution Act, 1867

[54] The respondents in this case challenge the constitutionality of s. 39 and argue that the provision is *ultra vires* Parliament because of the unwritten principles of the Canadian Constitution: the rule of law, the independence of the judiciary, and the separation of powers. Although the unwritten constitutional principles are capable of limiting government actions, I find that they do not do so in this case.

[55] The unwritten principles must be balanced against the principle of Parliamentary sovereignty. In *Commission des droits de la personne v. Attorney General of Canada*, [1982] 1 SCR 215, this Court upheld as constitutional s. 41(2) of the *Federal Court Act*, the predecessor to s. 39, which permitted the government to claim absolute privilege over a broader class of confidences.

[56] Recently, the Federal Court of Appeal considered the constitutional validity of s. 39 of the *Canada Evidence Act* in *Singh, supra*. On the basis of a thorough and compelling review of the principle of parliamentary sovereignty in the context of unwritten constitutional

principles, Strayer JA held that federal Crown privilege is part of valid federal law over which Parliament had the power to legislate. Strayer JA concluded at para. 36:

> ... [T]he rule of law cannot be taken to invalidate a statute which has the effect of allowing representatives of the Crown to identify certain documents as beyond disclosure: that is, the rule of law does not preclude a special law with a special result dealing with a special class of documents which, for long standing reasons based on constitutional principles such as responsible government, have been treated differently from private documents in a commercial law suit.

[57] I share the view of the Federal Court of Appeal that s. 39 does not offend the rule of law or the doctrines of separation of powers and the independence of the judiciary. It is well within the power of the legislature to enact laws, even laws which some would consider draconian, as long as it does not fundamentally alter or interfere with the relationship between the courts and the other branches of government.

[Justice L'Heureux-Dubé concurred in separate reasons.]

2. The Principle of Federalism

a. Overview

The basis for Confederation in 1867 was the agreement by the political leaders of the separate British colonies of Canada, New Brunswick, and Nova Scotia to divide sovereign legislative power between a federal government and regional or provincial governments, and to separate Canada into the provinces of Ontario and Quebec. As the Supreme Court stated in *Reference re Secession of Quebec* in 1998, the recognition of provincial legislatures with extensive areas of jurisdiction, principally over all private legal relationships under the rubric of "property and civil rights within the province," was the *sine qua non* of Confederation for the leaders and people of Quebec and the maritime provinces. The court recognized "federalism" as an unwritten principle of the Canadian Constitution, describing it as the means of recognizing regional cultural diversity at the founding of Canada, particularly with respect to the distinct nature of Quebec as a predominantly French-speaking society.

Reference re Secession of Quebec
[1998] 2 SCR 217

Federalism

[55] It is undisputed that Canada is a federal state. Yet many commentators have observed that, according to the precise terms of the *Constitution Act, 1867*, the federal system was only partial. See, e.g., K.C. Wheare, *Federal Government* (4th ed. 1963), at pp. 18-20. This was so because, on paper, the federal government retained sweeping powers which threatened to undermine the autonomy of the provinces. Here again, however, a review of the written provisions of the Constitution does not provide the entire picture. Our political

and constitutional practice has adhered to an underlying principle of federalism, and has interpreted the written provisions of the Constitution in this light. For example, although the federal power of disallowance [of provincial statutes] was included in the *Constitution Act, 1867*, the underlying principle of federalism triumphed early. Many constitutional scholars contend that the federal power of disallowance has been abandoned (e.g., P.W. Hogg, *Constitutional Law of Canada* (4th ed. 1997), at p. 120).

[56] In a federal system of government such as ours, political power is shared by two orders of government: the federal government on the one hand, and the provinces on the other. Each is assigned respective spheres of jurisdiction by the *Constitution Act, 1867*. See, e.g., *Liquidators of the Maritime Bank of Canada v. Receiver-General of New Brunswick*, [1892] AC 437 (PC), at pp. 441-42. It is up to the courts "to control the limits of the respective sovereignties": *Northern Telecom Canada Ltd. v. Communication Workers of Canada*, [1983] 1 SCR 733, at p. 741. In interpreting our Constitution, the courts have always been concerned with the federalism principle, inherent in the structure of our constitutional arrangements, which has from the beginning been the lodestar by which the courts have been guided.

[57] This underlying principle of federalism, then, has exercised a role of considerable importance in the interpretation of the written provisions of our Constitution. In the *Patriation Reference* ... , at pp. 905-9, we confirmed that the principle of federalism runs through the political and legal systems of Canada. Indeed, Martland and Ritchie JJ, dissenting in the *Patriation Reference*, at p. 821, considered federalism to be "the dominant principle of Canadian constitutional law." With the enactment of the Charter, that proposition may have less force than it once did, but there can be little doubt that the principle of federalism remains a central organizational theme of our Constitution. Less obviously, perhaps, but certainly of equal importance, federalism is a political and legal response to underlying social and political realities.

[58] The principle of federalism recognizes the diversity of the component parts of Confederation, and the autonomy of provincial governments to develop their societies within their respective spheres of jurisdiction. The federal structure of our country also facilitates democratic participation by distributing power to the government thought to be most suited to achieving the particular societal objective having regard to this diversity. The scheme of the *Constitution Act, 1867*, it was said in *Re the Initiative and Referendum Act*, [1919] AC 935 (PC), at p. 942, was

> not to weld the Provinces into one, nor to subordinate Provincial Governments to a central authority, but to establish a central government in which these Provinces should be represented, entrusted with exclusive authority only in affairs in which they had a common interest. Subject to this each Province was to retain its independence and autonomy and to be directly under the Crown as its head.

More recently, in *Haig v. Canada*, [1993] 2 SCR 995, at p. 1047, the majority of this Court held that differences between provinces "are a rational part of the political reality in the federal process." It was referring to the differential application of federal law in individual provinces, but the point applies more generally. A unanimous Court expressed similar views in *R v. S. (S.)*, [1990] 2 SCR 254, at pp. 287-88.

[59] The principle of federalism facilitates the pursuit of collective goals by cultural and linguistic minorities which form the majority within a particular province. This is the case in Quebec, where the majority of the population is French-speaking, and which possesses a distinct culture. This is not merely the result of chance. The social and demographic reality of Quebec explains the existence of the province of Quebec as a political unit and indeed, was one of the essential reasons for establishing a federal structure for the Canadian union in 1867. The experience of both Canada East and Canada West under the *Union Act, 1840* (UK), 3-4 Vict., c. 35, had not been satisfactory. The federal structure adopted at Confederation enabled French-speaking Canadians to form a numerical majority in the province of Quebec, and so exercise the considerable provincial powers conferred by the *Constitution Act, 1867* in such a way as to promote their language and culture. It also made provision for certain guaranteed representation within the federal Parliament itself.

[60] Federalism was also welcomed by Nova Scotia and New Brunswick, both of which also affirmed their will to protect their individual cultures and their autonomy over local matters. All new provinces joining the federation sought to achieve similar objectives, which are no less vigorously pursued by the provinces and territories as we approach the new millennium.

As noted, the principal textual source of this division of powers is found in ss. 91 and 92 of the *Constitution Act, 1867*, which set out lists of enumerated federal and provincial powers, respectively. Since the Privy Council decision of *Hodge v. The Queen* in 1883, the national and provincial legislatures have been understood as "coordinate" authorities, with equal sovereign status derived from the Constitution.

Sections 91 and 92 set out "subject matters," or areas of regulatory or legislative concern, that fall within the exclusive jurisdiction of the respective legislative bodies. Matters within federal jurisdiction include criminal law in s. 91(27), trade and commerce in s. 91(2), and banking in s. 91(15). Matters within provincial jurisdiction include hospitals (other than marine hospitals) in s. 92(7) and municipalities in s. 92(8). The most important provincial jurisdiction is that over "property and civil rights" in s. 92(13). This phrase, used in the *Quebec Act* of 1774 to refer to all private law matters (which by that statute reverted to the local French civil law tradition developed in New France before its cession to Britain in 1763), encompasses all matters of civil obligation, including contract, tort, and family law. For this reason, provinces have the more extensive jurisdiction over regulation of economic matters in Canada, other than those relating to international and interprovincial trade and commerce, which are understood to fall within s. 91(2). Section 93 of the *Constitution Act, 1867* confers jurisdiction over education to the provinces, while s. 95 grants a paramount authority to Parliament with respect to immigration.

The opening paragraph of s. 91 grants a residual law-making power to Parliament under the phrase "peace, order and good government of Canada" (colloquially known as POGG). This implies an exhaustive distribution of legislative powers between the two levels of legislature: until 1982, it was correct to say that there was no law that could not be enacted by either Parliament or the provincial legislatures. This principle has been modified by the adoption of the *Charter of Rights and Freedoms*, which places limits (the same limits) on both legislative levels.

For the first 115 years of Confederation, Canadian constitutional law largely concerned the elaboration by the judiciary of the boundaries and interrelationships between the federal and provincial jurisdictions established by these general terms. A significant part of the judicial discussion concerned the understanding of the relationship between the POGG power and the enumerated heads of power in s. 92, especially property and civil rights. Until 1949, the final court of appeal for Canadian law was the Judicial Committee of the Privy Council (JCPC), a subdivision of the British House of Lords responsible for appeals from the former colonies. The JCPC played a major role in the evolution of Canadian federalism. It became noted as an exponent of strong provincial powers and, in particular, for limiting POGG as a source of federal jurisdiction to circumstances of national crisis and emergency, such as occurred in wartime. For much of the period subsequent to 1949, the Supreme Court of Canada has modified this understanding and incrementally expanded the scope for federal authority and overlapping powers between the two levels of government. Given that the federal government appoints Supreme Court of Canada justices, this has on occasion caused discontent among provinces and led to calls for constitutional amendment to the appointment process for the court.

b. Federalism and Human Rights Legislation

Federalism means that regulatory authority over different aspects of Canadian society is divided between the federal and provincial governments. As a consequence, all 11 Canadian legislatures, as well as those of the Yukon, Northwest Territories, and Nunavut, have enacted human rights laws to govern those areas subject to their regulatory authority.

Most private activity falls within provincial authority under "property and civil rights" in s. 92(13) of the *Constitution Act, 1867*. However, certain sectors of the economy fall within federal authority—such as banking in s. 91(15), navigation and shipping in s. 91(10), and the military in s. 91(7). Within these sectors, employment relationships, as well as other important aspects of activity, are generally subject to federal authority as being incidental to their regulation. For this reason, provincial legislatures are unable to enact laws dealing with discrimination in these areas. Parliament has enacted the *Canadian Human Rights Act*, to cover these areas of the economy.

C. Executive Power

The executive branch replicates the duality created by federalism, with executives at the federal and provincial levels. Identifying the full and proper extent of the "executive" in Canada is a somewhat more difficult task than identifying the "legislature." The executive includes all ministries of government and their employees—the civil service. It also includes the armed forces and Crown corporations. It may include statutorily created bodies that carry out largely "governmental" functions. At some point, however, where the control of an entity is derived more from private sources, such as the membership of a registered society or corporation, than from ministerial sources, we are no longer dealing with the executive, but with an entity belonging to civil society. This line is not always easy to draw—institutions that lie at the margins may include universities and other post-secondary institutions, hospitals, and professional regulatory bodies. We discuss the composition of the executive in greater detail in chapter 5.

Commentators often argue that Canada's system of government is dominated by the executive branch, that the prime minister and premiers exercise an authority over their parties and over the legislatures that is unusual among western democracies. (See, for example, Jeffrey Simpson, *The Friendly Dictatorship: Reflections on Canadian Democracy* (Toronto: McClelland & Stewart, 2001).) While this may be true, it is largely a product of politics, not law.

In law, the executive branch is subordinate to the legislature. The relationship between the legislative and executive branches in Canada has two important features. First, subject to the relatively minor sources of power found in the "royal prerogative" and the Constitution, the executive branch derives any power it has solely from the laws or statutes passed by the legislature. That is, the executive must locate any authority it has to act in Canadian society from a statutory source. By way of statutes, legislators delegate elements of their sovereign power to executive actors, be that the federal or provincial Cabinet, a particular minister of the Crown, or a local public health official. The delegation is made on the terms of the statute, and can always be revoked by the legislature by amendment or repeal. In this sense, the executive in Canada (unlike that in the United States, where the president has many independent powers derived from the Constitution) is almost wholly dependent on and subordinate to the legislative branch for its authority to act.

The second feature of the relationship between the legislative and executive branches in Canada is that by constitutional convention, the executive is responsible to the legislature. This is the essential meaning of "responsible government" in the parliamentary tradition. Convention requires that the prime minister and his or her ministry command the support (or "confidence") of a majority of elected legislators. (As discussed in chapter 4, should the prime minister and his or her government lose the confidence of the legislature, they must either resign and a new government be formed from the existing membership of the House of Commons or seek a dissolution of Parliament and the holding of new elections.)

D. Judicial Power

The *Constitution Act, 1867* contains provisions on "Judicature" in ss. 96 to 101. Section 96 provides that the federal executive shall appoint the justices of the country's superior, county, and district courts. Although the power to appoint judges to these courts is assigned to the federal government, it is the provinces, exercising their authority over the "administration of justice" in s. 92(14) of the *Constitution Act, 1867*, that establish these courts in their respective jurisdiction. These courts are understood to exercise the inherent jurisdiction of superior, or King's courts, as understood in the British legal tradition. The superior courts in Canada are often referred to as "section 96 courts" in recognition that it is under this section of the *Constitution Act, 1867* that the judges are appointed. Each province also has a system of non-section 96 courts, to which the province has the authority to appoint judges.

Under s. 101, Parliament is accorded the authority to create courts for the "better administration of the laws of Canada"—understood to mean laws passed by Parliament itself. Using this authority, Parliament has enacted the *Federal Courts Act*, which establishes the trial level Federal Court of Canada and the Federal Court of Appeal. The Federal Courts' jurisdiction and power are statutory, not inherent, but they otherwise play a role similar to that of the provincial superior courts.

Section 101 also authorizes Parliament to create a general court of appeal for Canada. In 1875, Parliament enacted the *Supreme Court Act*, creating the Supreme Court of Canada to play this role. This ordinary federal statute, with amendments, remains the source of the Supreme Court's existence and role. The *Constitution Act, 1982* appears to have entrenched changes to the court's composition and the process for appointing its justices, but the Supreme Court otherwise does not have constitutional status.

The slender foundation in the text of the Constitution for the judicial system in Canada has not prevented the courts themselves from carving out an indispensable and essentially unassailable position in Canada's constitutional system. This position goes to what the Supreme Court of Canada has identified as the "core jurisdiction" of superior courts, which encompasses two crucial public law powers: (1) the jurisdiction to rule on the constitutional validity of all ordinary laws in Canada, and (2) the jurisdiction to supervise the activities of executive government and other statutorily delegated actors to ensure that they act within their statutory authority. The former role represents the superior courts' "constitutional law" jurisdiction; the latter role represents its "administrative law" jurisdiction.

1. *The Judiciary's Constitutional Law Jurisdiction*

As discussed above, the principle of constitutional supremacy presupposes a role for an adjudicative institution to rule on whether ordinary legislation has violated the limits on legislative power set out in the Constitution. The principal remedy adopted by the judiciary in constitutional cases has been that of declaring laws invalid and of no force and effect. Since the adoption of the *Charter of Rights and Freedoms*, the question of remedies has become somewhat more complex. Section 24 of the Charter authorizes "courts of competent jurisdiction" to grant remedies in individual circumstances for Charter breaches, including the exclusion from the criminal process of evidence obtained as a result of a breach where not to do so would "bring the administration of justice into disrepute." The question of what scope s. 24 may give for remedies in damages has received little elaboration by the courts to date.

2. *The Judiciary's Administrative Law Jurisdiction*

In Canada, superior courts exercise a supervisory jurisdiction with respect to exercises of executive government authority. This is the subject matter of administrative law. As earlier described, executive government derives all its authority to act from statutes (save and except for those few matters where authority is derived from royal prerogative). This implies that executive authority is limited by and to the jurisdiction granted by statutory delegation from the legislature. Just as the judiciary acts as the "umpire" with respect to claims that legislatures have exceeded their constitutional mandate, superior courts have historically assumed the role of ensuring that executive government acts within its delegated statutory authority. In practice, this role is performed by allowing all persons adversely affected by government action to petition the superior courts seeking "judicial review" of whether the executive official has acted within the bounds of his or her statutory power. This administrative law or judicial review jurisdiction is understood to be a matter of common law development, and therefore not itself dependent on being granted by legislatures.

The significance of this common law supervisory jurisdiction has been underlined by the Supreme Court of Canada's identification of judicial review of executive action as having constitutional status. In *Crevier v. Quebec*, [1981] 2 SCR 220, the court stated that judicial review of executive powers is a "hallmark" of s. 96 jurisdiction, and so cannot be withdrawn from those courts by provincial legislatures. In *MacMillan-Bloedel Ltd. v. Simpson*, [1995] 4 SCR 725, the court confirmed that Parliament is also constitutionally barred from infringing this "core jurisdiction" of s. 96 courts.

As noted, however, the federal government has the power to create s. 101 courts and thereby confer administrative law powers on a new "court." That is effectively what Parliament did in 1970 by creating the Federal Courts and conferring on them exclusive jurisdiction with respect to the supervision of federal statutory delegates. Since that time, administrative law jurisdiction in Canada has been divided between the Federal Courts and the provincial superior courts, roughly on the basis of whether the delegate in question is empowered under a federal or provincial statute.

We return to these topics in chapters 5 and 8.

3. The Principle of Judicial Independence

Judicial independence is a constitutional doctrine closely tied to the separation of powers. The Supreme Court has described judicial independence as the "lifeblood of constitutionalism in democratic societies": see *Beauregard v. Canada*, [1986] 2 SCR 56, at 70. It is "essential to the achievement and proper functioning of a free, just and democratic society based on the principles of constitutionalism and the rule of law": see *Mackin v. New Brunswick (Minister of Finance)*, [2002] 1 SCR 405, at para. 34.

Judicial independence ensures that "judges, as the arbiters of disputes, are at complete liberty to decide individual cases on their merits without interference": see *Ell v. Alberta*, [2003] 1 SCR 857, at para. 21. It insulates judges from retaliation from other branches of government for their decisions and guarantees that "the power of the state is exercised in accordance with the rule of law and the provisions of our Constitution. In this capacity, courts act as a shield against unwarranted deprivations by the state of the rights and freedoms of individuals": see *Ell*, at para. 22.

Judicial independence also preserves the separation of powers between the three branches of our democracy by "depoliticizing" the relationship between the judiciary and the other two branches: "the legislature and executive cannot, and cannot appear to, exert political pressure on the judiciary, and conversely ... members of the judiciary should exercise reserve in speaking out publicly on issues of general public policy that are or have the potential to come before the courts, that are the subject of political debate, and which do not relate to the proper administration of justice": see *Re Remuneration of Judges* (the "*Provincial Judges Reference*"), [1997] 3 SCR 3, at para. 140.

The actual content of judicial independence is discussed in detail in chapter 6.

III. PROCESSES OF CONSTITUTIONAL AMENDMENT
AND EVOLUTION

A constitution embodies legal stability, but it must also account and allow for change. The balance between the need to make a constitution difficult to amend, while still allowing it to evolve to meet the changing needs of the society it governs, is one of the great challenges of constitutional law. It has certainly been one of the great challenges of Canada's constitutional history.

A. The Amending Formula in Part V of the Constitution Act, 1982

The Canadian Constitution lacked any formal amending process until 1982. The framers of the *Constitution Act, 1867* did not include in the document any provisions addressing how the people or governments of the dominion could make amendments to the Constitution. This reflected their understanding of Canada as a colony of the United Kingdom. Just as the *Constitution Act, 1867* was a statute of the Imperial Parliament in London, so too its amendment was left to British parliamentarians. In effect, the "super-majority" required of Canadians with respect to amending their own constitution was the need to request that this be undertaken in London.

The project of patriating the Constitution and thereby accomplishing the last stage of national independence and sovereignty foundered for decades precisely over the failure to achieve agreement on a new, domestic amending formula. This was hardly surprising given that a debate over a constitutional amending process is a debate over political power. For many years, Quebec sought a veto over any constitutional change that would affect the powers of its government or touch on issues of language and culture. Other provinces either opposed Quebec's veto, or sought their own veto. After years of failing to achieve agreement, the federal government of Prime Minister Pierre Trudeau moved forward in 1980-81 with a unilateral proposal to patriate the Constitution with a domestic amending formula of its own design. This resulted in a constitutional crisis. In the *Patriation Reference* in 1981, the Supreme Court ruled that federal unilateralism, though lawful, breached a convention of the Constitution requiring "substantial" agreement of the provinces.

Representatives of the federal and provincial governments met in a constitutional conference in November 1981 and agreed on the terms of the *Constitution Act, 1982*, including the amending formula in part V of the Act. The formula did not include a veto for any single province. The government of Quebec, alone of all provinces, did not agree to the new Constitution, a position that has remained true for all succeeding governments of Quebec since that time. Nevertheless, in the *Quebec Veto Reference*, [1982] 2 SCR 793, the Supreme Court ruled that Quebec's agreement was not needed for purposes of meeting the "substantial agreement" standard, and the *Constitution Act, 1982* came into force and effect with respect to the entire country, Quebec included.

The process for amending the Constitution of Canada is set out in part V of the *Constitution Act, 1982*, which actually sets out five distinct amending formulas applying to different circumstances:

1. the general formula for all amendments not falling within formulas (2) through (5), which requires the agreement of Parliament and the legislatures of at least two-thirds of the provinces having at least 50 percent of the population of Canada (s. 38);
2. unanimity of Parliament and all provincial legislatures (s. 41);
3. Parliament, and the legislatures of just those provinces affected by an amendment (s. 43);
4. Parliament alone, with respect to its own institutions (s. 44); and
5. a provincial legislature alone, with respect to the provincial constitution (s. 45).

The amending formula clearly turns on federalism, in that the parties to any amendment are the federal and provincial legislatures. Similarly, amendment works through representative institutions. There is no role in the formula for popular initiatives, referenda, or constitutional conferences.

Constitution Act, 1982
Being Schedule B to the *Canada Act 1982* (UK), 1982, c. 11

Part V

Procedure for Amending Constitution of Canada

38(1) An amendment to the Constitution of Canada may be made by proclamation issued by the Governor General under the Great Seal of Canada where so authorized by

(a) resolutions of the Senate and House of Commons; and

(b) resolutions of the legislative assemblies of at least two-thirds of the provinces that have, in the aggregate, according to the then latest general census, at least fifty per cent of the population of all the provinces.

(2) An amendment made under subsection (1) that derogates from the legislative powers, the proprietary rights or any other rights or privileges of the legislature or government of a province shall require a resolution supported by a majority of the members of each of the Senate, the House of Commons and the legislative assemblies required under subsection (1).

(3) An amendment referred to in subsection (2) shall not have effect in a province the legislative assembly of which has expressed its dissent thereto by resolution supported by a majority of its members prior to the issue of the proclamation to which the amendment relates unless that legislative assembly, subsequently, by resolution supported by a majority of its members, revokes its dissent and authorizes the amendment.

(4) A resolution of dissent made for the purposes of subsection (3) may be revoked at any time before or after the issue of the proclamation to which it relates.

39(1) A proclamation shall not be issued under subsection 38(1) before the expiration of one year from the adoption of the resolution initiating the amendment procedure thereunder, unless the legislative assembly of each province has previously adopted a resolution of assent or dissent.

(2) A proclamation shall not be issued under subsection 38(1) after the expiration of three years from the adoption of the resolution initiating the amendment procedure thereunder.

40. Where an amendment is made under subsection 38(1) that transfers provincial legislative powers relating to education or other cultural matters from provincial legislatures to Parliament, Canada shall provide reasonable compensation to any province to which the amendment does not apply.

41. An amendment to the Constitution of Canada in relation to the following matters may be made by proclamation issued by the Governor General under the Great Seal of Canada only where authorized by resolutions of the Senate and House of Commons and of the legislative assembly of each province:

(a) the office of the Queen, the Governor General and the Lieutenant Governor of a province;

(b) the right of a province to a number of members in the House of Commons not less than the number of Senators by which the province is entitled to be represented at the time this Part comes into force;

(c) subject to section 43, the use of the English or the French language;

(d) the composition of the Supreme Court of Canada; and

(e) an amendment to this Part.

42(1) An amendment to the Constitution of Canada in relation to the following matters may be made only in accordance with subsection 38(1):

(a) the principle of proportionate representation of the provinces in the House of Commons prescribed by the Constitution of Canada;

(b) the powers of the Senate and the method of selecting Senators;

(c) the number of members by which a province is entitled to be represented in the Senate and the residence qualifications of Senators;

(d) subject to paragraph 41(d), the Supreme Court of Canada;

(e) the extension of existing provinces into the territories; and

(f) notwithstanding any other law or practice, the establishment of new provinces.

(2) Subsections 38(2) to (4) do not apply in respect of amendments in relation to matters referred to in subsection (1).

43. An amendment to the Constitution of Canada in relation to any provision that applies to one or more, but not all, provinces, including

(a) any alteration to boundaries between provinces, and

(b) any amendment to any provision that relates to the use of the English or the French language within a province,

may be made by proclamation issued by the Governor General under the Great Seal of Canada only where so authorized by resolutions of the Senate and House of Commons and of the legislative assembly of each province to which the amendment applies.

44. Subject to sections 41 and 42, Parliament may exclusively make laws amending the Constitution of Canada in relation to the executive government of Canada or the Senate and House of Commons.

45. Subject to section 41, the legislature of each province may exclusively make laws amending the constitution of the province.

46(1) The procedures for amendment under sections 38, 41, 42 and 43 may be initiated either by the Senate or the House of Commons or by the legislative assembly of a province.

(2) A resolution of assent made for the purposes of this Part may be revoked at any time before the issue of a proclamation authorized by it.

47(1) An amendment to the Constitution of Canada made by proclamation under section 38, 41, 42 or 43 may be made without a resolution of the Senate authorizing the issue of the proclamation if, within one hundred and eighty days after the adoption by the House of Commons of a resolution authorizing its issue, the Senate has not adopted such a resolution and if, at any time after the expiration of that period, the House of Commons again adopts the resolution.

(2) Any period when Parliament is prorogued or dissolved shall not be counted in computing the one hundred and eighty day period referred to in subsection (1).

48. The Queen's Privy Council for Canada shall advise the Governor General to issue a proclamation under this Part forthwith on the adoption of the resolutions required for an amendment made by proclamation under this Part.

―――――――――――

The adoption of a domestic amending formula in the Constitution after 115 years of Confederation left an important question unanswered: would the amending formula prove workable? The 30 years that have passed since 1982 have not provided a definitive answer to that question because Canadians have not succeeded in making any significant constitutional amendments in that period despite strenuous efforts to do so. In 1987, the federal government and the governments of all ten provinces agreed to a set of amendments known as the Meech Lake Accord, whose principal purpose was to reconcile the province of Quebec with the Constitution of Canada. Included in the Accord were proposed amendments to the Constitution that would recognize Quebec as a "distinct society" within Canada and limit the federal government's power to spend in areas of provincial jurisdiction. Public opposition to the Accord developed in several areas of the country, leading to a full-blown constitutional crisis. The three-year period set out in s. 39(2) of the *Constitution Act, 1982* expired before all legislatures passed resolutions endorsing the Accord, and it failed. This failure led to a renewed two-year effort to negotiate a new agreement on a wider package of amendments, including proposals for aboriginal self-government and an elected Senate. The Charlottetown Accord, as it was called, was put to a national referendum in October 1992. The Constitution does not contemplate referenda as part of the amending process, so the 1992 referendum was understood to be advisory in nature. Nevertheless, when majorities in Quebec and the western provinces rejected the Accord, the federal and provincial governments declined to proceed with the changes it proposed. Thus, five years of intense, often wrenching public debate, had achieved nothing with respect to what were viewed as the major issues in Canada's constitutional life. The fallout from these events included the referendum on secession in Quebec in 1995, the *Secession Reference* in 1998, and decisions by successive federal governments to avoid talk of constitutional reform if at all possible.

B. Judicial Interpretation and the "Living Tree"

The difficulty Canada has experienced in making formal amendments to the Constitution since 1982 should not be taken to mean that the Constitution is a static entity, unresponsive to changes in the society it purports to govern. This section and the next explore two recognized ways in which constitutional evolution occurs in Canada even in the absence of formal amendments to the text of the Constitution. The first of these involves an approach to interpretation that permits the judiciary to read constitutional text in light of changes in society and contemporary uses of language. While this "living tree" approach is well-accepted in Canadian jurisprudence, it is not uncontroversial.

Former US Chief Justice Charles Evans Hughes stated: "The Constitution is what the Judges say it is." This sounds at first like a declaration of unbridled judicial power. In another sense, it is merely a truism. The general language in which constitutions are written does not apply itself. It must be interpreted in order to be applied. As stated above, the very idea of constitutional supremacy calls for an adjudicative institution—a judiciary that has the authority to interpret and apply constitutional text to real world circumstances.

There are many different tools and techniques for textual interpretation, and few judges or lawyers employ only one. Nevertheless, in the field of constitutional interpretation, two general approaches are commonly conceived as the leading, and competing, schools. The first is known as the historical or originalist approach. At the risk of greatly oversimplifying this approach, proponents of originalism believe that constitutional text should be understood as having a single, unchanging meaning—the meaning intended by those who wrote and ratified the text. This provides the Constitution with needed stability. Should the meaning of the text cease to speak to the needs of contemporary society, then this problem should be addressed by amending the text. So long as formal amendment processes require the operation of democratic processes, the community will assume responsibility for constitutional evolution in the appropriate arena of political life.

The second approach is known under various names—sometimes the "progressive" or "living tree" approach. This is the alternative favoured by the Supreme Court of Canada. This approach conceives of the text of the Constitution as not being frozen in meaning to one time and place—partly because much of the text may never have had a single agreed-on meaning. Rather, it seeks to give a reasoned reading of the text that makes sense of it at the time it is being interpreted. This approach was first stated to be appropriate to Canadian constitutionalism by the Judicial Committee of the Privy Council in the famous "*Persons*" case in 1930 (*Edwards v. AG Canada*, [1930] AC 124, excerpted in chapter 2). Recall that, in this case, the Judicial Committee of the Privy Council reversed the Supreme Court of Canada's decision that since the word "persons" in 1867 was intended to refer only to men, women could not be "qualified persons" for the purpose of being appointed to the Senate. The Lords stated that the open-textured language of a constitution should be viewed as a "living tree" that is capable of growth and evolution. In this way, the judiciary assumes a modest role in keeping a constitution in tune with the times and making it less necessary for text to be amended.

The Supreme Court of Canada has used the living-tree metaphor on a number of occasions, including in the *Reference re Same-Sex Marriage*, [2004] 3 SCR 698. The court ruled unanimously that Parliament had the power to pass legislation changing the definition of civil marriage from an opposite- to a same-sex relationship, and in doing so rejected an originalist argument that the word "marriage" in s. 91(26) of the *Constitution Act, 1867* could only be defined in opposite-sex terms.

The progressive or living-tree approach may on occasion remove the necessity (or rather, relieve the political pressure) for constitutional amendment. It does not replace it. Nor does it take away from the significance of amending procedures as being the locus of fundamental issues of political power in society.

C. Unwritten Principles of the Constitution

Part V of the *Constitution Act, 1982* appears to provide a complete code for the process of constitutional amendment by Canada's governments. The federal government sought to rely on this understanding when it initiated a reference to the Supreme Court on the issue of whether Quebec (or, presumably, any other province) has the power under the Constitution to secede unilaterally from Canada. In 1995, the Parti Québécois (PQ) government of Quebec had come within 50,000 votes of winning a referendum on sovereignty. It appeared that the PQ government's assumption had been that a majority vote for sovereignty in a referendum would form the legal basis for secession without agreement of the rest of Canada. The reference by the federal government challenged this assumption. The government argued to the court that secession of a province necessarily involves amendment of the Constitution, and that this can only be effected through the processes set out in part V. It cannot be lawfully accomplished, the government argued, solely through a vote in a referendum. Referenda, after all, are not mentioned in part V and have no status other than as an informal means for governments to consult with their constituents.

The Supreme Court's subtle judgment in the *Secession Reference* managed to affirm much of this position, while at the same time establishing that the Constitution has a depth beyond the text and comprehends legal obligations not found in its text. As we have seen, the court identified four unwritten principles that are part of the "architecture" of the Constitution—the principles of democracy, federalism, constitutionalism and the rule of law, and protection of minority rights. The justices rejected the idea, advanced by counsel acting as *amicus curiae* on behalf of the sovereignist position, that the principle of democracy alone could justify basing a lawful secession on a referendum vote. The court found that democracy must be qualified by each of the other principles, which together meant that secession could be achieved only in accordance with part V. However, the court added, a vote representing a "clear majority" on a "clear question" in favour of secession would be sufficient to create a *legal* duty to negotiate on the part of the other parties to the federation. The court described this as a duty to negotiate the terms of secession in good faith, but not a duty to reach agreement on any particular terms, or at all. In this way, the court recognized a constitutional role for a referendum that nowhere appears in part V.

Reference re Secession of Quebec
[1998] 2 SCR 217

[83] Secession is the effort of a group or section of a state to withdraw itself from the political and constitutional authority of that state, with a view to achieving statehood for a new territorial unit on the international plane. In a federal state, secession typically takes the

form of a territorial unit seeking to withdraw from the federation. Secession is a legal act as much as a political one. By the terms of Question 1 of this Reference, we are asked to rule on the legality of unilateral secession "[u]nder the Constitution of Canada." This is an appropriate question, as the legality of unilateral secession must be evaluated, at least in the first instance, from the perspective of the domestic legal order of the state from which the unit seeks to withdraw. As we shall see below, it is also argued that international law is a relevant standard by which the legality of a purported act of secession may be measured.

[84] The secession of a province from Canada must be considered, in legal terms, to require an amendment to the Constitution, which perforce requires negotiation. The amendments necessary to achieve a secession could be radical and extensive. Some commentators have suggested that secession could be a change of such a magnitude that it could not be considered to be merely an amendment to the Constitution. We are not persuaded by this contention. It is of course true that the Constitution is silent as to the ability of a province to secede from Confederation but, although the Constitution neither expressly authorizes nor prohibits secession, an act of secession would purport to alter the governance of Canadian territory in a manner which undoubtedly is inconsistent with our current constitutional arrangements. The fact that those changes would be profound, or that they would purport to have a significance with respect to international law, does not negate their nature as amendments to the Constitution of Canada.

[85] The Constitution is the expression of the sovereignty of the people of Canada. It lies within the power of the people of Canada, acting through their various governments duly elected and recognized under the Constitution, to effect whatever constitutional arrangements are desired within Canadian territory, including, should it be so desired, the secession of Quebec from Canada. As this Court held in the *Manitoba Language Rights Reference* ... , at p. 745, "[t]he Constitution of a country is a statement of the will of the people to be governed in accordance with certain principles held as fundamental and certain prescriptions restrictive of the powers of the legislature and government." The manner in which such a political will could be formed and mobilized is a somewhat speculative exercise, though we are asked to assume the existence of such a political will for the purpose of answering the question before us. By the terms of this Reference, we have been asked to consider whether it would be constitutional in such a circumstance for the National Assembly, legislature or government of Quebec to effect the secession of Quebec from Canada *unilaterally*.

[86] The "unilateral" nature of the act is of cardinal importance and we must be clear as to what is understood by this term. In one sense, any step towards a constitutional amendment initiated by a single actor on the constitutional stage is "unilateral." We do not believe that this is the meaning contemplated by Question 1, nor is this the sense in which the term has been used in argument before us. Rather, what is claimed by a right to secede "unilaterally" is the right to effectuate secession without prior negotiations with the other provinces and the federal government. At issue is not the legality of the first step but the legality of the final act of purported unilateral secession. The supposed juridical basis for such an act is said to be a clear expression of democratic will in a referendum in the province of Quebec. This claim requires us to examine the possible juridical impact, if any, of such a referendum on the functioning of our Constitution, and on the claimed legality of a unilateral act of secession.

[87] Although the Constitution does not itself address the use of a referendum procedure, and the results of a referendum have no direct role or legal effect in our constitutional scheme, a referendum undoubtedly may provide a democratic method of ascertaining the views of the electorate on important political questions on a particular occasion. The democratic principle identified above would demand that considerable weight be given to a clear expression by the people of Quebec of their will to secede from Canada, even though a referendum, in itself and without more, has no direct legal effect, and could not in itself bring about unilateral secession. Our political institutions are premised on the democratic principle, and so an expression of the democratic will of the people of a province carries weight, in that it would confer legitimacy on the efforts of the government of Quebec to initiate the Constitution's amendment process in order to secede by constitutional means. In this context, we refer to a "clear" majority as a qualitative evaluation. The referendum result, if it is to be taken as an expression of the democratic will, must be free of ambiguity both in terms of the question asked and in terms of the support it achieves.

[88] The federalism principle, in conjunction with the democratic principle, dictates that the clear repudiation of the existing constitutional order and the clear expression of the desire to pursue secession by the population of a province would give rise to a reciprocal obligation on all parties to Confederation to negotiate constitutional changes to respond to that desire. The amendment of the Constitution begins with a political process undertaken pursuant to the Constitution itself. In Canada, the initiative for constitutional amendment is the responsibility of democratically elected representatives of the participants in Confederation. Those representatives may, of course, take their cue from a referendum, but in legal terms, constitution-making in Canada, as in many countries, is undertaken by the democratically elected representatives of the people. The corollary of a legitimate attempt by one participant in Confederation to seek an amendment to the Constitution is an obligation on all parties to come to the negotiating table. The clear repudiation by the people of Quebec of the existing constitutional order would confer legitimacy on demands for secession, and place an obligation on the other provinces and the federal government to acknowledge and respect that expression of democratic will by entering into negotiations and conducting them in accordance with the underlying constitutional principles already discussed.

[89] What is the content of this obligation to negotiate? At this juncture, we confront the difficult inter-relationship between substantive obligations flowing from the Constitution and questions of judicial competence and restraint in supervising or enforcing those obligations. This is mirrored by the distinction between the legality and the legitimacy of actions taken under the Constitution. We propose to focus first on the substantive obligations flowing from this obligation to negotiate; once the nature of those obligations has been described, it is easier to assess the appropriate means of enforcement of those obligations, and to comment on the distinction between legality and legitimacy.

[90] The conduct of the parties in such negotiations would be governed by the same constitutional principles which give rise to the duty to negotiate: federalism, democracy, constitutionalism and the rule of law, and the protection of minorities. Those principles lead us to reject two absolutist propositions. One of those propositions is that there would be a legal obligation on the other provinces and federal government to accede to the secession of a province, subject only to negotiation of the logistical details of secession. This proposition

is attributed either to the supposed implications of the democratic principle of the Constitution, or to the international law principle of self-determination of peoples.

[91] For both theoretical and practical reasons, we cannot accept this view. We hold that Quebec could not purport to invoke a right of self-determination such as to dictate the terms of a proposed secession to the other parties: that would not be a negotiation at all. As well, it would be naive to expect that the substantive goal of secession could readily be distinguished from the practical details of secession. The devil would be in the details. The democracy principle, as we have emphasized, cannot be invoked to trump the principles of federalism and rule of law, the rights of individuals and minorities, or the operation of democracy in the other provinces or in Canada as a whole. No negotiations could be effective if their ultimate outcome, secession, is cast as an absolute legal entitlement based upon an obligation to give effect to that act of secession in the Constitution. Such a foregone conclusion would actually undermine the obligation to negotiate and render it hollow.

[92] However, we are equally unable to accept the reverse proposition, that a clear expression of self-determination by the people of Quebec would impose no obligations upon the other provinces or the federal government. The continued existence and operation of the Canadian constitutional order cannot remain indifferent to the clear expression of a clear majority of Quebecers that they no longer wish to remain in Canada. This would amount to the assertion that other constitutionally recognized principles necessarily trump the clearly expressed democratic will of the people of Quebec. Such a proposition fails to give sufficient weight to the underlying constitutional principles that must inform the amendment process, including the principles of democracy and federalism. The rights of other provinces and the federal government cannot deny the right of the government of Quebec to pursue secession, should a clear majority of the people of Quebec choose that goal, so long as in doing so, Quebec respects the rights of others. Negotiations would be necessary to address the interests of the federal government, of Quebec and the other provinces, and other participants, as well as the rights of all Canadians both within and outside Quebec.

[93] Is the rejection of both of these propositions reconcilable? Yes, once it is realized that none of the rights or principles under discussion is absolute to the exclusion of the others. This observation suggests that other parties cannot exercise their rights in such a way as to amount to an absolute denial of Quebec's rights, and similarly, that so long as Quebec exercises its rights while respecting the rights of others, it may propose secession and seek to achieve it through negotiation. The negotiation process precipitated by a decision of a clear majority of the population of Quebec on a clear question to pursue secession would require the reconciliation of various rights and obligations by the representatives of two legitimate majorities, namely, the clear majority of the population of Quebec, and the clear majority of Canada as a whole, whatever that may be. There can be no suggestion that either of these majorities "trumps" the other. A political majority that does not act in accordance with the underlying constitutional principles we have identified puts at risk the legitimacy of the exercise of its rights.

[94] In such circumstances, the conduct of the parties assumes primary constitutional significance. The negotiation process must be conducted with an eye to the constitutional principles we have outlined, which must inform the actions of *all* the participants in the negotiation process.

[95] Refusal of a party to conduct negotiations in a manner consistent with constitutional principles and values would seriously put at risk the legitimacy of that party's assertion of its rights, and perhaps the negotiation process as a whole. Those who quite legitimately insist upon the importance of upholding the rule of law cannot at the same time be oblivious to the need to act in conformity with constitutional principles and values, and so do their part to contribute to the maintenance and promotion of an environment in which the rule of law may flourish.

[96] No one can predict the course that such negotiations might take. The possibility that they might not lead to an agreement amongst the parties must be recognized. Negotiations following a referendum vote in favour of seeking secession would inevitably address a wide range of issues, many of great import. After 131 years of Confederation, there exists, inevitably, a high level of integration in economic, political and social institutions across Canada. The vision of those who brought about Confederation was to create a unified country, not a loose alliance of autonomous provinces. Accordingly, while there are regional economic interests, which sometimes coincide with provincial boundaries, there are also national interests and enterprises (both public and private) that would face potential dismemberment. There is a national economy and a national debt. Arguments were raised before us regarding boundary issues. There are linguistic and cultural minorities, including aboriginal peoples, unevenly distributed across the country who look to the Constitution of Canada for the protection of their rights. Of course, secession would give rise to many issues of great complexity and difficulty. These would have to be resolved within the overall framework of the rule of law, thereby assuring Canadians resident in Quebec and elsewhere a measure of stability in what would likely be a period of considerable upheaval and uncertainty. Nobody seriously suggests that our national existence, seamless in so many aspects, could be effortlessly separated along what are now the provincial boundaries of Quebec. As the Attorney General of Saskatchewan put it in his oral submission:

> A nation is built when the communities that comprise it make commitments to it, when they forego choices and opportunities on behalf of a nation, … when the communities that comprise it make compromises, when they offer each other guarantees, when they make transfers and perhaps most pointedly, when they receive from others the benefits of national solidarity. The threads of a thousand acts of accommodation are the fabric of a nation. …

[97] In the circumstances, negotiations following such a referendum would undoubtedly be difficult. While the negotiators would have to contemplate the possibility of secession, there would be no absolute legal entitlement to it and no assumption that an agreement reconciling all relevant rights and obligations would actually be reached. It is foreseeable that even negotiations carried out in conformity with the underlying constitutional principles could reach an impasse. We need not speculate here as to what would then transpire. Under the Constitution, secession requires that an amendment be negotiated.

[98] The respective roles of the courts and political actors in discharging the constitutional obligations we have identified follows ineluctably from the foregoing observations. In the *Patriation Reference*, a distinction was drawn between the law of the Constitution, which, generally speaking, will be enforced by the courts, and other constitutional rules, such as the conventions of the Constitution, which carry only political sanctions. It is also

the case, however, that judicial intervention, even in relation to the *law* of the Constitution, is subject to the Court's appreciation of its proper role in the constitutional scheme.

[99] The notion of justiciability is, as we earlier pointed out in dealing with the preliminary objection, linked to the notion of appropriate judicial restraint. We earlier made reference to the discussion of justiciability in *Reference re Canada Assistance Plan* … , at p. 545:

> In exercising its discretion whether to determine a matter that is alleged to be non-justiciable, the Court's primary concern is to retain its proper role within the constitutional framework of our democratic form of government.

In *Operation Dismantle* … , at p. 459, it was pointed out that justiciability is a "doctrine … founded upon a concern with the appropriate role of the courts as the forum for the resolution of different types of disputes." An analogous doctrine of judicial restraint operates here. Also, as observed in *Canada (Auditor General) v. Canada (Minister of Energy, Mines and Resources)*, [1989] 2 SCR 49 (the *Auditor General's* case), at p. 91:

> There is an array of issues which calls for the exercise of judicial judgment on whether the questions are properly cognizable by the courts. Ultimately, such judgment depends on the appreciation by the judiciary of its own position in the constitutional scheme.

[100] The role of the Court in this Reference is limited to the identification of the relevant aspects of the Constitution in their broadest sense. We have interpreted the questions as relating to the constitutional framework within which political decisions may ultimately be made. Within that framework, the workings of the political process are complex and can only be resolved by means of political judgments and evaluations. The Court has no supervisory role over the political aspects of constitutional negotiations. Equally, the initial impetus for negotiation, namely a clear majority on a clear question in favour of secession, is subject only to political evaluation, and properly so. A right and a corresponding duty to negotiate secession cannot be built on an alleged expression of democratic will if the expression of democratic will is itself fraught with ambiguities. Only the political actors would have the information and expertise to make the appropriate judgment as to the point at which, and the circumstances in which, those ambiguities are resolved one way or the other.

[101] If the circumstances giving rise to the duty to negotiate were to arise, the distinction between the strong defence of legitimate interests and the taking of positions which, in fact, ignore the legitimate interests of others is one that also defies legal analysis. The Court would not have access to all of the information available to the political actors, and the methods appropriate for the search for truth in a court of law are ill-suited to getting to the bottom of constitutional negotiations. To the extent that the questions are political in nature, it is not the role of the judiciary to interpose its own views on the different negotiating positions of the parties, even were it invited to do so. Rather, it is the obligation of the elected representatives to give concrete form to the discharge of their constitutional obligations which only they and their electors can ultimately assess. The reconciliation of the various legitimate constitutional interests outlined above is necessarily committed to the political rather than the judicial realm, precisely because that reconciliation can only be achieved through the give and take of the negotiation process. Having established the legal framework, it would be for the democratically elected leadership of the various participants to resolve their differences.

[102] The non-justiciability of political issues that lack a legal component does not deprive the surrounding constitutional framework of its binding status, nor does this mean that constitutional obligations could be breached without incurring serious legal repercussions. Where there are legal rights there are remedies, but as we explained in the *Auditor General's* case, supra, at p. 90, and *New Brunswick Broadcasting* ... , the appropriate recourse in some circumstances lies through the workings of the political process rather than the courts.

[103] To the extent that a breach of the constitutional duty to negotiate in accordance with the principles described above undermines the legitimacy of a party's actions, it may have important ramifications at the international level. Thus, a failure of the duty to undertake negotiations and pursue them according to constitutional principles may undermine that government's claim to legitimacy which is generally a precondition for recognition by the international community. Conversely, violations of those principles by the federal or other provincial governments responding to the request for secession may undermine their legitimacy. Thus, a Quebec that had negotiated in conformity with constitutional principles and values in the face of unreasonable intransigence on the part of other participants at the federal or provincial level would be more likely to be recognized than a Quebec which did not itself act according to constitutional principles in the negotiation process. Both the legality of the acts of the parties to the negotiation process under Canadian law, and the perceived legitimacy of such action, would be important considerations in the recognition process. In this way, the adherence of the parties to the obligation to negotiate would be evaluated in an indirect manner on the international plane.

[104] Accordingly, the secession of Quebec from Canada cannot be accomplished by the National Assembly, the legislature or government of Quebec unilaterally, that is to say, without principled negotiations, and be considered a lawful act. Any attempt to effect the secession of a province from Canada must be undertaken pursuant to the Constitution of Canada, or else violate the Canadian legal order. However, the continued existence and operation of the Canadian constitutional order cannot remain unaffected by the unambiguous expression of a clear majority of Quebecers that they no longer wish to remain in Canada. The primary means by which that expression is given effect is the constitutional duty to negotiate in accordance with the constitutional principles that we have described herein. In the event secession negotiations are initiated, our Constitution, no less than our history, would call on the participants to work to reconcile the rights, obligations and legitimate aspirations of all Canadians within a framework that emphasizes constitutional responsibilities as much as it does constitutional rights.

[105] It will be noted that Question 1 does not ask how secession could be achieved in a constitutional manner, but addresses one form of secession only, namely unilateral secession. Although the applicability of various procedures to achieve lawful secession was raised in argument, each option would require us to assume the existence of facts that at this stage are unknown. In accordance with the usual rule of prudence in constitutional cases, we refrain from pronouncing on the applicability of any particular constitutional procedure to effect secession unless and until sufficiently clear facts exist to squarely raise an issue for judicial determination.

The Court's recognition of the protection of minorities as a principle of the Constitution clearly buttresses the importance of human rights laws and protections in Canada. The question whether this principle could support an obligation to negotiate with or consult a minority religious group in the course of amending the Constitution pursuant to part V of the *Constitution Act, 1982* was tested shortly after the *Secession Reference*. In *Hogan v. Newfoundland*, the Newfoundland Court of Appeal concluded that where an amendment is agreed to by the governments cited in the applicable part of the amending formula (in that case, the federal government and the government of Newfoundland under s. 43), they need not take any additional measures. Leave to appeal to the Supreme Court was refused.

Hogan v. Newfoundland (Attorney General)
2000 NFCA 12

CAMERON JA: [1] On January 8, 1998 the Governor General of Canada proclaimed into force an amendment to Term 17 of the Terms of Union between Canada and Newfoundland. This appeal examines the validity of that amendment. The appellants, Hogan et al., claiming to represent adherents of the Roman Catholic faith, assert that the amendment is unconstitutional and is in breach of contract. ...

· · ·

[3] To place this matter in perspective and to address the submissions of the appellants it is necessary to briefly recount some of the background of Term 17, recognizing all too well that any summary will not adequately portray to the reader the passion with which issues and events of the pre-confederation era were viewed by the citizens of Newfoundland, and that by concentrating on the matter of education there is a danger that one will lose sight of the complexity of the questions which were to be weighed by those voting in the referenda held prior to Newfoundland becoming part of Canada. One further caveat must be added. While it is open to this Court, as it was to the trial judge, to take judicial notice of the fact of Confederation which was, after all, accomplished by virtue of an Act of the United Kingdom Parliament, issues of fact relevant to this case cannot be decided on other than the evidence properly placed before the Court. Personal recollections, or historical research not placed in evidence, cannot be considered, nor can myths.

· · ·

[10] On July 31, 1997, the Premier of the Province of Newfoundland announced that a plebiscite would be held on September 2, 1997. The question was as follows:

Do you support a single school system where all children, regardless of their religious affiliation, attend at the same schools where opportunities for religious education and observances are provided?

[11] On August 25, one week before the vote, the proposed wording of the new Term 17 was released. It provided as follows:

(1) In lieu of section ninety-three of the *Constitution Act, 1867*, this section shall apply in respect of the Province of Newfoundland.

(2) In and for the Province of Newfoundland, the Legislature shall have exclusive authority to make laws in relation to education, but shall provide for courses in religion that are not specific to a religious denomination.

(3) Religious observances shall be permitted in a school where requested by parents.

[12] Seventy-two percent of those who voted in the September 1997 referendum favoured the proposed amendment. The proposal carried in 47 out of 48 electoral districts. The amendment resolution was passed unanimously by the Newfoundland House of Assembly. Following hearings before a Joint Committee of the House of Commons and the Senate, to which over sixty submissions were made, and a recommendation by the majority of the Joint Committee that the resolution be adopted, the resolution authorizing the amendment to Term 17 was passed by a majority vote in both Houses of Parliament. The Amendment was proclaimed on January 8, 1998.

· · ·

The Procedure for Amendment of the Constitution

[72] Three alternative arguments comprise this submission. These shall be considered under the headings: The Constitution Act; Obligation to Negotiate; and Rule of Law and Respect for Minorities.

(1) The Constitution Act

[73] In his text *Constitutional Law of Canada*, Professor Hogg states that "the new procedures in Part V of the *Constitution Act, 1982* constitute a complete code of legal (as opposed to conventional) rules which enable all parts of the "Constitution of Canada" to be amended" (p. 4-4). (See also: *Quebec Constitutional Amendment (No. 2)*, [1982] 2 SCR 793 at p. 806.) Part V provides five methods of amending the Constitution, which range from requiring the consent of the Senate, House of Commons and the Legislative Assemblies of all provinces (s. 41) to unilateral action by the Legislature of only one province (s. 45). Broadly speaking, the wider the focus of the amendment or the more critical the subject matter to the balance of rights and powers in Confederation, the more complex the procedure. For example, s. 41 applies to such things as amendments to the procedures for amendment themselves or the rights of provinces to certain numbers of members in the House of Commons, while s. 45 would permit the legislature of each province to make laws amending its constitution.

[74] The method specified in s. 43 was used for the amendment to Term 17 under consideration in this matter, as it had been for the two prior amendments to Term 17 ... . The appellants submit that the procedure under s. 38 was mandatory to change Term 17. Section 38 requires, in addition to resolution of the Senate and House of Commons, resolutions of two-thirds of the provinces that have at least 50% of the population before a change in the Constitution can be effected (sometimes called the seven-fifty formula). The seven-fifty formula is used for those amendments not covered by other amendment procedures as well as those cases where its use is specifically required. There is no suggestion that any of the other methods of amendment might have been appropriately used in this case.

[75] When it was pointed out by the respondents that, if in the context of this case the appellants were correct, the application of the seven-fifty formula would mean that Term 17 could be amended without the consent of Newfoundland, the appellants argued that there might be cases where the subject matter was such that two procedures might have to be followed.

[76] The characterization of Term 17 as a contract or a constitutional provision was discussed earlier. For the purpose of this part of the discussion it will be assumed, without deciding the point, that the amendment to Term 17 of the Terms of Union is a constitutional amendment of a minority right. What is the nature of this right? The rights granted by s. 93 were examined in *Reference Re Education Act (Que.)*, [1993] 2 SCR 511. At p. 539, Gonthier J discussed the content of the constitutional guarantee under s. 93 and noted that it "crystallizes the rights and privileges pertaining to denominational schools under the law in effect at the time of Confederation," which in the case of Quebec provided different rights for those in rural Quebec than for those in Quebec City and Montreal. He then added:

> Such a disparity in constitutional protection, whether within the same province or from sea to sea, would be ridiculous and even unacceptable if it applied to fundamental rights, but as Beetz J said in [*Greater Montreal Protestant School Board v. Quebec (Attorney General)*, [1989] 1 SCR 377] at p. 401:
>
> > While it may be rooted in notions of tolerance and diversity, the exception in s. 93 is not a blanket affirmation of freedom of religion or freedom of conscience.
>
> Beetz J went on to add that s. 93 "should not be construed as a Charter human right or freedom or, to use the expression of Professor Peter Hogg, a 'small bill of rights for the protection of minority religious groups.'"

[77] Iacobucci J, in *Adler*, adopted the same approach. That is, that s. 93 is a comprehensive code with respect to denominational rights and that other sections of the Constitution, in particular the Charter, ought not to be invoked in aid of interpretation of s. 93. He quotes with approval the words of Dickson CJ in *Mahe v. Alberta*, [1990] 1 SCR 342, at p. 369 where he said:

> … [I]t would be totally incongruous to invoke in aid of the interpretation of a provision which grants special rights to a select group of individuals, the principle of equality intended to be universally applicable to every individual.

Justice Iacobucci expressed the view that s. 93(1) was a comprehensive code of denominational school rights.

[78] Term 17 performs a similar function for Newfoundland as s. 93 does for 6 other provinces. The reasoning of the Supreme Court of Canada in interpreting s. 93 is equally applicable to this case. Term 17 cannot be equated with freedom of religion for the reasons already noted. Term 17, as it existed in 1949, granted special rights to certain classes of individuals but these cannot be described as fundamental rights, which are surely those which are basic to all individuals. Freedom of religion would be a fundamental right. However, the removal of state support for denominational schools (the primary result of the amendment to Term 17 under consideration) is not an interference with freedom of religion.

[79] The appellants concede that even fundamental rights may be amended. They suggest that, to determine which of the five procedures laid out in Part V is to apply to an
amendment to the Constitution, the proper approach is to examine not just the changes to
be made and the particular section to be amended, but also the effect of the proposed
amendment. The appellants suggest that this is best achieved by asking "How is the Constitution of Canada to be different after this amendment than it was before?"

[80] In the view of the appellants any effect on a matter which would require a more
complex amending procedure means that that more complex procedure must be used. …

[81] In the future, situations may arise which will require the enunciation of a detailed
method of analysis to aid in deciding which of the procedures for the amendment of the
Constitution specified in Part V is required. This case does not give rise to any such need.
On reading Part V, it is clear that the intent of the framers of the Constitution was to create
alternative methods of amendment, not cumulative methods. The procedures for amending
the Constitution are complex. The suggestion of the appellants would, because of minimal
even tangential effect, invoke a more complex procedure.

[82] If one asks the simply direct question, the one dictated by the wording of s. 43—is
the proposed amendment "in relation to any provision that applies to only one or more, but
not all, provinces" (in this case, only to the Province of Newfoundland)—the obvious, inescapable answer is "yes." This case is concerned with an amendment to Term 17 of the
Terms of Union. Term 17 did not exist prior to Newfoundland joining Confederation, it has
no application to any other province and was directed solely to the relationship between
Newfoundland and Canada. The proposed amendment does not include expanding its application to other provinces. Rather, it replaces the prior Term 17. While the nature of a
provision might have influenced the drafters of the Constitution when they were deciding
which of the procedures would be used to amend that provision, it is not part of the analysis
here. Whether Term 17 can be characterized as a minority right is not the question at issue.
It is not the type, nature or subject matter of provision being amended which is critical—it
is the scope of the application of the provision.

[83] However, as the analysis which follows will demonstrate, even if one accepted the
appellants' suggestion of considering the effect of the proposed amendment, the amendment procedure required in this case is that specified in s. 43. In their factum the appellants,
referring to s. 42 of the Constitution, maintain that the seven-fifty procedure is appropriate
as it is the one mandated in relation to the establishment of new provinces. Section 42(f) can
have no application in the circumstances of this case. We are not concerned with the establishment of a new province. Newfoundland has been a part of Canada for 50 years.

· · ·

[87] Further, the examples specifically noted in s. 43 as being open to amendment under
that section would indicate that the section is not intended to be limited to certain headings
or to matters that do not impact at all on other provinces. Section 43(b) provides that the
bilateral procedure applies to "any amendment to any provision that relates to the use of the
English or the French language within a province." On the reasoning used by the appellants
this provision should be amended under s. 41. Yet the framers chose to use the s. 43 procedure when the amendment related to the use of the French or English language within a
province.

[The Court of Appeal then rejected an argument that the *Charter of Rights and Freedoms* was being implicitly amended by the amendment to Term 17.]

. . .

[98] The appellants further contend that compliance with the provisions of Part V of the *Constitution Act, 1982* is not sufficient in the context of this case, that the nature of the rights being amended demands an additional step, the absence of which undermines the validity of an amendment which might otherwise be enacted in accordance with the *Constitution Act, 1982*. The origin of this submission is found in the appellant's interpretation of the *Reference re Secession of Quebec*.

— *(2) Obligation To Negotiate*

[99] In its decision in the *Secession Reference* the Supreme Court of Canada confirmed that four fundamental principles underlie the Constitution of this country: federalism; democracy; constitutionalism and the rule of law; and respect for minorities. All parties accept this proposition. The appellants argue that the rights granted to them under Term 17 comprise a minority right and that the *Secession Reference*, which counsel for the appellants describes as a case concerning constitutional amendments, supports the view that before any action to amend a constitutional minority right can take place there is an obligation on those who would do so to negotiate, not just with other governments, but also with those whose rights are being interfered with, an obligation which the appellants say was not met in this case.

. . .

[101] The *Constitution Act, 1982* does not specifically address the matter of secession, though, of course, it does provide methods for amendment of the Constitution. It is clear that the provisions which provide for unilateral action by a Legislature or Parliament would have no application to secession by a province. Therefore Question 1 is directed to what happens under Canadian constitutional law if one province attempted to secede from Confederation using a method not anticipated by the written Constitution. It is in that context that the statements of the Supreme Court of Canada must be viewed.

[102] The Court, referring in the *Secession Reference to the Provincial Court Judges Reference*, [1997] 3 SCR 3, confirmed that the Constitution is not limited to the written constitution. ...

[103] The appellants would take the conclusion of the Supreme Court of Canada that a clear expression by a majority of Quebecers that they no longer wish to remain in Canada gives rise to a duty on the parties to Confederation to negotiate in accordance with the constitutional principles referred to above and transform that duty into a constitutional requirement, superimposed on the amending process. It follows, they say, that the body which proposes any amendment respecting a minority right, which the appellants equate with a change respecting one of the fundamental principles, must negotiate with the minority affected prior to any attempt to effect an amendment.

[104] This position takes the *Secession Reference* far beyond what the Court said. First, the Court was describing a principled approach of dealing with problems or situations which are not expressly dealt with by the text of the Constitution. As Binnie J noted in

Re Eurig Estate (1998), 165 DLR (4th) 1 at para. 66, in the *Secession Reference* the Court affirmed that "implicit principles can and should be used to expound the Constitution, but they cannot alter the thrust of its explicit text." (See para. 53 of the *Secession Reference* which declares the primacy of the written constitution.) If the proper procedures specified by the Constitution are followed, there is no basis upon which to impose additional steps such as negotiation with those who might be particularly affected by the amendment to complete the amendment process.

(3) *Rule of Law and Respect for Minorities*

[105] At its core, this argument is that the actions of the Government of Newfoundland prior to the calling of the referendum of September 1997 and during the period from the calling of the referendum to the vote, including the method of conducting the vote, were in violation of the applicable legislation—the *Election Act*, RSN 1990, c. E-3, as amended, and were also in violation of the principle of protection of minority rights. None of the alleged deficiencies demonstrates a failure to meet all of the requirements specified in s. 43 of the *Constitution Act, 1982*. So then, this argument is based on the belief that even if s. 43 could otherwise be said to be the proper amending formula, there are aspects of this case, founded on constitutional principles, which make compliance with s. 43 insufficient to amend Term 17.

[106] While it is conceded that the amending procedure does not require a referendum, the appellants argue that having chosen to make a referendum a part of the process, the Government must abide by the rule of law, applicable laws and the requirements of the Charter and any failure to do so results in an invalid amendment. Here the appellants make an analogy to administrative law and ask that the Court focus not on the result, but on the procedure to determine if the basic rules were met.

[107] In *Reference re Secession of Quebec*, the Supreme Court of Canada emphasized the fact that the Court has no supervisory role over political aspects of constitutional negotiations. At para. [100] the Court added: "equally, the initial impetus for negotiation, namely a clear majority on a clear question in favour of secession, is subject only to political evaluation, and properly so." The comments of the Court were made in the context of a reference. However, the general approach is equally appropriate in this case.

[108] The submission of the AG Canada is that the following factors would fall into that political character, at least in relation to the validity of the *Constitution Amendment, 1998 (Newfoundland Act)*, and, therefore, that they have no place in the considerations to be made by this Court: (1) the Provincial Government's policy on educational reform; (2) the quality of the political debate regarding the proposed amendments; (3) the analysis of the results of the vote; (4) the balancing of interest of those favouring and those opposing the amendment; and (5) the specific motivations of members of the Legislative Assembly. The appellants agree respecting the first and third listed topics. As to the others, the appellants argue that the Court can and must examine the referendum process because it is undertaken under law and therefore should be subject to court scrutiny; that any violation of fundamental rights is also subject to court scrutiny and that the court is free, not to tell a member of the Legislature or Parliament how to vote, but to examine the express statements of the members to determine the significance of certain factors in that process. Specifically,

the appellants note that in their statements each member spoke of the referendum when describing their reasons for voting as they did. In other words, the appellants look to the "political" statements to support their submission that while the referendum may not have been constitutionally required, it was instrumental in the voting by the members of the legislative bodies.

[109] The Court has no role in examining the motivation of members of the Legislature or the Houses of Parliament in casting their votes. The interpretation of and weight to be given to the results of the referendum is a political matter. I would add further that, at least in respect of the members of the Senate and House of Commons, the very points made by the appellants in this case were made before the Joint Committee and specifically referred to in the report of the Committee which said:

> Some of the denominational interests that testified had specific criticisms of the referendum process. They argued that the original question left the impression that unidenominational education courses would be allowed, that the actual text of the proposed resolution was re-leased too late in the referendum process to allow for full debate, that religious denominations opposed to the amendment were denied government funding, and that scrutineers were not allowed. They also objected to government-funded advertising in favour to the resolution.

It cannot be said that the members of those bodies were unaware of the "deficiencies" pointed to by the appellants.

[110] Counsel for the appellants concedes that the trial judge dealt with the issue of unfairness only in the context of the spending issue. He did not deal with it on any other level. But these submissions were made and the appellants argue that this Court can make the necessary findings here.

[111] I agree that it is not the role of this Court to enter into the policy debate regarding the amendment of Term 17 and the subsequent measures taken respecting education in Newfoundland. The only task before this Court is the determination of the legal issues raised on the appeal.

[112] Once again the appellants turn to the *Secession Reference* as enunciating the principles upon which their submission is founded. They point, of course, to the four fundamental principles identified in that case, particularly the rule of law and respect for minorities. At para. [74] of that decision the Court identified three overlapping reasons for entrenching a constitution beyond the reach of simple majority rule:

> First, a constitution may provide an added safeguard for fundamental human rights and individual freedoms which might otherwise be susceptible to government interference. Although democratic government is generally solicitous of those rights, there are occasions when the majority will be tempted to ignore fundamental rights in order to accomplish collective goals more easily or effectively. Constitutional entrenchment ensures that those rights will be given due regard and protection. Second, a constitution may seek to ensure that vulnerable minority groups are endowed with the institutions and rights necessary to maintain and promote their identities against the assimilative pressures of the majority. And third, a constitution may provide for a division of political power that allocates political power amongst different levels of government. That purpose would be defeated if one of those democratically elected levels of

government could usurp the powers of the other simply by exercising its legislative power to allocate additional political power to itself unilaterally.

The appellants extract from these reasons the view that a role of the Constitution is the protection of minority groups from the whim of the majority and argue that once one places minority rights in the hands of the majority, it is a violation of the rule of law. They further argue that in this case the error of putting the minority rights in the hands of the majority, presumably by conducting a referendum in which all voters could participate, was compounded by failure to comply with the law respecting referenda, and the unfair way the Government of Newfoundland conducted the campaign.

[113] The appellants agree that minority rights can be removed under the Constitution. (Although if one follows the reasoning of not placing minority rights in the hands of the majority presumably a minority right could never be changed without the consent of that minority.) However, they submit that, even if the right can be removed under the bilateral formula, if the process of getting the resolutions is tainted by a violation of a principle that cannot be amended by s. 43, then the requirements have not been met and the amendment cannot stand. The logical result of this argument is that if no referendum had been held an amendment which followed the procedure set out in Part V for such amendments would be beyond challenge, but because the Government of Newfoundland made the decision to consult directly the electorate on the question of the amendment to Term 17, the amendment must be declared to have no force and effect.

[114] In support of their position that the four fundamental principles can be used in the way advocated by the appellants they cite the decisions of the Supreme Court of Canada in the *Provincial Court Judges Reference*, the *Secession Reference*, in *Re Manitoba Language Rights*, [1985] 1 SCR 721 and in *New Brunswick Broadcasting Co. v. Nova Scotia (Speaker, House of Assembly)* (1993), 100 DLR (4th) 212.

[The Court of Appeal proceeded to consider the applicability of each of these four cases.]

. . .

[121] Counsel for the appellant argues that if Part V of the Constitution was a complete answer to amendment of the Constitution, the Supreme Court of Canada would not have had to talk about fundamental principles in the *Secession Reference* and state there is a requirement to negotiate. He adds that if the complexity of constitutional amendment was intended to provide the protections required under the Constitution there would have been no need for the Supreme Court to refer to the principles underlying the Constitution. The Supreme Court of Canada imposed the additional step, the appellants argue, and the language used by the Court is not limited to the secession context, but is general.

[122] The appellants, however, concede that there could be amendments under 43(b) that would affect a minority right, but, they say, there could not be an amendment that violates the principle about the protection of minority rights. The appellants maintain that there is a difference between a provision that enhances minority rights and one that detracts from them because the principle is about the protection of them. Counsel for the appellant quotes para. [54] of the *Secession Reference* which states that the principles are binding upon the courts and governments, which the appellants argue means that the principles must be law, as only law would be binding upon the courts. Further, although other provisions of the

constitution cannot be used to trump each other the import of the appellants' position is that these broadly stated fundamental principles can trump a constitutional provision.

[123] Counsel for the appellant in his oral presentation stated clearly that the appellants do not suggest that the amendment to Term 17 "actually amends or purports to amend the fundamental principle relative to protection of minority rights." Rather he maintained the amendment to Term 17 and the procedure by which it was implemented is contrary to the fundamental principle respecting minority rights. However, he accepts that had Term 17 been amended by the unanimous procedure or, perhaps even the 7/50 procedure, he could not make this claim, because by the unanimous procedure the fundamental principle could be amended.

[124] The Supreme Court in the *Secession Reference* pointed to examples of specific constitutional provisions which reflect the underlying constitutional principle of protection of minorities. One of those was the protection of minority educational rights; another the protection of language rights, both of which are described as the product of negotiation and political compromise. A further example is, of course, the Charter provisions for the protection of minority rights. In the *Secession Reference*, the Court was merely illustrating how one of the fundamental principles is manifested in the written Constitution.

[125] In interpreting the Constitution of Canada, one cannot ignore the history of its development. There can be no denying the evolutionary (as opposed to revolutionary) nature of the creation of Canada. Indeed, long after Canada was recognized as an independent country, it continued to evolve and mature constitutionally. However, the fact that we now have constitutional documents to which we can refer collectively as the Constitution does not eliminate all reference to our largely unwritten constitutional past. Not every nuance of the powers of the different heads of government, for example, is written in the Constitution. Even with a written document, certain underlying assumptions will be seen as being self-evident and of constitutional stature. The *New Brunswick Broadcasting* case required the Court to express what was unwritten. Here the appellants would have this Court defeat a constitutionally mandated process by reference to the "fundamental or original principles." However, unlike the Provincial Court Judges Reference or the New Brunswick Broadcasting case, here the Court is being asked to read in requirements, not to confirm some long accepted unwritten principle of the Constitution but to limit the application of the amending provisions to a right that was granted by the written Constitution. This is not a case where the unwritten assumptions of educational rights need to be stated by the Courts. The rights are fully explored and stated in Term 17. Term 17 is a complete statement of the denominational education rights. No other term written or unwritten of the Constitution need be called upon to interpret Term 17 or to determine how it should be amended. Neither the rule of law nor respect for minorities prevents the application of s. 43 to the amendment of Term 17. The appellants' position ignores the inescapable fact that the Constitution entrusts minority rights to the majority. The structure is designed not to prevent constitutional amendment but to ensure, by making the process more difficult than the passage of an amendment to any other bill, that the rights are given "due regard and protection." The appropriate provision in Part V of the Constitution, having been complied with, the validity of the amendment to Term 17 cannot be questioned.

PART II

The Key Actors in Public Law

CHAPTER FOUR

Parliament and the Legislative Process

Having set the stage of Canadian public law, it is now time to examine in greater detail the key public law "actors": the legislature, the executive, and the judiciary. In this first chapter on this theme, we focus on law making and the lawmakers in our public law system. The most important law-making institutions in this country are, of course, the federal Parliament and provincial legislatures. Our focus here is on Parliament, although much of our discussion of this federal body applies equally to its provincial counterparts.

Section I of this chapter describes the separate institutions that comprise Parliament: the monarch and her delegate, the governor general; the Senate; and the House of Commons. It also describes how the Parliament is called into session, prorogued, and dissolved. Section II examines the role of several of the key actors in Parliament, including political parties, the speakers, and parliamentary committees. Finally, section III discusses "parliamentary law": the rules and procedures that guide Parliament's functioning. It then sets out the procedure by which parliamentary bills become statutes.

I. STRUCTURE AND OPERATION OF PARLIAMENT

A. Constituent Parts of the Parliament of Canada

What is Parliament and how does it function? Section 17 of the *Constitution Act, 1867* creates a "Parliament of Canada" consisting of "the Queen, an Upper House styled the Senate, and the House of Commons." In this first section we describe how the membership of these three components of Canada's Parliament is determined.

1. The Monarch and Governor General

The monarch—currently Queen Elizabeth II—plays a double role in the Canadian constitutional framework. Not only is the monarch part of the Parliament, the *Constitution Act, 1867* also vests the "Executive Government" in the Queen, a matter discussed further in chapter 5. The Queen is, in other words, Canada's official head of state. In practice, however, many of the Queen's powers are to be exercised by the governor general. Section 10 of the *Constitution Act, 1867* provides:

The Provisions of this Act referring to the Governor General extend and apply to the Governor General for the Time being of Canada, or other the Chief Executive Officer or Administrator for the Time being carrying on the Government of Canada *on behalf and in the Name of the Queen*, by whatever Title he is designated. [Emphasis added.]

Meanwhile, by letters patent issued by George VI in 1947, the governor general is "to exercise all powers and authorities lawfully belonging to Us in respect of Canada."

In contrast to many republican systems, the Canadian head of state is not elected. His or her identity depends, in the case of the monarch, on birth, and in the case of the governor general, on appointment.

a. Selecting the Monarch

The identity of the monarch—and thus of Canada's titular head of state—is determined in the United Kingdom according to rules of heredity and antiquated laws of succession, most notably the famous *Act of Settlement* of 1701. This venerable statute bars Catholics from assuming the Crown, and even precludes the monarch from marrying a Roman Catholic. Furthermore, the monarch must be in communion with the Church of England. The Act's dictates are clearly discriminatory, viewed from the optic of modern human rights law. It has, therefore, been challenged in Canadian courts as a violation of the *Canadian Charter of Rights and Freedoms*. Consider the following case, one that provides important insight into the constitutional status of the monarchy in Canada.

O'Donohue v. The Queen
(2003), 109 CRR (2d) 1 (Ont. SCJ); aff'd. [2005] OJ no. 965 (CA)

ROULEAU J: [1] The applicant, Tony O'Donohue, has brought the present application for a declaration that certain provisions of the *Act of Settlement, 1701*, are of no force or effect as they discriminate against Roman Catholics in violation of the equality provisions of the *Canadian Charter of Rights and Freedoms*. … [O]nly the issues of standing and justiciability are to be dealt with at this point. Should I grant the applicant standing and find justiciability the matter will proceed to be heard on the merits; if not, the application will be struck.

· · ·

[2] Mr. O'Donohue is a Canadian citizen and a Roman Catholic. He believes that certain provisions of the *Act of Settlement* are clearly discriminatory against Roman Catholic people and offensive to the Roman Catholic faith. For many years he has tried, through various political means, to have the *Act of Settlement* changed. He has had no success.

[3] The *Act of Settlement* is an imperial statute adopted by the United Kingdom in 1701. By its terms it provides that it is an act "established and declared" in the "Kingdoms of England, France and Ireland, and the dominions thereunto belonging." As a result it became and remains part of the laws of Canada.

[4] The *Act of Settlement* contains several provisions but one in particular addresses the difficult succession issues that led to civil war in England in the latter part of the 17th cen-

tury. This provision in effect provides that Roman Catholics cannot accede to the Crown of England, nor be married to someone who holds the Crown. …

[5] Mr. O'Donohue brings the present application to have those parts of the *Act of Settlement*, insofar as they refer to Roman Catholics and limit their rights, declared to be in breach of s. 15(1) of the *Canadian Charter of Rights and Freedoms* and of no force or effect. …

· · ·

[13] … [T]he determination of whether a matter is justiciable "is, first and foremost, a normative enquiry into the appropriateness as a matter of constitutional judicial policy of the courts deciding a given issue or, instead, deferring to other decision-making institutions of the polity." … "[T]here is an array of issues which calls for the exercise of judicial judgment on whether the questions are properly cognizable by the courts. Ultimately, such judgment depends on the appreciation by the judiciary of its own position in the constitutional scheme."

[14] The constitutional scheme of our democratic government consists of four branches: the Crown, the legislative body, the executive and the courts. As set out in *New Brunswick Broadcasting Co. v. Nova Scotia (Speaker of the House of Assembly)*, … "it is fundamental to the working of government as a whole that all these parts play their proper role. It is equally fundamental that no one of them overstep its bounds, that each show proper deference for the legitimate sphere of activity of the other."

[15] In the present case all parties acknowledge that if the impugned portions of the *Act of Settlement* have constitutional status then the matter is not justiciable. It is well settled that the Charter cannot be used to amend or trump another part of our constitution. …

[16] The respondents maintain that even if the impugned provisions of the *Act of Settlement* are not part of the Constitution, they clearly are part of the Rules of Succession. They argue that a finding that the Rules of Succession are justiciable would run contrary to the intent of Parliament and constitutional convention among the Commonwealth nations, and would be beyond the proper role of the courts within our constitutional framework.

[17] The impugned portions of the *Act of Settlement* are a key element of the rules governing succession to the British Crown. They were enacted following a long period of civil and religious strife. They confirmed that only the Protestant heirs of Princess Sophia, the Electoress of Hanover, are entitled to assume the throne. The Act of Settlement together with other statutes establish the legitimate heir to the British Crown. …

[18] Canada was established as a constitutional monarchy. This fundamental aspect of our constitutional structure is both recognized and maintained by the *Constitution Act, 1982*, being Schedule B to the *Canada Act 1982* (UK), 1982, c. 11. It is found, among other places, in the preamble to the Constitution.

[19] It is well recognized that the preamble to the Constitution identifies the organizing principles of our Constitution and can be used to fill in gaps in the express terms of the constitutional text … .

[20] The preamble to the *Constitution Act, 1867* … provides as follows:

Whereas the Provinces of Canada, Nova Scotia, and New Brunswick have expressed their Desire to be federally united into One Dominion under the Crown of the United Kingdom of

Great Britain and Ireland, with a Constitution similar in Principle to that of the United Kingdom. …

[21] This portion of the preamble confirms not only that Canada is a constitutional monarchy, but also that Canada is united under the Crown of the United Kingdom of Great Britain. A constitutional monarchy, where the monarch is shared with the United Kingdom and other Commonwealth countries, is, in my view, at the root of our constitutional structure.

[22] The role of the Queen is provided for in s. 9 of the *Constitution Act, 1867*, which reads as follows:

> The Executive Government and Authority of and over Canada is hereby declared to continue and be vested in the Queen.

[23] The office of the Queen is such a fundamental part of our constitutional structure that amendments to the Constitution in respect of that office require the unanimous consent of the federal and provincial governments (see s. 41(a) of the *Constitution Act, 1982*).

· · ·

[24] Since the Queen occupies such a central place in the Canadian Constitution, the respondents submit that the rules governing the succession to the throne are themselves essential to the proper functioning of this branch of our constitutional scheme. In the result, these rules are by necessity incorporated into the Constitution of Canada.

· · ·

[27] … [I]t is clear that Canada's structure as a constitutional monarchy and the principle of sharing the British monarch are fundamental to our constitutional framework. In light of the preamble's clear statement that we are to share the Crown with the United Kingdom, it is axiomatic that the rules of succession for the monarchy must be shared and be in symmetry with those of the United Kingdom and other Commonwealth countries. One cannot accept the monarch but reject the legitimacy or legality of the rules by which this monarch is selected.

· · ·

[29] If the courts were free to review and declare inoperative certain parts of the rules of succession, Canada could break symmetry with Great Britain, and could conceivably recognize a different monarch than does Great Britain. In fact, Canada could arguably reanimate the debate regarding the heir to the throne, an argument that was resolved by the *Act of Settlement*. This would clearly be contrary to settled intention, as demonstrated by our written Constitution, and would see the courts changing rather than protecting our fundamental constitutional structure.

[30] The fact that the rules of succession are part of our constitutional fabric is further supported by an analysis of the way in which these rules of succession have functioned within the Commonwealth.

[31] By the *Statute of Westminster, 1931* (UK) … the United Kingdom agreed that it would no longer impose British statutes on the various dominions without their accord. It also provided that the British monarch would continue to be the monarch of various Commonwealth countries including Canada. In order to recognize that the United Kingdom would no longer impose British statutes on the dominions, but also to ensure that the rules

of succession which had previously been imposed by the United Kingdom on those Commonwealth countries continued to be consistent, the British Parliament set out in the preamble to the *Statute of Westminster* the following:

> And whereas it is meet and proper to set out by way of preamble to this Act that, inasmuch as the Crown is the symbol of the free association of the members of the British Commonwealth of Nations, and as they are united by a common allegiance to the Crown, it would be in accord with the established constitutional position of all the members of the Commonwealth in relation to one another that any alteration in the law touching the Succession to the Throne or the Royal Style and Titles shall hereafter require the assent as well as of the Parliaments of all the Dominions as of the Parliament of the United Kingdom:

[32] The *Statute of Westminster* is a part of the Constitution of Canada by virtue of it being listed in the schedule to the Constitution (*Constitution Act, 1982*, s. 52(2)(b)).

[33] As a result of the *Statute of Westminster* it was recognized that any alterations in the rules of succession would no longer be imposed by Great Britain and, if symmetry among commonwealth countries were to be maintained, any changes to the rules of succession would have to be agreed to by all members of the Commonwealth. This arrangement can be compared to a treaty among the Commonwealth countries to share the monarchy under the existing rules and not to change the rules without the agreement of all signatories. While Canada as a sovereign nation is free to withdraw from the arrangement and no longer be united through common allegiance to the Crown, it cannot unilaterally change the rules of succession for all Commonwealth countries. Unilateral changes by Canada to the rules of succession, whether imposed by the court or otherwise, would be contrary to the commitment given in the *Statute of Westminster*, would break symmetry and breach the principle of union under the British Crown set out in the preamble to the *Constitution Act, 1867*. Such changes would, for all intents and purposes, bring about a fundamental change in the office of the Queen without securing the authorizations required pursuant to s. 41 of the *Constitution Act, 1982*.

. . .

[36] The impugned positions of the *Act of Settlement* are an integral part of the rules of succession that govern the selection of the monarch of Great Britain. By virtue of our constitutional structure whereby Canada is united under the Crown of Great Britain, the same rules of succession must apply for the selection of the King or Queen of Canada and the King or Queen of Great Britain. As stated by Prime Minister St. Laurent to the House of Commons during the debate on the bill altering the royal title:

> Her Majesty is now Queen of Canada but she is the Queen of Canada because she is Queen of the United Kingdom. … It is not a separate office … it is the sovereign who is recognized as the sovereign of the United Kingdom who is our Sovereign … .

[37] These rules of succession, and the requirement that they be the same as those of Great Britain, are necessary to the proper functioning of our constitutional monarchy and, therefore, the rules are not subject to Charter scrutiny.

[38] In the present case the court is being asked to apply the Charter not to rule on the validity of acts or decisions of the Crown, one of the branches of our government, but rather

to disrupt the core of how the monarchy functions, namely the rules by which succession is determined. To do this would make the constitutional principle of Union under the British Crown together with other Commonwealth countries unworkable, would defeat a manifest intention expressed in the preamble of our Constitution, and would have the courts over-step their role in our democratic structure.

[39] In conclusion, the *lis* raised in the present application is not justiciable and there is no serious issue to be tried. … The application is dismissed.

b. Selecting the Governor General

The governor general is selected closer to home. In practice, the monarch appoints the gov-ernor general. However, by Canadian constitutional convention, the Queen follows the Can-adian prime minister's recommendations in appointing the governor general. Thus, while she is customarily consulted in advance, the Queen takes her direction from what is known as an "instrument of advice"—essentially a personal letter from the prime minister. There are no legal criteria constraining the prime minister's choice for governor general. Convention probably dictates that only Canadians may now be appointed, and Canadian practice strongly favours alternating anglophone and francophone representatives. At base, however, the prime minister's selection is a political decision.

The first Canadian governors general were former diplomats or at least diplomat/politi-cians. Between 1979 and 1999, Canada's four governors general were former politicians. In three instances, these former members of Parliament were from the party in power at the time of the appointment, prompting some critics to suggest that the governor general's pos-ition had tumbled from diplomatic symbol to political patronage plum. Two recent appoint-ments—Prime Minister Chrétien's selection of apparently non-partisan Adrienne Clarkson and Prime Minister Martin's naming of Michaëlle Jean—followed yet another pattern: ap-pointment of non-political figures from the arts and media community representing Can-ada's burgeoning multicultural fabric. The current governor general, David Johnston, was a prominent academic prior to his appointment.

2. Senate

Unusually for a modern democracy, Canada has an *unelected* upper chamber of the federal legislature. Section 24 of the *Constitution Act, 1867* expressly anticipates the *appointment* of senators by the governor general:

> The Governor General shall from Time to Time, in the Queen's Name, by Instrument under the Great Seal of Canada, summon qualified Persons to the Senate; and, subject to the Provisions of this Act, every Person so summoned shall become and be a Member of the Senate and a Senator.

In exercising this power, the governor general follows the advice of the prime minister, as required by constitutional convention.

In the past, there was legal controversy over whether the reference to "persons" in s. 24 included women. This doubt—so peculiar to modern eyes—was resolved with a "yes" in the famous "*Persons*" case, decided by the Judicial Committee on the Privy Council as *Edwards v. AG of Canada*, [1930] AC 124, in 1929, reproduced in chapter 2. In that decision, Lord Sankey wrote:

> The exclusion of women from all public offices is a relic of days more barbarous than ours, but it must be remembered that the necessity of the times often forced on man customs which in later years were not necessary. …
>
> Customs are apt to develop into traditions which are stronger than law and remain unchallenged long after the reason for them has disappeared.
>
> The appeal to history therefore in this particular matter is not conclusive. …

The law lords then observed later in the decision:

> The *British North America Act* planted in Canada a living tree capable of growth and expansion within its natural limits. The object of the Act was to grant a Constitution to Canada. Like all written constitutions it has been subject to development through usage and convention. …
>
> Their Lordships do not conceive it to be the duty of this Board—it is certainly not their desire—to cut down the provisions of the Act by a narrow and technical construction, but rather to give it a large and liberal interpretation so that the Dominion to a great extent, but within certain fixed limits, may be mistress in her own house, as the provinces to a great extent, but within certain fixed limits, are mistresses in theirs.

While gender discrimination is no longer part of the Canadian Constitution, the appointments process continues to fuel substantial controversy—it has too often been treated as a means for the party in power to reward friends and supporters. Many proposals exist for senate reform, although none has been successful. Given this deadlock, several provincial governments have attempted to assert control over appointments. Most notably, Alberta enacted a *Senatorial Selection Act*, RSA 2000, c. S-5, providing for the direct election of senatorial candidates. Once selected by election, the provincial government is to submit the nominees' names to the federal government, identifying these individuals as persons who may be summoned to the Senate for the purpose of filling vacancies relating to Alberta.

This law has had only a modest impact on senator selections. Alberta has had three elections, in 1989, 1999, and 2004. Stan Waters was elected in 1989, and in fact was appointed to the Senate in 1990 by Prime Minister Mulroney, then trying to elicit provincial support for the Meech Lake accord. However, Prime Minister Chrétien declined to appoint the two so-called senators-in-waiting elected in 1999—Bert Brown and Ted Morton. In response, Mr. Brown sued in the Alberta courts seeking a declaration that the senatorial appointment provisions of the 1867 Act were contrary to democratic principles, as set out by the Supreme Court in the *Reference re Secession of Quebec*, discussed at length in chapter 3.

Brown v. Alberta
(1999), 177 DLR (4th) 349 (Alta. CA)

BY THE COURT:

Introduction

[1] The appellant, Bert Brown, commenced proceedings by originating notice seeking an order declaring the provisions of the *Constitution Act, 1867* … providing for the appointment of senators by the Governor General in Council to be contrary to democratic principles and that to conform with those principles, senators must be appointed in a manner consistent with the provisions of an Alberta statute, the *Senatorial Selection Act* … . He did not challenge the constitutionality of either statute nor assert any violation of the *Canadian Charter of Rights and Freedoms*. Indeed, he acknowledged that he was not alleging interference with any legal right.

[2] The Attorney General of Canada applied to strike out the originating notice. Paperny J found that the Court had no jurisdiction to grant the declaration sought because there was no legal interest engaged. She struck out the originating notice on the basis that it was "plain and obvious" that it could not succeed as it disclosed no cause of action.

[3] The appellant does not allege error by the chambers judge but says we should allow his appeal and grant the declaration because of statements made by the Supreme Court of Canada in a judgment released after the ruling in Queen's Bench, *Reference re Secession of Quebec*.

[4] The appellant was elected under the Alberta statute as a "senate nominee." He acknowledged that at the time of the appeal there were no vacancies in the Senate.

· · ·

[9] The chambers judge found that the underlying purpose of the appellant's application was to bring public attention to the issue of senatorial selection and to put public and political pressure on the Governor General to appoint to the Senate a person elected under the *Senatorial Selection Act*. She concluded that in light of this purpose, it would not be appropriate for the court to intervene because there was no justiciable or legal issue, that is, no rights of the parties would be affected. On this basis, the originating notice of motion was struck out.

· · ·

[12] The appellant asks us to declare the current senatorial appointment system undemocratic based on statements made by the Supreme Court of Canada in the *Quebec Secession Reference*. … Specifically, in view of the wide-ranging comments by the Supreme Court of Canada, and his election under the Alberta statute, he requests us to state that when there is an Alberta Senate vacancy, he has "the right to be considered." He does not use the word "right" in the legal sense or as a term of art. And, he does not ask that we issue an order that the Governor General consider him for appointment or find that he has a legal right to be appointed as a Senator. He does not directly challenge, on any legal basis, either the *Constitution Act, 1867* or provincial legislation.

· · ·

[20] The appellant's claim for a day in court is based on two pillars: first, the statements of the Supreme Court of Canada on political institutions and democratic principles, and second, his status as a "senate nominee," elected through a democratic process. He invites the Court to conclude that from these circumstances it is possible to find a legal issue in his case.

[21] The appellant relies on the following statement, amongst others, from the *Quebec Secession Reference*, at para. 87:

> Our political institutions are premised on the democratic principle, and so an expression of the democratic will of the people of a province carries weight, in that it would confer legitimacy on the efforts of the government of Quebec to initiate the Constitution's amendment process in order to secede by constitutional means.

[22] In his factum, the appellant argues:

> It is submitted that it is now distinctly arguable, in light of the Supreme Court's decision in the *Quebec Reference* that this case does raise a legal issue, and that, the Governor-General may have a duty to appoint to the Senate otherwise qualified persons who have been democratically elected, such as by the processes of the *Alberta Senatorial Selection Act*. The declaratory order requested in this case does not go so far as that; it merely asks for an order declaring that, to be consistent with the democratic principles, senators appointed from Alberta must be appointed on a basis consistent with the processes of the *Senatorial Selection Act*. ...

[23] It is true that in the *Quebec Secession Reference*, the Supreme Court articulated several principles and interpretive canons underlying the Constitution, including principles related to democracy and the democratic process. But the appellant does not show how or where those statements about democratic principles would change the law as to what constitutes a legal issue or allow this Court to find that his case raises a legal issue. It seems that the appellant is arguing that the nature of the remedy he seeks is such that he need not show there is a legal issue, as that requirement has, to date, been defined by the courts, or that he does not have as heavy a burden in doing so.

[24] The remedy he seeks from the court is an order declaring that senators appointed from Alberta "must be appointed" in a manner consistent with the processes of the *Senatorial Selection Act*. This claim, however, does not stand unqualified. He asserts that this procedure "must" be followed for an appointment to be "consistent with democratic principles." In other words, the appellant does not ask the court to declare that appointments made inconsistently with the *Senatorial Selection Act* are unconstitutional. Rather, he requests that the court declare that any such appointments would be undemocratic. In essence, he is asking the court to be an arbiter of the democratic character of senatorial appointment. He wants the court to look at the appointment process and to make a statement on whether or not the process is democratic. In order for the court to be able to make such a statement, it must have jurisdiction to do so. It will have jurisdiction only where there is a legal issue.

[25] We agree with the Crown that the appellant "seeks to invoke the democratic principle, *per se*, divorced of its interpretive role and devoid of legal issues, simply because a declaratory order from the Court would, in his view, 'have considerable persuasive effect, and it would confer democratic legitimacy on the *Senatorial Selection Act*.'" We do not view the Supreme Court's statements in the *Quebec Secession Reference* as modifying the existing

jurisprudence on what constitutes a legal issue. Accordingly, we cannot find that the appellant's originating notice, as it is presently structured, raises a legal issue as required by the existing law. ...

[26] ... The question before this Court is whether the appellant's originating notice, in its existing form and at this time, can be viewed as raising a legal issue. The *Quebec Secession Reference* does not change the law on the scope of the court's jurisdiction to grant declaratory relief, nor does it overrule existing authorities that set out what constitutes a "legal issue." We concur with the finding of the chambers judge that the appellant has not raised a legal issue based on the nature and extent of the relief he requests in his originating notice as it is presently structured. Thus, the court does not have jurisdiction to grant declaratory relief.

[27] Accordingly, we must dismiss the appeal.

In a second case, brought in the Federal Court, the Reform Party of Canada sought an interlocutory injunction to restrain the governor general from appointing a senator from Alberta, unless that person has been elected pursuant to the provisions of the *Senatorial Selection Act*.

Samson v. Attorney General of Canada
(1998), 165 DLR (4th) 342 (FCTD)

McGILLIS J: [1] The applicants have applied for an interlocutory injunction to restrain the Governor General of Canada from appointing to the Senate a qualified person from the Province of Alberta, unless that person has been elected pursuant to the provisions of the *Senatorial Selection Act*, RSA, c. S-11.5. ...

· · ·

[3] The threshold question to be considered on this application is whether the applicants have established that there is a serious issue to be tried in this matter.

[4] Sections 24 and 32 of the *Constitution Act, 1867* expressly confer on the Governor General the unfettered discretion to appoint qualified persons to the Senate. Those sections read as follows:

> 24. The Governor General shall from Time to Time, in the Queen's Name, by Instrument under the Great Seal of Canada, summon qualified Persons to the Senate; and, subject to the Provisions of this Act, every Person so summoned shall become and be a Member of the Senate and a Senator.
>
> 32. When a Vacancy happens in the Senate by Resignation, Death or otherwise, the Governor General shall by Summons to a fit and qualified Person fill the Vacancy.

[5] Under the express and unequivocal terms of sections 24 and 32 of the *Constitution Act, 1867*, the Governor General's power to appoint qualified persons to the Senate is purely discretionary. In other words, there are no procedural or other limitations restricting the exercise of the Governor General's discretionary constitutional power of appointment under sections 24 and 32. A limitation could only be imposed on that power by means of a constitutional amendment to sections 24 and 32, effected in accordance with the procedure

prescribed in Part V of the *Constitution Act, 1982*. In the circumstances, the Court cannot impose procedural or other limitations on the Governor General's express power of appointment to the Senate, or otherwise fetter the exercise of his discretion. ...

[6] The Governor General's constitutional power to appoint qualified persons to the Senate is also purely political in nature. In practice, the Governor General exercises his power of appointment on the advice and recommendation of the Governor-in-Council. In the event that the Governor-in-Council makes a recommendation which ignores the pending election to be held in Alberta under the provisions of the provincial *Senatorial Selection Act*, it proceeds at its own political peril. However, that is a purely political decision to be made by politicians, without the interference or intervention of the Court.

[7] Counsel for the applicants relied heavily in his submissions on various statements made by the Supreme Court of Canada in *Reference re Secession of Quebec* (no. 25506, August 20, 1998). In my opinion, nothing in that case supports the proposition that a court may ignore the express and unequivocal provisions of the *Constitution Act, 1867*. I also note in passing that the *Quebec Secession Case* dealt with a situation involving a constitutional void. In the present case, express and unequivocal constitutional provisions govern the appointment process to the Senate.

[8] Counsel for the applicants also submitted that the Governor General's appointment of Mr. Stan Waters of Alberta to the Senate in 1990, following his election under the provisions of the *Senatorial Selection Act*, constitutes a "precedent" or a "convention" which may alter the express terms of the *Constitution Act, 1867*. I cannot accept that argument. The fact the Governor General on one previous occasion, acting on the advice and recommendation of the Governor-in-Council of the day, appointed to the Senate a person who had been elected in Alberta under the *Senatorial Selection Act* does not constitute a "convention" which alters the express wording of the *Constitution Act, 1867*. It was simply a political decision made by the Government of the day at that particular time in our nation's history.

[9] In my opinion, the applicants' claim in this matter is political, and not legal, in nature. As a result, the relief which the applicants seek in their application may only be attained in the political arena by means of a constitutional amendment. I have therefore concluded that the applicants have failed to establish that the case raises a serious issue to be tried. In the circumstances, it is unnecessary for me to address the other two branches of the test.

[10] The application for an interlocutory injunction is dismissed.

Following the 2006 election, Prime Minister Harper promised to rethink the manner in which senators are selected, including opening the door to election of nominees under provincial Senate selection laws. These elected nominees could then be appointed to the Upper Chamber by the governor general. The Harper government has repeatedly tabled bills that would amend the *Constitution Act, 1867* to impose term limits on new senators, restricting their tenure to eight years. (The current Constitution allows senators to remain in office until age 75.) Additional legislation has been proposed that, in its latest form, would steer the prime minister to honour provincial senatorial selection laws in the recommendations on Senate appointments made to the governor general, opening the door to a Senate with an elected composition. These law projects have died repeatedly in Parliament for a number of reasons, and it remained unclear at the time of this writing whether any would succeed.

The Senate is also controversial in the degree to which it fails to reflect the notion of representation by population. Section 22 of the *Constitution Act, 1867* partitions Canada into four "divisions," entitled to equal representation in the Senate. These divisions are Ontario, Quebec, the Maritime provinces, and the Western provinces. Each province within these last two divisions, as well as the Northwest Territories and the Yukon, is to be represented by a specified number of senators. Pursuant to the *Constitution Act, 1999 (Nunavut)*, one senator represents Nunavut. The resulting Senate representation by province, when contrasted with the population of each province, produces striking imbalances. For instance, Nova Scotia senators comprise 9.52 percent of the Senate, while Nova Scotia has 2.82 percent of the Canadian population. This pattern recurs for all of the Atlantic provinces. In comparison, Ontario—with almost 39 percent of the population—has representation that amounts to just under 23 percent of the Senate. Alberta and British Columbia are also "underrepresented" by 5 and 7 percent, respectively.

Correcting this problem would require an amendment to the *Constitution Act, 1867* that, under the applicable constitutional amendment formula, would require approval by the federal Parliament and at least seven provinces that collectively have at least 50 percent of the Canadian population.

3. House of Commons

Unlike senators, members of the House of Commons are elected, a requirement anticipated by s. 37 of the *Constitution Act, 1867*. Elections to the House of Commons are run according to a rich blend of constitutional and statutory law. Section 3 of the Charter says, for instance, that "[e]very citizen of Canada has the right to vote in an election of members of the House of Commons or of a legislative assembly and to be qualified for membership therein." The precise manner in which members of Parliament are elected is governed by the *Canada Elections Act*, SC 2000, c. 9, a very detailed statute designed to guarantee fair electoral contests.

Consider the following overview of elections of members of Parliament to the House of Commons.

Elections Canada, *Canada's Electoral System*
(Ottawa: Chief Electoral Officer of Canada, 2001)

Representation in the House of Commons

Representation in the House of Commons is based on geographical divisions known as electoral districts, constituencies or ridings. Each riding elects one member to the House of Commons, and the number of ridings is established through a formula set out in the Constitution. Riding boundaries are established by independent commissions, taking into account population and social and economic links. New commissions are set up following each decennial (10-year) census to make any necessary revisions to existing boundaries, following criteria defined in the *Electoral Boundaries Readjustment Act*. The process of redefining electoral boundaries is called redistribution, and the results are recorded in a representation order. [The current number of districts—and thus of members of Parliament—is 308.]

. . .

First Past the Post

Canada's electoral system is referred to as a "single-member plurality" or "first-past-the-post" system. In every electoral district, the candidate with the most votes wins a seat in the House of Commons and represents that riding as its member of Parliament, or MP. This means that candidates need not receive more than 50 percent of the vote (an absolute majority) to be elected.

Do not assume that there is absolute voter parity between the ridings from which MPs are elected. Not every Canadian's vote is "worth" the same amount and, generally speaking, a vote is worth more in the less densely populated rural ridings than in the crowded urban electoral districts. Is such unevenness in a voter's capacity to influence elections consistent with s. 3 of the Charter? Consider the following case, which concerns provincial electoral districts in Saskatchewan.

Reference re Prov. Electoral Boundaries (Sask.)
[1991] 2 SCR 158

McLACHLIN J: This appeal involves a constitutional challenge to provincial electoral distribution in the province of Saskatchewan. My conclusion is that the electoral boundaries created by *The Representation Act, 1989*, SS 1989-90, c. R-20.2, do not violate the right to vote enshrined in s. 3 of the *Canadian Charter of Rights and Freedoms*.

I reach this conclusion through consideration of a number of subsidiary issues:

I   The Question to be Answered

. . .

III Defining the Right to Vote

IV Is the Right to Vote Violated by the Saskatchewan Boundaries?

V   Section l and Justification

I The Question to be Answered

This case comes to us as an appeal from a reference to the Saskatchewan Court of Appeal (1991), 90 Sask. R 174. The reference requested that court's opinion on the following questions:

In respect of the constituencies defined in the *Representation Act, 1989*:

(a)   Does the variance in the size of voter populations among those constituencies, as contemplated by s. 20 of *The Electoral Boundaries Commission Act*, … and recommended in the Saskatchewan *Electoral Boundaries Commission 1988 Final Report*, infringe or deny rights or freedoms guaranteed by the *Canadian Charter of Rights and Freedoms*? If so, in what particulars? Is any such limitation or denial of rights or freedoms justified by s. 1 of the *Canadian Charter of Rights and Freedoms*?

(b)   Does the distribution of those constituencies among urban, rural and northern areas, as contemplated by s. 14 of *The Electoral Boundaries Commission Act*, … and recommended in the Saskatchewan *Electoral Boundaries Commission 1988 Final Report*, infringe or deny rights or freedoms guaranteed by the *Canadian Charter of Rights and Freedoms*? If so, in what particulars? Is any such limitation or denial of rights or freedoms justified by s. 1 of the *Canadian Charter of Rights and Freedoms*?

Different views have been expressed as to what issues these questions raise. The appellant asserts that what is at issue is the constitutional validity of *The Representation Act, 1989*. The respondent contends that the question is not whether the Act was unconstitutional, but whether the electoral boundaries created pursuant to the Act violate the Charter.

I am of the view that it is the boundaries themselves which are at issue on this appeal. The questions focus, not on the Act, but on the constitutionality of "the variance in the size of voter populations among [the] constituencies" and "the distribution of those constituencies among urban, rural and northern areas." In so far as *The Representation Act, 1989* defines the constituencies, the validity of that Act is indirectly called into question. And in so far as *The Electoral Boundaries Commission Act* provides the criteria by which the boundaries are to be fixed, that Act may affect the answers given to the questions posed. But the basic question put to this Court is whether the variances and distribution reflected in the constituencies themselves violate the Charter guarantee of the right to vote.

. . .

III Defining the Right To Vote

Section 3 of the *Canadian Charter of Rights and Freedoms* reads as follows:

> 3. Every citizen of Canada has the right to vote in an election of members of the House of Commons or of a legislative assembly and to be qualified for membership therein.

The question is simply stated: What is meant by "the right to vote" in s. 3? Before addressing this question it is necessary to address the way the Court should go about determining the content of the right.

A. General Principles Applicable to Defining the Right

The content of a *Charter* right is to be determined in a broad and purposive way, having regard to historical and social context. As Dickson J (as he then was) said in *R v. Big M Drug Mart Ltd.*, [1985] 1 SCR 295, at p. 344:

In my view this analysis is to be undertaken, and the purpose of the right or freedom in question is to be sought by reference to the character and the larger objects of the *Charter* itself, to the language chosen to articulate the specific right or freedom, to the historical origins of the concepts enshrined, and where applicable, to the meaning and purpose of the other specific rights and freedoms with which it is associated within the text of the *Charter*. The interpretation should be, as the judgment in *Southam* emphasizes, a generous rather than a legalistic one, aimed at fulfilling the purpose of the guarantee and securing for individuals the full benefit of the *Charter*'s protection. At the same time it is important not to overshoot the actual purpose of the right or freedom in question, but to recall that the *Charter* was not enacted in a vacuum, and must therefore, as this Court's decision in *Law Society of Upper Canada v. Skapinker* ... illustrates, be placed in its proper linguistic, philosophic and historical contexts.

From this general statement of principle I turn to more particular considerations which bear relevance to this appeal.

The first of these is the doctrine that the *Charter* is engrafted onto the living tree that is the Canadian constitution ... . Thus, to borrow the words of Lord Sankey in *Edwards v. Attorney-General for Canada*, ... it must be viewed as "a living tree capable of growth and expansion within its natural limits."

The doctrine of the constitution as a living tree mandates that narrow technical approaches are to be eschewed ... . It also suggests that the past plays a critical but non-exclusive role in determining the content of the rights and freedoms granted by the *Charter*. The tree is rooted in past and present institutions, but must be capable of growth to meet the future. As Dickson J stated in *R v. Big M Drug Mart Ltd.* ... :

> ... the *Charter* is intended to set a standard upon which *present as well as future* legislation is to be tested. Therefore the meaning of the concept of freedom of conscience and religion is not to be determined solely by the degree to which that right was enjoyed by Canadians prior to the proclamation of the *Charter*. [Emphasis in original.]

This admonition is as apt in defining the right to vote as it is in defining freedom of religion. The right to vote, while rooted in and hence to some extent defined by historical and existing practices, cannot be viewed as frozen by particular historical anomalies. What must be sought is the broader philosophy underlying the historical development of the right to vote—a philosophy which is capable of explaining the past and animating the future.

This appeal also engages the general principle that practical considerations must be borne in mind in constitutional interpretation ... . Courts must be sensitive to what Frankfurter J (*McGowan v. Maryland*, 366 US 420 (1961)) calls "the practical living facts" to which a legislature must respond ... . This is nowhere more true than in considering the right to vote, where practical considerations such as social and physical geography may impact on the value of the citizen's right to vote.

Of final and critical importance to this appeal is the canon that in interpreting the individual rights conferred by the *Charter* the Court must be guided by the ideal of a "free and democratic society" upon which the *Charter* is founded. As Dickson CJ stated in *R v. Oakes* ... :

The Court must be guided by the values and principles essential to a free and democratic society which I believe embody, to name but a few, respect for the inherent dignity of the human person, commitment to social justice and equality, accommodation of a wide variety of beliefs, respect for cultural and group identity, and faith in social and political institutions which enhance the participation of individuals and groups in society.

The first task on an appeal such as this is to define the scope of the right to vote under s. 3 of the *Charter*. The second is to evaluate the existing electoral boundaries in the light of that definition to determine if they violate s. 3 of the *Charter*. If a violation is found, a third task arises—determining whether the limitation on the right is "demonstrably justified in a free and democratic society" and hence saved under s. 1 of the *Charter*. The general principles to which I have referred, while bearing particularly on the task of defining the ambit of the right, also animate the second and third steps of the analysis.

B. *The Focus of the Debate*

The question for resolution on this appeal can be summed up in one sentence: to what extent, if at all, does the right to vote enshrined in the *Charter* permit deviation from the "one person–one vote" rule? The answer to this question turns on what one sees as the purpose of s. 3. Those who start from the premise that the purpose of the section is to guarantee equality of voting power support the view that only minimal deviation from that ideal is possible. Those who start from the premise that the purpose of s. 3 is to guarantee effective representation see the right to vote as comprising many factors, of which equality is but one. The contest, as I see it, is most fundamentally between these two views, although the submissions before us vary in the emphasis they place on different factors and hence on where they would draw the line.

The Saskatchewan Court of Appeal, as I read its reasons, fell into the camp of those who see the purpose of s. 3 as guaranteeing equality of voting power *per se*. It suggested that the only deviation permissible from the ideal of equality under s. 3 is that required by the practical problems of ensuring that the number of voters in each constituency is mathematically equal on the day of voting … . On the basis of this definition, it found that the electoral boundaries in Saskatchewan violated s. 3 of the *Charter*. Other considerations, such as geography, historical boundaries and community interests, fell to be considered under s. 1. The court found that the boundaries were not justified under s. 1, except for the two northern ridings where population is extremely sparse.

In this Court, the respondent, supporting the judgment of the Court of Appeal, urged that the goal of s. 3 is equality of voting power, as nearly as may possibly be achieved. The appellant, while not going so far as to deny the importance of equality in a meaningful right to vote, urged that equality was but one of many factors relevant to the right to vote enshrined in s. 3 and that the fundamental purpose of s. 3 was not to ensure equality of voting power, but effective and fair representation conducive to good government. The interveners tended to ally themselves with one of these two positions, stressing their own particular perspectives. For example, Equal Justice for All urged no deviation from equality, except as might be justified in aid of disadvantaged groups, while the Attorney General for Alberta went so far as to deny equality's place as a "core" or "fundamental" value in assessing the right to vote.

C. *The Meaning of the Right To Vote*

It is my conclusion that the purpose of the right to vote enshrined in s. 3 of the *Charter* is not equality of voting power *per se*, but the right to "effective representation." Ours is a representative democracy. Each citizen is entitled to be *represented* in government. Representation comprehends the idea of having a voice in the deliberations of government as well as the idea of the right to bring one's grievances and concerns to the attention of one's government representative; as noted in *Dixon v. B.C. (A.G.)*, [1989] 4 WWR 393, at p. 413, elected representatives function in two roles—legislative and what has been termed the "ombudsman role."

What are the conditions of effective representation? The first is relative parity of voting power. A system which dilutes one citizen's vote unduly as compared with another citizen's vote runs the risk of providing inadequate representation to the citizen whose vote is diluted. The legislative power of the citizen whose vote is diluted will be reduced, as may be access to and assistance from his or her representative. The result will be uneven and unfair representation.

But parity of voting power, though of prime importance, is not the only factor to be taken into account in ensuring effective representation. Sir John A. Macdonald in introducing the *Act to re-adjust the Representation in the House of Commons*, SC l872, c. 13, recognized this fundamental fact (House of Commons Debates, Vol. III, 4th Sess., p. 926 (June 1, 1872)):

> … it will be found that, … while the principle of population was considered to a very great extent, other considerations were also held to have weight; so that different interests, classes and localities should be fairly represented, that the principle of numbers should not be the only one.

Notwithstanding the fact that the value of a citizen's vote should not be unduly diluted, it is a practical fact that effective representation often cannot be achieved without taking into account countervailing factors.

First, absolute parity is impossible. It is impossible to draw boundary lines which guarantee exactly the same number of voters in each district. Voters die, voters move. Even with the aid of frequent censuses, voter parity is impossible.

Secondly, such relative parity as may be possible of achievement may prove undesirable because it has the effect of detracting from the primary goal of effective representation. Factors like geography, community history, community interests and minority representation may need to be taken into account to ensure that our legislative assemblies effectively represent the diversity of our social mosaic. These are but examples of considerations which may justify departure from absolute voter parity in the pursuit of more effective representation; the list is not closed.

It emerges therefore that deviations from absolute voter parity may be justified on the grounds of practical impossibility or the provision of more effective representation. Beyond this, dilution of one citizen's vote as compared with another's should not be countenanced. I adhere to the proposition asserted in *Dixon, supra*, at p. 414, that "only those deviations should be admitted which can be justified on the ground that they contribute to better government of the populace as a whole, giving due weight to regional issues within the populace and geographic factors within the territory governed."

This view of the meaning of the right to vote in s. 3 of the *Charter* conforms with the general principles of interpretation discussed at the outset.

The first and most important rule is that the right must be interpreted in accordance with its purpose. As will be seen, there is little in the history or philosophy of Canadian democracy that suggests that the framers of the *Charter* in enacting s. 3 had as their ultimate goal the attainment of voter parity. That purpose would have represented a rejection of the existing system of electoral representation in this country. The circumstances leading to the adoption of the *Charter* negate any intention to reject existing democratic institutions. As noted in *Dixon, supra*, at p. 412: "There is no record of such fundamental institutional reform having been mentioned at the conferences that preceded the adoption of the [proposed] *Charter*." Nor was the issue raised by any of the plethora of interest groups making submissions in respect of voting rights during the prolonged Joint Senate and House of Commons Committee Hearings on the proposed *Charter*. The framers of the *Charter* had two distinct electoral models before them—the "one person–one vote" model espoused by the United States Supreme Court in *Baker v. Carr*, 369 US 186 (1962), *Karcher v. Daggett*, 462 US 725 (1983), and *Kirkpatrick v. Preisler*, 394 US 526 (1969), and the less radical, more pragmatic approach which had developed in England and in this country through the centuries and which was actually in place. In the absence of any supportive evidence to the contrary (as may be found in the United States in the speeches of the founding fathers), it would be wrong to infer that in enshrining the right to vote in our written constitution the intention was to adopt the American model. On the contrary, we should assume that the goal was to recognize the right affirmed in this country since the time of our first Prime Minister, Sir John A. Macdonald, to effective representation in a system which gives due weight to voter parity but admits other considerations where necessary.

I turn next to the history of our right to vote. As already noted, the history of our right to vote and the context in which it existed at the time the *Charter* was adopted support the conclusion that the purpose of the guarantee of the right to vote is not to effect perfect voter equality, in so far as that can be done, but the broader goal of guaranteeing effective representation. As I noted in *Dixon, supra*, at p. 409, democracy in Canada is rooted in a different history than in the United States:

> Its origins lie not in the debates of the founding fathers, but in the less absolute recesses of the British tradition. Our forefathers did not rebel against the English tradition of democratic government as did the Americans; on the contrary, they embraced it and changed it to suit their own perceptions and needs.

I went on to describe the Canadian tradition as one of evolutionary democracy moving in uneven steps toward the goal of universal suffrage and more effective representation, which even in its advanced stages tolerates deviation from voter parity in the interests of better representation:

> What is that tradition? It was a tradition of evolutionary democracy, of increasing widening of representation through the centuries. But it was also a tradition which, even in its more modern phases, accommodates significant deviation from the ideals of equal representation. Pragmatism, rather than conformity to a philosophical ideal, has been its watchword.

Other Commonwealth countries have affirmed the same tradition. Thus the Australian High Court rejected a "one person–one vote" approach in favour of an approach which permitted consideration of countervailing factors: *Attorney-General (Aus.); Ex rel. McKinlay v. Commonwealth* (1975), 135 CLR 1. Stephen J wrote, at p. 57:

> It is, then, quite apparent that representative democracy is descriptive of a whole spectrum of political institutions, each differing in countless respects yet answering to that generic description … .
>
> To contend that the presence of what is described as "as near as practicable equality of numbers" within electoral divisions is essential to representative democracy, to a legislature "chosen by the people," is to deny proper meaning to language and to ignore long chapters in the evolution of democratic institutions both in this country and overseas, in which, representative democracy having been attained, its details have undergone frequent changes in response to community pressures but have failed to possess this feature of equality of numbers on which the plaintiffs now insist.

See also Gibbs J, at p. 45 and Barwick CJ, at p. 25.

To return to the metaphor of the living tree, our system is rooted in the tradition of effective representation and not in the tradition of absolute or near absolute voter parity. It is this tradition that defines the general ambit of the right to vote. This is not to suggest, however, that inequities in our voting system are to be accepted merely because they have historical precedent. History is important in so far as it suggests that the philosophy underlying the development of the right to vote in this country is the broad goal of effective representation. It has nothing to do with the specious argument that historical anomalies and abuses can be used to justify continued anomalies and abuses, or to suggest that the right to vote should not be interpreted broadly and remedially as befits *Charter* rights. Departures from the Canadian ideal of effective representation may exist. Where they do, they will be found to violate s. 3 of the *Charter*.

I turn finally to the admonition that courts must be sensitive to practical considerations in interpreting *Charter* rights. The "practical living fact," to borrow Frankfurter J's phrase, is that effective representation and good government in this country compel those charged with setting electoral boundaries sometimes to take into account factors other than voter parity, such as geography and community interests. The problems of representing vast, sparsely populated territories, for example, may dictate somewhat lower voter populations in these districts; to insist on voter parity might deprive citizens with distinct interests of an effective voice in the legislative process as well as of effective assistance from their representatives in their "ombudsman" role. This is only one of a number of factors which may necessitate deviation from the "one person–one vote" rule in the interests of effective representation.

In the final analysis, the values and principles animating a free and democratic society are arguably best served by a definition that places effective representation at the heart of the right to vote. The concerns which Dickson CJ in *Oakes* associated with a free and democratic society—respect for the inherent dignity of the human person, commitment to social justice and equality, respect for cultural and group identity, and faith in social and political institutions which enhance the participation of individuals in society—are better met by an electoral system that focuses on effective representation than by one that focuses on mathematical parity. Respect for individual dignity and social equality mandate that citizen's votes not be unduly debased or diluted. But the need to recognize cultural and group identity and to enhance the participation of individuals in the electoral process and society requires that other concerns also be accommodated.

In summary, I am satisfied that the precepts which govern the interpretation of *Charter* rights support the conclusion that the right to vote should be defined as guaranteeing the right to effective representation. The concept of absolute voter parity does not accord with the development of the right to vote in the Canadian context and does not permit of sufficient flexibility to meet the practical difficulties inherent in representative government in a country such as Canada. In the end, it is the broader concept of effective representation which best serves the interests of a free and democratic society.

IV Do the Saskatchewan Boundaries Violate the Right To Vote?

· · ·

I turn then to the contention that the distribution of seats itself violates s. 3 of the *Charter*. As already noted, variances between southern seats fall within plus or minus 25 percent of the provincial quotient. Moreover, the distribution between urban and rural seats closely approximates the actual split between urban and rural population. It remains, however, to consider whether unjustifiable deviations exist with respect to particular ridings in the southern half of the province.

Before examining the electoral boundaries to determine if they are justified, it may be useful to mention some of the factors other than equality of voting power which figure in the analysis. One of the most important is the fact that it is more difficult to represent rural ridings than urban. The material before us suggests that not only are rural ridings harder to serve because of difficulty in transport and communications, but that rural voters make greater demands on their elected representatives, whether because of the absence of alternative resources to be found in urban centres or for other reasons. Thus the goal of effective representation may justify somewhat lower voter populations in rural areas. Another factor which figured prominently in the argument before us is geographic boundaries; rivers and municipal boundaries form natural community dividing lines and hence natural electoral boundaries. Yet another factor is growth projections. Given that the boundaries will govern for a number of years—the boundaries set in 1989, for example, may be in place until 1996 projected population changes within that period may justify a deviation from strict equality at the time the boundaries are drawn.

Against this background, I turn to the boundaries themselves.

· · ·

In summary, the evidence supplied by the province is sufficient to justify the existing electoral boundaries. In general, the discrepancies between urban and rural ridings is small, no more than one might expect given the greater difficulties associated with representing rural ridings. And discrepancies between particular ridings appear to be justified on the basis of factors such as geography, community interests and population growth patterns. It was not seriously suggested that the northern boundaries are inappropriate, given the sparse population and the difficulty of communication in the area. I conclude that a violation of s. 3 of the *Charter* has not been established.

In these circumstances, it is unnecessary to consider s. 1.

V Conclusion

I would allow the appeal and answer both Reference Questions in the negative.

As every observer of Canadian politics knows, elections are contested by political parties. A political party is a defined entity in s. 2 of the *Canada Elections Act*: a political party is "an organization one of whose fundamental purposes is to participate in public affairs by endorsing one or more of its members as candidates and supporting their election." Consider the following discussion of political parties by Canada's election administrator.

Elections Canada, *Canada's Electoral System*
(Ottawa: Chief Electoral Officer of Canada, 2001)

Any number of candidates may run for election in an electoral district, but each candidate may run in one electoral district only, either independently or under the banner of a registered or eligible political party. Each party may endorse only one candidate per riding. Candidates who run for election without party affiliation may be designated as "independent" or have no designation appear.

A political party is a group of people who together establish a constitution and by-laws, elect a leader and other officers, and endorse candidates for election to the House of Commons. To obtain the right to put the party name on the ballot, under the names of the candidates it endorses, a political party must register with the Chief Electoral Officer. ...

After an election, the party with the most elected representatives usually becomes the governing party. The leader of this party becomes the Prime Minister and chooses people (usually members of Parliament of his or her party) to head the various government departments. The party with the second largest number of MPs is called the "Official Opposition." All the elected candidates have a seat in the House of Commons, where they vote on draft legislation (called Bills) and thus have an influence on government policy.

Until recently, the *Canada Elections Act* required a registered party to run candidates in at least 50 electoral districts. This rule was struck down by the Supreme Court in 2003 in *Figueroa v. Canada*, [2003] 1 SCR 912. Consider the reasoning applied by the court and its vision of electoral democracy, and the role of political parties in it.

Figueroa v. Canada
[2003] 1 SCR 912, 2003 SCC 37

IACOBUCCI J (McLachlin CJ and Major, Bastarache, Binnie, and Arbour JJ concurring):

I. Introduction

[1] This appeal raises fundamental questions in respect of the democratic process in our country. More specifically, this appeal focuses on the purpose and meaning to be given to s. 3 of the *Canadian Charter of Rights and Freedoms*, which confers on each citizen the right to vote in the election of members of the House of Commons and the provincial legislative assemblies and to be qualified for membership therein. The issue is whether federal legislation that restricts access to certain benefits to political parties that have nominated candidates in at least 50 electoral districts violates s. 3. I conclude that it does and would therefore allow the appeal.

• • •

IV. Issues

[16] The question to be determined in this appeal is whether ss. 24(2), 24(3) and 28(2) of the *Elections Act* infringe s. 3 of the *Charter* by withholding from candidates nominated by political parties that have failed to satisfy the 50-candidate threshold the right to issue tax receipts for donations received outside the election period, the right to transfer unspent election funds to the party, and the right to list their party affiliation on the ballot papers—and, if so, whether that infringement is reasonable and demonstrably justified under s. 1 of the *Charter*.

• • •

V. Analysis

A. Does the 50-Candidate Threshold Violate Section 3 of the Charter?

[18] The first question to be determined in this appeal is whether the restriction on the right of candidates to issue tax receipts for donations received outside the election period, to transfer unspent election funds to the party, and to list their party affiliation on the ballot papers infringes s. 3 of the *Charter*. This requires the Court to perform two tasks. The first is to define the purpose of s. 3 of the *Charter*. The second is to evaluate the 50-candidate threshold in light of that definition in order to determine whether it violates s. 3 of the *Charter*.

(1) Section 3 of the Charter

[19] Under s. 3 of the *Charter*, "[e]very citizen of Canada has the right to vote in an election of members of the House of Commons or of a legislative assembly and to be qualified for membership therein." On its face, the scope of s. 3 is relatively narrow: it grants to each citizen no more than the bare right to vote and to run for office in the election of representatives of the federal and provincial legislative assemblies. But *Charter* analysis requires courts

to look beyond the words of the section. In the words of McLachlin CJBCSC (as she then was), "[m]ore is intended [in the right to vote] than the bare right to place a ballot in a box": *Dixon v. British Columbia (Attorney General)*, [1989] 4 WWR 393, at p. 403.

[20] In order to determine the scope of s. 3, the Court must first ascertain its purpose. … In interpreting the scope of a *Charter* right, courts must adopt a broad and purposive approach that seeks to ensure that duly enacted legislation is in harmony with the purposes of the *Charter*.

[21] This Court first considered the purpose of s. 3 in *Reference re Provincial Electoral Boundaries (Sask.)*, [1991] 2 SCR 158 ("*Saskatchewan Reference*"). In determining that s. 3 does not require absolute equality of voting power, McLachlin J held that the purpose of s. 3 is "effective representation" (p. 183). This Court has subsequently confirmed, on numerous occasions, that the purpose of s. 3 is effective representation. …

. . .

[25] But the right to effective representation contemplates more than the right to an effective representative in Parliament or a legislative assembly. … [T]he purpose of s. 3 includes not only the right of each citizen to have and to vote for an elected representative in Parliament or a legislative assembly, but also to the right of each citizen to play a meaningful role in the electoral process. This, in my view, is a more complete statement of the purpose of s. 3 of the *Charter*.

[26] Support for the proposition that s. 3 should be understood with reference to the right of each citizen to play a meaningful role in the electoral process, rather than the election of a particular form of government, is found in the fact that the rights of s. 3 are participatory in nature. Section 3 does not advert to the composition of Parliament subsequent to an election, but only to the right of each citizen to a certain level of participation in the electoral process. On its very face, then, the central focus of s. 3 is the right of each citizen to participate in the electoral process. This signifies that the right of each citizen to participate in the political life of the country is one that is of fundamental importance in a free and democratic society and suggests that s. 3 should be interpreted in a manner that ensures that this right of participation embraces a content commensurate with the importance of individual participation in the selection of elected representatives in a free and democratic state. Defining the purpose of s. 3 with reference to the right of each citizen to play a meaningful role in the electoral process, rather than the composition of Parliament subsequent to an election, better ensures that the right of participation that s. 3 explicitly protects is not construed too narrowly.

. . .

[28] As this Court frequently has acknowledged, the free flow of diverse opinions and ideas is of fundamental importance in a free and democratic society. … Put simply, full political debate ensures that ours is an open society with the benefit of a broad range of ideas and opinions. … This, in turn, ensures not only that policy makers are aware of a broad range of options, but also that the determination of social policy is sensitive to the needs and interests of a broad range of citizens.

[29] It thus follows that participation in the electoral process has an intrinsic value independent of its impact upon the actual outcome of elections. To be certain, the electoral process is the means by which elected representatives are selected and governments formed, but it is also the primary means by which the average citizen participates in the open debate

that animates the determination of social policy. The right to run for office provides each citizen with the opportunity to present certain ideas and opinions to the electorate as a viable policy option; the right to vote provides each citizen with the opportunity to express support for the ideas and opinions that a particular candidate endorses. In each instance, the democratic rights entrenched in s. 3 ensure that each citizen has an opportunity to express an opinion about the formation of social policy and the functioning of public institutions through participation in the electoral process.

[30] … Democracy, of course, is a form of government in which sovereign power resides in the people as a whole. In our system of democracy, this means that each citizen must have a genuine opportunity to take part in the governance of the country through participation in the selection of elected representatives. The fundamental purpose of s. 3, in my view, is to promote and protect the right of each citizen to play a meaningful role in the political life of the country. Absent such a right, ours would not be a true democracy.

· · ·

(2) Does the 50-Candidate Threshold Violate Section 3?

[38] Consequently, the essential question to be determined is whether the 50-candidate threshold interferes with the capacity of individual citizens to play a meaningful role in the electoral process. In order to answer this question, the Court must answer two prior questions. First, do the members and supporters of political parties that nominate fewer than 50 candidates play a meaningful role in the electoral process? And if so, does the restriction on the right to issue tax receipts for donations received outside the election period, to transfer unspent election funds to the party and to list their party affiliation on the ballot papers interfere with the capacity of the members and supporters of political parties that nominate fewer than 50 candidates to play a meaningful role in the electoral process?

(a) The Role of Political Parties That Nominate Candidates in Fewer Than 50 Electoral Districts

[39] … It is my conclusion that the ability of a political party to make a valuable contribution to the electoral process is not dependent upon its capacity to offer the electorate a genuine "government option." Rather, political parties enhance the meaningfulness of individual participation in the electoral process for reasons that transcend their capacity (or lack thereof) to participate in the governance of the country subsequent to an election. Irrespective of their capacity to influence the outcome of an election, political parties act as both a vehicle and outlet for the meaningful participation of individual citizens in the electoral process.

[40] With respect to the ability of a political party to act as an effective vehicle for the meaningful participation of individual citizens in the electoral process, it is important to note that political parties have a much greater capacity than any one citizen to participate in the open debate that the electoral process engenders. By doing so in a representative capacity, on behalf of their members and supporters, political parties act as a vehicle for the participation of individual citizens in the political life of the country. Political parties ensure that the ideas and opinions of their members and supporters are effectively represented in the open debate occasioned by the electoral process and presented to the electorate as a vi-

able option. If those ideas and opinions are not subsequently adopted by the government of the day, it is not because they have not been considered, but, rather, because they have received insufficient public support.

[41] Importantly, it is not only large political parties that are able to fulfil this function. It likely is true that a large party will be able to play a larger role in the open discourse of the electoral process, but it does not thereby follow that the capacity of a political party to represent the ideas and opinions of its members and supporters in the electoral process is dependent upon its capacity to offer the electorate a "government option." Large or small, all political parties are capable of introducing unique interests and concerns into the political discourse. Consequently, all political parties, whether large or small, are capable of acting as a vehicle for the participation of individual citizens in the public discourse that animates the determination of social policy.

[42] For example, marginal or regional parties tend to dissent from mainstream thinking and to bring to the attention of the general public issues and concerns that have not been adopted by national parties. They might exert less influence than the national parties, but still can be a most effective vehicle for the participation of individual citizens whose preferences have not been incorporated into the political platforms of national parties. It is better that an individual citizen have his or her ideas and concerns introduced into the open debate of the electoral process by a political party with a limited geographical base of support than not to have his or her ideas and concerns introduced into that debate by any political party at all.

[43] In respect of their ability to act as an effective outlet for the meaningful participation of individual citizens in the electoral process, the participation of political parties in the electoral process also provides individuals with the opportunity to express an opinion on governmental policy and the proper functioning of public institutions. A vote for a candidate nominated by a particular party is an expression of support for the platform or policy perspectives that the party endorses. The participation of political parties thereby enhances the capacity of individual citizens to express an opinion as to the type of country that they would like Canada to be through the exercise of the right to vote.

[44] Once again, the capacity of a political party to provide individual citizens with an opportunity to express an opinion on governmental policy and the proper functioning of public institutions is not dependent upon its capacity to participate in the governance of the country subsequent to an election. As the preceding paragraph suggests, participation as a voter is not only about the selection of elected representatives. Irrespective of its effect on the outcome of an election, a vote for a particular candidate is an expression of support for a particular approach or platform. Whether that vote contributes to the election of a candidate or not, each vote in support of that approach or platform increases the likelihood that the issues and concerns underlying that platform will be taken into account by those who ultimately implement policy, if not now then perhaps at some point in the future.

[45] As a consequence, there is no reason to think that political parties that have not satisfied the 50-candidate threshold do not act as an effective outlet for the meaningful participation of individual citizens in the electoral process. There is no correlation between the capacity of a political party to offer the electorate a government option and the capacity of a political party to formulate a unique policy platform for presentation to the general public. In each election, a significant number of citizens vote for candidates nominated by

registered parties in full awareness that the candidate has no realistic chance of winning a seat in Parliament—or that the party of which she or he is a member has no realistic chance of winning a majority of seats in the House of Commons. Just as these votes are not "wasted votes," votes for a political party that has not satisfied the 50-candidate threshold are not wasted votes either. As a public expression of individual support for certain perspectives and opinions, such votes are an integral component of a vital and dynamic democracy.

[46] It is thus my conclusion that the members and supporters of political parties that nominate candidates in fewer than 50 electoral districts do play a meaningful role in the electoral process. They are both a vehicle for the participation of individual citizens in the open debate occasioned by the electoral process and an outlet for the expression of support for political platforms that are different from those adopted by political parties with a broad base of support. The question that thus arises is whether the 50-candidate threshold interferes with the right of such citizens to play a meaningful role in the electoral process.

(b) The Impact of the 50-Candidate Threshold

[47] As outlined earlier, the effect of the 50-candidate threshold is to extend the benefits of registration only to those parties that have nominated candidates in 50 electoral districts. At issue in this appeal are the rights of candidates to issue tax receipts for donations received outside the election period, to transfer unspent election funds to the party and to include their party affiliation on the ballot papers. The question to be determined is whether withholding these benefits from candidates of parties who have not met the 50-candidate threshold undermines the right of each citizen to meaningful participation in the electoral process. In each instance, it is my opinion that the threshold does, in fact, have this effect.

· · ·

[58] For these reasons, I conclude that the 50-candidate threshold does infringe s. 3 of the *Charter*. It undermines both the capacity of individual citizens to influence policy by introducing ideas and opinions into the public discourse and debate through participation in the electoral process, and the capacity of individual citizens to exercise their right to vote in a manner that accurately reflects their preferences. In each instance, the threshold requirement is inconsistent with the purpose of s. 3 of the *Charter*: the preservation of the right of each citizen to play a meaningful role in the electoral process.

B. Is the Infringement Saved by Section 1 of the Charter?

[59] In order to justify the infringement of a *Charter* right under s. 1, the government must demonstrate that the limitation is reasonable and demonstrably justifiable in a free and democratic society. This involves a two-step analysis, pursuant to *Oakes* ... and related cases. ... Throughout this process the burden rests on the government. The government first must demonstrate that the objective of the legislation is sufficiently pressing and substantial to warrant violating a *Charter* right. The objectives must be neither "trivial" nor "discordant with the principles integral to a free and democratic society." ... Once this has been established, the government must then demonstrate that the infringement is proportionate, namely, that the legislation is rationally connected to the objective, that it minimally impairs the *Charter* right in question, and that the salutary benefits of the legislation outweigh the deleterious effects.

❦

· · ·

[61] In his factum, the Attorney General of Canada submits that the objective of the 50-candidate threshold is "to enhance the effectiveness of Canadian elections, in both their process *and* outcome" (emphasis in original). More specifically, the Attorney General submits that the 50-candidate threshold advances three separate goals: (i) to improve the effectiveness of the electoral process; (ii) to protect the integrity of the electoral financing regime; and (iii) to ensure that the process is able to deliver a viable outcome for our form of responsible government. To provide a more complete analysis of the federal government's arguments under s. 1, I deal with each objective advanced separately. Consequently, in the analysis below, I consider each of the proposed objectives in turn to determine first whether the government has demonstrated that any of the specific objectives is of pressing and substantial importance and, second, that the violation of s. 3 is proportionate.

[The majority concluded that the 50-candidate minimum was not saved by s. 1. As summarized in the official headnote:

> While the objective of ensuring the cost-efficiency of the tax credit scheme is pressing and substantial, the 50-candidate threshold does not meet the proportionality branch of the *Oakes* test. There is no connection whatsoever between the objective and the threshold requirement with respect to transfers of unspent election funds or listing party affiliations on ballot papers. Nor is the restriction on the right of political parties to issue tax receipts for donations received outside the election period rationally connected to the objective. The connection between legislation that has no impact upon either the number of citizens allowed to claim the tax credit or the size of the credit and the objective is tenuous at best. Moreover, the government has provided no evidence that the threshold actually improves the cost-efficiency of the tax credit scheme. The legislation also fails the minimal impairment test because cost savings can be achieved without violating s. 3. Further, any benefits associated with the reduced costs of the tax credit scheme do not outweigh the deleterious effects of this legislation.
>
> While preserving the integrity of the electoral process is a pressing and substantial concern in a free and democratic state, this objective provides no justification for the restriction on the right of candidates to list their party affiliation on the ballot papers. The same is true of the restriction on the right to issue tax credits and the right to transfer unspent election funds to the party. Furthermore, even if the restrictions on the right to issue the tax credit and the right to retain unspent election funds prevent the misuse of the electoral financing regime, the legislation fails the minimal impairment test. In each instance, the government has failed to demonstrate that it could not achieve the same results without violating s. 3 of the *Charter*.
>
> Lastly, articulating the objective as ensuring a viable outcome for responsible government in the form of majority governments is problematic. In any event, the 50-candidate threshold fails the rational connection test and its salutary benefits have not been shown to outweigh its deleterious effects.]

· · ·

[90] In the final analysis, I conclude both that the 50-candidate threshold is inconsistent with the right of each citizen to play a meaningful role in the electoral process, and that the government has failed to justify this violation.

B. Bringing the Constituent Elements of Parliament Together

A Parliament is not a permanent feature, meeting indefinitely. Canada has had 39 Parliaments since 1867, and at the time of this writing was in the midst of its 40th. Thus, federal Parliaments have been summoned 40 times and dissolved on 39 occasions. Elections to the House of Commons take place in the period after the dissolution of the old Parliament and the summoning of a new Parliament. During the life of a Parliament itself, most Parliaments have been "prorogued" between different "sessions" of that Parliament. In this section, we discuss the process of summoning, proroguing, and dissolving a Parliament.

1. Summoning

Section 38 of the *Constitution Act, 1867* empowers the governor general "from Time to Time, in the Queen's Name, by Instrument under the Great Seal of Canada, [to] summon and call together the House of Commons." However, this apparent discretion is greatly constrained by constitutional convention, and now the Charter.

By constitutional convention, the governor general calls Parliament to session on the advice of the prime minister. This convention is codified in the Writ of Election, enacted as Schedule 1 in the *Canada Elections Act*. This writ empowers the monarch (and thus the governor general) to set the date for a new Parliament "by and with the advice" of the prime minister.

Consider the events that follow soon after the summoning of a new Parliament.

House of Commons, *Précis of Procedure*
(Ottawa: House of Commons, 2003)

2(a) Formal Opening of a Parliament

The formal opening of the first session of a Parliament is distinguished from the opening of subsequent sessions by two preliminary proceedings: the taking and subscribing of the Oath of Allegiance by Members and the election of a Speaker. ...

At the hour of the formal opening of Parliament, the House receives the Usher of the Black Rod who reads a message requesting the immediate attendance of the House in the Senate Chamber. The meeting of Parliament in the Senate Chamber follows the practice established in Britain that no monarch, or monarch's representative, has entered the House of Commons since King Charles I in 1642, and that the place of the sovereign in Parliament is in the Upper House. The Speaker addresses the Governor General by an established formula stating that he or she has been elected by the House of Commons as Speaker and, for the Commons, "humbly claim[s] all their undoubted rights and privileges, especially that they may have freedom of speech in their debates, access to Your Excellency's person at all seasonable times, and that their proceedings may receive from Your Excellency the most favourable construction." On behalf of the Governor General, the Speaker of the Senate replies with a similarly stylized affirmation, including that he or she "grants, and upon all occasions will recognize and allow their constitutional privileges." This claiming of privileges, like many parliamentary ceremonies, has its origins in constitutional history when the

Commons were fighting for their privileges in the face of royal tyranny in Britain: the first record there of such a claim dates from 1554. Significant nowadays among those specified privileges is freedom of speech: anything said in the Senate, House of Commons or in committee as part of parliamentary business is not actionable in the courts.

2(b) Speech from the Throne

Following the claim to privileges and the reply, the Governor General reads the Speech from the Throne, imparting the causes of summoning Parliament, prior to which declaration neither House can proceed with any public business. The Speech from the Throne formally opens the first session and any subsequent sessions of a Parliament and marks the first occasion of "Parliament Assembled" in its three constituent parts: the Sovereign or the Sovereign's representative, the Senate, and the House of Commons. In the first session of a Parliament, after the Speech from the Throne, the Speaker and Members return to the House where the Speaker reports the claim to privileges and the reply, as well as the causes of the summoning of Parliament.

3. Address in Reply to the Speech from the Throne

When the House returns from the Senate after the Speech from the Throne, its business includes a routine motion by the Prime Minister that the Throne Speech be considered either that day or on some future day. On the specified day, the proceedings which result in the House of Commons' response to the Throne Speech—the Address in Reply to the Speech from the Throne—begin when a government Member not of the Ministry moves that an Address be presented to the Governor General (or more rarely, the Sovereign) "to offer our humble thanks … for the gracious speech which Your Excellency has addressed … ." Following the speech of another government private Member who seconds the motion, the House normally adjourns to the first of six (not necessarily consecutive) days for resuming debate on the motion and on any amendments.

As the motion itself is relatively unspecific, debate is very wide-ranging, providing one of the few opportunities for private Members to speak on topics of their choice. The normal rules of debate apply. All Members except the Prime Minister and the Leader of the Opposition are restricted to 20-minute speeches, followed by a 10-minute questions and comments period after each speech.

… On the first of the six days of formal debate (so-called Leaders' Day), the first speaker is the Leader of the Opposition, who may conclude by proposing an amendment to add words to the original motion. The Prime Minister speaks next, followed by the leader of the second largest party in opposition, who may offer a subamendment. Opposition amendments and subamendments entail direct questions of confidence in the Government. Again, given the unspecific nature of the main motion, the rule of relevance is not strictly applied to such "no-confidence" amendments. A procedurally acceptable amendment will add some specific element of its own; a subamendment may propose an addition to or deletion from the words of the amendment and must be relevant to it.

The House of Commons *Précis of Procedure* notes that opposition amendments to the address in reply to the speech from the throne constitute "direct questions of confidence in the Government." Thus, a failure by the government to carry an unamended address in reply likely constitutes a vote of no confidence, causing the government to fall. Confidence votes are discussed below.

2. Prorogation

Once summoned, a given Parliament is generally divided into several sessions, separated by a prorogation. A prorogation is again the prerogative of the governor general, acting on the advice of the prime minister. A prorogation (or, for that matter, a dissolution of Parliament, pending an election) may not endure indefinitely, however. Section 5 of the Charter provides that "[t]here shall be a sitting of Parliament and of each legislature at least once every twelve months." Put another way, Parliament cannot be entirely sidelined. Consider the implications of prorogation.

House of Commons, *Précis of Procedure*
(Ottawa: House of Commons, 2003)

Prorogation ends a session, but does not dissolve Parliament; the Speaker is still in office for all purposes during a period of prorogation. Similarly, the Prime Minister, Ministers and Parliamentary Secretaries remain in office and all Members of the House retain their full rights and privileges.

Prorogation, like dissolution, abolishes all pending legislation and quashes further committee activity. Thus, no committee can sit after a prorogation and any bill of a previous session, in order to be proceeded with, must, in principle, be introduced again as a new bill. However, Standing Order 86.1 makes special provision for reinstating Private Members' bills at the same stage they had reached at the end of a previous session. On occasion, with the agreement of the House, government bills have also been reinstated, by way of a motion, at the same stage they had reached in the previous session.

Committee work may also be revived either by motion in the House, or, if a study was undertaken under the authority of a committee's permanent mandate as established in the Standing Orders, by motion in committee.

While pending legislation is abolished by prorogation, any outstanding Orders or Addresses of the House for returns or papers are not; rather, they are brought down during the following session without renewal of the Order. The same is true, for example, for government responses to committee reports where requested, and for responses to petitions. These Orders are in force from one session to another, but are ended by dissolution.

Parliament can be prorogued through a speech by the Governor General in the Senate Chamber, although this is merely a convention and not required by any Standing Order or statute. ...

Parliament may also be prorogued by proclamation published in the *Canada Gazette*. In recent years, Parliament has been prorogued while the House is adjourned by this method, with the date of the new session being fixed in the proclamation. This date can be changed by means of a further proclamation. The House has also in the past adjourned for a period of time, reconvened, and Parliament has been prorogued shortly thereafter by proclamation with the new session opening soon afterward.

Between a prorogation and the next session of the same Parliament, the House is said to be "in recess," although the word is often loosely used to refer to a long adjournment. "Adjournment," however, is technically the termination by the House of its own sitting (by motion or pursuant to Standing or Special Orders) for any period of time within a session. Unlike dissolution and prorogation, adjournment does not quash all pending proceedings. At the next sitting, the House transacts the business previously appointed and all proceedings resume at the stage at which they were left before the adjournment.

———————————————

Whether a governor general has the power to refuse a prorogation requested by the prime minister was a matter of some importance in 2008, during what might be labelled the "prorogation crisis." In a nutshell, the opposition political parties were galvanized in late 2008 by (depending on who you believe) the Conservative government's apparent indifference to an emerging global economic crisis or its proposal to eliminate part of the political party subsidies (the most significant effect of which would have been felt by the relatively cash-poor opposition parties and not the Conservatives). The opposition parties proposed something of an ad hoc coalition and combined to table a motion of non-confidence in the government. As discussed below, if a non-confidence motion is carried in the Commons, the government falls. In the 40th minority Parliament, the opposition parties together controlled a majority of votes in the Commons and, voting in a block, they would have been sure to succeed in the non-confidence motion. Since Parliament had only recently reconvened after the fall 2008 election, they obviously anticipated that, should the government fall, the coalition would first be invited to form a new government before the governor general opted to dissolve Parliament and return to the polls.

To stave off a vote on the non-confidence motion, Prime Minister Harper postponed voting on the measure for a week and then subsequently asked the governor general to prorogue Parliament, a highly unorthodox request in such a young Parliament. Since the move was so clearly designed to prevent (or at least delay) a planned non-confidence vote, a difficult question arose as to whether a government could escape the judgment of Parliament by forcing its closure during the period of prorogation. The opposition parties urged that the governor general not grant the prorogation—and collectively signalled to the governor general that all three parties had lost confidence in the government and that the Liberals and NDP had agreed to form a new government, with the support of the Bloc Québécois, if the Conservatives fell. In the end, however, the governor general agreed to prorogue Parliament and, by the time Parliament returned nearly eight weeks later, the opposition coalition had collapsed, removing the immediate threat to the Conservative government.

These actions prompted a debate both in academia and more generally on whether the governor general had acted properly in granting the prorogation request, with some observers concluding that she had not, while others suggested that she had. See, for example, the collection of essays compiled in Peter H. Russell and Lorne Sossin, eds., *Parliamentary Democracy in Crisis* (Toronto: University of Toronto Press, 2009) and the discussion and works cited in Craig Forcese and Aaron Freeman, *The Laws of Government: The Legal Foundations of Canadian Democracy*, 2nd ed. (Toronto: Irwin Law, 2011), chapter 5.

3. Dissolution

Both the *Constitution Act, 1867* (s. 5) and the Charter (s. 4(1)) limit the duration of a Commons to five years (except in times of war or insurrection). These provisions mean that (without such a war or insurrection) Parliament must be dissolved and elections must happen at least every five years. Almost always, however, Parliaments do not last five years, and the governor general acts at a time of the prime minister's choosing in dissolving a Parliament. This dissolution prompts a new electoral cycle, governed by the *Canada Elections Act*. (In the federal Parliament, there are now fixed election dates every four years. However, as with the 2008 election, the governor general retains his or her constitutional power to dissolve Parliament before these fixed dates.)

There are, however, instances where a prime minister might be *forced* by constitutional convention to seek a dissolution from the governor general at a time not of his or her choosing. Constitutional convention requires a prime minister to resign his or her government *or* seek parliamentary dissolution after a "no confidence" vote by the House. Without a no confidence vote in the House, it seems unlikely that the governor general has the power to dissolve Parliament when opposed by the prime minister.

Nevertheless, it is not always clear where a vote in the House of Commons is one of no confidence. Consider the views of the 1985 "McGrath committee."

Special Committee on the Reform of the House of Commons, *Report*
(Ottawa: Canadian Government Publishing Centre,
Supply and Services Canada, June 1985)

The confidence of the House of Commons in the governing party lies at the heart of what we have come to know as responsible government. This form of government requires that the cabinet be responsible for its actions to an elected legislature. It implies necessarily that there be a policy-making body of ministers bound to provide unanimous advice to the Sovereign; that the public service be under the control of political leaders responsible to the legislature; and that both the executive and the legislature be responsible to the people.

Ministerial responsibility, along with the fusion of the executive and legislative branches, are distinguishing features of responsible government. The rules relating to these features are not set down in the Constitution. They are governed by convention, precedent and common sense. There is no single definition of ministerial responsibility; there are, in fact, three parts to the doctrine.

First there is the responsibility of a minister to the Queen or the Governor General; this is often overlooked, but it is basic to our constitutional order. Governments are not elected but appointed, and ministers serve not for a term, but until they die, resign or are dismissed.

Second, there is the individual responsibility of a minister to the House. This revolves around the questions of when a minister should offer his or her resignation and when should it be accepted or asked for. The answers seem to turn on the personal and political relationship between the minister and the prime minister. The principle is accepted, however, that where there is personal culpability on the part of a minister, in the form of private or public conduct regarded as unbecoming and unworthy of a minister of the Crown, the minister should resign.

The third responsibility is that of the ministry collectively to the House. If the confidence of the House is lost, it spells the end for the ministry unless the government is granted a dissolution and is sustained by the electorate.

Confidence from an Historical Perspective

The standing of a government in the House and the passage of its legislative program have come to be regarded as essential parts of responsible government. This was not always the case. In the nineteenth century political parties gained importance. This led to significant changes in the United Kingdom and in Canada as the parties, and particularly the leaders, appealed for votes in an enlarged and increasingly pluralistic electorate. The task of the House of Commons was reduced to voting on the legislation and estimates presented to it by the government.

The rarity of defeats of government measures in Great Britain (except in the minority situation in 1924) led rapidly to the development of a constitutional myth that every vote was a test of confidence. Any dissenting or cross-voting members on the government side were seen to be placing the government in jeopardy or risking dissolution of the House. In recent years, there has been more and more cross-party voting. In the seven-year period between April 1972 and April 1979, there were sixty-five defeats of government measures in the British House. This was not the end of responsible government. The government did not cease to govern. It was simply forced to modify or abandon some of its policies in deference to the House. Even with the large government majorities in recent years, there has not been a return to the inflexibility of the executive that marked earlier administrations. This kind of flexibility is not unlike what existed in early Canadian parliaments in the time of Sir John A. Macdonald when government measures were defeated a number of times without the government falling.

Recent British experience makes it clear that at present losing a vote, even on a financial measure, is not automatically a matter of non-confidence entailing either resignation of the government or a dissolution of the Commons. The government can decide how it will treat its loss. Whatever a government may say or imply in order to intimidate its own parliamentary supporters, a lost vote in itself does not involve resignation or dissolution.

The same phenomenon of lost votes that took place in Great Britain in the 1970s was also evident in Canada during that same period and, to a lesser extent, even earlier. At the start of the first session of the twenty-ninth parliament Prime Minister Trudeau said, "Some things for us will be questions of confidence. Some things would mean the demise of the government. … But I hasten to add that other questions, if they go against us, will not be interpreted by the government as a defeat of the government. We shall accept amendments."

The minority government of Pierre Trudeau lost eight of eighty-one recorded votes between 1972 and 1974. Setting aside the vote of May 8, 1974, which brought down the government, four of the lost votes were on government bills, two were on motions pertaining to parliamentary committees, and one was on a supply item, specifically on a supplementary estimate of $19,000 for Information Canada.

The minority governments of Lester Pearson lost three votes. Two were on appeals of a ruling made by the Speaker. The third came February 19, 1968. A vote ended with the defeat on third reading of Bill C-193 respecting income tax. This vote was regarded as sufficiently serious to require the government to introduce a motion to the effect that the House did not consider its vote of February 19 as a vote of non-confidence in the government. The motion was passed, after debate, on February 28.

It is clear from both British and Canadian experience that a government that has lost a vote in the House on a matter of confidence faces the choice of resigning or asking for dissolution. A government that has lost a vote on some other matter may remain in office and may choose to ask for a vote of confidence.

Since every vote in the House is not a matter of confidence, it is not true that a government that loses a vote in the House can simply have the House dissolved. As a rule, the Governor General accepts the advice of the prime minister. In certain cases, however, the Governor General is justified in refusing an immediate request for dissolution. ...

Precedent shows that responsible government does not break down and government does not become unworkable when the executive bows to the wishes of the House on a wide variety of matters in a wide variety of circumstances. It is useful by way of summary to place government defeats into three categories, noting that each one invites a different response from the government.

A government defeated on a vote of confidence is expected to resign or seek a dissolution. Three types of votes can be termed confidence votes. First, there are explicitly worded votes of confidence. These state expressly that the House has or has not confidence in the government. Next are motions made votes of confidence by a declaration of the government. The government may declare that if defeated on a particular motion before the House, even one that is not an explicitly worded vote of confidence, it will resign or seek a dissolution. Then there are implicit votes of confidence. Traditionally, certain matters have been deemed to involve confidence, even though not declared to be so by the prior statement of the government. Falling within this category is the granting of supply. Failure to grant supply is regarded as the established means by which the House can demonstrate its lack of confidence in the ministry. However, it should be noted that a single defeat on a specific estimate would not in itself constitute a vote of non-confidence. In fact, because of the multiplicity of votes on all the aspects of supply, this is largely a category that has fallen into disuse. One could argue that this type of defeat actually belongs in the category of defeats that are not votes of confidence.

The second category is lost votes on items central to government policy but not made matters of confidence prior to the vote. The government in this case can either seek an explicit vote of confidence from the House or resign or request a dissolution. If the government opted for resignation or asked for dissolution, this would make the lost vote one of confidence retrospectively. There should normally be few votes that fall into this category.

The last group is votes on items not at the heart of government policy; these are obviously the most numerous during any parliament. Although a lost vote on second reading of a major bill might fall within the second category mentioned above, a loss on one or more of the many divisions during the committee and report stages would usually fall within this third classification. …

In conclusion, we offer several observations. Although they can have no legal effect in our system of government, they should serve as an indication of the direction in which this committee believes the House of Commons should develop.

- A government should be careful before it declares or designates a vote as one of confidence. It should confine such declarations to measures central to its administration.
- While a defeat on supply is a serious matter, elimination or reduction of an estimate can be accepted. If a government wishes, it can designate a succeeding vote as a test of confidence or move a direct vote of confidence.
- Defeats on matters not essential to the government's program do not require it to arrange a vote of confidence, whether directly or on some procedural or collateral motion.
- Temporary loss of control of the business of the House does not call for any response from the government whether by resignation or by asking for a vote of confidence.

Note one of the McGrath committee observations: "As a rule, the Governor General accepts the advice of the prime minister. In certain cases, however, the Governor General is justified in refusing an immediate request for dissolution." In 1926, Governor General Byng called upon Conservative leader Arthur Meighen to form a government when Prime Minister Mackenzie King resigned after being refused dissolution. King had sought this dissolution to pre-empt a lost confidence vote for his minority Liberal government, held together in a precarious coalition with the Progressives in a Parliament produced via an election held only eight months before (and in session for an even briefer period of six months). When Meighen's government quickly collapsed and Parliament was dissolved, King campaigned on Lord Byng's failure to respond to his original dissolution request, soundly defeating the Conservatives.

It seems almost certain, however, that Byng acted in keeping with constitutional convention: a governor general may refuse a dissolution in the wake of the resignation of (at least a minority) government, where another prime-minister-apparent is able to command the confidence of the Commons, whether this person comes from the opposition or from within the governing party. Indeed, the governor general may have a constitutional duty to exercise this power of refusal.

The exercise of this "reserve" power is likely most legitimate where a government seeks a dissolution soon after an election. In comparison, use of the reserve power to refuse dissolution is less appropriate if exercised several years into a Parliament, at a time near its natural expiry. In those circumstances, it is better for the question of government leadership to be decided by the people in an election. For a discussion of reserve powers, see Andrew Heard, *Canadian Constitutional Conventions* (Toronto: Oxford University Press, 1991), at 23-24; Eugene A. Forsey and G.C. Eglington, *The Question of Confidence in Responsible Government* (Ottawa: Special Committee on the Reform of the House of Commons, 1985), at 152 et seq.

II. KEY ACTORS IN PARLIAMENT

While in session, parliamentary procedures implicate several key actors, including political parties, the Speaker, and parliamentary committees. We discuss each of these players in turn.

A. Political Parties

As noted above, political parties are a recognized entity in Canadian election law. Politically, parties act to marshal collective resources in the hope of achieving electoral success. Parties are also, however, the partial product of two *legal* aspects of parliamentary democracy.

First, decision making in Parliament depends on swaying a majority of votes in each chamber. For instance, the Commons makes decisions through the device of motions, basically a question put to the House by the Speaker in response to a proposition made by a member. There are several different species of motion, each governed by its own procedural niceties. Eventually, however, all motions are debated, amended, superseded, adopted, negatived, or withdrawn. (A "superseded" motion is one replaced by another motion.) The success of a motion is determined by whether it attracts a majority of votes.

There is a constitutional reason for this. Consider s. 49 of the *Constitution Act, 1867*: "Questions arising in the House of Commons shall be decided by a *Majority* of Voices other than that of the Speaker, and when the Voices are equal, but not otherwise, the Speaker shall have a Vote" (emphasis added). Note also s. 36: "Questions arising in the Senate shall be decided by a *Majority* of Voices, and the Speaker shall in all Cases have a Vote, and when the Voices are equal the Decision shall be deemed to be in the Negative" (emphasis added). These rules encourage parliamentarians to organize as political parties: entities that command the loyalty of their members and, if those members are elected in sufficient numbers, allow control of a majority of the Commons.

A second constitutional motivation for parties stems from the confidence convention: by constitutional convention, the individual commanding the confidence of the Commons (that is, its majority) is appointed prime minister. Thus, party control of a majority of the House brings with it executive power.

Both of these legal considerations ensure that Westminster parliamentary systems are preoccupied (and sometimes obsessed) with maintaining "party discipline"—the *en bloc* votes of party members (or at least a coalition of different party members) sufficient to constitute a majority. In this environment, individual members of Parliament are not always (or, in some Parliaments, even usually) able to vote their conscience. Instead, they may be obliged to toe the party line. Indeed, party backbench members of Parliament are sometimes described derisively as little more than voting machines. Prime Minister Trudeau famously observed that members of Parliament were "nobodies" 50 yards from the Commons. Other commentators have referred to backbenchers in the governing party as "trained seals." See, for instance, editorial, "MPs No Longer Trained Seals," *Halifax Daily News*, October 14, 2002, at 11; Charles Gordon, "At Last, Backbench Liberals Who Don't Want To Be Trained Seals," *Ottawa Citizen*, March 1, 2003, at B6.

In the result, there has been substantial discussion of a so-called democratic deficit in federal politics—that Parliaments (or at least Parliaments in which a single party controls a majority of seats in the House of Commons) play a paltry, secondary role in Canadian governance because of party discipline. Assembled in 2003, parliamentarians reviewing the question of parliamentary reform complained that

> the House of Commons and the Senate are no longer places in which meaningful debate occurs. The impetus to get the government's business through and the strongly enforced party discipline have combined to limit the number of voices heard in Parliament. In most matters of public debate, Canadians have many different points of view, while only a limited number of views are expressed within the walls of Parliament—largely as a result of party discipline. Parliament must put the richness of opinion that exists in the Canadian public to the service of the Canadian public by allowing for those multiple voices to be heard in Parliament.

(Ottawa: Library of Parliament, *The Parliament We Want: Parliamentarians' Views on Parliamentary Reform*, 2003; http://www.parl.gc.ca/Content/LOP/ResearchPublications/cp5-e.htm.)

Put another way, Parliament has become a place for ramming through government policy, not querying its merits. In the middle part of the last decade, there seemed to be some support for the idea of more "free votes" in Parliament—circumstances in which MPs voted their conscience, not just as the party leader dictated. However, by the time of this writing, the free vote reforms seem to have evaporated. In the words of a 2007 report of the Library of Parliament, "the cycle of procedural reform that began in 2004 appears to have stalled, at least while current minority government conditions persist" (Ottawa: Library of Parliament, *Parliamentary Reform and the House of Commons*, PRB 07-43E (Oct. 5, 2007), at 4).

The political affiliation of a given parliamentarian is a matter of politics, not law. There is no requirement that a parliamentarian be a member of a party, or that a party have a certain number of members. However, so-called official party status is reserved for parties possessing a minimum number of members in the Commons. Thus, once a party claims the allegiance of at least 12 members, certain benefits flow to it. Within the chamber of the Commons, these include membership on the Commons Board of Internal Economy and additional allowances for the party leader, whip, and house leader sitting in the Commons. Furthermore, recognized parties are able to tap into caucus research funds authorized by that Commons Board.

In Commons proceedings themselves, once the 12-MP threshold is reached, party members are then entitled to sit together, have their party affiliation noted with their name in the official records and on television broadcasts of proceedings, and are allowed a larger number of questions during Question Period.

B. The Speaker

Further key players in Parliament are the Speakers of the two houses of Parliament. In the Commons, the Speaker is a member of Parliament elected to the Speaker's position by other MPs. The manner of his or her selection, and many of his or her powers, are set out in the "standing orders" of the House of Commons. These standing orders are internal procedural rules established by the Commons pursuant to its parliamentary "privileges" and discussed further below. Consider the following discussion of the Speaker's selection and function.

House of Commons, *Précis of Procedure*
(Ottawa: House of Commons, 2003)

1(a) The Speaker

The Member elected by other Members to be Speaker assumes the position of highest authority in the House, and represents the Commons in all its powers, proceedings and dignity. The duties of the office fall into three categories. First, the Speaker acts as the spokesperson of the House in its relations with the Crown, the Senate and authorities outside Parliament. Second, the Speaker presides over the sittings of the House and enforces the observance of all rules for the preservation of order and the conduct of business. Third, the Speaker has extensive responsibilities relating to the administration of the House of Commons. ...

The Speaker as Spokesperson

For centuries in Britain, the Speaker's primary duty was to represent the House and to protect its interests with the Crown. While the position has evolved so that presiding over debate is now considered the primary role, certain activities continue to reflect the earlier function as petitioner for and guardian of the privileges of Members. This aspect of the Speaker's role is best exemplified when, shortly after being elected, the Speaker leads the House to the Senate to inform the Governor General that the Commons has elected a Speaker according to law, to claim the privileges on behalf of the House and to receive the Speech from the Throne. During a parliamentary session, the Speaker may from time to time lead the House to the Senate whenever the traditional ceremony for Royal Assent to legislation passed by the House and Senate is to be used. It is also the Speaker who orally transmits to Members messages received from the Sovereign, the Governor General or the Senate when required. Similarly, the Speaker communicates resolutions of thanks, sympathy, censure or reprimand in the name of the House to any outside body or agent. Whenever a vacancy occurs in the membership of the House, it is the Speaker's responsibility to issue a warrant to the Chief Electoral Officer for a writ of election.

The Speaker as Presiding Officer

The Speaker's principal duty as presiding officer is to maintain order in debate and to apply and interpret the practices and traditions of the House. To do this, the Speaker must rely on the Standing Orders—the written rules of the House—precedents and various procedural authorities. The Speaker's actions must always be and appear to be impartial; for this reason, the Speaker never participates in debate. In overseeing the conduct of the House, the Speaker seeks to maintain the balance between two fundamental operating principles of Parliament: to allow the majority to secure the transaction of business in an orderly manner and to protect the right of the minority to be heard.

Maintaining Order

The Standing Orders [of the House of Commons] set down only in general terms the authority of the Speaker to maintain order and decorum in the House. One rule states simply that "the Speaker shall preserve order and decorum, and shall decide questions of order." In practice, the authority of the Speaker is wide-ranging, affecting such matters as Members' dress, disturbances on the floor or in the Galleries as well as the conduct of proceedings and the rules of debate. Since debate is the means by which most motions are considered, the practices here are, in fact, quite specific. For example, all debate is addressed to the Speaker, not to other Members; even during Question Period, questions are addressed through the Chair. It is the Speaker who possesses the authority to recognize participants in the debate, and who can call to order any Member who indulges in repetition or irrelevant arguments.

The strongest penalty the Speaker can use against a Member is to "name" the Member, and the threat of naming is usually enough to ensure respect for the Speaker's authority. A Member is named for disregarding the authority of the Speaker when, for example, the Member has refused a request to withdraw unparliamentary language, to desist in irrelevant or repetitious debate, or to stop interrupting a Member who is addressing the House. Persisting in any other disorderly conduct when warned by the Speaker to desist is also a defiance of the authority of the Chair which can lead to naming.

Before naming a Member, the Speaker usually warns him or her several times that in not obeying the Chair, he or she risks being named. If the Member apologizes to the general satisfaction of the Speaker, the incident is usually considered closed and no other measure is taken. If the Member is named, however, the Speaker has two options: he or she may immediately order the offending Member to withdraw from the Chamber for the balance of the day's sitting; alternatively, the Speaker may simply wait for the House to take whatever disciplinary action it deems appropriate. The first is an option introduced in February 1986, and since its adoption, has been used exclusively as a disciplinary measure consequent upon naming. However, should the Speaker choose the second alternative, another Member—usually the Government House Leader—will immediately propose a motion to suspend the offending Member. Such a motion is neither debatable nor amendable. Once the motion for suspension has been proposed, the Speaker will put the question. If the motion carries, the Member must withdraw from the Chamber and is also prevented from sitting in Committees of the Whole and in legislative, standing or special committees for the duration of the suspension.

Legal Status of the Speaker

Provision for the Speakership in Canada is assured not only by tradition and convention, but also by the Constitution. Section 44 of the *Constitution Act, 1867* stipulates that the House of Commons once assembled after a general election "shall proceed with all practicable speed to elect one of its Members to be Speaker." Section 46 states that the Speaker shall preside over all meetings of the House. Sections 45 and 47 treat the matter of vacancy or prolonged absence of the Speaker, and section 49 sanctions the casting vote of the Chair in cases where there is a tie vote among Members on a question before the House.

The *Parliament of Canada Act* specifies the administrative duties of the Speaker and the Deputy Speaker. Other statutes refer to the Speaker with regard to such things as the receiving and tabling of reports and returns and the Speaker's role in House resolutions.

Election of the Speaker

At the beginning of a Parliament when the House first assembles, Members are summoned to the Senate by the Deputy of the Governor General, through a message delivered to the House by the Usher of the Black Rod. Preceded by the Clerk of the House, the Members go to the Upper Chamber where they are informed that "the Deputy … does not see fit to declare the causes of his [or her] summoning the present Parliament of Canada until the Speaker of the House of Commons shall have been chosen according to Law … ."

On June 27, 1985, the House adopted changes to the Standing Orders, providing for the election of the Speaker by secret ballot. The election process is the first order of business at the opening of the first session of a Parliament, or in the event of the resignation of the incumbent Speaker, or a vacancy in the office for any other reason.

The election of the Speaker at the opening of a Parliament is presided over by the Member who has the longest period of unbroken service and who is not a member of the Cabinet, nor holds any office within the House. In the case of a resignation, the incumbent Speaker presides over the proceedings to choose his or her successor. Before proceeding with the election of a Speaker, the Member presiding invites candidates for the office of the Speaker to address the House for not more than five minutes.

The names of all eligible Members of Parliament, who have not indicated that they do not wish to be considered for the position, appear on the list of candidates. Party leaders and Cabinet Ministers are prohibited from posing their candidacy for the speakership. In voting for the Speaker, Members write the name of their choice on the ballot. Voting continues until one Member receives a majority of the votes cast. After each ballot, the name(s) of the Member(s) who received the least number of votes and the names of all Members who received 5% or less of the total number of votes cast are dropped from the list of candidates.

C. Parliamentary Committees

Parliamentary committees are subsets of Parliament tasked with much of the detailed work in Parliament. Consider the following description of committee functions and membership.

House of Commons, *Précis of Procedure*
(Ottawa: House of Commons, 2003)

14. Committees

The House of Commons delegates most of the detailed study of proposed legislation and the scrutiny of government policy and programs to its committees. In delegating these responsibilities, the House of Commons establishes specific terms of reference for their work through Standing Orders or, from time to time, by Special Orders of the House.

14(a) Types of Committees

There are various types of committees.

Committees of the Whole (House)—As the name suggests, such committees are composed of the entire membership of the House of Commons. They are established by the Standing Orders and examine appropriation bills, or, from time to time, the House may refer other bills to Committee of the Whole to expedite their passage. ...

Standing committees—These are committees appointed for the life of a Parliament to deal with subjects of continuing concern to the House. There are currently 18 standing committees as established by the Standing Orders. ... For the most part, they parallel the government departments whose policy development, program administration and budgetary estimates they examine. Occasionally, the House may decide to send special inquiries to standing committees.

Legislative committees—Legislative Committees are created on an *ad hoc* basis to examine bills in detail, and may report only the bill, with or without amendments, to the House. In recent times however, most bills have been sent to standing committees for examination.

Special committees—Sometimes referred to as "task forces," special committees are appointed on an *ad hoc* basis by the House to study specific matters. Each special committee is established by a motion specifying its purpose and powers.

Joint committees—These committees are composed of members of both the House of Commons and the Senate. They may be appointed under the Standing Orders of each House (Standing Joint) or they may be created by special resolutions of the two Houses (Special Joint).

Subcommittees—Standing committees are free to delegate some part of their mandate or a particular task to a smaller group. They do this by creating subcommittees. They may delegate their responsibilities to subcommittees created with the exception of the power to report directly to the House. Special committees may be given the power to create subcommittees if the House so decides, but legislative committees may only create a subcommittee on their agenda, commonly called a steering committee.

14(b) Powers of Committees

Committees are given different kinds of powers by the House of Commons in relation to their specific tasks.

Standing Committees

The powers of a standing committee are set out in the Standing Orders as follows:

- to examine matters referred to it by the House;
- to report to the House from time to time;
- to send for persons, papers and records;
- to sit while the House is sitting or stands adjourned;
- to sit jointly with other standing committees;
- to print necessary papers and evidence; and
- to delegate to a subcommittee any of its powers except the power to report to the House.

Standing committees are also empowered by the Standing Orders to study and report on all matters relating to the mandate, management and operation of government departments assigned to them; to review all Order in Council appointments referred to them; and to examine all permanently referred reports. ...

Legislative Committees

The powers of a legislative committee are set out in Standing Orders 113(5) and 120 as follows:

- to examine and inquire into the bill referred to it by the House;
- to report the bill with or without amendments;

and except when the House otherwise orders:

- to send for persons whom the committee deems to be competent to appear as witnesses on technical matters;
- to send for papers and records;
- to sit when the House is sitting or stands adjourned;
- to print necessary papers and evidence; and
- to retain the services of expert and technical staff.

As discussed earlier, a legislative committee is only permitted to establish a subcommittee on agenda and procedure, to which it may delegate only the power to schedule meetings, to call for government officials and technical witnesses and to send for papers and records, subject to the approval of the main committee. As legislative committees have a very specific mandate, that is the consideration of a bill, they do not require subcommittees for other than planning purposes.

Special Committees

The powers of a special committee are those set out in its Order of Reference and do not include those listed in the Standing Orders unless specified in the Order of Reference. Like standing committees, special committees may also request additional powers by means of a report to the House if they have the permission to report from "time to time."

General

All committees are empowered to retain the services of such expert, professional, technical or clerical staff as may be necessary. Additional powers, such as the power to travel, may also be granted by means of an Order of Reference from the House.

As this extract suggests, committees are potentially quite powerful actors, and indeed where witnesses before them are uncooperative, may draw upon Parliament's contempt powers. The latter are part of Parliament's parliamentary privilege, a concept described below. As described by Joseph Maingot, this means that "[a]ny act or omission that obstructs or impedes either House of Parliament in the performance of its functions, or that obstructs or impedes any Member or officer of such House in the discharge of his duty, or that has a tendency, directly or indirectly, to produce such results may be treated as contempt even though there is no precedent of the offence." (Joseph P. Maingot, *Parliamentary Privilege in Canada*, 2nd ed. (Montreal: McGill-Queen's University Press, 1997), at 193.)

In April 2008, the House of Commons agreed to a motion holding a then-RCMP deputy commissioner "in contempt of Parliament for providing false and misleading testimony to the House of Commons Standing Committee on Public Accounts on February 21, 2007; and that the House of Commons take no further action as this finding of contempt is, in and of itself, a very serious sanction" (House of Commons, *Journals*, No. 76, 39th Parl., 2d sess. (April 10, 2008)). The move followed a Commons public account committee probe into the mismanagement of the RCMP's pension and insurance plans, and criticism by that committee of the officer's apparently contradictory (and, in the eyes of parliamentarians, "misleading" or perhaps "untruthful") evidence on the issue (House of Commons Standing Committee on Public Accounts, Third Report, 39th Parl., 1st sess. (February 2008), at 10). The event had significant implications for the officer's reputation. She retired from the RCMP only months later ("RCMP Officer Retires After Contempt Citation" *Globe and Mail* (November 8, 2008), at A13).

The contempt citation ultimately issued by the Commons was controversial, with critics raising serious concerns about the level of due process accorded by parliamentarians to the RCMP officer. (See, for example, Kathryn May, "Mountie Found in Contempt" *Gazette* [Montreal] (April 11, 2008), at A10; Kathryn May, "Parliamentary Privilege Used as a 'Sword' Against Citizens, Political Experts Warn" *Ottawa Citizen* (April 24, 2008), at A1.) The lawyer for the officer asserted that "[t]his process is fundamentally flawed. … There's no due process in it. We have what are, in effect, amateur fact-finders operating in an environment where there is no due process for the witness" (Steve Rennie, "Find Mountie in Contempt, Panel Advises" *Winnipeg Free Press* (February 13, 2008), at A7). The parliamentary law counsel contested this view, arguing that "the process was fair, even when measured by legal standards that don't apply, and as fair as it ought to have been in view of the nature of the proceedings" (Rob Walsh, "Fairness in Committees" (Summer 2008) *Canadian Parliamentary Review* 23, at 26).

III. PARLIAMENTARY PROCEDURE

How does Parliament perform its law-making functions? In this section we begin by examining the sources of law governing the parliamentary law-making function, before reviewing the actual procedure followed in converting a bill (a law project) into a statute (a binding piece of legislation).

A. Sources of Parliamentary Law

"Parliamentary law"—the rules determining parliamentary procedure—flows from an array of sources: the Constitution; assorted statutes such as the *Parliament of Canada Act*, RSC 1985, c. P-1; the standing orders; and assorted usages, customs, and precedents, as assessed by the Speaker. In the sections that follow, we highlight some of this parliamentary law.

1. Constitutional and Legislative Basis: Parliamentary Privilege

The starting point for understanding "parliamentary law" is the Constitution. The Canadian Constitution incorporates British parliamentary traditions via the preamble to the *Constitution Act, 1867*. This Act endows Canada with "a Constitution similar in Principle to that of the United Kingdom." The 1867 Act also speaks of Parliament possessing parliamentary "privileges," as does the *Parliament of Canada Act*.

"Parliamentary privileges" are those rights "necessary to ensure that legislatures can perform their functions, free from interference by the Crown and the courts": *Provincial Judges Reference*, [1997] 3 SCR 3, at para. 10. "Privilege," in this context, often means "the legal exemption from some duty, burden, attendance or liability to which others are subject": see *New Brunswick Broadcasting Co. v. Nova Scotia*, [1993] 1 SCR 319, at para. 117, per McLachlin J. Consider the Supreme Court of Canada's most recent analysis of "parliamentary privilege," its scope, and the role of the courts in deciding its existence.

Canada (House of Commons) v. Vaid
[2005] 1 SCR 667, 2005 SCC 30

BINNIE J: [1] The former Speaker of the House of Commons, the Honourable Gilbert Parent, is accused of constructively dismissing his chauffeur, Mr. Satnam Vaid, for reasons that amount to workplace discrimination and harassment under the *Canadian Human Rights Act*. ... The issue on this appeal is whether it is open to the Canadian Human Rights Tribunal to investigate Mr. Vaid's complaint.

[2] The former Speaker denies any impropriety, but he joins the House of Commons in a preliminary objection that the hiring and firing of House employees are "internal affairs" which may not be questioned or reviewed by any tribunal or court outside the House itself. This immunity, the appellants say, emerged from the struggle for independence by the House of Commons from the prerogatives of the King, the authority of the Royal courts of law, and the special rights of the House of Lords reaching back in part to the time of the Tudor Kings and Queens in the 16th century. The appellants contend that these hard-won powers and immunities, collectively referred to as the privileges of Parliament, permit the Senate and the House to conduct their employee relations free from interference from the Canadian Human Rights Commission or any other body outside Parliament itself.

[3] The respondent Canadian Human Rights Commission, which seeks to investigate Mr. Vaid's allegations, says it is unthinkable that Parliament would seek to deny its employees the benefit of labour and human rights protections which Parliament itself has imposed on every other federal employer.

[4] There are few issues as important to our constitutional equilibrium as the relationship between the legislature and the other branches of the State on which the Constitution has conferred powers, namely the executive and the courts. The resolution of this issue is especially important when the action of the Speaker sought to be immunized from outside scrutiny is directed against a stranger to the House (i.e., not a Member or official) who is remote from the legislative functions that parliamentary privilege was originally designed to protect. ... The purpose of privilege is to recognize Parliament's *exclusive* jurisdiction to

deal with complaints within its privileged sphere of activity. The proper focus, in my view, is not the grounds on which a particular privilege is exercised, but the prior question of the existence and scope of the privilege asserted by Parliament in the first place.

[5] Focussing, then, on the scope of the claimed privilege, the respondents argue that the duties of the Speaker's chauffeur appear too remote from the legislative function of the House and that the respondent Vaid's dismissal is not immunized from external review by virtue of parliamentary privilege. …

. . .

[20] It is a wise principle that the courts and Parliament strive to respect each other's role in the conduct of public affairs. Parliament, for its part, refrains from commenting on matters before the courts under the *sub judice* rule. The courts, for their part, are careful not to interfere with the workings of Parliament. None of the parties to this proceeding questions the pre-eminent importance of the House of Commons as "the grand inquest of the nation." Nor is doubt thrown by any party on the need for its legislative activities to proceed unimpeded by any external body or institution, including the courts. It would be intolerable, for example, if a member of the House of Commons who was overlooked by the Speaker at question period could invoke the investigatory powers of the Canadian Human Rights Commission with a complaint that the Speaker's choice of another member of the House discriminated on some ground prohibited by the *Canadian Human Rights Act*, or to seek a ruling from the ordinary courts that the Speaker's choice violated the member's guarantee of free speech under the Charter. These are truly matters "internal to the House" to be resolved by its own procedures. Quite apart from the potential interference by outsiders in the direction of the House, such external intervention would inevitably create delays, disruption, uncertainties and costs which would hold up the nation's business and on that account would be unacceptable even if, in the end, the Speaker's rulings were vindicated as entirely proper.

[21] Parliamentary privilege, therefore, is one of the ways in which the fundamental constitutional separation of powers is respected. In Canada, the principle has its roots in the preamble to our *Constitution Act, 1867* which calls for "a Constitution similar in Principle to that of the United Kingdom." Each of the branches of the State is vouchsafed a measure of autonomy from the others. Parliamentary privilege was partially codified in art. 9 of the UK *Bill of Rights* of 1689. … Parliamentary privilege is a principle common to all countries based on the Westminster system, and has a loose counterpart in the Speech or Debate Clause of the United States Constitution, art. 1, §6, cl. 1.

[22] The respondent Vaid does not quarrel either with the existence or the importance of parliamentary privilege. His argument is that the Speaker's attempt to treat his dismissal from his job as chauffeur as an expression of such lofty doctrine is to overreach, if not trivialize, its true role and function. Even if the employment arrangements of some employees closely connected to the legislative process are covered by privilege, the respondents argue that the Speaker goes too far in attempting to throw the mantle of this ancient doctrine over the dealings of the House with such support staff as chauffeurs, picture framers, locksmiths, car park administrators, catering staff and others who play comparable supporting roles on Parliament Hill.

[23] Over the years, the assertion of parliamentary privilege has varied in its scope and extent. …

[24] It is evident that there have been variations in the extent of privilege asserted by Parliament over the years, as well as a difference on occasion between the scope of a privilege asserted by Parliamentarians and the scope of a privilege the courts have recognized as justified. … In resolving such conflicts it is important that both Parliament and the courts respect "the legitimate sphere of activity of the other":

> Our democratic government consists of several branches: the Crown, as represented by the Governor General and the provincial counterparts of that office; the legislative body; the executive; and the courts. It is fundamental to the working of government as a whole that all these parts play their proper role. It is equally fundamental that no one of them overstep its bounds, that each show proper deference for the legitimate sphere of activity of the other. (*New Brunswick Broadcasting Co. v. Nova Scotia (Speaker of the House of Assembly)*, [1993] 1 SCR 319, *per* McLachlin J, at p. 389)

• • •

[29] While there are some significant differences between privilege at the federal level, for which specific provision is made in s. 18 of the *Constitution Act, 1867*, and privilege at the provincial level, which has a different constitutional underpinning, many of the relevant issues concerning privilege were resolved in *New Brunswick Broadcasting* and earlier cases, and there is no need to repeat the analysis here. For present purposes, it is sufficient to state a number of propositions that are now accepted both by the courts and by the parliamentary experts.

1. Legislative bodies created by the *Constitution Act, 1867* do not constitute enclaves shielded from the ordinary law of the land. "The tradition of curial deference does not extend to everything a legislative assembly might do, but is firmly attached to certain specific activities of legislative assemblies, i.e., the so-called privileges of such bodies." … Privilege "does not embrace and protect activities of *individuals*, whether members or non-members, simply because they take place within the precincts of Parliament." …

2. Parliamentary privilege in the Canadian context is the sum of the privileges, immunities and powers enjoyed by the Senate, the House of Commons and provincial legislative assemblies, and by each member individually, without which they could not discharge their functions. …

3. Parliamentary privilege does not create a gap in the general public law of Canada but is an important part of it, inherited from the Parliament at Westminster by virtue of the preamble to the *Constitution Act, 1867* and in the case of the Canadian Parliament, through s. 18 of the same Act. …

4. Parliamentary privilege includes "the *necessary immunity* that the law provides for Members of Parliament, and for Members of the legislatures of each of the ten provinces … *in order for these legislators to do their legislative work*." … The idea of necessity is thus linked to the autonomy required by legislative assemblies and their members to do their job.

5. The historical foundation of every privilege of Parliament is necessity. If a sphere of the legislative body's activity could be left to be dealt with under the ordinary law of the land without interfering with the assembly's ability to fulfill its constitutional

functions, then immunity would be unnecessary and the claimed privilege would not exist. …

6. When the existence of a category (or sphere of activity) for which inherent privilege is claimed (at least at the provincial level) is put in issue, the court must not only look at the historical roots of the claim but also to determine whether the category of inherent privilege *continues* to be necessary to the functioning of the legislative body today. Parliamentary history, while highly relevant, is not conclusive. …

7. "Necessity" in this context is to be read broadly. The time-honoured test, derived from the law and custom of Parliament at Westminster, is what "the dignity and efficiency of the House" require: "If a matter falls within this necessary sphere of matters without which the *dignity and efficiency of the House* cannot be upheld, courts will not inquire into questions concerning such privilege. All such questions will instead fall to the exclusive jurisdiction of the legislative body." …

8. Proof of necessity may rest in part in "shewing that it has been long exercised and acquiesced in" (*Stockdale v. Hansard*, at p. 1189). The party who seeks to rely on the immunity provided by parliamentary privilege has the onus of establishing its existence. …

9. Proof of necessity is required only to establish the existence and scope of a *category* of privilege. Once the category (or sphere of activity) is established, it is for Parliament, not the courts, to determine whether in a particular case the *exercise* of the privilege is necessary or appropriate. In other words, within categories of privilege, Parliament is the judge of the occasion and manner of its exercise and such exercise is not reviewable by the courts: "Each specific instance of *the exercise* of a privilege need not be shown to be necessary." …

10. "Categories" include freedom of speech … ; control by the Houses of Parliament over "debates or proceedings in Parliament" (as guaranteed by the *Bill of Rights* of 1689) including day-to-day procedure in the House … ; the power to exclude strangers from proceedings … ; disciplinary authority over members … ; and non-members who interfere with the discharge of parliamentary duties … , including immunity of members from subpoenas during a parliamentary session. … Such general categories have historically been considered to be justified by the exigencies of parliamentary work.

11. The role of the courts is to ensure that a claim of privilege does not immunize from the ordinary law the consequences of conduct by Parliament or its officers and employees that exceeds the necessary scope of the category of privilege. …

12. Courts are apt to look more closely at cases in which claims to privilege have an impact on persons outside the legislative assembly than at those which involve matters entirely internal to the legislature. …

· · ·

[41] Parliamentary privilege is *defined* by the degree of autonomy necessary to perform Parliament's constitutional function. …

· · ·

[43] While much latitude is left to each House of Parliament, such a purposive approach to the definition of privilege implies important limits. There is general recognition, for

example, that privilege attaches to "proceedings in Parliament." Nevertheless, … not "*every-thing that is said or done within the Chamber during the transaction of business forms part of proceedings in Parliament.* Particular words or acts may be entirely unrelated to any business which is in course of transaction, or is in a more general sense before the House as having been ordered to come before it in due course." … "Particular words or acts may be entirely unrelated to any business being transacted or ordered to come before the House in due course."

· · ·

[45] Parliament's sovereignty when engaged in the performance of its legislative duties is undoubted … .

[46] All of these sources point in the direction of a similar conclusion. In order to sustain a claim of parliamentary privilege, the assembly or member seeking its immunity must show that the sphere of activity for which privilege is claimed is so closely and directly connected with the fulfillment by the assembly or its members of their functions as a legislative and deliberative body, including the assembly's work in holding the government to account, that outside interference would undermine the level of autonomy required to enable the assembly and its members to do their work with dignity and efficiency.

· · ·

[52] I therefore turn to the appellants' contention that "the power of the Speaker of the House of Commons to hire, manage and dismiss House employees is among the constitutionally entrenched parliamentary privileges over which the House has exclusive jurisdiction. This exclusive jurisdiction extends to the investigation and adjudication of workplace discrimination claims" … .

· · ·

[70] [Having also reviewed Canadian authority and found it silent on the issue,] I conclude that British authority does not establish that the House of Commons at Westminster is immunized by privilege in the conduct of *all* labour relations with *all* employees irrespective of whether those categories of employees have any connection (or nexus) with its legislative or deliberative functions, or its role in holding the government accountable.

· · ·

[72] [Turning to the "necessity test,"] [t]he employment roster of the House of Commons in 2005 is very different from that of 1867. In the early period, the House of Commons had only 66 permanent staff and 67 sessional employees. At present, according to the Human Resources Section of the House of Commons, there are 2377 employees. These include many departments and services unknown in 1867. The Library of Parliament alone employs 298 people, more than twice the total number of House employees in 1867. The Information Services for the House now has 573 employees. Not all of these greatly expanded services relate directly to the House's function as a legislative and deliberative body. Parliamentary Precinct Services employs over 800 staff including a locksmith, an interior designer, various curators, five carpenters, a massage therapist, two picture framers, a chief of parking operations and two traffic constables. Parliamentary Corporate Services includes several kitchen chefs, lesser cooks and helpers, three dishwashers/potwashers and other catering support staff. There is no doubt that the House of Commons regards *all* of its employees as helpful but the question is whether that definition of the scope of the privilege it asserts is too broad. Is the management of *all* employees … "so closely and directly con-

nected with proceedings in Parliament that intervention by the courts would be inconsistent with Parliament's sovereignty as a legislative and deliberative assembly"? … In other words, can it be said that immunity from outside scrutiny in the management of *all* service employees is such that without it … the House and its members "could not discharge their functions"? …

* * *

[75] I have no doubt that privilege attaches to the House's relations with *some* of its employees, but the appellants have insisted on the broadest possible coverage without leading any evidence to justify such a sweeping immunity, or a lesser immunity, or indeed any evidence of necessity at all. We are required to make a pragmatic assessment but we have been given no evidence on which a privilege of more modest scope could be delineated. …

[76] The appellants having failed to establish the privilege in the broad and all-inclusive terms asserted, the respondents are entitled to have the appeal disposed of according to the ordinary employment and human rights law that Parliament has enacted with respect to employees within federal legislative jurisdiction.

2. Standing Orders

In *Vaid*, the Supreme Court grappled with privilege as a source of potential immunity of parliamentarians from human rights law. As the discussion in that case suggests, however, parliamentary privilege is a broad concept that extends beyond these immunity issues. It includes Parliament's power "to establish rules of procedure for itself and to enforce them," without external interference (House of Commons, *Beauchesne's Rules and Forms of the House of Commons of Canada*, 6th ed. (Toronto: Carswell, 1989), at 14). Courts have specifically held that Canada's legislatures has the power to administer that part of the statute law relating to its internal procedure, as well as to determine the content of such things as Standing Orders on Procedure, without any intervention from the courts. See *Carter v. Alberta* (2002), 222 DLR (4th) 40, at 48 (Alta. CA), citing Maingot, *Parliamentary Privilege in Canada*, 2nd ed. (Montreal: McGill-Queen's University Press, 1997), at 183-87; *Ontario (Speaker of the Legislative Assembly) v. Ontario Human Rights Commission* (2001), 54 OR (3d) 595 (CA), at para. 48.

Parliament has exercised this internal governance right. Both houses of the federal Parliament have promulgated their own rules of procedure. We focus on the standing orders of the House of Commons, but broadly speaking, these Commons rules are replicated in the Senate's own procedural code.

The standing orders are rules of procedure adopted by at least a simple majority vote of the members of the Commons. They constitute a fairly comprehensive code of Commons operations, including in relation to Commons law making. The orders, however, do not anticipate every circumstance, and their meaning often requires interpretation. For this reason, order 1 of the standing orders provides that where the orders are silent, "procedural questions shall be decided by the Speaker or Chair, whose decisions shall be based on the usages, forms, customs, and precedents of the House of Commons of Canada and on parliamentary tradition in Canada and other jurisdictions, so far as they may be applicable to the House."

We turn now to examining how these standing orders and other legal standards govern law making in Parliament.

B. Parliamentary Law Making

Our discussion of parliamentary law making focuses on both substance and procedure. Substantively, what is the scope of Parliament's law-making jurisdiction? Procedurally, what process does Parliament follow?

1. The Scope of Parliament's Law-Making Jurisdiction

Parliamentary supremacy, discussed in chapter 3, means that Parliament and its provincial counterparts are the only truly sovereign body in Canadian constitutional law. In its classic form, supremacy means that Parliament is the source of all power and Parliament has the jurisdiction "to make or unmake any law whatever": see Albert Venn Dicey, *Introduction to the Study of the Law of the Constitution*, 10th ed. (Toronto: Macmillan, 1961), at 39.

Of course, in Canada, there is no full federal parliamentary supremacy. Parliament is subordinated to other constraints in the Constitution, most notably the division of powers between the federal and provincial governments in the *Constitution Act, 1867* and constitutionally protected individual rights and liberties found in the Charter. But so long as it falls within these constitutional bounds, Parliament may make any law on any topic it wishes, as an exercise of its parliamentary supremacy. See discussion in *Babcock v. Canada*, [2002] 3 SCR 3, at para. 57, excerpted in chapter 3.

a. The Power To Pass Bad Laws

Does this parliamentary supremacy also mean that Parliament is free to pass careless, unwise, or ill-motivated statutes, so long as these flaws do not also constitute constitutional violations? The answer is "yes." Consider the following cases.

Bacon v. Saskatchewan Crop Insurance Corp.
(1999), 180 Sask. R 20 (CA)

WAKELING JA (for the court): [1] This appeal calls into question the legality of the Gross Revenue Insurance Program (GRIP) as it was applied in 1992 by the Saskatchewan Crop Insurance Corporation (SCIC). The appellants are Wayne Bacon and Gary Svenkeson who sued as representatives of three hundred and eighty six farmers who were registered under GRIP 91 and took exception to the manner in which GRIP 92 had been legislatively imposed upon them by virtue of the passage of amendments to *The Agricultural Safety Net Act*, SS 1990-91 c. A-14.2 as amended SS 1992, c. 51. The appellants brought this action against SCIC and the Government of Saskatchewan (Government) to set aside the legislation establishing GRIP 92 and seeking damages.

· · ·

[3] ... [T]he government felt it was necessary to change the concept of GRIP 91 and structure a new program referred to as GRIP 92 intended for the next year. ... [T]he government [also] felt compelled to pass *The Farm Income Insurance Legislation Amendment Act*, 1992, SS 1992 c. 51. The purpose of this legislation was to establish the changed terms

of the GRIP 1991 contract for the year 1992 and to extinguish any claims for breach of contract that might otherwise arise as a result of this change. This Amendment Act was assented to on August 24, 1992 but was effective January 1, 1991.

[4] At trial, the appellants contended the Government had no authority to pass this legislation as governments, like everyone else, are subject to the law. The rule of law is a concept or principle so fundamental that even governments are not exempt from its application. This meant the laws of the land, including those relating to contractual obligations, are as binding upon the government as upon the public. As a consequence, the Government had no legal authority to pass legislation imposing a new contract and extinguishing the right to sue for the breach of the earlier contract.

· · ·

[7] The argument advanced by the appellants can be best understood by a reference to the following opening paragraphs of their factum:

> It should be established clearly at the outset what this case is not about. This case is not about the *Canadian Charter of Rights and Freedoms.* …
>
> Secondly, this case is not about the division of powers in the Constitution between the federal and provincial governments. It is acknowledged that this case involves property and civil rights within the province. It is further acknowledged that this is within the jurisdiction of the Government of Saskatchewan in the context as this case as presented, and there will be no argument advanced by the Plaintiffs that the facts of this case suggest that in somehow the legislation challenged is contrary to the aspect of the division of powers within the Constitution.
>
> This case is about the Rule of Law in the democratic society. The concept of the Rule of Law, will be submitted as something far more basic to the interaction of state and individual than either the Charter of Rights, or the division of federal and provincial powers.
>
> The Rule of Law was a legal concept that pre-dates the notion of a formal written Constitution, and which provides the basis for the common law control over the state in its interaction with individuals.

· · ·

[11] The Government … contends the role of Parliament (which is a word I use to include legislatures) is supreme when acting within its constitutional limits, as was the case in this instance. For this reason, the question of whether the passage of the legislation was an arbitrary use of power need not be asked.

· · ·

[15] The appellants found their case on the contention that a new and more enlightened approach to the concept of the supremacy of Parliament has now emerged based on a greater respect for the rule of law. The freshness of this new approach was acknowledged in this fashion in their factum:

> The phrase "rule of law" has been developed and expanded as the concept of democracy continues to change to suit the continuing needs and aspirations of the public.

[16] The start of this evolutionary process is said to have its foundation in the Magna Carta which contained the statement "the King is under no man save God and the Law." This may, indeed, be a cornerstone for the concept of the rule of law, but fails to be of great

assistance to the appellant since it does nothing to restrict the supremacy of Parliament as being the principal source of the law.

[17] The appellants then turn to the comments of the Supreme Court justices in *Roncarelli v. Duplessis* … as being a more recent application of the doctrine of the rule of law. In this case, the actions of Duplessis (who was at the time both the Premier and Attorney General of Quebec) were set aside as being arbitrary and without lawful authority.

[18] This is an example of where the courts have acted to prevent the arbitrary use of power by a public official which was unsupported by legislative authority, even though that official was of the highest rank. The appellants contend this judgment is the modern cornerstone for the development of the emerging concept of the importance of the rule of law. I am unable to see it in this light. The judgment issued nearly 40 years ago as an instance where an abuse of power by an official was found to be contrary to the concept of the rule of law and to date it has never been applied as anything more than an illustration of the application of the rule of law to prevent officials from acting arbitrarily without the support of lawful authority.

• • •

[23] The appellants [also rely on] the most recent pronouncements of the Supreme Court as contained in the *Reference re Secession of Quebec* which did not bring into question the extent of the supremacy of Parliament but did require a consideration of the nature of federalism as it exists in Canada. …

• • •

[25] … They interpret the statement "the law is supreme over the acts of both government and private persons" [found in the case] as being an unequivocal indication the government has no more right to avoid its contractual obligations then does a private person.

[26] This is not what I take from this statement. It is nothing more than an acceptance that the law as it exists is applicable to both government and private persons. It is a fundamental statement of the obligation of governments which is not challenged by any of the parties to this appeal. However, the law, including the common law, is subject to change by legislation and when changed it is this changed law which is the "one law for all." The law, which is applicable to us all, cannot be taken as static and unchangeable. It is forever evolving and Parliament plays a major role in its development. There is no statement in the *Secession* case which would suggest otherwise.

• • •

[30] The protection we treasure as a democratic country with the rule of law as "a fundamental postulate" of our constitution is twofold. Protection is provided by our courts against arbitrary and unlawful actions by officials while protection against arbitrary legislation is provided by the democratic process of calling our legislators into regular periods of accountability through the ballot box. This concept of the rule of law is not in any way restricted by the Supreme Court's statement that nobody including governments is beyond the law. That statement is a reference to the law as it exists from time to time and does not create a restriction on Parliament's right to make laws, but is only a recognition that when they are made they are then applicable to all, including governments.

• • •

[36] … [T]he public's protection from the arbitrary use of power by officials is provided by the Courts in situations such as was dealt with in *Roncarelli v. Duplessis*, but the public's

protection from the arbitrary use of power by the elected legislators is the ballot box. We place our confidence in the Courts to the extent they will recognize and deal with arbitrary actions of officials not supported by law but we place our confidence in the democratic process of elections to deal with the arbitrary use of legislative powers. These are separate and distinct threats to our freedom and have separate and distinct protections. To say that since the courts do a good job in providing protection in one area against the arbitrary use of power by officials they must also do it in relation to the passage of arbitrary legislation is to misunderstand the democratic process by downgrading the importance of holding a government responsible to the will of the electors.

. . .

[39] In the result, I find that there is no basis to challenge the validity of the legislation which was used to impose the GRIP 92 contract and to extinguish the right to challenge its application through reliance upon the usual common law remedies.

The Saskatchewan Court of Appeal's reasoning in *Bacon* has been followed by other courts. In *PSAC v. Canada* (2000), 192 FTR 23 (TD), at issue was the justiciability of a union's complaint about a statute ordering striking workers back to the job. The union argued that that the legislation was contrary to the rule of law because it was arbitrary and was passed in bad faith. The court held that this argument disclosed no legal foundation for the lawsuit. In arriving at this decision it made these observations:

> Unlike the Parliament at Westminster, the Parliament of Canada is not supreme. It has never been so. The division of powers found in sections 91 and 92 of the *Constitution Act, 1867* (formerly the *British North America Act*) identified certain subjects in respect of which Parliament could not legislate. Federal legislation which touched upon matters reserved to the provinces was struck down. Since the advent of the *Canadian Charter of Rights and Freedoms* (the "Charter"), Parliament has been further constrained in that it cannot legislate in ways which infringe the rights enumerated in the Charter. Legislation which did so has been declared invalid.
>
> … On the basis of the conventional view that Parliament's sovereignty is limited only by the division of powers in the *Constitution Act, 1867* and the enumerated rights in the *Canadian Charter of Rights and Freedoms*, I find that the plaintiff does not have a cause of action arising from breach of the rule of law.

Indeed, even when it is alleged that an ill-intentioned ministry tricked Parliament into enacting legislation, the courts will not probe that statute's promulgation. Consider the following decision.

Turner v. Canada
[1992] 3 FC 458 (CA)

MAHONEY JA: [1] This is an appeal from a decision of the Trial Division … which struck out the substantive allegations of the statement of claim herein, preserving only those paragraphs identifying the parties and claiming relief. The learned Trial Judge refused, however, to dismiss the action as against any of the individual defendants: the Prime Minister and three named Ministers of the Crown, and gave the respondent [plaintiff] leave to amend the statement of claim. The appellants say the Trial Judge erred in not dismissing the action entirely as the statement of claim discloses no reasonable cause of action and also in not dismissing it as against the named individuals for want of jurisdiction.

· · ·

[3] It is pleaded that the respondent was engaged in a lawsuit with another party in the Yukon Supreme Court when an amendment to the *Yukon Quartz Mining Act* … , having retroactive effect, deprived him of his defence in the action and led him to an unfavourable settlement. It alleges that the Ministers "through their negligence and outright connivance" caused the enactment of legislation which abridged his rights and injured him and he claims damages therefor.

[4] The fundamental allegations iterated and reiterated throughout the pleading are that Parliament was tortiously misled to enact the retroactive amendment and that the respondent was denied a fair hearing by surreptitious procedures adopted by Parliament. That procedural fairness is not required in a legislative process is well established. …

[5] Both the *Canadian Bill of Rights* and the *Canadian Charter of Rights and Freedoms* are pleaded. In our opinion, while those may undoubtedly affect the validity and construction of legislation, … they do not bear on the process of legislating. This action is not framed on the basis that the impugned legislation is invalid or inoperative but as a claim for damages as a result of the tainted process whereby it is said to have been enacted. That brings Parliamentary sovereignty squarely into issue.

[6] The elements of that sovereignty enunciated by Lord Simon in *Pickin v. British Railways Board* …

> [Firstly, this (Parliamentary sovereignty)] involves that … the courts in this country have no power to declare enacted law to be invalid. …
>
>   A second concomitant of the sovereignty of Parliament is that the Houses of Parliament enjoy certain privileges. These are vouchsafed so that Parliament can fulfil its key functions in our system of democratic government. …
>
>   … Among the privileges of the Houses of Parliament is the exclusive right to determine the regularity of their own internal proceedings. …
>
>   It is well known that in the past there have been dangerous strains between the law courts and Parliament—dangerous because each institution has its own particular role to play in our constitution, and because collision between the two institutions is likely to impair their power to vouchsafe those constitutional rights for which citizens depend on them. So for many years Parliament and the courts have each been astute to respect the sphere of action and the privileges of the other—Parliament, for example, by its *sub judice* rule, the courts by taking care to exclude evidence which might amount to infringement of parliamentary privilege. …
>
> · · ·
>
>   [Thirdly, a] further practical consideration is that if there is evidence that Parliament may have been misled into an enactment, Parliament might well—indeed, would be likely to—wish to conduct its own inquiry. It would be unthinkable that two inquiries—one parliamentary and the other forensic—should proceed concurrently, conceivably arriving at different conclusions; and a parliamentary examination of parliamentary procedures and of the actions and understandings of officers of Parliament would seem to be clearly more satisfactory than one conducted in a court of law—quite apart from considerations of Parliamentary privilege.

The second and third of those elements are pertinent here, the first not at all since the validity of the legislation is not questioned.

[7] We are all of a view that an action against Her Majesty based on allegations that Parliament has been induced to enact legislation by the tortious acts and omissions of Ministers of the Crown is not justiciable. The appeal will be allowed with costs, the statement of claim entirely struck out and the action dismissed with costs.

Still, even if Parliament is competent to pass bad (but still constitutionally valid) laws, it is not to be presumed that it means to do so. Parliament may strip away contractual rights, for instance, but to do so it must be emphatic. Consider the Supreme Court of Canada's views in the following case.

Wells v. Newfoundland
[1999] 3 SCR 199

MAJOR J: [1] This appeal deals with the position of the Crown and its senior civil servants who hold tenured appointments subject to good behaviour. Are such office-holders owed compensation in the event that their positions are eliminated by legislation? There is no dispute that Parliament and the provincial legislatures have the authority to structure the public service as they see fit, and to eliminate or alter positions in the process. But can it escape the financial consequences for doing so without explicitly extinguishing the rights they have abrogated? I conclude that they cannot.

· · ·

[2] In August 1985, the respondent Andrew Wells, was appointed as a member of the Public Utilities Board ("Board") with the designation Commissioner (Consumer Representative) under the provisions of the *Public Utilities Act*, RSN 1970, c. 322 ("1970 Act"). …

· · ·

[4] The respondent's tenure proved to be a short and turbulent one. On April 6, 1988, the Executive Council of the Government of Newfoundland ordered the Departments of Justice and Transportation and the Treasury Board Secretariat to assess the continuing need for the Board.

· · ·

[6] All the foregoing factors resulted in a substantially decreased workload for the Board given its loss of jurisdiction over two areas of authority that had previously accounted for a substantial amount of its work. The assessment recommended a differently constituted Board with fewer Commissioners, and that the respondent's position be replaced by an office of Consumer Advocate in the Department of Consumer Affairs and Communications or the Department of Justice.

[7] In the wake of this review, a new *Public Utilities Act* was tabled. The respondent was informed by the Minister of Justice that the government intended to act on the recommendations of the review and that on "the balance of probabilities" his position would be abolished. On December 18, 1989, the Newfoundland House of Assembly passed Bill 44, which comprehensively restructured the Board, reduced the number of Commissioners

from six to three, and abolished the Consumer Representative position. Under its provisions, all existing commissioners were to cease holding office, but remained eligible for re-appointment to limited positions on the new Board.

[8] This Bill was proclaimed into force on February 16, 1990, as the *Public Utilities Act, 1989,* ... and the respondent ceased to hold office on that date. ...

· · ·

[37] The appellant Crown asserts that even if it breached the respondent's contract of employment by eliminating his position, it was entitled to do so as an exercise of its unfettered sovereign power. ...

[38] The Crown's argument is that no matter what the terms of the respondent's engagement may have been, the legislature retained the power to eliminate his position.

· · ·

[41] ... [T]here is no question that the Government of Newfoundland had the authority to restructure or eliminate the Board. There is a crucial distinction, however, between the Crown legislatively avoiding a contract, and altogether escaping the legal consequences of doing so. While the legislature may have the extraordinary power of passing a law to specifically deny compensation to an aggrieved individual with whom it has broken an agreement, clear and explicit statutory language would be required to extinguish existing rights previously conferred on that party. ...

[42] The respondent's contractual rights relating to his employment as a Commissioner were acquired under the *Public Utilities Act,* and its repeal did not, of itself, strip him of those rights. ... The government was free to pass such a bill and they were equally free to pass a bill which would have explicitly denied the respondent compensation. ... However, since no such Act was passed, the respondent's basic contractual rights to severance pay remain.

· · ·

[46] In a nation governed by the rule of law, we assume that the government will honour its obligations unless it explicitly exercises its power not to. In the absence of a clear express intent to abrogate rights and obligations—rights of the highest importance to the individual—those rights remain in force. To argue the opposite is to say that the government is bound only by its whim, not its word. In Canada this is unacceptable, and does not accord with the nation's understanding of the relationship between the state and its citizens.

· · ·

[50] The appellant Crown argues that the respondent's contract was frustrated by the passage of the new Act, which made further employment of Wells in his previous position impossible. ...

[51] The obvious objection to this submission is that self-induced frustration does not excuse non-performance. ... The Crown responds that the separation of powers between the legislative and executive branches means that a legislative act which bars the executive from performing pending contractual obligations does not constitute self-induced frustration, as these branches are independent entities.

[52] The doctrine of separation of powers is an essential feature of our constitution. It maintains a separation of powers between the judiciary and the other two branches, legislature and the executive, and to some extent between the legislature and the executive. ... The government cannot, however, rely on this formal separation to avoid the consequences

of its own actions. While the legislature retains the power to expressly terminate a contract without compensation, it is disingenuous for the executive to assert that the legislative enactment of its own agenda constitutes a frustrating act beyond its control.

[53] On a practical level, it is recognized that the same individuals control both the executive and the legislative branches of government. As this Court observed in *Attorney General of Quebec v. Blaikie*, … "There is thus a considerable degree of integration between the Legislature and the Government. … [I]t is the Government which, through its majority, does in practice control the operations of the elected branch of the Legislature on a day to day basis." Similarly, in *Reference re Canada Assistance Plan*, … Sopinka J said:

> … [T]he true executive power lies in the Cabinet. And since the Cabinet controls the government, there is in practice a degree of overlap among the terms "government," "Cabinet" and "executive." … In practice, the bulk of the new legislation is initiated by the government.

[54] The separation of powers is not a rigid and absolute structure. The Court should not be blind to the reality of Canadian governance that, except in certain rare cases, the executive frequently and *de facto* controls the legislature. The new *Public Utilities Act* in Newfoundland was a government bill, introduced by a member, as directed by Cabinet Directive C 328-'89. Therefore, the same "directing minds," namely the executive, were responsible for both the respondent's appointment and his termination. Moreover, since a number of positions equivalent to that previously held by the respondent were created under the new Act, the executive could have re-appointed him and remedied its breach of contract. This continues to demonstrate the futility of the frustration argument in the circumstances of this case.

[55] The Crown had a contractual obligation to the respondent, which it breached by eliminating his position. As his right to seek damages for that breach was not taken from him by legislation, he is entitled to compensation.

b. *The Power To Follow Unfair Procedures*

The discussion above underscores that not every ill that afflicts a statute may be cured by the courts, even in a system where Parliament's sovereignty is constrained by a constitution. More than that, it is also true that in reviewing the *process* by which Parliament makes its laws, courts are even more reluctant to impose standards on the legislative branch. Certainly, the *Constitution Act, 1867* does specify some requirements for the legislative process: matters are to be decided in both the Senate and the Commons by a majority of votes; the quorum of the Senate is 15 senators, including the speaker, and of the Commons, 20 members; money bills must originate in the Commons; bills must be in French and English; and all bills require royal assent. (*Constitution Act, 1867*, ss. 36, 49, 35, 48, 53, 133, and 55, respectively.)

But so long as these prerequisites are met, courts have no role in querying the procedure Parliament selects in passing its law. Any effort by courts to scrutinize the procedure by which laws are passed by Parliament would quickly trench on parliamentary privilege. The internal procedure immunized from external court scrutiny includes the manner in which Parliament passes Acts. In the British parliamentary tradition, it is for "Parliament to lay down the procedures which are to be followed before a Bill can become an Act": see Lord Morris of Borth-y-Gest in *Pickin v. British Railways Board*, [1974] AC 765, at 790 (HL), cited with approval in *Martin v. Ontario*, [2004] OJ no. 2247 (Sup. Ct.), at para. 21. These are all matters of parliamentary privilege.

Does this mean that Parliament would be free to act unfairly—perhaps by passing a law without any notice to those implicated by it? The answer is likely "yes." The Supreme Court has implied that "three readings in the Senate and House of Commons" is a procedure due any citizen of Canada by "[l]ong-standing parliamentary tradition": see *Authorson v. Canada (Attorney General)*, [2003] 2 SCR 40, at para. 37. However, nothing constitutionalizes this practice. Canadians are not entitled to any sort of due process or procedural fairness in the law-making process.

Consider how the Supreme Court addressed this issue in *Wells v. Newfoundland*. Recall that here, Wells was arguing that legislative changes eliminating the board of which he was a member violated employment rights and entitled him to compensation. Ultimately successful for the reasons outlined in the extract above, another of his arguments failed:

> [57] The thrust of the respondent's submission was that since he lost his job as a result of governmental action, he had a right to fairness in the making of that decision. Procedurally unfair or arbitrary decisions by government lack the force of law and are reviewable by the courts. …
>
> • • •
>
> [59] Both the decision to restructure the Board, and the subsequent decision not to reappoint the respondent, were *bona fide* decisions. The decision to restructure the Board was deliberated and enacted by the elected legislature of the Province of Newfoundland. This is fatal to the respondent's argument on bad faith, as legislative decision making is not subject to any known duty of fairness. Legislatures are subject to constitutional requirements for valid lawmaking, but within their constitutional boundaries, they can do as they see fit. The wisdom and value of legislative decisions are subject only to review by the electorate. The judgment in *Reference re Canada Assistance Plan* [(B.C.), [1991] 2 SCR 525] … was conclusive on this point in stating that: "the rules governing procedural fairness do not apply to a body exercising purely legislative functions." …
>
> [60] In *Reference re Amendment of Constitution of Canada*, [[1981] 1 SCR 753] … it was stated … :
>
>> How Houses of Parliament proceed, how a provincial legislative assembly proceeds is in either case a matter of self-definition, subject to any overriding constitutional or self-imposed statutory or indoor prescription. It is unnecessary here to embark on any historical review of the "court" aspect of Parliament and the immunity of its procedures from judicial review. *Courts come into the picture when legislation is enacted and not before* (unless references are made to them for their opinion on a bill or a proposed enactment). [Emphasis added.]
>
> [61] The respondent's loss resulted from a legitimately enacted "legislative and general" decision, not an "administrative and specific" one. … While the impact on him may be singularly severe, it did not constitute a direct and intentional attack upon his interests. His position is no different in kind than that of an unhappy tax-payer who is out-of-pocket as a result of a newly enacted budget, or an impoverished welfare recipient whose benefits are reduced as a result of a legislative changes in eligibility criteria. This was not a personal matter, it was a legislative policy choice. …

In *Authorson v. Canada*, a group of disabled veterans and their representatives sued the federal government for payment of interest on pension monies held and managed by the government on their behalf over many years, alleging this to constitute a breach of fiduciary duty. The government conceded that it had owed such a duty, and had breached it by failing to pay interest. However, the attorney general defended the claim on the basis that Parliament had passed legislation denying any such claim for monies owed prior to 1990, effectively expropriating the claim without compensation. The veterans argued that the *Canadian Bill of Rights*, an ordinary statute passed by Parliament in 1960, and described by the Supreme Court as "quasi-constitutional" in nature, applied to the expropriating legislation and obligated Parliament both to engage in a fair process before adopting the legislation and, as a matter of substantive law, prohibited expropriation without compensation. The veterans cited in particular the reference to "due process" in s. 1(a) of the *Canadian Bill of Rights*:

> 1. It is hereby recognized and declared that in Canada there have existed and shall continue to exist without discrimination by reason of race, national origin, colour, religion or sex, the following human rights and fundamental freedoms, namely,
>
>> (a) the right of the individual to life, liberty, security of the person and enjoyment of property, and the right not to be deprived thereof except by due process of law;

The court rejected this argument, as follows.

Authorson v. Canada (Attorney General)
[2003] 2 SCR 40

MAJOR J: [1] The deceased respondent, Authorson, a disabled veteran of World War II, was the representative of a large class of disabled veterans of Canada's military forces. He died in 2002, but the action continues to be prosecuted by his litigation administrator and guardian.

[2] This litigation raises difficult questions. The government of Canada, through the appellant, the Attorney General of Canada, agrees that throughout the relevant time it acted as a fiduciary for each of the veterans, that the funds owed the veterans and administered by the government were rarely credited with interest, and that a full accounting was never made to the respondent.

[3] It is not in dispute that the respondent is owed interest, and that this omission continued until legislation changing government practice was enacted in 1990. The appellant, while agreeing that the respondent is owed money, argues that Parliament has, by enacting legislation to that effect, made the debt unenforceable.

[4] The respondent submits that the *Canadian Bill of Rights*, SC 1960, c. 44 (reproduced in RSC 1985, App. III) (the "*Bill of Rights*"), ensures him due process in the expropriation of his property. The appellant's position is that the expropriative legislation was a valid exercise of its legislative power, and that no remedy exists.

· · ·

[14] Does the *Bill of Rights* require that Parliament give just compensation to the veterans? The governmental expropriation of property without compensation is discouraged by

our common law tradition, but it is allowed when Parliament uses clear and unambiguous language to do so.

[15] The *Department of Veterans Affairs Act*, s. 5.1(4) takes a property claim from a vulnerable group, in disregard of the Crown's fiduciary duty to disabled veterans. However, that taking is within the power of Parliament. The appeal has to be allowed.

· · ·

(1) Procedural Rights in Legislative Enactment

[39] As well, see *Wells v. Newfoundland*, [1999] 3 SCR 199, at para. 59:

> ... [L]egislative decision making is not subject to any known duty of fairness. Legislatures are subject to constitutional requirements for valid law-making, but within their constitutional boundaries, they can do as they see fit. The wisdom and value of legislative decisions are subject only to review by the electorate. The judgment in *Reference re Canada Assistance Plan* ... was conclusive on this point in stating that: "the rules governing procedural fairness do not apply to a body exercising purely legislative functions."

[40] The submission that a court can compel Parliament to change its legislative procedures based on the *Bill of Rights* must fail. The *Bill of Rights* purports to guide the proper interpretation of every "law of Canada," which s. 5 of the *Bill of Rights* defines to mean "an Act of the Parliament of Canada enacted before or after the coming into force of this Act." Court interference with the legislative process is not an interpretation of an already enacted law.

[41] Due process protections cannot interfere with the right of the legislative branch to determine its own procedure. For the *Bill of Rights* to confer such a power would effectively amend the Canadian constitution, which, in the preamble to the *Constitution Act, 1867*, enshrines a constitution similar in principle to that of the United Kingdom. In the United Kingdom, no such pre-legislative procedural rights have existed. From that, it follows that the *Bill of Rights* does not authorize such power.

· · ·

V. Conclusion

[62] The respondent and the class of disabled veterans it represents are owed decades of interest on their pension and benefit funds. The Crown does not dispute these findings. But Parliament has chosen for undisclosed reasons to lawfully deny the veterans, to whom the Crown owed a fiduciary duty, these benefits whether legal, equitable or fiduciary. The due process protections of property in the *Bill of Rights* do not grant procedural rights in the process of legislative enactment. They do confer certain rights to notice and an opportunity to make submissions in the adjudication of individual rights and obligations, but no such rights are at issue in this appeal.

[63] While the due process guarantees may have some substantive content not apparent in this appeal, there is no due process right against duly enacted legislation unambiguously expropriating property interests.

c. Ethics in Law Making

The discussion to this point suggests that no prudential constraints exist on Parliament, other than those found in the Constitution. But a word of caution should be voiced about the latitude Parliament has to pass laws as it wills. Parliament may be sovereign, but individual parliamentarians are not. A parliamentarian induced by the prospect of financial gain to vote one way or another in performing his or her law-making functions is subject to sanction in a number of different ways. Ethics rules exist both in statutory law and in the internal procedural rules governing each house of Parliament. Consider the following discussion.

Margaret Young, *Conflict-of-Interest Rules for Federal Legislators*
Law and Government Division, Parliamentary Research Branch
(Ottawa: Library of Parliament, December 2003)

Issue Definition

Conflict of interest is one aspect of public-sector ethics, and Canadian legislatures and governments have developed legislation and codes of conduct that show a wide variety of approaches to the issue. This paper will focus on the most important developments at the federal level. Although the emphasis here is on federal legislators, other federal public officials—such as public-service workers and judges as well as members of administrative agencies, tribunals and Crown corporations—are also affected by conflict-of-interest rules.

Our society expects that individuals should be as free as possible to pursue their economic goals, but also expects that those in positions of public trust should not act in their public capacity on matters in which they have a personal economic interest. Even an appearance of a conflict affects the public's confidence in office holders generally.

Some suggest that Parliament should adopt more comprehensive rules covering conflict of interest. Others are concerned that such a step would deter qualified or desirable people from running for public office. The difficulty of striking a balance, while also protecting the privacy interests of legislators, helps to explain why all four bills on this issue presented in the 33rd and 34th Parliaments died on the *Order Paper*, and why a Parliamentary Committee Report in the subsequent Parliament was not acted upon until the 37th Parliament.

Background and Analysis

There are a number of possible definitions of conflict of interest. Mr. Justice W.D. Parker, who presided at the inquiry into conflict-of-interest allegations against Sinclair Stevens, defined a *real* conflict of interest as a "situation in which a minister of the Crown has knowledge of a private economic interest that is sufficient to influence the exercise of his or her public duties and responsibilities." A *potential* conflict of interest, on the other hand, exists where a minister "finds himself or herself in a situation in which the existence of some private economic interest could influence the exercise of his or her public duties or responsibilities … provided that he or she has not yet exercised such duty or responsibility." A potential conflict becomes a real conflict where the Minister does not dispose of relevant assets or withdraw from certain public duties or decisions. Mr. Justice Parker also talked about an *apparent* conflict of interest, which "exists when there is a reasonable apprehension, which reasonably well-informed persons could properly have, that a conflict of interest exists," even if, in fact, there is neither a potential nor a real conflict. Some definitions concentrate on "decision-making" rather than "situations," while some regimes prefer to leave the term undefined.

The principles underlying conflict-of-interest rules are impartiality and integrity: a decision-maker cannot be perceived as being impartial and acting with integrity if he or she could derive a personal benefit from a decision. Public confidence in governmental institutions is closely allied to public belief that decisions will be taken and laws will be enacted, and subsequently applied and administered, fairly and objectively, free of personal biases and considerations. That said, it is not clear how far the principle of impartiality extends, particularly when partisan politics are involved. Nor is it clear that the personal interests involved are necessarily purely economic ones.

Today, governments intervene in virtually all sectors of the economy, either through direct control or through regulatory agencies, safety and health legislation, tariff and tax policies, or federal subsidies. Thus, it is not unusual for legislation introduced in Parliament to affect the general economic interests of Members of Parliament in some way.

Some conflicts are unavoidable. An *inherent conflict* arises out of the position of the Parliamentarian as an individual in society, i.e., as a homeowner, parent or consumer. Parliament continually deals with legislation affecting these interests and, as the Parliamentarian is affected like other citizens, there is a low risk of an adverse consequence. Also unavoidable is the *representative interest* conflict which arises when Members share personal interests, for example in farming, fishing and resource development, with the constituency electing them. Other interests, however, may in some cases substantially affect the independence of a legislator, particularly when he or she enters Cabinet. Family businesses pose problems, but so do a wide range of assets, liabilities and financial interests. Conflict-of-interest rules generally deal with these latter kinds of interests.

To what extent, then, should a Parliamentarian be able to retain personal economic and other interests? The rules must not be so stringent as to discourage persons of ability and experience from entering public life, yet must be stringent enough to deter unethical practices and maintain the good reputation of Parliament and its Members. The rules also must make some distinctions between Private Members and senators, who individually may have little influence over the decision-making process, and Cabinet Ministers and their staff.

A. Techniques of Control

A number of methods are available to control conflicts of interest.

- *Disclosure* requires that legislators reveal their assets, typically first confidentially to a designated official, and then publicly so that a personal interest becomes public knowledge and Parliamentarians are inhibited from acting for their personal benefit. Public disclosure also informs the legislator's constituents and colleagues of the situation so that they can consider its implications.
- *Avoidance* requires legislators to *divest* themselves of interests or relationships that might impair their judgement, either by a sale at arm's length or by use of a trust ad-

ministered by a trustee independently of the legislator; in the latter case, it must be ensured that the trust is beyond the Parliamentarian's control.

- *Withdrawal* (also called *recusal*) requires Parliamentarians to refrain from acting on matters in which they have personal financial interests.

Typically, conflict-of-interest regimes incorporate a combination of the above controls.

B. Types of Interests

The more common types of interests that can put a legislator into a conflict situation are outlined below.

- *Investments:* Investments usually considered unlikely to give rise to a conflict of interest include government bonds, guaranteed investment certificates and open-ended mutual funds. Even here, conflicts may arise; for example, the Commissioner in Ontario has ruled that the Treasurer should not hold provincial bonds because he is responsible for setting the interest rates. Which investments that present conflicts are suitable for placing in a trust? Should the value of any retained interests be disclosed? Should shareholdings of Parliamentarians be restricted to a percentage of total issued shares in a company? Any arbitrary percentage set might be insignificant where there were only a few shareholders, but could result in effective control of a company if shares were widely held.
- *Debts:* Liabilities, as well as assets, are potential sources of conflict, because the creditors of persons in public office may give the appearance of having influence over their debtors.
- *Corporate Positions:* A legislator may find that Parliament is considering measures that would affect him or her as an officer, director or employee of a company or affect the interests of the company. As a director, he or she is required to act in the best interests of the company, yet as a legislator he or she is required to act in the best interests of the public.
- *Outside Employment:* To what extent should Parliamentarians be able to carry on their law practices, businesses, or other types of employment? Cabinet Ministers are now prohibited from such activities. Should there be a restriction on the amount of money that can be earned from outside employment? Parliamentarians dealing with laws that may affect their business clients could be put in a position opposed to the best interests of the public. A legislator might attract more clients if the latter believed he or she would increase their influence with the federal government. Should Parliamentarians be able to profit in this way from their status?
- *Lobbying:* Dealing with government officials on behalf of constituents is a normal function of legislators. What about legislators who use their position to further personal interests or who are paid to act on behalf of others? Should they be able to make representations or appear before government boards or commissions or federal courts in their personal capacity, or would the appearance of influence be too strong? What is the position of legislators who receive indirect benefits as lawyers, employees, or financial advisors of persons or companies for whom they act? Is it sufficient for legislators to reveal their interests to government officials with whom they correspond, or

must they avoid any contact with such persons and bodies except in the course of their duties as representatives of their constituents?

- *Government Contracts and Activities:* Should legislators be able to participate with other Canadians in government programs, or would the appearance of influence be too strong and the possibility of conflict too high? To what extent should Parliamentarians be allowed to own or invest in businesses that have government contracts?
- *Gifts and Honoraria:* Should legislators be permitted to accept free vacation trips or other gifts from acquaintances, businesses or foreign governments? Should there be a restriction on the amount that can be accepted? Should disclosure be the only requirement? "Honoraria" can be disguised gifts.
- *Inside Information:* Are controls necessary to deter legislators from using for personal advantage any information that comes to them in their official capacity?
- *Spouse and Dependent Children:* To what extent should the above interests be controlled if they are held by those with close family ties to the Parliamentarian? The legislator is as likely to be influenced by family interests as by his or her own.

C. Statutory and Parliamentary Rules

Most conflict-of-interest rules for federal legislators are found in three Acts of Parliament (the *Criminal Code*, the *Parliament of Canada Act* and the *Canada Elections Act*) and in the Standing Orders of the House of Commons and Rules of the Senate.

[In 2006, Parliament enacted the Conservative government's comprehensive *Federal Accountability Act.*, SC 2006, c. 9. A core component of the latter is the *Conflict of Interest Act*, SC 2006, c. 9, s. 2, an ethics instrument that applies to senior level executive officials, including ministers.]

Bribery, the most extreme form of conflict of interest, is a criminal offence. The *Criminal Code* provides for 14 years' imprisonment for a Parliamentarian who accepts or attempts to obtain any form of valuable consideration for doing or omitting to do anything in his or her official capacity. ... The *Parliament of Canada Act* prohibits a Parliamentarian from receiving outside compensation for services rendered on any matter before the House, the Senate or their committees. The Act excludes persons with remunerated employment in the federal government and certain officials at the provincial level from being eligible as Members of the House of Commons, although there are exceptions. The *Parliament of Canada Act* makes a Member of a provincial legislative assembly ineligible to be a Member of the House of Commons. The *Canada Elections Act* disqualifies the above office holders from candidacy for the House of Commons as well as Members of the Council of the Northwest Territories, the Council of the Yukon Territory or the Legislative Assembly of Nunavut, and certain office holders who are not entitled to vote.

The most significant ethics instrument governing the day-to-day activities of federal members of Parliament is the *Conflict of Interest Code for Members of the House of Commons*, introduced as part of the Commons standing orders in 2004.

Conflict of Interest Code for Members of the House of Commons
House of Commons, *Standing Orders*, Appendix
(Ottawa: House of Commons, 2004, as amended)

Purposes

1. The purposes of this Code are to

(a) maintain and enhance public confidence and trust in the integrity of Members as well as the respect and confidence that society places in the House of Commons as an institution;

(b) demonstrate to the public that Members are held to standards that place the public interest ahead of their private interests and to provide a transparent system by which the public may judge this to be the case;

(c) provide for greater certainty and guidance for Members in how to reconcile their private interests with their public duties and functions; and

(d) foster consensus among Members by establishing common standards and by providing the means by which questions relating to proper conduct may be answered by an independent, non-partisan adviser.

Principles

2. Given that service in Parliament is a public trust, the House of Commons recognizes and declares that Members are expected

(a) to serve the public interest and represent constituents to the best of their abilities;

(b) to fulfill their public duties with honesty and uphold the highest standards so as to avoid real or apparent conflicts of interests, and maintain and enhance public confidence and trust in the integrity of each Member and in the House of Commons;

(c) to perform their official duties and functions and arrange their private affairs in a manner that bears the closest public scrutiny, an obligation that may not be fully discharged by simply acting within the law;

(d) to arrange their private affairs so that foreseeable real or apparent conflicts of interest may be prevented from arising, but if such a conflict does arise, to resolve it in a way that protects the public interest; and

(e) not to accept any gift or benefit connected with their position that might reasonably be seen to compromise their personal judgment or integrity except in accordance with the provisions of this Code.

Interpretation

Definitions

3(1) The following definitions apply in this Code.

"all-party caucus" means a caucus open to all political parties.

"benefit" means

(a) an amount of money if there is no obligation to repay it; and

(b) a service or property, or the use of property or money that is provided without charge or at less than its commercial value, other than a service provided by a volunteer working on behalf of a Member;

but does not include a benefit received from a riding association or a political party.

"Commissioner" means the Conflict of Interest and Ethics Commissioner appointed under section 81 of the *Parliament of Canada Act.*

"common-law partner," with respect to a Member, means a person who is cohabiting with the Member in a conjugal relationship, having so cohabited for a period of at least one year.

"spouse," with respect to a Member, does not include a person from whom the Member is separated where all support obligations and family property have been dealt with by a separation agreement or by a court order.

Furthering private interests

(2) Subject to subsection (3), a Member is considered to further a person's private interests, including his or her own private interests, when the Member's actions result, directly or indirectly, in any of the following
(a) an increase in, or the preservation of, the value of the person's assets;
(b) the extinguishment, or reduction in the amount, of the person's liabilities;
(c) the acquisition of a financial interest by the person;
(d) an increase in the person's income from a source referred to in subsection 21(2);
(e) the person becoming a director or officer in a corporation, association or trade union; and
(f) the person becoming a partner in a partnership.

Not furthering private interests

(3) For the purpose of this Code, a Member is not considered to further his or her own private interests or the interests of another person if the matter in question
(a) is of general application;
(b) affects the Member or the other person as one of a broad class of the public;
(b.1) consists of being a party to a legal action relating to actions of the Member as a Member of Parliament; or
(c) concerns the remuneration or benefits of the Member as provided under an Act of Parliament.

Family members

(4) The following are the members of a Member's family for the purposes of this Code:
(a) the Member's spouse or common-law partner; and
(b) a son or daughter of the Member, or a son or daughter of the Member's spouse or common-law partner, who has not reached the age of 18 years or who has reached that age but is primarily dependent on the Member or the Member's spouse or common-law partner for financial support.

Interpretation: purposes and principles

3.1 In interpreting and applying Members' obligations under this Code, the Commissioner may have regard to the purposes and principles in sections 1 and 2.

Application

Application to Members

4. The provisions of this Code apply to conflicts of interest of all Members of the House of Commons when carrying out the duties and functions of their office as Members of the House, including Members who are ministers of the Crown or parliamentary secretaries.

Assisting constituents

5. A Member does not breach this Code if the Member's activity is one in which Members normally and properly engage on behalf of constituents.

Jurisdiction of the Board of Internal Economy

6. Nothing in this Code affects the jurisdiction of the Board of Internal Economy of the House of Commons to determine the propriety of the use of any funds, goods, services or premises made available to Members for carrying out their parliamentary duties and functions.

Activities outside Parliament

7. Nothing in this Code prevents Members who are not ministers of the Crown or parliamentary secretaries from any of the following, as long as they are able to fulfill their obligations under this Code:
    (a) engaging in employment or in the practice of a profession;
    (b) carrying on a business;
    (c) being a director or officer in a corporation, association, trade union or non-profit organization; and
    (d) being a partner in a partnership.

Rules of Conduct

Furthering private interests

8. When performing parliamentary duties and functions, a Member shall not act in any way to further his or her private interests or those of a member of the Member's family, or to improperly further another person's or entity's private interests.

Using influence

9. A Member shall not use his or her position as a Member to influence a decision of another person so as to further the Member's private interests or those of a member of his or her family, or to improperly further another person's or entity's private interests.

Insider information

10(1) A Member shall not use information obtained in his or her position as a Member that is not generally available to the public to further the Member's private interests or those of a member of his or her family, or to improperly further another person's or entity's private interests.

Information not to be communicated

(2) A Member shall not communicate information referred to in subsection (1) to another person if the Member knows, or reasonably ought to know, that the information may be used to further the Member's private interests or those of a member of his or her family, or to improperly further another person's or entity's private interests.

Attempts

11. A Member shall not attempt to engage in any of the activities prohibited under sections 8 to 10.

Disclosure of a private interest: House and committee

12(1) A Member who has a private interest that might be affected by a matter that is before the House of Commons or a committee of which the Member is a member shall, if present during consideration of the matter, disclose orally or in writing the general nature of the private interest at the first opportunity. The general nature of the private interest shall be disclosed forthwith in writing to the Clerk of the House.

Subsequent disclosure

(2) If a Member becomes aware at a later date of a private interest that should have been disclosed in the circumstances of subsection (1), the Member shall make the required disclosure forthwith.

Disclosure recorded

(3) The Clerk of the House shall cause the disclosure to be recorded in the Journals and shall send the disclosure to the Commissioner, who shall file it with the Member's public disclosure documents.

Disclosure of a private interest: other circumstances

(4) In any circumstances other than those in subsection (1) that involve the Member's parliamentary duties and functions, a Member who has a private interest that might be affected shall disclose orally or in writing the general nature of the private interest at the first opportunity to the party concerned. The Member shall also file a notice in writing concerning the private interest with the Commissioner, who shall file it with the Member's public disclosure documents.

Debate and voting

13. A Member shall not participate in debate on or vote on a question in which he or she has a private interest.

Private interest

13.1 For the purpose of sections 12 and 13, "private interest" means those interests that can be furthered in subsection 3(2), but does not include the matters listed in subsection 3(3).

Prohibition: gifts and other benefits

14(1) Neither a Member nor any member of a Member's family shall accept, directly or indirectly, any gift or other benefit, except compensation authorized by law, that might reasonably be seen to have been given to influence the Member in the exercise of a duty or function of his or her office.

(1.1) For greater certainty, subsection (1) applies to gifts or other benefits:

(a) related to attendance at a charitable or political event; and

(b) received from an all-party caucus established in relation to a particular subject or interest.

Exception

(2) Despite subsection (1), a Member or a member of a Member's family may accept gifts or other benefits received as a normal expression of courtesy or protocol, or within the customary standards of hospitality that normally accompany the Member's position.

Statement: gift or other benefit

(3) If gifts or other benefits that are related to the Member's position are accepted under this section and have a value of $500 or more, or if the total value of all such gifts or benefits received from one source in a 12-month period is $500 or more, the Member shall, within 60 days after receiving the gifts or other benefits, or after that total value is exceeded, file with the Commissioner a statement disclosing the nature of the gifts or other benefits, their source and the circumstances under which they were given.

Exception

(4) Any disclosure made pursuant to the requirements of section 15 does not need to be disclosed as a gift or other benefit under subsection (3).

Sponsored travel

15(0.1) Despite subsection 14(1), a Member may accept, for the Member and guests of the Member, sponsored travel that arises from or relates to his or her position.

Statement: sponsored travel

(1) If travel costs exceed $500 and those costs are not wholly or substantially paid from the Consolidated Revenue Fund or by the Member personally, his or her political party or any interparliamentary association or friendship group recognized by the House, the Member shall, within 60 days after the end of the trip, file a statement with the Commissioner disclosing the trip.

Content of statement

(2) The statement shall disclose the name of the person or organization paying the travel costs, the name of any person accompanying the Member, the destination or destinations, the purpose and length of the trip, the nature of the benefits received and the value, including supporting documents for transportation and accommodation.

Publication

(3) By March 31 of each year, the Commissioner shall prepare a list of all sponsored travel for the previous calendar year, including the details set out in subsection (2), and the Speaker shall lay the list upon the Table when the House next sits.

Government contracts

16(1) A Member shall not knowingly be a party, directly or through a subcontract, to a contract with the Government of Canada or any federal agency or body under which the Member receives a benefit unless the Commissioner is of the opinion that the contract is unlikely to affect the Member's obligations under this Code.

Clarification

(2) A Member may participate in a program operated or funded, in whole or in part, by the Government of Canada under which the Member receives a benefit if
　　(a) the Member meets the eligibility requirements of the program;
　　(b) the Member does not receive any preferential treatment with respect to his or her participation; and
　　(c) the Member does not receive any special benefit not available to other participants.

Public corporations

17(1) A Member is not prohibited from owning securities in a public corporation that contracts with the Government of Canada unless the Commissioner is of the opinion that the size of the holdings is so significant that it is likely to affect the Member's obligations under this Code.

Trust

(2) If the Commissioner is of the opinion that the Member's obligations under this Code are likely to be affected under the circumstances of subsection (1), the Member may comply

with the Code by placing the securities in a trust under such terms established in section 19 as the Commissioner considers appropriate.

Partnerships and private corporations

18. A Member shall not have an interest in a partnership or in a private corporation that is a party, directly or through a subcontract, to a contract with the Government of Canada under which the partnership or corporation receives a benefit unless the Commissioner is of the opinion that the interest is unlikely to affect the Member's obligations under this Code.

Pre-existing contracts

19(1) Sections 16 and 18 do not apply to a contract that existed before the Member's election to the House of Commons, but they do apply to its renewal or extension.

Trust

(2) Section 18 does not apply if the Member has entrusted his or her interest in a partnership or in a private corporation that is a party to a contract with the Government of Canada under which the partnership or corporation receives a benefit to one or more trustees on all of the following terms:

(a) the provisions of the trust have been approved by the Commissioner;

(b) the trustees are at arm's length from the Member and have been approved by the Commissioner;

(c) the trustees may not consult with the Member with respect to managing the trust, but they may consult with the Commissioner;

(d) the trustees may, however, consult with the Member, with the approval of the Commissioner and in his or her presence if an extraordinary event is likely to materially affect the trust property;

(e) in the case of an interest in a corporation, the Member shall resign any position of director or officer in the corporation;

(f) the trustees shall provide the Commissioner with a written annual report at the same time as the Member files his or her annual disclosure statement setting out the nature of the trust property, the value of that property, the trust's net income for the preceding year and the trustees' fees, if any; and

(g) the trustees shall give the Member sufficient information to permit the Member to submit returns as required by the Income Tax Act and give the same information to the Canada Customs and Revenue Agency.

Interest acquired by inheritance

(3) Sections 16 to 18 do not apply to an interest acquired by inheritance until the first anniversary date of the acquisition.

Disclosure statement

20(1) A Member shall, within 60 days after the notice of his or her election to the House of Commons is published in the Canada Gazette, and annually on or before a date established by the Commissioner, file with the Commissioner a full statement disclosing the Member's private interests and the private interests of the members of the Member's family.

Reasonable efforts

(2) Information relating to the private interests of the members of the Member's family shall be to the best of the Member's knowledge, information and belief. The Member shall make reasonable efforts to determine such information.

Confidentiality

(3) The Commissioner shall keep the statement confidential.

Content of disclosure statement

21(1) The statement shall
(a) identify and state the value of each asset or liability of the Member and the members of the Member's family that;
(i) in the case of a credit card balance, exceeds $10,000 and has been outstanding for more than six months;
(ii) in all other cases, exceeds $10,000;
(b) state the amount and indicate the source of any income greater than $1,000 that the Member and the members of the Member's family have received during the preceding 12 months and are entitled to receive during the next 12 months;
(b.1) Notwithstanding paragraph (b), every Member shall disclose to the Commissioner every trust known to the Member from which he or she could, currently or in the future, either directly or indirectly, derive a benefit or income;
(c) state all benefits that the Member and the members of the Member's family, and any private corporation in which the Member or a member of the Member's family has an interest, have received during the preceding 12 months, and those that the Member and the members of the Member's family or corporation are entitled to receive during the next 12 months, as a result of being a party, directly or through a subcontract, to a contract with the Government of Canada, and describe the subject-matter and nature of each such contract or subcontract;
(c.1) For the purpose of paragraph (1)(c), benefits include compensation resulting from expropriation by the Government of Canada;
(d) if the statement mentions a private corporation,
(i) include any information about the corporation's activities and sources of income that the Member is able to obtain by making reasonable inquiries,
(ii) state the names of any other corporations with which that corporation is affiliated, and

(iii) list the names and addresses of all persons who have an interest in the corporation;

(iv) list the real property or immovables owned by the private corporation.

(e) list the directorships or offices in a corporation, trade or professional association or trade union held by the Member or a member of the Member's family and list all partnerships in which he or she or a member of his or her family is a partner; and

(f) include any other information that the Commissioner may require.

Source of income

(2) For the purposes of paragraph (1)(b), a source of income is

(a) in the case of income from employment, the employer;

(b) in the case of income from a contract, the party with whom the contract is made; and

(c) in the case of income arising from a business or profession, that business or profession.

Statement: material change

(3) The Member shall file a statement reporting any material change to the information required under subsection (1) to the Commissioner within 60 days after the change.

Meeting with the Commissioner

22. After reviewing a Member's statement filed under section 20 or subsection 21(3), the Commissioner may require that the Member meet with the Commissioner, and may request the attendance of any of the members of the Member's family, if available, to ensure that adequate disclosure has been made and to discuss the Member's obligations under this Code.

Disclosure summary

23(1) The Commissioner shall prepare a disclosure summary based on each Member's statement filed under section 21 and submit it to the member for review.

Public inspection

(2) Each summary is to be placed on file at the office of the Commissioner and made available for public inspection during normal business hours, and posted on the website of the Commissioner. Each summary shall also be available to the public, on request, by fax or mail.

Content of disclosure summary

24(1) The summary shall

(a) subject to subsection (3), set out the source and nature, but not the value, of the income, assets and liabilities referred to in the Member's statement filed under section 20;

(b) identify any contracts or subcontracts referred to in paragraph 21(1)(c) and describe their subject-matter and nature;

(c) list the names of any affiliated corporations referred to in that statement;

(d) include a copy of any statements of disclosure filed by the Member under subsections 14(3), 15(1) and 21(3);

(e) list the positions and corporations, trade or professional associations and trade unions disclosed under paragraph 21(1)(e); and

(f) list any trusts disclosed under paragraph 21(1)(b.1).

Categorization of interests

(2) An interest in a partnership or corporation may be qualified in the summary by the word "nominal," "significant" or "controlling" if, in the opinion of the Commissioner, it is in the public interest to do so.

Items not to be disclosed

(3) The following shall not be set out in the summary:

(a) an asset or liability with a value of less than $10,000;

(b) a source of income of less than $10,000 during the 12 months before the relevant date;

(c) real property or immovables that the Member uses as a principal residence or uses principally for recreational purposes;

(d) personal property or movable property that the Member uses primarily for transportation, household, educational, recreational, social or aesthetic purposes;

(e) cash on hand or on deposit with a financial institution that is entitled to accept deposits;

(f) fixed-value securities issued or guaranteed by a government or by a government agency;

(g) a registered retirement savings plan that is not self-administered or self-directed;

(h) investments in a registered retirement savings plan that is self-administered or self-directed that would not be publicly disclosed under this section if held outside the plan;

(i) an interest in a pension plan, employee benefit plan, annuity or life insurance policy;

(j) an investment in an open-ended mutual fund;

(k) a guaranteed investment certificate or similar financial instrument;

(k.1) any information relating to the place or manner of employment of a son or daughter of the Member, or a son or daughter of the Member's spouse or common-law partner; and

(l) any other asset, liability or source of income that the Commissioner determines should not be disclosed because

(i) the information is not relevant to the purposes of this Code, or

(ii) a departure from the general principle of public disclosure is justified in the circumstances.

Evasion

25. A Member shall not take any action that has as its purpose the circumvention of the Member's obligations under this Code.

Opinions

Request for opinion

26(1) In response to a request in writing from a Member on any matter respecting the Member's obligations under this Code, the Commissioner shall provide the Member with a written opinion containing any recommendations that the Commissioner considers appropriate.

Confidentiality

(2) The opinion is confidential and may be made public only by the Member, with his or her written consent or if the Member has made the opinion public.

Opinion binding

(3) An opinion given by the Commissioner to a Member is binding on the Commissioner in relation to any subsequent consideration of the subject-matter of the opinion so long as all the relevant facts that were known to the Member were disclosed to the Commissioner.

Publication

(4) Nothing in this section prevents the Commissioner from publishing opinions for the guidance of Members, provided that no details are included that could identify the Member.

Timely response

(5) In this section and in any other situation in which a Member seeks an opinion from the Commissioner, the Commissioner shall provide the opinion in a timely manner.

Inquiries

Request for an inquiry

27(1) A Member who has reasonable grounds to believe that another Member has not complied with his or her obligations under this Code may request that the Commissioner conduct an inquiry into the matter.

Form of request

(2) The request shall be in writing, signed, and shall identify the alleged non-compliance and set out the reasonable grounds for that belief.

Direction by the House

(3) The House may, by way of resolution, direct the Commissioner to conduct an inquiry to determine whether a Member has complied with his or her obligations under this Code.

Notice

(3.1) The Commissioner shall forward without delay the request for an inquiry to the Member who is the subject of the request and afford the Member 30 days to respond.

Preliminary review

(3.2) The Commissioner shall:
(a) conduct a preliminary review of the request and the response to determine if an inquiry is warranted; and
(b) notify in writing both Members of the Commissioner's decision within 15 working days of receiving the response.

Initiative of Commissioner

(4) If, after giving the Member concerned written notice and 30 days to respond to the Commissioner's concerns, the Commissioner has reasonable grounds to believe that a Member has not complied with his or her obligations under this Code, the Commissioner may, on his or her own initiative, conduct an inquiry to determine whether the Member has complied with his or her obligations under this Code.

Public comments

(5.1) Other than to confirm that a request for an inquiry has been received, or that a preliminary review or inquiry has commenced, or been completed, the Commissioner shall make no public comments relating to any preliminary review or inquiry.

Non-meritorious requests

(6) If the Commissioner is of the opinion that a request for an inquiry was frivolous or vexatious or was not made in good faith, the Commissioner shall so state in dismissing the request in a report under section 28(6) and may recommend that further action be considered against the Member who made the request.

Inquiry to be private

(7) The Commissioner shall conduct an inquiry in private and with due dispatch, provided that at all appropriate stages throughout the inquiry the Commissioner shall give the Member reasonable opportunity to be present and to make representations to the Commissioner in writing or in person by counsel or by any other representative.

Cooperation

(8) Members shall cooperate with the Commissioner with respect to any inquiry.

Report to the House

28(1) Forthwith following an inquiry, the Commissioner shall report to the Speaker, who shall present the report to the House when it next sits.

Report to be public

(2) The report of the Commissioner shall be made available to the public upon tabling in the House, or, during a period of adjournment or prorogation, upon its receipt by the Speaker.

Report after dissolution

(3) During the period following a dissolution of Parliament, the Commissioner shall make the report public.

No contravention

(4) If the Commissioner concludes that there was no contravention of this Code, the Commissioner shall so state in the report.

Mitigated contravention

(5) If the Commissioner concludes that a Member has not complied with an obligation under this Code but that the Member took all reasonable measures to prevent the non-compliance, or that the non-compliance was trivial or occurred through inadvertence or an error in judgment made in good faith, the Commissioner shall so state in the report and may recommend that no sanction be imposed.

Sanctions

(6) If the Commissioner concludes that a Member has not complied with an obligation under this Code, and that none of the circumstances in subsection (5) apply, or is of the opinion that a request for an inquiry was frivolous or vexatious or was not made in good faith, the Commissioner shall so state in the report and may recommend appropriate sanctions.

Reasons

(7) The Commissioner shall include in the report reasons for any conclusions and recommendations.

General recommendations

(8) The Commissioner may include in his or her report any recommendations arising from the matter that concern the general interpretation of this Code and any recommendations for revision of this Code that the Commissioner considers relevant to its purpose and spirit.

Right to speak

(9) Within 10 sitting days after the tabling of the report of the Commissioner in the House of Commons, the Member who is the subject of the report shall have a right to make a statement in the House immediately following Question Period, provided that he or she shall not speak for more than 20 minutes.

Deemed concurrence

(10) A motion to concur in a report referred to in subsection (4) or (5) may be moved during Routine Proceedings. If no such motion has been moved and disposed of within 30 sitting days after the day on which the report was tabled, a motion to concur in the report shall be deemed to have been moved and adopted at the expiry of that time.

Report to be considered

(11) A motion respecting a report referred to in subsection (6) may be moved during Routine Proceedings, when it shall be considered for no more than two hours, after which the Speaker shall interrupt any proceedings then before the House and put forthwith and successively, without further debate or amendment, every question necessary to dispose of the motion. During debate on the motion, no Member shall speak more than once or longer than ten minutes.

Vote

(12) If no motion pursuant to subsection (11) has been previously moved and disposed of, a motion to concur in the report shall be deemed to have been moved on the 30th sitting day after the day on which the report was tabled, and the Speaker shall immediately put every question necessary to dispose of the motion.

Referral back

(13) At any point before the House has dealt with the report, whether by deemed disposition or otherwise, the House may refer it back to the Commissioner for further consideration, with instruction.

Suspension of inquiry

29(1) The Commissioner shall immediately suspend the inquiry into a matter if
    (a) there are reasonable grounds to believe that the Member has committed an offence under an Act of Parliament, in which case the Commissioner shall notify the proper authorities of the Commissioner's belief; or
    (b) it is discovered that:
        (i) the act or omission under investigation is also the subject of an investigation to determine if an offence under an Act of Parliament has been committed, or
        (ii) a charge has been laid with respect to that act or omission.

Inquiry continued

(2) The Commissioner shall not continue his or her inquiry until the other investigation or the charge regarding the act or omission has been finally disposed of.

2. Parliament's Law-Making Procedure

If Parliament is free to determine its own procedure and pass laws as it pleases within its constitutional zone of jurisdiction, what rules does it, in fact, follow? The law-making process is governed mostly by the rules of procedure of each chamber of Parliament—for example, the standing orders of the House of Commons. Consider the following description of the means by which Parliament makes laws.

House of Commons, *Précis of Procedure*
(Ottawa: House of Commons, 2003)

11. The Legislative Process

There are two main types of bills: public and private. In general, a public bill is concerned with matters of public policy, while a private bill relates to matters of a particular interest or benefit to a person or persons, including corporations. Because the legislative process of a private bill is somewhat different, it is discussed separately at the end of this chapter.

11(a) Public Bills

There are two types of public bills: government public bills introduced and sponsored by a Minister, and private Members' public bills sponsored by a private Member. These may be further divided into those that are of a financial nature and those that are not. A bill for the appropriation of any part of the public revenue or for taxation must be accompanied by a Royal Recommendation. Such bills require additional procedures for passage in the House. ...

Government bills originating in the House are numbered from C-1 to C-200 in the order in which they are introduced. They may be considered each day during Government Orders in any sequence the Government determines.

Private Members' public bills, on the other hand, may be considered only during Private Members' Hour, a period limited to one hour per day, five days per week (Mondays from 11:00 a.m. to 12:00 noon, Tuesdays, Wednesdays and Thursdays from 5:30 p.m. to 6:30 p.m., and Fridays from 1:30 p.m. to 2:30 p.m.). ... Such bills originating in the House are numbered from C-201 to C-1000 in the order in which they are introduced, and are considered in the order established by a draw and as set forth in the Standing Orders. ...

Before a bill becomes law, it goes through the following stages: (1) Once the appropriate notice has been given, a Member is given leave of the House to introduce the bill; (2) the bill is read a first time and printed; (3) the bill is read a second time; (4) the bill is referred to committee; (5) the bill is considered in committee and reported back to the House; (6) the House concurs in the bill at report stage; (7) the bill is read a third time and passed by the House; (8) the bill goes through stages in the Senate approximately the same as those in the House; (9) finally, the bill receives Royal Assent.

In February 1994, new rules were adopted to give the House more flexibility in dealing with legislation. While all bills must still go through the same stages, the new rules allow the House to vary the order in which bills pass through these stages. The new options for the legislative process are described in section 11(c).

11(b) Stages of a Bill—The Traditional Legislative Process

Introduction

To introduce a public bill, a Member must give 48 hours' written notice and then, by motion, obtain leave to introduce the bill. This motion is automatically adopted without debate, amendment or question put. A private Member introducing a bill then will normally make a short speech explaining the purpose of his or her bill. Normally, a Minister introducing a government bill does not speak at this time. However, the Standing Orders were modified in 2001 changing the order of Routine Proceedings so that "Introduction of Government Bills" comes just before "Statements by Ministers." This change allows Ministers to make a brief explanation of a bill in the House following its introduction. …

First Reading

First reading follows immediately and is also automatically adopted without debate, amendment or question put. The order for the printing of the bill is included in the motion. Following that, the Speaker asks: "When shall the bill be read a second time?" to which the response is generally: "At the next sitting of the House." This formality allows the bill to be placed on the *Order Paper* for second reading. It is also at this stage that a specific bill number is assigned to legislation.

Second Reading

Second reading is the most important stage in the passage of a bill. It is then that the principle and object of the bill are debated and either accepted or rejected. The clauses of the bill are not discussed in detail at this stage.

Three types of amendments may be proposed to the motion for second reading. The first is the six months' hoist: "That Bill [number and title] be not now read a second time but that it be read a second time this day six months hence." If the amendment is adopted, the bill is withdrawn for the remainder of the current session. The second type is the reasoned amendment, which expresses specific reasons for opposing second reading. Finally, an amendment may be introduced to refer the subject-matter to a committee before the principle of the bill is approved. Such an amendment would read: "That the bill be not now read a second time but that the order be discharged, the bill withdrawn and the subject-matter referred to the Standing Committee on … ." No amendments may be made to the bill itself at this stage.

Committee Stage

The Standing Orders provide that a bill be read twice and then referred to a committee. Appropriation bills, authorizing the withdrawal of funds from the Consolidated Revenue Fund, are referred to a Committee of the Whole [a plenary of all the members of the Commons]; other types of bills are generally referred to a standing, special or legislative committee specified in the motion for second reading. The committee then considers the bill clause-by-clause. Amendments to the text of the bill are considered at this stage.

Before beginning clause-by-clause study, the committee usually hears the Member or Minister sponsoring the bill and may also receive testimony from outside witnesses. Amendments in committee must be in keeping with the principle of the bill as agreed to at second reading in the House. Generally, the committee may make amendments to any part of a bill (*i.e.*, the title, preamble, clauses or schedules). Clauses and/or schedules may be omitted and new ones added. After a committee has completed its consideration of a bill, it orders that the bill be reported to the House.

Report Stage

The House undertook a thorough revision of its legislative process in 1968, which resulted in the modern rules where bills are sent to committee for detailed examination. The committee's study is followed by an opportunity for further consideration in the House in what is known as report stage. At this stage, Members—particularly those who were not on the committee—may propose amendments, after giving notice, to the text of the bill as it was reported by the committee. Unlike committee stage where the bill is considered clause-by-clause, there is no debate at report stage unless notices of amendment are given, and debate is to be relevant to these amendments. …

When deliberations at report stage are concluded, a motion is moved that the bill (with any amendments) be concurred in. The question is put immediately, without amendment or debate. If no amendments are put down for consideration at report stage, this stage becomes more of a formality, and report and third reading stages may then occur on the same day.

Third Reading

Debate at third reading begins when the Order of the Day is called, the motion being "That Bill … be now read a third time and do pass." The basic principles governing the acceptability of amendments at third reading are that they be strictly relevant to the bill and do not contradict the principle of the bill as passed at second reading. The same types of amendments as may be proposed at second reading may also be proposed at third reading; that is, the six months' hoist and the reasoned amendment. In addition, an amendment may be proposed to refer the bill back to committee to be further amended in a specific area or to reconsider a certain clause or clauses.

Passage by the Senate

In order for a bill to receive Royal Assent and become law, it must be passed in identical form by both Houses. Accordingly, after a bill has been passed by the House of Commons, a message is sent to the Senate requesting that the bill be passed by the Upper Chamber, where procedures for passage of a bill are similar to those in the House. If the Senate passes the bill without any amendment, a message to that effect is sent to inform the House of Commons and unless it contains financial provisions, the bill is not returned to the House.

If there are amendments to the bill, the Senate communicates this to the House by message. Twenty-four hours' written notice is required for any motion respecting Senate amendments to a bill. In the House, consideration of Senate amendments appears on the Orders of the Day and proceeds under a motion moved by the sponsor of the bill. If the Houses wishes to agree to the Senate amendments, the motion is as follows: "That the amendments made by the Senate to Bill ... be now read a second time and concurred in." If the motion is adopted, a message is sent informing the Senate accordingly, and the bill is returned to the Senate for Royal Assent.

If the House does not wish to agree to the Senate amendments, it adopts a motion stating the reasons for its disagreement, which it communicates to the Senate. If the Senate wishes the amendments to stand nonetheless, it sends a message to this effect to the House, which then accepts or rejects them. If it is impossible for an agreement to be reached by exchanging messages, the House that has possession of the bill may ask that a conference be held, although this practice has fallen into disuse.

Royal Assent and Proclamation

The *Constitution Act, 1867* states that the approval of the Crown, signified by Royal Assent, is required for any bill to become law after passage by both Houses. The ceremony of Royal Assent is one of the oldest of all parliamentary proceedings and brings together the three constituent parts of Parliament: the Crown (represented by the Governor General), the Senate, and the House of Commons. Until recently, Royal Assent was always given to bills by means of the traditional ceremony outlined below. However, in 2002, legislation was passed providing for an alternative procedure for signifying Royal Assent to bills. Bill S-34, assented to on the June 4, 2002 and now Chapter 15 of the Statutes of Canada, permits Royal Assent to be given by written procedure as well as by the traditional ceremony.

Royal Assent is given to a bill when it has been passed in exactly the same form by both Houses; it is at this stage that a bill becomes law. The bill comes into force on the day of Assent, unless otherwise provided in the bill itself. Provision is sometimes made for coming into force on a certain day or a day to be fixed by order of the Governor in Council, and parts of bills may be brought into force at different times.

During the traditional ceremony, the Governor General may appear in person to give Royal Assent to major pieces of legislation and at prorogation. However, a Deputy in the person of the Chief Justice of Canada or a Puisne Judge of the Supreme Court normally represents the Governor General at other times. On all occasions, the Speaker or the Deputy Speaker is present at the bar of the Senate Chamber where the ceremony takes place.

The office of the Governor General, acting at the request of the Government, notifies the House by letter usually on the day of the event or one or two days before Royal Assent is to be given. The message is read by the Speaker to the House. It is a notice only and does not constitute a summons, which comes when the Usher of the Black Rod appears in the Chamber to request the attendance of Members in the Senate.

A quorum is not necessary for the Speaker to take the Chair when Black Rod is at the door; if the House is sitting in Committee of the Whole, the Speaker immediately takes the Chair. After knocking, entering and delivering the summons, Black Rod returns to the Senate, followed by the Sergeant-at-Arms with the Mace, the Speaker, the Table Officers and the Members, all of whom assemble at the bar of the Senate.

The ceremony for Royal Assent consists of the reading by the Senate Clerk, officially styled Clerk of the Parliaments, of the titles of the bill or bills to be approved. The formula of assent is then pronounced by the Senate Clerk on behalf of the Crown's representative. … The Clerk of the Parliaments, in the name of the Sovereign, then thanks the House for its loyalty and benevolence and announces the Royal Assent. At the conclusion of the ceremony, the Speaker returns to the House and reports what has just occurred. The proceeding usually takes 15 or 20 minutes, after which the House resumes the business interrupted by the arrival of Black Rod or adjourns the sitting.

The written procedure for signifying Royal Assent to bills adopted in 2002, preserves the traditional ceremony outlined above by requiring that it be used twice in each calendar year, including for the first appropriation bill in each session. An Act that has been given Royal Assent in written form is deemed assented to on the day on which the two Houses of Parliament have been notified of the written declaration by their respective Speakers.

11(c) Stages of a Bill—Variations on the Traditional Legislative Process

All bills that come before the House of Commons must, in some way, pass through the same legislative stages in order to become law. Amendments to the Standing Orders adopted in February 1994 added two new options to the traditional legislative process. …

(i) Committee Prepares and Brings in a Bill

The Standing Orders provide that a motion to appoint or instruct a committee to prepare a bill may be moved by a Minister or by a private Member. However, the procedures to be followed in each instance are not entirely the same.

A Minister who wants to instruct a committee to prepare and bring in a bill must give 48 hours' written notice of the motion he or she intends to move. Once the notice period has passed, the motion will be placed on the Order Paper under "Government Orders." When it is called by the government it may be debated for a maximum of 90 minutes, after which the Speaker will interrupt debate and put all questions necessary to dispose of the motion. …

The adoption by the House of a motion to concur in a report of a committee instructed to prepare and bring in a bill is an order to bring in the bill. …

(ii) Committee Study of a Bill Before Second Reading

Tradition dictates that the adoption of the motion for second reading of a bill defines the principle contained in the bill and therefore limits the scope of the amendments that may be made to the bill in committee and at report stage. On occasions where the House has wanted to expand the purposes of the bill after second reading, it has generally been unable to do so because, with the adoption of the second reading motion, the principle of the bill had already been defined. By referring a bill to committee before the principle has been adopted by the House, the House gives itself more flexibility to review and fine-tune the legislation. In recognition of this, changes to the Standing Orders adopted in February 1994 defined the procedures by which the House could refer a bill to a committee for detailed examination before second reading.

A Minister wishing to move that a government bill be referred to a committee for study before second reading will, immediately after the reading of the Order of the Day for the second reading of the bill, and after notifying representatives of the opposition parties, propose a motion that the bill be referred to a standing, special or legislative committee. Under the rules of the House, there may be up to three hours of debate on the motion, the motion is not amendable, and there is a specific speaking order for Members of the different parties. At the end of three hours, or when no other Member rises to speak, the Speaker will put the question to the House. If the motion is adopted, the bill will be referred to the committee for study.

Generally speaking, the committee will conduct its clause-by-clause examination of the bill subject to the same rules and procedures governing the committee study of bills after second reading. However, the scope of the amendments that can be made to the bill is much wider. At the conclusion of its study, the committee will report the bill to the House, with or without amendments. The report stage of this bill cannot be taken up until three sitting days after the bill is reported to the House.

When the bill is reported back to the House, what follows is essentially a combined report and second reading stage. Members of the House can offer amendments to the legislation, just as at report stage after second reading, and the same procedures for dealing with amendments will be followed. … When the proceedings at report stage have been concluded, a motion "That the bill, as amended, be concurred in at report stage and be read a second time" or "That the bill be concurred in at report stage and read a second time" will be put and disposed of without debate or amendment. When the bill has been concurred in and read a second time, it shall be set down for third reading and passage at the next sitting of the House.

11(d) Private Bills

A bill designed to exempt an individual or group of individuals from the application of the law is a private bill. Private bills are subject to special rules in both Houses of Parliament, however, most private bills originate in the Senate where the fees and charges imposed on the promoter are less.

The progress of private legislation as prescribed by the Standing Orders is somewhat different than for public bills in that a private bill is introduced by means of a petition signed by the interested parties and presented in the House by a Member who has agreed to sponsor it. "Parliamentary agents" are authorized to promote private bills and find sponsors; Members are forbidden to act as parliamentary agents or to accept payment for presenting bills. The petition must be favourably reported upon by either the Examiner of Petitions or the Standing Committee on Procedure and House Affairs. The sponsor must deposit a printed copy of the bill with the Clerk of the House.

After approval of the petition, private bills are tabled, read a first time, printed, and ordered for second reading. Private bills from the Senate accompanied by messages requesting passage are deemed to have been read a first time and are ordered for second reading. Such bills are automatically placed on the order of precedence established for Private Members' Business and are automatically made votable. As in the case of a public bill, debate at the second reading is on the general principle and expediency of the bill.

Notice of private bills must be posted in the lobbies of the Parliament buildings before consideration in a committee, but the procedures for hearing witnesses and proposing amendments in committee are otherwise virtually identical for public and private bills. However, when an amendment that might harm parties concerned is moved to a private bill, adequate notice must be given, and both the promoters of the bill and those opposed to it may be represented by counsel. Another difference in procedure gives an extra vote to the chairman of a committee considering a private bill: he or she votes to break a tie like any other chairman, but also votes on the motion like the other members.

The committee must report to the House on all bills referred to it. Amendments may be made to the bill, lack of evidence to support the preamble may be noted, and adherence to the rules governing notice may be commented on. Consideration of the report by the House is the same for private and public bills, as are the rules governing third reading.

Any further amendments adopted by the Senate are referred to the committee that considered the bill initially. If accepted, the amendments are read in the House a second time and, once agreed to, are returned to the Senate with a message informing that Chamber accordingly. If the committee reports unfavourably, the House may continue to insist on its own amendments in its message to the other Chamber. If an impasse occurs, a conference between the two Chambers may be requested.

CHAPTER FIVE

The Exercise of Executive Authority

Notwithstanding the absence of a rigid separation-of-powers doctrine in Canada, it is still useful to speak about a distinct executive branch of government. The executive branch refers to those institutions in government that are responsible for implementing and enforcing laws, whether those laws are formulated by the legislature or, in the case of the common law, by the judiciary.

Following from that broad definition, the executive branch is not a single institution, but rather it consists of a highly varied assortment of institutions and officials ranging from constitutionally recognized positions, such as the governor general and the Privy Council (and in effect, Cabinet), to entities that operate at arm's length from the formal government apparatus, but nevertheless perform governmental functions. Examples of the latter include independent boards and tribunals, professional regulatory bodies, and Crown corporations. It is not uncommon for legal commentators to draw a distinction between the executive branch, consisting of those officials with a direct connection to the government, sometimes referred to as the "political executive," and the wider constellation of administrative institutions and officials. This chapter uses the term "executive" in a broad sense and interchangeably with the term "administrative."

While the institutional arrangements used for the exercise of executive authority are wide ranging, a coherent set of legal principles establishing the boundaries of executive powers and the manner by which executive powers are to be exercised has developed. This body of jurisprudence is referred to as administrative law, and in the common law provinces is largely (although not exclusively) a creature of the common law. In Quebec, the structure of the executive is similar to that found in the other common law jurisdictions in Canada, although the field of administrative law in Quebec, following the French tradition, is much more inclusive, covering matters such as government contracts, public sector employment, and public finance that are not typically considered as part of the core of administrative law in common law systems.

At the heart of administrative law is a requirement that government officials exercise their powers in furtherance of public, not private, interests. As we suggested in the prior chapter, a similar expectation underlies the exercise of legislative powers, but in the case of legislators public preferences are made known, and the creation of public policy is legitimized, through democratic processes. However, with some notable exceptions, most administrative officials are not elected.

In cases where administrative officials exercise narrow powers that are carefully defined through legislation, the democratic legitimacy of administrative decisions is derived from the close relationship between administrative officials and the legislature. In circumstances where administrative officials exercise broader discretion, there are much greater concerns in relation to whether administrative discretion is being exercised in a manner that is fair to those affected by the decision and in a way that has sufficient regard to the public interest. To a significant degree the legal rules that have developed in administrative law have arisen so as to constrain the exercise of administrative discretion in ways that respect the intentions of the legislative branch and promote outcomes that take the public interest into account.

This chapter identifies and describes the various institutions and officials that make up the executive branch of government and the roles that administrative institutions play in the implementation and development of public policy in Canada. In section I, we place the discussion that follows in historical context by highlighting the notable rise of the "administrative state," and the swelling of executive size and powers. In section II, we define the executive branch and examine the functions of the Crown, the ministry, the public service, independent administrative agencies, Crown corporations, municipalities, and enforcement officials. In section III, we highlight the sources of executive powers, and some of the legal limitations associated with their exercise. Section IV describes the principal roles and functions of executive authority. The discussion on the limits to the exercise of delegated authority is continued in chapter 8, which addresses the legal rules respecting the obligation on administrative decision-makers to act fairly, and the rules controlling the exercise of discretion. As these rules also engage questions regarding the supervisory role of the courts, these issues are best considered in the context of judicial review of administrative action in chapter 8.

I. THE RISE OF THE ADMINISTRATIVE STATE IN CANADA

The executive branch of government is not in itself a recent development. Indeed, the *Constitution Act, 1867* recognizes the formal (and rudimentary) institutions of the federal executive in ss. 9 through 16 and the provincial executive in ss. 58 through 68. At this early stage of the development of the federal and provincial governance structures, the role of government was conceived in much narrower terms. As a consequence, the executive branches of the federal and provincial governments were both smaller in size and much less extensive in their scope. However, as the excerpt below describes, over the past century the role of government has undergone a significant transformation. As the role of government expanded, so did the need for a more decentralized, expert-driven bureaucracy. One of the implications of this transformation is a more attenuated link between decision-makers and elected officials.

Law Reform Commission of Canada, "Independent Administrative Agencies"
Working Paper 25 (Ottawa: Law Reform Commission of Canada, 1980)

The emergence of a complex federal administrative structure in Canada, including independent agencies which refine and apply the law under the aegis of special statutory powers, is not the product of a well-defined approach or design. The growth of this structure is best described as an aspect of the evolution of government rather than as a planned constitutional development. It takes its shape from pragmatic responses to emerging problems over the years. In some situations, especially in the early years, the choice of certain types of governmental bodies to perform particular functions may have been the product of a reasoned general approach. But the choice in many cases seems to have been *ad hoc*. The selection of a non-departmental rather than a departmental body to regulate, or an administrative tribunal rather than the courts to adjudicate, appears to have been influenced, more often than not, by the exigencies of the case and existing institutional precedents than by an overall plan or any particular attitudes respecting one type of governmental body rather than another.

· · ·

A. The Traditional Legal Context

Government in a general sense includes two functions—law-making and administration. Under our system, Parliament makes the laws which are carried forward by the executive and the public service. Both functions, legislative and executive, are actively directed by the governing party through the Cabinet. Ours is a system of responsible government which is based on the concept that the government collectively, and Ministers of the Crown individually, must account to Parliament for governmental action under their control.

The courts function independently as arbiters of the law in accordance with fundamental constitutional relationships which have evolved over the centuries and were inherited from Great Britain. Some of these constitutional relationships are reflected in the *British North America Act*, 1867; others—such as the independence of the courts—are firmly established by custom or tradition. Fundamental too is the "rule of law," that society shall be governed through principled decision-making rather than by the arbitrary fiat of an individual or group. While Parliament, its role as legislator with the limits of federal jurisdiction, is supreme in the sense that it can easily repeal or amend any ordinary law, in practice it normally feels compelled to respect the basic laws or constitutional conventions about such matters as the relationships between the legislature, the executive and the courts. These well-accepted propositions (which, while trite, can stand repetition from time to time) take us towards a less well defined area between law and politics—the field of public administration.

· · ·

Today, it is impossible for elected representatives effectively to supervise all aspects of the public business. Substantial areas of government are managed by officials who are only remotely responsible to Ministers or to Parliament and who have little direct contact with the public. Industries are controlled and regulated, taxes are levied, welfare grants are dispensed, and land is expropriated by bureaucracies which are never required to stand for election. This expansion of government has conferred on government appointees and public servants great legislative, administrative and sometimes judicial power. The courts have attempted to adapt the principles of administrative law, first developed through judicial review of lower tribunals at a time when Justices of the Peace were still the main administrators in the English countryside, to contemporary conditions where comprehensive standards are needed to limit or structure the powers of public officials who enjoy wide authority under delegated legislation. Given the scope of current governmental operations and the degree of discretionary power exercised by administrative authorities, it is clear that sources of law additional to judicial ones will have to be depended upon if administrative law is to be bolstered to meet existing needs and to ensure that governmental action is carried out fairly, effectively and responsibly.

B. *The Expansion of Government*

. . .

The need for novel administrative structures reflecting the character of government functions in a young and developing country first became apparent in Canada in connection with the nascent railway industry. Even before Confederation the Province of Canada had resorted to a type of nondepartmental regulatory body when it enacted a *Railway Act* in 1851 under which regulatory functions, principally the approval of rates, were assigned to a Board of Railway Commissioners, although in fact the functions were assumed by four Cabinet Ministers. This device, known after Confederation as the Railway Committee of the Privy Council, persisted until 1903.

However, a debate over whether Cabinet Ministers should be replaced by full-time semi-independent officials began as early as the 1880's. The idea of establishing a railway regulatory commission to take over the function of rate-making from the Cabinet committee was considered but rejected in the Galt Royal Commission Report of 1888. That Commission was reluctant to recommend the model of the recently established United States Interstate Commerce Commission, which it regarded as untried, and ventured the view that a commission format was inconsistent with the Canadian system of responsible government, ignoring the fact that the British Parliament was also then experimenting with a commission model. But the problems associated with the employment of Cabinet Ministers as regulators did not go unnoticed by the Galt Commission. The fact that Railway Committee members served only part-time and were based in Ottawa, their lack of expertise and their vulnerability to political pressure were sensed as limitations on their effectiveness.

. . .

Generally, there was less inclination at that time to involve the federal public service in complex programs. To a large extent the public service performed ministerial functions and gave support to more direct public service programs offered in the provinces. More specifically, the tradition of patronage in the public service of the day gave rise to fears that designated departmental personnel might have inappropriate backgrounds or lack the technical capacity to deal with the kinds of issues being raised in the context of railway regulation. Also, adjudicative functions were largely foreign to departments, and the considerations which supported the removal of these duties from the Cabinet Committee probably precluded as well their being vested in a department. In retrospect, it is interesting to speculate on the question whether the present *pot-pourri* of independent agencies would exist today if a professional and non-partisan Canadian federal public service had been available at the turn of the century to take up the slack from Cabinet ministers.

. . .

The *Railway Act* of 1903 … opted for a new administrative agency, the Board of Railway Commissioners, which appears to have served as a model for later legislative initiatives vesting all kinds of governmental functions in independent agencies. It is noteworthy, however, that the Act provided for an important measure of judicial and political control. There was an appeal to the courts on questions of law or jurisdiction, and the Governor in Council was authorized, either on petition or of its own motion, to vary or rescind any order, decision or rule of the Board. Thorny issues about the appropriate institutional relationships to establish between Cabinet, independent agencies, and individual ministers in charge of related departments still remain to be adequately dealt with today.

Within six years Canada again used a regulatory commission model to establish by treaty, jointly with the United States, the International Joint Commission to replace the International Waterways Commission, which had been a purely investigatory body. It marked a further important step in establishing a framework for government regulation in Canada similar in many respects to the type concurrently being set up in the United States. The practice of appointing experts to decide rather than merely to advise was becoming firmly established. There was much faith displayed at the time in the recruitment by government of specialists, especially those with backgrounds in business affairs, to bring their knowledge to bear on certain economic and political issues. The approach was again followed in 1912, when the *Canada Grain Act* established a Board of Grain Commissioners charged with the administration of terminal warehouses and generally all matters related to the inspection, weighing, trading and storage of grain.

This was a period during our history when marked changes were taking place in the economy and in society at large. By 1900 the major economic and political problems which had precipitated Confederation had been resolved, the frontiers had been established and guaranteed, transportation and communication links had been forged and our national political and legal institutions had been established. During the first part of this century there was intense economic development, stimulated by waves of immigration, integration with the American economy, the assumption of responsibility in international affairs and the forced expansion of World War I. Immigration, which had been a mere 49,000 in 1901, rose to a phenomenal 402,000 in 1913. At the same time people were moving to the cities, especially Montreal, Toronto, Vancouver and Winnipeg.

C. *World War I—Growth of Government Controls*

With the advent of World War I and the commitment of Canada to the war effort, there was marked intervention in the economy by the federal government, including rent and price control, the prevention of hoarding, and the control of the marketing of Canada's principal products. This led to the creation of many administrative agencies such as the Board of Grain Supervisors (succeeded in 1919 by the Canadian Wheat Board), the Food Control Board (later the Canada Food Board), the Wage Trade Board, and municipal Fair Price Committees.

The government also took major initiatives in the health and welfare fields for the first time, although certain measures tangential to Agriculture, Immigration and Indian Affairs operations had been previously adopted. A Board of Pension Commissioners was established in 1916, to be replaced by the existing Canadian Pension Commission in 1933. The Department of Soldiers Civil Re-establishment was created in 1918, and the Department of Health in 1919. They were consolidated in 1928, only to be split again into Veterans Affairs and National Health and Welfare in 1944.

To finance the expansion of the public sector, direct taxation was introduced, first under the rubric of an excess business profits tax in 1916, and then in the much more significant form of an income tax on individuals and corporations in 1917. The income tax has greatly increased since then, and has provided guaranteed means for bureaucratic growth.

It was also during the War, fifteen years after the installation of the first major regulatory agency, that the Union Government under Robert Borden placed the federal civil service on a truly professional footing by the *Civil Service Act*, 1918. The Civil Service Commission, which had been given statutory powers over personnel in 1908, saw these powers expanded under the new legislation. At this point, the Commission assumed responsibility to pass upon the qualifications of candidates for admission to and classification, transfer and promotion in, the civil service. For the first time, it was explicitly provided that, save in exceptional cases provided for under the statute, neither the Governor in Council nor any minister, officer of the Crown, board or commission would have the power to appoint or promote anyone to a position in the civil service. It should be noted, however, that most independent agencies created in the years after the War were exempted from the provisions of the Act.

A final significant step taken by the Union Government was the passage of the *Public Service Rearrangement and Transfer of Duties Act* in 1918. As expanded in 1925, the Act provides that the Governor in Council may transfer any powers, duties or functions or the control or supervision of any part of the public service from one Minister to any other Minister, or from one department or portion of the public service to another. The Governor in Council may also amalgamate any two or more departments under one Minister of the Crown and under one deputy minister. Although a final section of the Act provided that all orders made under the authority of the Act must be tabled in the House of Commons, since the *Regulations Act* was passed in 1950 no such orders are required to be tabled in the House. In recent years the executive has carried out numerous administrative reorganizations with minimal consultation. However, the practice has remained that any new departments or agencies have to be established by statute and, at least as a matter of courtesy, major reorganizations of existing departments and agencies have been ratified through legislation.

D. The Inter-War Period

. . .

The period following the War until the depression of the "30's" was one in which the federal government generally refrained from extensive new activities. A contributing factor to this quiescence was that the government was burdened with war debts and the obligations resulting from its absorption of the railways which became the Canadian National Railways (CNR). This latter step was to serve as a model for other public sector enterprises to become at least partially integrated with Canadian governmental structures. By 1939, fifteen Crown-owned companies had been created to operate in the fields of rail, ship and air transportation, banking and credit, harbour administration and commodity marketing.

The rapid dismantling of war-time controls should not obscure their long-term effects. Professional civil servants had acquired expertise in performing complex tasks which far outstripped the involvement of their predecessors who, only a few years before, had been primarily involved in merely ministerial functions. The stage was set for departments to assume, in the long run, functions which up to that time might have been assigned only to specialist boards or commissions. As the Rowell-Sirois Report put it:

> People saw how governments could mould their lives and civil servants learned how to do it. …
> The belief grew that governments could and should use their powers to improve social condi-
> tions. The war-time experience with the regulation and direction of enterprise was an import-
> ant factor in bringing on the wide extension of government control which economic and social
> chaos seemed to make desirable.

Economic and social pressures, this time in the form of the Great Depression, comprised the motivating factor behind renewed federal legislative efforts in the "30's." The flurry of Canadian "New Deal" legislation in 1935 saw the creation of a number of regulatory and adjudicatory agencies, but several of these became entangled in constitutional difficulties. One such casualty was federal legislation to provide unemployment insurance, but the federal government later re-enacted legislation in this field, following a constitutional amendment in 1940, to create a commission with tripartite labour, business and govern-ment representation to oversee the functioning of a special Unemployment Insurance Account contributed to by employers and employees. Other casualties included several measures governing labour relations. Constitutional difficulties also frustrated several joint federal-provincial attempts to regulate marketing. Ultimately, various techniques, such as administrative delegation, were devised to overcome these difficulties, but these had cer-tainly not been extensively developed when World War II again pushed constitutional dis-tinctions into the background.

By no means were all the Crown entities created at this time unconstitutional, however. For example, the Canadian Broadcasting Corporation (CBC), created in 1932, regulated private radio and television broadcasting along with carrying on its own activities in the field until 1958. At that time an independent government agency, the Board of Broadcast Governors, later to give way in turn to the Canadian Radio Television Commission, was created to regulate the broadcasting industry. Administrative reforms also continued in areas of activity where the federal government had been active previously. In 1931, the Tariff Board was created as an independent agency to carry out advisory and quasi-judicial func-tions: first, it was to conduct inquiries into matters relating to tariffs and trade; second, it was to assume appellate functions previously handled by a departmental committee under the Minister of Finance which had been called the Board of Customs. In 1935, the Canadian Wheat Board was given the responsibility for marketing wheat in interprovincial and export trade. In 1936 the National Harbours Board was created, and the Departments of Railway and Canals and the Marine were merged with the Civil Aviation Branch of the Department of National Defence in a new Department of Transport. Trans-Canada Airlines, the precur-sor of Air Canada, was created in 1938. Also in 1938, the Board of Railway Commissioners, which had survived the vicissitudes of time and political criticism, was reconstituted as the Board of Transport Commissioners.

E. World War II and Its Aftermath

World War II again saw the federal government adopting close and detailed control over the economy. In many cases the chosen instrument of control was a Crown Corporation which itself "went into business"—for example, Eldorado Mining and Refining, the Polymer Corporation, the Industrial Development Bank, and Defence Construction Ltd., to name a few. The technique of control through public ownership rather than regulation was, of course, not new, and has continued to be used. One has only to mention the CNR, the CBC and Air Canada to appreciate the importance of this type of entity. The distinction between government economic controls through the activities of Crown corporations, as opposed to controls through the use of regulatory mechanisms, is not always so clear-cut as these instances would seem to suggest, however. Thus such hybrid equities as the Bank of Canada and the Canadian Wheat Board combine both public ownership and regulatory functions.

· · ·

Governmental organizations continued to proliferate in the post-war period. Further specialized bodies such as the Atomic Energy Control Board (1946) were set up. Canadian involvement in the setting up of NATO, the maintenance of a Department of Defence Production and the commitment of about one-third of the federal budget to defence matters, led to a substantial expansion of the federal public service during the early years of the Cold War.

During the economic booms of 1946-49 and the Korean War period, a network of marketing boards spread across the country. When, in 1952, the Supreme Court of Canada decided in the case of *PEI Potato Marketing Board v. Willis*, [1952] 2 SCR 392, 4 DLR (2d) 146, that regulatory power within the jurisdiction of the federal government could validly be delegated to boards created and operated by a provincial government, and vice versa, by implication this encouraged the creation of yet more independent administrative agencies, in the interests of cooperative federalism.

Welfare state activities blossomed. At the federal level, the Family Allowances Plan (1944), the Old Age Security Pension (1952) and the Canada Pension Plan (1965) joined the earlier established veterans' allowance and unemployment insurance benefits programs. Government intervention was also marked in respect of disposition and use of manpower, perhaps encouraged by large waves of immigrants. More recently, a rising tide of regulations, service and subsidization endeavours has added to the growth of government to the point where at least forty per cent of gross national income is expended on state-related activities. The number of civil servants has at least doubled since the end of World War II. In the words of John H. Deutsch writing in 1968:

> The life of the public service is closely bound up with the role of the state in society. One of the most striking features of the history of our time has been the large and persistent increase in the activities of government. Over the hundred-year span of Canada's history, the changes have been truly remarkable. During this period, Canada's working population has increased about seven and a half times, but the number of employees in the public service of the federal government has risen by approximately one hundred times. In 1867, less than one out of every hundred of the working population was employed by all governments—federal, provincial, and municipal. Today at least one in every eight is on a government payroll. At the time of Confederation, total government expenditures were in the order of 5 per cent of the total gross national production. Today, they are in the order of 32 per cent.

Since the Law Reform Commission of Canada published this report in 1980, the trend of growing size and pervasiveness of government activity has continued. In 2009, total public sector employment was in excess of 3.5 million, out of a total employment of over 16 million, and total government expenditures exceeded $600 billion compared with a gross domestic product of approximately $1.3 trillion. In the 1990s there was some movement toward the privatization of government services. This trend saw the government divest ownership in Crown corporations such as Air Canada and Petro-Canada, and also saw the increased delivery of government services by private actors.

II. THE EXECUTIVE BRANCH DEFINED

A. The Crown

Section 9 of the *Constitution Act, 1867* states: "The Executive Government and Authority of and over Canada is hereby declared to continue and be vested in the Queen." As a formal matter then, the entire authority of the executive branch is vested in the monarchy. Consequently, "the Crown," as a symbol of the monarchy, is a reference to the executive itself.

The Crown is the formal legal entity of government and, like other entities possessing a legal personality, the Crown is the bearer of both legal rights and legal obligations. In this regard, the "Crown" has the capacity to own property, enter into contracts and to sue and be sued. In the context of federalism, the Crown is divisible in the sense that the governments of the provinces and the federal government are each themselves distinct legal entities, notwithstanding the identification of each with the same monarch. Consequently, legal obligations attaching to one level of government cannot be attributed to another level of government by virtue of their respective executive powers being rooted in a common monarch. In order to clearly identify which executive body is being referred to in legal and other official documents, it is common to refer to the "Crown in the right of Canada," in the case of the federal government, and the "Crown in the right" of New Brunswick or Alberta, as the case may be, in relation to provincial governments.

The identification of the government with the Crown speaks only to the formal legal status of the executive. The Queen herself does not exercise authority over matters of public policy in Canada, or for that matter in the United Kingdom. First, by Letters Patent issued by George VI in 1947, the governor general is "to exercise all powers and authorities lawfully belonging to Us [the monarch] in respect of Canada." Consequently, it is commonplace in both the *Constitution Act, 1867* and in many provincial statutes to see references to powers exercised by the "Governor General in Council," or the "Lieutenant General in Council."

However, in a system of representative government like Canada's, the Crown's representative is not as potent as these provisions imply. As discussed in chapter 4, the Queen appoints the governor general and lieutenant governors to act as her representatives, although by constitutional convention these appointments are now made on the advice of the prime minister, whose advice the Queen is bound to follow. In turn, the governor general and the lieutenant governors for each province are bound by constitutional convention to exercise their powers with the advice of the Cabinet of their respective government. (This requirement is also alluded to, in part, in the *Constitution Act, 1867* in ss. 12 and 65 addressing the powers of the governor general and the lieutenant governor, respectively.)

As discussed further below, "Cabinet" is the collective decision-making committee comprising the prime minister (or premier) and his or her ministers. However, the 1867 Act never actually mentions "Cabinet." Instead, the reference is to the "Queen's Privy Council." Thus, s. 13 provides that references to the "Governor General in Council" in the 1867 Act "shall be construed as referring to the Governor General acting by and with the Advice of the Queen's Privy Council for Canada." (An identical provision is found in the federal *Interpretation Act*, guiding interpretation of federal statutes.) Under s. 11 of the 1867 Act, the Privy Council is a body to "aid and advise in the Government of Canada."

The Privy Council is not technically the same thing as the federal Cabinet. The governor general swears in privy councillors for life. Cabinet ministers serve in their Cabinet capacity for a much shorter tenure. Furthermore, the governor general often swears in other, "distinguished" Canadians to the Privy Council (including, in the past, the provincial premiers). As a consequence, all Cabinet ministers are privy councillors, but not all (or even a majority) of privy councillors are sitting Cabinet ministers.

Nevertheless, by constitutional convention, only those privy councillors who are also presently in Cabinet are entitled to exercise the powers of the Privy Council. For this reason, where powers in the 1867 Act are exercisable by the "Governor General in Council" or the "Lieutenant Governor in Council," they are in effect exercised by federal and provincial cabinets, respectively.

B. The Prime Minister and Cabinet

Ministers and the prime minister together comprise the "ministry," a category sometimes also referred to colloquially as the government. The terms "ministry" and "Cabinet" are usually used interchangeably. However, a minister is not automatically a Cabinet member. The question of who obtains a seat at the Cabinet table is a political matter for the prime minister to decide.

The prime minister is the first among equals in the ministry. It is the prime minister who presides over Cabinet. He or she has the sole authority to determine who the governor general swears in as a minister, who sits in Cabinet, and what portfolio within Cabinet that person holds. And all ministerial appointments are "at the pleasure" of the prime minister—meaning the prime minister has unfettered authority to compel the removal of ministers.

By constitutional convention, the prime minister also possesses authority to exercise so-called personal prerogatives. For example, the prime minister selects people to fill some important appointments that (technically) are made by the governor general (such as appointments to the Senate and the appointment of chief justices). As noted in chapter 4, it is the prime minister who advises the governor general as to the dissolution of Parliament, effectively giving the prime minister the power to control the timing of elections.

Formally, beyond these powers, the prime minister does not hold a privileged position within Cabinet in the sense that he or she can formulate policy or exercise decision-making powers independently of Cabinet. As a political matter, however, the prime minister exercises considerable influence.

Cabinet is, in the words of Peter Hogg, "in most matters the supreme executive authority": see Peter Hogg, *Constitutional Law of Canada*, 3rd ed. (Toronto: Carswell, 1992). It is Cabinet that determines the legislative agenda of the government in Parliament and it is Cabinet and its ministers that are responsible for the administration of the individual departments of the government.

The separation of the executive branch from the legislative branch is not, however, absolute. The constitutional convention of "responsible government" lies at the foundation of Canadian governance. Two key elements of responsible government should be noted. First, in a system of responsible government, Cabinet members are drawn from the legislative branch, almost always the House of Commons for the federal Cabinet. Ministers may hold office pending election to the Commons or while a senator, but all ministers are expected to also be members of the legislature.

Second, under the system of responsible government, the ministry is accountable to the legislative branch both collectively and individually. Collective responsibility requires that the ministry maintain the confidence of the Parliament. Individual ministerial responsibility requires that each minister be answerable in Parliament for the activities of his or her department.

In addition to their Cabinet responsibilities, Cabinet ministers have administrative responsibility for departments under their charge, which may often include specific powers to make decisions affecting the rights of individuals. For example, under s. 40 of the federal *Extradition Act*, SC 1999, c. 18, the federal minister of justice has wide-ranging discretion to make decisions respecting orders of surrender of persons to other jurisdictions to face prosecution for a crime committed in that other state; a discretion that must be exercised "personally"— meaning it cannot be delegated to another department official.

At times, the multiple roles of ministerial officials can give rise to claims of conflict. In *Idziak v. Canada (Minister of Justice)*, [1992] 3 SCR 631, it was argued that the minister of justice's involvement in the two-step extradition process raised questions of bias. Before a suspect can be extradited, there is a hearing before a judge in order to determine whether there is a sufficient factual and legal basis to support extradition (that is, that a crime was committed in the jurisdiction seeking extradition), and a further determination made by the minister as to whether the person must be surrendered. The minister of justice, in his capacity as the head of the Justice Department, oversees the prosecution in the extradition hearing, and is personally required to make a determination on the order of surrender. The Supreme Court of Canada, in rejecting the claim of bias, emphasizes the distinct nature of the competing ministerial roles:

> It has been seen that the extradition process has two distinct phases. The first, the judicial phase, encompasses the court proceedings which determine whether a factual and legal basis for extradition exists. If that process results in the issuance of a warrant of committal, then the second phase is activated. There, the Minister of Justice exercises his or her discretion in determining whether to issue a warrant of surrender. The first decision-making phase is certainly judicial in its nature and warrants the application of the full panoply of procedural safeguards. By contrast, the second decision-making process is political in its nature. The Minister must weigh the representations of the fugitive against Canada's international treaty obligations.
>
> • • •
>
> Parliament chose to give discretionary authority to the Minister of Justice. It is the Minister who must consider the good faith and honour of this country in its relations with other states. It is the Minister who has the expert knowledge of the political ramifications of an extradition

decision. In administrative law terms, the Minister's review should be characterized as being at the extreme legislative end of the *continuum* of administrative decision-making.

The appellant contends that a dual role has been allotted to the Minister of Justice by the *Extradition Act*. The Act requires the Minister to conduct the prosecution of the extradition hearing at the judicial phase and then to act as adjudicator in the ministerial phase. These roles are said to be mutually incompatible and to raise an apprehension of bias on their face. This contention fails to recognize either the clear division that lies between the phases of the extradition process, each of which serves a distinct function, or to take into account the separation of personnel involved in the two phases.

It is correct that the Minister of Justice has the responsibility to ensure the prosecution of the extradition proceedings and that to do so the Minister must appoint agents to act in the interest of the requesting state. However the decision to issue a warrant of surrender involves completely different considerations from those reached by a court in an extradition hearing. The extradition hearing is clearly judicial in its nature while the actions of the Minister of Justice in considering whether to issue a warrant of surrender are primarily political in nature. This is certainly not a case of a single official's acting as both judge and prosecutor in the same case. At the judicial phase the fugitive possesses the full panoply of procedural protection available in a court of law. At the ministerial phase, there is no longer a *lis* in existence. The fugitive has by then been judicially committed for extradition. The Act simply grants to the Minister a discretion as to whether to execute the judicially approved extradition by issuing a warrant of surrender.

C. The Public Service

The employees of the various ministries of the government, often referred to as civil servants, are also part of the executive branch. Unlike the political members of the executive, the civil servants are politically neutral and as such continue their employment with the government regardless of the political fortunes of the government of the day. The concept of a professional and neutral civil service seeks to draw a notional line between the political responsibilities of the minister in charge of the department and the administrative responsibilities of the civil service. Kenneth Kernaghan, a political scientist, identifies three principles that structure the relationship between the civil service and political officials within the government: ministerial responsibility, political neutrality, and public service anonymity: see Kenneth Kernaghan, *The Future Role of a Professional Non-Partisan Public Service in Ontario* (Panel on the Role of Government, Research Paper Series no. 13, 2003).

Ministerial responsibility requires that the presiding minister be held politically accountable for all matters arising within the department, including policy decisions by civil servants. Political neutrality requires that civil servants carry out their responsibilities loyally to the government in power without regard for the civil servant's own political views. Related to this, public servants are (at least in the classic model) restricted in their ability to engage in partisan political activities and cannot express publicly their personal views on policy issues. Public service anonymity, which follows as a consequence of the first two principles, provides that bureaucrats should be held accountable to their political overseers, but are not answerable to Parliament: see Kernaghan, above, at 3-11.

While the principles regarding public service neutrality have been traditionally understood as constitutional conventions, and therefore acting as political but not legal constraints, Professor Lorne Sossin has argued that there exists in Canadian administrative and constitutional law a dense web of legal norms concerning "bureaucratic independence" that "includes, but is not limited to, the protection of the neutrality of the civil service, the protection of the whistle-blowing exception to the duty of loyalty, the protection against improper political interference in administrative decision making, the preservation of the rule of law, and the maintenance of objective guarantees of separation from the political executive, including the merit principle for hiring and promotion [protection against patronage] and security of tenure": see Lorne Sossin, "Speaking Truth to Power? The Search for Bureaucratic Independence in Canada" (2005), 55 *UTLJ* 1, at 57-58.

As these comments suggest, the loyalty owed by civil servants is not boundless, but requires that civil servants refrain from public criticism of government policies. In *Fraser v. Canada*, excerpted below, the appellant, who was an employee of Revenue Canada, was discharged after repeatedly criticizing the government's policies regarding metrification. On a review of the original decision, the appellant argued that the duty to refrain from criticism only extends to areas related to the civil servants' direct responsibilities. In upholding the original decision of an adjudicator of the Public Service Staff Relations Board (a tribunal established to consider employment issues in the federal civil service), the Supreme Court comments on the particular nature of public service employment.

Fraser v. Canada (Public Service Staff Relations Board)
[1985] 2 SCR 455

DICKSON CJ: ... It is true that Mr. Fraser's major criticisms were directed against two policies, the metric conversion program and the Charter. It is also true that his job and the policies of his department did not bear on these two policies. But it does not follow that the Adjudicator erred in law in finding that Mr. Fraser's criticisms were related to his job. A job in the public service has two dimensions, one relating to the employee's tasks and how he or she performs them, the other relating to the perception of a job held by the public. In my opinion, the Adjudicator appreciated these two dimensions. His discussion on this point is in these terms:

> When Mr. Fraser suggested on the Floyd Patterson radio hot-line program on February 5, 1982 that the Prime Minister in the conduct of the nation would prefer to act in a similar manner to the present regime in Poland, he adversely affected his own ability to conduct the affairs of the department in which he worked. For example, a corporate taxpayer who is selected as the subject of an audit by Mr. Fraser who also assigns the auditor to examine his records might well speculate about the reasons for having been selected and be concerned about the professionalism of the exercise. Surely a relatively influential official of Revenue Canada who publicly and vehemently accuses his employer, the Government of Canada, and the Prime Minister of autocratic and coercive behaviour is unlikely to instill confidence in a clientele that has a right to expect impartial and judicious treatment. And if a taxpayer's reservations were to be perceived by an auditor as an obstacle to an effective investigation, Revenue Canada officials could then rely on the widest and most far-reaching instruments of search and seizure. In this context Mr. Lowe's concern about the public's perception of Revenue Canada merits some attention. A

public servant simply cannot be allowed under the rubric of free speech to cultivate distrust of the employer amongst members of the constituency whom he is obliged to serve. I am satisfied that Mr. Fraser cast doubt on his effectiveness as a Government employee once he escalated his criticism of Government policy to a point and in a form that far exceeded the issues of general public interest that he espoused before February 1, 1982. Or, more succinctly, his incipient and persistent campaign in opposition to the incumbent Government conflicted with the continuation of his employment relationship. Once that situation arose he either had to cease his activities or resign from the position he occupied.

This analysis and conclusion, namely that Mr. Fraser's criticisms were job-related, is, in my view, correct in law. I say this because of the importance and necessity of an impartial and effective public service. There is in Canada a separation of powers among the three branches of government—the legislature, the executive and the judiciary. In broad terms, the role of the judiciary is, of course, to interpret and apply the law; the role of the legislature is to decide upon and enunciate policy; the role of the executive is to administer and implement that policy.

The federal public service in Canada is part of the executive branch of Government. As such, its fundamental task is to administer and implement policy. In order to do this well, the public service must employ people with certain important characteristics. Knowledge is one, fairness another, integrity a third.

As the Adjudicator indicated, a further characteristic is loyalty. As a general rule, federal public servants should be loyal to their employer, the Government of Canada. The loyalty owed is to the Government of Canada, not the political party in power at any one time. A public servant need not vote for the governing party. Nor need he or she publicly espouse its policies. And indeed, in some circumstances a public servant may actively and publicly express opposition to the policies of a government. This would be appropriate if, for example, the Government were engaged in illegal acts, or if its policies jeopardized the life, health or safety of the public servant or others, or if the public servant's criticism had no impact on his or her ability to perform effectively the duties of a public servant or on the public perception of that ability. But, having stated these qualifications (and there may be others), it is my view that a public servant must not engage, as the appellant did in the present case, in sustained and highly visible attacks on major Government policies. In conducting himself in this way the appellant, in my view, displayed a lack of loyalty to the Government that was inconsistent with his duties as an employee of the Government.

As the Adjudicator pointed out, there is a powerful reason for this general requirement of loyalty, namely the public interest in both the actual, and apparent, impartiality of the public service. The benefits that flow from this impartiality have been well-described by the MacDonnell Commission. Although the description relates to the political activities of public servants in the United Kingdom, it touches on values shared with the public service in Canada:

> Speaking generally, we think that if restrictions on the political activities of public servants were withdrawn two results would probably follow. The public might cease to believe, as we think they do now with reason believe, in the impartiality of the permanent Civil Service; and Ministers might cease to feel the well-merited confidence which they possess at present in the loyal and faithful support of their official subordinates; indeed they might be led to scrutinise the

utterances or writings of such subordinates and to select for positions of confidence only those whose sentiments were known to be in political sympathy with their own.

If this were so, the system of recruitment by open competition would provide but a frail barrier against Ministerial patronage in all but the earlier years of service; the Civil Service would cease to be in fact an impartial, non-political body, capable of loyal service to all Ministers and parties alike; the change would soon affect the public estimation of the Service, and the result would be destructive of what undoubtedly is at present one of the greatest advantages of our administrative system, and one of the most honourable traditions of our public life.

See paragraphs 10-11 of c. 11 of MacDonnell Committee quoted in *Re Ontario Public Service Employees Union and Attorney-General for Ontario* (1980), 31 OR (2d) 321 (CA), at p. 329.

There is in Canada, in my opinion, a similar tradition surrounding our public service. The tradition emphasizes the characteristics of impartiality, neutrality, fairness and integrity. A person entering the public service or one already employed there must know, or at least be deemed to know, that employment in the public service involves acceptance of certain restraints. One of the most important of those restraints is to exercise caution when it comes to making criticisms of the Government.

———————————————

A related issue to the matter of public service loyalty is the extent to which members of the civil service can engage in partisan political activities. The statutes governing public service employment include restrictions on the kinds of political activities that certain bureaucrats can participate in: see *Public Service Employment Act*, SC 2003, c. 22, ss. 111-117. These types of statutory restrictions have been the subject of judicial scrutiny, most notably in two Supreme Court of Canada decisions, *OPSEU v. Ontario (Attorney General)*, [1987] 2 SCR 2 and *Osborne v. Canada (Treasury Board)*, [1991] 2 SCR 69. Both cases acknowledged the existence of a constitutional convention of public service neutrality and affirmed its importance as a principle of executive governance. In the *OPSEU* case, Ontario legislation restricting provincial civil servants' political activities, including activities in federal politics, was upheld as valid provincial legislation, but the legislation was not subject to Charter scrutiny in that case.

In *Osborne*, the question whether such restrictions were consistent with the Charter was considered, and resulted in the federal statutory restrictions being struck down as contrary to the right of free expression. Of particular concern to the court was that the legislation, which applied to all civil servants, was overinclusive because it failed to make distinctions between the kinds of work the employee may be involved in and his or her level of responsibility within the civil service. The restrictions on political activities now apply only to senior members of the bureaucracy.

D. Independent Administrative Agencies

As a matter of express constitutional recognition and constitutional convention, the formal executive bodies are limited to the governor general and lieutenant governors, the federal and provincial Cabinets, and the system of governmental departments and ministries that are overseen by individual ministers, including the civil service. However, executive functions are extensively carried out by a variety of bodies that have a measure of independence from the government. This naturally leads to the question of why it is seen as necessary or desirable to establish bodies that are independent from the government to carry out governmental functions. There is no single answer to this question. However, the reasons for establishing administrative bodies will determine the structure and form of the body created.

The legislature may determine that certain decisions are best made on a principled basis and therefore should be insulated from considerations of political expediency. This is often the case where decisions affect the legal rights of many individuals and there is merit in having those rights determined in a consistent manner. In this regard, the government may create a specialized tribunal to adjudicate individual cases free from direct government oversight. Here the role of an administrative body approaches that of the judiciary; although, in the case of administrative tribunals, the scope of cases heard is limited to a defined subject area. As an example, the Immigration and Refugee Board of Canada hears only matters relating to immigration admissibility and refugee claims.

A similar justification underlies the creation of independent agencies to administer government entitlement disputes. Here, one of the parties to the dispute is the government itself, which militates in favour of an independent and impartial decision-maker. In other, often economic matters, insulation from political forces is seen as desirable to ensure that long-term goals are not compromised by short-term political interests or the undue influence of interest groups. The creation of the Bank of Canada to oversee currency and related macroeconomic issues is a prominent example of such a body. In other cases, there will be a need for a particular kind of expertise that is best undertaken by a specialized body staffed by experts. In this regard, independence may facilitate specialization because of the restricted mandate of an administrative agency, as opposed to a government department. Finally, some public services requiring close cooperation and coordination between different jurisdictions can be delivered by multijurisdictional agencies. One such agency is the Canada–Newfoundland and Labrador Offshore Petroleum Board; another, addressing Canada–United States transboundary water issues, is the International Joint Commission.

Independent administrative bodies appear in a broad range of forms depending on their function. The nomenclature used to identify independent agencies is sometimes confusing in that a variety of terms, such as board, commission, authority, council, and agency, are used to describe administrative bodies, although the use of different terms does not necessarily signify different functions or structures. An administrative body is the product of the legislative instrument that creates it. In this regard there are few restrictions placed on legislators who want to create an administrative body and delegate powers to it. The provisions establishing the Canadian Human Rights Commission are typical of the statutory provisions used to create an independent administrative body.

Canadian Human Rights Act
RSC 1985, c. H-6, ss. 26-27

26(1) A commission is hereby established to be known as the Canadian Human Rights Commission, in this Part and Part III referred to as the "Commission," consisting of a Chief Commissioner, a Deputy Chief Commissioner and not less than three or more than six other members, to be appointed by the Governor in Council.

(2) The Chief Commissioner and Deputy Chief Commissioner are full-time members of the Commission and the other members may be appointed as full-time or part-time members of the Commission.

(3) Each full-time member of the Commission may be appointed for a term not exceeding seven years and each part-time member may be appointed for a term not exceeding three years.

(4) Each member of the Commission holds office during good behaviour but may be removed by the Governor in Council on address of the Senate and House of Commons.

(5) A member of the Commission is eligible to be re-appointed in the same or another capacity.

27(1) In addition to its duties under Part III with respect to complaints regarding discriminatory practices, the Commission is generally responsible for the administration of this Part and Parts I and III and

(a) shall develop and conduct information programs to foster public understanding of this Act and of the role and activities of the Commission thereunder and to foster public recognition of the principle described in section 2;

(b) shall undertake or sponsor research programs relating to its duties and functions under this Act and respecting the principle described in section 2;

(c) shall maintain close liaison with similar bodies or authorities in the provinces in order to foster common policies and practices and to avoid conflicts respecting the handling of complaints in cases of overlapping jurisdiction;

(d) shall perform duties and functions to be performed by it pursuant to any agreement entered into under subsection 28(2);

(e) may consider such recommendations, suggestions and requests concerning human rights and freedoms as it receives from any source and, where deemed by the Commission to be appropriate, include in a report referred to in section 61 reference to and comment on any such recommendation, suggestion or request;

(f) shall carry out or cause to be carried out such studies concerning human rights and freedoms as may be referred to it by the Minister of Justice and include in a report referred to in section 61 a report setting out the results of each such study together with such recommendations in relation thereto as it considers appropriate;

(g) may review any regulations, rules, orders, by-laws and other instruments made pursuant to an Act of Parliament and, where deemed by the Commission to be appropriate, include in a report referred to in section 61 reference to and comment on any provision thereof that in its opinion is inconsistent with the principle described in section 2; and

(h) shall, so far as is practical and consistent with the application of Part III, try by persuasion, publicity or any other means that it considers appropriate to discourage and reduce discriminatory practices referred to in sections 5 to 14.1.

(2) The Commission may, on application or on its own initiative, by order, issue a guideline setting out the extent to which and the manner in which, in the opinion of the Commission, any provision of this Act applies in a class of cases described in the guideline.

(3) A guideline issued under subsection (2) is, until it is revoked or modified, binding on the Commission and any member or panel assigned under subsection 49(2) with respect

to the resolution of a complaint under Part III regarding a case falling within the description contained in the guideline.

(4) Each guideline issued under subsection (2) shall be published in Part II of the *Canada Gazette*.

The Canadian Human Rights Commission is a creation of the federal Parliament, with the commissioners themselves being appointed by the governor in council (in effect, Cabinet). The independence of the commission is established through the provision of security of tenure to the commissioners who may only be removed upon the address of both Houses. Independence is also established through the assignment of powers under s. 27, which can be exercised without political oversight. A further provision of the *Canadian Human Rights Act*, s. 61, requires that the commission submit an annual report to Parliament detailing the commission's activities. In this way, the commission has some direct accountability to Parliament.

Section 27 confers on the commission broad powers to carry out its statutory mandate, including the ability to undertake, at its initiative, reviews of regulatory instruments for the purpose of ensuring their adherence to the anti-discriminatory purposes of the Act and to enact binding guidelines regarding the application of the Act. These powers are to be exercised without direct oversight by political officials. The provision of a degree of discretion exercisable by the commission further contributes to the commission's independence because the commission has the authority to develop policies and procedures largely unfettered by senior political officials, including the minister of justice, who is responsible for the Act. The commission has the authority to investigate human rights complaints against the federal government, making independence from the government critical to the legitimacy of the commission.

In addition to creating the commission, the *Canadian Human Rights Act* also creates a further independent body called the Canadian Human Rights Tribunal, which has the responsibility of holding, at the request of the commission, inquiries into human rights complaints filed with the commission. The tribunal is independent from the commission and fulfills a different role in the overall scheme under the Act. Whereas the commission has wide-ranging powers to investigate discriminatory practices and to seek the resolution of human rights complaints—which include as noted above the exercise of policy creation functions and administrative functions—the tribunal acts in a quasi-judicial capacity inquiring into human rights complaints. The commission has the authority to appear before the tribunal, and in doing so it is required to represent the "public interest."

Provincial human rights legislation has created similar independent administrative bodies to those created under the *Canadian Human Rights Act*.

Does this discussion mean that adjudicative administrative bodies must be independent, as a constitutional matter? The answer is usually "no." Certainly, there are circumstances where independence may be required. For example, s. 7 of the Charter bars deprivation of life, liberty, or security of the person in the absence of fundamental justice. Likewise, the *Canadian Bill of Rights*—a 1960 statute of Parliament that purports to trump all inconsistent federal laws—guarantees in s. 2(e) that no law may "deprive a person of the right to a fair hearing in accordance with the principles of fundamental justice for the determination of his rights and obligations." The Supreme Court has recognized that where a body exercises power of a sort triggering these provisions, some measure of independence may be required of that organization. Thus, in *Ocean Port Hotel Ltd. v. British Columbia (General Manager, Liquor Control and Licensing Branch)*, the Supreme Court drew a distinction between administrative tribunals and decision-makers, as emanations of the executive that must take their policy direction from the legislature, and the courts, which are protected by the constitutional principle of judicial independence.

Ocean Port Hotel Ltd. v. British Columbia (General Manager, Liquor Control and Licensing Branch)
[2001] 2 SCR 781

McLACHLIN CJ (for the court): [1] This appeal raises a critical but largely unexplored issue of administrative law: the degree of independence required of members sitting on administrative tribunals empowered to impose penalties. As the intervening Attorneys General emphasize, this is an issue that implicates the structures of administrative bodies across the nation. ...

. . .

[8] Before the Court of Appeal, Ocean Port argued for the first time that the Board lacked sufficient independence to make the ruling and impose the penalty it had, and that as a result the decision must be set aside. It also objected to the order on the grounds that: (1) the Board relied on hearsay, irrelevant evidence and insufficient evidence to support the allegations against Ocean Port, in contravention of the principles of natural justice and its duty of fairness; (2) the Board erred in law in its application of s. 10(3) of the *Evidence Act*, RSBC 1996, c. 124; and (3) the jurisdiction of the General Manager under the Act was limited to matters of compliance and could not ground a decision on an "offence," a power reserved to the courts.

. . .

III. Legislation

[15] [The *Liquor Control Act* states:]

30(1) The Liquor Appeal Board is continued consisting of a chair and other members the Lieutenant Governor in Council may appoint.
(2) The chair and the members of the appeal board
    (a) serve at the pleasure of the Lieutenant Governor in Council, and
    (b) are entitled to
        (i) receive the remuneration set by the Lieutenant Governor in Council, and
        (ii) be paid reasonable expenses incurred in carrying out their duties as members of the appeal board.

. . .

IV. Discussion

[18] This appeal concerns the independence of the Liquor Appeal Board. The Court of Appeal concluded that members of the Board lacked the necessary guarantees of independence required of administrative decision makers imposing penalties. More specifically, it held that the tenure enjoyed by Board members—appointed "at the pleasure" of the executive to serve on a part-time basis—was insufficiently secure to preserve the appearance of their independence. As a consequence, it set aside the Board's decision in the present case.

[19] The appellant, with the support of the intervening Attorneys General, argues that this reasoning disregards a fundamental principle of law: absent a constitutional challenge, a statutory regime prevails over common law principles of natural justice. The *Act* expressly provides for the appointment of Board members at the pleasure of the Lieutenant Governor in Council. The decision of the Court of Appeal, the appellant contends, effectively struck down this validly enacted provision without reference to constitutional principle or authority. In essence, the Court of Appeal elevated a principle of natural justice to constitutional status. In so doing, it committed a clear error of law.

[20] This conclusion, in my view, is inescapable. It is well established that, absent constitutional constraints, the degree of independence required of a particular government decision maker or tribunal is determined by its enabling statute. It is the legislature or Parliament that determines the degree of independence required of tribunal members. The statute must be construed as a whole to determine the degree of independence the legislature intended.

[21] Confronted with silent or ambiguous legislation, courts generally infer that Parliament or the legislature intended the tribunal's process to comport with principles of natural justice: *Minister of National Revenue v. Coopers and Lybrand*, [1979] 1 SCR 495, at p. 503; *Law Society of Upper Canada v. French*, [1975] 2 SCR 767, at pp. 783-84. In such circumstances, administrative tribunals may be bound by the requirement of an independent and impartial decision maker, one of the fundamental principles of natural justice: *Matsqui* ... (per Lamer CJ and Sopinka J); *Régie* ... , at para. 39; *Katz v. Vancouver Stock Exchange*, [1996] 3 SCR 405. Indeed, courts will not lightly assume that legislators intended to enact procedures that run contrary to this principle, although the precise standard of independence required will depend "on all the circumstances, and in particular on the language of the statute under which the agency acts, the nature of the task it performs and the type of decision it is required to make": *Régie*, at para. 39.

[22] However, like all principles of natural justice, the degree of independence required of tribunal members may be ousted by express statutory language or necessary implication. See generally: *Innisfil (Corporation of the Township of) v. Corporation of the Township of Vespra*, [1981] 2 SCR 145; *Brosseau v. Alberta Securities Commission*, [1989] 1 SCR 301; *Ringrose v. College of Physicians and Surgeons (Alberta)*, [1977] 1 SCR 814; *Kane v. Board of Governors of the University of British Columbia*, [1980] 1 SCR 1105. Ultimately, it is Parliament or the legislature that determines the nature of a tribunal's relationship to the executive. It is not open to a court to apply a common law rule in the face of clear statutory direction. Courts engaged in judicial review of administrative decisions must defer to the legislator's intention in assessing the degree of independence required of the tribunal in question.

[23] This principle reflects the fundamental distinction between administrative tribunals and courts. Superior courts, by virtue of their role as courts of inherent jurisdiction, are constitutionally required to possess objective guarantees of both individual and institutional independence. The same constitutional imperative applies to the provincial courts: *Reference re Remuneration of Judges of the Provincial Court of Prince Edward Island*, [1997] 3 SCR 3 (the "*Provincial Court Judges Reference*"). Historically, the requirement of judicial independence developed to demarcate the fundamental division between the judiciary and the executive. It protected, and continues to protect, the impartiality of judges—both in fact and perception—by insulating them from external influence, most notably the influence of the executive: *Beauregard v. Canada*, [1986] 2 SCR 56, at p. 69; *Régie*, at para. 61.

[24] Administrative tribunals, by contrast, lack this constitutional distinction from the executive. They are, in fact, created precisely for the purpose of implementing government policy. Implementation of that policy may require them to make quasi-judicial decisions. They thus may be seen as spanning the constitutional divide between the executive and judicial branches of government. However, given their primary policy-making function, it is properly the role and responsibility of Parliament and the legislatures to determine the composition and structure required by a tribunal to discharge the responsibilities bestowed upon it. While tribunals may sometimes attract Charter requirements of independence, as a general rule they do not. Thus, the degree of independence required of a particular tribunal is a matter of discerning the intention of Parliament or the legislature and, absent constitutional constraints, this choice must be respected.

[25] In the present case, the legislature of British Columbia spoke directly to the nature of appointments to the Liquor Appeal Board. Pursuant to s. 30(2)(a) of the Act, the chair and members of the Board "serve at the pleasure of the Lieutenant Governor in Council." In practice, members are appointed for a one-year term (pursuant to an Order-in-Council), and serve on a part-time basis. All members but the chair are paid on a per diem basis. The chair establishes panels of one or three members to hear matters before the Board "as the chair considers advisable": s. 30(5).

. . .

[27] In my view, the legislature's intention that Board members should serve at pleasure, as expressed through s. 30(2)(a) of the Act, is unequivocal. As such, it does not permit the argument that the statute is ambiguous and hence should be read as imposing a higher degree of independence to meet the requirements of natural justice, if indeed a higher standard is required. It is easy to imagine more exacting safeguards of independence—longer, fixed-term appointments; full-time appointments; a panel selection process for appointing members to panels instead of the Chair's discretion. However, in each case one must face the question: "Is this what the legislature intended?" Given the legislature's willingness to countenance "at pleasure" appointments with full knowledge of the processes and penalties involved, it is impossible to answer this question in the affirmative. Huddart JA concluded that the tenure enjoyed by Board members was "no better than an appointment at pleasure" (para. 27). However, this is precisely the standard of independence required by the Act. Where the intention of the legislature, as here, is unequivocal, there is no room to import common law doctrines of independence, "however inviting it may be for a Court to do so": *Re W. D. Latimer Co. and Bray* (1974), 6 OR (2d) 129 (CA), at p. 137.

. . .

[29] Nor is a constitutional guarantee of independence implicated in the present case. The respondent does not argue that the proceedings before the Board engage a right to an independent tribunal under ss. 7 or 11(d) of the *Canadian Charter of Rights and Freedoms*. Instead, it contends that the preamble to the *Constitution Act, 1867* mandates a minimum degree of independence for at least some administrative tribunals. In support, the respondent invokes Lamer CJ's discussion of judicial independence in the *Provincial Court Judges Reference*. In that case, Lamer CJ, writing for the majority, concluded that "judicial independence is at root an *unwritten* constitutional principle … recognized and affirmed by the preamble to the *Constitution Act, 1867*" (para. 83 (emphasis in original)). The respondent argues that the same principle binds administrative tribunals exercising adjudicative functions.

[30] With respect, I find no support for this proposition in the Provincial Court Judges Reference. The language and reasoning of the decision are confined to the superior and provincial courts. Lamer CJ addressed the issue of judicial independence; that is, the independence of the courts of law comprising the judicial branch of government. Nowhere in his reasons does he extend his comments to tribunals other than courts of law.

[31] Nor does the rationale for locating a constitutional guarantee of independence in the preamble to the *Constitution Act, 1867* extend, as a matter of principle, to administrative tribunals. Lamer CJ's reasoning rests on the preamble's reference to a constitutional system "similar in Principle to that of the United Kingdom." Applied to the modern Canadian context, this guarantee extends to provincial courts (at para. 106):

> The historical origins of the protection of judicial independence in the United Kingdom, and thus in the Canadian Constitution, can be traced to the *Act of Settlement of 1701*. As we said in *Valente* … , at p. 693, that Act was the "historical inspiration" for the judicature provisions of the *Constitution Act, 1867*. Admittedly, the Act only extends protection to judges of the English superior courts. However … judicial independence [has] grown into a principle that now extends to all courts, not just the superior courts of this country.

These comments circumscribe the requirement of independence, as a constitutional imperative emanating from the preamble, to the provincial and superior courts.

[32] Lamer CJ also supported his conclusion with reference to the traditional division between the executive, the legislature and the judiciary. The preservation of this tripartite constitutional structure, he argued, requires a constitutional guarantee of an independent judiciary. The classical division between court and state does not, however, compel the same conclusion in relation to the independence of administrative tribunals. As discussed, such tribunals span the constitutional divide between the judiciary and the executive. While they may possess adjudicative functions, they ultimately operate as part of the executive branch of government, under the mandate of the legislature. They are not courts, and do not occupy the same constitutional role as courts.

[33] The Constitution is an organic instrument, and must be interpreted flexibly to reflect changing circumstances: *Attorney-General for Ontario v. Attorney-General for Canada*, [1947] AC 127 (PC). Indeed, in the *Provincial Court Judges Reference*, Lamer CJ relied on this principle to extend the tradition of independent superior courts (derived from the constitution of the United Kingdom) to all courts, stating that "our Constitution has evolved over time" (para. 106). However, I can find no basis upon which to extend the constitutional

guarantee of judicial independence that animated the *Provincial Court Judges Reference* to the Liquor Appeal Board. The Board is not a court, nor does it approach the constitutional role of the courts. It is first and foremost a licensing body. The suspension complained of was an incident of the Board's licensing function. Licences are granted on condition of compliance with the Act, and can be suspended for non-compliance. The exercise of power here at issue falls squarely within the executive power of the provincial government.

The *Ocean Port* case did not settle the matter of the degree of independence required of administrative tribunals as a general proposition because the Supreme Court of Canada's analysis requires a close consideration of the actual functions of the administrative body and the intent of the legislature in creating the administrative body. The issue was revisited in *Bell Canada v. Canadian Telephone Employees Association*, [2003] 1 SCR 884, where a decision of the Canadian Human Rights Tribunal was challenged on the basis of the lack of independence of the tribunal stemming from the ability of the Canadian Human Rights Commission to issue guidelines that bound the tribunal and the power of the tribunal chair to extend tribunal members' terms in ongoing inquiries. Seizing on the Supreme Court of Canada's statement in *Ocean Port* that administrative tribunals "may be seen as spanning the constitutional divide between executive and judicial branches of government" (para. 24), the Supreme Court of Canada in *Bell Canada* goes on to consider the precise nature of the tribunal:

[21] … Some administrative tribunals are closer to the executive end of the spectrum: their primary purpose is to develop, or supervise the implementation of, particular government policies. Such tribunals may require little by way of procedural protections. Other tribunals, however, are closer to the judicial end of the spectrum: their primary purpose is to adjudicate disputes through some form of hearing. Tribunals at this end of the spectrum may possess court-like powers and procedures. These powers may bring with them stringent requirements of procedural fairness, including a higher requirement of independence (see *Newfoundland Telephone* [[1992] 1 SCR 623], at p. 638 *per* Cory J, and *Russell v. Duke of Norfolk*, [1949] 1 All ER 109 (CA)).

[22] To say that tribunals span the divide between the executive and the judicial branches of government is *not* to imply that there are only two types of tribunals—those that are quasi-judicial and require the full panoply of procedural protections, and those that are quasi-executive and require much less. A tribunal may have a number of different functions, one of which is to conduct fair and impartial hearings in a manner similar to that of the courts, and yet another of which is to see that certain government policies are furthered. In ascertaining the content of the requirements of procedural fairness that bind a particular tribunal, consideration must be given to *all* of the functions of that tribunal. It is not adequate to characterize a tribunal as "quasi-judicial" on the basis of one of its functions, while treating another aspect of the legislative scheme creating this tribunal—such as the requirement that the tribunal follow interpretive guidelines that are laid down by a specialized body with expertise in that area of law—as though this second aspect of the legislative scheme were external to the true purpose of the tribunal. All aspects of the tribunal's structure, as laid out in its enabling statute, must be examined, and an attempt must be made to determine precisely what combination of functions the legislature intended that tribunal to serve, and what procedural protections are appropriate for a body that has these particular functions.

[23] The main function of the Canadian Human Rights Tribunal is adjudicative. It conducts formal hearings into complaints that have been referred to it by the Commission. It has many of the powers of a court. It is empowered to find facts, to interpret and apply the law to the facts before it, and to award appropriate remedies. Moreover, its hearings have much the same structure as a formal trial before a court. The parties before the Tribunal lead evidence, call and cross-examine witnesses, and make submissions on how the law should be applied to the facts. The Tribunal is not involved in crafting policy, nor does it undertake its own independent investigations of complaints: the investigative and policy-making functions have deliberately been assigned by the legislature to a different body, the Commission.

In this case, the Supreme Court of Canada held that in light of these functions "the Tribunal, though not bound to the highest standard of independence by the unwritten constitutional principle of adjudicative independence, must act impartially and meet a relatively high standard of independence, both at common law and under s. 2(e) of the *Canadian Bill of Rights*" (para. 31).

Part of the challenge to the Canadian Human Rights Tribunal's impartiality arose from the commission's dual role as a creator of guidelines that are binding on the tribunal and as a party that appears before the tribunal.

[40] ... Bell objects that Parliament has placed in one and the same body the function of formulating guidelines, investigating complaints, and acting as prosecutor before the Tribunal. Bell is correct in suggesting that the Commission shares these functions. However, this overlapping of different functions in a single administrative agency is not unusual, and does not on its own give rise to a reasonable apprehension of bias (see [*2747-3174 Québec Inc. v. Quebec (Régie des permis d'alcool)*, [1996] 3 SCR 919], at paras. 46-48, *per* Gonthier J; *Newfoundland Telephone*, *supra*, at p. 635, *per* Cory J; *Brosseau v. Alberta Securities Commission*, [1989] 1 SCR 301). As McLachlin CJ observed in *Ocean Port*, [[2001] 2 SCR 781], at para. 41, "[t]he overlapping of investigative, prosecutorial and adjudicative functions in a single agency is frequently necessary for [an administrative agency] to effectively perform its intended role."

[41] Indeed, it may be that the overlapping of functions in the Commission is the legislature's way of ensuring that both the Commission and the Tribunal are able to perform their intended roles. In *Public Service Alliance*, [[2000] 1 FC 146 (TD)], Evans J noted that although it was unusual for Parliament to have conferred the power to make subordinate legislation on the Commission and not the Governor in Council, Parliament must have contemplated that "the expertise that the Commission will have acquired in the discharge of its statutory responsibilities for human rights research and public education, and for processing complaints up to the point of adjudication" (para. 140) was necessary in the formulation of the guidelines, and was more important than certain other goals. In our view, Evans J's conjecture regarding Parliamentary intent is correct. The Commission is responsible, among other things, for maintaining close liaisons with similar bodies in the provinces, for considering recommendations from public interest groups and any other bodies, and for developing programs of public education (s. 27(1)). These collaborative and educational responsibilities afford it extensive awareness of the needs of the public, and extensive knowledge of developments in anti-discrimination law at the federal and provincial levels. Placing the guideline power in the hands of the Commission may therefore have been Parliament's way of ensuring that the Act would be interpreted in a manner that was sensitive to the needs of

the public and to developments across the country, and hence, that it would be interpreted by the Tribunal in the manner that best furthered the aims of the Act as a whole.

[42] This point is related to our earlier discussion of the importance of considering the aims of the Act as a whole, in assessing whether the requirement of impartiality has been met. We noted there that the Act's ultimate aim of identifying and rectifying instances of discrimination would only be furthered if ambiguities in the Act were interpreted in a manner that furthered, rather than frustrated, the identification of discriminatory practices. If, as the Act suggests, this can best be accomplished by giving the Commission the power to make interpretive guidelines that bind the Tribunal, then the overlapping of functions in the Commission plays an important role. It does not result in a lack of impartiality, but rather helps to ensure that the Tribunal applies the Act in the manner that is most likely to fulfill the Act's ultimate purpose.

What the Supreme Court of Canada recognizes in the above excerpt is the desirability in many instances of creating executive entities that are capable of exercising multiple and overlapping functions that respond to the regulatory demands at hand. Often administrative bodies can be created that are better placed than the legislature to address the particular requirements of a regulatory scheme owing to their expertise, flexibility, independence, efficiency, or combination thereof, as the case may be.

E. Crown Corporations

The Canadian Human Rights Commission is not created as a separate legal entity, although it does have statutory authority to enact internal bylaws and to enter into contracts concerning matters related to the commission's mandate. However, it is not uncommon for administrative bodies to be created that have a legal personality separate from the government. The principle justification for the creation of Crown corporations is that where there is a strong commercial aspect to the government service, it may require that decisions be made free from political influences that may unduly interfere with commercial objectives. Additionally, the commercial nature of some activities may be ill-suited to government departmental structures and the related rules respecting financial matters, such as controls on the expenditure of public funds and the management of debt. The use of Crown corporations should also be understood as a distinct form of regulation that arises from direct ownership, as opposed to the imposition of regulatory controls on private entities.

Of course, if Crown corporations were solely concerned with commercial objectives, there would be little incentive to resort to the creation of a Crown corporation, as opposed to a wholly private sector approach. It follows that Crown corporations will have public objectives. In some instances, the Crown corporation may have an express regulatory mandate, as is the case with the Bank of Canada. Alternatively, the Crown corporation may deliver services that are considered to be of public importance; examples include Canada Post, VIA Rail, and the provision of electrical power generation and distribution by provincial Crown corporations. In some cases, the government may decide that the justification for providing a service through a Crown corporation can no longer be maintained, resulting in the elimination or privatization of the Crown corporation, as was the case with Petro-Canada and Air Canada.

The private and public objectives of Crown corporations require the government to balance the operational benefits of independence and the need for accountability. Given the diversity of the size, mandates, and sources of funding of Crown corporations, a "one size fits all" approach to accountability is difficult. The primary vehicle for accountability of federal Crown corporations is the *Financial Administration Act*, RSC 1985, c. F-11, which imposes standardized governance and accountability requirements on listed Crown corporations, including approval of annual corporate plans, capital budgets, and in some cases operating budgets. The government has in many cases the authority of appointment over corporate directors and key corporate officers. The *Financial Administration Act* also provides authority for the government to intervene in the management of a Crown corporation by directing the board of directors to follow a particular course of action where such action is in the public interest. This authority, called a "directive power," is an extraordinary power and requires the appropriate minister to consult with the board of directors of the affected Crown corporation in advance of the issuance of the directive and to table the directive in both Houses once issued.

F. Enforcement Bodies: Police and Prosecutors

The executive branch of the government, in addition to being responsible for the implementation of government policy, is required to enforce those policies that have the force of law. The enforcement duties of the executive fall primarily on the police, to maintain order and to investigate illegal conduct, and to prosecutors. Policing functions are the responsibility of both the provincial and federal governments. Provincial police, including those employed by municipal police forces, have the authority to investigate matters in relation to both provincial laws and federal criminal laws. The federal police force, the Royal Canadian Mounted Police, has the authority to police federal statutes (although provincial policing bodies have primary enforcement responsibility for offences under the *Criminal Code*), police the federal territories and, in much of Canada, to provide police services in provinces under contract. Both the federal government and the provinces have prosecutorial power, exercised by their respective attorneys general.

While enforcement agencies in Canada derive their authority from legislation, they hold a unique legal position with the broader executive framework. In common law, police and prosecutors have been distinguished from other civil servants in that in their enforcement duties they are not subject to political oversight in the sense that they must exercise their powers without direction from political officials or in furtherance of partisan political activities. On the other hand, police and prosecutors cannot operate without accountability for their actions. The two case excerpts that follow consider the tension between accountability and independence in the context of enforcement.

In the first excerpt, *R v. Campbell*, the police engineered a "reverse sting" operation by arranging the sale of narcotics to the accused and then charging them with conspiracy to traffic. A stay of proceedings was sought on the basis that the police had engaged in a serious breach of the law. In response, the Crown argued that any illegal conduct should be subject to Crown immunity from statutory offences. In the course of considering this argument, the Supreme Court of Canada considered the nature of the relationship between the police and the Crown. At the heart of this consideration was the degree to which the RCMP is independent from the political executive.

In the second excerpt, *Krieger v. Law Society (Alberta)*, the petitioner, Krieger, was a Crown prosecutor who was subject to a complaint to the Law Society, which stemmed from Krieger's conduct during a prosecution. Krieger sought to prevent the Law Society from reviewing the matter on the basis that to do so would interfere with the exercise of prosecutorial discretion. In this case, the independence of Crown prosecutors from political interference lay beneath the petitioner's claim not to be subject to regulatory oversight by the Law Society.

R v. Campbell
[1999] 1 SCR 565

BINNIE J: ... [27] The Crown's attempt to identify the RCMP with the Crown for immunity purposes misconceives the relationship between the police and the executive government when the police are engaged in law enforcement. A police officer investigating a crime is not acting as a government functionary or as an agent of anybody. He or she occupies a public office initially defined by the common law and subsequently set out in various statutes. In the case of the RCMP, one of the relevant statutes is now the *Royal Canadian Mounted Police Act*, RSC 1985, c. R-10.

[28] Under the authority of that Act, it is true, RCMP officers perform a myriad of functions apart from the investigation of crimes. These include, by way of examples, purely ceremonial duties, the protection of Canadian dignitaries and foreign diplomats and activities associated with crime prevention. Some of these functions bring the RCMP into a closer relationship to the Crown than others. The *Department of the Solicitor General Act*, RSC 1985, c. S-13, provides that the Solicitor General's powers, duties and functions extend to matters relating to the RCMP over which Parliament has jurisdiction, and that have not been assigned to another department. Section 5 of the *Royal Canadian Mounted Police Act* provides for the governance of the RCMP as follows:

> 5(1) The Governor in Council may appoint an officer, to be known as the Commissioner of the Royal Canadian Mounted Police, who, under the direction of the [Solicitor General], has the control and management of the Force and all matters connected therewith.

[29] It is therefore possible that in one or other of its roles the RCMP could be acting in an agency relationship with the Crown. In this appeal, however, we are concerned only with the status of an RCMP officer in the course of a criminal investigation, and in that regard the police are independent of the control of the executive government. The importance of this principle, which itself underpins the rule of law, was recognized by this Court in relation to municipal forces as long ago as *McCleave v. Moncton (City)* (1902), 32 SCR 106 (SCC). That was a civil case, having to do with potential municipal liability for police negligence, but in the course of his judgment Strong CJ cited with approval the following proposition, at pp. 108-09:

> Police officers can in no respect be regarded as agents or officers of the city. Their duties are of a public nature. Their appointment is devolved on cities and towns by the legislature as a

convenient mode of exercising a function of government, but this does not render them liable for their unlawful or negligent acts. The detection and arrest of offenders, the preservation of the public peace, the enforcement of the laws, and other similar powers and duties with which police officers and constables are entrusted are derived from the law, and not from the city or town under which they hold their appointment.

[30] At about the same time, the High Court of Australia rejected the notion that a police constable was an agent of the Crown so as to enjoy immunity against a civil action for wrongful arrest. Griffith CJ had this to say in *Enever v. R* (1906), 3 CLR 969 (Australia HC) at p. 977:

> Now, the powers of a constable, *quâ* peace officer, whether conferred by common or statute law, are exercised by him by virtue of his office, and cannot be exercised on the responsibility of any person but himself. If he arrests on suspicion of felony, the suspicion must be his suspicion, and must be reasonable to him. If he arrests in a case in which the arrest may be made on view, the view must be his view, not that of someone else. ... A constable, therefore, when acting as a peace officer, is not exercising a delegated authority, but an original authority, and the general law of agency has no application.

[31] Over 70 years later, Laskin CJ in *Nicholson v. Haldimand-Norfolk (Regional Municipality) Commissioners of Police* (1978), [1979] 1 SCR 311 (SCC) at p. 322, speaking with reference to the status of a probationary police constable, affirmed that "we are dealing with *the holder of a public office*, engaged in duties connected with the maintenance of public order and preservation of the peace, important values in any society" (emphasis added). See also *Ridge v. Baldwin* (1963), [1964] AC 40 (UK HL) at p. 65.

[32] Similar sentiments were expressed by the Judicial Committee of the Privy Council in *Attorney General for New South Wales v. Perpetual Trustee Co.*, [1955] AC 457 (Australia PC), another civil case dealing with the vicarious liability of the Crown, in which Lord Viscount Simonds stated, at pp. 489-90:

> [A constable's] authority is original, not delegated, and is exercised at his own discretion by virtue of his office: he is a ministerial officer exercising statutory rights independently of contract. The essential difference is recognized in the fact that his relationship to the Government is not in ordinary parlance described as that of servant and master.

[33] While for certain purposes the Commissioner of the RCMP reports to the Solicitor General, the Commissioner is not to be considered a servant or agent of the government while engaged in a criminal investigation. The Commissioner is not subject to political direction. Like every other police officer similarly engaged, he is answerable to the law and, no doubt, to his conscience. As Lord Denning put it in relation to the Commissioner of Police in *R v. Metropolitan Police Commissioner*, [1968] 1 All ER 763 (Eng. CA), at p. 769:

> I have no hesitation, however, in holding that, *like every constable in the land, he [the Commissioner of Police] should be, and is, independent of the executive*. He is not subject to the orders of the Secretary of State, save that under the *Police Act 1964* the Secretary of State can call on him to give a report, or to retire in the interests of efficiency. I hold it to be the duty of the Commissioner of Police, as it is of every chief constable, to enforce the law of the land. He must take steps so to post his men that crimes may be detected; and that honest citizens may go about

their affairs in peace. He must decide whether or not suspected persons are to be prosecuted; and, if need be, bring the prosecution or see that it is brought; *but in all these things he is not the servant of anyone, save of the law itself.* No Minister of the Crown can tell him that he must, or must not, keep observation on this place or that; or that he must, or must not, prosecute this man or that one. Nor can any police authority tell him so. The responsibility for law enforcement lies on him. He is answerable to the law and to the law alone. [Emphasis added.]

Krieger v. Law Society (Alberta)
[2002] 3 SCR 372

IACOBUCCI and MAJOR JJ: … [23] Prior to considering the specific questions raised by this appeal, we believe it is useful to discuss the nature and development of the Attorney General's office in Canada. Although we ultimately conclude that the Law Society retains jurisdiction over the alleged misconduct at the bottom of this dispute, the respondents rightly observed the unique and important role of the Attorney General and his agents as distinct from private lawyers.

[24] The office of Attorney General started in England as early as the thirteenth century as the King's Attorney. In essence, the Attorney General exercised on the King's behalf the prerogative to bring and terminate prosecutions. See J.L.J. Edwards, *The Law Officers of the Crown* (London: Sweet and Maxwell, 1964), at pp. 12-14; Law Reform Commission of Canada, Working Paper 62, *Controlling Criminal Prosecutions: The Attorney General and the Crown Prosecutor* (Ottawa: The Commission, 1990). Although there are great differences between the constitution of the Canadian and English offices of Attorney General, the power to manage prosecutions of individuals for criminal acts has changed little since these early times and between these countries. …

[25] Although prosecutions were predominantly brought privately in England until 1879, the original power of the Attorney General was and is of initiating, managing and terminating both private and public prosecutions. This power finds its source in the Attorney General's general role as the official legal advisor to the Crown.

[26] In Canada, the office of the Attorney General is one with constitutional dimensions recognized in the *Constitution Act, 1867*. Although the specific duties conventionally exercised by the Attorney General are not enumerated, s. 135 of that Act provides for the extension of the authority and duties of that office as existing prior to Confederation. A similar provision applicable to the Attorney General of Alberta is found in the *Alberta Act*, SC 1905, c. 3 (reprinted in RSC 1985, App. II, No. 20), at s. 16(1). Furthermore, s. 63 of the *Constitution Act, 1867* requires that the cabinets of Quebec and Ontario include in their membership the Attorneys General.

[27] Attorneys General in this country are, of course, charged with duties beyond the management of prosecutions. As in England, they serve as Law Officers to their respective legislatures, and are responsible for providing legal advice to the various government departments. Unlike England, the Attorney General is also the Minister of Justice and is generally responsible for drafting the legislation tabled by the government of the day. The numerous other duties of the provincial and federal Attorneys General are broadly outlined in the various Acts establishing the Departments of Justice in each jurisdiction.

· · ·

[29] The gravity of the power to bring, manage and terminate prosecutions, which lies at the heart of the Attorney General's role, has given rise to an expectation that he or she will be in this respect fully independent from the political pressures of the government. In the UK, this concern has resulted in the long tradition that the Attorney General not sit as a member of Cabinet. See Edwards, *supra*, at pp. 174-76. Unlike the UK, Cabinet membership prevails in this country. However, the concern remains the same, and is amplified by the fact that the Attorney General is not only a member of Cabinet but also Minister of Justice, and in that role holds a position with partisan political aspects. Membership in Cabinet makes the principle of independence in prosecutorial functions perhaps even more important in this country than in the UK.

[30] It is a constitutional principle in this country that the Attorney General must act independently of partisan concerns when supervising prosecutorial decisions. Support for this view can be found in Law Reform Commission of Canada, *supra*, at pp. 9-11. See also Binnie J in *R v. Regan* (2002), 2002 SCC 12 (SCC), at paras. 157-158 (dissenting on another point).

[31] This side of the Attorney General's independence finds further form in the principle that courts will not interfere with his exercise of executive authority, as reflected in the prosecutorial decision-making process. In *R v. Power*, [1994] 1 SCR 601 (SCC), L'Heureux-Dubé J said, at pp. 621-23:

> It is manifest that, as a matter of principle and policy, courts should not interfere with prosecutorial discretion. This appears clearly to stem from the respect of separation of powers and the rule of law. Under the doctrine of separation of powers, criminal law is in the domain of the executive.
>
> Donna C. Morgan in "Controlling Prosecutorial Powers—Judicial Review, Abuse of Process and Section 7 of The Charter" (1986-87), 29 *Crim. LQ* 15, at pp. 20-21, probes the origins of prosecutorial powers:
>
>> Most (prosecutorial powers) derive … from the royal prerogative, defined by Dicey as the residue of discretionary or arbitrary authority residing in the hands of the Crown at any given time. Prerogative powers are essentially those granted by the common law to the Crown that are not shared by the Crown's subjects. While executive action carried out under their aegis conforms with the rule of law, prerogative powers are subject to the supremacy of Parliament, since they may be curtailed or abolished by statute.
>>
>> · · ·
>
> In "Prosecutorial Discretion: A Reply to David Vanek" (1987-88), 30 *Crim. LQ* 378, at pp. 378-80, J.A. Ramsay expands on the rationale underlying judicial deference to prosecutorial discretion:
>
>> · · ·
>
>> It is fundamental to our system of justice that criminal proceedings be conducted in public before an independent and impartial tribunal. *If the court is to review the prosecutor's exercise of his discretion the court becomes a supervising prosecutor. It ceases to be an independent tribunal.* [Emphasis in original.]

[32] The court's acknowledgment of the Attorney General's independence from judicial review in the sphere of prosecutorial discretion has its strongest source in the fundamental principle of the rule of law under our Constitution. Subject to the abuse of process doctrine, supervising one litigant's decision-making process—rather than the conduct of litigants before the court—is beyond the legitimate reach of the court. In *Hoem v. Law Society (British Columbia)* (1985), 20 CCC (3d) 239 (BC CA), Esson JA, for the court, observed, at p. 254, that:

> The independence of the Attorney-General, in deciding fairly who should be prosecuted, is also a hallmark of a free society. Just as the independence of the bar within its proper sphere must be respected, so must the independence of the Attorney-General.

We agree with these comments. The quasi-judicial function of the Attorney General cannot be subjected to interference from parties who are not as competent to consider the various factors involved in making a decision to prosecute. To subject such decisions to political interference, or to judicial supervision, could erode the integrity of our system of prosecution. Clearly drawn constitutional lines are necessary in areas subject to such grave potential conflict.

In both *R v. Campbell* and *Krieger v. Law Society (Alberta)*, the Supreme Court of Canada is careful not to view the relationship between enforcement authorities and political branches of government in absolute terms. In *Campbell*, the court's finding of police independence is limited to the police in the exercise of their law enforcement functions. Similarly, in *Krieger*, the court distinguishes between activities that go directly to the exercise of prosecutorial discretion, which ought not to be reviewable, and activities, such as a prosecutor's tactics and conduct in court, which may properly be the subject of review by professional regulatory bodies like the Law Society.

The relationship between police action and political officials has also been the subject of other recent controversies, such as the treatment of protestors by the RCMP during the Asia-Pacific Economic Cooperation Conference in Vancouver in 1997 and the shooting of aboriginal protestor Dudley George at Ipperwash Provincial Park in Ontario in 1995 during a police confrontation, both of which resulted in commission inquiries. In these cases, both commissions had to grapple with where to draw the line between protecting against undue political interference with police activities and ensuring political accountability for police activities. Professor Kent Roach, in a background research paper prepared for the Ipperwash Inquiry, summarizes the tensions between independence and accountability in the following terms:

> In support of a broader understanding of police independence is considerable scepticism about all forms of political intervention in policing and of the distinction between exchanging information and exerting influence. The role of central agencies in events such as APEC also raises questions about whether traditions of Ministerial responsibility are viable given the complexity of modern governance. ...
>
>   Nevertheless, there are still some reasons to be cautious about embracing a doctrine of full police independence. In support of limiting police independence to the criminal investigation core are the dangers of the police making questionable policy decisions in the name of police

expertise and independence. There is also the democratic importance of promoting informed and meaningful debate about how the police interact with their fellow citizens. The case for transparent and accountable democratic control and responsibility over policing may be particularly strong [in the case of] police relations with Aboriginal people, because they involve [the] broader question of whether the government respects Aboriginal rights. ... The case for democratic policing is also strengthened [should] legal methods of holding the police accountable for the way they police demonstrations prove to be inadequate. Police complaints, Charter and civil litigation, and criminal prosecutions are blunt and after the fact methods [used] to control police conduct. We should be cautious about giving up on democratic control of the police and the traditions of responsible government.

If the democratic policing model is to be viable, however, steps should be taken to ensure that political intervention in policing is more transparent so that the responsible Minister can be held accountable for any guidance given to the police. Legislative reform to recognize police independence with respect to criminal investigations and providing for written and public guidelines and directives for other policy matters might strike an appropriate balance between the goals of police independence and the ultimate accountability of both the police and the responsible minister to both the people and the law. Such a process could make clear for the public, the police, and the courts, the exact influence elected politicians have had on policing decisions. Should such a process be dismissed as too onerous and too visible by the responsible officials, or as inconsistent with the complexities of modern governance and policing, [then] much of the democratic justification for political involvement in policing would be taken away. If our elected representatives are to influence policing, they should be prepared to do so in an open and accountable manner. If transparently democratic policing (outside the core of independent police investigation) fails, [then] the alternatives are full police independence or governmental policing. In other words, we will have to decide whether to place our trust in the police or our trust in governments that may not be held accountable for their influence on the police. Such a choice would not be a happy one to have to make in a democracy.

(Kent Roach, "Four Models of Police-Government Relationships" in M. Beare and T. Murray, eds., *Police and Government Relations: Who's Calling the Shots?* (Toronto: University of Toronto Press, 2007), at 75-76.)

G. Municipalities and Other Elected Subordinate Bodies

The predominant model for independent administrative bodies is for the political executive to directly appoint or create a system of appointments for members of administrative bodies. However, in many cases it is desirable that service delivery account for local circumstances and local values. Consequently, there exist in Canada and elsewhere administrative bodies, such as municipalities and school boards, that provide for the direct election of the governing body. Despite the presence of elected officials, and a broad policy-making function, bodies such as municipalities are not a distinct level of government in the sense of being a constitutionally recognized level of government within Canada. Ultimately, like other independent administrative bodies, municipal powers are subject to the regulatory qualifications that superior levels of government place on them, including the radical restructuring or even elimination of municipalities. In *East York (Borough) v. Ontario (Attorney General)*

(1997), 153 DLR (4th) 299 (Ont. CA), a decision by the Ontario government to amalgamate a number of municipalities into a single municipal government (the Toronto "megacity") was challenged on the basis that such a radical alteration required the consent of the affected local governments. In rejecting this argument, the court was unequivocal about the subordinate status of municipal governments, holding in essence that municipalities, as creations of the province, may be altered by the province without constraint.

Because municipalities are governed by elected officials and because they exercise broad plenary powers, municipalities are unlike most other forms of independent administrative bodies, where officials are appointed by senior levels of government. The legal significance of an administrative body with direct lines of democratic accountability was considered by the Supreme Court of Canada in *Shell Canada Products Ltd. v. Vancouver (City)*, a case concerning the legal authority of a municipality to refuse to do business with companies that had business ties to South Africa during the apartheid era.

Shell Canada Products Ltd. v. Vancouver (City)
[1994] 1 SCR 231

[This legal proceeding arose out of an application by Shell Canada Products Ltd. to quash resolutions passed by Vancouver City Council that directed staff not to conduct business with Shell Canada as long as Shell continued to do business in South Africa on the basis, *inter alia*, that the resolutions were beyond the power of the municipality to make. The municipality argued that a provision stating that the "Council may provide for the good rule and government of the city" authorized the resolution. The majority, relying on a longstanding rule that municipal authority could only be exercised in relation to activities that fell within municipal purposes, held that the extraterritorial purpose of the resolutions was improper. In a dissenting judgment, McLachlin J (as she then was) considered the question of permissible municipal purposes in light of the democratic nature of municipal government.]

McLACHLIN J: … Recent commentary suggests an emerging consensus that courts must respect the responsibility of elected municipal bodies to serve the people who elected them and exercise caution to avoid substituting their views of what is best for the citizens for those of municipal councils. Barring clear demonstration that a municipal decision was beyond its powers, courts should not so hold. In cases where powers are not expressly conferred but may be implied, courts must be prepared to adopt the "benevolent construction" which this Court referred to in *Greenbaum* [[1993] 1 SCR 674], and confer the powers by reasonable implication. Whatever rules of construction are applied, they must not be used to usurp the legitimate role of municipal bodies as community representatives.

Such an approach serves a number of purposes which the narrow interventionist approach does not. First, it adheres to the fundamental axiom that courts must accord proper respect to the democratic responsibilities of elected municipal officials and the rights of those who elect them. This is important to the continued healthy functioning of democracy at the municipal level. If municipalities are to be able to respond to the needs and wishes of their citizens, they must be given broad jurisdiction to make local decisions reflecting local values.

Second, a generous approach to municipal powers will aid the efficient functioning of municipal bodies and avoid the costs and uncertainty attendant on excessive litigation. Excessive judicial interference in municipal decision-making can have the unintended and unfortunate result of large amounts of public funds being expended by municipal councils in the attempt to defend the validity of their exercise of statutory powers. The object of judicial review of municipal powers should be to accord municipalities the autonomy to undertake their activities without judicial interference unless clearly warranted.

Thirdly, a generous approach to municipal powers is arguably more in keeping with the true nature of modern municipalities. As McDonald [Ann McDonald, "In the Public Interest: Judicial Review of Local Government" (1983), 9 *Queen's LJ* 62] asserts (at p. 100), the municipal corporation "has come a long way from its origins in a rural age of simple government demands." She and other commentators (see [Stanley M. Makuch, *Canadian Municipal and Planning Law* (Toronto: Carswell, 1983) and Sue Arrowsmith, *Government Procurement and Judicial Review* (Toronto: Carswell, 1988)]) advocate that municipal councils should be free to define for themselves, as much as possible, the scope of their statutory authority. Excessive judicial interference in the decisions of elected municipal councils may, as this case illustrates, have the effect of confining modern municipalities in the straitjackets of tradition. This rationale for a restrained approach to judicial intervention in the decisions of municipal bodies is eloquently set out by McDonald (at pp. 100-101):

> Once elected ... the council is entrusted with responsibility for governing, not just in the interest of those who elected them, but in the interest of the community generally, that is, *in the public interest*. This is a fairly vague and controversial concept, however. It is a generalized judgment of what is best for individuals, *as a part of a community*. From the perspective of particular individuals and interest groups, the public interest may be conceived differently and, as amongst them, views of the public interest will inevitably conflict. A council making its decision on the public interest will identify and weigh a wide variety of competing considerations: the demands of various interested parties, the advice of its experts, data from its own research resources. And it will undoubtedly be influenced by the preferences expressed by the electorate. The decision is ultimately a matter of choice and what a council decides is necessarily its own collective perception of the public interest.
>
> The voters of a community give their elected council members the final judgment in this controversy. Whether the councillors are right or wrong in their judgment depends on the vantage point of the person making this assessment, but in any event, this is the decision they were elected to make. There may, in fact, be no right or wrong in the matter. Persons displeased with a council's decision have "a remedy at the polls." [Footnote omitted.]
>
> It is not the court's function to make these decisions—either directly or indirectly. Primary responsibility for deciding the welfare of the community belongs to the municipal corporation. If the courts take upon themselves the judgment of the rightness or wrongness of council's decisions in these matters, they, as a body having no connection with local inhabitants, usurp the choice which the inhabitants conferred, by democratic process, on the council. If the courts are to interfere in this process, they must have a positive justification for doing so and that justification must relate to their own peculiar nature and function. [Emphasis in original.]

. . .

The question is whether City Council's motives in this case fall outside the area of the City's legitimate concern. The *Vancouver Charter* [SBC 1953, c. 55] empowers Council to "provide for the good rule and government of the city": s. 189. My colleague and I agree that this clause permits Vancouver City Council to enact measures for the benefit or welfare of the inhabitants of the City. We part company on what this phrase includes.

My colleague adopts a narrow view of the welfare of the inhabitants of the City. He asserts that the City's Resolutions effect a purpose "without any identifiable benefit to its inhabitants" (p. 23 [p. 280]) and speaks of "matters external to the interests of the citizens" (p. 21 [p. 279]). He appears to define "municipal purposes" essentially in terms of provision of basic services to the inhabitants of the City.

I would cast the proper functions of a municipality in a larger mould. The term "welfare of the citizens," it seems to me, is capable of embracing not only their immediate needs, but also the psychological welfare of the citizens as members of a community who have an interest in expressing their identity as a community. Our language recognizes this: we speak of civic spirit, of city pride. This suggests that City Council may properly take measures related to fostering and maintaining this sense of community identity and pride. Among such measures may be found community expression of disapproval or approval of different types of conduct, wherever it is found. The right of free expression, one of the most fundamental values of our society, may be exercised individually or collectively. Are the citizens of a city to be prevented from expressing through their elected representatives their disapproval of conduct which they feel to be improper? Are they to be forced to do business with a firm whose conduct they see as objectionable, simply because the conduct occurs outside the territorial boundaries of the city? Can the desire of the citizens' elected representatives to express their views on such matters and to withdraw support for the conduct to which they object by refusing to do business with its perpetrators be said to be totally unrelated to the welfare and interests of the citizens of the city? To all these questions I would answer no.

. . .

As discussed earlier, scholars are critical of the frequency with which courts disguise an assessment for reasonableness in the cloak of a review for vires. On one view of my colleague's reasons, they do this very thing. Sopinka J correctly states that the reasonableness of the Resolutions is not in issue, only the power of the City to pass them (p. 15 [pp. 274]). Yet he goes on to hold that the Resolutions must fall because they are "based on matters external to the interests of the citizens of the municipality" (p. 21 [p. 279]). But that is the very question at stake. What *is* external to the interests of the citizens? What conversely, is in their interests? The City councillors, after hearing both sides, took one view—a view which many other municipal councils have taken. My colleague takes another. In my view, it is the Council's judgment which should prevail. To repeat the words of Estey J in *Kuchma v. Tache (Rural Municipality)* [[1945] SCR 234] (at p. 243):

> Upon the question of public interest, courts have recognized that the municipal council, familiar with local conditions, is in the best position of all parties to determine what is or is not in the public interest. …

In summary on the first issue, I am satisfied that the purposes of City Council in resolving not to do business with Shell were proper and fell within the powers of the City under the *Vancouver Charter*.

In the majority decision in *Shell v. Vancouver*, Sopinka J was less willing to see the purposes of municipal government in such broad terms, preferring instead to see municipal purposes as having to relate more directly to matters within the boundaries of the local area. Whereas Justice McLachlin was inclined to see the municipalities as a distinct form of administrative decision-maker in light of its democratic structure, Justice Sopinka was more circumspect about deferring to democratic entities, noting (at para. 95):

> The suggestion that the only remedy is at the polls is of no value to the minority, who would be left with no remedy, and Council could continue to enlarge its statutory powers as long as it was able to retain its majority support. The public policy in favour of restricting a municipality to its statutory powers exists as much for the minority as for the majority.

Of particular concern in this case was the open-ended nature of the authorizing provision relied on by the City of Vancouver in support of its action, which could be taken to confer an almost limitless authority if not checked by the courts. In a subsequent case, *114957 Canada Ltée (Spraytech, Société d'arrosage) v. Hudson (Town)*, [2001] 2 SCR 241, addressing municipal authority, Justice LeBel (at para. 53) sought to draw a line between the kinds of popular concerns that could properly become the subject of municipal legislation:

> It appears to be sound legislative and administrative policy, under such [broadly worded] provisions, to grant local governments a residual authority to deal with the unforeseen or changing circumstances, and to address emerging or changing issues concerning the welfare of the local community living within their territory. Nevertheless, such a provision cannot be construed as an open and unlimited grant of provincial powers. It is not enough that a particular issue has become a pressing concern in the opinion of a local community. This concern must relate to problems that engage the community as a local entity, not a member of the broader polity. It must be closely related to the immediate interests of the community within the territorial limits defined by the legislature in a matter where local governments may usefully intervene.

The *Spraytech* case also introduced the concept of "subsidiarity" into governance-related legal disputes. Subsidiarity is described by the Supreme Court of Canada as "the proposition that law-making and implementation are often best achieved at a level of government that is not only effective, but also closest to the citizens affected and thus most responsive to their needs, to local distinctiveness, and to population diversity" (para. 3). In the *Spraytech* case, the principle was relied upon in support of an expansive approach to the interpretation of municipal powers. There is an implicit empirical assumption with the principle of subsidiarity that local governments are more democratically responsive, although such a claim seems hardly beyond contention, particularly in light of low voter turnout rates in municipal elections.

III. SOURCES OF EXECUTIVE POWER

Where does executive power come from? As we have already discussed, all executive power (except the limited authority existing in the *Constitution Act, 1867* or by virtue of constitutional convention) flows from the royal prerogative and statutory delegation.

A. Prerogative Powers

Prerogative powers are those powers exercisable by the Crown that do not arise from a statutory grant of power to the Crown. Prerogative powers are residual in the sense that historically the power of the Crown pre-existed that of the legislature and as a result prerogative powers are those powers that have remained with the Crown.

In exercising prerogative powers, the Crown is restricted to executive acts. Consequently, the Crown cannot exercise legislative powers pursuant to its prerogative, nor can it exercise judicial powers.

The prerogative powers themselves are not static in the sense that these powers will remain undiminished over time. To the contrary, where the legislature enacts a statute in relation to a matter previously exercised through prerogative powers, the statute has the effect of superseding the prerogative power. The ability of the legislature to abolish prerogative powers derives from parliamentary supremacy, the superior position of the legislature in our constitutional system.

At the present time the powers exercised by way of prerogative include many of the Crown's powers of appointment, and powers relating to foreign affairs, such as declarations of war, the appointment of ambassadors, and the issuing of passports.

There has been some legal debate over who in the executive can exercise prerogative powers and whether prerogative powers can be subjected to judicial oversight. These questions are considered in the following excerpt from *Black v. Chrétien*, a case involving a decision by the prime minister to recommend against the conferral of a foreign honour on a Canadian citizen, Conrad Black.

Black v. Chrétien
(2001), 199 DLR (4th) 228 (Ont. CA)

LASKIN JA: … [23] The motions judge concluded that the Prime Minister's communication with the Queen was an exercise of the prerogative power to grant honours and conduct foreign affairs. I agree with the motions judge that Prime Minister Chrétien was exercising a prerogative power, although I rest my own conclusion on the honours prerogative alone.

[24] Mr. Black submits that the motions judge erred in his conclusion for four reasons. First, because Mr. Black did not plead that the Prime Minister exercised a Crown prerogative, the motions judge should not have concluded that he did. Second, in Canada the Prime Minister does not have the power to exercise the Crown prerogative, only the Governor-General does. Third, the actions of Prime Minister Chrétien pleaded in the statement of claim were not an exercise of the Crown prerogative, either in relation to the granting of honours or the conduct of foreign affairs, but an unsolicited personal intervention in which

the Prime Minister gave wrong legal advice. Fourth, in Canada the prerogative power to conduct foreign affairs has been displaced by the *Department of Foreign Affairs and International Trade Act*, RSC 1985 c. E-22.

[25] To put these submissions in context, I will briefly review the nature of the Crown's prerogative power. According to Professor Dicey, the Crown prerogative is "the residue of discretionary or arbitrary authority, which at any given time is left in the hands of the Crown." Dicey, *Introduction to the Study of the Law of the Constitution* 10th ed. (London: Macmillan, 1959) at p. 424. Dicey's broad definition has been explicitly adopted by the Supreme Court of Canada and the House of Lords. See *Effect of Exercise of Royal Prerogative of Mercy upon Deportation Proceedings, Re*, [1933] SCR 269 (SCC), at 272-73 and *Attorney General v. De Keyser's Royal Hotel Ltd.*, [1920] AC 508 (UK HL), at 526. See also Peter Hogg and Patrick Monahan, *Liability of the Crown* 3rd ed. (Toronto: Carswell, 2000) at p. 15.

[26] The prerogative is a branch of the common law because decisions of courts determine both its existence and its extent. In short, the prerogative consists of "the powers and privileges accorded by the common law to the Crown." Peter Hogg, *Constitutional Law in Canada* Loose-Leaf Edition (Toronto: Carswell, 1995) at 1.9. See also *Case of Proclamations* (1611), 77 ER 1352 (Eng. KB). The Crown prerogative has descended from England to the Commonwealth. As Professor Cox has recently observed, "it is clear that the major prerogatives apply throughout the Commonwealth, and are applied as a pure question of law." N. Cox, *The Dichotomy of Legal Theory and Political Reality: The Honours Prerogative and Imperial Unity*, 14 Australian Journal of Law and Society (1998-99) 15 at 19.

[27] Despite its broad reach, the Crown prerogative can be limited or displaced by statute. See *Parliament of Canada Act*, RSC 1985 c. P-1 s. 4. Once a statute occupies ground formerly occupied by the prerogative, the prerogative goes into abeyance. The Crown may no longer act under the prerogative, but must act under and subject to the conditions imposed by the statute. *AG v. DeKeyser's Royal Hotel, supra*. In England and Canada, legislation has severely curtailed the scope of the Crown prerogative. Dean Hogg comments that statutory displacement of the prerogative has had the effect of "shrinking the prerogative powers of the Crown down to a very narrow compass." *Supra*. Professor Wade agrees:

> [I]n the course of constitutional history the Crown's prerogative powers have been stripped away, and for administrative purposes the prerogative is now a much-attenuated remnant. Numerous statutes have expressly restricted it, and even where a statute merely overlaps it the doctrine is that the prerogative goes into abeyance. E.C.S. Wade, *Administrative Law*, 6th ed. (Oxford: Clarendon Press, 1988) at pp. 240-41.

Nonetheless, as I will discuss, the granting of honours has never been displaced by statute in Canada and therefore continues to be a Crown prerogative in this country.

· · ·

[31] Mr. Black's second submission is that the Prime Minister cannot exercise the Crown prerogative. He submits that in Canada, only the Governor-General can exercise the prerogative. I find no support for this proposition in theory or in practice. Admittedly, the Governor-General is the Queen's permanent representative in Canada. The 1947 *Letters Patent Constituting the Office of the Governor-General* is the instrument by which the Monarch delegates her prerogative powers for application in Canada. The *Letters Patent* empowers the Governor-General "to exercise all powers and authorities lawfully belonging to Us in

respect of Canada." By convention, the Governor-General exercises her powers on the advice of the Prime Minister or Cabinet. Although the Governor-General retains discretion to refuse to follow this advice, in Canada that discretion has been exercised only in the most exceptional circumstances. See Paul Lordon, Q.C., *Crown Law* (Toronto: Butterworths, 1991) at p. 70.

[32] Still, nothing in the *Letters Patent* or the case law requires that all prerogative powers be exercised exclusively by the Governor-General. As members of the Privy Council, the Prime Minister and other Ministers of the Crown may also exercise the Crown prerogative. See Lordon, *supra*, at p. 71. The reasons of Wilson J in *Operation Dismantle* affirm that prerogative power may be exercised by cabinet ministers and therefore does not lie exclusively with the Governor-General. Similarly, in England the prerogative "[was] gradually relocated from the Monarch in person to the Monarch's advisors or ministers. Hence it made increasing sense to refer to those powers as belonging to the Crown ... ." Bridgid Hadfield, *Judicial Review and the Prerogative Power* in M. Sunkin and S. Payne, *The Nature of the Crown* (Oxford: Oxford University Press, 1999) at p. 199. This gradual relocation of the prerogative is consistent with Professor Wade's general view of the Crown prerogative as an "instrument of government." Commentary on Dicey's *Introduction to the Study of the Law of the Constitution* 9th ed. (London: Macmillan, 1950). The conduct of foreign affairs, for example, "is an executive act of government in which neither the Queen nor Parliament has any part." F.A. Mann, *Foreign Affairs in English Courts* (Oxford: Clarendon Press, 1986) at p. 2. See also *Barton v. Commonwealth (Australia)* (1974), 48 ALJR 161 (Australia HC), at 172.

[33] Counsel for the respondents points out that if Mr. Black were correct, the Prime Minister—whose powers are not enumerated in any statute—would have no legal authority to speak for Canada on foreign affairs. This proposition is, on its face, absurd. I therefore reject Mr. Black's submission that only the Governor-General can exercise prerogative powers in Canada. I conclude that the Prime Minister and the Government of Canada can exercise the Crown prerogative as well.

· · ·

Second Issue: Is the Prerogative Power Exercised by the Prime Minister Reviewable in the Courts?

[42] This is the main question on this appeal. The motions judge concluded at p. 541 that Mr. Black's complaint about the Prime Minister was not justiciable. He wrote: "It is not within the power of the court to decide whether or not the advice of the PM about the prerogative honour to be conferred or denied upon Black was right or wrong. It is not for the court to give its opinion on the advice tendered by the PM to another country. These are non-justiciable decisions for which the PM is politically accountable to Parliament and the electorate, not the courts."

[43] Mr. Black submits that the motions judge erred in concluding that Prime Minister Chrétien's exercise of the honours prerogative was not reviewable by the court. The amended statement of claim pleads that the Prime Minister gave the Queen wrong legal advice, which detrimentally affected Mr. Black. Mr. Black argues that had the advice been given under a statutory power, it would have been subject to judicial review; it should similarly be subject to judicial review if given under a prerogative power.

[44] I agree with Mr. Black that the source of the power—statute or prerogative—should not determine whether the action complained of is reviewable. However, in my view, the action complained of in this case—giving advice to the Queen or communicating to her Canada's policy on the conferral of an honour on a Canadian citizen—is not justiciable. Even if the advice was wrong or given carelessly or negligently, it is not reviewable in the courts. I therefore agree with the motions judge's conclusion.

[45] Under the law that existed at least into the 1960s, the court's power to judicially review the prerogative was very limited. The court could determine whether a prerogative power existed and, if so, what its scope was, and whether it had been superseded by statute. However, once a court established the existence and scope of a prerogative power, it could not review how that power was exercised. See S. DeSmith, H. Woolf and J. Jowell, *DeSmith, Woolf & Jowell's Principles of Judicial Review* (London: Sweet & Maxwell, 1999) at p. 175 and *DeKeyser's Royal Hotel, supra*. The appropriateness or adequacy of the grounds for its exercise, even whether the procedures used were fair, were not reviewable. The courts insisted that the source of the power—the prerogative—precluded judicial scrutiny of its exercise. The underlying rationale for this narrow review of the prerogative was that exercises of prerogative power ordinarily raised questions courts were not qualified or competent to answer.

[46] Even this narrow view of the court's role in reviewing the prerogative power now has to be modified in Canada because of the *Canadian Charter of Rights and Freedoms*. By s. 32(1)(a), the *Charter* applies to Parliament and the Government of Canada in respect of all matters within the authority of Parliament. The Crown prerogative lies within the authority of Parliament. Therefore, if an individual claims that the exercise of a prerogative power violates that individual's *Charter* rights, the court has a duty to decide the claim. See *Operation Dismantle* ... . However, Mr. Black does not assert any *Charter* claim.

[47] Apart from the *Charter*, the expanding scope of judicial review and of Crown liability make it no longer tenable to hold that the exercise of a prerogative power is insulated from judicial review merely because it is a prerogative and not a statutory power. The preferable approach is that adopted by the House of Lords in the *Civil Service Unions* case ... . There, the House of Lords emphasized that the controlling consideration in determining whether the exercise of a prerogative power is judicially reviewable is its subject matter, not its source. If, in the words of Lord Roskill, the subject matter of the prerogative power is "amenable to the judicial process," it is reviewable; if not, it is not reviewable. Lord Roskill provided content to this subject matter test of reviewability by explaining that the exercise of the prerogative will be amenable to the judicial process if it affects the rights of individuals. Again, in his words at p. 417:

> ... If the executive in pursuance of the statutory power does an act affecting the rights of the citizen, it is beyond question that in principle the manner of the exercise of that power may today be challenged on one or more of the three grounds which I have mentioned earlier in this speech. If the executive instead of acting under a statutory power acts under a prerogative power and in particular a prerogative power delegated to the respondent under article 4 of the Order in Council of 1982, so as to affect the rights of the citizen, I am unable to see, subject to what I shall say later, that there is any logical reason why the fact that the source of the power is the prerogative and not statute should today deprive the citizen of that right of challenge to

the manner of its exercise which he would possess were the source of the power statutory. In either case the act in question is the act of the executive… .

· · ·

[51] Under the test set out by the House of Lords, the exercise of the prerogative will be justiciable, or amenable to the judicial process, if its subject matter affects the rights or legitimate expectations of an individual. Where the rights or legitimate expectations of an individual are affected, the court is both competent and qualified to judicially review the exercise of the prerogative.

[52] Thus, the basic question in this case is whether the Prime Minister's exercise of the honours prerogative affected a right or legitimate expectation enjoyed by Mr. Black and is therefore judicially reviewable. To put this question in context, I will briefly discuss prerogative powers that lie at the opposite ends of the spectrum of judicial reviewability. At one end of the spectrum lie executive decisions to sign a treaty or to declare war. These are matters of "high policy." *R v. Secretary of State for Foreign & Commonwealth Affairs* (1988), [1989] 1 All ER 655 (Eng. CA), at 660, *per* Taylor LJ. Where matters of high policy are concerned, public policy and public interest considerations far outweigh the rights of individuals or their legitimate expectations. In my view, apart from *Charter* claims, these decisions are not judicially reviewable.

[53] At the other end of the spectrum lie decisions like the refusal of a passport or the exercise of mercy. The power to grant or withhold a passport continues to be a prerogative power. A passport is the property of the Government of Canada, and no person, strictly speaking, has a legal right to one. However, common sense dictates that a refusal to issue a passport for improper reasons or without affording the applicant procedural fairness should be judicially reviewable. This was the position taken by the English Court of Appeal in *R v. Secretary of State for Foreign & Commonwealth Affairs, ex parte Everett, supra*. Two passages from that case are worth highlighting. O'Connor LJ wrote at p. 658:

> The judge held that the issue of a passport fell into an entirely different category. That seems common sense. It is a familiar document to all citizens who travel in the world and it would seem obvious to me that the exercise of the prerogative, because there is no doubt that passports are issued under the royal prerogative in the discretion of the Secretary of State, is an area where common sense tells one that, if for some reason a passport is wrongly refused for a bad reason, the court should be able to inquire into it. I would reject the submission made on behalf of the Secretary of State that the judge was wrong to review the case.

And Taylor LJ wrote at p. 660:

> … At the top of the scale of executive functions under the prerogative are matters of high policy, of which examples were given by their Lordships: making treaties, making law, dissolving Parliament, mobilising the armed forces. Clearly those matters, and no doubt a number of others, are not justiciable. But the grant or refusal of a passport is in a quite different category. It is a matter of administrative decision, affecting the rights of individuals and their freedom of travel. It raises issues which are just as justiciable as, for example, the issues arising in immigration cases … .

· · ·

[60] The refusal to grant an honour is far removed from the refusal to grant a passport or a pardon, where important individual interests are at stake. Unlike the refusal of a peerage, the refusal of a passport or a pardon has real adverse consequences for the person affected. Here, no important individual interests are at stake. Mr. Black's rights were not affected, however broadly "rights" are construed. No Canadian citizen has a right to an honour.

[61] And no Canadian citizen can have a legitimate expectation of receiving an honour. In Canada the doctrine of legitimate expectations informs the duty of procedural fairness; it gives no substantive rights. *Baker v. Canada (Minister of Citizenship & Immigration)* (1999), 174 DLR (4th) 193 (SCC), at 212-14. See also *Civil Service Unions*, per Lord Diplock at p. 408-9. Here Mr. Black does not assert that he was denied procedural fairness. Indeed, he had no procedural rights.

[62] But even if the doctrine of legitimate expectations could give substantive rights, neither Mr. Black nor any other Canadian citizen can claim a legitimate expectation of receiving an honour. The receipt of an honour lies entirely within the discretion of the conferring body. The conferral of the honour at issue in this case, a British peerage, is a discretionary favour bestowed by the Queen. It engages no liberty, no property, no economic interests. It enjoys no procedural protection. It does not have a sufficient legal component to warrant the court's intervention. Instead, it involves "moral and political considerations which it is not within the province of the courts to assess." See *Operation Dismantle* ... , per Dickson J at p. 465.

[63] In other words, the discretion to confer or refuse to confer an honour is the kind of discretion that is not reviewable by the court. In this case, the court has even less reason to intervene because the decision whether to confer a British peerage on Mr. Black rests not with Prime Minister Chrétien, but with the Queen. At its highest, all the Prime Minister could do was give the Queen advice not to confer a peerage on Mr. Black.

[64] For these reasons, I agree with the motions judge that Prime Minister Chrétien's exercise of the honours prerogative by giving advice to the Queen about granting Mr. Black's peerage is not justiciable and therefore not judicially reviewable.

[65] Once Prime Minister Chrétien's exercise of the honours prerogative is found to be beyond review by the courts, how the Prime Minister exercised the prerogative is also beyond review. Even if the advice was wrong or careless or negligent, even if his motives were questionable, they cannot be challenged by judicial review. To paraphrase Dickson J in *Thorne's Hardware* ... , at p. 112: "It is neither our duty nor our right" to investigate the Prime Minister's motives or his reasons for his advice. Therefore, the declaratory relief and the tort claims asserted by Mr. Black cannot succeed. For these reasons, I would dismiss his appeal.

B. Statutory Powers

Far and away the vast majority of executive powers originate from a delegation of authority by the legislature by statute. The provisions from the *Canadian Human Rights Act*, excerpted above, are illustrative of the typical form of delegation. Here the statute creates the administrative body, in this case the Canadian Human Rights Commission, and enumerates the specific powers to be exercised it. The authority of the commission is determined solely by the statutory grant because as an administrative body the commission has no inherent powers.

There are few restraints on the legislature's ability to delegate powers to administrative bodies. For example, unlike the exercise of prerogative powers, which are restricted to executive functions, there are no functional restrictions on delegated powers. Consequently, it is common for the legislature to delegate even extensive legislative and adjudicatory functions to administrative bodies.

The principle of parliamentary sovereignty recognizes that the ability of parliament to enact legislation delegating the exercise of authority to some other body, be it Cabinet or an independent administrative body, is qualified only by constitutional considerations, such as the constraints found in the *Canadian Charter of Rights and Freedoms* and those relating to the division of powers.

In other words, the legislature cannot in law delegate powers that exceed the legislature's own powers. The application of the Charter to the executive is expressly confirmed by s. 32 of the Charter:

> Actions of the executive which breach individual *Charter* rights can and will be set aside, whether or not they are mandated by statute.

For example, where s. 7 applies (that is, where life, liberty, or security of the person is imperilled), the doctrine of "unconstitutional vagueness" may invalidate a statutory provision (and statutory delegation) either because that provision "(1) ... fails to give those who might come within the ambit of the provision fair notice of the consequences of their conduct; or (2) ... fails to adequately limit law enforcement discretion": see *Suresh v. Canada*, [2002] 1 SCR 3, at para. 81.

Another recurring argument that is made in relation to delegation is that a delegation must not amount to a complete abdication of legislative authority. This argument was considered by the Supreme Court of Canada in *Re Gray* (1918), 57 SCR 150, a case that considered the sweeping delegation of authority to the governor general in council under the *War Measures Act, 1914*.

Re Gray
(1918), 57 SCR 150

[This case concerned the legality of changes to statutory conscription rules that were enacted by Cabinet pursuant to a general delegation of powers. The delegation in question provided that

> [t]he Governor-in-Council shall have power to do and authorize such acts and things, and to make from time to time such orders and regulations, as he may by reason of the existence of real or apprehended war, invasion or insurrection, deem necessary or advisable for the security, defence, peace, order and welfare of Canada; .

In rejecting the argument that the delegation amounted to an unconstitutional abdication of legislative powers to the executive, the chief justice made the following comments:]

ANGLIN CJ: ... The practice of authorizing administrative bodies to make regulations to carry out the object of an Act, instead of setting out all the details in the Act itself, is well known and its legality is unquestioned. But it is said that the power to make such regulations could not constitutionally be granted to such an extent as to enable the express provisions of a statute to be amended or repealed; that under the constitution Parliament alone is to make laws, the Governor in Council to execute them, and the Court to interpret them; that it follows that no one of these fundamental branches of government can constitutionally either delegate or accept the functions of any other branch.

In view of *Rex v. Halliday*, [1917] AC 260, 86 LJKB 1119, I do not think this broad proposition can be maintained. Parliament cannot, indeed, abdicate its functions, but within reasonable limits at any rate it can delegate its powers to the executive government. Such powers must necessarily be subject to determination at any time by Parliament, and needless to say the acts of the executive, under its delegated authority, must fall within the ambit of the legislative pronouncement by which its authority is measured.

It is true that Lord Dunedin, in the case referred to, said:

> The British constitution has entrusted to the two Houses of Parliament, subject to the assent of the King, an absolute power untrammelled by any written instrument, obedience to which may be compelled by some judicial body.

That, undoubtedly, is not the case in this country, which has its constitution founded in the Imperial statute, *The BNA Act*, 1867. I cannot, however, find anything in that constitutional Act which, so far as material to the question now under consideration, would impose any limitation on the authority of the Parliament of Canada to which the Imperial Parliament is not subject.

. . .

It seems to me obvious that Parliament intended, as the language used implies, to clothe the executive with the widest powers in time of danger. Taken literally, the language of the section contains unlimited powers. Parliament expressly enacted that, when need arises, the executive may for the common defence make such orders and regulations as they may deem necessary or advisable for the security, peace, order and welfare of Canada. The enlightened men who framed that section, and the members of Parliament who adopted it, were providing for a very great emergency, and they must be understood to have employed words in their natural sense, and to have intended what they have said. There is no doubt, in my opinion, that the regulation in question was passed to provide for the security and welfare of Canada and it is therefore *intra vires* of the statute under which it purports to be made.

. . .

There are obvious objections of a political character to the practice of executive legislation in this country because of local conditions. But these objections should have been urged when the regulations were submitted to Parliament for its approval, or better still when *The War Measures Act* was being discussed. Parliament was the delegating authority, and it was for that body to put any limitations on the power conferred upon the executive. I am not aware that the authority to pass these regulations was questioned by a vote in either house. Our legislators were no doubt impressed in the hour of peril with the conviction that the safety of the country is the supreme law against which no other law can prevail. It is our clear duty to give effect to their patriotic intention.

[Chief Justice Anglin was equally emphatic in his rejection of the argument that the delegation amounted to an abdication.]

A complete abdication by Parliament of its legislative functions is something so inconceivable that the constitutionality of an attempt to do anything of the kind need not be considered. Short of such an abdication, any limited delegation would seem to be within the ambit of a legislative jurisdiction certainly as wide as that of which it has been said by incontrovertible authority that it is

> as plenary and as ample … as the Imperial Parliament in the plentitude of its powers possessed and could bestow. [*Hodge v. Reg.*, 9 App. Cas. 117, at p. 133, 53 LJPC.]

I am of the opinion that it was within the legislative authority of the Parliament of Canada to delegate to the Governor in Council the power to enact the impugned orders in council. To hold otherwise would be very materially to restrict the legislative powers of Parliament.

It is important to note that neither the Chief Justice nor Justice Anglin rejects the existence of a constitutional principle that denies the legislature the power to fully divest itself of its legislative powers. However, in light of the wide scope of the delegation in *Re Gray*, it is difficult to conceive of a delegation, short of one that purports to be of a permanent nature, that would offend this principle. The provinces were also found to possess a similarly wide authority to delegate legislative functions in *Hodge v. The Queen* (1883), 9 App. Cas. 117, quoted in *Re Gray* above.

A related principle that constrains the ability of legislatures to delegate authority requires that neither the federal Parliament nor the provincial legislatures may delegate legislative powers to the other. The basis of this rule is that an inter-delegation would upset the constitutional division of powers contained in ss. 91 and 92 of the *Constitution Act, 1867*. In the *Nova Scotia Inter-delegation* case, the Supreme Court of Canada was required to consider the constitutionality of a scheme by which provincial powers regarding employment matters would be delegated to the federal Parliament and certain taxation powers would be delegated from Parliament to the Nova Scotia legislature in order to facilitate an unemployment insurance scheme.

A-G NS v. A-G Can. (Nova Scotia Inter-delegation)
[1951] SCR 31

RAND J: … [60] Can either of these legislative bodies, then, confer upon the other or can the latter accept and exercise in such a subsidiary manner legislative power vested in the former? They are bodies of co-ordinate rank; in constitutional theory, legislative enactment is that of the Sovereign in Parliament and in Legislature, to each of which, as legislative organs of a federal union, has been given exclusive authority over specified matters in a distribution of total legislative subject-matter. Delegation has its source in the necessities of legislation; it has become an essential to completeness and adaptability of much of statutory law; but if one legislature is adequate, by its own action, to enactment, so, surely, is the other; in the proposed bill, there is no suggestion of authorizing Parliament, as delegate, in turn to sub-delegate to agencies of its own, and the practical ground of delegation is absent. But even where the broadest authority is intended, can we seriously imagine the Imperial Parliament, in the implication of the power to delegate, intending to include delegation by and to each other? These bodies were created solely for the purposes of the constitution by which each, in the traditions and conventions of the English Parliamentary system, was to legislate, in accordance with its debate and judgment, on the matters assigned to it and on no other. To imply a power to shift this debate and this judgment of either to the other is to permit the substance of transfer to take place, a dealing with and in jurisdiction utterly foreign to the conception of a federal organization.

[61] So exercising delegated powers would not only be incompatible with the constitutional function with which Nova Scotia is endowed and an affront to constitutional principle and practice, it would violate, also, the interest in the substance of Dominion legislation which both the people and the legislative bodies of the other provinces possess. In a unitary state, that question does not arise; but it seems to be quite evident that such legislative absolutism, except in respects in which, by the terms express or implied of the constituting Act, only one jurisdiction is concerned, is incompatible with federal reality. If a matter affects only one, it would not be a subject for delegation to the other; matters of possible delegation, by that fact, imply a common interest. Dominion legislation in relation to employment in Nova Scotia enacted by the legislature may affect interests outside of Nova Scotia; by delegation Nova Scotia might impose an indirect tax upon citizens of Alberta in respect of matters arising in Nova Scotia; or it might place restrictions on foreign or interprovincial trade affecting Nova Scotia which impinge on interests in Ontario. The incidence of laws of that nature is intended by the constitution to be determined by the deliberations of Parliament and not of any Legislature. In the generality of actual delegation to its own agencies, Parliament, recognizing the need of the legislation, lays down the broad scheme and indicates the principles, purposes and scope of the subsidiary details to be supplied by the delegate: under the mode of enactment now being considered, the real and substantial analysis and weighing of the political considerations which would decide the actual provisions adopted, would be given by persons chosen to represent local interests.

[62] Since neither is a creature nor a subordinate body of the other, the question is not only or chiefly whether one can delegate, but whether the other can accept. Delegation implies subordination and in *Hodge v. The Queen* (*supra*), the following observations (at p. 132) appear:

> Within these limits of subjects and area the local legislature is supreme, and has the same authority as the Imperial Parliament, or the parliament of the Dominion, would have had under like circumstances to confide to a municipal institution or body of its own creation authority to make by-laws or resolutions as to subjects specified in the enactment, and with the object of carrying the enactment into operation and effect.

· · ·

It was argued at the bar that a legislature committing important regulations to agents or delegates effaces itself. That is not so. It retains its powers intact, and can, whenever it pleases, destroy the agency it has created and set up another, or take the matter directly into his own hands. How far it shall seek the aid of subordinate agencies, and how long it shall continue them, are matters for each legislature, and not for Courts of Law, to decide.

[63] Subordination, as so considered, is constitutional subordination and not that implied in the relation of delegate. Sovereign states can and do confer and accept temporary transfers of jurisdiction under which they enact their own laws within the territory of others; but the exercise of delegation by one for another would be an incongruity; for the enactments of a state are of its own laws, not those of another state.

[64] Subordination implies duty: delegation is not made to be accepted or acted upon at the will of the delegate; it is ancillary to legislation which the appropriate legislature thinks desirable; and a duty to act either by enacting or by exercising a conferred discretion not, at the particular time, to act, rests upon the delegate. No such duty could be imposed upon or accepted by a co-ordinate legislature and the proposed bill does no more than to proffer authority to be exercised by the delegate solely of its own volition and, for its own purposes, as a discretionary privilege. Even in the case of virtually unlimited delegation as under the Poor Act of England, assuming that degree to be open to Canadian legislatures, the delegate is directly amenable to his principal for his execution of the authority.

. . .

[67] The practical consequences of the proposed measure, a matter which the Courts may take into account, entail the danger, through continued exercise of delegated power, of prescriptive claims based on conditions and relations established in reliance on the delegation. Possession here as elsewhere would be nine points of law and disruptive controversy might easily result. The power of revocation might in fact become no more feasible, practically, than amendment of the Act of 1867 of its own volition by the British Parliament.

[68] I would, therefore, dismiss the appeal with costs.

Shortly after deciding the *Nova Scotia Inter-delegation* case, the Supreme Court of Canada was presented with another inter-delegation scheme, except in this case the delegations were made, not directly from one legislature to another, but from Parliament to a provincially created administrative body. Here the object of the scheme was to confer comprehensive regulatory authority to market potatoes from PEI to the provincial marketing board, which required the federal Parliament to delegate powers relating to the export and interprovincial trade in PEI potatoes to the marketing board, a provincial administrative body. This form of inter-delegation was found to be unobjectionable on the basis that the inter-delegation was to an administrative body, as opposed to the legislature itself: see *PEI Potato Marketing Board v. Willis*, [1952] 2 SCR 392. The principal policy basis behind the distinction between invalid legislative inter-delegation and valid administrative inter-delegation relates to the democratic expectations of the legislature, which must be seen to be acting free of allegiances to other bodies, as opposed to those of an administrative body, where the recipient of authority is expected to exercise that power in accordance with the requirements of the delegating body.

One further constitutional restriction that may intrude on the power of a legislative body to delegate authority to an administrative body concerns whether the conferral of judicial functions on administrative tribunals interferes with the jurisdiction of the superior courts as defined by ss. 96 to 100 of the *Constitution Act, 1867*. Again, in the absence of a general separation-of-powers doctrine in Canada, there is no overarching prohibition against administrative tribunals exercising judicial functions. Instead, the prohibition is against bodies that are not constituted in accordance with the requirements of ss. 96 to 100—namely, appointed by the governor general, from the ranks of the bar and with security of tenure and security of salaries, exercising the powers of a superior court as contemplated under s. 96.

The difficulty has been determining with any exactitude what the powers of a s. 96 court are. To answer this question, the Supreme Court of Canada has developed a three-part test, enunciated first in *Re Residential Tenancies Act*, [1981] 1 SCR 714. We return to this issue in chapter 6.

C. Limits on the Exercise of Delegated Authority

While the constraints on the ability of the legislative branch to delegate authority are minimal, once authority is delegated to an administrative actor, the law imposes a rigorous set of limitations on the exercise of power by the recipient of delegated authority. The overarching principle that governs the exercise of delegated authority is that it must be exercised within the confines of the delegation itself. Recipients of delegated authority have no inherent jurisdiction to act. Their sole source of power (excepting those bodies that exercise prerogative powers or powers under the Constitution) derives from the statutory delegation.

Consequently, any act done outside the boundaries of the statutory grant is without legal authority and unlawful—that is, it is *ultra vires*. Jurisdiction in this sense relates to *what* powers are exercised, but there also exists a set of rules that dictate *how* delegated power must be exercised. These latter rules are also jurisdictional in the sense that a delegated authority is only authorized to exercise powers in ways that conform to these requirements. Put another way, an administrative agency may embark on an inquiry properly within its statutory mandate, but in carrying out the inquiry, the agency may nevertheless act without proper legal basis due to a failure to abide by the requirements of procedural fairness or abuses of discretion.

The rule that a delegated authority can exercise only those powers that are granted to it is conceptually straightforward and tends to turn on questions of the interpretation of the authorizing legislation. For example, in *Shell v. Vancouver* (excerpted above), there was no disagreement on the general rule that administrative bodies, in that case municipalities, "must stay within the powers conferred on them by provincial statutes" (per Sopinka J). However, McLachlin J and the majority disagreed in respect of the proper interpretation of the statutory provision relied upon in support of the municipality's decision, with McLachlin being more willing to take a "benevolent" (expansive) interpretive approach.

Determining whether an administrative act or decision is properly clothed with jurisdiction may require a consideration of whether the decision-maker has complied with applicable statutory conditions or whether a certain set of required factual circumstances is present. Consider the facts of *Bell v. Ontario (Human Rights Commission)*, [1971] SCR 756. At issue was whether the Ontario Human Rights Commission could exercise its authority in relation to a discrimination complaint involving the renting of accommodation. The commission's powers over discrimination matters were in relation to a "self-contained dwelling unit." In deciding that the commission was properly prevented from initiating proceedings, the Supreme Court of Canada held that the commission's jurisdiction was dependent upon the preliminary finding that the allegation of discrimination was in relation to a "self-contained dwelling unit," and the commission could not proceed in circumstances where that preliminary condition was not established.

A related jurisdictional rule requires that delegated authority must be exercised by the specific delegate to whom the authority is granted. This rule is captured in the Latin maxim *delegatus non potest delegare* described by Kerwin J in *Reference re Regulations in Relation to Chemicals*, [1943] SCR 1:

> The statute does not in express terms provide for delegation and the maxim *delegatus non potest delegare* is invoked to support a construction as would deny any implication of such an authority.
>
> The general principle is stated in Broom's Legal Maxims at page 570, as follows:
>
> > This principle is that a delegated authority cannot be re-delegated: *delegata potestas non potest delegari*, that is, one agent cannot lawfully appoint another to perform the duties of his agency. This rule applies wherever the authority involves a trust or discretion in the agent for the exercise of which he is selected, but does not apply where it involves no matter of discretion, and it is immaterial whether the act be done by one person or another, and the original agent remains responsible to the principal.
>
> The principle thus stated is somewhat qualified by Broom, at page 572, as follows:
>
> > Although, however, a deputy cannot, according to the above rule, transfer his entire powers to another, yet a deputy possessing general powers may, in many cases, constitute another person his servant or bailiff, for the purpose of doing some particular act; provided, of course, that such act be within the scope of his own legitimate authority.

And again:

> The rule as to delegated functions must, moreover, be understood with this necessary qualification, that, in the particular case, no power to re-delegate such functions has been given. Such an authority to employ a deputy may be either express or implied by the recognised usage of trade.
>
> The maxim is most frequently applied in matters pertaining to principal and agent but it is also applied in respect of legislative grants of authority; for example in *Re Behari Lal et al.*, it was held that the power conferred on the Governor General in Council by section 30 of the *Immigration Act* to prohibit the landing of immigrants of a specified class could not be delegated to the Minister of the Interior. Mr. Justice Clement said:
>
> > … In my opinion, nothing short of express words would avail to enable His Excellency in Council to delegate to another or others a power of this nature, the exercise of which is conditioned upon his consideration of its necessity or expediency.
>
> Again in *Geraghty v. Porter*, it was held that a delegated power of legislation must be exercised strictly in accordance with the powers creating it; and in the absence of express power so to do the authority cannot be delegated to any other person or body.
>
> The maxim, however, is at most a rule of construction, subject to qualifications, some of which are referred to by Broom.

> In the case of a statute, there, of course, must be a consideration of the language of the whole enactment and of its purposes and objects.

One important qualification to the rule against subdelegation, alluded to above, is that matters that are "merely administrative" may lawfully be subdelegated. In this context, "merely administrative" matters are those that do not involve the exercise of substantial amounts of discretion. This exception is in keeping with the overall purpose of the rule that recognizes that where the legislature entrusted decision-making powers to a certain official or body, then those powers should be exercised specifically by that delegate. In cases where there is little or no discretion to exercise, it should not matter who the decision-maker is because the outcomes are dictated by the scheme itself.

It should also be observed that a delegate may subdelegate where the power to subdelegate is specifically provided for in the statute.

The determination of the legality of the exercise of administrative authority is the function of the courts. The supervisory role of the courts raises complex issues concerning the conditions under which the judicial branch should interfere with decisions taken by the executive branch. These issues are taken up in chapter 8.

IV. THE NATURE AND FUNCTION OF DELEGATED POWERS

In light of the limited number of restrictions that are placed on the ability of the legislature to delegate authority to executive bodies, it should come as no surprise that, in practice, delegated authority has been granted in virtually every area of public policy. Although there is no accepted typology classifying the various forms of delegated power, it is common for commentators on administrative law to discuss administrative powers in terms of legislative, judicial, and administrative functions.

The characterization of the exercise of delegated authority in terms of function has historic legal significance in that many of the rules respecting the exercise of delegated authority varied depending on the nature of the powers exercised. For example, common law courts developed a set of procedural requirements, referred to as the rules of natural justice, that applied to decisions that were characterized as judicial or quasi-judicial, but not to those decisions that were classified as legislative or administrative in nature. Thus, how an administrative power was classified determined to a significant degree the manner by which that power had to be exercised.

In the last 25 years, the use of these classifications as a basis to determine the availability of procedural rights and remedies has given way to an approach that recognizes that a general duty to be fair is owed by a broader range of administrative decision-makers and is related to matters beyond simply the identity of the decision-maker, such as the type of interest affected and nature of the decision itself. Despite the courts' current de-emphasis on functional distinctions, it remains helpful to review the major types of decisions commonly made by administrative decision-makers.

A. Rule Making

The rise in the use of executive bodies to create rules of general application parallels the more general rise of administrative bodies. The most pervasive form of administrative rule making is the regulation-making power that is delegated to the Cabinet through the governor in council. However, administrative rule making is not restricted to this form. Regulation-making power is often delegated to other bodies, other than Cabinet. For instance, municipal bylaws are another prevalent form of delegated legislation, as are agency-developed policies and guidelines.

The legal effect of delegated legislation is determined by the parent legislation. In the case of regulations and municipal bylaws, these instruments are as effective as legislation in the sense that they give rise to legally enforceable obligations. However, delegated legislation, sometimes referred to as "subordinate legislation," is considered inferior to statutes; a conflict between a statute and delegated legislation is always resolved in favour in the statutory provision. In this context, a conflict is said to arise only in cases of direct conflict—that is, where compliance with both enactments is not possible. No conflict arises where delegated legislation, such as a municipal bylaw, imposes more onerous regulatory requirements than those enacted by a superior legislative body. See, for example, *114957 Canada Ltée (Spraytech, Société d'arrosage) v. Hudson (Town)*, [2001] 2 SCR 241.

The benefits of resorting to delegated forms of legislation relate chiefly to the relative flexibility of regulations. The statutory process is much more cumbersome and time consuming than the process for enacting regulations, and regulations are, consequently, preferred in situations that require adjustment of rules over time or detailed consultation with specific stakeholder groups. In many cases, it is impossible for legislators to know in advance the range of circumstances that will require specialized rules. Instead of amending or enlarging statutes in response to unforeseen cases, legislators often prefer to delegate the authority to enact rules to those persons who are charged with the implementation of the statutes, such as the minister (usually acting through Cabinet) or an agency. Delegated rule-making authority also allows for rule creation by those persons with specialized knowledge of the regulatory field, which legislators will generally lack. The result is a system of rule making that is more flexible, more responsive, and more sensitive to the regulatory context to be addressed.

The *Canadian Human Rights Act* again provides a helpful example. In the provision granting powers to the Canadian Human Rights Commission (set out above in section II.D), the commission is granted the authority to issue binding guidelines. This power allows the commission, the body that is most familiar with the application of the Act, to create more specific rules respecting the application of the Act in order to better guide the commission's decision-making process. Recall the excerpts from *Bell Canada v. Canadian Telephone Employees Association*, [2003] 1 SCR 884 cited above where the Supreme Court of Canada noted the commission's superior ability to make interpretive guidelines in order to ensure that the *Canadian Human Rights Act* is applied in ways that are supportive of the Act's goal of identifying and rectifying discrimination.

The expansive use of delegated legislation has led to concerns over the amount of scrutiny by elected officials and the public that regulations receive. The multiple readings of a bill in the legislature and the committee process in practice ensure that there is opportunity for interested groups and opposition politicians to consider the contents of a bill before it passes into law. Regulations, on the other hand, can be enacted by Cabinet without prior notice or consultation. These concerns were identified in an early consideration of the role of delegated rule making by a House of Commons Special Committee on Statutory Instruments (Third Report, *Journals*, October 22, 1969), at 1411:

> The more fundamental of the criticism can be summarized as follows: the parliamentary tendency to enact statutes in skeleton form, leaving the "details" to be filled in by regulations—such regulations bring often the very matters that are of most importance to the citizen; uncertainty in enabling statutes as to the extent of the area regulations are intended to cover; sweeping or subjective terms used in enabling acts which exclude the judicial control of the regulations made under their authority; lack of public debate, and inadequate consultation of all interested parties before the making of the regulations; lack of precision in the form and content of the regulations; inadequate publicity given to the regulations after they are made; inadequate parliamentary control over the regulations; and the danger that civil servants may be transformed into our masters.

To date, the courts have not generally been willing to extend the administrative law procedural obligations relating to notice and the opportunity to be heard to the executive's rule-making functions. That said, it should be noted that the courts have been more willing to impose procedural obligations in rule-making processes where the legislative outcomes have a particular impact on specific individuals. For example, where land-use bylaws particularly affect the property rights of individual landowners, the courts look past the formal legislative nature of the decision in imposing procedural obligations on municipal councils. See, for example, *Homex Realty and Development Co. v. Wyoming (Village)*, [1989] 2 SCR 1011.

In practice, regulation making is usually a fairly open activity, by virtue of government policy and some statutory law. In particular, the *Statutory Instruments Act*, RSC 1985, c. S-22 and the *Statutory Instruments Regulations* set out the basic legal requirements that must be followed in connection with the enactment of subordinate legislation, which includes an examination of the instrument to ensure its legality, and the registration and publication of the instrument in the *Canada Gazette*. The enabling legislation may also contain further specific requirements.

The principal policy document governing the federal regulatory process is the 2007 *Cabinet Directive on Streamlining Regulation* (at http://www.tbs-sct.gc.ca/ri-qr/directive/ directive01-eng.asp), which sets out requirements for the assessment of regulatory proposals and for procedures of notice and consultation. As a general rule, federal regulations are to be prepublished in the *Canada Gazette* and provide for a 30-day comment period, although Cabinet may exempt proposals from that requirement. The regulatory assessment process itself can be quite extensive, and is intended to achieve the following stated objectives:

- **protect and advance the public interest** in health, safety and security, the quality of the environment, and the social and economic well-being of Canadians, as expressed by Parliament in legislation;
- **promote a fair and competitive market economy** that encourages entrepreneurship, investment, and innovation;

- **make decisions based on evidence** and the best available knowledge and science in Canada and worldwide, while recognizing that the application of precaution may be necessary when there is an absence of full scientific certainty and a risk of serious or irreversible harm;
- **create accessible, understandable, and responsive** regulation through inclusiveness, transparency, accountability, and public scrutiny;
- **advance the efficiency and effectiveness** of regulation by ascertaining that the benefits of regulation justify the costs, by focussing human and financial resources where they can do the most good, and by demonstrating tangible results for Canadians; and
- **require timeliness, policy coherence, and minimal duplication** throughout the regulatory process by consulting, coordinating, and cooperating across the federal government, with other governments in Canada and abroad, and with businesses and Canadians.

The actual creation of the statutory instrument is accomplished through an executive order signed by the governor in council, minister, or authorized person. The statutory instrument only becomes legally effective once it is regist ered by the clerk of the Privy Council and published in the *Canada Gazette, unless the instrument is subject to an express statutory exemption*.

Note that beginning in 1986 the Commons standing orders included a "disallowance" procedure, allowing the House to issue an order revoking the statutory instrument. Pursuant to s. 19.1 of the *Statutory Instruments Act*, the joint committee may "make a report to the Senate and the House of Commons containing only a resolution that all or any portion of a *regulation* that stands permanently referred to the committee be revoked" (emphasis added). This resolution is deemed adopted unless within 15 sitting days "a Minister files with the Speaker of that House a motion to the effect that the resolution not be adopted." If such a motion is introduced, the matter is then debated, and if Parliament adopts a resolution that "all or any portion of a regulation be revoked, the authority authorized to make the regulation shall revoke the regulation or portion of the regulation no later than 30 days, or any longer period that may be specified in the resolution."

B. Dispute Resolution

It is common for administrative agencies to be created in order to hear and decide specific kinds of disputes. In some cases, administrative tribunals are very similar in their form to courts in that they adjudicate claims between competing parties strictly on the basis of existing law, they cannot initiate proceedings themselves, and they are given similar powers to courts, such as the power to summon witnesses and to award costs. In some cases, distinct tribunals are created to hear appeals by parties dissatisfied with a decision from an administrative decision-maker of first instance.

On the other hand, administrative dispute resolution mechanisms do not always take a highly legalized form. Indeed, one justification for the use of administrative dispute resolution over courts is that the formalities associated with formal court proceedings can be dispensed with, making administrative tribunals more open to public participation. There is also greater flexibility in determining who the decision-makers may be. For example, membership in a tribunal is often not restricted to lawyers, but may include experts in the policy area of the tribunal.

In addition, the use of administrative tribunals may afford greater flexibility in the range of considerations that decision-makers may take into account. Courts are restricted in resolving disputes in accordance with the rules of law and equity, but are not to engage in policy making. Administrative tribunals can, on the other hand, be designed such that tribunal members have broad discretion to determine and apply public policy. The Ontario Court of Appeal in *Cloverdale Shopping Centre Ltd. v. Etobicoke (Township)*, [1966] 2 OR 439 (CA), discusses the nature of the Ontario Municipal Board's adjudicatory function in the following terms:

> The function of the Board as well as the function of the Minister is administrative in character. The decision to be made transcends the interests of the immediate parties.
>
> • • •
>
> The Minister or the Board is not deciding a *lis* in the sense that the issue is confined to those for or against the proposal but he or it has to consider the safety, welfare and convenience, *i.e.*, the interests, of the public in the municipalities affected. In doing so the Minister or equally the Board is required to "act judicially" but not beyond the sense that the parties are to be accorded a full and fair hearing and their submissions considered. When this has been accorded to the parties, the decision—an administrative decision—has then to be made. The decision is not a decision upon the objections to the proposal; those objections may be, and frequently are, of validity and importance; they may, however, be overruled upon the larger considerations of administrative policy.
>
> • • •
>
> With no offence intended, it is trite to say that the Board in its general operation as well as in the case at bar pursues "hybrid" functions and it is perhaps because of the varied and important duties conferred upon the Board by numerous statutes that confusion may well arise as to its exact functions in a particular kind of case. Reference need only be made in this regard to the varied duties and functions of the Board in hearing, for example, assessment appeals, applications for annexation of additional territory to a municipality, arbitrations for the award of damages in connection with the compulsory taking of land. In discharging some of these functions the Board throughout the proceedings will be required to act judicially, in others to act administratively and in still others to discharge the "hybrid" functions. … In the case at bar the evidence and the very reasons of the Board disclose that the Board considered in connection with the application, the matters mentioned in the Act such as the health, safety, convenience or welfare of the inhabitants of the area and the requirements for land uses, communications and public services—*i.e.*, the "standards or principles" as appellants put it, envisioned by the Act. Having so considered such matters and the objections to alteration of the official plan, the Board proceeded to its administrative decision. Save in the limited field which has already been discussed, that administrative decision is not open to review by the Court. …

C. Benefit or Obligation Determination

The most prevalent, and the most diverse, group of administrative decision-makers are those empowered to determine whether a person will be granted a particular public benefit, such as a welfare entitlement or the issuance of a licence, will be subject to a tax or other obligation, or will be assessed a penalty.

Benefit determinations will often have distributive consequences that require decision-makers to confer a certain benefit, such as a broadcast licence, on some but not on others, raising fairness concerns. In addition, benefit determination may require decision-makers to attach complex sets of conditions to an approval, as is the case with many land-use or environmental approvals.

Obligation determinations may raise slightly different issues than benefit determinations. They are usually initiated by the imposing agency, leaving an affected person to take affirmative steps to protect his or her interests, if he or she feels aggrieved. As noted in relation to the dispute resolution functions of administrative decision-makers, in cases where the imposition potentially has a significant impact on the affected person, the scheme may provide an administrative avenue for further consideration, such as a right of appeal to an administrative tribunal or other administrative official.

The desire for fairness in individual cases is often in conflict with the need for administrative efficiency. In many cases, benefit and obligation determinations need to occur on a very large scale given the high number of applications involved. For example, in 2009-10 the Immigration and Refugee Board made 25,000 refugee determinations, leaving 63,000 claims pending. This often results in decisions being taken by persons with little or no direct contact with the affected person and with important discretionary decisions being made by low-level decision-makers within the agencies.

D. Enforcement Decisions

A final area of delegated authority is those decisions and activities that are required to promote compliance with legal obligations, including criminal and quasi-criminal enforcement proceedings. The executive branches of government use police and prosecutors to investigate and prosecute violations of statutory and regulatory requirements, most commonly through the courts. It is quite common for statutes to confer investigatory powers on other administrative officials for the purposes of a particular scheme and to confer upon them special powers such as the right to conduct searches and interviews and to require the production of documents.

Where reasonable grounds for violations of legal requirements are found by this body, the statute may empower the investigator to lay an information in order to initiate proceedings before a court pursuant to a statutory offence provision. Alternatively, the scheme may provide that a penalty be imposed directly by the investigating agency or by an administrative tribunal after hearing evidence. An example of the latter approach is found in the *Canadian Human Rights Act*, where the Canadian Human Rights Tribunal is authorized to conduct inquiries into complaints. Where those complaints are substantiated, the tribunal is empowered to impose remedial sanctions against the subject of the complaint.

E. Overlapping Functions

It should perhaps be apparent from these discussions that any one administrative body may carry out a variety of administrative functions. Again taking the Canadian Human Rights Commission as an example, the commission engages in rule making in issuing guidelines, it has investigatory powers in connection with discriminatory-practices complaints, and it has decision-making powers, such as the authority to dismiss a complaint, that affect the rights of individuals. Similarly, while some decisions are easily recognizable as being of a legislative or judicial character, many others defy classification in functional terms. As noted, tribunals may be structured in ways that are similar to courts, but may engage in policy creation. Conversely, an ostensibly legislative body may have to exercise its powers of decision in accordance with certain procedural requirements due to the nature of the interests affected. The legal requirements that qualify the exercise of delegated power are taken up in chapter 8.

CHAPTER SIX

The Courts and the Judiciary

We turn now to a detailed discussion of the structure of the Canadian court system and the composition of the judiciary. Section I of this chapter provides an overview of the structure of the Canadian court system, including the constitutional foundation for the judiciary in Canada. Section II describes the process by which judges are appointed to the bench, with a special emphasis on the federal judiciary. Section III examines in detail the concept of judicial independence, focusing on the security of tenure, financial independence and administrative independence of Canada's judges.

I. STRUCTURE OF THE CANADIAN COURT SYSTEM

A. Constitutional Framework of the Judiciary

The starting point in understanding the Canadian court system is the *Constitution Act, 1867*. As we have noted throughout this book, this instrument creates the basic institutions of the Canadian government and divides power between the federal and provincial levels of government. In relation to the judiciary, it crafts a court system that straddles the federal–provincial division of powers. To this end, s. 92(14) of the 1867 Act gives exclusive power to the provincial legislatures with respect to:

> The Administration of Justice in the Province, including the Constitution, Maintenance, and Organization of Provincial Courts, both of Civil and of Criminal Jurisdiction, and including Procedure in Civil Matters in those Courts.

And yet s. 96 provides that "[t]he Governor General shall appoint the Judges of the Superior, District, and County Courts in each Province … ." As noted in chapter 3, the generic name for these s. 96 courts is "superior courts" or, more correctly, "provincial superior courts." In addition to being responsible for appointing the judges in these superior courts, the federal government is also responsible for paying their salaries. Section 100 reads: "The Salaries, Allowances, and Pensions of the Judges of the Superior, District, and County Courts … shall be fixed and provided by the Parliament of Canada."

All told, these provisions mean that the provincial governments create s. 96 courts, but it is the federal government that appoints the judges to these "superior" courts and pays their salaries. This peculiar arrangement—courts created by the provinces and judges appointed by the federal government—reflects efforts by the framers of the 1867 Act to maintain federal control over a key source of patronage. See the discussion in Martin Friedland, *A Place*

Apart: Judicial Independence and Accountability in Canada (Ottawa: Canadian Judicial Council, 1995), at 234.

The provincial superior courts are not the only courts of the land. Under the authority given in s. 101 of the *Constitution Act, 1867*, the federal government has created the Supreme Court as the "general court of appeal for Canada." It also created the Federal Court, the Federal Court of Appeal, and the Tax Court of Canada. Section 101 reads:

> The Parliament of Canada may, notwithstanding anything in this Act, from Time to Time provide for the Constitution, Maintenance, and Organization of a General Court of Appeal for Canada, and for the Establishment of any additional Courts for the better Administration of the Laws of Canada.

Each of these s. 101 courts is created by federal statute. Thus, the Supreme Court is created by the *Supreme Court Act*, RSC 1985, c. S-26, the Federal Courts by the *Federal Courts Act*, RSC 1985, c. F-7, and the Tax Court by the *Tax Court of Canada Act*, RSC 1985, c. T-2.

The provinces, meanwhile, appoint and pay the salaries of the judges of the "provincial" courts—that is, courts that are not superior courts that provinces may choose to create from time to time.

An obvious question is this: in what circumstances may the provinces create these "provincial" courts that are not s. 96 courts? If provinces were free to create non-s. 96 courts readily, over time one might expect that superior courts would disappear, and along with them, the federal judicial selection process. As we have suggested before, the Supreme Court of Canada has repeatedly guarded against this possibility, employing s. 96 to limit provincial (and now federal) powers to strip jurisdiction from the superior courts. Consider the concerns voiced by the Supreme Court in *Re Residential Tenancies Act*, [1981] 1 SCR 714:

> As Professor Hogg has noted in his work on *Constitutional Law of Canada* (1977), p. 129, there is no general "separation of powers" in the *British North America Act, 1867*. Our Constitution does not separate the legislative, executive, and judicial functions and insist that each branch of government exercise only its own function. Thus it is clear that the Legislature of Ontario may confer non-judicial functions on the courts of Ontario and, subject to s. 96 of the *BNA Act*, which lies at the heart of the present appeal, confer judicial functions on a body which is not a court.
>
> Under s. 92(14) of the *BNA Act* the provincial legislatures have the legislative power in relation to the administration of justice in the province. This is a wide power but subject to subtraction of ss. 96 to 100 in favour of the federal authority. Under s. 96 the Governor General has the sole power to appoint the judges of the Superior, District and County Courts in each province. Under s. 97 the judges who are to be appointed to the Superior, District and County Courts are to be selected from the respective bars of each province. Under s. 100 the Parliament of Canada is obliged to fix and provide for their salaries. Section 92(14) and ss. 96 to 100 represent one of the important compromises of the Fathers of Confederation. It is plain that what was sought to be achieved through this compromise, and the intended effect of s. 96, would be destroyed if a province could pass legislation creating a tribunal, appoint members thereto, and then confer on the tribunal the jurisdiction of the superior courts. What was conceived as a strong constitutional base for national unity, through a unitary judicial system, would be gravely undermined. Section 96 has thus come to be regarded as limiting provincial competence to make appointments to a

tribunal exercising s. 96 judicial powers and therefore as implicitly limiting provincial competence to endow a provincial tribunal with such powers.

Consider also this passage from *Reference re Remuneration of Judges of the Provincial Court of Prince Edward Island*, [1997] 3 SCR 3, at para. 88 (*Provincial Judges Reference*):

> Section 96 seems to do no more than confer the power to appoint judges of the superior, district, and county courts. It is a staffing provision, and is once again a subtraction from the power of the provinces under s. 92(14). However, through a process of judicial interpretation, s. 96 has come to guarantee the core jurisdiction of the courts which come within the scope of that provision. In the past, this development has often been expressed as a logical inference from the express terms of s. 96. Assuming that the goal of s. 96 was the creation of "a unitary judicial system," that goal would have been undermined "if a province could pass legislation creating a tribunal, appoint members thereto, and then confer on the tribunal the jurisdiction of the superior courts": *Re Residential Tenancies Act, 1979*, [1981] 1 SCR 714, at p. 728. However, as I recently confirmed, s. 96 restricts not only the legislative competence of provincial legislatures, but of Parliament as well: *MacMillan Bloedel, supra*. The rationale for the provision has also shifted, away from the protection of national unity, to the maintenance of the rule of law through the protection of the judicial role.

In *Re Residential Tenancies Act*, the issue there was whether a province was encroaching on the federal government's s. 96 power to appoint judges by creating its own quasi-judicial body to adjudicate in an area of jurisdiction that belongs to the superior courts. In response, the Supreme Court established a three-part test for determining whether the provincial grant of power is valid. The first part requires a consideration of whether the powers exercised by the impugned provincial tribunal conformed to those that were under the "exclusive jurisdiction" of a s. 96 court at the time of Confederation. Consequently, powers shared with inferior courts at Confederation fall outside the area addressed in this first question, and can validly be exercised by a provincial tribunal.

If the powers were found to fall under the exclusive jurisdiction of a s. 96 court at Confederation, one must ask whether the power in question is to be exercised in a judicial manner—that is, do the tribunal's proceedings concern a *lis* (a dispute) that is to be determined on solely legal, as opposed to policy, grounds?

Finally, the third part of the test requires a consideration of whether the "institutional setting" itself is fundamentally judicial. Here the inquiry looks at whether the tribunal is ancillary to a broader administrative scheme. Only where a tribunal is found not to be ancillary to an administrative scheme will the tribunal's authority be found to be unconstitutional.

Cases that have modified the test are *McEvoy v. Attorney General for New Brunswick*, [1983] 1 SCR 704; *Sobeys Stores Ltd. v. Yeomans*, [1989] 1 SCR 238; *Reference re Young Offenders Act (PEI)*, [1991] 1 SCR 252; and *MacMillan Bloedel Ltd. v. Simpson*, [1995] 4 SCR 725. These cases establish that the superior courts are a fundamental institution protected by our Constitution through the interpretation of s. 96. The provinces cannot enact legislation to encroach on their core jurisdiction, nor may the federal Parliament.

B. Overview of the Current Canadian Court System

The result of these constitutional provisions is a complicated Canadian court system.

Department of Justice of Canada, *Canada's Court System*
(Ottawa: Department of Justice, 2009)

How the Courts Are Organized

There are basically four levels of court in Canada. First there are provincial/territorial courts, which handle the great majority of cases that come into the system. Second are the provincial/territorial superior courts. These courts deal with more serious crimes and also take appeals from provincial/territorial court judgments. On the same level, but responsible for different issues, is the Federal Court. At the next level are the provincial/territorial courts of appeal and the Federal Court of Appeal, while the highest level is occupied by the Supreme Court of Canada. ...

Provincial/Territorial Courts

Each province and territory, with the exception of Nunavut, has a provincial/territorial court, and these courts hear cases involving either federal or provincial/territorial laws. (In Nunavut, there is no territorial court—matters that would normally be heard at that level are heard by the Nunavut Court of Justice, which is a superior court.) The names and divisions of these courts may vary from place to place, but their role is the same. Provincial/territorial courts deal with most criminal offences, family law matters (except divorce), young persons in conflict with the law (from 12 to 17 years old), traffic violations, provincial/territorial regulatory offences, and claims involving money, up to a certain amount (set by the jurisdiction in question). Private disputes involving limited sums of money may also be dealt with at this level in Small Claims courts. In addition, all preliminary inquiries—hearings to determine whether there is enough evidence to justify a full trial in serious criminal cases—take place before the provincial/territorial courts.

A number of courts at this level are dedicated exclusively to particular types of offences or groups of offenders. One example is the Drug Treatment Court (DTC) program, which began in Toronto in 1998, followed over several years by Vancouver, Edmonton, Regina, Winnipeg, and Ottawa. The object of the DTCs is to address the needs of non-violent offenders who are charged with criminal offences that were motivated by their addiction. Those who qualify are offered an intensive combination of judicial supervision and treatment for their dependence, drawing on a range of community support services.

Youth courts handle cases where a young person, from 12 to 17 years old, is charged with an offence under federal youth justice laws. Procedures in youth court provide protections appropriate to the age of the accused, including privacy protections. Courts at either the provincial/territorial or superior court level can be designated youth courts.

Some provinces and territories (such as Ontario, Manitoba, Alberta and the Yukon) have established Domestic Violence Courts in order to improve the response of the justice system

Outline of Canada's Court System

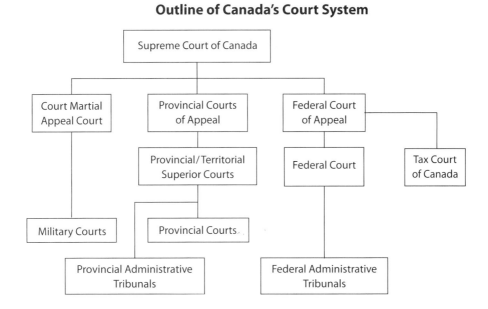

to incidents of spousal abuse by decreasing court processing time; increasing conviction rates; providing a focal point for programs and services for victims and offenders; and, in some cases, allowing for the specialization of police, Crown prosecutors and the judiciary in domestic violence matters.

Provincial/Territorial Superior Courts

Each province and territory has superior courts. These courts are known by various names, including Superior Court of Justice, Supreme Court (not to be confused with the Supreme Court of Canada), and Court of Queen's Bench. But while the names may differ, the court system is essentially the same across the country, with the exception, again, of Nunavut, where the Nunavut Court of Justice deals with both territorial and superior court matters.

The superior courts have "inherent jurisdiction," which means that they can hear cases in any area except those that are specifically limited to another level of court. The superior courts try the most serious criminal and civil cases, including divorce cases and cases that involve large amounts of money (the minimum is set by the province or territory in question).

In most provinces and territories, the superior court has special divisions, such as the family division. Some have established specialized family courts at the superior court level to deal exclusively with certain family law matters, including divorce and property claims. The superior courts also act as a court of first appeal for the underlying court system that provinces and territories maintain.

Although superior courts are administered by the provinces and territories, the judges are appointed and paid by the federal government.

Courts of Appeal

Each province and territory has a court of appeal or appellate division that hears appeals from decisions of the superior courts and provincial/territorial courts. The number of judges on these courts may vary from one jurisdiction to another, but a court of appeal usually sits as a panel of three. The courts of appeal also hear constitutional questions that may be raised in appeals involving individuals, governments, or governmental agencies.

The Federal Courts

The Federal Court and Federal Court of Appeal are essentially superior courts with civil jurisdiction. However, since the Courts were created by an Act of Parliament, they can only deal with matters specified in federal statutes (laws). In contrast, provincial and territorial superior courts have jurisdiction in all matters except those specifically excluded by a statute.

The Federal Court is the trial-level court; appeals from it are heard by the Federal Court of Appeal. While based in Ottawa, the judges of both Courts conduct hearings across the country. The Courts' jurisdiction includes interprovincial and federal-provincial disputes, intellectual property proceedings (e.g., copyright), citizenship appeals, *Competition Act* cases, and cases involving Crown corporations or departments of the Government of Canada. As well, only these Courts have jurisdiction to review decisions, orders and other administrative actions of federal boards, commissions and tribunals; these bodies may refer any question of law, jurisdiction or practice to one of the Courts at any stage of a proceeding.

For certain matters, such as maritime law, a case may be brought either before the Federal Court or Federal Court of Appeal, or before a provincial or territorial superior court. In this respect, the Federal Court and the Federal Court of Appeal share jurisdiction with the superior courts.

Specialized Federal Courts

In order to deal more effectively with certain areas of the law, the federal government has created specialized courts, notably the Tax Court of Canada and courts that serve the Military Justice System. These courts have been created by statute and can only decide matters that fall within the jurisdiction given to them by statute.

The Tax Court of Canada

The Tax Court of Canada gives individuals and companies an opportunity to settle disagreements with the federal government on matters arising under federal tax and revenue legislation. The Tax Court of Canada primarily hears disputes between the federal government and taxpayers after the taxpayer has gone through all other options provided for by the *Income Tax Act*. The Tax Court is independent of the Canada Revenue Agency and all other government departments. Its headquarters are in Ottawa, and it has regional offices in Montreal, Toronto and Vancouver.

Military Courts

Military courts, or courts martial, were established under the *National Defence Act* to hear cases involving the Code of Service Discipline. The Code applies to all members of the Canadian Forces as well as civilians who accompany the Forces on active service. It lays out a system of disciplinary offences designed to further the good order and proper functioning of the Canadian Forces.

The Court Martial Appeal Court hears appeals from military courts. Its function is comparable to that of a provincial/territorial appeal court, and it has the same powers as a superior court. Judges in the Court Martial Appeal Court are selected from the Federal Courts and other superior courts throughout the country. Like other courts of appeal, the Court Martial Appeal Court hears cases as a panel of three.

TRIAL BY JURY

Under the *Canadian Charter of Rights and Freedoms*, individuals accused of the most serious criminal offences generally have the right to choose to be tried by a jury or by a judge alone. A jury is a group of people, chosen from the community, who assess the facts of a case after a judge explains the law to them. They then make a decision based on their assessment. Sentencing, however, is left to the judge. Trial by jury is also available in some civil litigation, but is rarely used.

The Supreme Court of Canada

The Supreme Court of Canada is the final court of appeal from all other Canadian courts. The Supreme Court has jurisdiction over disputes in all areas of the law, including constitutional law, administrative law, criminal law and civil law.

The Court consists of a Chief Justice and eight other judges, all appointed by the federal government. The *Supreme Court Act* requires that at least three judges must come from Quebec. Traditionally, of the other six judges, three come from Ontario, two from western Canada, and one from the Atlantic provinces. The Supreme Court sits in Ottawa for three sessions a year—winter, spring and fall.

Before a case can reach the Supreme Court of Canada, it must have used up all available appeals at other levels of court. Even then, the Court must grant permission or "leave" to appeal before it will hear the case. Leave applications are usually made in writing and reviewed by three members of the Court, who then grant or deny the request without providing reasons for the decision. Leave to appeal is not given routinely—it is granted only if the case involves a question of public importance; if it raises an important issue of law or mixed law and fact; or if the matter is, for any other reason, significant enough to be considered by the country's Supreme Court.

In certain situations, however, the right to appeal is automatic. For instance, no leave is required in criminal cases where a judge on the panel of a court of appeal has dissented on how the law should be interpreted. Similarly, where a court of appeal has found someone guilty who had been acquitted at the original trial, that person automatically has the right to appeal to the Supreme Court.

The Supreme Court of Canada also plays a special role as adviser to the federal government. The government may ask the Court to consider questions on any important matter of law or fact, especially concerning interpretation of the Constitution. It may also be asked questions on the interpretation of federal or provincial/territorial legislation or the powers of Parliament or the legislatures. (Provincial and territorial courts of appeal may also be asked to hear references from their respective governments.)

New Approaches

The Nunavut Court of Justice

When the territory of Nunavut was established in 1999, a new kind of court in Canada was created as well. The Nunavut Court of Justice combines the power of the superior trial court and the territorial court so that the same judge can hear all cases that arise in the territory. In Nunavut, most of the communities are small and isolated from the capital of Iqaluit, so the court travels to them "on circuit." The circuit court includes a judge, a clerk, a court reporter, a prosecutor, and at least one defence attorney. Court workers and Crown witness coordinators might also travel with the circuit court, depending on the cases to be heard. Interpreters are hired in the communities when possible, or travel with the circuit court when necessary. In addition to holding regular sessions in Iqaluit, the court flies to most communities in Nunavut at intervals that range from six weeks to two years, depending on the number of cases.

Unified Family Courts

Unified family courts, found in several provinces, permit all aspects of family law to be dealt with in a single court with specialized judges and services. The unified family courts consist of superior court judges, who hear matters of both provincial/territorial and federal jurisdiction. These courts encourage the use of constructive, non-adversarial techniques to resolve issues, and provide access to a range of support services, often through community organizations. These services differ from province to province but typically include such programs as parent-education sessions, mediation, and counselling.

Sentencing Circles

Sentencing circles, pioneered in the Yukon Territorial Court in the early 1990s, are now used in much of the country, mostly at the provincial/territorial court level and in cases involving Aboriginal offenders and victims. Sentencing circles are part of the court process, though not courts in themselves, and they can be a valuable means of getting input and advice from the community to help the judge set an appropriate and effective sentence.

Sentencing circles generally operate as follows: After a finding or admission of guilt, the court invites interested members of the community to join the judge, prosecutor, defence counsel, police, social service providers, community elders, along with the offender, the victim and their families and supporters, and meet in a circle to discuss the offence, factors that may have contributed to it, sentencing options, and ways of reintegrating the offender into the community. Everyone is given the chance to speak. Often the circle will suggest a restorative community sentence involving some form of restitution to the victim, community service, and/or treatment or counselling. Sometimes members of the circle will offer to help ensure that the offender lives up to the obligations of the community sentence, while others may offer to provide support to the victim.

It is important to note, though, that sentencing circles do sometimes recommend a period of custody. Moreover, the judge is not bound to accept the circle's recommendations.

II. JUDICIAL APPOINTMENTS

Given that courts play such a fundamental role in preserving our constitutional order, the natural question this observation raises is: Are the right people selected to be judges? The manner in which judges are chosen has been an issue of some controversy, especially at the federal level. In this section, we look at the judicial selection process.

A. A Range of Models

Judicial selection processes vary internationally. It is worth commencing our discussion by contemplating three alternative (or sometimes mixed) models. These models are: (1) confirmation hearings; (2) nominating committees; and (3) direct elections. Consider how each of these approaches is employed to varying degrees in the United States.

US Department of Justice, *State Court Organization 1998*
(NCJ 178932) (Washington, DC: US Department of Justice, 2000)

How judges are selected and their terms of service on the bench differ sharply between the federal and state courts, and the differences among states are often nearly as significant. All federal judges are nominated by the President and serve "during good behavior" once confirmed by the US Senate unless they resign or are impeached and convicted by the US Congress. State court judges are likely to face an election as a part of their selection process and to serve fixed terms, which for [courts of final appeal] justices range between six and 14 years (15 years in the District of Columbia). Only Rhode Island offers appellate judges lifetime appointments, while the judges of the New Hampshire and Massachusetts Supreme Courts serve until age 70.

Judicial selection occurs for three purposes in the state courts: to fill an unexpired term upon the retirement, resignation, or death of an incumbent judge; to select for a full term (often referred to as the initial selection); and at the end of a term. …

One marker for examining the diverse selection methods adopted by the states is the "Missouri Plan." In 1940 the State of Missouri amended its constitution to establish a state-wide nominating committee for appellate judgeships and circuit-level commissions for general jurisdiction trial court judgeships. A judge, representatives of the state bar association, and nonlawyers appointed by the governor make up the commissions. The governor must appoint one of a commission's three nominees to fill a vacancy. The new appointee then faces a retention election in one year's time, running against his or her own record, and then further retention elections at 12-year intervals. Thirty-nine states use some form of judicial nominating commission in judicial selection, which became popular in the 1970s ... , although only 16 combine such a commission with retention elections on the Missouri model.

This description of the US system prompts further observations. First, note the prevalence of electoral models for state court judges. Few Canadian critics would support a system of election for our judges, even those who advocate "democratization" of the judiciary.

One problem is that election campaigns require financing. Who is most likely to contribute to such campaigns? When lawyers make financial contributions to a person who is "running for judge," do they expect favoured treatment in the courtroom if the judge is successful? Even the perception of the judge favouring a "supporter" detracts from the perception of judicial impartiality.

Another problem is that in deciding cases or rendering sentences, the judge may be inclined to court public sentiment rather than to make the "right," but unpopular, decision. This could be especially tempting when the next election is imminent. During a campaign, the judge might also appeal to public sentiment, establishing personal constraints on future decision making. Both of these problems raise questions of judicial independence, a key concept addressed below.

Second, note the US federal process: executive appointment following Senate confirmation. In the United States, at the federal level, there are district courts, district appellate courts, and the Supreme Court. Federal judges are appointed in accordance with article II, s. 2 of the US Constitution, which anticipates the participation of the US Senate in a confirmation process:

> [The President] ... shall nominate, and by and with the Advice and Consent of the Senate, shall appoint ... Judges of the Supreme Court, and all other Officers of the United States.

The nomination and confirmation process may be summarized as follows:

> Supreme Court justices, court of appeals judges, and district court judges are nominated by the President and confirmed by the United States Senate, as stated in the Constitution. The names of potential nominees often are recommended by senators or sometimes members of the House who are of the President's political party. The Senate Judiciary Committee typically conducts confirmation hearings for each nominee.

(Administrative Office of the US Courts, *Federal Judges*, available at http://www.uscourts.gov/faq.html.) Senate confirmation has sometimes been a highly political process, a point we return to below.

Third, note how the Missouri model (with or without subsequent "retention" elections) depends on a nomination or short-listing committee process. The executive appoints a judge from the short list developed by the committee. Other jurisdictions have employed variations on this nomination process. Consider these provisions of the South African Constitution.

178. Judicial Service Commission

1. There is a Judicial Service Commission consisting of—

    a. the Chief Justice, who presides at meetings of the Commission;

    b. the President of the Supreme Court of Appeal;

    c. one Judge President designated by the Judges President;

    d. the Cabinet member responsible for the administration of justice, or an alternate designated by that Cabinet member;

    e. two practising advocates nominated from within the advocates' profession to represent the profession as a whole, and appointed by the President;

    f. two practising attorneys nominated from within the attorneys' profession to represent the profession as a whole, and appointed by the President;

    g. one teacher of law designated by teachers of law at South African universities;

    h. six persons designated by the National Assembly from among its members, at least three of whom must be members of opposition parties represented in the Assembly;

    i. four permanent delegates to the National Council of Provinces designated together by the Council with a supporting vote of at least six provinces;

    j. four persons designated by the President as head of the national executive, after consulting the leaders of all the parties in the National Assembly; and

    k. when considering matters relating to a specific High Court, the Judge President of that Court and the Premier of the province concerned, or an alternate designated by each of them. …

174. Appointment of judicial officers

1. Any appropriately qualified woman or man who is a fit and proper person may be appointed as a judicial officer. Any person to be appointed to the Constitutional Court must also be a South African citizen.

2. The need for the judiciary to reflect broadly the racial and gender composition of South Africa must be considered when judicial officers are appointed.

3. The President as head of the national executive, after consulting the Judicial Service Commission and the leader of parties represented in the National Assembly, appoints the Chief Justice and the Deputy Chief Justice and, after consulting the Judicial Service Commission, appoints the President and Deputy President of the Supreme Court of Appeal.

4. The other judges of the Constitutional Court are appointed by the President, as head of the national executive, after consulting the Chief Justice and the leaders of parties represented in the National Assembly, in accordance with the following procedure:

    a. The Judicial Service Commission must prepare a list of nominees with three names more than the number of appointments to be made, and submit the list to the President.

    b. The President may make appointments from the list, and must advise the Judicial Service Commission, with reasons, if any of the nominees are unacceptable and any appointment remains to be made.

    c. The Judicial Service Commission must supplement the list with further nominees and the President must make the remaining appointments from the supplemented list.

5. At all times, at least four members of the Constitutional Court must be persons who were judges at the time they were appointed to the Constitutional Court.

6. The President must appoint the judges of all other courts on the advice of the Judicial Service Commission.

7. Other judicial officers must be appointed in terms of an Act of Parliament which must ensure that the appointment, promotion, transfer or dismissal of, or disciplinary steps against, these judicial officers take place without favour or prejudice.

8. Before judicial officers begin to perform their functions, they must take an oath or affirm, in accordance with Schedule 2, that they will uphold and protect the Constitution.

B. Provincial Judicial Appointment Process

We turn now to the Canadian judicial selection processes. Without exception, Canadian judges are selected by the executive branch, often following a short-listing process involving an advisory committee.

For provincially/territorially appointed judges, the process of choosing judges varies depending on the province/territory. The basic model is built on an advisory committee composed of a mixture of members from the legal community and laypersons. The committee accepts applications and interviews candidates before submitting a list of recommendations to the provincial attorney general.

By way of illustration, in Ontario, the Judicial Appointments Advisory Committee is described on the organization's website as follows:

> The Legislation requires the composition of the Committee to reflect the diversity of Ontario's population, including gender, geography, racial and cultural minorities. In addition to seven (7) lay members who are appointed by the Attorney General, six (6) from the legal community are appointed by the Chief Justice of the Ontario Court of Justice, the Law Society of Upper Canada, Canadian Bar Association—Ontario and the County and District Law Presidents' Association respectively. All members serve for a term of three (3) years.

The system operates on an application basis:

> Vacancies on the Bench are advertised in the *Ontario Reports* as the need arises. Candidates must submit 14 copies of a prescribed application form. These applications are reviewed by the Committee and a short list is prepared. The Judicial Appointments Advisory Committee meets to select candidates for interviews from the short list.
>
> After reference checks, confidential inquiries and interviews, the Committee sends a ranked list of its recommendations to the Attorney General who is required to make the appointment from that list.

(Government of Ontario, *Where Do Judges Come From? The Process of Appointment of Ontario Court Judges*, available at http://www.ontariocourts.on.ca/judicial_appointments/where.htm.)

The criteria for evaluating candidates are analogous to those applicable at the federal level in relation to personal and professional qualities and experience (discussed below). In addition, the following considerations are applied:

Community Awareness
- A commitment to public service.
- Awareness of and an interest in knowing more about the social problems that give rise to cases coming before the courts.

- Sensitivity to changes in social values relating to criminal and family matters.
- Interest in methods of dispute resolution alternatives to formal adjudication and interest in community resources available for participating in the disposition of cases.

Demographics

- The Judiciary of the Ontario Court of Justice should be reasonably representative of the population it serves. This requires overcoming the under-representation in the judicial complement of women, visible, cultural, and racial minorities and persons with a disability.

When the Ontario process was adopted, the attorney general at the time, Ian Scott QC, undertook to make recommendations to the Cabinet based exclusively on a very short list recommended by the advisory committee. That undertaking was respected. Subsequent attorneys general have, generally, followed this practice. As a result, political patronage is seldom identified as a criticism of these appointments.

The other provinces and territories did not immediately emulate the bold step forward taken by Attorney General Scott, but a variety of similar committees and procedures have evolved. The exception is Nunavut, which has a unified superior and territorial court called the Nunavut Court of Justice. Judges are appointed to that court by the federal government.

A recent, dramatic and rather bizarre turn of events in Quebec could encourage all provinces to review their appointments processes. Marc Bellemare was the minister of justice for Quebec in 2003 and 2004. Some six years after he left that office, he publicly stated that fundraisers for the Quebec Liberal Party had directly influenced the appointment of three judges while he was minister and that Premier Charest was complicit in forcing him to cooperate. The premier quickly established a public inquiry to address the allegations and started a personal action for defamation against Bellemare.

Former Supreme Court of Canada Justice Michel Bastarache was appointed as commissioner and was accused of bias by Bellemare in public hearings that attracted widespread publicity in Quebec. He reported in January 2011, and concluded that Bellemare had not been forced to act against his will in recommending the three appointments in question.

Perhaps more importantly, the report identified many deficiencies in the process for selecting judges that left it vulnerable to inappropriate influences. The absence of adequate standards, problems related to confidentiality, and flaws in the procedures of the selection committee were among the deficiencies noted in the report. The related recommendations should provide valuable guidance for future reforms in other jurisdictions as well as in Quebec.

C. Federal Judicial Appointment Process

The process by which the federal government appoints superior court judges varies. Section 96 court, Federal Court, and Tax Court judges are appointed by the governor in council (effectively, the Cabinet) usually following review of candidates by an advisory committee. No such advisory committee has existed for Supreme Court of Canada appointments. Instead, Supreme Court justices have traditionally been simply appointed by the governor in council.

1. Non-Supreme Court of Canada Appointments

a. Overview

The Office of the Commissioner for Federal Judicial Affairs oversees the federal judicial appointment process for s. 96 courts, the Federal Courts, and the Tax Court. Consider its discussion of the appointment process, as established by the Harper government in 2006.

Office of the Commissioner for Federal Judicial Affairs,
Process for an Application for Appointment
(Ottawa: Office of the Commissioner for Federal Judicial Affairs, 2009), online:
http://www.fja.gc.ca/appointments-nominations/process-regime-eng.html

*1. Commissioner for Federal Judicial Affairs Canada and
Executive Director, Judicial Appointments*

The Commissioner for Federal Judicial Affairs Canada has the overall responsibility for the administration of the appointments process on behalf of the Minister of Justice. The Commissioner is expected to carry out his responsibilities in such a way as to ensure that the system treats all candidates for judicial office fairly and equally. The Commissioner's responsibility is exercised directly or by his delegate, the Executive Director, Judicial Appointments.

It is the Commissioner's or the Executive Director, Judicial Appointments' particular responsibility, on behalf of the Minister, to ensure that all assessments are completed expeditiously and thoroughly.

2. Expression of Interest and Eligibility

Qualified lawyers and persons holding provincial or territorial judicial office who wish to be considered for appointment as a judge of a superior court in a province or territory or of the Federal Court of Appeal, the Federal Court or Tax Court of Canada must apply to the Commissioner for Federal Judicial Affairs Canada.

Persons interested in applying for Federal Judicial Appointment must complete

1. **Personal History Form**, which provides the basic data for the subsequent assessment of, or comment on the candidature by the appropriate advisory committee. Candidates should ensure that this form is completed in full and in accordance with the instructions provided. All information received is treated confidentially.
2. **Authorization Form**, which allows the Executive Director to obtain a statement of their current and past standing with the law societies in which they hold or have held membership.
3. **Background Check Consent Form**. Background checks will be conducted only if the Minister of Justice wants to appoint you to a judicial position following your assessment and recommendation by the Judicial Advisory Committee. A background check is required prior to any appointment to a public office.

. . .

In addition to candidates themselves, members of the legal community and all other interested persons and organizations are invited to nominate persons they consider qualified for judicial office; nominees will be contacted by the Commissioner to ascertain whether they wish to be considered for a judicial appointment.

The statutory qualifications for appointment are set out in the *Judges Act*, the *Federal Courts Act* and *Tax Court of Canada Act*. Generally, they require 10 years at the bar of a province or territory, or a combination of 10 years at the bar and in the subsequent exercise of powers and duties of a judicial nature on a full-time basis in a position held pursuant to a law of Canada or of a province or territory. Appointments to a provincial superior court are made only from members of the bar of that province, as required by the *Constitution Act, 1867*. Appointments to the superior courts of the three territories are open to all persons who meet the qualifications for appointment within their own province or territory.

Upon determining that a candidate meets the threshold constitutional and statutory criteria for a federal judicial appointment, the Executive Director, Judicial Appointments will forward the candidate's file to the appropriate committee for assessment (lawyers) or for comment (provincial or territorial court judges—see below). This file also includes the law society report concerning the candidate's current or past standing.

3. *Provincial and Territorial Court Judges*

Provincial or territorial court judges who wish to be candidates must also notify the Commissioner of their interest in a federal judicial appointment by completing a Personal History Form for judges. These candidates are not assessed by the advisory committees, but their files are submitted to the appropriate committee for comments which are then provided to the Minister of Justice, including the results of any confidential consultations undertaken by the committee. These comments are confidential and provided to the Minister only; they are not binding on the Minister, and the names of these candidates are automatically placed on the list of those available for appointment. They must, however, renew their expression of interest **every five years** failing which, their names will be withdrawn from the list.

4. *Judicial Advisory Committees*

Independent judicial advisory committees constitute the heart of the appointments process. It is the committees who have the responsibility of assessing the qualifications for appointment of the lawyers who apply. There is at least one committee in each province and territory; because of their larger population, Ontario has three regionally based committees and Quebec has two. Candidates are assessed by the regional committee established for the judicial district of their practice or occupation, or by the committee judged most appropriate by the Commissioner. Each committee consists of eight members representing the bench, the bar, law enforcement associations and the general public:

- a nominee of the provincial or territorial law society;
- a nominee of the provincial or territorial branch of the Canadian Bar Association;
- a judge nominated by the Chief Justice or senior judge of the province or territory;
- a nominee of the provincial Attorney General or territorial Minister of Justice;

- a nominee of the law enforcement community; and
- 3 nominees of the federal Minister of Justice representing the general public.

Each nominator is asked by the federal Minister of Justice to submit a list of names from whom an appointment to the relevant committee can be made. The Minister, with the assistance of the Commissioner for Federal Judicial Affairs Canada, then selects persons to serve on each committee who reflect factors appropriate to the jurisdiction, including geography, gender, language and multiculturalism. Committee members are appointed by the Minister of Justice to serve a three-year term, with the possibility of a single renewal.

The Minister meets periodically with the Chairs of all the committees for an exchange of views concerning the operation of the process.

Administrative support for the work of the committees, including information sessions and guidelines concerning confidentiality and other committee procedures, is provided by the Judicial Appointments Secretariat of the Office of the Commissioner.

All committee proceedings and consultations take place on a confidential basis.

5. *Judicial Advisory Committee for the Tax Court of Canada*

This Committee is comprised of 5 members: one nominee who is a judge of the Tax Court of Canada and four nominees of the Minister of Justice in consultation with the Chief Justice of the Tax Court. Selection of the members of the Advisory Committee for the Tax Court of Canada takes into consideration Canada's linguistic and geographic diversity. Committee terms are for 3 years.

Please note that an application for the Tax Court of Canada that includes an application for another court or courts will be sent to the Advisory Committee for the Tax Court, as well as to the relevant Advisory Committee for any other jurisdiction.

6. *Assessments and Confidentiality*

Extensive consultations in both the legal and non-legal community are undertaken by the committee in respect of each applicant.

Professional competence and overall merit are the primary qualifications. Committee members are provided with Assessment Criteria—see separate document—for evaluating fitness for the bench; these relate to professional competence and experience, personal characteristics, and potential impediments to appointment. Committees are encouraged to respect diversity and to give due consideration to all legal experience, including that outside a mainstream legal practice. Broad consultations by the committees, and community involvement through these consultations, are essential elements of the process.

The committees are asked to assess candidates on the basis of two categories—"recommended" or "unable to recommend" for appointment. These categories reflect the advisory nature of the committee process. Once the assessment has been completed, candidates are notified of the date they were assessed by the committee but are not provided with the results of the assessment. The results are kept confidential and solely for the Minister's use.

The committees set their own agenda as required, depending on the number of applications received and the judicial vacancies to be filled by the Minister of Justice. When completing and submitting their application, candidates should consider that definite Committee meeting dates are not always set in advance and it may take several months to process an application before sending it to the committee for assessment.

Following receipt of the committee's assessment, the Minister may at his discretion seek further information from the committee on any candidate. On those occasions when a committee's advice may be contrary to the information received from other sources by the Minister, the Minister may ask the committee for a reassessment of the candidate.

NOTE: Provincial and Territorial court judges are the only candidates who are not assessed by the committees. However, Committees will provide the Minister with a commentary on each such candidate.

7. *Duration of Assessments*

Lawyer candidates are notified of the date they were assessed by the committee, and assessments are valid for a period of two years from that date. During that time, a "recommended" candidate remains on the list of those available for judicial appointment by the Minister of Justice. If a lawyer candidate continues to be interested in being considered for appointment **after** the above two-year expiry date, a new Personal History Form must be submitted during the three months preceding the expiry date. In that case a new committee assessment is undertaken, and a candidate remains on the list until the new assessment is completed. A new Personal History Form can also be submitted after the expiry date, but in that case a previous assessment will cease to be valid.

Each candidate's assessment must be certified by the Commissioner or the Executive Director Judicial Appointments prior to its submission to the Minister of Justice.

The files of all candidates are maintained in a separate and confidential data bank in the Commissioner's office, for the sole use of the Minister of Justice.

8. *Appointments*

Federal judicial appointments are made by the Governor General acting on the advice of the federal Cabinet. A recommendation for appointment is made to Cabinet by the Minister of Justice with respect to the appointment of *puisne* judges, and by the Prime Minister with respect to the appointment of Chief Justices and Associate Chief Justices.

The recommendation to Cabinet is made from amongst the names which have been previously reported by the committees to the Minister.

Before recommending an appointment to Cabinet, the Minister may consult with members of the judiciary and the bar, with his or her appropriate provincial or territorial counterparts, as well as with members of the public. With respect to provincial and territorial court judges who apply for appointment to a superior court, the Minister may consult with that candidate's current Chief Judge as well as with the Chief Justice of the court for which the candidate is being considered. The Minister also welcomes the advice of any group or individuals on the considerations which should be taken into account when filling current vacancies.

The title "Honourable" is conferred on the new judge upon appointment.

As the discussion above indicates, ultimately, appointments must be made by the governor in council as required by s. 96 of the *Constitution Act, 1867* or the statutes governing the s. 101 courts. The recommendation for appointment as a judge is made to Cabinet by the minister of justice. Historically, political patronage played a prominent role in Canadian judicial appointments. The system described above is presented to the public as placing merit and objectivity above repaying political favours. But the government retains a broad discretion in making appointments, and skepticism and criticism persist.

b. Criticisms of the Non-Supreme Court Federal Appointment Process

It was not until the 1960s that any process at all was established to assist the minister of justice in deciding upon what recommendations to make to the Cabinet. A variety of changes have been made to the "advisory system" over the years. In 1994, Justice Minister Allan Rock committed to appointing only persons who received a "recommended" or "highly recommended" assessment from the evaluating committee. Such a commitment is not legally binding but could be embarrassing to ignore.

There is no requirement in law for the government to follow the recommendations of any advisory committee. (And an argument could be made that an attempt to impose such a legal requirement would be prohibited by s. 96, at least for provincial superior court judges.) The federal appointment process is established as a matter of "policy" rather than law.

The criticism of this approach was that it left too wide a range from which to select. The category of "recommended" provides a lower threshold than does "highly recommended," so it does not encourage a standard of excellence. Under this system, it is possible that a Cabinet minister from Nova Scotia could pressure the minister of justice to recommend a lawyer from that province who is not as highly rated by the committee, simply because the lawyer is a loyal political supporter of that Cabinet minister. Provided that the lawyer meets the "recommended" criterion, the minister of justice may make such a recommendation and assert that the process has been followed. Consider this newspaper report:

> More than 60 per cent of the 93 lawyers who received federal judicial appointments in Ontario, Alberta and Saskatchewan since 2000 donated exclusively to the [governing] Liberal party in the three to five years before securing their $220,000-per-annum posts.
>
> Just a handful donated exclusively to the Conservatives or New Democrats during the same period, according to a CanWest News Service analysis of the appointments.
>
> Individual annual donations tended to be small, ranging from $100 to a few thousand dollars, an examination of Elections Canada political donation records reveals as the Gomery inquiry considers allegations that the Liberals handed out federal judgeships as rewards for party loyalists in Quebec.

(Cristin Schmitz, with files from Lisa Tuominen, Peter O'Neil, and Graeme Hamilton, "Federal Judges Often Liberal Donors, Survey Finds" *Ottawa Citizen* (May 6, 2005), at A5.)

A 2010 study by Postmedia News and the *Ottawa Citizen* revealed that the Harper government appointed dozens of judges who donated to the Conservative Party prior to their appointments. Professor Jacob Ziegel's research (referenced below) also showed that a majority of judges appointed as chief justices had Conservative links prior to being appointed to the bench.

Calls for changes to the process have been made by various bar associations, independent public policy organizations, and legal scholars. In a report on the Federal Judicial Appointment Process (October 2005), the Canadian Bar Association states: "Some modifications would strengthen the process to ensure that it is open and transparent, and results in judicial appointments based solely on merit and which are ultimately representative of the diversity of Canadian society."

Prior to 2006 (when the appointments process described above was adopted), public criticism focused on:

- the failure to favour "highly recommended" over "recommended" candidates;
- the failure to provide greater accountability in this respect by identifying the number of candidates in and selected from each such category; and
- the broad discretion remaining in the government to make political patronage a significant factor in judicial selection.

The process adopted in 2006 was announced in November, not long after the election of the first Harper minority government.

Rather than giving a higher priority to the "highly recommended" category, it was simply abolished. Candidates would be assessed simply as "recommended" or "not recommended." Further controversy was generated by the addition of a law enforcement representative to the advisory committee and the designation of the judicial nominee as chair, who would only vote in the event of a tie. This means that the three government nominees together with the law enforcement nominee would outnumber the three nominees form the legal profession.

The judicial selection process has been the subject of a great deal of analysis and debate, with a variety of models throughout Western democracies. One of the most recent and promising is in Great Britain. There, the Judicial Appointments Commission is established by statute, with mechanisms to ensure its influence. The following is taken from its website at http://jac.judiciary.gov.uk.

Selection Policy

This section of the website provides information on JAC selection policy.

The independent Judicial Appointments Commission (JAC) selects candidates for judicial office on merit, through fair and open competition from the widest range of eligible candidates. We were set up to maintain and strengthen Judicial independence by taking responsibility for selecting candidates for Judicial Office out of the hands of the Lord Chancellor while making the appointments process clearer and more accountable.

Under the Constitutional Reform Act 2005 the JAC has a responsibility to develop and implement our own selection processes. We have very specific duties in the selection of Judges and Tribunal members, both legal and non-legal. Our key statutory responsibilities are:

- to select candidates solely on merit;
- to select only people of good character;
- to have regard to the need to encourage diversity in the range of persons available for selection for appointments.

Our role is to select and recommend candidates, not to appoint them. For each vacancy, Commissioners select one candidate to recommend to the Lord Chancellor for appointment. The Lord Chancellor can accept or reject a recommendation, or ask for it to be reconsidered. If he does so he is required to provide his reasons in writing to the Commission. He can only exercise that power once for each candidate and cannot select an alternative candidate.

Since October 2006, we have been using a new system for selecting Judges, and new criteria for what makes a good judge. It developed a set of Qualities and Abilities against which to measure judges, and a new system for selecting judges.

2. Supreme Court Appointments

Notably, none of the appointment processes described above apply to the Supreme Court of Canada, the highest court of the land. As a direct consequence, calls for changes to the federal appointments process have been especially persistent in relation to appointments to the Supreme Court. This relates to the great influence that the court's decisions may have on public policy, especially in the post-Charter era. It is argued that because the Supreme Court is, in effect, "legislating," it should be more accountable to the public through the appointment process. Some authors have argued that the court must be "democratized" by requiring public scrutiny of potential appointees. This might include the questioning of potential appointees by a parliamentary committee. Consider the views of Professor Ted Morton, one the most active critics of the status quo:

[W]hen a national court of appeal is given the function of constitutional review, of supervising the laws passed by Parliament, it is no longer simply enforcing laws; it is also making law. In a 21st century democracy, law-making institutions are expected to be accountable and representative, not independent. ...

As for warnings that the public parliamentary hearings would politicize the court, it's a little late in the day for that kind of political prudery. There is already intense behind-the-scenes lobbying for Supreme Court appointments. ...

The current system, rather than preventing the politicization of the appointment process, as its defenders would have us believe, simply drives the politics underground, beyond public knowledge and public scrutiny. ...

The Constitution belongs to all Canadians. You, the members of Parliament, represent all the Canadian people in all their diversity. You would be well within your democratic mandate and the tradition of parliamentary democracy to adopt reforms that make the Supreme Court, in its Constitution, reflect your own diversity. There is no reason to continue with a system in which a party that receives only 40% of the votes makes 100% of the appointments to our country's highest court.

(Submissions, Standing Committee on Justice, Human Rights, Public Safety and Emergency Preparedness, *Evidence* (April 1, 2004).)

Others have argued that the concept of "democratization" is misplaced in relation to the judiciary. Judges should not be "accountable" to any constituency but must be free to decide each case in accordance with their view of the law and their own conscience. While judges may have predilections, their role requires that they allow any personal views to be overcome by the requirements of the particular case they are deciding. Since the vast majority of

Supreme Court appointments are made from the appellate courts, appointees already have a "track record." The public has easy access to information on how they have decided cases, how well they write, and how productive they have been.

Further, US-style confirmation hearings have been criticized as political theatre. A recent critique by Professor Edward Ratushny describes some of their worst features:

> It is obvious that the confirmation requirement of the US Constitution was intended to impose a legislative restraint on the President's power of appointment. It is also obvious that the confirmation process has evolved into a highly politicized exercise. Some hearings have degenerated into grossly political spectacles that have little to do with the professional qualifications of the nominees or their ability to serve as judges.

(Edward Ratushny, "Confirmation Hearings for Supreme Court of Canada Appointments: Not a Good Idea!" in Pierre Thibault et al., eds., *Essays in Honour of Gérald-A. Beaudoin: The Challenges of Constitutionalism* (Cowansville, QC: Yvon Blais, 2002), at 411.)

For reasons like these, the Canadian Bar Association, for one, is strongly opposed to a US-style confirmation hearing process:

> [As the CBA has argued in the past,] public confirmation hearings similar to the US by a Parliamentary Committee risked politicizing the process and could deter prospective judges from putting their names forward. A US-type confirmatory process seeks to predetermine how a prospective judge would decide cases. With the advent of the *Charter* and the increase in judicial consideration of socio-political issues, there were increased concerns that political influence could impact on the appointment of judges.
>
> The CBA is strongly opposed to any system which would expose judges to Parliamentary criticism of their judgments, or cross-examination on their beliefs or preferences or judicial opinions, or any measure which would give to Canadians the mistaken impression that the judicial branch answers to the legislative branch.

(Canadian Bar Association, *Supreme Court Appointments Process* (March 2004), at 8.)

In response, supporters of a form of public hearings for nominees in Canada take the view that some of the most controversial hearings in the United States were "aberrations" rather than the norm and that, in any event, we should be able to adopt the concept without all of its worst features. Consider the views of Professor Jacob Ziegel:

> The horror stories the critics have in mind [in relation to the US system] no doubt are the confirmation hearings of Robert H. Bork and Clarence Thomas before the US Senate. However, they overlook the fact that public questioning of candidates is a relatively recent innovation in proceedings by the Senate Judiciary Committee and that there were exceptional features about the Bork and Thomas cases. The more recent nominees that have appeared before the Judiciary Committee have been approved without difficulty and they have not complained about unfair treatment. The nominees have reserved the right not to answer questions concerning their position on future cases that could come before the Supreme Court, and that right is generally conceded. If it was deemed appropriate or necessary in the Canadian context, rules could also be adopted to delimit the scope of a nominee's examination before the parliamentary committee.

(Jacob Ziegel, "Merit Selection and Democratization of Appointments to the Supreme Court of Canada," *Choices* (Institute for Research on Public Policy, June 1999), at 10.)

In 2005, in response to demands for a more transparent process, the minister of justice launched a "Proposal To Reform the Supreme Court of Canada Appointments Process," which, the minister announced on August 8, 2005, would be used in filling the vacancy created by the retirement of Mr. Justice John C. Major.

Minister of Justice, *Proposal To Reform the*
Supreme Court of Canada Appointments Process
(Ottawa: Department of Justice, April 2005)

A number of overarching principles have informed the development of the Government's proposal for a revised process.

Merit

The overriding objective of the appointments process must continue to be to ensure that the best candidates are appointed, based on merit. The Government has developed and applied criteria … . These should continue to provide appropriate benchmarks for assessing candidates for judicial office—both at the Supreme Court of Canada and other federally appointed courts. The needs of the Court in terms of expertise are also an important consideration.

Within this framework and to the extent possible, the Supreme Court of Canada bench should reflect the diversity of Canadian society. A diverse bench ensures that different and plural perspectives are brought to bear on the resolution of disputes.

Constitutional Framework for Appointments

Any revised appointments process must be rooted in the recognition that the appointment of Supreme Court judges is within the constitutional authority of the Governor-in-Council. This ensures that the executive branch of government remains responsible and accountable for the exercise of this important power.

Judicial Independence and the Integrity of the Courts

The system should protect and promote the reality and perception of judicial independence. The independence of the judiciary is essential for the rule of law and a cornerstone of our legal system. Judicial independence ensures that legal claims are adjudicated by fair, impartial and open-minded judges who are not beholden to any group, interest or stated public position. By the same token, the system should preserve the integrity of the Supreme Court of Canada and the court system. The judiciary is an institution that is vital for the maintenance of the rule of law and the health of Canada's democracy. Any reforms must be mindful of the impact that public commentary may have on the reputation of individual judges and the potential loss of public confidence necessary to discharge their judicial functions. This could also have the effect of deterring excellent candidates from allowing their names to be considered.

Transparency

The system should be more transparent. Transparency is accomplished by enhancing public knowledge and understanding of the process and can be seen as a goal in itself. Another goal of transparency is to ensure public confidence that appointments are made for legitimate reasons that are not linked to political favouritism. The Government agrees with the Justice Committee that transparency does not require candidates to be subject to direct, public questioning.

Parliamentary Input

The Government has clearly committed itself to ensuring meaningful Parliamentary input. Parliamentarians are the representatives of Canadians and are therefore in a unique position to contribute to the transparency of the advisory committee process. …

Provincial Input

The federal government has consistently acknowledged the importance of provincial input through consultation with appropriate provincial Chief Justices, Attorneys General, provincial bar leaders, and other interested provincial bodies that may wish to make recommendations. …

· · ·

II. Overview of Proposal

The Government's proposal consists of a four-stage process.

   a. The Minister would conduct consultations as under the current process (with the Chief Justice of Canada, the provincial attorneys general in the region, the chief justices in the region, the local law societies and the Canadian Bar Association). From these consultations, an initial list of candidates would be developed. Ordinarily, the list would be between five and eight names, depending on the size of the region.

   b. An advisory committee would be established as each vacancy arises to reflect the regional nature of the appointments. The advisory committee would assess, on a strictly confidential basis, the merit of candidates provided to it by the Minister. The work of the Committee would be based on a written mandate from the Minister and established criteria. The Committee would provide an unranked short list of three candidates with an assessment of their merit and a full record of the consultations conducted.

   c. The Minister would complete such further consultations as considered necessary and provide his advice to the Prime Minister. The Prime Minister would make his recommendation to Cabinet and, in all but the most exceptional circumstances, the appointment would be made from the short list.

   d. The Minister would appear before the Justice Committee after the appointment to explain the appointment process and the professional and personal qualities of the appointee.

The composition of the advisory committee employed in stage (b) is described as follows:

> The Advisory Committee will include a Member of Parliament from each recognized party, a retired judge and, from the region where the vacancy arises, a nominee of the provincial Attorneys General, a nominee of the law societies and two prominent Canadians who are neither lawyers nor judges. A new Advisory Committee will be formed each time a Supreme Court vacancy occurs.

The Conservative Party opposed the Liberal plan, taking a strong position in favour of more active parliamentary involvement in Supreme Court judge selection. In its dissent to a 2004 parliamentary committee report on the issue, the Conservative Party recommended that "[t]here must be Parliamentary ratification of the chosen nominee": see Commons Standing Committee on Justice, Human Rights, Public Safety and Emergency Preparedness, *Improving the Supreme Court of Canada* (May 2004).

In early 2006, Conservative Prime Minister Harper announced a hybrid selection process, incorporating elements of the Liberal plan plus pseudo-parliamentary questioning of the nominee. Thus, the prime minister nominated Mr. Justice Rothstein based on the short list of candidates compiled by the preceding Liberal government. However, before Justice Rothstein was formally appointed to the Supreme Court, a special committee comprising members of Parliament and including the new minister of justice questioned him in a public (and televised) hearing. Also present was Professor Peter Hogg, an eminent constitutional scholar. Professor Hogg played a quasi-refereeing role, apprising committee members of the constraints the nominee faced in answering questions that would require him to prejudge cases that he might subsequently adjudicate. Nevertheless, critics such as the Canadian Bar Association denounced the process, noting that open questioning of judicial nominees would ultimately impair judicial independence by forcing candidates to take positions on exactly these sorts of issues. The committee was restrained, however, in its questioning of Mr. Justice Rothstein, and the process seemed to please most observers. Whether future proceedings following this pattern will be equally congenial remains to be seen.

The subsequent Supreme Court appointment did not provide much guidance as it took a circuitous route through some interesting political manoeuvres. On April 9, 2008, Justice Michel Bastarache announced that he would retire at the end of the next Court session on June 30. He would be only 61 upon retiring, but had been on the court for over a decade and was a member of the New Brunswick Court of Appeal prior to that. His advance notice would allow the government to select his replacement prior to the following session of the court on the second Tuesday of October.

According to the tradition described above, this appointment would come from the Atlantic provinces, and the premier of Newfoundland and Labrador said publicly that it was the first appointment from his jurisdiction and was long overdue. But a superb candidate was sitting on the Nova Scotia Court of Appeal. Justice Thomas Cromwell had served for ten years on this court, where he demonstrated excellent legal analysis, judgment writing diligence, industry, and courtesy. Prior to going directly to the appellate court, he had established an excellent reputation as a law professor and author. On top of all of these qualifications, he had served for three years as executive legal officer to former Chief Justice Antonio Lamer. He was fully bilingual and had a thorough knowledge of the workings of the court. Journalistic interviews with knowledgeable lawyers, law professors, and others consistently identified him as an outstanding candidate.

In May, Justice Minister Rob Nicholson announced that he would gather a list of names and submit them to a panel of five MPs (two Conservatives and one from each of the opposition parties). This panel would then select three names from which the prime minister would select his "nominee." This person would then appear before a parliamentary committee as Justice Rothstein had done. However, no progress appeared to occur and Parliament recessed on June 25 with a scheduled return date of September 15. Over the summer there was much speculation of a fall election and a fair amount of campaigning.

On September 5, Prime Minister Harper announced that his "nominee" would be Cromwell and that his appointment would still be subject to his appearance before a parliamentary committee. The advisory panel of MPs played no role in this choice. On September 7, the election was announced for October 14 and the Conservatives were returned with a (stronger) minority.

Parliament convened on November 18 with rumours swirling of an opposition coalition in the making. On December 1, the opposition parties announced an agreement that would see a Liberal–NDP coalition supported by the Bloc Québécois. They announced publicly that they would combine to support a non-confidence motion to bring down the government on December 8. They were prepared to avoid another election by forming a new government.

As discussed in chapter 4, the prime minister responded with a bold pre-emptive strike by asking the governor general to prorogue Parliament. This was highly unusual since an election had just been held and Parliament had been sitting for less than three weeks. However, the request was granted and Parliament would not reopen for business until January 26, 2009, which would provide sufficient time for the opposition alliance to dissipate.

Meanwhile, the Supreme Court had been left in a very difficult position. It had already gone through the entire fall session with only eight judges, meaning it had to sit as seven to ensure a majority decision. The overriding contribution and responsibility of this court is to provide future guidance as to the state of the law on matters of transcending importance. Certainty will be elusive if the court divides by four judges to three since adding the additional judges could reverse the majority by five to four. The *Supreme Court Act* required that the court commence its next session on January 22, 2009.

On December 21, 2008, the prime minister announced that he would bypass the intended parliamentary hearings in order to proceed immediately with the Cromwell appointment. Justice Cromwell was appointed to widespread acclaim and joined the court for the January term.

The significance of Supreme Court appointments will come to the fore in the immediate future with four imminent mandatory retirements: Justices Fish (2013), Binnie (2014), LeBel (2014), and Rothstein (2015). All of these and other judges of the court also could take early retirement, as did Justice Bastarache. The related appointments will have a great impact on the character of the court for many years.

Indeed, just as we were going to press, both Justices Binnie and Charron announced their early retirement. In a press release dated May 13, 2011, Prime Minister Harper responded by announcing that the minister of justice would commence consultations to establish a list of qualified candidates. This list would then be reviewed by a "selection panel" composed of five members of Parliament: three Conservatives, one NDP, and one Liberal. This panel would then submit an unranked list of six candidates to the government.

The next step would be for the prime minister to select two persons as his choices from this short list. These two "nominees" would be required to appear at a public hearing before an ad hoc parliamentary committee to respond to questions from the members of Parliament who are on the committee. Finally, the government would formally appoint the two nominees on the recommendation of the prime minister. This process would be similar to that adopted for the appointment of Justice Rothstein in 2006.

III. JUDICIAL INDEPENDENCE

No discussion of the Canadian court system is complete without an examination of the concept of "judicial independence." Put simply, judicial independence is the notion that judges are at arm's length from the other branches of government. In *British Columbia v. Imperial Tobacco Canada Ltd.*, [2005] 2 SCR 473, at para. 45, the Supreme Court described judicial independence as follows:

> Judicial independence consists essentially in the freedom "to render decisions based solely on the requirements of the law and justice": *Mackin v. New Brunswick (Minister of Finance)*, [2002] 1 SCR 405, 2002 SCC 13, at para. 37. It requires that the judiciary be left free to act without improper "interference from any other entity" ...—i.e. that the executive and legislative branches of government not "impinge on the essential 'authority and function' ... of the court" (*MacKeigan v. Hickman*, [1989] 2 SCR 796, at pp. 827-28).

A. Sources and Scope

Judicial independence is a richly constitutional concept. Sections 96 to 100 of the *Constitution Act, 1867* provide for the appointment, tenure, and remuneration of federally appointed judges. We have already discussed how s. 96 has been interpreted by the courts as not merely indicating who has the power of appointment, but also establishing the superior courts as a fundamental institution protected by our Constitution. The scope of ss. 99 and 100 also has been elaborated by judicial interpretation to further protect judicial independence.

Section 99 specifies the tenure of office of superior court judges as follows:

> (1) Subject to subsection two of this section, the Judges of the Superior Courts shall hold office during good behaviour, but shall be removable by the Governor General on Address of the Senate and House of Commons.
>
> (2) A Judge of a Superior Court, whether appointed before or after the coming into force of this section, shall cease to hold office upon attaining the age of seventy-five years. ...

In other words, federally appointed superior court judges are removable only for breach of "good behaviour," until the mandatory retirement age of 75. As we shall see, physical or mental incapacity—that is, the inability to act as a judge—has been interpreted to be a breach of "good behaviour."

Meanwhile, s. 100 indicates that the "salaries, allowances and pensions" of superior court judges "shall be fixed and provided by the Parliament of Canada." This provision has been interpreted by the Supreme Court as guaranteeing the "financial security of judges of the superior, district, and county courts": see *Provincial Judges Reference*, [1997] 3 SCR 3, at para. 84.

Note, however, that these *Constitution Act, 1867* provisions apply only to superior courts. Does that mean that judicial independence does not exist as a constitutional matter for other courts, such as provincial courts? The answer is "no" for several reasons. Most obviously, s. 11(d) of the Charter imposes a requirement for judicial independence in certain circumstances:

> 11. Any person charged with an offence has the right
>   (d) to be presumed innocent until proven guilty according to law in a fair and public hearing by an independent and impartial tribunal.

Since most criminal cases are tried by provincially appointed judges, this Charter provision requires that these courts and the individual judges that are appointed to provincial courts be "independent and impartial." Otherwise, an accused person facing trial before such a court would be entitled to a stay of proceedings for the denial of the Charter right under s. 11(d).

The meaning of "an independent and impartial tribunal" in s. 11(d) received extensive consideration through the 1980s and early 1990s. In this period, the Supreme Court of Canada developed the concept of "institutional independence," referring to those requirements that must be in place in order for the judiciary to be sufficiently independent of pressures from the other branches of the state in order to meet this standard. Three such requirements were identified by the court: (1) security of tenure; (2) financial security; and (3) administrative control or independence with respect to the management of court business. Each of these three features was subject to elaboration.

Most notably, in the mid-1990s, a political and legal crisis arose with respect to the issue of "financial security" of the provincial court, or non-s. 96 judiciary across the country. In a period of severe budgetary constraint, several provincial governments imposed salary freezes or rollbacks on their provincial civil services, and included in these regimes the provincial court judiciary. In several provinces, criminal accused made claims that these unilateral moves by executive governments with respect to judicial salaries violated the parameters of "financial security" of judges, and denied them trials before independent tribunals. A number of such challenges succeeded. A reference case came before the Supreme Court of Canada dealing with the situations in three provinces: Alberta, Manitoba, and Prince Edward Island. The court majority recognized that the issues in the case could be resolved solely within the context of interpreting and applying s. 11(d). Nevertheless, the majority took the opportunity to consider the constitutional status of the judiciary as a whole, and not merely in its criminal law jurisdiction. The court majority recognized an unwritten principle of judicial independence in the Constitution.

Portions of the majority judgment are reproduced here for their enunciation of the principle of judicial independence in our Constitution. Other portions are included below under section C, related more specifically to financial security. Finally, the dissenting judgment is reproduced in chapter 8.

**Reference re Remuneration of Judges of the Provincial Court of
Prince Edward Island et al. (the "Provincial Judges Reference")**
[1997] 3 SCR 3

LAMER CJ (L'Heureux-Dubé, Sopinka, Gonthier, Cory, and Iacobucci JJ concurring):

I. Introduction

[1] The four appeals handed down today ... raise a range of issues relating to the independence of provincial courts, but are united by a single issue: whether and how the guarantee of judicial independence in s. 11(d) of the *Canadian Charter of Rights and Freedoms* restricts the manner by and the extent to which provincial governments and legislatures can reduce the salaries of provincial court judges. Moreover, in my respectful opinion, they implicate the broader question of whether the constitutional home of judicial independence lies in the express provisions of the *Constitution Acts, 1867 to 1982*, or exterior to the sections of those documents. I am cognizant of the length of these reasons. Although it would have been possible to issue a set of separate but interrelated judgments, since many of the parties intervened in each other's cases, I find it convenient to deal with these four appeals in one set of reasons. ...

• • •

[9] ... Judicial independence is valued because it serves important societal goals—it is a means to secure those goals.

[10] One of these goals is the maintenance of public confidence in the impartiality of the judiciary, which is essential to the effectiveness of the court system. Independence contributes to the perception that justice will be done in individual cases. Another social goal served by judicial independence is the maintenance of the rule of law, one aspect of which is the constitutional principle that the exercise of all public power must find its ultimate source in a legal rule.

• • •

[82] These appeals were all argued on the basis of s. 11(d), the *Charter*'s guarantee of judicial independence and impartiality. From its express terms, s. 11(d) is a right of limited application—it only applies to persons accused of offences. Despite s. 11(d)'s limited scope, there is no doubt that the appeals can and should be resolved on the basis of that provision. To a large extent, the Court is the prisoner of the case which the parties and interveners have presented to us, and the arguments that have been raised, and the evidence that we have before us, have largely been directed at s. 11(d). In particular, the two references from PEI are explicitly framed in terms of s. 11(d), and if we are to answer the questions contained therein, we must direct ourselves to that section of the Constitution.

[83] Nevertheless, while the thrust of the submissions was directed at s. 11(d), the respondent Wickman in *Campbell et al.* and the appellants in the PEI references, in their written submissions, the respondent Attorney General of PEI, in its oral submissions, and the intervener Attorney General of Canada, in response to a question from Iacobucci J, addressed the larger question of where the constitutional home of judicial independence lies, to which I now turn. Notwithstanding the presence of s. 11(d) of the *Charter*, and ss. 96-100 of the *Constitution Act, 1867*, I am of the view that judicial independence is at root an un-

written constitutional principle, in the sense that it is exterior to the particular sections of the Constitution Acts. The existence of that principle, whose origins can be traced to the *Act of Settlement of 1701*, is recognized and affirmed by the preamble to the *Constitution Act, 1867*. The specific provisions of the *Constitution Acts, 1867* to *1982*, merely "elaborate that principle in the institutional apparatus which they create or contemplate": *Switzman v. Elbling*, [1957] SCR 285, at p. 306, per Rand J.

[84] I arrive at this conclusion, in part, by considering the tenability of the opposite position—that the Canadian Constitution already contains explicit provisions which are directed at the protection of judicial independence, and that those provisions are exhaustive of the matter. Section 11(d) of the *Charter*, as I have mentioned above, protects the independence of a wide range of courts and tribunals which exercise jurisdiction over offences. Moreover, since well before the enactment of the *Charter*, ss. 96-100 of the *Constitution Act, 1867* separately and in combination, have protected and continue to protect the independence of provincial superior courts: *Cooper* … , at para. 11; *MacMillan Bloedel Ltd. v. Simpson*, [1995] 4 SCR 725, at para. 10. More specifically, s. 99 guarantees the security of tenure of superior court judges; s. 100 guarantees the financial security of judges of the superior, district, and county courts; and s. 96 has come to guarantee the core jurisdiction of superior, district, and county courts against legislative encroachment, which I also take to be a guarantee of judicial independence.

[85] However, upon closer examination, there are serious limitations to the view that the express provisions of the Constitution comprise an exhaustive and definitive code for the protection of judicial independence. The first and most serious problem is that the range of courts whose independence is protected by the written provisions of the Constitution contains large gaps. Sections 96-100, for example, only protect the independence of judges of the superior, district, and county courts, and even then, not in a uniform or consistent manner. Thus, while ss. 96 and 100 protect the core jurisdiction and the financial security, respectively, of all three types of courts (superior, district, and county), s. 99, on its terms, only protects the security of tenure of superior court judges. Moreover, ss. 96-100 do not apply to provincially appointed inferior courts, otherwise known as provincial courts.

[86] To some extent, the gaps in the scope of protection provided by ss. 96-100 are offset by the application of s. 11(d), which applies to a range of tribunals and courts, including provincial courts. However, by its express terms, s. 11(d) is limited in scope as well—it only extends the envelope of constitutional protection to bodies which exercise jurisdiction over offences. As a result, when those courts exercise civil jurisdiction, their independence would not seem to be guaranteed. The independence of provincial courts adjudicating in family law matters, for example, would not be constitutionally protected. The independence of superior courts, by contrast, when hearing exactly the same cases, would be constitutionally guaranteed.

[87] The second problem with reading s. 11(d) of the *Charter* and ss. 96-100 of the *Constitution Act, 1867* as an exhaustive code of judicial independence is that some of those provisions, by their terms, do not appear to speak to this objective. Section 100, for example, provides that Parliament shall fix and provide the salaries of superior, district, and county court judges. It is therefore, in an important sense, a subtraction from provincial jurisdiction over the administration of justice under s. 92(14). Moreover, read in the light of the *Act of Settlement of 1701*, it is a partial guarantee of financial security, inasmuch as it vests

responsibility for setting judicial remuneration with Parliament, which must act through the public means of legislative enactment, not the executive. However, on its plain language, it only places Parliament under the obligation to provide salaries to the judges covered by that provision, which would in itself not safeguard the judiciary against political interference through economic manipulation. Nevertheless, as I develop in these reasons, with reference to *Beauregard*, s. 100 also requires that Parliament must provide salaries that are adequate, and that changes or freezes to judicial remuneration be made only after recourse to a constitutionally mandated procedure.

[88]   A perusal of the language of s. 96 reveals the same difficulty:

> 96. The Governor General shall appoint the Judges of the Superior, District, and County Courts in each Province, except those of the Courts of Probate in Nova Scotia and New Brunswick.

Section 96 seems to do no more than confer the power to appoint judges of the superior, district, and county courts. It is a staffing provision, and is once again a subtraction from the power of the provinces under s. 92(14). However, through a process of judicial interpretation, s. 96 has come to guarantee the core jurisdiction of the courts which come within the scope of that provision. In the past, this development has often been expressed as a logical inference from the express terms of s. 96. Assuming that the goal of s. 96 was the creation of "a unitary judicial system," that goal would have been undermined "if a province could pass legislation creating a tribunal, appoint members thereto, and then confer on the tribunal the jurisdiction of the superior courts": *Re Residential Tenancies Act, 1979*, [1981] 1 SCR 714, at p. 728. However, as I recently confirmed, s. 96 restricts not only the legislative competence of provincial legislatures, but of Parliament as well: *MacMillan Bloedel, supra*. The rationale for the provision has also shifted, away from the protection of national unity, to the maintenance of the rule of law through the protection of the judicial role.

[89]   The point which emerges from this brief discussion is that the interpretation of ss. 96 and 100 has come a long way from what those provisions actually say. This jurisprudential evolution undermines the force of the argument that the written text of the Constitution is comprehensive and definitive in its protection of judicial independence. The only way to explain the interpretation of ss. 96 and 100, in fact, is by reference to a deeper set of unwritten understandings which are not found on the face of the document itself.

[90]   The proposition that the Canadian Constitution embraces unwritten norms was recently confirmed by this Court in *New Brunswick Broadcasting Co. v. Nova Scotia (Speaker of the House of Assembly)*, [1993] 1 SCR 319. In that case, the Court found it constitutional for the Nova Scotia House of Assembly to refuse the media the right to record and broadcast legislative proceedings. The media advanced a claim based on s. 2(b) of the *Charter*, which protects, inter alia, "freedom of the press and other media of communication." McLachlin J, speaking for a majority of the Court, found that the refusal of the Assembly was an exercise of that Assembly's unwritten legislative privileges, that the Constitution of Canada constitutionalized those privileges, and that the constitutional status of those privileges therefore precluded the application of the *Charter*.

. . .

[94] In my opinion, the existence of many of the unwritten rules of the Canadian Constitution can be explained by reference to the preamble of the *Constitution Act, 1867*. The relevant paragraph states in full:

> Whereas the Provinces of Canada, Nova Scotia, and New Brunswick have expressed their Desire to be federally united into One Dominion under the Crown of the United Kingdom of Great Britain and Ireland, with a Constitution similar in Principle to that of the United Kingdom:

Although the preamble has been cited by this Court on many occasions, its legal effect has never been fully explained. On the one hand, although the preamble is clearly part of the Constitution, it is equally clear that it "has no enacting force": *Reference re Resolution to Amend the Constitution*, [1981] 1 SCR 753, at p. 805 (joint majority reasons). In other words, strictly speaking, it is not a source of positive law, in contrast to the provisions which follow it.

[95] But the preamble does have important legal effects. Under normal circumstances, preambles can be used to identify the purpose of a statute, and also as an aid to construing ambiguous statutory language: *Driedger on the Construction of Statutes* (3rd ed. 1994), by R. Sullivan, at p. 261. The preamble to the *Constitution Act, 1867* certainly operates in this fashion. However, in my view, it goes even further. In the words of Rand J, the preamble articulates "the political theory which the Act embodies": *Switzman* … , at p. 306. It recognizes and affirms the basic principles which are the very source of the substantive provisions of the *Constitution Act, 1867*. As I have said above, those provisions merely elaborate those organizing principles in the institutional apparatus they create or contemplate. As such, the preamble is not only a key to construing the express provisions of the *Constitution Act, 1867*, but also invites the use of those organizing principles to fill out gaps in the express terms of the constitutional scheme. It is the means by which the underlying logic of the Act can be given the force of law.

[96] What are the organizing principles of the *Constitution Act, 1867*, as expressed in the preamble? The preamble speaks of the desire of the founding provinces "to be federally united into One Dominion," and thus, addresses the structure of the division of powers. Moreover, by its reference to "a Constitution similar in Principle to that of the United Kingdom," the preamble indicates that the legal and institutional structure of constitutional democracy in Canada should be similar to that of the legal regime out of which the Canadian Constitution emerged. To my mind, both of these aspects of the preamble explain many of the cases in which the Court has, through the normal process of constitutional interpretation, stated some fundamental rules of Canadian constitutional law which are not found in the express terms of the *Constitution Act, 1867*.

. . .

[The court discusses its previous jurisprudence concerning the use of the preamble of the *Constitution Act, 1867* to infer basic rules of Canadian constitutional law.]

[104] These examples—the doctrines of full faith and credit and paramountcy, the remedial innovation of suspended declarations of invalidity, the recognition of the constitutional status of the privileges of provincial legislatures, the vesting of the power to regulate

political speech within federal jurisdiction, and the inferral of implied limits on legislative sovereignty with respect to political speech—illustrate the special legal effect of the pre-amble. The preamble identifies the organizing principles of the *Constitution Act, 1867*, and invites the courts to turn those principles into the premises of a constitutional argument that culminates in the filling of gaps in the express terms of the constitutional text.

[105] The same approach applies to the protection of judicial independence. In fact, this point was already decided in *Beauregard*, and, unless and until it is reversed, we are gov-erned by that decision today. In that case (at p. 72), a unanimous Court held that the pre-amble of the *Constitution Act, 1867*, and in particular, its reference to "a Constitution similar in Principle to that of the United Kingdom," was "textual recognition" of the principle of judicial independence. Although in that case, it fell to us to interpret s. 100 of the *Constitu-tion Act, 1867*, the comments I have just reiterated were not limited by reference to that provision, and the courts which it protects.

[106] The historical origins of the protection of judicial independence in the United Kingdom, and thus in the Canadian Constitution, can be traced to the *Act of Settlement of 1701*. As we said in *Valente, supra*, at p. 693, that Act was the "historical inspiration" for the judicature provisions of the *Constitution Act, 1867*. Admittedly, the Act only extends protec-tion to judges of the English superior courts. However, our Constitution has evolved over time. In the same way that our understanding of rights and freedoms has grown, such that they have now been expressly entrenched through the enactment of the *Constitution Act, 1982*, so too has judicial independence grown into a principle that now extends to all courts, not just the superior courts of this country.

[107] I also support this conclusion on the basis of the presence of s. 11(d) of the *Char-ter*, an express provision which protects the independence of provincial court judges only when those courts exercise jurisdiction in relation to offences. As I said earlier, the express provisions of the Constitution should be understood as elaborations of the underlying, unwritten, and organizing principles found in the preamble to the *Constitution Act, 1867*. Even though s. 11(d) is found in the newer part of our Constitution, the *Charter*, it can be understood in this way, since the Constitution is to be read as a unified whole: *Reference re Bill 30, An Act to amend the Education Act (Ont.)*, [1987] 1 SCR 1148, at p. 1206. An analogy can be drawn between the express reference in the preamble of the *Constitution Act, 1982* to the rule of law and the implicit inclusion of that principle in the *Constitution Act, 1867*: *Reference re Manitoba Language Rights, supra*, at p. 750. Section 11(d), far from indicating that judicial independence is constitutionally enshrined for provincial courts only when those courts exercise jurisdiction over offences, is proof of the existence of a general prin-ciple of judicial independence that applies to all courts no matter what kind of cases they hear.

[108] I reinforce this conclusion by reference to the central place that courts hold within the Canadian system of government. In *OPSEU*, … Beetz J linked limitations on legislative sovereignty over political speech with "the existence of certain political institutions" as part of the "basic structure of our Constitution" (p. 57). However, political institutions are only one part of the basic structure of the Canadian Constitution. As this Court has said before, there are three branches of government—the legislature, the executive, and the judiciary: *Fraser v. Public Service Staff Relations Board*, [1985] 2 SCR 455, at p. 469; *R v. Power*, [1994] 1 SCR 601, at p. 620. Courts, in other words, are equally "definitional to the Canadian

understanding of constitutionalism" (*Cooper* … , at para. 11) as are political institutions. It follows that the same constitutional imperative—the preservation of the basic structure—which led Beetz J to limit the power of legislatures to affect the operation of political institutions, also extends protection to the judicial institutions of our constitutional system. By implication, the jurisdiction of the provinces over "courts," as that term is used in s. 92(14) of the *Constitution Act, 1867*, contains within it an implied limitation that the independence of those courts cannot be undermined.

[109] In conclusion, the express provisions of the *Constitution Act, 1867* and the *Charter* are not an exhaustive written code for the protection of judicial independence in Canada. Judicial independence is an unwritten norm, recognized and affirmed by the preamble to the *Constitution Act, 1867*. In fact, it is in that preamble, which serves as the grand entrance hall to the castle of the Constitution, that the true source of our commitment to this foundational principle is located.

The Supreme Court returned to this issue in the case of *Ell v. Alberta*, [2003] 1 SCR 857, 2003 SCC 35. There the issue related to the application of the principle of judicial independence to the office of justice of the peace. Justice Major wrote:

> [3] The principle of judicial independence must be interpreted in light of the public interests it is meant to protect: a strong and independent judiciary capable of upholding the rule of law and our constitutional order, and public confidence in the administration of justice. The reforms in this case reflect a good faith and considered decision of the Legislature that was intended to promote these interests. As a result, the legislation does not undermine the perception of independence in the mind of a reasonable and informed person, and is respectful of the principle of judicial independence.
>
> · · ·
>
> [18] Judicial independence has been recognized as "the lifeblood of constitutionalism in democratic societies": see *Beauregard v. Canada*, [1986] 2 SCR 56, at p. 70, per Dickson CJ. It requires objective conditions that ensure the judiciary's freedom to act without interference from any other entity. The principle finds explicit constitutional reference in ss. 96 to 100 of the *Constitution Act, 1867* and s. 11(d) of the *Canadian Charter of Rights and Freedoms*. The application of these provisions is limited: the former to judges of superior courts, and the latter to courts and tribunals that determine the guilt of those charged with criminal offences: see *Reference re Remuneration of Judges of the Provincial Court of Prince Edward Island*, [1997] 3 SCR 3 ("*Provincial Court Judges Reference*"), at para. 84, per Lamer CJ. The respondents do not fall into either of these categories. Nonetheless, as this Court has recognized, the principle of judicial independence extends beyond the limited scope of the above provisions.
>
> · · ·
>
> [20] Historically, the principle of judicial independence was confined to the superior courts. As a result of the expansion of judicial duties beyond that realm, it is now accepted that all courts fall within the principle's embrace. See *Provincial Court Judges Reference, supra*, at para. 106:
>
> > … [O]ur Constitution has evolved over time. In the same way that our understanding of rights and freedoms has grown, such that they have now been expressly entrenched through the enactment of the *Constitution Act, 1982*, so too has judicial independence

grown into a principle that now extends to all courts, not just the superior courts of this country.

The scope of the unwritten principle of independence must be interpreted in accordance with its underlying purposes. In this appeal, its extension to the office held by the respondents depends on whether they exercise judicial functions that relate to the bases upon which the principle is founded.

In the result, the court held that the justices of the peace were "constitutionally required to be independent in the exercise of their duties."

B. Assessing Independence

Before turning to the precise content of the independence requirement, it should be asked how this independence is measured. For the Supreme Court, "[t]he general test for the presence or absence of independence consists in asking whether a reasonable person who is fully informed of all the circumstances would consider that a particular court enjoyed the necessary independent status." *Mackin v. New Brunswick (Minister of Finance)*, [2002] 1 SCR 405, at para. 38. Thus, independence includes both a requirement of actual independence, and also conditions sufficient to give rise to a reasonable perception of independence on the part of a reasonable and well-informed person.

In *Canada (Minister of Citizenship and Immigration) v. Tobiass*, [1997] 3 SCR 391 the Supreme Court considered whether judicial independence had been impaired by a private meeting between a senior Department of Justice official and the chief justice of the Federal Court in relation to delay in the hearing of certain cases in which the Justice Department was a litigant. The court wrote:

> [42] This appeal presents three issues. … The second is whether judicial independence, or the appearance of it, suffered as a result of the meeting between Mr. Thompson and Isaac CJ. The third is whether, if any damage was done to the appearance of judicial independence, the trial judge properly exercised his discretion to enter a stay of proceedings.
>
> • • •
>
> [67] We conclude that the meeting between Mr. Thompson and Isaac CJ and the subsequent conduct of officials of the Department of Justice did indeed cause damage to the appearance of judicial independence. The question remains as to the extent of that damage and how it should be weighed in considering whether a stay should be granted in these significant and important proceedings.
>
> [68] The independence of judges has two aspects: an institutional aspect and a personal aspect. As Le Dain J wrote in *Valente v. The Queen*, [1985] 2 SCR 673, at p. 691:
>
> > … the word "independent" in s. 11(d) of the *Charter* is to be understood as referring to the status or relationship of judicial independence as well as to the state of mind or attitude of the tribunal in the actual exercise of its judicial function.

The parties agree that it is the personal aspect of judicial independence—what is sometimes called "impartiality"—that is at issue here. No one alleges, and indeed there is no credible evidence to suggest, that the integrity of the Federal Court as an institution has been compromised.

[69] Though it is very important that the judiciary should actually remain independent, it is equally important that the judiciary should be seen to be independent. In our view, there is not sufficient evidence to support the conclusion that the Chief Justice and the Associate Chief Justice did not in fact remain independent. However, the evidence does compel us to conclude that the appearance of judicial independence suffered significantly as a result of what happened on March 1, 1996.

[70] The test for determining whether the appearance of judicial independence has been maintained is an objective one. The question is whether a well-informed and reasonable observer would perceive that judicial independence has been compromised. As Lamer CJ wrote in *R v. Lippé*, [1991] 2 SCR 114, at p. 139, "[t]he overall objective of guaranteeing judicial independence is to ensure a reasonable perception of impartiality."

[71] The essence of judicial independence is freedom from outside interference. Dickson CJ, in *Beauregard v. Canada*, [1986] 2 SCR 56, described the concept in these words, at p. 69:

> Historically, the generally accepted core of the principle of judicial independence has been the complete liberty of individual judges to hear and decide the cases that come before them: no outsider—be it government, pressure group, individual or even another judge—should interfere in fact, or attempt to interfere, with the way in which a judge conducts his or her case and makes his or her decision. This core continues to be central to the principle of judicial independence.

[72] What emerges from all of this is a simple test for determining whether the appearance of judicial independence has been maintained: whether a reasonable observer would perceive that the court was able to conduct its business free from the interference of the government and of other judges.

The outcome of this case is discussed below.

C. Dimensions and Core Characteristics

What does judicial independence require? In the *Provincial Judges Reference*, Chief Justice Lamer also provided a conceptual analysis of judicial independence:

> [118] The three core characteristics of judicial independence—security of tenure, financial security, and administrative independence—should be contrasted with what I have termed the two dimensions of judicial independence. In *Valente*, Le Dain J drew a distinction between two dimensions of judicial independence, the individual independence of a judge and the institutional or collective independence of the court or tribunal of which that judge is a member. In other words, while individual independence attaches to individual judges, institutional or collective independence attaches to the court or tribunal as an institutional entity. The two different dimensions of judicial independence are related in the following way (*Valente* ... , at p. 687):
>
> > The relationship between these two aspects of judicial independence is that an individual judge may enjoy the essential conditions of judicial independence but if the court or tribunal over which he or she presides is not independent of the other branches of

government, in what is essential to its function, he or she cannot be said to be an independent tribunal.

[119] It is necessary to explain the relationship between the three core characteristics and the two dimensions of judicial independence, because Le Dain J did not fully do so in *Valente*. For example, he stated that security of tenure was part of the individual independence of a court or tribunal, whereas administrative independence was identified with institutional or collective independence. However, the core characteristics of judicial independence, and the dimensions of judicial independence, are two very different concepts. The core characteristics of judicial independence are distinct facets of the definition of judicial independence. Security of tenure, financial security, and administrative independence come together to constitute judicial independence. By contrast, the dimensions of judicial independence indicate which entity—the individual judge or the court or tribunal to which he or she belongs—is protected by a particular core characteristic.

[120] The conceptual distinction between the core characteristics and the dimensions of judicial independence suggests that it may be possible for a core characteristic to have both an individual and an institutional or collective dimension. To be sure, sometimes a core characteristic only attaches to a particular dimension of judicial independence; administrative independence, for example, only attaches to the court as an institution (although sometimes it may be exercised on behalf of a court by its chief judge or justice). However, this need not always be the case. The guarantee of security of tenure, for example, may have a collective or institutional dimension, such that only a body composed of judges may recommend the removal of a judge. However, I need not decide that particular point here.

These three core characteristics of security of tenure, financial security, and administrative independence are discussed in turn below.

1. Security of Tenure

Constitutionally protected security of tenure has both an individual and an institutional dimension. Individual security of tenure means that judges may not be dismissed by the executive before the age of retirement except for misconduct or disability. Thus, a judge may only be removed from office for a reason relating to his or her capacity to perform his or her judicial duties. Arbitrary removal is prohibited: see *Mackin*, [2002] 1 SCR 405, at paras. 42 and 43.

Institutionally, before a judge may be removed for cause, "there must be a judicial inquiry to establish that such cause exists, at which the judge affected must be afforded an opportunity to be heard": see *Re Therrien*, [2001] 2 SCR 3, at para. 39. Superior court judges are removable only by a joint address of the House of Commons and the Senate, per s. 99 of the *Constitution Act, 1867*: see *Ell*, [2003] 1 SCR 857, at para. 31.

In the early years after Confederation, only four cases came before Parliament seeking removal, the last of which concluded in 1881. None were successful. In the 1960s, the case of Justice Leo Landreville was referred to a royal commission before coming before Parliament. He ultimately resigned, but his case has been described as a "travesty of justice" and a demonstration of the inadequacy of Parliament as a vehicle for investigating allegations of judicial misconduct: see William Kaplan, *Bad Judgment: The Case of Mr. Justice Leo A. Landreville* (Toronto: University of Toronto Press, 1996).

In 1971, the *Judges Act*, RSC 1985, c. J-1 was amended to establish the Canadian Judicial Council (CJC) as the body responsible for investigating complaints about the conduct of federally appointed judges. If the council concludes that removal of a judge is warranted, it makes a report to the minister of justice, who may introduce a motion before Parliament. Authority to recommend removal of a judge from office is found in s. 69(3) of the *Judges Act*:

> The Governor in Council may, on the recommendation of the Minister, after receipt of a report described in subsection 65(1) in relation to an inquiry under this section in connection with a person who may be removed from office by the Governor in Council other than on an address of the Senate or House of Commons or on a joint address of the Senate and House of Commons, by order, remove the person from office.

In practice, every judge facing convincing allegations of misconduct has resigned at some stage of the council's proceedings rather than going before Parliament for an ultimate determination.

Consider this description of the CJC complaints process.

Canadian Judicial Council, *About the Council*
(Ottawa: CJC, 2011), online: http://www.cjc-ccm.gc.ca/
english/about_en.asp

Mandate and Powers

Parliament created the Canadian Judicial Council in 1971. The objectives of the Council, as mandated by the *Judges Act*, are to promote efficiency, uniformity, and accountability, and to improve the quality of judicial service in all superior courts of Canada. The Council has authority over the work of more than 1,100 federally appointed judges.

How does the Council work?

The Canadian Judicial Council itself is made up of 39 members and is chaired by the Chief Justice of the Supreme Court of Canada, the Right Honourable Beverley McLachlin. Council membership consists of the chief justices, associate chief justices, and some senior judges from provincial and federal superior courts across the country.

The chief justices of each province are responsible for the day-to-day administration of justice within their own jurisdictions across Canada. Full meetings more than twice a year would be impossible, so the Council's committee system allows members to work on a regular basis in smaller groups that focus on the issues that affect Canada's justice system. Some committees are permanent, standing committees; others are formed from time to time to deal with specific issues or projects.

What powers does the Council have?

Canadians rightly demand a high degree of professionalism and good conduct from their judges. They also need judges who are independent and able to give judgments in court without fear of retaliation or punishment. To help achieve this goal, the Canadian Judicial

Council was granted power under the *Judges Act* to investigate complaints made by members of the public and the Attorney General about the conduct (not the decisions) of federally appointed judges. After its investigation of a complaint, the Council can make recommendations, including removing a judge from office.

Conduct of Judges

We expect the highest standards of conduct from our judges. If a judge's conduct does not meet our expected high standards and is not suitable to be a member of the judiciary, the Canadian Judicial Council has a process for reviewing the alleged inappropriate conduct and, if necessary, for removing the judge from office.

What is the Council's role in reviewing judicial conduct?

Under the *Judges Act*, the Canadian Judicial Council has the authority to investigate complaints about federally appointed judges in Canada. These are judges from federal courts and higher levels of provincial courts.

By directing complaints to the Canadian Judicial Council, Parliament acknowledges that the public must have a way to voice its concerns about judges. At the same time, the system must allow judges to respond to allegations of misconduct in a fair way. The entire process must be efficient, fair, and objective.

The procedure for making a complaint about a judge's conduct is described fully in the complaints section of this website. Any member of the public, the Minister of Justice, or provincial Attorneys General, can make a complaint about a federally appointed judge to the Council. Provided the complaint is about a judge's conduct (not a judge's decision in a court case), is in writing, and is about a specific federally appointed judge, the Council will take the complaint and review the matter.

The Council may handle the complaint in a variety of ways, from asking the judge to respond to the complaint, to holding a full inquiry into the matter. In very serious cases, the Council can recommend to Parliament that a judge be removed from office.

The Council cannot investigate general complaints about the justice system, the courts, or the judiciary as a whole. It cannot change judicial decisions in court cases, compensate individuals, grant appeals, or address demands for a new trial.

The Canadian Judicial Council does not have jurisdiction over the lower levels of provincial courts, such as those that hear small claims disputes, and some family and criminal matters. If a member of the public wants to make a complaint about a judge in one of those courts, the complaint must be directed to the judicial council in that judge's province or territory.

· · ·

Judicial Conduct

How is judicial conduct defined?

Judicial conduct (a judge's conduct/behaviour) refers to the high standard of personal conduct that is expected of judges, both in court and in public. If a judge is not suitable to be a member of the judiciary, the justice system provides for a way to review the judge's behaviour and recommend a course of action.

There is an important distinction between a judge's personal conduct in or outside of a courtroom and a decision that a judge makes in a particular court case. If a federally appointed judge's behaviour is not appropriate, you can make a complaint to the Canadian Judicial Council. If you believe that the judge reached the wrong decision in your court case, you may appeal to a higher court to review that decision.

Principles of judicial conduct

. . .

We expect judges to maintain a high standard of conduct, both inside and outside the courtroom. When someone believes that a judge's behaviour (not their decision) is of concern, or that a judge is not fit to sit on the Bench, a complaint can be made to the Canadian Judicial Council. In very serious cases, Parliament can remove a judge from office.

. . .

What is the Canadian Judicial Council's role?

If a federally appointed judge has breached the standard of good behaviour and is not suitable to be a member of the judiciary, only Parliament can remove the judge from office. And, under the *Judges Act*, Parliament has assigned the process to review alleged breaches of conduct to the Canadian Judicial Council.

By directing complaints to the Canadian Judicial Council, Parliament acknowledges that the public must have a way to voice its concerns about judges. At the same time, the system must allow judges to respond to allegations of misconduct in a fair manner. The process must be efficient, fair, and objective.

A matter for appeal or a complaint?

In brief, the Canadian Judicial Council investigates complaints about an individual judge's inappropriate conduct, not a judge's decision in a court case.

Every year, judges in Canadian courts make hundreds of thousands of decisions on matters ranging from procedural issues to determining important points of law. When one party in a legal dispute thinks the judge made the wrong decision, the justice system allows that person to appeal to a higher court. For example, if you think that a judge of the Ontario Superior Court of Justice reached the wrong decision in your case, you can appeal the decision to the Ontario Court of Appeal.

Judges can make mistakes. An appeal court can reverse or vary the decision made by the judge who heard the case. The fact that an appeal court overturns a judge's decision does not mean that the judge's conduct was improper or that the judge should be removed from office. It simply means that the appeal court believed the judge made a mistake about the law or the facts of the case.

All judges are expected to uphold a high standard of personal conduct, both inside and outside the courtroom. So, aside from the decision the judge reaches in your case, the judge must be impartial when hearing your case, be respectful and courteous throughout the proceedings, and maintain a high standard of integrity. For example, it is appropriate for members of the public to ask the Council to investigate complaints about judges who are thought to have shown biases based on race, gender, or religion. Complaints can arise from judges' comments in the courtroom, from speeches or interviews given outside the courtroom.

If you are concerned about the conduct of a federally appointed judge, think carefully about the kind of action you may take:

- If you believe the judge made the wrong decision in your case, consider appealing your case to a higher court.
- If you believe a judge's conduct was improper, either during your case or in public, consider making a complaint to the Canadian Judicial Council.

• • •

Making a Complaint

Who can make a complaint?

Any member of the public can make a complaint to the Council. Provided the complaint is about judicial conduct, is made in writing, and is about a specific federally appointed judge, the Council will review the matter.

Although the Minister of Justice or a provincial Attorney General can initiate a formal inquiry about a federally appointed judge, most complaints come from the general public.

If a provincial Attorney General or the Minister of Justice of Canada submits a complaint, the Council must appoint an Inquiry Committee to consider whether a recommendation should be made to the Minister of Justice to remove the judge from office. The Inquiry Committee must hold a hearing, normally in public. The Council then considers the report of the Inquiry Committee and makes a recommendation to the Minister of Justice.

In accordance with the complaints process, the Canadian Judicial Council can also initiate an inquiry into a judge's conduct.

Who can you make a complaint against?

The Canadian Judicial Council has the authority to investigate complaints only about federally appointed judges in Canada. These are judges from federal courts and higher levels of courts in each province.

The Council cannot investigate general complaints about the justice system, the courts, or the judiciary as a whole. It cannot change judicial decisions in court cases, compensate individuals, grant appeals, or address demands for a new trial.

The Canadian Judicial Council does not have jurisdiction over the lower levels of provincial courts, such as those that hear small claims disputes, and some family and criminal matters. If you want to make a complaint about a judge in one of those courts, you must direct your complaint to the judicial council in your province or territory.

The Canadian Judicial Council does not have the authority to investigate complaints against court staff or lawyers. Complaints about court staff should be made to the court administration office of the courthouse in question. Complaints about lawyers should be made to the Law Society in your province or territory.

How do I make a complaint?

The Canadian Judicial Council seeks to ensure a fair process when a complaint is made against a judge. Every complaint is considered seriously and conscientiously.

You do not have to be represented by a lawyer if you want to make a complaint about a judge. You do not need to use a special form to make a complaint to the Council. There is no fee charged and no deadline for making a complaint. The Council requires only that a complaint be:

- in writing;
- about a named, federally appointed judge; and
- about the conduct of a judge and not their decision.

You can write a letter to the Canadian Judicial Council, and send it by regular mail (Canadian Judicial Council, Ottawa, Ontario, K1A 0W8) or by email [info@cjc-ccm.gc.ca]. Your letter should include:

- your name and address;
- the name of the judge you are making a complaint against; and
- a description of the judge's conduct that you believe was inappropriate.

What happens after I make a complaint?

The Council is committed to reviewing complaints about the conduct of judges in a way that is sensitive to the person making the complaint, fair to the judge who the complaint was about, and credible to the judiciary and the public. While the public must have a way to voice its concerns about members of the judiciary, the judges must be given an opportunity to respond to the allegation of misconduct. The complaint procedure is set out fully in the Canadian Judicial Council's Complaint Procedures.

The Council takes complaints very seriously and deals with them as quickly as possible. Out of the 200 or so complaints received every year, the Council concludes the majority of them within three months.

Step 1: review of complaint
A member of the Council's Judicial Conduct Committee first reviews the complaint. Many complaints are dismissed because they do not meet the criteria for review. For example, some complaints are about a judge's decision in a case, not his or her conduct; others may be about a provincially appointed judge, rather than a federally appointed judge.

Step 2: investigation of the complaint
When the Council further investigates, a copy of the complaint is sent to the judge in question and the chief justice of that judge's province, with a request for comments. The Complainant may also be asked to provide additional comments.

Some complaints contain serious allegations of inappropriate conduct against a judge and must be further investigated by the Council. Such cases may be investigated with the assistance of a lawyer from outside the Council. This person is chosen for their expertise and reputation in the legal community. The lawyer may interview the judge, the complainant, and others who are connected with the situation, and prepare a report.

Step 3: the Review Panel
If the complaint is not immediately resolved, the matter may be handed over to a Review Panel for further study. The Review Panel is composed of up to five members, who are all judges. If the Review Panel concludes that the complaint has merit, but is not serious enough to move to the next stage (formal hearing by the Inquiry Committee), the Review Panel may close the file with an expression of concern, or may recommend counselling for the judge, or other similar remedial actions.

Step 4: Inquiry Committee
If the complaint might be serious enough to warrant the judge's removal from office, the Review Panel can decide that there should be an Inquiry Committee to hear the matter. The Inquiry Committee is composed of Council members and senior lawyers.

If the complaint comes from a provincial Attorney General or the Minster of Justice of Canada, the matter may go directly to an Inquiry Committee.

The Inquiry Committee can conduct its own investigation into the complaint, and hear from the judge, the person who made the complaint, and others. The Inquiry Committee normally holds a public hearing, where the judge and the person who complained can attend and give evidence about the matter that led to the complaint. The Inquiry Committee prepares a report, which goes to the full Canadian Judicial Council for discussion.

Step 5: recommendations
After considering the Inquiry Committee's report, the Council must decide whether the judge's conduct has rendered the judge "incapacitated or disabled from the due execution of the office of judge."

Council may recommend to Parliament (through the Minister of Justice) that the judge be removed from office. Parliament has never had to face such a situation, but sometimes a judge will retire or resign before that step is taken.

Step 6: notice of the decision
When the complaint has been considered and a decision is reached, the Council will advise the person who complained of its decision in writing.

For an analysis of the role of the council in dealing with judicial misconduct, including five case studies, see Ed Ratushny, "Speaking as Judges: How Far Can They Go?" (2000), 11 *NJCL* 293.

The reports of formal inquiry committees established by the CJC are available on its website at http://www.cjc-ccm.gc.ca. An inquiry committee of the council conducts a formal public hearing into the allegations of misconduct and reports to the full council. The council, in turn, may then make a report to the minister of justice. Consider the 1996 report of the CJC in relation to Justice Bienvenue.

Report of the Canadian Judicial Council to the Minister of Justice Under Section 63(1) of the Judges Act Concerning the Conduct of Mr. Justice Jean Bienvenue of the Superior Court of Quebec in R v. T. Théberge
(Ottawa: CJC, October 1996)

The majority of the Canadian Judicial Council, consisting of:

Chief Justice Lamer (Chief Justice of Canada), Chief Justice Clarke (Nova Scotia), Associate Chief Justice Deslongchamps (Quebec), Associate Chief Justice Dohm (British Columbia), Chief Justice Esson (British Columbia), Chief Justice Fraser (Alberta), Chief Justice Glube (Nova Scotia), Chief Justice Gushue (Newfoundland), Chief Justice Hewak (Manitoba), Mr. Justice Hudson (Yukon Territory), Chief Justice Lemieux (Quebec), Chief Justice LeSage (Ontario), Chief Justice MacPherson (Saskatchewan), Chief Justice McEachern (British Columbia), Chief Justice McMurtry (Ontario), Associate Chief Justice Mercier (Manitoba), Chief Justice Moore (Alberta), Associate Chief Justice Morden (Ontario), Associate Chief Justice Oliphant (Manitoba), Associate Chief Justice Palmeter (Nova Scotia), Chief Justice Scott (Manitoba), and Associate Chief Justice Wachowich (Alberta),

is of the opinion that Mr. Justice Bienvenue has become incapacitated or disabled from the due execution of the office of judge and recommends that he be removed from the office of judge of the Superior Court of Quebec. The majority except Chief Justice McEachern rely on sections 65(2)(b), (c) and (d) of the *Judges Act*; their reasons are attached. In separate concurring reasons, which will follow at a later date, Chief Justice McEachern relies only on section 65(2)(d).

The following members of the Council dissent from this decision:

Chief Justice Bayda (Saskatchewan), Chief Justice Carruthers (Prince Edward Island), Associate Chief Judge Christie (Tax Court of Canada), Chief Justice Hickman (Newfoundland), Chief Justice Hoyt (New Brunswick), Chief Justice MacDonald (Prince Edward Island), and Associate Chief Justice Smith (Ontario).

for reasons to follow at a later date.

Antonio Lamer
Chairman
September 20, 1996

Reasons of All Majority Members Except Chief Justice McEachern

We are in substantial agreement with the conclusions stated by the majority of the Inquiry Committee under the heading "Recommendation" in its report dated June 25, 1996, as follows:

If the judge's meeting with the jury after the verdict [in which he made comments critical of its performance] had been an isolated occurrence, we would merely have expressed our disapproval of this violation of paragraphs 65(2)(b) and (c) of the Act, on the assumption that such an occurrence would not happen again. The judge's remarks about women and his deepseated ideas behind those remarks legitimately cast doubt on his impartiality in the execution of his judicial office. Yet impartiality is the essence of the office of judge. Accordingly, this violation led us to conduct a further analysis to determine whether Mr. Justice Bienvenue had become incapacitated or disabled from the due execution of the office of judge.

That analysis required us to review all the incidents that marked Tracy Théberge's trial or occurred after that trial. We also particularly took account of Mr. Justice Bienvenue's testimony at the inquiry. We find that the judge has shown an aggravating lack of sensitivity to the communities and individuals offended by his remarks or conduct. In addition—the evidence could not be any clearer—Mr. Justice Bienvenue does not intend to change his behaviour in any way.

Because of his conduct during all the incidents that marked Tracy Théberge's trial, Mr. Justice Bienvenue has undermined public confidence in him and strongly contributed to destroying public confidence in the judicial system. In our view, this is the conclusion that would be reached by a reasonable and informed person.

Combining the test used by the Committee of the Canadian Judicial Council in the *Marshall* case and that applied by the Supreme Court to assess judicial impartiality and independence, we believe that if Mr. Justice Bienvenue were to preside over a case, a reasonable and informed person, viewing the matter realistically and practically—and having thought the matter through—would have a reasonable apprehension that the judge would not execute his office with the objectivity, impartiality and independence that the public is entitled to expect from a judge.

We are therefore of the opinion that Mr. Justice Bienvenue has breached the duty of good behaviour under section 99 of the *Constitution Act, 1867* and has become incapacitated or disabled from the due execution of the office of judge for the reasons set out in paragraphs 65(2)(b), (c) and (d) of the *Judges Act*:

- having been guilty of misconduct,
- having failed in the due execution of that office,
- having been placed, by his conduct, in a position incompatible with the due execution of that office,

and we recommend that he be removed from office.

We are, however, of the view that the question whether Mr. Justice Bienvenue breached the duty of good behaviour under s. 99 of the *Constitution Act, 1867*, is one exclusively for consideration by Parliament. We have, therefore, only addressed the provisions of s. 65 of the *Judges Act*.

The totality of the matters dealt with by the Inquiry Committee demonstrably support the majority Committee's conclusion that "Mr. Justice Bienvenue has shown an almost complete lack of sensitivity to the communities and individuals offended by his remarks." Interwoven throughout the evidence is a complete lack of appreciation by Mr. Justice Bienvenue of the duties and responsibilities of a judge.

It is important to note that the majority emphasized that: "In addition—the evidence cannot be any clearer—Mr. Justice Bienvenue does not intend to change his behaviour in any way."

No attempt has been made by Mr. Justice Bienvenue since the delivery of the report of the Inquiry Committee to indicate any intention on his part to, in fact, change his behaviour.

It is essential to the integrity of the administration of justice that the public have confidence in the impartiality of the judiciary. We agree with the majority of the Inquiry Committee that the public can no longer reasonably have such confidence in Mr. Justice Bienvenue.

Concurring Reasons of Chief Justice McEachern

September 27, 1996

I agree with the recommendation of the majority of my colleagues that the Honourable Mr. Justice Bienvenue of the Superior Court of Quebec has become incapacitated or disabled from the due performance of his office of judge but I would limit the basis for this finding to s. 65(2)(d), that is to say by having been placed by his conduct or otherwise in a position incompatible with the due execution of his office.

The standard of proof in this matter is the civil standard of a balance of probabilities. Because of the importance of the issues, the grounds must be powerfully persuasive.

Applying that standard, I am unable to find that Mr. Justice Bienvenue is biased against Jewish persons. His unfortunate and entirely inaccurate comment about the Holocaust in the sentencing proceedings was a highly insensitive, inappropriate and very bad analogy that should not have been used to assist him to describe the nature of the offence with which he was dealing. I note that his apology to the Jewish community satisfied those organizations who reported, after meeting with the judge, that they observed no evidence of anti-Semitism in his attitude.

I depart from the reasons of the majority only because, with all possible deference and respect, I do not wish to base my concurrence on any grounds except the reasonable apprehension he has created, by his words and conduct, that he may permit his strongly held beliefs about the relative qualities of men and women to affect the decisions he may be called upon to decide in the course of his judicial duties.

To put it more bluntly, it is my view that in many cases that arise for decision in the course of the work of a busy court, litigants whose cases are assigned to Mr. Justice Bienvenue, both men and women, may reasonably apprehend, and be fearful, that in some cases he will stereotype women worse than men, and in other cases he will stereotype women better than men.

These simplistic views, when they intrude into legal proceedings, breach the fundamental equality requirements of the Constitution of Canada and the ordinary fairness expectations of litigants in our courts. I wish emphatically to record that there can be no reasonable expectation that judges must all have the same views about all matters. This case, however, crosses the line because Mr. Justice Bienvenue expressed, and later reaffirmed, his idiosyncratic views at a crucial stage in the sentencing proceedings he was conducting and thereby created a reasonable apprehension that his unusual views did play a part in reaching the sentence he imposed.

Moreover, as the evidence shows, Mr. Justice Bienvenue made it clear that he still held firmly to such views at the time of the Inquiry hearings, and he thereby lent support to the reasonable apprehension created by his sentencing remarks that other litigants would risk unfairness in his court.

Because it is unnecessary to go further, I disavow reliance upon any of the other grounds apparently relied upon by the Inquiry Committee, singly or cumulatively, as sufficient grounds for a recommendation for removal even though it appears that Mr. Justice Bienvenue, in the closing days of the trial in question, was conducting himself in a manner other than what is expected of federally appointed judges. It is unnecessary to decide how those other grounds should be classified or what varying degrees of seriousness should be assigned to them.

Reasons of the Minority by Chief Justice Bayda

October 1, 1996

The issue in these proceedings before the Canadian Judicial Council is whether, to use the words of the majority of the Inquiry Committee, "an individual who has been a judge for almost 20 years and whose integrity has not been questioned" did, by his conduct during a three-week murder trial, and by his conduct in speaking to the news media after the trial, demonstrate that he has become incapacitated or disabled from the due execution of his judicial duties and, for that reason, ought to be removed from office.

Sections 65(2)(b), (c) and (d) of the *Judges Act* are the governing provisions:

> 65(2) Where, in the opinion of the Council, the judge in respect of whom an inquiry or investigation has been made has become incapacitated or disabled from the due execution of the office of judge by reason of
>
> . . .
>
> (b) having been guilty of misconduct,
>
> (c) having failed in the due execution of that office, or
>
> (d) having been placed, by his conduct or otherwise, in a position incompatible with the due execution of that office,
>
> the Council, in its report to the Minister under subsection (1), may recommend that the judge be removed from office.

They must be read in conjunction with and interpreted in the light of s. 99 of the *Constitution Act*:

> 99. The judges of the superior courts shall hold office during good behaviour but shall be removable by the governor general on address of the Senate and House of Commons.

The proceedings were initiated by a letter from the Minister of Justice of Canada to Council and a letter from the Minister of Justice of Quebec to Council requesting Council to inquire, pursuant to the *Judges Act*, into the conduct of the judge in question, Mr. Justice Bienvenue of the Superior Court of Quebec, during and after the murder trial of Ms. Tracy Théberge.

An Inquiry Committee established in accordance with the *Judges Act*, and comprising three members of Council and two lawyers appointed by the Minister of Justice of Canada, inquired into the judge's conduct. They heard 19 witnesses including the judge, as well as submissions from independent counsel, and the judge's counsel. The Committee considered the matter and prepared a majority and a minority report.

Four members signed the former and one the latter. The reports were filed with the Council. The majority made findings of fact and law and ultimately concluded as follows:

> We are therefore of the opinion that Mr. Justice Jean Bienvenue has breached the duty of good behaviour under section 99 of the *Constitution Act, 1867* and has become incapacitated or disabled from the due execution of the office of judge for the reasons set out in paragraphs 65(2)(b),(c) and (d) of the *Judges Act*:
>
> - having been guilty of misconduct,
> - having failed in the due execution of that office,
> - having been placed, by his conduct, in a position incompatible with the due execution of that office, and we recommend that he be removed from office.

After considering the two reports and further written submissions from both counsel, the Judicial Council reached a decision—not unanimous—to recommend to the Minister that Mr. Justice Bienvenue be removed from office for essentially the reasons given by the majority of the Inquiry Committee. The lack of unanimity has given rise to three reports by Council, one by the majority, excluding Chief Justice McEachern, one by Chief Justice McEachern supporting the majority decision, and this report by the minority. The Council did not hear any oral evidence or any oral submissions. Mr. Justice Bienvenue, although given the opportunity, did not appear before Council.

The majority of the Inquiry Committee made certain findings of primary fact which we accept. We do not, however, accept the Committee's crucial conclusory findings, either of law or fact. The findings of primary fact to which we refer are these:

1. the "Kleenex" remarks to a female juror;
2. certain uncomplimentary remarks about a parking attendant;
3. certain inappropriate comments to a female reporter concerning her attire;
4. remarks to a court official in the judge's private chambers about the jury's competence and about the accused's colour and sexual orientation;
5. meeting of the judge with the jurors after the verdict;
6. remarks by the judge during sentencing concerning women in general (and about men) and separate remarks concerning the victims of the Holocaust;
7. events that occurred after sentencing.

It is the sixth and seventh of these, insofar as they particularly concern women, that were the true focus of the Inquiry Committee and of Council. It is fair to say that the remarks about women were the catalytic force which precipitated the decision to recommend removal.

Had those remarks not been made, the improprieties of conduct reflected in the remainder of the primary facts (1 to 5) taken separately and cumulatively, would not have been a sufficient basis for the decision to recommend removal. They may have given rise to some form of sanction, perhaps even a severe disapproval, but not removal.

It is clear from the Committee's majority report that, while the majority did not brush aside these other improprieties, they were used mainly as a buttress to the conclusion the majority reached regarding the consequences that are to flow from the remarks concerning women in general. It is for these reasons that we will emphasize the aspect of the Committee's report that pertains to the remarks about women—remarks that none of us believes to be true or appropriate for use by a judge.

The judge said this about women in his sentencing remarks:

> IT HAS always been said, and correctly so, that when—women—whom I have always considered the noblest beings in creation and the noblest (*sic*) of the two sexes of the human race—it is said that when women ascend the scale of virtues, they reach higher than men, and I have always believed this. AND it is also said, and this too I believe, that when they decide to degrade themselves, they sink to depths to which even the vilest man could not sink.
>
> ALAS, YOU ARE indeed in the image of these women so famous in history: the Delilahs, the Salome, Charlotte Corday, Mata Hari and how many others who have been a sad part of our history and have debased the profile of women. You are one of them, and you are the clearest living example of them that I have seen.

After the trial was completed the judge repeated some of these remarks several times to various news media. During the hearing before the Inquiry Committee the judge reaffirmed his belief in the truth of these remarks. The judge intimated that the genesis for the belief was his cultural and religious upbringing and the reality that a like belief has been held by many thinkers over the centuries. He made it quite clear that he would not readily be disabused of that belief.

The first point to note is that the misconduct alleged against the judge consists of words spoken by the judge in the context of a judicial proceeding. It is important to keep that context in mind. A judge performing his or her judicial function acts in a very different capacity from a judge who chooses to speak extra-judicially on a certain subject. A judge performing his or her judicial function needs to examine all sides of a particular question, not only the side favoured by one party to the proceeding or the side favoured by a large segment of the population who may have an interest in the proceeding. He or she needs to give full consideration to *individual* interests and should, generally speaking, be more concerned with protecting those individual interests than with pursuing communal goals. The area of communal goals is better left to the legislature whose job it is to enunciate general policy and enact the means to achieve the policy goals, and to the executive branch of government whose job it is to carry into effect such legislative policy.

In the course of examining all sides of a question and giving full consideration to individual interests, a judge is apt to play the role of a devil's advocate, to think out loud and to use language—sometimes appropriate, sometimes inappropriate—that one side or some segment of society may find unacceptable. For example—a judge may feel it necessary in the interests of justice, to tell a litigant that he or she is an "unmitigated liar" or that society will no longer put up with the litigant's "brutal propensities" or "lawless attitude" and so on. Anyone familiar with judicial proceedings will readily recognize this sort of exercise and ought to be very loathe to restrict judges from engaging in it.

Moreover, it is important and sometimes essential that a judge speak his or her mind, giving full reasons for reaching a decision. Not only is this important to litigants it is also important to courts of appeal reviewing the judge's decision. They ought to be in a position of some certainty if they are to rule on whether a judge erred in his or her conclusions and if so where the error occurred. Any restriction that inspires judges to keep their reasons to themselves, generally speaking, should be discouraged, as it does not auger well for the administration of justice. And lastly, in this respect, it is important to keep in mind that remarks made in the course of a judicial proceeding are subject to the scrutiny of a court of appeal and any injustice created by reason of a judge's unacceptable belief is correctable.

It logically follows that from the standpoint of disciplinary consequences which ought to flow from a judge's improper remarks, remarks made during judicial proceedings ought not to be judged as harshly as those made extra-judicially. That, of course, does not mean a judge can with impunity say whatever he or she wants during a judicial proceeding, but it does mean that the boundaries are different for the two contexts. Did the judge cross the boundary in the present case? It is necessary to consider this question from two perspectives: substance and perception.

In our respectful view the belief voiced by the judge reflected a predilection or predisposition, even a bias perhaps, regarding both men and women that is unacceptable to many people in our society and actually repugnant to some, perhaps many. The basic question that needs to be examined is this: What effect, if any, does the "having" of this predilection, predisposition, or bias by a judge, have upon the ability and the capacity of a judge to perform his or her judicial functions?

Every judge knows, and every reasonably informed person not a judge who approaches the issue objectively ought to know, that like every other member of the human species all judges have certain predilections. Judges are not—and society does not want them to be—intellectual eunuchs devoid of any philosophy of life, of society, of government or of law and a judge's world is the same as the public's—a world of realism rather than a world of idealism. The critical question is not: Does the judge have a predilection? Rather the critical question is: Is the judge able and prepared to set the predilection aside and not *put it to work* in the exercise of his or her judicial functions?

Where the misconduct alleged against a judge centres on some unacceptable predilection the judge is said to have, what is the threshold for determining whether the judge is guilty of misconduct, or has failed in the due execution of the office of a judge, or has been placed in a position incompatible with the due execution of this office? The threshold is not whether there is proof the judge in fact *has* that predilection. Nor is the threshold whether the judge is able or intends to shed the predilection. Shedding the predilection or not shedding it is still a question of "having" or "not having" the predilection. The threshold has to go beyond "having." It is whether there is proof the judge has in fact recurringly in the past *put the predilection to work* to the detriment of litigants or in all likelihood intends in the future to recurringly put it to work to the detriment of litigants.

If merely "having" a predilection were sufficient, it is not difficult to envision consequences resembling kafkaesque scenarios, and questions that are downright disturbing. Would judges' past writings, speeches, judgments, etc. be scrutinized to detect evidence of certain kinds of unacceptable predilections? Would the results produce a proliferation of Inquiry Committees looking into the "conduct" of misspoken judges? Would some sort of "thought" police become a reality? Would judgments need to be tailored and crafted with care and precision heretofore not imagined? Does society want its judges to become easier shooting targets for certain disenchanted segments of society? Does the making of judges into easier shooting targets enhance or diminish the administration of justice in the eyes of the reasonably informed members of society? Will judges be prompted to cull from their judicial vocabularies such Shakespearian phrases as "pure as Caesar's wife," and such pedestrian everyday expressions as "christian charity" or "godlike features" which, until now, have simply rolled off one's tongue?

Our form of democratic society envisages a judiciary unfettered in its ability to think and unhobbled in its capacity to hold views that do not accord with those of the mainstream. To be removed from office for merely "having" a predilection or predisposition or bias flies in the face of the legitimacy of that unfettered and unhobbled judiciary.

The next question which needs to be examined is this: What is the proof in the present case of Mr. Justice Bienvenue's "having" the predilection *and* "putting it to work to the detriment of litigants." When he spoke the impugned words in the course of sentencing, he clearly affirmed that he had the predilection. When he spoke to the media in the days after the trial he reiterated the words. This amounted to nothing more than a re-affirmation that he has the predilection. When confronted before the Inquiry Committee he again re-affirmed he has the predilection. He also confirmed that he either would not or could not readily shed it. But as noted, not shedding it does not put the analysis past the "having" stage. The threshold stage is putting the predilection to work to the detriment of litigants.

Is there proof that Mr. Justice Bienvenue put this predilection to work before the Théberge case took place? The answer is *no*. The only evidence in this regard is that upon which the Inquiry Committee found Mr. Justice Bienvenue to be "an individual who has been a judge for almost 20 years and whose integrity has not been questioned." It must be remembered that the terms of reference of the Inquiry Committee did not include an investigation of Mr. Justice Bienvenue's conduct preceding the Théberge case.

Is there proof that Mr. Justice Bienvenue put the predilection to work in the Théberge case to the detriment of Ms. Théberge? Again, in our respectful view, the answer is *no*. The Committee made no finding of fact that would assist in this respect. The only item of evidence that may be interpreted as tending to show that predilection at work is the decision by Mr. Justice Bienvenue to impose a 14-year parole ineligibility on Ms. Théberge's life sentence despite the jury's recommendation of the minimum 10-year period of ineligibility. Whether it is *possible* for that circumstance to be interpreted as the predilection at work is one thing. Whether *in fact* it should be interpreted that way is quite another. There is not the slightest indication that given the viciousness of the killing the judge would not have made an identical ruling had the offender been a male rather than a female. Even if the judge's ruling can be shown to be the predilection at work, this is only one instance of that happening. One instance is hardly evidence of recurrence. Furthermore, the way to correct that one instance is—as has been done—to refer this justiciable matter to the Court of Appeal. That is where the matter rightfully belongs. This one instance is hardly a matter for the Canadian Judicial Council to use as a spearhead for a recommendation consisting of the draconian step of an irrevocable removal of the judge from office.

That leaves for determination the presence of proof of whether Mr. Justice Bienvenue intends in the future to "recurringly put the predilection to work to the detriment of litigants." In our respectful view there is not the slightest evidence of the judge's future intent in respect of putting his predilection to work. There is, as noted earlier, evidence of his inability or disinclination to shed his predilection (perhaps even evidence of his reluctance to express contrition) but, also as noted, all that is evidence of "having" not of "putting the predilection to work"—a distinctly different factor. When the Inquiry Committee found "In addition—the evidence could not be any clearer—Mr. Justice Bienvenue does not intend to change his behaviour in any way," it must have confused "behaviour" with "having." It could not have been referring to "putting the predilection to work" because there was no evidence of his "putting the predilection to work" in the past. And since there was no evidence it makes no sense to talk about "no change" to that "behaviour." The Committee was obviously confusing "having" with "behaviour" or referring to some other kind of behaviour. There is no presumption in law or in the realm of common sense that having a predilection and being disinclined or unable to shed it will automatically mean that the judge will put the predilection to work to the detriment of the litigants either at every opportunity or from time to time. To make the presumption in this case is unfair to Mr. Justice Bienvenue and puts at risk every other judge in the country against whom a like presumption might be made in respect of whatever general predisposition it is the judge may have. The presumption that ought to be made is that the judge, as judges have been doing from time immemorial, will engage his or her professionalism and will set aside such predispositions as often as is required. The presumption should prevail unless there is evidence to the contrary.

In summary it is our respectful view the majority of the Inquiry Committee made two critical interrelated errors.

The first is this: The majority did not make the crucial distinction between "having" a predilection and "putting it to work to the detriment of litigants." This is evident in at least two conclusory findings made by the Committee:

> Because of his [having] ideas about both women and men, Mr. Justice Bienvenue's impartiality in the execution of his judicial office has legitimately been called into question.
>
> • • •
>
> Like anyone else, a judge can have a bad day. In this case, the breaches of ethics brought to our attention—the *judge's repeated remarks about women* and the comments he made to the jurors after their verdict—are serious and, as with the other incidents alleged against him, have not been retracted by him. We are therefore not dealing here merely with strong language. (italics added)

The second is this: The majority found that having a predilection and being unable or disinclined to shed it is the same as putting the predilection to work. Alternatively the majority applied a presumption that being unable or disinclined to shed the predilection is automatically followed not by a setting aside of the predilection but by putting the predilection to work to the detriment of litigants.

In our respectful view the majority of this Council repeated those same two errors. In its report it says, "No attempt has been made by Mr. Justice Bienvenue since the delivery of the report of the Inquiry Committee to indicate any intention on his part to, in fact, change his behaviour." (One gets the distinct impression the majority would have been prepared to absolve Mr. Justice Bienvenue had he shown some contrition or expressed penitence.) Although it is not entirely clear, it would appear that when the majority of Council speaks of "behaviour" they mean "having" the predilection concerning women. When they speak of "change" they mean shedding the predilection concerning women. By "behaviour" they do not mean and could not mean "putting the predilection to work" because there is no evidence of the predilection being put to work in the past. The corollary, of course, is that there could be no "change" to "putting the predilection to work."

The foregoing analysis deals primarily with the issue from the perspective of *substance*. From that perspective, the basic question should properly read: What effect, if any, does the "having" of the predilection by a judge, have upon the *actual* ability and the *actual* capacity of a judge to perform his or her judicial function? The answer as we have seen is none.

From the perspective of *perception* the basic question becomes: What effect, if any, does the "having" of the predilection by a judge have upon the *perceived* ability and the *perceived* capacity of a judge to perform his or her judicial function? The majority of the Committee reached this conclusion:

> Because of his conduct during all the incidents that marked Tracy Théberge's trial, Mr. Justice Bienvenue has undermined public confidence in him and strongly contributed to destroying public confidence in the judicial system. In our view, this is the conclusion that would be reached by a reasonable and informed person.
>
> Combining the test used by the Committee of the Canadian Judicial Council in the *Marshall* case and that applied by the Supreme Court to assess judicial impartiality and independence, we believe that if Mr. Justice Bienvenue were to preside over a case, a reasonable and informed person, viewing the matter realistically and practically—and having thought the matter through—would have a reasonable apprehension that the judge would not execute his office with the objectivity, impartiality and independence that the public is entitled to expect from a judge.

The majority of Council agreed.

With the greatest of deference to both the majority of the Committee and the majority of Council we strongly disagree that a reasonable and informed person would assess the remarks concerning women in this harsh fashion and would in the end have the complete lack of confidence and the reasonable apprehension described by the majority of the Committee (and agreed with by the majority of the Council) to the point where he or she would vote to remove Mr. Justice Bienvenue from office.

A reasonable and informed person by definition would make the assessment and view all of the issues objectively. That means the person would need to set aside any biases, predilections or predispositions he or she had, and not "put them to work" in making the assessment. A reasonable, informed and objective person would need to consider a series of relevant factors and would likely ask and answer questions such as these:

1. Is having a predilection enough to render a judge incapable, or must there be more? For example, must there be a "putting to work" of the predilection? We have already seen where "having" alone leads. A reasonable, informed, objective person should easily be able to come to the same conclusion.
2. Where did Mr. Justice Bienvenue get these ideas? A reasonable, informed and objective person would know that the ideas reflected in Mr. Justice Bienvenue's words have been around for centuries. One does not need to be a biblical scholar to know that both the Old and New Testaments are replete with thinking not unlike that reflected in Mr. Justice Bienvenue's words. If he was brought up in a Judeo-Christian culture, and he apparently was, it is not difficult to understand why he would think this way.

He, of course, is far from alone in having these outdated beliefs. Some institutions in our society continue to promote this sort of thinking.

A reasonable, informed and objective person will quickly recognize that Mr. Justice Bienvenue is continuing to trade in a variant of the stereotypical view about the essential personalities and characteristics of men and women. The view, once orthodox and mainstream was universally held by leaders and other members of society including our law makers—parliamentarians and judges—and our appointers of judges. It found expression in our many institutions such as our schools and churches, in our many intellectual, social, cultural and sport associations, and, in our laws—both statutory and judge-made. To quickly remind oneself of the type of laws that prevailed, one needs only to read such recent decisions by the Supreme Court of Canada as *R v. Seaboyer*, [1991] 2 SCR 577 and *R v. Butler*, [1992] 1 SCR 452 and some custody cases espousing principles, as for example those embodied in the "tender years doctrine" (see *Talsky v. Talsky*, [1976] 2 SCR 292).

The stereotypical view is the progenitor of what is now considered idiosyncratic thinking and a bias, predisposition or predilection unfavourable to women. A reasonable, informed and objective person who encounters someone in authority who is continuing to trade in the view may be concerned, disappointed, perhaps even surprised. But given the view's recent pervading, universal, long-term reign and its continuing currency in some circles, he or she would hardly be "shocked"—to borrow a term from the *Marshall* test referred to by the Committee.

3. But this is 1996, is it right for judges to have these kinds of outmoded views and beliefs? The answer is no, but the shift from what was orthodox and mainstream to what is now unorthodox and passé is an evolutionary one, not a precipitous one reminiscent of a revolution. It is only in relatively recent times that the evolution has been making progress. Some judges were quick to adjust and adapt. Others have not been so quick. In order to consummate and complete the evolution now well underway should one resort to a "sledge hammer" approach to beat into submission the remaining judges who still think that way? Or should one opt for a more sophisticated and in the end a more practical approach respecting Mr. Justice Bienvenue and the remaining judges? A reasonable, informed and objective person would have no difficulty in answering the first question in the negative and the second in the affirmative.

4. Is there some way other than removal from office that one could use to ensure that Mr. Justice Bienvenue does not continue to trade in his stereotypical belief (thereby running the risk of putting his predilection to work)? Social context education is clearly a viable avenue and in the end a very real practical approach. There was no evidence before the Committee or before Council that Mr. Justice Bienvenue has been putting his predilection to work during the past twenty years he has been a judge. (As noted his past conduct before the Théberge trial took place was not before the Committee or Council.) With proper and repeated education, there should be very little difficulty ensuring his predilection is not "put to work." Indeed with proper education and time he may even become convinced that his belief is bad, and should that occur one would not need to be concerned about his putting to work the predilection it reflects. A reasonable, informed and objective person would likely

conclude that it is much too early to say that he is so irredeemable that one should metaphorically "put him behind bars and throw away the key."

5. Does the fact the words were spoken by Mr. Justice Bienvenue in court and not extra-judicially make a difference? A reasonable, informed and objective person would after reflection conclude that there is a difference, for the reasons outlined earlier. He or she would conclude that any injustice resulting from the words spoken on this one occasion should properly be dealt with by a court of appeal and not by a disciplinary body. Had there been a pattern of such conduct—a recurrence—the matter might need to be viewed in a different light. But there is no evidence of such a pattern.

6. Does the removal of one judge for speaking unacceptable words solve what may be a minor (in terms of numbers) institutional problem? In the decision to remove the judge in these circumstances, is there an element of "judicial cleansing," something in the nature of a "judicial crucifixion" in expiation of past and future "sins of the judiciary," a purported reconciliation of the judiciary with the public? One would hope not but one is not entirely sure.

7. Does removing Mr. Justice Bienvenue for "having" a predilection affecting men and women mean that other judges having other predilections, such as predilections favourable or unfavourable towards abortion, environmental despoiling, big business, the media, governmental bureaucracy, gambling, gun control and so on, ought also to be removed? Would it make any difference if the judge not only held a predilection concerning a subject matter but a bias against the persons involved with the subject matter (e.g. abortionists, pro-lifers, polluters, bureaucrats, gamblers, etc.)? Were the answers to the first and perhaps the second question "yes" the ranks of the judiciary would be depleted quite dramatically. A reasonable, informed and objective person would appreciate the total undesirability of the consequence to society of removal for having such predilections and biases but, more important, would conclude that judges should be presumed to be able and willing to set aside their predilections and biases.

This series of questions is not intended as an exhaustive list. There are other questions that may need to be considered. In the result we are confident that a reasonable and informed person, viewing and assessing the circumstances objectively would not acquire an apprehension and a lack of confidence of the type described by the majority of the Committee and the majority of Council.

It is unfortunate that the majority of the Committee treated itself as a court and the proceedings before it as a court proceeding where there is a *lis inter partes* rather than as a tribunal with no *lis* before it but whose primary role was a search for truth (as the Supreme Court of Canada held in *Ruffo v. Conseil de la magistrature*, [1995] 4 SCR 267).

Had the Committee not overlooked this aspect of its *raison d'être* it would not have excluded a consideration of the results of a poll Mr. Justice Bienvenue's counsel sought to introduce. We, as members of Council, would very much have liked to interpret the results of that poll for ourselves rather than have been left in the dark. The poll may have been a better source of information than the editorial writers for some of the Quebec press whose views were readily available to all Council members.

The majority of the Committee in its report said this: "Under the Act, this Committee is responsible for assessing the judge's conduct." The Committee seemed to overlook the fact that s. 65(2) of the *Judges Act* places that responsibility on Council. As Council members, we would have appreciated any help we could get, including poll results, to which we could have ascribed whatever weight we thought proper, in order to make a proper assessment of the state of the public's confidence in the judiciary and public's apprehension or lack of it, concerning Mr. Justice Bienvenue.

In our respectful view too much emphasis was placed by the majority of both the Committee and the Council upon what judges think the public's reaction ought to be rather than upon what the public's reaction actually was. In a matter as serious as the one concerning the removal of a judge, the public whose judges we are, ought to have more direct say, even at this stage of the proceedings, about what is their apprehension of bias and their lack of confidence or otherwise in the judiciary.

To this point we have dealt only with the remarks concerning men and women and have not dealt with any of the other improprieties found by the Committee. In our respectful view those other improprieties—the buttress for the decision to remove—when put into the crucible of scrutiny either separately or cumulatively fare no better than the remarks concerning men and women—the main pillar for the decision to remove. If the main pillar falls, the buttresses either fall or are considerably diminished in importance from the standpoint of a decision to remove.

The only conduct other than the remarks concerning women and men that could possibly fall into a category serious enough to consider removing a judge from office were the remarks concerning Jews and the Holocaust.

It is clear from the evidence considered by the Committee that these remarks, after due explanation and apology by Mr. Justice Bienvenue, did not raise in the minds of those most closely affected by them the lack of public confidence in the judiciary or the apprehension of bias held by the Committee to have been raised by the other improprieties. Although the remarks were flagrantly insensitive, hurtful, and grossly inappropriate, the Committee did not find any misconduct on the part of Mr. Justice Bienvenue attributable to the remarks concerning Jews and the Holocaust. In our respectful view this was a proper finding. By making no reference to this matter in its report the majority of Council appears to have agreed with the Committee's finding as well.

In view of the decision reached by the majority of Council it was not necessary for us, the minority, to consider whether Mr. Justice Bienvenue's conduct, taken as a whole, during the trial of Ms. Théberge ought to attract some sanction other than removal from office. And we, of course, make no finding in that respect. We are, however, prepared to say that, given the primary facts found by the Committee, we found the conduct of Mr. Justice Bienvenue, taken as a whole, unacceptable, insensitive, and of a type that we do not at all condone.

Before closing we desire to raise three procedural questions that were not put before either the Inquiry Committee or Council. We raise the questions not because we have made any decisions relating to them (we have not) but as suggestions for Council to consider sometime in the future in an effort to improve our disciplinary procedures.

One wonders whether the Inquiry Committee, essentially a fact finding, investigative tribunal, would not have been well advised, given the circumstances of the present case, to canvass the entire federally-appointed judiciary to seek the judiciary's opinion on the relevant questions of the public's lack of confidence and reasonable apprehension and the resultant incapacity or disability of the judge to further perform his judicial functions. As a fact finding body with no *lis* before it, is not the Committee (and ultimately Council) entitled to all the intelligent help it can get on issues like these? The results of the "canvass" would simply have been another "primary fact" available to the Committee and Council to consider. The results would not have been determinative. Rules of evidence governing court procedure should not hold sway where no *lis* is involved. Somehow it does not seem right or advisable for the Committee or Council to arrogate to itself all the wisdom necessary to decide an issue as troubling and as far reaching as the removal of a long-serving federally-appointed judge, particularly where the service is described as "with integrity." Moreover, is there not a similarity in process between a canvass of approximately 950 judges and a vote of 399 members of the House of Commons and the Senate acting under s. 99 of the *Constitution Act*?

The second suggestion pertains to the Committee's power, right, or obligation to recommend removal. There is some doubt whether it has this power, right, or obligation under the Act. If the Committee does have it, perhaps it should not. Council members considering any disciplinary measure as serious as removal should approach the issue with a completely open mind and should not feel strait-jacketed by a Committee's recommendation. Perhaps the Committee ought to be what the law says it ought to be, namely, a fact finding, investigative body, leaving it to Council to decide whether any sanctions or further steps should flow from the facts found by the Committee. Perhaps the Committee should be entitled to say: "We think there is nothing here for Council to consider" or "we think there is something here for Council to consider," in much the same way that a judge sitting on a preliminary inquiry finds that there is sufficient evidence for a matter to proceed to trial or that there is no sufficient evidence.

It may well be that Council's position in relation to the Minister of Justice and Parliament should be similar to the position we suggest for the Committee in relation to Council.

The third suggestion relates to the composition of the Inquiry Committee provided for in s. 63(3) of the *Judges Act*. This subsection vests in the Minister of Justice for Canada the power to appoint to the Inquiry Committee "such members, if any, of the bar of a province, as may be designated by the Minister." Apart from the constitutional issue which the presence of such a power raises (considered in the *Gratton* inquiry), there is some question about the propriety—from the standpoint of fairness—of the Minister's having or exercising such a power where the Minister instituted the inquiry pursuant to s. 63(1). It is unusual to say the least for a complainant to have the power to appoint a percentage—in the present case 40%—of the adjudicators or assessors who are required to examine and rule upon certain issues arising out of the complaint while the person complained against has no such similar power.

These three suggestions raise issues that we think ought to be explored further.

Upon learning of the recommendation of the council majority, Justice Bienvenue resigned as a judge.

The reports of two inquiry committees in 2008 and the consequent reports of the council to the minister of justice provide fertile ground for further exploring the boundaries of security of tenure. Both involved the potential removal of Ontario Superior Court judges and address the same fundamental issue of whether the judge can continue to sit or whether public confidence in the judge and the judiciary requires removal.

The questionable conduct of Justice Theodore Matlow arose out of his involvement as a citizen in a community movement, including a group known as Friends of the Village, to oppose certain commercial development in a Toronto neighborhood. The following excerpt from the report of the Inquiry Committee reflects some of their concerns about his conduct:

> [152] The Inquiry Committee determines that Justice Matlow's overall conduct in organizing and leading the Friends, his assumption of the role of president, spokesperson and, on occasion, advocate of the Friends, his conduct in seeking to personally be a party and as a result being made a party in the OMB application of First Spadina, his conduct in providing guidance, advice and assistance in the application by some members of the Friends to the Superior Court of Justice, and his conduct in assisting in preparation of the supporting affidavit to which was attached copies of letters from him to the Mayor of the City and the Attorney General of Ontario, constitutes conduct that is highly inappropriate for a judge.

(Inquiry Committee Decisions, Matlow (December 2008), Inquiry Committee Report (May 28, 2008).)

This conduct did not arise out of his judicial duties but did not conform to the ethical principles expected to govern judges' behaviour even in their private lives. The five members of the Inquiry Committee unanimously concluded that his removal from the office of judge was warranted.

The conduct of Justice Paul Cosgrove arose out his judicial role in the course of conducting proceedings related to a murder trial. In effect, the judge turned the criminal proceedings into an ill-conceived and distorted investigation into the role of the Crown. The four members of the majority of the Inquiry Committee stated:

> 164. In our opinion, the conduct of the judge referred to in this part in failing to exercise restraint and in abusing the powers of his office is conduct which meets the strict test set out above in Marshall. This conclusion does not rest on the appearance of bias or on the judge's incompetence in failing to control the trial. It rests rather on his words and conduct, in abusing judicial independence and acting beyond the powers of a judge.

(Inquiry Committee Decisions, Cosgrove (March 2009), Inquiry Committee Report (November 27, 2008).)

They concluded that the conduct called for a recommendation for his removal from office. The dissenting member was of the view that the judge understood the gravity of his conduct and would avoid such conduct in future. A strong admonition would allow the public to continue to have confidence in him as a judge.

The council had no difficulty in unanimously accepting the advice of the majority of the Inquiry Committee in Cosgrove and unanimously recommended to the minister of justice that he be removed from office. Upon learning of this report, Cosgrove resigned (Inquiry Committee Report Decisions, Cosgrove (March 2009), Report of the CJC to the Minister of Justice).

In contrast, the majority of the council in Matlow rejected the unanimous advice of the Inquiry Committee and recommended to the minister of justice that he not be removed from office. A minority of four chief justices unanimously endorsed the advice of the Inquiry Committee and would have recommended removal (Inquiry Committee Decisions, Matlow (December 2008), Report of the CJC to the Minister of Justice).

2. Financial Security

Financial security relates to the pay judges receive for performing their job. It protects against an "unscrupulous government" that "could utilize its authority to set judges' salaries as a vehicle to influence the course and outcome of adjudication": see *Provincial Judges Reference*, at para. 145.

The *Provincial Judges Reference* was sparked by a climate in which a number of provincial governments were implementing policies of financial restraint. The remuneration of provincially appointed judges made them a politically vulnerable target since their salaries are high in relation to the average citizen. However, they are low in relation to federally appointed judges and to the more successful practising lawyers. Some provinces sought to reduce these judicial salaries. One province retroactively repealed its legislation requiring it to accept the recommendations of an advisory committee on judicial salaries. It may be a fair assumption that underlying the Supreme Court's decision in this case was a concern about ongoing and unseemly confrontations between the executive and judicial branches over judicial remuneration.

The Supreme Court addressed the problem in this way.

Reference re Remuneration of Judges of the Provincial Court of Prince Edward Island et al. ("Provincial Judges Reference")
[1997] 3 SCR 3

LAMER CJ: [121] What I do propose, however, is that financial security has both an individual and an institutional or collective dimension. *Valente* only talked about the individual dimension of financial security, when it stated that salaries must be established by law and not allow for executive interference in a manner which could "affect the independence of the individual judge" (p. 706). Similarly, in *Généreux*, speaking for a majority of this Court, I applied *Valente* and held that performance-related pay for the conduct of judge advocates and members of a General Court Martial during the Court Martial violated s. 11(d), because it could reasonably lead to the perception that those individuals might alter their conduct during a hearing in order to favour the military establishment.

[122] However, *Valente* did not preclude a finding that, and did not decide whether, financial security has a collective or institutional dimension as well. That is the issue we must address today. But in order to determine whether financial security has a collective or institutional dimension, and if so, what collective or institutional financial security looks like, we must first understand what the institutional independence of the judiciary is. I emphasize this point because, as will become apparent, the conclusion I arrive at regarding the collective or institutional dimension of financial security builds upon traditional understandings

of the proper constitutional relationship between the judiciary, the executive, and the legislature.

· · ·

[130] … Independence of the judiciary implies not only that a judge should be free from executive or legislative encroachment and from political pressures and entanglements but also that he should be removed from financial or business entanglement likely to affect or rather to seem to affect him in the exercise of his judicial functions.

[131] Given the importance of the institutional or collective dimension of judicial independence generally, what is the institutional or collective dimension of financial security? To my mind, financial security for the courts as an institution has three components, which all flow from the constitutional imperative that, to the extent possible, the relationship between the judiciary and the other branches of government be depoliticized. As I explain below, in the context of institutional or collective financial security, this imperative demands that the courts both be free and appear to be free from political interference through economic manipulation by the other branches of government, and that they not become entangled in the politics of remuneration from the public purse.

[132] I begin by stating these components in summary fashion.

[133] First, as a general constitutional principle, the salaries of provincial court judges can be reduced, increased, or frozen, either as part of an overall economic measure which affects the salaries of all or some persons who are remunerated from public funds, or as part of a measure which is directed at provincial court judges as a class. However, any changes to or freezes in judicial remuneration require prior recourse to a special process, which is independent, effective, and objective, for determining judicial remuneration, to avoid the possibility of, or the appearance of, political interference through economic manipulation. What judicial independence requires is an independent body, along the lines of the bodies that exist in many provinces and at the federal level to set or recommend the levels of judicial remuneration. Those bodies are often referred to as commissions, and for the sake of convenience, we will refer to the independent body required by s. 11(d) as a commission as well. Governments are constitutionally bound to go through the commission process. The recommendations of the commission would not be binding on the executive or the legislature. Nevertheless, though those recommendations are non-binding, they should not be set aside lightly, and, if the executive or the legislature chooses to depart from them, it has to justify its decision—if need be, in a court of law. As I explain below, when governments propose to single out judges as a class for a pay reduction, the burden of justification will be heavy.

[134] Second, under no circumstances is it permissible for the judiciary—not only collectively through representative organizations, but also as individuals—to engage in negotiations over remuneration with the executive or representatives of the legislature. Any such negotiations would be fundamentally at odds with judicial independence. As I explain below, salary negotiations are indelibly political, because remuneration from the public purse is an inherently political issue. Moreover, negotiations would undermine the appearance of judicial independence, because the Crown is almost always a party to criminal prosecutions before provincial courts, and because salary negotiations engender a set of expectations about the behaviour of parties to those negotiations which are inimical to judicial independence. When I refer to negotiations, I utilize that term as it is traditionally understood

in the labour relations context. Negotiations over remuneration and benefits, in colloquial terms, are a form of "horse-trading." The prohibition on negotiations therefore does not preclude expressions of concern or representations by chief justices and chief judges, and organizations that represent judges, to governments regarding the adequacy of judicial remuneration.

[135]   Third, and finally, any reductions to judicial remuneration, including *de facto* reductions through the erosion of judicial salaries by inflation, cannot take those salaries below a basic minimum level of remuneration which is required for the office of a judge. Public confidence in the independence of the judiciary would be undermined if judges were paid at such a low rate that they could be perceived as susceptible to political pressure through economic manipulation, as is witnessed in many countries.

· · ·

[166]   Although provincial executives and legislatures, as the case may be, are constitutionally permitted to change or freeze judicial remuneration, those decisions have the potential to jeopardize judicial independence. The imperative of protecting the courts from political interference through economic manipulation is served by interposing an independent body—a judicial compensation commission—between the judiciary and the other branches of government. The constitutional function of this body is to depoliticize the process of determining changes or freezes to judicial remuneration. This objective would be achieved by setting that body the specific task of issuing a report on the salaries and benefits of judges to the executive and the legislature, responding to the particular proposals made by the government to increase, reduce, or freeze judges' salaries.

[167]   I do not wish to dictate the exact shape and powers of the independent commission here. These questions of detailed institutional design are better left to the executive and the legislature, although it would be helpful if they consulted the provincial judiciary prior to creating these bodies. Moreover, different provinces should be free to choose procedures and arrangements which are suitable to their needs and particular circumstances. Within the parameters of s. 11(d), there must be scope for local choice, because jurisdiction over provincial courts has been assigned to the provinces by the *Constitution Act, 1867*. This is one reason why we held in *Valente*, supra, at p. 694, that "[t]he standard of judicial independence for purposes of s. 11(d) cannot be a standard of uniform provisions."

· · ·

[169]   The commissions charged with the responsibility of dealing with the issue of judicial remuneration must meet three general criteria. They must be independent, objective, and effective. I will address these criteria in turn, by reference, where possible, to commissions which already exist in many Canadian provinces to set or recommend the levels of judicial remuneration.

[170]   First and foremost, these commissions must be independent. The rationale for independence flows from the constitutional function performed by these commissions— they serve as an institutional sieve, to prevent the setting or freezing of judicial remuneration from being used as a means to exert political pressure through the economic manipulation of the judiciary. It would undermine that goal if the independent commissions were under the control of the executive or the legislature.

[171]   There are several different aspects to the independence required of salary commissions. First, the members of these bodies must have some kind of security of tenure. In this

context, security of tenure means that the members of commissions should serve for a fixed term, which may vary in length. ... In my opinion, s. 11(d) does not impose any restrictions on the membership of these commissions. Although the independence of these commissions would be better served by ensuring that their membership stood apart from the three branches of government, as is the case in Ontario (*Courts of Justice Act*, Schedule, para. 11), this is not required by the Constitution.

[172] Under ideal circumstances, it would be desirable if appointments to the salary commission were not made by any of the three branches of government, in order to guarantee the independence of its members. However, the members of that body would then have to be appointed by a body which must in turn be independent, and so on. This is clearly not a practical solution, and thus is not required by s. 11(d). As we said in *Valente* ... , at p. 692:

> It would not be feasible ... to apply the most rigorous and elaborate conditions of judicial independence to the constitutional requirement of independence in s. 11(d) of the Charter ... .

What s. 11(d) requires instead is that the appointments not be entirely controlled by any one of the branches of government. The commission should have members appointed by the judiciary, on the one hand, and the legislature and the executive, on the other. The judiciary's nominees may, for example, be chosen either by the provincial judges' association, as is the case in Ontario (*Courts of Justice Act*, Schedule, para. 6), or by the Chief Judge of the Provincial Court in consultation with the provincial judges' association, as in British Columbia (*Provincial Court Act*, s. 7.1(2)). The exact mechanism is for provincial governments to determine. Likewise, the nominees of the executive and the legislature may be chosen by the Lieutenant Governor in Council, although appointments by the Attorney General as in British Columbia (*Provincial Court Act*, s. 7.1(2)), or conceivably by the legislature itself, are entirely permissible.

[173] In addition to being independent, the salary commissions must be objective. They must make recommendations on judges' remuneration by reference to objective criteria, not political expediencies. The goal is to present "an objective and fair set of recommendations dictated by the public interest" (Canada, Department of Justice, *Report and Recommendations of the 1995 Commission on Judges' Salaries and Benefits* (1996), at p. 7). Although s. 11(d) does not require it, the commission's objectivity can be promoted by ensuring that it is fully informed before deliberating and making its recommendations. This can be best achieved by requiring that the commission receive and consider submissions from the judiciary, the executive, and the legislature. In Ontario, for example, the Provincial Judges' Remuneration Commission is bound to consider submissions from the provincial judges' association and the government (*Courts of Justice Act*, Schedule, para. 20). Moreover, I recommend (but do not require) that the objectivity of the commission be ensured by including in the enabling legislation or regulations a list of relevant factors to guide the commission's deliberations. These factors need not be exhaustive. A list of relevant factors might include, for example, increases in the cost of living, the need to ensure that judges' salaries remain adequate, as well as the need to attract excellent candidates to the judiciary.

[174] Finally, and most importantly, the commission must also be effective. The effectiveness of these bodies must be guaranteed in a number of ways. First, there is a constitutional obligation for governments not to change (either by reducing or increasing) or freeze

judicial remuneration until they have received the report of the salary commission. Changes or freezes of this nature secured without going through the commission process are unconstitutional. The commission must convene to consider and report on the proposed change or freeze. Second, in order to guard against the possibility that government inaction might lead to a reduction in judges' real salaries because of inflation, and that inaction could therefore be used as a means of economic manipulation, the commission must convene if a fixed period of time has elapsed since its last report, in order to consider the adequacy of judges' salaries in light of the cost of living and other relevant factors, and issue a recommendation in its report. Although the exact length of the period is for provincial governments to determine, I would suggest a period of three to five years.

[175] Third, the reports of the commission must have a meaningful effect on the determination of judicial salaries. Provinces which have created salary commissions have adopted three different ways of giving such effect to these reports. One is to make a report of the commission binding, so that the government is bound by the commission's decision. Ontario, for example, requires that a report be implemented by the Lieutenant Governor in Council within 60 days, and gives a report of the Provincial Judges' Remuneration Commission statutory force (*Courts of Justice Act*, Schedule, para. 27). Another way of dealing with a report is the negative resolution procedure, whereby the report is laid before the legislature and its recommendations are implemented unless the legislature votes to reject or amend them. This is the model which has been adopted in British Columbia (*Provincial Court Act*, s. 7.1(10)) and Newfoundland (*Provincial Court Act*, 1991, s. 28(7)). The final way of giving effect to a report is the affirmative resolution procedure, whereby a report is laid before but need not be adopted by the legislature. As I shall explain below, until the adoption of Bill 22, this was very similar to the procedure followed in Manitoba (*Provincial Court Act*, s. 11.1(6)).

· · ·

[185] By laying down a set of guidelines to assist provincial legislatures in designing judicial compensation commissions, I do not intend to lay down a particular institutional framework in constitutional stone. What s. 11(d) requires is an institutional sieve between the judiciary and the other branches of government. Commissions are merely a means to that end. In the future, governments may create new institutional arrangements which can serve the same end, but in a different way. As long as those institutions meet the three cardinal requirements of independence, effectiveness, and objectivity, s. 11(d) will be complied with.

In *Provincial Court Judges' Assn. of New Brunswick v. New Brunswick et al.*, 2005 SCC 44, the court revisited and somewhat amended the test it established in the 1997 case. In that case, "Provincial Court judges in New Brunswick, Ontario and Quebec, justices of the peace in Alberta and municipal court judges in Quebec sought judicial review of their provincial governments' decisions to reject certain compensation commission recommendations relating to their salaries and benefits" (at 45).

Provincial Court Judges' Assn. of New Brunswick v. New Brunswick (Minister of Justice); Ontario Judges' Assn. v. Ontario (Management Board); Bodner v. Alberta; Conférence des juges du Québec v. Quebec (Attorney General); Minc v. Quebec (Attorney General)
[2005] 2 SCR 286, 2005 SCC 44

THE COURT: [3] … In the *Reference re Remuneration of Judges of the Provincial Court of Prince Edward Island*, [1997] 3 SCR 3 ("*Reference*"), this Court held that independent commissions were required to improve the process designed to ensure judicial independence but that the commissions' recommendations need not be binding. These commissions were intended to remove the amount of judges' remuneration from the political sphere and to avoid confrontation between governments and the judiciary. The *Reference* has not provided the anticipated solution, and more is needed.

· · ·

[21] A commission's report is consultative. The government may turn it into something more. Unless the legislature provides that the report is binding, the government retains the power to depart from the commission's recommendations as long as it justifies its decision with rational reasons. These rational reasons must be included in the government's response to the commission's recommendations.

· · ·

[25] The government can reject or vary the commission's recommendations, provided that legitimate reasons are given. Reasons that are complete and that deal with the commission's recommendations in a meaningful way will meet the standard of rationality. Legitimate reasons must be compatible with the common law and the Constitution. The government must deal with the issues at stake in good faith. Bald expressions of rejection or disapproval are inadequate. Instead, the reasons must show that the commission's recommendations have been taken into account and must be based on facts and sound reasoning. They must state in what respect and to what extent they depart from the recommendations, articulating the grounds for rejection or variation. The reasons should reveal a consideration of the judicial office and an intention to deal with it appropriately. They must preclude any suggestion of attempting to manipulate the judiciary. The reasons must reflect the underlying public interest in having a commission process, being the depoliticization of the remuneration process and the need to preserve judicial independence.

The court concluded that the rejection of commission recommendations met the "rationality" test in New Brunswick, Ontario, and Alberta, but not in Quebec.

Chief Justice Lamer's decision in the *Provincial Judges Reference* was the subject of harsh criticism by notable academics, including Professor Peter Hogg. In a rejoinder, Professors Daphne Gilbert and Ed Ratushny take issue with Professor Hogg and argue that such criticism is unfounded and unfair to Chief Justice Lamer.

See D. Gilbert and E. Ratushny, "The Lamer Legacy for Judicial Independence" in *The Sacred Fire/Le Feu Sacre*, Adam Dodek and Daniel Jutras, eds. (Markham, ON: LexisNexis, 2009).

3. Administrative Independence

The last component of judicial independence is "administrative independence." Put simply, administrative independence requires that courts themselves have control over the administrative decisions "that bear directly and immediately on the exercise of the judicial function," such as "assignment of judges, sittings of the court, and court lists—as well as the related matters of allocation of court rooms and direction of the administrative staff engaged in carrying out these functions": see *Provincial Judges Reference*, [1997] 3 SCR 3, at para. 117. This requirement is met generally in the statutes creating the various courts, which assign to judges themselves these administrative roles. See, for example, *Supreme Court Act*, s. 97; *Federal Courts Act*, ss. 15 and 16.

Administrative independence was at issue in the *Tobiass* case discussed above. Recall that the Supreme Court was asked to consider whether judicial independence (or at least the perception of that independence) had been impaired by a private meeting between a senior Department of Justice official and the chief justice of the Federal Court. This meeting concerned a delay in the hearing of certain cases in which the Justice Department was a litigant. The court concluded that at least the appearance of independence was transgressed, for the following reasons.

Canada (Minister of Citizenship and Immigration) v. Tobiass
[1997] 3 SCR 391

THE COURT: ... [74] First, and as a general rule of conduct, counsel for one party should not discuss a particular case with a judge except with the knowledge and preferably with the participation of counsel for the other parties to the case. ... The meeting between Mr. Thompson and the Chief Justice, at which counsel for the appellants were not present, violated this rule and was clearly inappropriate, and this despite the fact that the occasion for the meeting was a highly legitimate concern about the exceedingly slow progress of the cases.

[75] Second, and again as a general rule, a judge should not accede to the demands of one party without giving counsel for the other parties a chance to present their views. It was therefore clearly wrong, and seriously so, for the Chief Justice to speak to the Associate Chief Justice at the instance of Mr. Thompson. ... [A] chief justice is responsible for the expeditious progress of cases through his or her court and may under certain circumstances be obligated to take steps to correct tardiness. Yet, the actions of Isaac CJ were more in the nature of a response to a party rather than to a problem. Thus, an action that might have been innocuous and even obligatory under other circumstances acquired an air of impropriety as a result of the events that preceded it. Quite simply, it was inappropriate.

[76] In similar fashion, by responding as he did to the Chief Justice's intervention without the participation of counsel for the appellants, Jerome ACJ acted inappropriately. We believe that there is ample evidence that might lead a reasonable observer to conclude that the Associate Chief Justice was not able to conduct the appellants' cases free from the interference of the federal Department of Justice and of the Chief Justice of his court. Before March 1, 1996, the Associate Chief Justice was content with the pace at which the appellants'

cases were advancing through his court. Indeed, even after Mr. Amerasinghe wrote to the Court Administrator to complain about the slow pace of the proceedings, the Associate Chief Justice resolved not to expedite consideration of the preliminary motions. Instead, he insisted on hearing oral argument according to the original, exceedingly dilatory schedule. It was only after the March 1, 1996 meeting between Mr. Thompson and the Chief Justice that Jerome ACJ acquired an appreciation of the Government's position. In his letter of March 1, 1996, the Chief Justice wrote:

> As regards the three cases about which you wrote, *the Associate Chief Justice says firstly, that he did not fully appreciate until he read your letter, the urgency of dealing with these matters as expeditiously as the Government would like.* However, now that he is aware he will devote one week from 15 May to deal with these cases not only with respect to the preliminary points but also with respect to the merits. Finally, he has authorized me to say that additional cases of this class coming into the Court will be given the highest priority in light of the concerns expressed in your letter. [Emphasis added.]

[77] Subsequent developments confirmed that the Associate Chief Justice had indeed finally received the Government's message. On April 10, 1996, the Associate Chief Justice retreated from his earlier position and announced that he would set aside sufficient time in May to dispose of all the preliminary issues in the appellants' cases. He also indicated that he would bring the cases to a final conclusion by July.

[78] We do not see how a reasonable observer could fail at least to wonder whether the Government, through Mr. Thompson, had succeeded in influencing the Associate Chief Justice to take a position more favourable to the Government's interests than he would otherwise have done. Making this conclusion even more likely is the undertaking of the Chief Justice and the Associate Chief Justice to Mr. Thompson that all reasonable steps would be taken to avoid a reference to the Supreme Court of Canada.

[79] The respondent tries to resist this conclusion by saying that the impetus to efficiency came not from Mr. Thompson and the Government but from the Chief Justice. The Chief Justice, the respondent says, was duty-bound to look into what was, by any objective standard, a serious delay in proceedings in his court. The respondent thus offers the Chief Justice as a kind of *novus actus interveniens* who stands between the Government and the Associate Chief Justice and, by the propriety of his own intentions, severs what would otherwise be an improper link between them.

[80] What the respondent's submission overlooks is that the Chief Justice was not able to exercise his administrative function entirely free from outside interference. Mr. Thompson approached the Chief Justice and told him that if the Associate Chief Justice did not pick up the pace, the Federal Court would face the embarrassment of having the Government go "over its head" to this Court. The Chief Justice's letter to Mr. Thompson suggests that this "threat" carried some weight with him and with the Associate Chief Justice as well:

> I have discussed your concerns with the Associate Chief Justice and, like me, he is prepared to take all reasonable steps possible to avoid a Reference to the Supreme Court of Canada on these matters.

It is reasonable to suppose that the threat of appeal to a higher authority influenced the Chief Justice and Associate Chief Justice to act in a way that would otherwise have been unpalatable to them. In this we agree entirely with Stone JA [in the Federal Court of Appeal], who found that "an informed person would conclude that this decision, by which the hearing of all preliminary motions and the trials would be compressed into a relatively short time frame, would redound to the disadvantage of the individual respondents [now appellants] and was taken so as 'to avoid' a reference to the Supreme Court" (p. 868). To interfere with the scheduling of cases because of delay is one thing but to pledge to take all reasonable steps to avoid a reference to the Supreme Court of Canada is quite another. It is wrong and improper for a judge to give such an undertaking. What is pertinent is to avoid delays, not to avoid appeals or recourse to higher courts.

[81] However, the respondent is quite right to observe that the delay in the Federal Court—Trial Division was inordinate and arguably inexcusable, and posed a real problem for the Department of Justice and for the Chief Justice. The fact is that in the space of a year, the Associate Chief Justice heard only one day of argument, and that on a preliminary motion. In our view, the Associate Chief Justice's dilatoriness defies explanation. The appellants attempt nevertheless to explain it, saying that the Associate Chief Justice had reason to delay the proceedings until judgment had been given by himself in a case called *Nemsila*, which might have cast some light on citizenship revocation cases generally. The Chief Justice for his part mentioned the *Nemsila* case in his letter of March 1, 1996, though he did not attempt to offer it as a justification for delay in the appellants' cases.

[82] However, even accepting that there was reason to await the rendering of judgment in *Nemsila*, the proper procedure would have been to hear argument on the appellants' motion and, if necessary, to reserve judgment. To call three cases to a halt awaiting the outcome of another case strikes us as a procedure calculated to create unnecessary delay. The appellants also point out that the respondent was not ready to proceed to a hearing on the merits. Apparently the respondent had not finished translating certain witness statements. But no one has suggested that the matter should have been brought to a conclusion on the merits before May 15, 1996, only that some progress should have been made toward resolving the preliminary questions before that date, and to settle the preliminary questions would not have required that all the witness statements should be available. Therefore, the fact that the respondent was not yet ready to proceed to trial cannot excuse the delay in the Associate Chief Justice's consideration of the preliminary questions.

[83] What all this means is that Mr. Thompson went to the Chief Justice with a legitimate grievance. This fact does not excuse what Mr. Thompson did—he assuredly chose an impermissible means of presenting his grievance—but it does cast into very real doubt the sinister interpretation that the appellants have attempted to place on his conduct. Given the vexing delay that the respondent had faced in the Trial Division, it is quite understandable that Mr. Thompson would have wished to do something about it. We believe that Mr. Thompson's motives were proper. It was his judgment that is questionable. What Mr. Thompson did was not wicked or done in bad faith. It is enough to say that what he did was inappropriate. As senior counsel in the Department of Justice, he arranged to speak privately—without opposing counsel present—to the Chief Justice, concerning cases which were pending. This he should not have done.

· · ·

[85] In short, the evidence supports the conclusion that the appearance of judicial independence suffered a serious affront as a result of the March 1, 1996 meeting between Mr.

Thompson and Isaac CJ. This affront very seriously compromised the appearance of judicial independence. A reasonable observer apprised of the workings of the Federal Court and of all the circumstances would perceive that the Chief Justice and the Associate Chief Justice were improperly and unduly influenced by a senior officer of the Department of Justice. However, there is no persuasive evidence of bad faith on the part of any of the actors in this drama, nor is there any solid evidence that the independence of the judges in question was actually compromised.

[Despite this finding, the Supreme Court did not uphold the trial judge's decision to order a stay of proceedings, but instead required that the proceedings be conducted by a trial division judge who was not tainted by the improper communications between the Court and the Department of Justice.]

PART III

Interplay Between the Courts and the Political Branches of Government

CHAPTER SEVEN

Statutory Interpretation

In this chapter and the next, we shift from a discussion of the structure and function of Canadian public law institutions to a closer examination of how the legislative, executive, and judicial branches interact with one another. Our focus here is on the relationship between the courts and the other branches of government—the legislature and the executive.

As we have suggested repeatedly, parliamentary supremacy is an important element of Canadian public law. Nevertheless, there is a threshold in Canadian constitutional law—a point at which parliamentary supremacy gives way to "constitutional" supremacy.

So long as Parliament or its provincial counterparts observe the binding constitutional limits on their jurisdiction, they are supreme and the courts must simply interpret and carry out their dictates as expressed in their acts. However, if a legislature wanders beyond its constitutional limits, it must be subordinated by the courts to the Constitution. Here, courts do two things. First, they determine the exact nature and scope of the constitutional limits, by interpreting the written Constitution and sometimes by discerning unwritten constitutional principles by which the legislature must abide. In this respect, they perform a constitutionalized interpretation role. Second, they decide whether a given statute has exceeded the constitutional limits determined through interpretation. If it has, they provide a remedy. Normally, the remedy is to declare that the offending legislation is invalid and has no force or effect.

Quite apart from this practice of direct judicial review, the courts often engage in indirect review when they interpret legislation in light of common law constitutional values such as respect for individual autonomy and private property rights. In such cases the courts presume that the legislature, in enacting a particular provision, did not intend to violate long-recognized constitutional values or authorize its delegates to do so.

Given these constitutional judicial review functions, it is arguable that Canadian democracy rests on a de facto system of judicial supremacy. For some, the power exercised by judges in carrying out their review functions is deeply problematic. Others welcome this check on the untrammelled power of the legislature. Clearly, the separation of powers between the judicial and the legislative branch is critically important to Canadian democracy—and often provokes heated debate.

Somewhat less controversial is the relationship between the courts and the executive. Like the legislature, the executive is constrained by the Constitution, and policed by the courts accordingly. Recall also that the executive has only limited legal powers, primarily those delegated to it by the legislature by statute. The courts are charged with ensuring that the executive does not stray beyond the scope of those powers. In this manner, the courts serve as the legislature's foot soldiers, preventing the executive from usurping power not accorded to it by the legislative branch.

Chapter 8 examines judicial review of both legislative and executive action. In this chapter, we focus on the rules of statutory interpretation: the doctrines that direct how courts should interpret the legislative will expressed in statutes and regulations. Section I provides an overview of statutory interpretation as a distinct field of legal inquiry, examining the sources of interpretation law and a summary of the sort of problems with which statutory interpretation grapples. Section II examines in detail the key statutory interpretation doctrines. Section III provides examples of these rules in action.

I. OVERVIEW OF STATUTORY INTERPRETATION

A. Introduction

There are thousands of federal and provincial statutes governing virtually every aspect of human activity. Paradoxically, although this legislation is by far the most important source of law in modern democratic states, little attention is paid to statutory interpretation in North American law schools outside Quebec. The theory and methodology of statutory interpretation is a challenging subject, as extensive and complex as the theory and methodology of the common law. Yet common law is the focus of most standard first-year courses—property, contracts, and torts. And even the so-called public law subjects—constitutional law and criminal law—are generally taught through case law, using common law methodology. In most law schools, the knowledge and skills required to master statutory interpretation are addressed perfunctorily as part of an introduction to a public law course or a research and writing course. Some law schools offer upper-year courses in statutory interpretation or legal drafting. These courses are worth their weight in gold.

Although statutory interpretation is generally addressed in the context of public law, there is no area of law that is not governed at least in part by legislation. In tort law, think of the *Occupiers Liability Act*; in contract law, think of the *Consumer Protection Act*; in property law, think of the *Personal Property Security Act*. These days, family law, succession law, corporate and commercial law, employment and labour law, intellectual property law, insurance law, environmental law, health law, and professional self-government (the self-regulation of professionals like doctors, teachers, accountants, and lawyers)—and more—are all grounded in legislation.

Furthermore, the skills required to read legislation and resolve interpretation disputes are also needed to deal with private law documents such as contracts, collective agreements, wills, and trusts. They are also needed to deal with the Constitution Acts against which ordinary legislation is tested as well as treaties with aboriginal peoples and international agreements. All these texts rely on language to set out legally binding rules. To determine the content of the rule, it is necessary to interpret the language of the text.

B. Sources of Interpretation Law

There are three main sources of interpretation law: interpretation acts, interpretation rules in individual statutes and regulations (and in Quebec, in civil codes), and, most importantly, the common law.

1. Interpretation Acts

Under the separation-of-powers doctrine, the role of the legislature is to make law, while the role of the judiciary is to interpret law, test its validity, and apply it to particular facts. However, it is open to a sovereign legislature to issue instructions on how particular legislation, or legislation in general, is to be interpreted.

Every Canadian jurisdiction has an *Interpretation Act* that contains various rules applicable to statutes in general. The federal Act, for example, has rules respecting corporations, offences, evidence, the appointment of civil servants, the exercise of administrative powers, reports to Parliament, the coming into force of legislation, the impact of amendment and repeal, how to calculate majorities and time periods, and more. It also contains a list of defined terms that are found throughout the federal statute book, such as "bank," "holiday," "person," "month," and "Her Majesty." These definitions apply unless the context indicates otherwise. Interpretation rules are also found in general acts governing the making of regulations (at the federal level, the *Statutory Instruments Act*, RSC 1985, c. S-22) and statute revisions (at the federal level, the *Legislation Revision and Consolidation Act*, RSC 1985, c. S-20). The following excerpt from the federal *Interpretation Act* is typical of what is found in this type of legislation. Note that the federal Act applies only to federal legislation; provincial or territorial legislation is governed by the relevant provincial or territorial Act.

Interpretation Act
RSC 1985, c. I-21

Territorial operation

8(1) Every enactment applies to the whole of Canada, unless a contrary intention is expressed in the enactment.

. . .

Duality of legal traditions and application of provincial law

8.1 Both the common law and the civil law are equally authoritative and recognized sources of the law of property and civil rights in Canada and, unless otherwise provided by law, if in interpreting an enactment it is necessary to refer to a province's rules, principles or concepts forming part of the law of property and civil rights, reference must be made to the rules, principles and concepts in force in the province at the time the enactment is being applied.

Terminology

8.2 Unless otherwise provided by law, when an enactment contains both civil law and common law terminology, or terminology that has a different meaning in the civil law and the common law, the civil law terminology or meaning is to be adopted in the Province of

Quebec and the common law terminology or meaning is to be adopted in the other provinces.

. . .

Law always speaking

10. The law shall be considered as always speaking, and where a matter or thing is expressed in the present tense, it shall be applied to the circumstances as they arise, so that effect may be given to the enactment according to its true spirit, intent and meaning.

"Shall" and "may"

11. The expression "shall" is to be construed as imperative and the expression "may" as permissive.

Enactments deemed remedial

12. Every enactment is deemed remedial, and shall be given such fair, large and liberal construction and interpretation as best ensures the attainment of its objects.

Preamble

13. The preamble of an enactment shall be read as a part of the enactment intended to assist in explaining its purport and object.

Marginal notes and historical references

14. Marginal notes and references to former enactments that appear after the end of a section or other division in an enactment form no part of the enactment, but are inserted for convenience of reference only.

Application of definitions and interpretation rules

15(1) Definitions or rules of interpretation in an enactment apply to all the provisions of the enactment, including the provisions that contain those definitions or rules of interpretation.

Interpretation sections subject to exceptions

15(2) Where an enactment contains an interpretation section or provision, it shall be read and construed

(a) as being applicable only if a contrary intention does not appear; and

(b) as being applicable to all other enactments relating to the same subject-matter unless a contrary intention appears.

Words in regulations

16. Where an enactment confers power to make regulations, expressions used in the regulations have the same respective meanings as in the enactment conferring the power.

Her Majesty not bound or affected unless stated

17. No enactment is binding on Her Majesty or affects Her Majesty or Her Majesty's rights or prerogatives in any manner, except as mentioned or referred to in the enactment.

2. Interpretation Rules in Acts and Regulations

Individual acts and regulations often contain definitions, application provisions, purpose statements, and the like. Definitions tell interpreters how particular words used in the legislation are to be understood; application sections indicate the scope of the legislation in terms of space (territorial application), time (temporal application), persons affected (for example, Her Majesty), and subject matter (some things may be excepted). Preambles and purpose statements, at the beginning of statutes, indicate the reasons for the new legislation—the concerns addressed, the values reflected in the legislation, and the anticipated benefits. Commencement and transitional provisions, at the end of statutes, indicate when the legislation will commence or come into force and how it will apply to situations in progress. The following excerpt from the *Canadian Human Rights Act* contains a number of such provisions.

Canadian Human Rights Act
RSC 1985, c. H-6

Purpose

2. The purpose of this Act is to extend the laws in Canada to give effect, within the purview of matters coming within the legislative authority of Parliament, to the principle that all individuals should have an opportunity equal with other individuals to make for themselves the lives that they are able and wish to have and to have their needs accommodated, consistent with their duties and obligations as members of society, without being hindered in or prevented from doing so by discriminatory practices based on race, national or ethnic origin, colour, religion, age, sex, sexual orientation, marital status, family status, disability or conviction for an offence for which a pardon has been granted.

· · ·

Definitions

25. In this Act,

· · ·

"disability" means any previous or existing mental or physical disability and includes disfigurement and previous or existing dependence on alcohol or a drug;

"employee organization" includes a trade union or other organization of employees or a local, the purposes of which include the negotiation of terms and conditions of employment on behalf of employees.

· · ·

Limitation

62(1) This Part and Parts I and II do not apply to or in respect of any superannuation or pension fund or plan established by an Act of Parliament enacted before March 1, 1978.

· · ·

Binding on Her Majesty

66(1) This Act is binding on Her Majesty in right of Canada, except in matters respecting the Yukon Government or the Government of the Northwest Territories or Nunavut.

3. Common Law Rules

Apart from legislative directives of the sort described above, statutory interpretation is rooted in the common law, in a body of principles, presumptions, and conventions known as the "rules of statutory interpretation." Strictly speaking, these rules are not binding in the way that the rules of the *Criminal Code* are binding. Rather, they operate as guidelines. They offer interpreters a checklist of relevant considerations, suggesting various lines of inquiry and ensuring that no possibility has been overlooked. They are relied on by counsel in developing arguments and by judges to justify outcomes in interpretation disputes. The following extracts from *Sullivan on the Construction of Statutes* provide an introduction to the common law development of statutory interpretation and the current common law approach.

Ruth Sullivan, *Sullivan on the Construction of Statutes*
5th ed. (Markham, ON: Butterworths, 2008), at 4-7

The evolution of statutory interpretation. [Modern interpretive practice in Canada] is the culmination of centuries of statutory interpretation by common law courts. Historically, those courts recognized and practised four distinct approaches to statutory interpretation. First, there was the approach known as "equitable construction" which subsequently evolved into "the mischief rule." The definitive exposition of this approach is found in *Heydon's Case* [(1584), 3 Co. Rep. 7a, 76 ER 637] where the court described the task of interpreting statutes in the following expansive terms:

> ... [T]he office of all the Judges is always to make such construction as shall suppress the mischief [for which the common law did not provide] and advance the remedy [chosen by Parliament to cure the disease of the commonwealth], and to suppress subtle inventions and evasions for continuance of the mischief, *pro privato commodo*, and to add force and life to the cure and remedy, according to the true intent of the makers of the Act, *pro bono publico*. [Ibid., at 638 (ER)]

In equitable construction, the words of the legislative text are less important than achieving Parliament's actual intentions. Accordingly, legislation is construed so as to promote legislative purpose, cure any over- or under-inclusions in the implementing provisions and suppress attempts by citizens to avoid the intended impact of the legislation. This approach was appropriate in an era when judges were active participants in law-making and texts were not expected to dictate outcomes because they were both inaccessible and unreliable. ... (For many centuries, legislation was recorded by hand on a Parliamentary roll, and the clerk who did the recording controlled such matters as headings, marginal notes and punctuation. Before the printing press made accurate reproduction possible and inexpensive, copies of legislation were hard to come by and inevitably contained numerous variations and mistakes.) ...

By the 18th century, with the establishment of Parliament as a separate and primary source of power, there was less room for equitable construction. At the same time, however, judges were strongly influenced by the natural law theory espoused by Locke at the end of the 17th century. As Corry [J.A. Corry, "Administrative Law and the Interpretation of Statutes" (1936), 1 *UTLJ* 286, at 296-97] explains:

> The Stuart theory of the state was laid low in the revolution of 1688, and a new constitution and a new political theory took its place. The new political theory was fashioned by Locke who found in reason clear proof that men have certain rights which are beyond the reach of all governments … . This theory justified the revolution and became an article of faith in the eighteenth century [when] there grew to full flower that intense attachment of the common law to the liberty and the property of individuals … . Some things were so contrary to reason that Parliament could not be deemed to have intended them unless the words were painfully clear.

This belief in reason and fundamental rights founded upon reason became the basis for the doctrine of strict construction and for a number of new presumptions aimed at preserving the life, liberty and property of citizens from state interference.

In the 19th and 20th centuries two doctrines dominated judicial thinking: parliamentary sovereignty and the rule of law. These doctrines paved the way for literal construction and the evolution of both the "plain meaning rule" and the "golden rule." Under the plain meaning rule, a court is obliged to stick to the literal meaning of the legislative text in so far as that meaning is clear. As explained by Chief Justice Tindal in the *Sussex Peerage* case [(1844), 11 Cl. & Fin. 85, 8 ER 1034]:

> My Lords, the only rule for the construction of Acts of Parliament is that they should be construed according to the intent of the Parliament which passed the Act. If the words of the statute are in themselves precise and unambiguous, then no more can be necessary than to expound those words in their natural and ordinary sense. The words themselves alone do, in such case, best declare the intention of the lawgiver.

If the words of a legislative text are clear and unambiguous, the court must apply them as written despite any contrary evidence of legislative intent and regardless of consequences.

Most proponents of the plain meaning rule follow Chief Justice Tindal's lead in suggesting that courts should adhere to the plain meaning of the text because it offers the best evidence of the lawgiver's intent. Another justification for sticking to the plain meaning is rule of law and the need for certainty and predictability. Citizens should be able to rely on the apparent meaning of the legislation that governs them. [This justification would be compelling were it not for the fact that individuals form different impressions of what a text means and have different intuitions about how "plain" their particular impression is.] …

The uncompromising character of the plain meaning rule was emphasized by Lamer CJ in *R v. McIntosh* [[1995] 1 SCR 686, at para. 34] when he wrote:

> [W]here, by the use of clear and unequivocal language capable of only one meaning, anything is enacted by the legislature, it must be enforced however harsh or absurd or contrary to common sense the result may be … . The fact that a provision gives rise to absurd results is not, in my opinion, sufficient to declare it ambiguous and then embark upon a broad-ranging interpretative analysis.

In *McIntosh*, the majority conceded that its reading of the legislation led to absurd results that no rational legislature could have intended. But because the meaning (in their view) was plain, they refused to look at any evidence of legislative intent other than the text itself.

While many courts and judges profess to be strongly committed to the plain meaning rule, this commitment inevitably wavers when the consequences of applying the apparent meaning of a text are found to be intolerable. In such cases, resort is had to the so-called golden rule, which permits courts to depart from the ordinary meaning of a text to avoid absurd consequences. As explained by Lord Wensleydale in *Grey v. Pearson* [(1857), 6 HL Cas. 61, at 106, 10 ER 1216, at 1234]:

> [T]he grammatical and ordinary sense of the words is to be adhered to, unless that would lead to some absurdity or some repugnance or inconsistency with the rest of the instrument, in which case the grammatical and ordinary sense of the words may be modified so as to avoid that absurdity and inconsistency, but no further.

The golden rule is grounded in the supervisory and mediating roles of the courts. Courts supervise the other players in the system by ensuring that those who exercise powers conferred by the legislature do so within the limits of those powers. Courts also complete the act of law-making by mediating between the rule as enacted—which is an abstraction, a mere string of words—and the facts of the case in so far as they are known. As the Supreme Court of Canada noted in the *Secession Reference*, the judicial mandate in a constitutional democracy involves not only respect for democratic institutions—the most important of which is the legislature—but also adherence to the rule of law and other common law values [*Reference re Secession of Quebec*, [1998] 2 SCR 217, at 247]. The legitimacy of courts derives in part from their duty to ensure an appropriate observance of, and balance among, these (sometimes conflicting) norms.

Although the inconsistency between the plain meaning rule and the golden rule is evident, there are few judges who do not rely on both as need arises. There is a point at which even the most committed literalist is prepared to sacrifice literal meaning to avoid the unthinkable. In *R v. McIntosh*, [[1995] 1 SCR 686] Lamer CJ refused to depart from what he took to be the plain meaning of the text even though it led to results which he conceded were absurd. But in other judgments, both before and after *McIntosh*, he was prepared to abandon the plain meaning of a text if it seemed the right thing to do. In *R v. Paul*, [1982] 1 SCR 621, at 662, for example, he relied on the following passage from Maxwell to virtually redraft s. 645(4)(c) of the *Criminal Code*:

1. Modification of the Language to Meet the Intention

Where the language of a statute, in its ordinary and grammatical construction, leads to a manifest contradiction of the apparent purpose of the enactment, or to some inconvenience or absurdity which can hardly have been intended, a construction may be put upon it which modifies the meaning of the words and even the structure of the sentence. This may be done by departing from the rules of grammar, by giving an unusual meaning to particular words, or by rejecting them altogether, on the ground that the legislature could not possibly have intended what its words signify.

[[1982] 1 SCR 621, at 662 citing P. St. J. Langan, *Maxwell on the Interpretation of Statutes*, 12th ed. (London: Sweet & Maxwell, 1969), at 228.] This willingness to modify meaning or sentence structure in order to avoid absurd results seems to be an unavoidable aspect of interpretation. Although the legislature is sovereign, it is not omniscient; it cannot envisage and provide for (or against) every possible application of its general rules. It must rely on official interpreters to mediate between the text and the facts in particular cases so as to ensure an outcome that does not bring the law into disrepute.

Each of the approaches described above—equitable construction, presumed intent, the plain meaning rule and the golden rule—emphasizes a particular aspect of interpretation that at one time or another was taken to be all-important. Under the modern principle, described below, these approaches are integrated.

———————————

In 1974, Elmer Driedger, a legislative drafter with the federal Department of Justice, published an influential text entitled *The Construction of Statutes* (Toronto: Butterworths, 1974) in which, after reviewing the evolution of statutory interpretation described above, he reached the following conclusion (at 67):

> Today there is only one principle or approach, namely, the words of an Act are to be read in their entire context, in their grammatical and ordinary sense harmoniously with the scheme of the Act, the object of the Act, and the intention of Parliament.

Driedger's principle or approach has been dubbed "the modern principle" and has been relied on in innumerable decisions by Canadian courts as the preferred approach to interpretation. (For critical analysis of the modern principle and how it is applied, see Beaulac and Côté, "Driedger's Modern Principle at the Supreme Court of Canada: Interpretation, Justification, Legitimization" (2006), 40 *Themis* 131-72, and Sullivan, "Statutory Interpretation in the Supreme Court of Canada" (1998-99), 30 *Ottawa L Rev.* 177.)

The following extract from *Sullivan on the Construction of Statutes* draws attention to the chief features of the modern principle.

Ruth Sullivan, *Sullivan on the Construction of Statutes*
5th ed. (Markham, ON: Butterworths, 2008), at 1-3

The chief significance of the modern principle is its insistence on the complex, multidimensional character of statutory interpretation. The first dimension emphasized is textual meaning. Although texts issue from an author and a particular set of circumstances, once published they are detached from their origin and take on a life of their own—one over which the reader has substantial control. Recent research in psycholinguistics has shown that the way readers understand the words of a text depends on the expectations they bring to their reading. These expectations are rooted in linguistic competence and shared linguistic convention; they are also dependent on the wide-ranging knowledge, beliefs, values and experience that readers have stored in their brain. The content of a reader's memory constitutes the most important context in which a text is read and influences in particular his or her impression of ordinary meaning—what Driedger calls the grammatical and ordinary sense of the words.

A second dimension endorsed by the modern principle is legislative intent. All texts, indeed all utterances, are made for a reason. Authors want to communicate their thoughts and they may further want their readers to adopt different views or adjust their conduct. A cooperative reader tries to discover what the author had in mind. In the case of legislation, the law-maker wants to communicate the law that it intended to enact because that law, as set out in the successive provisions of a statute or regulation, is the means chosen by the law-maker to achieve a set of desired goals. Law-abiding readers (including those who administer or enforce the legislation and those who resolve disputes) try to identify the intended goals of the legislation and the means devised to achieve those goals, so that they can act accordingly. This aspect of interpretation is captured in Driedger's reference to the scheme and object of the Act and the intention of Parliament.

A third dimension of interpretation referred to in the modern principle is compliance with established legal norms. These norms are part of the "entire context" in which the words of an Act must be read. They are also an integral part of legislative intent, as that concept is explained by Driedger. In the second edition he wrote:

> It may be convenient to regard "intention of Parliament" as composed of four elements, namely
>
> - the expressed intention—the intention expressed by the enacted words;
> - the implied intention—the intention that may legitimately be implied from the enacted words;
> - the presumed intention—the intention that the courts will in the absence of an indication to the contrary impute to Parliament; and
> - the declared intention—the intention that Parliament itself has said may be or must be or must not be imputed to it.

[Elmer A. Driedger, *The Construction of Statutes*, 2d ed. (Toronto: Butterworths, 1983), at p. 106. (Bullets added.)]

Presumed intention embraces the entire body of evolving legal norms which contribute to the legal context in which official interpretation occurs. These norms are found in Constitution Acts, in constitutional and quasi-constitutional legislation and in international law, both customary and conventional. Their primary source, however, is the common law. [This is true even in Quebec in matters of public law, which is derived from common law sources. In matters of private law, the *Civil Code of Quebec* is the primary source of legal norms.] Over the centuries courts have identified certain values that are deserving of legal protection and these have become the basis for strict and liberal construction doctrine and the presumptions of legislation intent. These norms are an important part of the context in which legislation is made and read.

The modern principle says that the words of a legislative text must be read in their ordinary sense *harmoniously* with the scheme and objects of the Act and the intention of the legislature. In an easy case textual meaning, legislative intent and relevant norms all support a single interpretation. In hard cases, however, these dimensions are vague or obscure or point in different directions. In the hardest cases, the textual meaning seems plain, but cogent evidence of legislative intent (actual or presumed) makes the plain meaning unacceptable. If the modern principle has a weakness, it is its failure to acknowledge and address the dilemma created by hard cases.

The modern principle may also be criticized for encouraging the assumption that statutory interpretation consists of resolving doubt about the meaning of particular words. As indicated by the materials that follow, a significant number of interpretation disputes turn on issues other than the meaning of words.

C. Range of Interpretation Issues

There is more to statutory interpretation than disputes about the meaning of the legislative text. Sometimes the meaning is clear, but there is a gap in the legislative scheme and the question is whether the court can do anything about it. Sometimes there is overlap between a clear provision and the common law and the issue is whether both apply. Many disputes are about the circumstances in which a court should update a statute or decline to apply a legislative rule even though its meaning appears to be clear. In short, determining the meaning of words in a legislative text is an important task of interpreters, a necessary first task, but it is only part of the work of interpretation. (This account of the several types of argument available to interpreters, and the claims associated with each, is based on Ruth Sullivan, "Statutory Interpretation in a Nutshell" (2003), 82 *Can. Bar Rev.* 51, at 64-65.)

Table 1 indicates the range of issues that arise in statutory interpretation and how they are addressed.

Table 1 Issues Arising in Statutory Interpretation

Type of problem	Type of argument in response
Ambiguous, vague, or incomplete text	Disputed meaning
Evolving context	Static versus dynamic interpretation
Overinclusive text	Non-application
Underinclusive text	Incorrigible gap in legislative scheme, or supplement with common law rule or remedy
Contradictory or incoherent text	Corrigible mistake
Overlapping provisions	No conflict: Overlap versus exhaustive code
Conflict: Paramountcy rule

In a *disputed meaning argument*, the interpreter claims that, properly interpreted, the provision in question has a particular preferred meaning. He or she must establish that this preferred meaning is the ordinary meaning, an intended technical meaning, or at least a plausible meaning. If the legislation is bilingual, the interpreter must address both language versions.

For instance, in *Perrier Group of Canada Inc. v. Canada*, [1996] 1 FC 586 (CA), the court had to decide whether the carbonated water sold under the Perrier label was a "beverage" within the meaning of the *Excise Tax Act*. Perrier Group argued that "beverage" meant a manufactured drink, produced by mixing ingredients, and therefore excluded naturally carbonated water. The minister of revenue argued that "beverage" meant any liquid fit for human consumption and therefore included water. The court preferred the minister's understanding of the term.

In a *static versus dynamic interpretation argument*, the interpreter claims that the text should be interpreted as it would have been when the text was first enacted (static interpretation) or interpreted in light of current understanding of language and social conditions (dynamic interpretation).

For instance, in *Harvard College v. Canada (Commissioner of Patents)*, [2004] 4 SCR 45, the issue was whether the so-called oncomouse was an "invention" within the definition of the *Patent Act*, which included "any new and useful art, process, machine, manufacture or composition of matter." Even though a genetically altered mouse could be thought of as a "composition of matter," the majority preferred a static interpretation. The Court held that Parliament had not contemplated the patenting of higher life forms when it drafted the definition of "invention." Such a "radical departure from the traditional patent regime" could not be effected through interpretation but required legislative intervention.

In a *non-application argument*, the interpreter identifies a reason not to apply a provision to the facts even though, given its ordinary meaning, it would otherwise apply. A provision may be "read down" in this way for any number of reasons—to promote legislative purpose, to avoid absurdity, or to comply with the presumptions of legislative intent.

For example, in *Re Vabalis* (1983), 2 DLR (4th) 382 (Ont. CA), a married woman applied to change her name from Vabalis to Vabals under Ontario's *Change of Name Act*, RSO 1980, c. 6. Section 4(1) of the Act provided as follows:

> A married person applying for a change of surname shall also apply for a change of the surnames of his or her spouse and all unmarried minor children of the husband or of the marriage.

Since Ms. Vabalis had not adopted her husband's name when she married, applying this provision to her would have required her husband, whose surname was different, to change his name to Vabals. The court held that this requirement was absurd and should be limited to married applicants who have the same surname as the spouse. In effect, the court narrowed the scope of the provision by reading in words of qualification:

> A married person who applies for a change of surname *and has the same surname as his or her spouse* shall also apply for a change of the surname of his or her spouse.

In an *incorrigible gap argument*, the interpreter claims that the legislation as drafted cannot apply to the facts even though, given its purpose, it probably should apply; whether this omission is deliberate or inadvertent, the court has no jurisdiction to fill a gap in a legislative scheme or otherwise enlarge the scope of legislation.

In *Beattie v. National Frontier Insurance Co.* (2003), 68 OR (3d) 60 (CA), an insured claimed no-fault accident benefits under Ontario's statutory scheme. Under the regulations, a claimant who was driving a vehicle at the time of the accident was ineligible for certain benefits if he or she

- knew the vehicle was uninsured,
- did not have a valid driver's licence, or
- was operating the vehicle without the owner's consent.

In addition, s. 30(4) provided that if the claimant "was engaged in ... an act for which [he or she] is charged with a criminal offence," the insurer was obliged to hold in trust any amounts payable under the scheme until the charge is finally disposed of, at which time the amounts …

  (c) shall be returned to the insurer, if the [claimant] is found guilty of the offence … ; or

  (d) shall be paid to the [claimant], if … not found guilty.

Beattie was found guilty of impaired driving, and he conceded that under s. 30(4)(c), the benefits paid into trust pending his conviction had to be returned to the insurer. However, he claimed post-conviction benefits on the ground that there was nothing in the legislation that prevented him from receiving those benefits.

The court reluctantly agreed. Although it was clear that the lawmaker had intended to deny benefits to a person in Beattie's position, there was a gap in the legislative scheme. Section 30(4) dealt exclusively with benefits payable before disposition of the charge, and there was nothing in the Act or regulations denying a claimant access to benefits once he or she was convicted of an offence.

In a *supplementation argument*, the interpreter concedes that the legislation as drafted does not apply, but claims that the common law does apply so as to supplement the under-inclusive legislation. Supplementation arguments are generally successful when the court relies on its *parens patriae* jurisdiction or its inherent jurisdiction to control its own process.

For example, in *Beson v. Director of Child Welfare for Newfoundland*, [1982] 2 SCR 716, the court acknowledged that although the province's *Adoption of Children Act* created various appeals to the Adoption Appeal Board, it apparently did not provide for an appeal in the circumstances of the case. Wilson J wrote:

> If the Besons had indeed no right of appeal under the statute … there is a gap in the legislative scheme which the Newfoundland courts could have filled by an exercise of their *parens patriae* jurisdiction.

In a *corrigible mistake argument*, the interpreter claims that the provision in question contains a drafting mistake, which must be corrected before determining whether the provision applies to the facts. He or she must establish what the legislature clearly intended and what the text would have said had it been properly drafted. This problem arises quite often in interpreting bilingual legislation when the two versions say different things.

In *Morishita v. Richmond (Township)* (1990), 67 DLR (4th) (BCCA), the court had to interpret a provision in a municipal bylaw that referred to s. 4 of the bylaw. Since the reference to s. 4 was incoherent, while the reference to s. 5 made good sense, the court concluded that the lawmaker had intended to refer to s. 5 and it interpreted the bylaw accordingly.

In the absence of conflict, if two or more provisions apply to the same facts, each is to be applied as written. Although not articulated as such, the courts work with a *presumption of overlap*. Any law, whether common law or legislation, which could apply is presumed to apply in the absence of evidence to the contrary.

In an *exhaustive code argument*, the interpreter concedes that the overlap between legislative provisions or between legislation and the common law does not create a conflict, but claims that a particular Act or provision was meant to apply exhaustively, to the exclusion of other law, whether statutory or common law.

In *Gendron v. Supply & Services Union of PSAC, Loc. 50057*, [1990] 1 SCR 1298, the issue was whether a union member could bring an action against the union for breaching the common law duty of fair representation. The court ruled that the duties owed by unions to union members were set out in the *Canada Labour Code* and, on this issue at least, the statute was meant to be an exhaustive code, displacing recourse to the common law.

In a *paramountcy argument*, the interpreter claims that there is a conflict between two provisions or between a provision and the common law and that one takes precedence over the other on the basis of some principled reason—for example, legislation prevails over the common law or the specific prevails over the general.

In *Insurance Corporation of BC v. Heerspink*, [1982] 2 SCR 145, Heerspink challenged the statutory right of an insurance company to terminate an insurance contract upon giving 15 days' notice without establishing any cause. BC's *Human Rights Code* provided that persons could not be denied a "service … customarily available to the public … unless a reasonable cause exists for such denial." Reconciling this apparent conflict, Lamer J (as he then was) wrote, at 178:

> When the subject matter of a law is said to be the comprehensive statement of the "human rights" of the people living in the jurisdiction, then there is no doubt in my mind that the people of that jurisdiction have through their legislature clearly indicated that they consider that law, and the values it endeavours to buttress and protect are, save their constitutional laws, more important than all others. Therefore, short of that legislature speaking to the contrary in express and unequivocal language in the Code or in some other enactment, it is intended that the Code supersede all other laws when conflict arises.

Obviously, the types of argument surveyed above are not mutually exclusive. The issues that arise in applying legislation to a given set of facts can often be framed in more than one way. How an issue is framed is rhetorically significant and can often affect the outcome of a case.

II. AN OVERVIEW OF THE RULES OF STATUTORY INTERPRETATION

Numerous rules exist to guide statutory interpretation, the most important of which are reviewed below.

A. Rules About Meaning

The first thing an interpreter must do is read the text and form an impression of its meaning. The following rules address this task:

- *Ordinary meaning rule.* Ordinary meaning is the meaning that spontaneously comes to the mind of a competent reader upon reading a legislative text. This is presumed to be the meaning intended by Parliament. However, the presumption can be rebutted by evidence suggesting that some other meaning was intended.
- *Technical meaning rule.* It is presumed that legislatures use words in their popular, non-technical sense. However, when legislation deals with a specialized subject and uses language that people governed by the legislation would understand in a specialized way, that specialized understanding is preferred over ordinary usage.
- *Shared meaning rule.* If there is a discrepancy between the versions of a bilingual statute, the meaning that is shared by both versions is presumed to be the intended mean-

ing. If the English version could be interpreted in two ways and the French version in only one of those ways, the shared meaning would be the meaning of the French version. If the English version is broader than the French version, the shared meaning would be the French version. (This aspect of the shared meaning rule has come in for criticism by academics. See, for example, Ruth Sullivan, "An Alternative to the Shared Meaning Rule as Formulated in *R. v. Daoust* and *The Law of Bilingual Interpretation*," forthcoming in *Ottawa L Rev.*) The presumption in favour of the shared meaning is rebutted by evidence suggesting that some other meaning was intended.

- *Original meaning rule.* The meaning of the words used in a legislative text is fixed at the time of enactment, but its application to facts over time is not fixed. In static interpretation, the text is applied as it would have been when the legislation was first enacted. In dynamic interpretation, the text is applied in light of circumstances and assumptions existing at the time of application. Language that is technical, concrete, and specific tends to attract a static interpretation; language that is general or abstract attracts a dynamic interpretation.
- *Plausible meaning rule.* If the ordinary meaning of a text is rejected to give effect to the actual or presumed intentions of the legislature, the meaning adopted must be one that the text is capable of bearing. This rule is sometimes honoured in the breach. For example, in *Paul v. The Queen*, [1982] 1 SCR 621, SCJ no. 32, the Supreme Court of Canada concluded that a criminal prosecution "before the same court *at the same sittings*" should be interpreted to mean a criminal prosecution "before the same judge." Lamer J acknowledged that this interpretation disregarded the meaning of the words "at the same sittings," but was nonetheless prepared to adopt this interpretation in order to adapt the provision to the current method of dealing with criminal prosecutions.

The following judgment illustrates the application of the technical meaning rule.

Re Witts and Attorney General for British Columbia
(1982), 138 DLR (3d) 555 (BCSC)

[The petitioner Witts bought a horse at a "claiming race," believing it to be a colt as described in the racing program and racing form. Although the horse's racing career was undistinguished, Witts intended to use the horse for breeding purposes because of its excellent blood lines. After taking possession of the horse, Witts discovered that it was a gelding and therefore useless for breeding. Witts tried to rescind his purchase by objecting to the race stewards under the *Horse Racing Rules and Regulations*, BC Reg. 62/70. Witts's objection was based on the fact that a horse held out to be a colt turned out to be a gelding. Under the Racing Rules, close examination of a horse to be purchased in a claiming race was prohibited and title vested in the buyer whatever the condition of the horse. Under rule 11.01(kk) no objection to a claim based on the sex or age of a claimed horse could be entertained by the stewards. Witts's objection was rejected by the stewards on the ground that it was based on the sex of the horse. His appeal to the Racing Commission was dismissed. He then applied to the Superior Court for judicial review of the commission's decision.]

WALLACE J: The petitioner applies for an order, pursuant to the *Judicial Review Procedure Act*, RSBC 1979, c. 209, reversing a ruling of the British Columbia Racing Commission because of error.

· · ·

In reaching their decision the stewards applied Rule 1.01, definition of "horse" [am. BC Reg. 215/74, s. 1] and Rule 11.01(kk) of BC Reg. 62/70 of the *Horse Racing Act*, which read:

> "horse" includes a stallion, mare, gelding, colt, or filly;

· · ·

>   (kk) No objection to a claim based on the sex or age of the claimed horse shall be entertained by the Stewards.

· · ·

Argument

The petitioner says an error was made [by the stewards and the commission] in construing Rule 11.01(kk) and in failing to recognize and apply the appropriate principles of equity and fairness.

The rules and regulations of the *Horse Racing Act* provide in the interpretation s. 1.01 that

> "age" as applied to a horse, shall be calculated from January 1st of the year in which it was foaled.

Thus, counsel urged, where a meaning differing from the common meaning of a word was intended, the Lieutenant-Governor in Council passed the required regulation to achieve that objective. "Sex" is not defined in the interpretation section and, since no special meaning is attributed to the word by the regulations, counsel submits the general rule, that statutes are presumed to use words in their popular sense, should be applied. Accordingly, one must turn to the dictionaries for the common and ordinary meaning of the term. The *Shorter Oxford Dictionary* provides this definition:

> Sex—either of the two divisions of organic beings distinguished as male and female respectively. Quality in respect of being male or female. 3. The distinction between male and female in general.

In the instant case the petitioner asserts that the misrepresentation of "colt" or "gelding" relates to the absence of reproductive organs and not to the sex of the animal. Accordingly, he submits the commission erred on the face of the record in declining jurisdiction on the ground that the protest was based on the sex of the claimed horse.

· · ·

The position of the respondent is best stated by reference to para. 4 of the affidavit of Mr. Joseph Horton, a racing steward for some years:

> ... In the world of horse racing, the sex of a horse is either a stallion, colt, gelding, ridgling, mare, or filly and in all my seven years of supervising claiming races I have never heard of any trainer or owner stating the sex of his/her horse to be other than one of the foregoing. In fact,

I have never heard of a horse to be referred to as a male horse or a female horse from anyone having knowledge of horses. ...

. . .

Counsel for the respondent refers to the decision of *Unwin v. Hanson*, [1891] 2 QB 115 at p. 119, where Esher MR sets out the following principle of construction:

Now when we have to consider the construction of words such as this occurring in Acts of Parliament we must treat the question thus: If the Act is directed at dealing with matters affecting everybody generally, the words used have the meaning attached to them in the common and ordinary use of language. If the Act is one passed with reference to a particular trade, business, or transaction, and words are used which everybody conversant with that trade, business, or transaction, knows and understands to have a particular meaning in it, then the words are to be construed as having that particular meaning, though it may differ from the common or ordinary meaning of the words. For instance, the "waist" or the "skin" are well-known terms as applied to a ship, and nobody would think of their meaning the waist or the skin of a person when they are used in an Act of Parliament dealing with ships.

Counsel points out that the affidavits of Mr. Mooney and Mr. Horton reveal that, when speaking to individuals in the world of horse-racing, the sex of a horse is described as either stallion, colt, gelding, ridgling, mare or filly, and never as a male or female horse. This evidence is supported by the reference to the sex of this horse as a colt or gelding in the entry blank and certificate of registration, official record, racing programme and racing form.

. . .

Ruling

. . .

Turning now to the remaining issue: the appropriate construction to be placed on the word "sex" as used in the Rule 11.01(kk). I find the word is capable of being used in two ways: one being the common meaning of a male or female animal, the other being a particular meaning as used by persons conversant with horse-racing to designate whether the animal is a colt, gelding, stallion, ridgling, mare, or filly.

It would appear the regulations pertaining to claiming races are designed to provide, primarily, a market-place for racing horses and, secondly, to ensure that horses of equal ability compete in the same races. Moreover, the regulations are designed to establish with certainty, and unconditionally, that a person who successfully claims a horse thereafter owns that horse—neither the owner nor the claimant can attempt to avoid the transfer of title which takes place at the moment the race is started by raising, after the race has been run, a condition of the offer or acceptance. ...

To permit the transfer of title to be questioned on any ground, other than fraud, might well negate the whole object of a claiming race which places, upon the owner, the risk that the horse may be purchased for the entered price—and, upon the purchaser, the risk that the horse he has purchased may be defective in some respect and less desirable than he considered it to be when he filed his claim.

. . .

Accordingly, I find that the commission did not err in concluding the petitioner's protest in this case was based on the "sex" of a horse as that term is understood in the racing fraternity and the protest was barred by Rule 11.01(kk).

The petitioner is therefore left to seek a remedy for any loss he has suffered from those responsible for the publication of the erroneous information contained in the official forms upon which he was required to rely when seeking information upon which to formulate his claim.

I consider this litigation has arisen in large part because of the failure of the regulation to adequately define the extended or special meaning of the term "sex" as was done for the term "age." Accordingly, I consider it a proper case in which there should not be an award of costs to the successful respondent.

Petition dismissed.

_____

Several points about the technical meaning rule are worth noting. First, a person who claims that a legislative text has a technical meaning different from its popular, non-technical meaning has the burden of establishing

- the technical meaning of the word or expression, and
- that the technical meaning was intended in this context.

As the *Witts* case illustrates, evidence of technical meaning is offered by experts in the relevant field through testimony or affidavit evidence.

Second, legal terms of art are considered technical terms. If a word or expression has both a popular meaning and a legal meaning, the former is presumed. For obvious reasons, the courts do not require expert testimony to establish the legal meaning of a word or expression.

B. Presumptions Relied On To Analyze the Meaning of a Text

Courts make a number of (idealized) assumptions about the way legislation is drafted, which influence the way the finished product is interpreted. The following are the most important of these assumptions.

- *Straightforward expression.* The legislature chooses the clearest, simplest, and most direct way of stating its meaning.
- *Uniform expression.* The legislature uses the same words and techniques to express the same meaning and different words and techniques to express different meanings.
- *No tautology/no redundancy ("the legislature does not legislate in vain").* There are no superfluous words in legislation; every word, every feature of the text is there for a reason and plays a meaningful role in the legislative scheme.
- *Internal coherence.* All the provisions of a legislative text fit together logically and work together coherently to achieve the purposes of the legislation.

These assumptions are the basis of a number of so-called maxims of interpretation, including:

- *Implied exclusion (expressio unius est exclusio alterius).* If something is not mentioned in circumstances where one would expect it to be mentioned, it is impliedly excluded.
- *Associated words (noscitur a sociis).* The meaning of a word or phrase is affected by the other words or phrases with which it is linked in a sentence.
- *Limited class (ejusdem generis).* When a list of things that all belong to an identifiable class is followed by a more general term, the general term may be read down to include only other things within the identifiable class. For example, in the phrase "ice skating, sledding, skiing, and other sports," "sports" may be read down to include only sports that are played in winter.
- *The legislature would have said "x."* A legitimate basis for rejecting a proposed interpretation is to point out that had the legislature intended the proposed interpretation, it would have framed the legislation in a different way, as it did elsewhere in the Act or regulation or elsewhere in the statute book.

In the *Witts* case, the petitioner appealed (unsuccessfully) to the implied exclusion rule. He argued that when the legislature wished to depart from the ordinary meaning of a word, it did so expressly by setting out its preferred definition of the term, as evidenced by the definition of "age" in the regulation. Since "sex" was not defined, it should be given its ordinary meaning. This argument did not succeed because when regulations govern a specialized activity carried out by persons who understand terms in a particular way in the context of their specialized activity, the terms (considered "technical terms" or "terms of art") are often understood to have their specialized meaning.

The following judgment illustrates reliance on the ordinary meaning rule, the associated words rule, and the no tautology rule.

R v. Daoust
[2004] 1 SCR 217

[As part of an investigation of pawn brokers suspected of accepting and selling stolen merchandise, the Quebec City police set up an operation using an undercover officer. The officer went to D's establishment on four different occasions to sell goods, which he hinted were stolen. Each transaction ended with the merchandise being accepted for a sum of money. On the final occasion, D told the officer that this would be the last time they would do business together, to which B, the establishment's manager, added, "We can't always be helping you to steal." B and D were charged under s. 462.31 of the *Criminal Code* with having transferred the possession of property with the intent to conceal or convert it, knowing that it was obtained as a result of the commission of an enterprise crime offence. At trial, they were found guilty. The Court of Appeal set aside the convictions on the ground that the *actus reus* of the offence had not been made out.]

BASTARACHE J:

. . .

Legislation

462.31(1) Every one commits an offence who uses, transfers the possession of, sends or delivers to any person or place, transports, transmits, alters, disposes of or otherwise deals with, in any manner and by any means, any property or any proceeds of any property with intent to conceal or convert that property or those proceeds, knowing or believing that all or a part of that property or of those proceeds was obtained or derived directly or indirectly as a result of

(a) the commission in Canada of an enterprise crime offence or a designated substance offence; or

(b) an act or omission anywhere that, if it had occurred in Canada, would have constituted an enterprise crime offence or a designated substance offence.

462.31(1) Est coupable d'une infraction quiconque—de quelque façon que ce soit—utilise, enlève, envoie, livre à une personne ou à un endroit, transporte, modifie ou aliène des biens ou leurs produits—ou en transfère la possession—dans l'intention de les cacher ou de les convertir sachant ou croyant qu'ils ont été obtenus ou proviennent, en totalité ou en partie, directement ou indirectement :

a) soit de la perpétration, au Canada, d'une infraction de criminalité organisée ou d'une infraction désignée;

b) soit d'un acte ou d'une omission survenu à l'extérieur du Canada qui, au Canada, aurait constitué une infraction de criminalité organisée ou une infraction désignée.

. . .

(3) Was the Purchase a "Transfer of Possession" Within the Meaning of Section 462.31 Cr. C.?

[48] The following question now arises: does one "transfer the possession" of property in the context of laundering proceeds of crime if one buys the property with the intention of converting it? The Court of Appeal answered this question in the negative, and I believe its interpretation is the correct one in this case. The Court of Appeal held that s. 462.31, as drafted, does not apply to the receiver of the property (at para. 14):

> Read as a whole, *s. 462.31 appears to me to be aimed at the person who, having the control or possession of the proceeds of a crime, carries out any of the prohibited activities*—uses the proceeds, transfers their possession, transports them, alters them or disposes of them—with the prohibited knowledge and intent, to which I shall return presently. [Emphasis added.]

[49] Section 462.31 contains a list of acts that are essentially unilateral ones. The "transfer of possession" is the act of the person who has the control or possession of the object and then tries to pass it on to another. This interpretation is compatible with the ordinary meaning of the word "transfer/*transfert*," that is, [TRANSLATION] "[a]ct whereby a person transmits a right to another": *Le Nouveau Petit Robert* (2002); [TRANSLATION] "[t]ransmission of a right from one holder to another": Gérard Cornu, ed., *Vocabulaire juridique* (8th ed. 2000); "[a]ny mode of disposing of or parting with an asset or an interest in an asset": *Black's Law Dictionary* (7th ed. 1999). Although "transfer/*transfert*" necessarily implies a relationship between two persons and that a beneficiary of the transfer is an essential element of carrying it out, the offence is not aimed at the beneficiary. This is demonstrated by the text

of s. 462.31 itself, which criminalizes the act of "deliver[ing] to any person or place." This clarification highlights the fact that Parliament intended that this provision apply only to the party originally having control of the property, rather than both parties.

[50] The word "transfer" (*transfert*) must therefore be given its ordinary meaning, this despite the presence of the expression "in any manner and by any means" (*de quelque façon que ce soit*) in s. 462.31. The appellant argues that the inclusion of this expression demonstrates Parliament's intent that the terms in s. 462.31, including the word "transfer," be given a large and liberal interpretation. I cannot accept this argument. The words "in any manner and by any means" do not add to the number of activities constituting a transfer of possession. Rather, they qualify the methods by which it is possible to execute the transfer, leaving unanswered the question as to whom this provision is intended to apply. For example, within the meaning of s. 462.31, the transportation of property could include any mode of transportation, be it boat, airplane, car or any other ("in any manner and by any means"). In other words, one of the elements of the *actus reus* enumerated in s. 462.31 must be present, but the manner in which this element is carried out is unimportant. The activities criminalized by this provision all concern the same person, that is, the person who originally has the object in his or her possession and seeks to dispose of it.

[51] The appellant also argued that both versions of s. 462.31 show an unequivocal intent to encompass all positive acts committed in relation to criminally obtained property for the purpose of converting or concealing it. However, upon examining the list of prohibited acts in this provision, it would appear that all these acts are of the same nature or category and apply only to the person with control over the property. For example, the verbs "sell" (*vendre*), "give" (*donner*), "exchange" (*échanger*) and "dispose of" (*se départir*) are close in meaning to the enumerated acts. However, the word "purchase" (*achat*) has an altogether different meaning, so this Court could not interpret a series of terms as including that word when it does not share their common meaning. For this reason, buying or receiving property or similar acts involving the person who accepts or acquires the property do not constitute elements of the offence of laundering proceeds of crime. This is an application of the *noscitur a sociis* rule. According to that rule, the meaning of a term may be revealed by its association with other terms where the latter may not be read in isolation: Côté ... , at p. 313, and *Minister of Municipal Affairs of the Province of New Brunswick v. Canaport Ltd.*, [1976] 2 SCR 599, at p. 604.

[52] This interpretation is supported by a reading of s. 354 *Cr. C.*, which already prohibits the possession of criminally obtained property:

> 354(1) Every one commits an offence who has in his possession any property or thing or any proceeds of any property or thing knowing that all or part of the property or thing or of the proceeds was obtained by or derived directly or indirectly from
>> (a) the commission in Canada of an offence punishable by indictment; or
>> (b) an act or omission anywhere that, if it had occurred in Canada, would have constituted an offence punishable by indictment.

This provision is aimed specifically at persons who receive or accept property despite knowing it to be of illicit origin. It would thus be redundant to interpret the word "*transfer*" in s. 462.31 as including the act of purchasing or possessing property when another provision of the *Criminal Code* already prohibits that act. Although a statute may be redundant, the contrary is presumed: Côté … , at p. 278; *R v. Chartrand*, [1994] 2 SCR 864. It must therefore be presumed that s. 462.31 criminalizes different behaviours, since Parliament does not speak in vain: *Bell ExpressVu* … , at para. 37; *Canada (Attorney General) v. Mossop*, [1993] 1 SCR 554, at p. 617; *Quebec (Attorney General) v. Carrières Ste-Thérèse Ltée*, [1985] 1 SCR 831, at p. 838.

[53] In the present case, the evidence shows that the respondents bought the merchandise believing it to be stolen. However, in light of the foregoing, the act of purchasing this merchandise is not the equivalent of "transfers the possession of," which is the element of the offence specified in the indictment and which the Crown must prove. For this reason, it is my opinion that the respondents did not transfer the possession of the property within the meaning of s. 462.31.

[The Court dismissed the appeal.]

In *Daoust*, the court supports its understanding of "transfer" by claiming that it is the ordinary meaning of the word. It implicitly relies on the presumption in favour of ordinary meaning. To reject ordinary meaning, the court would have to establish that there were cogent grounds to believe that some other meaning was intended.

The ordinary meaning of a word or phrase is *not* its dictionary meaning, but rather the meaning that spontaneously comes to mind when the word or phrase is read in its immediate context. The immediate context consists of the other words in the sentence plus the complex store of knowledge, impressions, assumptions, and values the reader brings to the text. Given the diverse experience of readers, which gives rise to different knowledge, impressions, assumptions, and values, is it possible to suppose that ordinary meaning is the same for everyone?

To determine the ordinary meaning of language, courts rely on their own linguistic intuitions. Since personal intuition is an unsatisfactory basis for establishing matters of fact in a lawsuit, it is common for litigants and courts to appeal to dictionaries. However, notice that dictionaries can only indicate a range of the meanings a word is capable of bearing; they can never indicate what a word means in a particular context.

Bastarache J relies on both ordinary language dictionaries and *Black's Law Dictionary* to establish the ordinary meaning of "transfer." In so far as *Black's* sets out technical legal meanings, this methodology is problematic. Bastarache J does not consider whether "transfer" might have a specialized legal meaning that differs from its ordinary meaning.

Bastarache J also invokes the associated words rule and the no redundancy rule. Do you find the arguments based on these rules persuasive?

C. Purpose and Scheme Analysis

All legislation is enacted for a purpose—to achieve a particular outcome by imposing new obligations or prohibitions or creating new rights or privileges. This feature of legislation is reflected in the following rules:

- *Legislative purpose.* Interpreters must always try to determine the purposes of legislation and, in so far as the text permits, adopt an interpretation that promotes or is at
  least consistent with those purposes. Interpretations that would tend to defeat legislative purpose are considered absurd.

  The vaguer the language of the legislative text, the more discretion is conferred on
  the tribunal or court that applies it, and the greater is the importance of purpose in
  adopting an appropriate interpretation.
- *Interpretation acts.* The *Interpretation Act* of every Canadian jurisdiction includes a provision that directs interpreters to give every enactment "such fair, large and liberal
  construction and interpretation as best ensures the attainment of its objects." In other
  words, an interpretation that promotes the purpose of legislation is to be preferred over
  strict construction. Notice, however, that when legislation has been drafted in an overly
  broad fashion, a narrow interpretation will be one that best ensures the attainment of
  its objects.
- *Legislative scheme.* The provisions of an act are presumed to work together as parts of
  a coherent scheme designed to implement the legislature's goals. It is often helpful to
  look at the titles, headings, and subheadings and at the sequence of marginal or sec-
  tional notes to get an indication of the scheme.

  To determine how a particular provision contributes to the scheme, ask yourself why
  the provision was included—what does it add to the other provisions, how does it
  qualify or limit them, what was the underlying rationale? Knowing how a provision
  contributes to a scheme generally is a good indicator of how it should be interpreted.

R v. Chartrand
[1994] 2 SCR 864

[The accused, aged 43, invited a child to accompany him in his car so that he could take
photographs of him. The child agreed. They drove approximately 3 kilometres, stopping
occasionally to take pictures. The child's father found the accused and the child at one of the
spots where they stopped. The accused claimed that he was taking pictures of the child as a
surprise for the child's parents. The accused was charged with abduction of a person under
14 years of age (s. 281 of the *Criminal Code*).

Section 281 of the Code reads as follows:

> 281. Every one who, not being the parent, guardian or person having the lawful care or
> charge of a person under the age of fourteen years, unlawfully takes, entices away, conceals,
> detains, receives or harbours that person with intent to deprive a parent or guardian, or any
> other person who has the lawful care or charge of that person, of the possession of that person
> is guilty of an indictable offence and liable to imprisonment for a term not exceeding ten years.

> 281. Quiconque, n'étant pas le père, la mère, le tuteur ou une personne ayant la garde ou la
> charge légale d'une personne âgée de moins de quatorze ans, enlève, entraîne, retient, reçoit,
> cache ou héberge cette personne avec l'intention de priver de la possession de celle-ci le père,
> la mère, le tuteur ou une autre personne ayant la garde ou la charge légale de cette personne est
> coupable d'un acte criminel et passible d'un emprisonnement maximal de dix ans.

The issues before the Court were the meaning of the word "unlawfully" in s. 281, and the significance of the fact that the word "unlawfully" appears in the English version of s. 281 but the French equivalent "illégalement" does not appear in the French version.]

L'HEUREUX-DUBÉ J (for the Court): ... I propose to deal with that issue by looking at the legislative history of the section, its purpose and context as well as the wording of the statute and the interpretation given by the jurisprudence to the word "unlawfully." I conclude that, in light of the history and purpose of the 1982 amendments and the context in which they were enacted, the word "unlawfully" as it is used in s. 281 does not require the commission of an additional unlawful act. Rather, it represents verbal surplusage that enunciates no more than the general defences, justifications, and excuses already available under the Code.

[L'Heureux-Dubé J began by reviewing the historical evolution of the abduction provisions currently found in the *Criminal Code*. She noted that the offence of abduction was first introduced into the Code of 1892, which made it an offence for anyone to unlawfully entice away or detain or harbour a child. However, a separate subsection provided that lawful possession by a parent or other person was a defence.

In 1982 the abduction provisions were amended to distinguish between abduction by parents and by strangers. In the amended provisions the word "unlawfully" did not appear in the offence of abduction by parents; it was retained in the offence of abduction by strangers in the English version but deleted in the French version. The subsection creating a defence of lawful possession disappeared altogether.

L'Heureux-Dubé J found that the words "unlawfully"/"illégalement" were excluded from the offence of abduction by parents because Parliament wanted to prohibit the practice of a parent taking away his or her own children without the knowledge and consent of the other parent. Since parents legally have possession of their children, such abductions would not be "unlawful" unless the children were taken in violation of a court order. Therefore, it was necessary to delete the requirement of "unlawful."

However, the reason for excluding "illégalement" from the offence of abduction by strangers in the French version while leaving the word "unlawfully" in the English version was not clear. In an effort to clarify Parliament's intention, L'Heureux-Dubé J turned to the purpose of the provision.]

(2) Purpose and Context

In this examination of the purpose of s. 281, it is necessary to look at the whole scheme designed by Parliament to deal with such related offences as kidnapping, hostage taking and abduction, more precisely, ss. 279 to 286 of the Code. Those sections deal with the whole range of related offences. Sections 279 and 279.1 deal respectively with kidnapping and hostage taking of a person. Section 280 deals with abduction of a person under sixteen, and ss. 281 to 283 deal with abduction of a person under fourteen. In the first two offences, pursuant to ss. 279 and 279.1, the consent to the guilty act of the person abducted could be a defence while in the other four offences, pursuant to s. 286, the consent of the young person is not a defence. More particularly, pursuant to s. 284, in the offences defined by ss. 281 to 283, only the consent of the parents (guardians, etc.) of the child may be a defence. Thus, in ss. 279 and 279.1, the focus is on the person abducted while, in ss. 281 to 283, the focus is on the parents (guardians, etc.) since only their consent, and not that of the taken child, could constitute a defence. Therefore, it would appear that ss. 279 and 279.1 are offences against the person abducted, while ss. 281 to 283 are mainly offences against the rights of the parents (guardians, etc.) of the abducted child.

The wording of ss. 281 to 283 leads us to a similar conclusion. All three sections specify that the taking must be with intent to deprive the parent, guardian or person who has the lawful care or charge of the child. This conclusion was also reached in *Re Bigelow and The Queen* (1982), 69 CCC (2d) 204 (Ont. CA), at p. 213, leave to appeal to the Supreme Court of Canada refused, [1982] 2 SCR v, in which a father was accused of detaining his child contrary to s. 250 (now s. 281):

> The gravamen of the offence under s. 250(1) is interference with the custodial rights of the mother by intentionally depriving her of those rights by "detaining" the child … . Although s. 250 is placed in Part VI of the Criminal Code under the heading of "Offences Against the Person and Reputation" *it is not an offence against the person of the child. … In reality it is an offence against the custodial rights of the mother.* [Emphasis added.]

Seen in that context, the purpose of s. 281 is to secure the right and ability of parents (guardians, etc.) to exercise control over their children (those children for whom they act as guardians, etc.) for the protection of those children, and at the same time to prevent the risk of harm to children by diminishing their vulnerability. It is also a recognition by Parliament that children are best protected by the supervision of their parents (guardians, etc.).

That purpose is still more apparent from the social context in which those amendments were adopted and the mischief they were intended to cure. Concerns were voiced at the time by numerous groups as to the security of children in Canada and the fact that the offence of abduction in s. 250, as it was prior to the 1982 amendments, did not adequately protect against parental abduction. (See *Minutes of Proceedings and Evidence* of the Standing Committee on Justice and Legal Affairs of June 3, 1982, at p. 93:31; brief from Abducted Children's Rights of Canada on "Child Abduction" appended to the Minutes of June 3, 1982, at p. 93A:1; comments at p. 78:9 of the Minutes of April 27, 1982; J.-L. Baudouin, "L'enlevement et la non-representation d'enfants a la lumiere du nouveau droit civil quebecois, du droit federal et du droit international" (1982-1983), 17 RJT 151; *R v. Cook* … , at p. 479; and *Ewaschuk* … , at p. 195.) To alleviate the confusion which arose under that section, and to render the law more effective regarding the abduction of children, Parliament found it more appropriate to distinguish between parental and stranger abductions and to adopt different rules for each type of abduction. (See *House of Commons Debates*, vol. X, 1st Sess., 32nd Parl., July 7-8, 1981, at pp. 11300, 11344 and 11348; and *House of Commons Debates*, vol. XIII, 1st Sess., 32nd Parl., December 17, 1981, at p. 14187.)

The broad aim of criminal law is to prevent harm to society (W.R. LaFave and A.W. Scott, *Criminal Law* (2nd ed. 1986), at p. 10; A.W. Mewett and M. Manning, *Criminal Law* (2nd ed. 1985), at p. 14). Since the wording of the section does not suggest otherwise, s. 281 must be interpreted in a manner which conforms with this aim, here the prevention of harm to, and protection of, children. A glance at the social context in which this legislation must be interpreted sets the stage for our purposive and contextual approach to s. 281 of the Code.

Each year, in Canada, hundreds of children are abducted by strangers from playgrounds, parks, school yards and streets:

> In 1989, 1,003 abductions were reported to the police. These incidents were equally likely to involve abduction of a person under 14 years of age by a person who is not a guardian (36%) and abduction by a parent or guardian in contravention of a custody order (36%).

(*Juristat* from Statistics Canada, vol. 10, No. 15 (October 1990), at p. 7.)

The number of children abducted by strangers is reported to be 61 in 1993 (Royal Canadian Mounted Police, *1993 Annual Report on Canada's Missing Children*). That figure may understate the magnitude of the problem of child abduction since children who have been abducted by strangers will generally be listed in the "unknown" category until a witness has informed the authorities that he or she has actually seen the child being taken by an individual. In this "unknown" category, by contrast, there were 9,959 cases reported in 1993. Although many first time runaways are no doubt counted in this category, a fair number of such children may have been children abducted by strangers. Regardless of the precise statistics, the abduction of children by strangers is a sad reality and a great concern to society: one is too many. (See also, R.J. McDonald, "Missing Children," in *Canadian Social Trends*, No. 24 (Spring 1992), at pp. 2-5.)

That the legislation was designed to curb such social ill cannot be doubted. The purpose of s. 281—to protect children from abduction—reflects a societal interest in the security of children in that it both prevents and deters the abduction of children by strangers. This accords with public policy. Viewed in the light of its purpose and context, such legislation has a broad scope and the restrictive interpretation of s. 281 of the Code proposed by the respondent does not seem to be particularly attractive.

Important as they are, however, the legislative history, the purpose and the context of s. 281 of the Code are, in the end, tributary to the wording of the statute and the case law which has interpreted that section, a matter I will now turn to.

(3) The Wording of the Statute and the Interpretation Given by Jurisprudence to the Word "Unlawfully"

What does an "unlawful" taking mean in s. 281 of the Code? The *Dictionary of Canadian Law* (1991), at pp. 1120-21, referring to *Archbold Pleading, Evidence and Practice in Criminal Cases* (43rd ed. 1988), at p. 1342, defines the word "unlawfully" as "[w]ithout a lawful reason or excuse." *Black's Law Dictionary* (6th ed. 1990), at p. 1536, referring to *State v. Noble*, 563 P.2d 1153 (NM 1977), at p. 1157, equates the term "unlawful" with the expression "without excuse or justification." That interpretation has been retained in a number of cases. (See, for instance, *R v. Wasyl Kapij* (1905), 1 WLR 130, at p. 136, interpreting the word "unlawfully" in the context of the offence of unlawfully obstructing or preventing a clergyman from celebrating a divine service.)

In cases dealing more specifically with parental abduction under s. 250, as it read before the 1982 amendments, "unlawfully" has been equated with, amongst other things, "without lawful authority" in the sense of absence of parental authority over the child or "without lawful justification, authority or excuse." (See: Ewaschuk … , at p. 179; Johnstone … , at

p. 273; *R v. Van Herk* ... , at p. 363; *R v. Enkirch* (1982), 1 CCC (3d) 165 (Alta. CA); *R v. Cook* ... , at p. 475; *R v. Horsford* ... , at p. 480; *R v. Kosowan* ... ; and *R v. Falvo* ... .)

It is appropriate to interpret the expression "unlawfully" as meaning "without lawful justification, authority or excuse," as that term is used in s. 281 of the *Criminal Code*; this interpretation is in accord with the purpose of the section which is to prevent and punish strangers intending to deprive a parent (guardian, etc.) of his or her child (the child for whom they act as guardian, etc.). To require that an additional unlawful act occur beyond the physical act of taking the child is at cross-purposes with the mischief Parliament wanted to cure; such an interpretation would not adequately achieve the goal of prevention, and the rights of the parents could not be vindicated. This is especially true given the fact that when a stranger abducts a child, he or she often just "takes" the child in a non-violent manner. At the same time, this interpretation accords with the protection of those persons who innocently take a child out of the control of a parent (guardian, etc.), and who may well be able to provide justification for their conduct. Surely, the aim and purpose of the section cannot be to convict people who have a lawful justification for taking children such as an honourable purpose by a good samaritan.

. . .

In the case of s. 281, given its legislative history, its purpose, the context in which it was enacted and, most particularly, the absence of the word "unlawfully" (*illégalement*) in the French text of s. 281, it is my view that the word "unlawfully" in the English text of s. 281 was carried over from the 1892 legislation under less "modern drafting styles" and the word is "surplusage, merely indicating the existence of general defences in crime." Retaining that word in the English text was a mere oversight and the French text reflects the true intent of Parliament when, in 1982, it redrafted s. 250 (now s. 281) to apply only to abduction by strangers. The fact that the word "unlawfully" does not appear in s. 250.1 (now s. 282) and 250.2 (now s. 283) provides further support for this conclusion.

As a consequence, there was no necessity for the Crown to prove an additional unlawful act or some element of unlawfulness beyond the taking of a child by a person who did not have lawful authority over that child. The trial judge was in error in so interpreting s. 281 of the Code.

Notice the several ways in which L'Heureux-Dubé J determines the purpose of s. 281. First she analyzes the similarities and differences among the several provisions dealing with abduction and infers the rationale for each provision. Next she considers the social context in which the legislation was amended and the mischief it was meant to cure. She also relies on legislative history, law review articles, case law, and government publications. Finally, she refers to the purpose of criminal law generally, citing as authority a number of standard texts.

Notice also that L'Heureux-Dubé J relies on both a disputed word argument ("unlawfully" in s. 281 means without lawful excuse) and a corrigible mistake argument (retaining "unlawfully" in the English text was a mere oversight—a mistake). Why was it appropriate to bring the French and English versions in line by eliminating "unlawfully" from the English version rather than adding "illégalement" to the French version?

D. Mistakes and Gaps in the Legislative Scheme

- *Corrigible mistakes.* Although the legislature is presumed not to make mistakes, the presumption is rebutted by persuasive evidence that the text does not accurately reflect the rule the legislature intended to enact. The courts have jurisdiction to correct such mistakes, unless the mistake amounts to a gap in the legislative scheme.
- *Incorrigible gaps.* The courts almost always deny jurisdiction to cure a gap in a legislative scheme or to otherwise cure underinclusive provisions by making them apply to facts outside the ambit of the language of the text. Curing an underinclusive scheme or provision amounts to "reading in," which is generally considered a form of judicial legislation, as opposed to "reading down," which is not.
- *Supplementing legislation by reliance on common law (or the Civil Code).* Although the courts cannot cure underinclusive legislation by expanding its scope beyond what the text allows, it can rely on supplemental sources of law to complement what the legislative scheme provides. In doing so, it must often address the difficult question of the relationship between statute law and the common law.

E. Presumptions of Legislative Intent

The presumptions of legislative intent are formal expressions of evolving common law norms. One of the recurring issues in statutory interpretation is whether the courts should apply the same rules and techniques to all legislation, regardless of its subject matter or purpose. Historically, the courts have distinguished between legislation that takes away the freedom or property of an individual or otherwise interferes with his or her rights on the one hand, and legislation designed to cure mischief, advance religion, or otherwise confer benefits on the other. Legislation that interferes with individual rights or freedoms is considered "penal" and attracts a "strict" construction. Legislation that cures mischief or confers benefits is considered "remedial" and attracts a "liberal" construction.

When legislation is strictly construed, the emphasis is on the wording of the text: general terms are read down, conditions of application are fully enforced, and ambiguities are resolved in favour of non-application. When legislation is liberally construed, the focus is on achieving the benevolent purpose of the legislation: general principles are applied as fully as their wording permits, while exceptions and qualifications are strictly interpreted. If doubts or ambiguities arise, they are resolved in favour of the person seeking the benefit of the statute.

Provisions like s. 12 of the federal *Interpretation Act* were clearly enacted to eliminate the distinction between penal and remedial legislation by deeming all legislation to be remedial. This was an effort by legislators in the late 19th century to push back against the judicial tendency to deem all legislation to be penal. Courts today are far less likely to invoke strict construction than were courts in the past, but the distinction continues to figure in modern statutory interpretation. It is fair to say that most modern courts are prepared to adopt a

- strict construction of criminal law;
- strict construction of laws that expropriate private property;
- strict construction of exceptions to well-established legal principles;

- liberal construction of quasi-constitutional legislation such as human rights codes; and
- liberal construction of social welfare legislation.

The courts also control legislative initiatives by imputing to the legislature an intention to abide by norms that the courts consider important. These are the so-called presumptions of legislative intent.

The following list of presumptions is not exhaustive:

- presumed compliance with constitutional law and constitutional law values;
- presumed compliance with international law;
- presumed continuation of common law;
- presumed compliance with rule of law;
- presumed non-interference with common law rights;
- presumption against the extraterritorial application of legislation;
- presumption against the retroactive application of legislation;
- presumption against interference with vested rights (both common law and statutory); and
- presumption against applying legislation to the Crown and its agents.

The courts have also developed special rules to deal with special situations. For example, legislation dealing with First Nations is to be interpreted in their favour.

F. Avoiding Absurdity

It is presumed that the legislature does not intend its legislation to produce absurd consequences. Therefore, an interpretation that avoids such consequences is preferred over one that does not. The clearer and more precise a text seems to be, the greater the absurdity required to depart from its ordinary meaning. The greater the absurdity that flows from a particular interpretation, the more justified an interpreter is in rejecting it. The following are some of the forms of absurdity that the legislature is presumed to avoid:

- irrational distinctions (treating like things differently or different things the same way);
- irrational, contradictory, or anomalous effects;
- defeating the purpose of the legislation;
- undermining the efficient application of legislation; and
- violating important norms of justice or fairness.

G. Relation to Other Legislation and Other Sources of Law

- *Constitutional law.* It is presumed that legislatures intend to enact constitutionally valid law and in particular to comply with any limitations on their jurisdiction set out in the various Constitution Acts. For this reason an interpretation that renders legislation valid is preferred over one that does not. However, this presumption must not be used to defeat the clear intentions of the legislature. Legislatures sometimes do intend to restrict a Charter right or freedom in order to achieve an important goal, and they are entitled to do so if the restriction can be justified under s. 1. This possibility must not be taken away through interpretation.

- *Regulations.* Regulations must be read in light of their enabling provision and their enabling legislation as a whole. The regulations and enabling legislation are presumed to constitute an integrated scheme. Interpretation provisions in the enabling legislation (such as definitions or application provisions) are presumed to apply to regulations and other instruments made under the enabling legislation.
- *Related legislation (statutes in pari materia).* Statutes dealing with the same subject matter must be read together and are presumed to offer a coherent and consistent treatment of the subject. Sometimes such statutes form a single, integrated scheme; sometimes they create distinct but overlapping schemes. Interpretation provisions in one statute are presumed to apply to related statutes.
- *The statute book.* Even if statutes do not relate to the same subject, it is often useful to compare provisions in different enactments that deal with a particular matter—for example, limitation of action provisions or search and seizure provisions. Given that drafters are presumed to be consistent in their use of language and techniques, the similarities and differences among the provisions can form the basis for inferring legislative intent.
- *Common law.* Provincial legislation (outside Quebec) sometimes incorporates common law concepts or terms; and federal legislation sometimes incorporates common law and civil law concepts or terms. In such cases, resort to common law (or civil law) sources is appropriate to determine the meaning of the concept or term.

  Legislation may also "codify" common law rules or principles—that is, give statutory form to pre-existing common law. In these cases, too, resort to common law sources may be appropriate. However, sometimes the purpose of the legislation is to modify or displace the common law. Legislation that is intended to displace and preclude further resort to the common law is often labelled "a complete code." With respect to offences, the *Criminal Code* is a complete code, but with respect to defences it is not.
- *International law.* It is presumed that legislatures, provincial as well as federal, intend to comply with international law, both customary and conventional. This presumption operates most strongly in the case of implementing legislation—that is, legislation enacted for the purpose of making an international agreement an effective part of domestic law. However, the presumption has also been applied to help resolve ambiguities in non-implementing legislation.

H. Extrinsic Aids

Resolving interpretation issues can often be assisted by so-called extrinsic aids, including the following:

- *Legislative source.* Consists of agreements that the legislation in question is intended to implement or of legislation (whether domestic or foreign) on which the legislation has been modelled in whole or in part.
- *Legislative history.* Consists of material formally brought to the attention of the legislature during the legislative process, including ministerial statements, committee reports, recorded debates, and tabled background material.

- *Legislative evolution.* Consists of the successive amendments and re-enactments a provision has undergone from its initial enactment to the time of application; note that subsequent evolution is not considered a legitimate aid.
- *Expert opinion.* Consists of precedent, administrative opinion, and scholarly legal publications, as well as expert testimony.

The rules governing the admissibility and use of this material are complex and in a state of flux. In practice, the courts tend to accept whatever material is offered, provided it is relevant to the issue before the court and will not take the other party by surprise. However, appellate courts have not gone out of their way to establish clear principles and guidelines in this area. Courts sometimes decline to look at this material if it contradicts what appears to be the "plain meaning" of the legislative text.

III. SOME ILLUSTRATIONS

The cases set out below illustrate how the courts tackle statutory interpretation. The *McIntosh* case is lengthy and complex and requires careful reading. As you read it, try to identify the type of problem that the majority and dissent think they are facing. Also, try to identify which "rules" of statutory interpretation they rely on in their reasoning.

R v. McIntosh
[1995] 1 SCR 686

LAMER CJ:

[The accused, a disc jockey, had given the deceased, who lived in the same neighbourhood, some sound equipment to repair. Over the next eight months the accused made several attempts to retrieve his equipment, but the deceased actively avoided him. On the day of the killing, the accused's girlfriend saw the deceased working outside and informed the accused. The accused obtained a kitchen knife and approached the deceased. Words were exchanged. According to the accused, the deceased pushed him, and a struggle ensued. Then the deceased picked up a dolly, raised it to head level, and came at the accused. The accused reacted by stabbing the deceased with the kitchen knife. At his trial on a charge of second degree murder, the accused took the position that the stabbing of the deceased was an act of self-defence.]

. . .

II. *Relevant Statutory Provisions*

Criminal Code, RSC 1985, c. C-46
Defence of Person
self-defence against unprovoked assault
   34(1) *Every one who is unlawfully assaulted without having provoked the assault is justified in repelling force by force if* the force he uses is not intended to cause death or grievous bodily harm and is no more than is necessary to enable him to defend himself. [Emphasis added.]

extent of justification

(2) *Every one who is unlawfully assaulted and who causes death or grievous bodily harm in repelling the assault is justified if*

(a) he causes it under reasonable apprehension of death or grievous bodily harm from the violence with which the assault was originally made or with which the assailant pursues his purposes; and

(b) he believes, on reasonable grounds, that he cannot otherwise preserve himself from death or grievous bodily harm. [Emphasis added.]

self-defence in case of aggression

35. *Every one who* has without justification assaulted another but did not commence the assault with intent to cause death or grievous bodily harm, or *has without justification provoked an assault on himself by another, may justify the use of force subsequent to the assault if*

(a) he uses the force

(i) under reasonable apprehension of death or grievous bodily harm from the violence of the person whom he has assaulted or provoked, and

(ii) in the belief, on reasonable grounds, that it is necessary in order to preserve himself from death or grievous bodily harm;

(b) he did not, at any time before the necessity of preserving himself from death or grievous bodily harm arose, endeavour to cause death or grievous bodily harm; *and*

(c) *he declined further conflict and quitted or retreated from it as far as it was feasible to do so* before the necessity of preserving himself from death or grievous bodily harm arose. [Emphasis added.]

provocation

36. Provocation includes, for the purposes of sections 34 and 35, provocation by blows, words or gestures.

preventing assault

37(1) Every one is justified in using force to defend himself or any one under his protection from assault, if he uses no more force than is necessary to prevent the assault or the repetition of it.

extent of justification

(2) Nothing in this section shall be deemed to justify the wilful infliction of any hurt or mischief that is excessive, having regard to the nature of the assault that the force used was intended to prevent.

IV. *Analysis*

A. *Introduction*

[14] This case raises a question of pure statutory interpretation: Is the self-defence justification in s. 34(2) of the *Criminal Code* available where an accused is an initial aggressor, having provoked the assault against which he claims to have defended himself? The trial judge, Moldaver J, construed s. 34(2) as not applying in such a circumstance. The Ontario Court of Appeal disagreed.

[15] The conflict between ss. 34 and 35 is obvious on the face of the provisions. Section 34(1) begins with the statement, "Every one who is unlawfully assaulted without having provoked the assault … ." In contrast, s. 34(2) begins, "Every one who is unlawfully assaulted … ." Missing from s. 34(2) is any reference to the condition, "without having provoked the assault." The fact that there is no non-provocation requirement in s. 34(2) becomes important when one refers to s. 35, which explicitly applies where an accused has "without justification provoked an assault … ." Therefore, both ss. 34(2) and 35 appear to be available to initial aggressors. Hence, the issue arises in this case of whether the respondent, as an initial aggressor raising self-defence, may avail himself of s. 34(2), or should be required instead to meet the more onerous conditions of s. 35.

[16] As a preliminary comment, I would observe that ss. 34 and 35 of the *Criminal Code* are highly technical, excessively detailed provisions deserving of much criticism. These provisions overlap, and are internally inconsistent in certain respects. Moreover, their relationship to s. 37 (as discussed below) is unclear. It is to be expected that trial judges may encounter difficulties in explaining the provisions to a jury, and that jurors may find them confusing. The case at bar demonstrates this. During counsel's objections to his charge on ss. 34 and 35, the trial judge commented, "Well, it seems to me these sections of the Criminal Code are unbelievably confusing." I agree with this observation.

[17] Despite the best efforts of counsel in the case at bar to reconcile ss. 34 and 35 in a coherent manner, I am of the view that any interpretation which attempts to make sense of the provisions will have some undesirable or illogical results. It is clear that legislative action is required to clarify the *Criminal Code*'s self-defence regime.

B. Did the Trial Judge Err in Charging the Jury That Section 34(2) of the Criminal Code Is Not Available to an Initial Aggressor?

(i) Section 34(2) Is Not Ambiguous

[18] In resolving the interpretive issue raised by the Crown, I take as my starting point the proposition that where no ambiguity arises on the face of a statutory provision, then its clear words should be given effect. … Where the language of the statute is plain and admits of only one meaning, the task of interpretation does not arise (*Maxwell on the Interpretation of Statutes* (12th ed. 1969), at p. 29).

[19] While s. 34(1) includes the statement "without having provoked the assault," s. 34(2) does not. Section 34(2) is clear, and I fail to see how anyone could conclude that it is, on its face, ambiguous in any way. Therefore, taking s. 34(2) in isolation, it is clearly available to an initial aggressor.

[20] The Crown has asked this Court to read into s. 34(2) the words "without having provoked the assault." The Crown submits that by taking into consideration the common law of self-defence, legislative history, related *Criminal Code* provisions, margin notes, and public policy, it becomes clear that Parliament could not have intended s. 34(2) to be available to initial aggressors. Parliament's failure to include the words "without having provoked the assault" in s. 34(2) was an oversight, which the Crown is asking this Court to correct.

· · ·

[23] The Crown argues that it was Parliament's intention that neither s. 34(1) nor s. 34(2) be available to initial aggressors, and that it was a mere oversight that the words

chosen in s. 34(2) do not give effect to this intention. I would have thought it would be equally persuasive to argue that Parliament intended both ss. 34(1) and (2) to be available to initial aggressors, and that Parliament's mistake was in *including* the words "without having provoked the assault" in s. 34(1).

[24] Parliament's intention becomes even more cloudy when one refers to s. 45 of the 1892 *Criminal Code*, SC 1892, c. 29, which was the forerunner of ss. 34(1) and 34(2):

> 45. Every one unlawfully assaulted, not having provoked such assault, is justified in repelling force by force, if the force he uses is not meant to cause death or grievous bodily harm, and is no more than is necessary for the purpose of self-defence; *and every one so assaulted* is justified, though he causes death or grievous bodily harm, if he causes it under reasonable apprehension of death or grievous bodily harm from the violence with which the assault was originally made or with which the assailant pursues his purpose, and if he believes, on reasonable grounds, that he cannot otherwise preserve himself from death or grievous bodily harm. [Emphasis added.]

There is a clear ambiguity in this provision. Does the expression "every one so assaulted" refer to "[e]very one unlawfully assaulted," or to "[e]very one unlawfully assaulted, not having provoked such assault"? This question is academic, since Parliament appears to have resolved the ambiguity in its 1955 revision of the *Criminal Code*, SC 1953-54, c. 51. The first part of the former s. 45 was renumbered s. 34(1), and the second part became s. 34(2). The new s. 34(2) omitted any reference to a non-provocation requirement.

[25] If Parliament's intention is to be implied from its legislative actions, then there is a compelling argument that Parliament intended s. 34(2) to be available to initial aggressors. When Parliament revised the *Criminal Code* in 1955, it could have included a provocation requirement in s. 34(2). The result would then be similar to s. 48(2) of the New Zealand *Crimes Act 1961*, SNZ 1961, No. 43 (repealed and substituted 1980, No. 63, s. 2) which was virtually identical to s. 34(2) save that it included an express non-provocation requirement:

> 48. ...
> (2) Every one unlawfully assaulted, *not having provoked the assault*, is justified in repelling force by force although in so doing he causes death or grievous bodily harm, if ... . [Emphasis added.]

The fact that Parliament did not choose this route is the best and only evidence we have of legislative intention, and this evidence certainly does not support the Crown's position.

[26] ... The Crown is asking this Court to read words into s. 34(2) which are simply not there. In my view, to do so would be tantamount to *amending* s. 34(2), which is a legislative and not a judicial function. The contextual approach provides no basis for the courts to engage in legislative amendment.

· · ·

[29] It is a principle of statutory interpretation that where two interpretations of a provision which affects the liberty of a subject are available, one of which is more favourable to an accused, then the court should adopt this favourable interpretation. By this same reasoning, where such a provision is, on its face, favourable to an accused, then I do not think that

a court should engage in the interpretive process advocated by the Crown for the sole purpose of narrowing the provision and making it less favourable to the accused. Section 34(2), on its face, is available to the respondent. It was, with respect, an error for the trial judge to narrow the provision in order to preclude the respondent from relying on it.

• • •

(ii) Even Though Section 34(2) May Give Rise to Absurd Results, the Crown's Interpretation Cannot Be Adopted

[31] It is important to reiterate that there is no ambiguity on the face of s. 34(2). The Crown's argument that the provision is ambiguous relies on legislative history, the common law, public policy, margin notes, and the relationship between ss. 34 and 35. The Crown alleges that it would be absurd to make s. 34(2) available to initial aggressors when s. 35 so clearly applies. Parliament, the Crown submits, could not have intended such an absurd result, and therefore the provision cannot mean what it says. …

• • •

[34] … I would adopt the following proposition: where, by the use of clear and unequivocal language capable of only one meaning, anything is enacted by the legislature, it must be enforced however harsh or absurd or contrary to common sense the result may be (*Maxwell on the Interpretation of Statutes*, supra, at p. 29). The fact that a provision gives rise to absurd results is not, in my opinion, sufficient to declare it ambiguous and then embark upon a broad-ranging interpretive analysis.

• • •

[38] … Under s. 19 of the *Criminal Code*, ignorance of the law is no excuse to criminal liability. Our criminal justice system presumes that everyone knows the law. Yet we can hardly sustain such a presumption if courts adopt interpretations of penal provisions which rely on the reading-in of words which do not appear on the face of the provisions. How can a citizen possibly know the law in such a circumstance?

• • •

[40] I would agree that some absurdity flows from giving effect to the terms of s. 34(2). One is struck, for example, by the fact that if s. 34(2) is available to an initial aggressor who has killed or committed grievous bodily harm, then that accused may be in a better position to raise self-defence than an initial aggressor whose assault was less serious. This is because the less serious aggressor could not take advantage of the broader defence in s. 34(2), as that provision is only available to an accused who "causes death or grievous bodily harm." Section 34(1) would not be available since it is explicitly limited to those who have not provoked an assault. Therefore, the less serious aggressor could only have recourse to s. 35, which imposes a retreat requirement. It is, in my opinion, anomalous that an accused who commits the most serious act has the broadest defence.

[41] Even though I agree with the Crown that the interpretation of s. 34(2) which makes it available to initial aggressors may be somewhat illogical in light of s. 35, and may lead to some absurdity, I do not believe that such considerations should lead this Court to narrow a statutory defence. Parliament, after all, has the right to legislate illogically (assuming that this does not raise constitutional concerns). And if Parliament is not satisfied with the judicial application of its illogical enactments, then Parliament may amend them accordingly.

[42] … Although I appreciate the efforts of the Crown to underscore the problems with the *Criminal Code*'s self-defence regime through a broad historical, academic and policy-based analysis, I suspect that very few citizens are equipped to engage in this kind of interpretive approach. Rare will be the citizen who will read ss. 34 and 35, and recognize the logical inconsistencies as between the two provisions. Rarer still will be the citizen who will read the provisions and conclude that they are inconsistent with the common law, or with Parliament's intention in 1892, or with margin notes. Given that citizens have to live with the *Criminal Code*, and with judicial interpretations of the provisions of the *Code*, I am of the view that s. 34(2) must be interpreted according to its plain terms. It is therefore available where an accused is an initial aggressor, having provoked the assault against which he claims to have defended himself.

• • •

Conclusion

[47] With respect, Moldaver J erred in instructing the jury at the respondent's trial that s. 34(2) was not available to an initial aggressor. I therefore am in agreement with the Ontario Court of Appeal. The appeal is dismissed, the respondent's conviction set aside and a new trial.

McLACHLIN J (La Forest, L'Heureux-Dubé, and Gonthier JJ concurring in dissent):

Introduction

[48] This case raises the issue of whether a person who provokes another person to assault him can rely on the defence of self-defence, notwithstanding the fact that he failed to retreat from the assault he provoked. The Chief Justice would answer this question in the affirmative. I, with respect, take a different view.

• • •

[50] It was open to the jury to find, in this scenario, that McIntosh had provoked the assault by threatening the deceased while armed with a knife. This raised the question of which of the self-defence provisions of the *Criminal Code* apply to a person who provokes the aggression that led to the killing. The answer depends on the interpretation accorded to ss. 34 and 35 of the *Criminal Code*, RSC, 1985, c. C-46, which codify self-defence in Canada. Section 35 clearly applies where the accused initiated the aggression; however, it contains a requirement that the accused have attempted to retreat, and might not have assisted McIntosh. Sections 34(1) and 34(2), on the other hand, contain no requirement to retreat. Section 34(1) clearly does not apply to the initial aggressor. The debate, in these circumstances, focused on s. 34(2). If McIntosh could avail himself of s. 34(2), he would be entitled to rely on self-defence, notwithstanding findings that he provoked the fight and did not retreat.

• • •

Analysis

1. Does Section 34(2) of the Criminal Code Apply to a Person Who Provokes an Attack?

[53] McIntosh raises one main argument. It is this. Section 34(1) states expressly that it does not apply to people who have provoked the assault from which they defended themselves. Section 34(2), by contrast, does not expressly exclude provokers. Therefore, s. 34(2) must be read as applying to people who have provoked the assault from which they defended themselves. In order to prevent s. 34(2) from applying to initial aggressors, it would be necessary to "read in" to s. 34(2) the phrase found in s. 34(1): "without having provoked the assault." On this basis, it is argued that the provisions contain no ambiguity. It is further argued that even if they did contain an ambiguity, it must be resolved in favour of the accused, following the principle that an ambiguity in penal provisions should be resolved in the manner most favourable to accused persons.

. . .

[57] At first blush the argument seems attractive that the absence of the phrase "without having provoked the assault" in s. 34(2) makes it applicable to all cases of self-defence, even those where the accused provoked the attack. Yet, a closer look at the language, history and policy of ss. 34 and 35 of the *Criminal Code* suggests that this argument should not prevail.

[58] The Chief Justice starts from the premise that "the language of the statute is plain and admits of only one meaning" (p. 697). From this he concludes that "the task of interpretation does not arise" (p. 697). I cannot agree. First, the language is not, with respect, plain. The facial ambiguity of s. 34(2) is amply attested by the different interpretations which it has been given by different courts. But even if the words were plain, the task of interpretation cannot be avoided. As *Driedger on the Construction of Statutes* (3rd ed. 1994) puts it at p. 4, "no modern court would consider it appropriate to adopt that meaning, however 'plain,' without first going through the work of interpretation."

[59] The point of departure for interpretation is not the "plain meaning" of the words, but the intention of the legislature. The classic statement of the "plain meaning" rule, in the *Sussex Peerage Case* (1844), 11 C & F 85, 8 ER 1034 (HL), at p. 1057, makes this clear: "the only rule for the construction of Acts of Parliament is, that they should be construed according to the intent of the Parliament which passed the Act." To quote *Driedger, supra*, at p. 3: "The purpose of the legislation must be taken into account, even where the meaning appears to be clear, and so must the consequences." As Lamer CJ put it in *R v. Z. (D.A.)*, [1992] 2 SCR 1025, at p. 1042: "the express words used by Parliament must be interpreted not only in their ordinary sense but also in the context of the scheme and purpose of the legislation." The plain meaning of the words, if such exists, is a secondary interpretative principle aimed at discerning the intention of the legislator. If the words admit of only one meaning, they may indeed "best declare the intention of the lawgiver" as suggested in the *Sussex Peerage Case* at p. 1057, but even here it is the intention, and not the "plain meaning," which is conclusive. But if, as in the case of s. 34(2), the words permit of doubt as to the intention of Parliament, other matters must be looked to to determine that intention.

[60] I also depart from the Chief Justice on his application of the proposition that "where two interpretations of a provision which affects the liberty of a subject are available,

one of which is more favourable to an accused, then the court should adopt this favourable interpretation" (p. 702). This Court in *Marcotte v. Deputy Attorney General for Canada*, [1976] 1 SCR 108, at p. 115, made it clear that this rule of construction applies only where "real ambiguities are found, or doubts of substance arise" (*per* Dickson J (as he then was)). If the intention of Parliament can be ascertained with reasonable precision, the rule has no place. As La Forest J put it in *R v. Deruelle*, [1992] 2 SCR 663, at pp. 676-77:

> In the court below, the majority suggested that any ambiguity in a penal provision should be resolved in favour of the accused. ... While it is true that s. 254(3) is not a model of clarity, in this instance the intent of Parliament is sufficiently clear that there is no need for the aid of that canon of statutory construction.

[61] In summary, then, I take the view that this Court cannot evade the task of interpreting s. 34(2). The Court's task is to determine the intention of Parliament. The words of the section, taken alone, do not provide a clear and conclusive indication of Parliament's intention. It is therefore necessary to look further to determine Parliament's intention to the history of the section and the practical problems and absurdities which may result from interpreting the section one way or the other. These considerations lead, in my respectful view, to the inescapable conclusion that Parliament intended s. 34(2) to apply only to unprovoked assaults. This in turn leads to the conclusion that the trial judge was correct in declining to leave s. 34(2) with the jury.

The History of Section 34(2)

[62] Self-defence at common law rested on a fundamental distinction between cases where no fault was attributable to the killer, and cases where the killing was partly induced by some fault of the killer. Where the killer was not at fault—that is where he had not provoked the aggression—the homicide was called "justifiable homicide." Where blame could be laid on the killer, as where he had provoked the aggression, on the other hand, the homicide was called "excusable homicide." (See E.H. East, *A Treatise of the Pleas of the Crown* (1803), vol. 1; William Blackstone, *Commentaries on the Laws of England* (1769), Book IV.)

[63] Justifiable homicide and excusable homicide attracted different duties. In the case of justifiable homicide, or homicide in defending an unprovoked attack, the killer could stand his ground and was not obliged to retreat in order to rely on the defence of self-defence. In the case of excusable homicide, on the other hand, the killer must have retreated as far as possible in attempting to escape the threat which necessitated homicide, before he could claim self-defence. In other words, unprovoked attacks imposed no duty to retreat. Provoked attacks did impose a duty to retreat.

[64] The two situations recognized at common law—justifiable homicide and excusable homicide—were codified in the first Canadian *Criminal Code* in 1892, SC 1892, c. 29, in ss. 45 and 46. Section 45 when enacted in 1892 differed from its modern equivalent, s. 34, in that it was not divided into two subsections. Rather, it consisted of two parts divided by a semicolon. The wording too was slightly different. Its wording indicated that the phrase at the heart of this appeal—"not having provoked the assault"—was applicable to both halves of the section. Section 45 read:

Self-defence against unprovoked assault

45. Every one unlawfully assaulted, not having provoked such assault, is justified in repelling force by force, if the force he uses is not meant to cause death or grievous bodily harm, and is no more than is necessary for the purpose of self-defence; and every one so assaulted is justified, though he causes death or grievous bodily harm, if he causes it under reasonable apprehension of death or grievous bodily harm from the violence with which the assault was originally made or with which the assailant pursues his purpose, and if he believes, on reasonable grounds, that he cannot otherwise preserve himself from death or grievous bodily harm.

[65] The 1892 *Code* was clear and conformed to the common law on which it was based. An accused who had not provoked the assault was a person "unlawfully assaulted." He was entitled to stand his ground and need not retreat. An accused who had provoked the assault, on the other hand, was covered by s. 46 and could not claim to have acted in self-defence unless he retreated.

[66] In 1906 the *Criminal Code* underwent a general revision. One of the policies of the revision was to divide longer provisions into subsections. In accordance with this policy, s. 45 became s. 53(1) and (2). The wording, however, remained identical. The marginal note to s. 53(1) read "Self defence. Assault.," and the marginal note to s. 53(2) read "Extent justified." In 1927, while the section remained identical in wording and numbering, the marginal note to s. 53(1) reverted to "Self-defence against unprovoked assault."

[67] In 1955, in the course of another general revision, SC 1953-54, c. 51, s. 53 became s. 34. The words "Every one so assaulted is justified, though he causes" in the second subsection were removed, and the words "Every one who is unlawfully assaulted and who causes" were substituted. The second subsection was further divided into two paragraphs, but all else remained the same. Section 35, like the former s. 46, dealt with provoked assault. As might be expected, s. 34 imposed no requirement of retreat; s. 35 did. Thus the common law distinction between justifiable homicide and excusable homicide was carried forward.

[68] One incongruity, however, emerged with the 1955 revision. The phrase "so assaulted" in the second part of the old s. 45 had clearly referred back to the phrase in the first part "unlawfully assaulted, not having provoked such assault." In 1955, however, when "Every one so assaulted" was replaced in the severed subsection by "Every one who is unlawfully assaulted," the clear reference back that had been present in the older versions became less clear. The phrase "not having provoked such assault," which in the old s. 45 had modified or explained the term "unlawfully assaulted" in both the first and second part of the section, was thus effectively deleted from s. 34(2).

[69] History provides no explanation for why the explanatory phrase was omitted from s. 34(2). Certainly there is no suggestion that Parliament was attempting to change the law of self-defence. The more likely explanation, given the history of the changes, is inadvertence. In the process of breaking the old s. 45 into two subsections and later substituting new words for the old connector "so assaulted," and in the context of the significant task of a general revision of the entire *Code*, the need to insert the modifying phrase "not having provoked such assault" in the newly worded subsection was overlooked.

[70] The marginal notes accompanying ss. 34 and 35 support the view that the omission of the phrase "without having provoked the assault" in the 1955 *Code* was inadvertent and that Parliament continued to intend that s. 34 would apply to unprovoked assaults and s. 35

to provoked assaults. The note for s. 34 is "Self-defence against unprovoked assault/Extent of justification," for s. 35 "Self-defence in case of aggression," namely assault or provocation. While marginal notes are not part of the legislative act of Parliament, and hence are not conclusive support in interpretation, I agree with the view of Wilson J in *R v. Wigglesworth*, [1987] 2 SCR 541, at pp. 556-58, that they may be of some limited use in gleaning the intention of the enactment. Inasmuch as they do indicate an intention, they clearly support the interpretation suggested by the above discussion.

[71] Parliament's retention of the phrase "unlawfully assaulted" in both s. 34(1) and s. 34(2) provides yet further confirmation of the view that Parliament did not intend to remove the long-standing distinction between provoked and unprovoked assault. The meaning of that phrase, in the context of the two sections, is indicated by its conjunction with the phrase "not having provoked such assault" which modified "unlawfully assaulted" in the 1892 codification. This phrase in the 1892 codification suggests that "unlawfully assaulted" in the context of that section meant "not having provoked such assault." There is no reason to suppose that the meaning of the phrase "unlawfully assaulted" changed in the intervening years. If so, then on its plain wording s. 34(2) applies only to an unprovoked assault, even in the absence of the phrase "without having provoked the assault."

[72] Parliament's intention to retain the long-standing distinction between provoked and unprovoked assault in the context of self-defence is also confirmed by the fact that neither s. 34(1) nor s. 34(2) imposes a duty to retreat, indicating that these provisions deal with the common law category of justifiable homicide, contrasted with the excusable homicide of s. 35.

[73] Taking all this into account, can it be said that Parliament intended to change the meaning of s. 34(2) in the 1955 codification, thus abrogating sixty years of statutory criminal law, based on hundreds of years of the common law? I suggest not. To effect such a significant change, Parliament would have made its intention clear. This it did not do. If the word "unlawful" is given its proper meaning, it is unnecessary to read anything into the section to conclude that it does not apply to provoked assaults. Alternatively, if it were necessary to read in the phrase "without having provoked the assault," this would be justified. *Driedger*, at p. 106, states that a court will be justified in making minor amendments or substituting one phrase for another where a drafting error is evidenced by the fact that the provision leads to a result that cannot have been intended. Redrafting a provision, it suggests at p. 108, is acceptable where the following three factors are present: (1) a manifest absurdity; (2) a traceable error; and (3) an obvious correction. All three conditions are filled in the case at bar. In a similar vein, Pierre-André Côté, *The Interpretation of Legislation in Canada* (2nd ed. 1991), suggests that words may be read in to "express what is already implied by the statute" (p. 232). This condition too is met in the case of s. 34(2).

[74] The argument that Parliament intended to effect a change to the law of self-defence in 1955 rests finally on the presumption that a change in wording is intended to effect substantive change. But this presumption is weak and easily rebutted in Canada, where making formal improvements to the statute book is a minor industry. This is particularly the case where, as in this case, there is evidence of a drafting error: *Driedger*, at pp. 450-51.

[75] I conclude that the intention of Parliament is clear and that s. 34(2), read in its historical context, applies only to unprovoked assaults.

• • •

Policy Considerations

[79] The interpretation of ss. 34 and 35 which I have suggested is supported by policy considerations. The Crown argues that it would be absurd to make s. 34(2) available to aggressors when s. 35 so clearly applies. Parliament, it argues, could not have intended such a result. More practically, as the Chief Justice notes, the sections read as McIntosh urges may lead to absurd results. If s. 34(2) is available to an initial aggressor who has killed or committed grievous bodily harm, then that accused may be in a better position to raise self-defence than an initial aggressor whose assault was less serious; since s. 34(2) is only available to an aggressor who "causes death or grievous bodily harm," the less serious aggressor would not fall under its ambit. The less serious aggressor, forced to rely on s. 35, would have no defence in the absence of retreat. It is anomalous, to use the Chief Justice's word, that an accused whose conduct is the more serious has the broader defence.

. . .

[81] While I agree with the Chief Justice that Parliament can legislate illogically if it so desires, I believe that the courts should not quickly make the assumption that it intends to do so. Absent a clear indication to the contrary, the courts must impute a rational intent to Parliament. …

[82] Not only is the result McIntosh argues for anomalous; to my mind it is unwise and unjust. … The obligation to retreat from provoked assault has stood the test of time. It should not lightly be discarded. Life is precious; the justification for taking it must be defined with care and circumspection.

Conclusion on Section 34(2)

[83] In summary, the history, the wording and the policy underlying s. 34(2) all point to one conclusion: Parliament did not intend it to apply to provoked assault. It follows that the trial judge did not err in limiting s. 34(2) in this way in his instructions to the jury.

. . .

I would allow the appeal and restore the conviction.

Lamer CJ sees the interpretation problem arising in *McIntosh* as one of disputed meaning, while McLachlin J sees it as a corrigible mistake. Are there other possibilities? For example, might the issue be characterized as a conflict between overlapping provisions?

Given that Lamer CJ agrees with the trial judge's comment that these provisions are "unbelievably confusing," is it cogent to claim they are "plain"? What rule of interpretation does he implicitly rely on in concluding that s. 34(2) is plain? On his interpretation, what meaning should be given to the word "unlawfully" in ss. 34(1) and (2)?

Do you share Lamer CJ's concern that potential defendants who read ss. 34 and 35 would be unfairly taken by surprise if the court were to limit s. 34(2) to defendants who did not provoke the assault?

Do you agree with McLachlin J that the words "without having provoked the assault" are missing from s. 34(1) because a mistake was made in the course of a statute revision? Assuming that such a mistake was made, is it appropriate for the court to "correct" it by changing the wording of the text?

Do you agree with McLachlin J that "unlawfully" in ss. 34(1) and (2) means "without having provoked the assault"? Arguably, this is inconsistent with the no redundancy rule. But drafting in the 19th century tended to be more detailed and redundant than modern drafting. Should the courts take this sort of consideration into account when interpreting legislation?

The majority and dissenting judgments in *McIntosh* illustrate the clash between the textualist and intentionalist approaches to interpretation. Lamer CJ insists that courts must give effect to the "plain meaning" of a legislative text, even if this leads to absurdity. McLachlin J (as she then was) believes that the judicial mandate is to give effect to Parliament's intent, as inferred not only from the language of the text but also from aids such as the evolution of the legislation from common law to its current formulation.

In your opinion, which judgment is more persuasive? Why?

The following is the leading case on statutory interpretation. It sets out the preferred approach of the Supreme Court of Canada and has been cited for this purpose in countless subsequent judgments. In reading the case, once again notice how the court characterizes the type of interpretation problem it is facing and notice as well the particular rules of statutory interpretation relied on.

Re Rizzo and Rizzo Shoes Ltd.
[1998] 1 SCR 27

[In April 1989 a petition in bankruptcy was filed against Rizzo Shoes Ltd. and it was ordered into bankruptcy. As a result, Rizzo's employees lost their employment and a trustee assumed control of the corporation's property. The trustee was responsible for liquidating the property and distributing the proceeds among the corporation's debtors. A claim was made on behalf of Rizzo's former employees for termination and severance pay said to be owing under Ontario's *Employment Standards Act*, RSO 1980, c. 137 as a result of employment loss. The trustee disallowed the claim on the ground that the bankruptcy of an employer does not constitute a dismissal from employment and therefore no entitlement to severance, termination, or vacation pay arose under the Act. On appeal, the Ontario Court (General Division) reversed the trustee's decision, but on further appeal, the Ontario Court of Appeal restored it. The employees appealed to the Supreme Court of Canada.]

IACOBUCCI J (for the Court): [1] This is an appeal by the former employees of a now bankrupt employer from an order disallowing their claims for termination pay (including vacation pay thereon) and severance pay. The case turns on an issue of statutory interpretation. Specifically, the appeal decides whether, under the relevant legislation in effect at the time of the bankruptcy, employees are entitled to claim termination and severance payments where their employment has been terminated by reason of their employer's bankruptcy.

. . .

2. Relevant Statutory Provisions

[6] The relevant versions of the *Bankruptcy Act* (now the *Bankruptcy and Insolvency Act*) and the *Employment Standards Act* for the purposes of this appeal are RSC, 1985, c. B-3 (the "BA"), and RSO 1980, c. 137, as amended to April 14, 1989 (the "ESA") respectively.

Employment Standards Act, RSO 1980, c. 137, as amended:

40(1) No employer shall terminate the employment of an employee who has been employed for three months or more unless the employee gives,

(a) one weeks notice in writing to the employee if his or her period of employment is less than one year;

(b) two weeks notice in writing to the employee if his or her period of employment is one year or more but less than three years;

(c) three weeks notice in writing to the employee if his or her period of employment is three years or more but less than four years;

(d) four weeks notice in writing to the employee if his or her period of employment is four years or more but less than five years;

(e) five weeks notice in writing to the employee if his or her period of employment is five years or more but less than six years;

(f) six weeks notice in writing to the employee if his or her period of employment is six years or more but less than seven years;

(g) seven weeks notice in writing to the employee if his or her period of employment is seven years or more but less than eight years;

(h) eight weeks notice in writing to the employee if his or her period of employment is eight years or more,

and such notice has expired.

. . .

(7) Where the employment of an employee is terminated contrary to this section,

(a) the employer shall pay termination pay in an amount equal to the wages that the employee would have been entitled to receive at his regular rate for a regular non-overtime work week for the period of notice prescribed by subsection (1) or (2), and any wages to which he is entitled;

. . .

40a ...

(1a) Where,

(a) fifty or more employees have their employment terminated by an employer in a period of six months or less and the terminations are caused by the permanent discontinuance of all or part of the business of the employer at an establishment; or

(b) one or more employees have their employment terminated by an employer with a payroll of $2.5 million or more,

the employer shall pay severance pay to each employee whose employment has been terminated and who has been employed by the employer for five or more years.

Employment Standards Amendment Act, 1981, SO 1981, c. 22

2(1) Part XII of the said Act is amended by adding thereto the following section:

. . .

(3) Section 40a of the said Act does not apply to an employer who became a bankrupt or an insolvent person within the meaning of the *Bankruptcy Act* (Canada) and whose assets have been distributed among his creditors or to an employer whose proposal within the meaning of the *Bankruptcy Act* (Canada) has been accepted by his creditors in the period from and including the 1st day of January, 1981, to and including the day immediately before the day this Act receives Royal Assent.

Bankruptcy Act, RSC, 1985, c. B-3

121(1) All debts and liabilities, present or future, to which the bankrupt is subject at the date of the bankruptcy or to which he may become subject before his discharge by reason of any obligation incurred before the date of the bankruptcy shall be deemed to be claims provable in proceedings under this Act.

Interpretation Act, RSO 1990, c. I.11

10. Every Act shall be deemed to be remedial, whether its immediate purport is to direct the doing of anything that the Legislature deems to be for the public good or to prevent or punish the doing of any thing that it deems to be contrary to the public good, and shall accordingly receive such fair, large and liberal construction and interpretation as will best ensure the attainment of the object of the Act according to its true intent, meaning and spirit.

· · ·

17. The repeal or amendment of an Act shall be deemed not to be or to involve any declaration as to the previous state of the law.

· · ·

4. Issues

[17] This appeal raises one issue: does the termination of employment caused by the bankruptcy of an employer give rise to a claim provable in bankruptcy for termination pay and severance pay in accordance with the provisions of the ESA?

5. Analysis

[18] The statutory obligation upon employers to provide both termination pay and severance pay is governed by ss. 40 and 40a of the ESA, respectively. The Court of Appeal noted that the plain language of those provisions suggests that termination pay and severance pay are payable only when the employer terminates the employment. For example, the opening words of s. 40(1) are: "No employer shall terminate the employment of an employee … ." Similarly, s. 40a(1a) begins with the words, "Where … fifty or more employees have their employment terminated by an employer … ." Therefore, the question on which this appeal turns is whether, when bankruptcy occurs, the employment can be said to be terminated "by an employer."

[19] The Court of Appeal answered this question in the negative, holding that, where an employer is petitioned into bankruptcy by a creditor, the employment of its employees is not terminated "by an employer," but rather by operation of law. Thus, the Court of Appeal reasoned that, in the circumstances of the present case, the ESA termination pay and severance pay provisions were not applicable and no obligations arose. In answer, the appellants submit that the phrase "terminated by an employer" is best interpreted as reflecting a dis-

tinction between involuntary and voluntary termination of employment. It is their position that this language was intended to relieve employers of their obligation to pay termination and severance pay when employees leave their jobs voluntarily. However, the appellants maintain that where an employee's employment is involuntarily terminated by reason of their employer's bankruptcy, this constitutes termination "by an employer" for the purpose of triggering entitlement to termination and severance pay under the ESA.

[20] At the heart of this conflict is an issue of statutory interpretation. Consistent with the findings of the Court of Appeal, the plain meaning of the words of the provisions here in question appears to restrict the obligation to pay termination and severance pay to those employers who have actively terminated the employment of their employees. At first blush, bankruptcy does not fit comfortably into this interpretation. However, with respect, I believe this analysis is incomplete.

[21] Although much has been written about the interpretation of legislation (see, e.g., Ruth Sullivan, *Statutory Interpretation* (1997); Ruth Sullivan, *Driedger on the Construction of Statutes* (3rd ed. 1994) (hereinafter "*Construction of Statutes*"); Pierre-André Côté, *The Interpretation of Legislation in Canada* (2nd ed. 1991)), Elmer Driedger in *Construction of Statutes* (2nd ed. 1983) best encapsulates the approach upon which I prefer to rely. He recognizes that statutory interpretation cannot be founded on the wording of the legislation alone. At p. 87 he states:

> Today there is only one principle or approach, namely, the words of an Act are to be read in their entire context and in their grammatical and ordinary sense harmoniously with the scheme of the Act, the object of the Act, and the intention of Parliament.

· · ·

[22] I also rely upon s. 10 of the *Interpretation Act*, RSO 1980, c. 219, which provides that every Act "shall be deemed to be remedial" and directs that every Act shall "receive such fair, large and liberal construction and interpretation as will best ensure the attainment of the object of the Act according to its true intent, meaning and spirit."

[23] Although the Court of Appeal looked to the plain meaning of the specific provisions in question in the present case, with respect, I believe that the court did not pay sufficient attention to the scheme of the ESA, its object or the intention of the legislature; nor was the context of the words in issue appropriately recognized. I now turn to a discussion of these issues.

[24] In *Machtinger v. HOJ Industries Ltd.*, [1992] 1 SCR 986, at p. 1002, the majority of this Court recognized the importance that our society accords to employment and the fundamental role that it has assumed in the life of the individual. The manner in which employment can be terminated was said to be equally important (see also *Wallace v. United Grain Growers Ltd.*, [1997] 3 SCR 701). It was in this context that the majority in *Machtinger* described, at p. 1003, the object of the ESA as being the protection of "… the interests of employees by requiring employers to comply with certain minimum standards, including minimum periods of notice of termination." Accordingly, the majority concluded, at p. 1003, that, "… an interpretation of the Act which encourages employers to comply with the minimum requirements of the Act, and so extends its protections to as many employees as possible, is to be favoured over one that does not."

[25] The objects of the termination and severance pay provisions themselves are also broadly premised upon the need to protect employees. Section 40 of the ESA requires employers to give their employees reasonable notice of termination based upon length of service. One of the primary purposes of this notice period is to provide employees with an opportunity to take preparatory measures and seek alternative employment. It follows that s. 40(7)(a), which provides for termination pay in lieu of notice when an employer has failed to give the required statutory notice, is intended to "cushion" employees against the adverse effects of economic dislocation likely to follow from the absence of an opportunity to search for alternative employment. (Innis Christie, Geoffrey England and Brent Cotter, *Employment Law in Canada* (2nd ed. 1993), at pp. 572-81.)

[26] Similarly, s. 40a, which provides for severance pay, acts to compensate long-serving employees for their years of service and investment in the employer's business and for the special losses they suffer when their employment terminates. In *R v. TNT Canada Inc.* (1996), 27 OR (3d) 546, Robins JA quoted with approval at pp. 556-57 from the words of D.D. Carter in the course of an employment standards determination in *Re Telegram Publishing Co. v. Zwelling* (1972), 1 LAC (2d) 1 (Ont.), at p. 19, wherein he described the role of severance pay as follows:

> Severance pay recognizes that an employee does make an investment in his employer's business—the extent of this investment being directly related to the length of the employee's service. This investment is the seniority that the employee builds up during his years of service. ... Upon termination of the employment relationship, this investment of years of service is lost, and the employee must start to rebuild seniority at another place of work. The severance pay, based on length of service, is some compensation for this loss of investment.

[27] In my opinion, the consequences or effects which result from the Court of Appeal's interpretation of ss. 40 and 40a of the ESA are incompatible with both the object of the Act and with the object of the termination and severance pay provisions themselves. It is a well established principle of statutory interpretation that the legislature does not intend to produce absurd consequences. According to Côté, supra, an interpretation can be considered absurd if it leads to ridiculous or frivolous consequences, if it is extremely unreasonable or inequitable, if it is illogical or incoherent, or if it is incompatible with other provisions or with the object of the legislative enactment (at pp. 378-80). Sullivan echoes these comments noting that a label of absurdity can be attached to interpretations which defeat the purpose of a statute or render some aspect of it pointless or futile (Sullivan, *Construction of Statutes*, supra, at p. 88).

[28] The trial judge properly noted that, if the ESA termination and severance pay provisions do not apply in circumstances of bankruptcy, those employees "fortunate" enough to have been dismissed the day before a bankruptcy would be entitled to such payments, but those terminated on the day the bankruptcy becomes final would not be so entitled. In my view, the absurdity of this consequence is particularly evident in a unionized workplace where seniority is a factor in determining the order of lay-off. The more senior the employee, the larger the investment he or she has made in the employer and the greater the entitlement to termination and severance pay. However, it is the more senior personnel who are likely to be employed up until the time of the bankruptcy and who would thereby lose their entitlements to these payments.

[29] If the Court of Appeal's interpretation of the termination and severance pay provisions is correct, it would be acceptable to distinguish between employees merely on the basis of the timing of their dismissal. It seems to me that such a result would arbitrarily deprive some employees of a means to cope with the economic dislocation caused by unemployment. In this way the protections of the ESA would be limited rather than extended, thereby defeating the intended working of the legislation. In my opinion, this is an unreasonable result.

[30] In addition to the termination and severance pay provisions, both the appellants and the respondent relied upon various other sections of the ESA to advance their arguments regarding the intention of the legislature. In my view, although the majority of these sections offer little interpretive assistance, one transitional provision is particularly instructive. In 1981, s. 2(1) of the ESAA introduced s. 40a, the severance pay provision, to the ESA. Section 2(2) deemed that provision to come into force on January 1, 1981. Section 2(3), the transitional provision in question provided as follows:

> 2. ...
>
> (3) Section 40a of the said Act does not apply to an employer who became a bankrupt or an insolvent person within the meaning of the *Bankruptcy Act* (Canada) and whose assets have been distributed among his creditors or to an employer whose proposal within the meaning of the *Bankruptcy Act* (Canada) has been accepted by his creditors in the period from and including the 1st day of January, 1981, to and including the day immediately before the day this Act receives Royal Assent.

[31] The Court of Appeal found that it was neither necessary nor appropriate to determine the intention of the legislature in enacting this provisional subsection. Nevertheless, the court took the position that the intention of the legislature as evidenced by the introductory words of ss. 40 and 40a was clear, namely, that termination by reason of a bankruptcy will not trigger the severance and termination pay obligations of the ESA. The court held that this intention remained unchanged by the introduction of the transitional provision. With respect, I do not agree with either of these findings. Firstly, in my opinion, the use of legislative history as a tool for determining the intention of the legislature is an entirely appropriate exercise and one which has often been employed by this Court (see, e.g., *R v. Vasil*, [1981] 1 SCR 469, at p. 487; *Paul v. The Queen*, [1982] 1 SCR 621, at pp. 635, 653 and 660). Secondly, I believe that the transitional provision indicates that the Legislature intended that termination and severance pay obligations should arise upon an employer's bankruptcy.

[32] In my view, by extending an exemption to employers who became bankrupt and lost control of their assets between the coming into force of the amendment and its receipt of royal assent, s. 2(3) necessarily implies that the severance pay obligation does in fact extend to bankrupt employers. It seems to me that, if this were not the case, no readily apparent purpose would be served by this transitional provision.

[33] I find support for my conclusion in the decision of Saunders J in *Royal Dressed Meats Inc. ... . Having reviewed s. 2(3) of the ESAA, he commented as follows (at p. 89):

> ... any doubt about the intention of the Ontario Legislature has been put to rest, in my opinion, by the transitional provision which introduced severance payments into the ESA. ... it seems to me an inescapable inference that the legislature intended liability for severance payments to

arise on a bankruptcy. That intention would, in my opinion, extend to termination payments which are similar in character.

[34] This interpretation is also consistent with statements made by the Minister of Labour at the time he introduced the 1981 amendments to the ESA. With regard to the new severance pay provision he stated:

> The circumstances surrounding a closure will govern the applicability of the severance pay legislation in some defined situations. For example, a bankrupt or insolvent firm will still be required to pay severance pay to employees to the extent that assets are available to satisfy their claims.
>
> • • •
>
> ... [T]he proposed severance pay measures will, as I indicated earlier, be retroactive to January 1 of this year. That retroactive provision, however, will not apply in those cases of bankruptcy and insolvency where the assets have already been distributed or where an agreement on a proposal to creditors has already been reached.
>
> (*Legislature of Ontario Debates*, 1st sess., 32nd Parl., June 4, 1981, at pp. 1236-37.)

Moreover, in the legislative debates regarding the proposed amendments the Minister stated:

> For purposes of retroactivity, severance pay will not apply to bankruptcies under the Bankruptcy Act where assets have been distributed. However, once this act receives royal assent, employees in bankruptcy closures will be covered by the severance pay provisions.
>
> (*Legislature of Ontario Debates*, 1st sess., 32nd Parl., June 16, 1981, at p. 1699.)

[35] Although the frailties of Hansard evidence are many, this Court has recognized that it can play a limited role in the interpretation of legislation. Writing for the Court in *R v. Morgentaler*, [1993] 3 SCR 463, at p. 484, Sopinka J stated:

> ... until recently the courts have balked at admitting evidence of legislative debates and speeches. ... The main criticism of such evidence has been that it cannot represent the "intent" of the legislature, an incorporeal body, but that is equally true of other forms of legislative history. Provided that the court remains mindful of the limited reliability and weight of Hansard evidence, it should be admitted as relevant to both the background and the purpose of legislation.

[36] Finally, with regard to the scheme of the legislation, since the ESA is a mechanism for providing minimum benefits and standards to protect the interests of employees, it can be characterized as benefits-conferring legislation. As such, according to several decisions of this Court, it ought to be interpreted in a broad and generous manner. Any doubt arising from difficulties of language should be resolved in favour of the claimant (see, e.g., *Abrahams v. Attorney General of Canada*, [1983] 1 SCR 2, at p. 10; *Hills v. Canada (Attorney General)*, [1988] 1 SCR 513, at p. 537). It seems to me that, by limiting its analysis to the plain meaning of ss. 40 and 40a of the ESA, the Court of Appeal adopted an overly restrictive approach that is inconsistent with the scheme of the Act.

• • •

[40] As I see the matter, when the express words of ss. 40 and 40a of the ESA are examined in their entire context, there is ample support for the conclusion that the words "terminated by the employer" must be interpreted to include termination resulting from the bankruptcy of the employer. Using the broad and generous approach to interpretation appropriate for benefits-conferring legislation, I believe that these words can reasonably bear that construction (see *R v. Z. (D.A.)*, [1992] 2 SCR 1025). I also note that the intention of the Legislature as evidenced in s. 2(3) of the ESAA, clearly favours this interpretation. Further, in my opinion, to deny employees the right to claim ESA termination and severance pay where their termination has resulted from their employer's bankruptcy, would be inconsistent with the purpose of the termination and severance pay provisions and would undermine the object of the ESA, namely, to protect the interests of as many employees as possible.

[41] In my view, the impetus behind the termination of employment has no bearing upon the ability of the dismissed employee to cope with the sudden economic dislocation caused by unemployment. As all dismissed employees are equally in need of the protections provided by the ESA, any distinction between employees whose termination resulted from the bankruptcy of their employer and those who have been terminated for some other reason would be arbitrary and inequitable. Further, I believe that such an interpretation would defeat the true meaning, intent and spirit of the ESA. Therefore, I conclude that termination as a result of an employer's bankruptcy does give rise to an unsecured claim provable in bankruptcy pursuant to s. 121 of the BA for termination and severance pay in accordance with ss. 40 and 40a of the ESA. Because of this conclusion, I do not find it necessary to address the alternative finding of the trial judge as to the applicability of s. 7(5) of the ESA.

[42] I note that subsequent to the Rizzo bankruptcy, the termination and severance pay provisions of the ESA underwent another amendment. Sections 74(1) and 75(1) of the *Labour Relations and Employment Statute Law Amendment Act*, 1995, SO 1995, c. 1, amend those provisions so that they now expressly provide that where employment is terminated by operation of law as a result of the bankruptcy of the employer, the employer will be deemed to have terminated the employment. However, s. 17 of the *Interpretation Act* directs that, "[t]he repeal or amendment of an Act shall be deemed not to be or to involve any declaration as to the previous state of the law." As a result, I note that the subsequent change in the legislation has played no role in determining the present appeal.

6. *Disposition and Costs*

[43] I would allow the appeal and set aside paragraph 1 of the order of the Court of Appeal. In lieu thereof, I would substitute an order declaring that Rizzo's former employees are entitled to make claims for termination pay (including vacation pay due thereon) and severance pay as unsecured creditors.

———————————

Iacobucci J appears to agree with the Ontario Court of Appeal that the language of ss. 40 and 40a of the *Employment Standards Act* plainly excludes loss of employment caused by bankruptcy. To reach this conclusion, what specific language does he rely on? Do you agree with his assessment of this language?

Notice that determining whether a text is "plain" or "ambiguous" is a linguistic judgment based on personal intuition. Are judges better equipped than others to make such judgments? Would it be appropriate for courts to rely on linguists to assist them in determining whether a text is clear or ambiguous?

In *McIntosh*, Lamer CJ complained that "[t]he Crown is asking this Court to read words into s. 34(2) which are simply not there. In my view, to do so would be tantamount to *amending* s. 34(2), which is a legislative and not a judicial function." In *Rizzo*, Iacobucci J appears to disregard certain words in the text—for example, "by the employer" in s. 40a. Is this a permissible interpretation? Or does it amount to amending the legislation?

In addressing this question it is useful to distinguish between reading down and reading in as these concepts are used in statutory interpretation. Reading down refers to accepting an interpretation of a provision that is narrower in scope than the ordinary meaning of the text would support. When a provision is read down, words of limitation or qualification are effectively added to the text, for one of the following reasons:

- the court is giving effect to limitations or qualifications that are implicit in the text or the scheme of the legislation; it is, therefore, giving effect to the legislature's intent;
- the court is refusing to apply the legislation to situations that are outside the mischief the legislation was meant to address; it is, therefore, refusing to exceed the legislature's intent; or
- the court is relying on a presumption of legislative intent.

In each case, the additional words narrow rather than enlarge the scope of the provision and are meant to reflect the legislature's intent.

When a court reads in, it expands the scope of a legislative provision or fills a gap in a legislative scheme, thus making the legislation apply to facts that it would not otherwise encompass given the limits of the language used in the provision or scheme. One way to read in is to ignore words of qualification or limitation in the Act; another is to add words of expansion to the Act. Usually, courts refuse to read in, on the ground that it amounts to amendment rather than interpretation. Rightly or wrongly, courts associate enlarging the scope of a text with amendment. In the *Rizzo* case, did Iacobucci J rely on reading in?

In its judgment in *Rizzo* the Supreme Court of Canada appears to repudiate the textualist approach endorsed by a majority of the court in *McIntosh*. Notice that both Lamer CJ's judgment in *McIntosh* and Iacobucci J's judgment in *Rizzo* purport to be consistent with Driedger's modern principle. What does this say about the principle?

In both *McIntosh* and *Rizzo*, the court fails to examine the French version of the legislation. In more recent years the court has served notice that it expects counsel to consider both language versions of bilingual legislation when arguing interpretation issues before the court. Its current position on bilingual interpretation is set out and applied in the *Medovarski* case.

Medovarski v. Canada (**Minister of Citizenship and Immigration**)
[2005] 2 SCR 639, 2005 SCC 51

McLACHLIN CJ (for the court):

1. Introduction

[1] The core question on these appeals is whether s. 196, a transitional provision of the *Immigration and Refugee Protection Act*, SC 2001, c. 27 (*IRPA*), removes the right to appeal an order for removal to the Immigration Appeal Division (IAD), in the case of persons deemed inadmissible for serious criminality (i.e. sentenced to six months or more of imprisonment). The old statute (*Immigration Act*, RSC 1985, c. I-2) granted this right of appeal. The new statute does not for those imprisoned over two years. The transitional provision took away the right to appeal an order for removal unless a party had, under the old Act, been "granted a stay." The old Act provided for two kinds of stays: automatic stays and actively ordered stays. The appellants enjoyed only an automatic statutory stay. If the phrase "granted a stay" indicates both kinds of stays, the appellants' right to appeal is preserved. Conversely, if it indicates only actively ordered stays, the appellants' right to appeal is removed.

[2] The appellants are Olga Medovarski and Julio Esteban. Ms. Medovarski was sentenced to two years of imprisonment for criminal negligence causing death while driving a car when intoxicated. Mr. Esteban was sentenced to four years in prison for conspiracy to traffic cocaine. Both were ordered deported. Medovarski and Esteban each appealed to the Immigration Appeal Division of the Immigration and Refugee Board and their removal orders were automatically stayed. Both of those appeals were discontinued as a result of the transitional provisions of the *IRPA*. …

[3] I conclude, as did the majority of the Federal Court of Appeal, that "granted a stay" indicates only actively granted stays, and s. 196 of the *IRPA* therefore removes the appellants' right to appeal the order for their removal for serious criminality. The applicable principles of statutory interpretation permit no other conclusion. The appellants' argument that this result is unfair does not displace this conclusion. The section, properly interpreted, establishes that Parliament intended to deny a right of appeal to persons in the appellants' circumstances. Accordingly, I would dismiss the appeals.

2. Legislation

[4] The transitional provisions of the *IRPA* include ss. 192 and 196:

> 192. If a notice of appeal has been filed with the Immigration Appeal Division immediately before the coming into force of this section, the appeal shall be continued under the former Act by the Immigration Appeal Division of the Board.

> 196. Despite section 192, an appeal made to the Immigration Appeal Division before the coming into force of this section *shall be discontinued if the appellant has not been granted a stay under the former Act* and the appeal could not have been made because of *section 64 of this Act*.

[5] Section 64 of the *IRPA* expressly removes a right to appeal for those inadmissible on the grounds of serious criminality:

> 64(1) No appeal may be made to the Immigration Appeal Division by a foreign national or their sponsor or by a permanent resident if the foreign national or permanent resident has been found to be *inadmissible on grounds of security, violating human or international rights, serious criminality or organized criminality.*
>
> (2) For the purpose of subsection (1), serious criminality must be with respect to a crime that was punished in Canada by a term of imprisonment of *at least two years.*

[6] The appellants, Medovarski and Esteban fall within the scope of the current s. 64 which alters the legislative regime to ensure that they have no right of appeal under the *IRPA.*

[7] However, the appellants argue that since they filed a notice of appeal, which resulted in the removal order being automatically stayed pursuant to s. 49(1)(b) of the former Act, their appeal should not be discontinued under s. 196.

> 49(1) Subject to subsection (1.1), the execution of a removal order made against a person is stayed. …
>
> (b) *in any case where an appeal from the order has been filed with the Appeal Division,* until the appeal has been heard and disposed of or has been declared by the Appeal Division to be abandoned;

$$\cdots$$

3. Analysis

[8] The words of this statute, like any other, must be interpreted having regard to the object, text and context of the provision, considered together: E.A. Driedger, *Construction of Statutes* (2nd ed. 1983), at p. 87. In interpreting s. 196 to determine whether it eliminates appeals for permanent residents for whom a stay from an order for removal had been granted, I consider the purpose of the *IRPA* and its transitional provisions, the French and English text of s. 196, the legislative context of s. 196, and the need to interpret the provision to avoid an absurd, illogical or redundant result. Finally, I deal with concerns about unfairness to the appellants caused by the transition to the new *IRPA.*

3.1 Purpose of the Section 196 Transitional Provisions

[9] The *IRPA* enacted a series of provisions intended to facilitate the removal of permanent residents who have engaged in serious criminality. This intent is reflected in the objectives of the *IRPA*, the provisions of the *IRPA* governing permanent residents and the legislative hearings preceding the enactment of the *IRPA.*

[10] The objectives as expressed in the *IRPA* indicate an intent to prioritize security. This objective is given effect by preventing the entry of applicants with criminal records, by removing applicants with such records from Canada, and by emphasizing the obligation of permanent residents to behave lawfully while in Canada. This marks a change from the focus in the predecessor statute, which emphasized the successful integration of applicants more than security: e.g. see s. 3(1)(i) of the *IRPA* versus s. 3(j) of the former Act; s. 3(1)(e) of the *IRPA* versus s. 3(d) of the former Act; s. 3(1)(h) of the *IRPA* versus s. 3(i) of the former Act. Viewed collectively, the objectives of the *IRPA* and its provisions concerning

permanent residents, communicate a strong desire to treat criminals and security threats less leniently than under the former Act.

[11] In keeping with these objectives, the *IRPA* creates a new scheme whereby persons sentenced to more than six months in prison are inadmissible: *IRPA*, s. 36(1)(a). If they have been sentenced to a prison term of more than two years then they are denied a right to appeal their removal order: *IRPA*, s. 64. Provisions allowing judicial review mitigate the finality of these provisions, as do appeals under humanitarian and compassionate grounds and pre-removal risk assessments. However, the Act is clear: a prison term of over six months will bar entry to Canada; a prison term of over two years bans an appeal.

[12] In introducing the *IRPA*, the Minister emphasized that the purpose of provisions such as s. 64 was to remove the right to appeal by serious criminals. She voiced the concern that "those who pose a security risk to Canada be removed from our country as quickly as possible."

[13] In summary, the provisions of the *IRPA* and the Minister's comments indicate that the purpose of enacting the *IRPA*, and in particular s. 64, was to efficiently remove criminals sentenced to prison terms over six months from the country. Since s. 196 explicitly refers to s. 64 (barring appeals by serious criminals), it seems that the transitional provisions should be interpreted in light of these legislative objectives.

· · ·

3.2 The Text of Section 196

[18] The next step is to consider the terms of s. 196. The Minister and majority of the Federal Court of Appeal conclude that the use of the term "granted" indicates an actively ordered, as opposed to an automatic stay. This is supported by the *Concise Oxford English Dictionary*'s definition of the term "grant" which defines it as: "give (a right, property, etc.) formally or legally to … legal conveyance or formal conferment" (p. 620). This definition supports a deliberate act. The English version of s. 196 suggests that it applies only to stays actively granted. This said, it is possible to argue, for instance, that statutes can "grant" a right of appeal and that consequently the English version of s. 196 is not as clear as the Minister contends.

[19] Against this, the appellants raise the French version of s. 196, the meaning of which is even less clear. The French text of s. 196 states:

Malgré l'article 192, il est mis fin à l'affaire portée en appel devant la Section d'appel de l'immigration si l'intéressé est, alors *qu'il ne fait pas l'objet d'un sursis au titre de l'ancienne loi*, visé par la restriction du droit d'appel prévue par l'article 64 de la présente loi.

[20] It is argued that the French version broadly applies to all appeals that are not the "*objet*" of a stay, including statutory stays. However, again the matter is not entirely clear. "*[L]'objet d'un sursis au titre de l'ancienne loi*" is broader and more passive than the English version, which refers to "granting" a stay. The appellants argue that beneficiaries of automatic stays under the old Act are "*objets*" of a stay. Again, however, the matter is not entirely clear. On this interpretation it can be argued that the condition imposed by s. 196 would have little meaning (see below). Further, the companion s. 197 refers to "an appellant who has been granted a stay under the former Act" who "breaches a condition of the stay." It uses

the same language as s. 196. But s. 197 can only refer to an actively ordered stay since conditions are not imposed in an automatic stay, suggesting that s. 196 refers to an actively ordered stay.

[21] The result is that we are dealing with an English version which arguably applies only to actively granted stays, although admitting of ambiguity, and a French version which arguably applies to all stays, whether statutory or granted, although again admitting of ambiguity.

[22] Other uses of the word "stay" in the old and new Acts provide little assistance; the term is used in a variety of different ways depending on the context.

3.3 Principles of French and English Statutory Interpretation

[23] There is some conflict in the lower courts and between the parties as to the approach that should be adopted with respect to conflicting French and English versions of legislation. However, this dispute was addressed and resolved by this Court in *R v. Daoust*, [2004] 1 SCR 217, 2004 SCC 6, supported by earlier decisions, particularly *Schreiber v. Canada (Attorney General)*, [2002] 3 SCR 269, 2002 SCC 62. These cases, while not cited by the Federal Court of Appeal, guide the analysis of bilingual statutes.

[24] In interpreting bilingual statutes, the statutory interpretation should begin with a search for the shared meaning between the two versions: P.A. Côté, *The Interpretation of Legislation in Canada* (3rd ed. 2000), at p. 327. In *Daoust*, Bastarache J held for the Court that the interpretation of bilingual statutes is subject to a two-part procedure.

[25] First, one must apply the rules of statutory interpretation to determine whether or not there is an apparent discordance, and if so, whether there is a common meaning between the French and English versions. "[W]here one of the two versions is broader than the other, the common meaning would favour the more restricted or limited meaning": *Schreiber*, at para. 56, *per* LeBel J. *Schreiber* concerned a discrepancy between the French version of s. 6(a) of the *State Immunity Act*, RSC 1985, c. S-18, which stated that the exception to state immunity is narrowly "*décès*" or "*dommages corporels*," compared to the broader English "death" or "personal injury." Given the conflict between the two provisions the Court adopted the clearer and more restrictive French version. The common meaning is the version that is plain and not ambiguous. If neither version is ambiguous, or if they both are, the common meaning is normally the narrower version: *Daoust*, at paras. 28-29.

[26] Second, one must determine if the common meaning is consistent with Parliament's intent: *Daoust*, at para. 30.

[27] I now turn to the application of these principles to the facts in this case.

[28] If the English version of s. 196 is interpreted as applying only to actively granted stays, and if the French version is read as referring to all stays, including automatic ones, the two versions are inconsistent. One then looks for the common meaning, which is normally the narrower meaning. In this case, the narrower version is the English version of s. 196. This suggests that the English meaning prevails, and the provision is confined to actively granted stays.

[29] If both the English and French versions are seen as ambiguous, the result is the same. One reconciles them at the first step by finding the common meaning, which again is the narrower meaning.

[30] The final step asks whether the results comport with Parliament's intent. Here they do. The narrower interpretation accords with Parliament's general object of abolishing appeals where a permanent resident has been found inadmissible on the grounds of serious criminality and is sentenced to a prison term of over two years, while preserving appeals in cases where the merits were such that a stay is ordered.

3.4 Avoidance of Redundancy

[31] As we have seen, consideration of the purpose and language of s. 196 tend to suggest that it was intended to apply only to actively granted stays. This conclusion is reinforced by the absurd effect of the interpretation advocated by the appellants. If s. 196 applies to automatic stays, then it effectively becomes redundant and is reduced to an essentially meaningless statutory provision.

[32] The appellants' interpretation results in three related problems.

[33] First, s. 192 provides that appeals are continued "[i]f a notice of appeal has been filed … ." Section 49(1)(b) of the former Act automatically stayed the execution of a removal order once the appeal has been filed. This would mean that the appellants' removal orders were automatically stayed by the simple act of filing an appeal. They argue that this should result in their appeals being continued pursuant to s. 192 of the *IRPA*. However, s. 196 states that "[d]espite s. 192, an appeal made to the Immigration Appeal Division … shall be discontinued if the appellant has not been granted a stay." Since the appellant has already automatically been granted a stay under s. 49(1)(b), requiring that a stay be granted for the operation of s. 196 would make no sense since an automatic stay is already in place. Further, the use of "if" or "*si*" in s. 196 creates a condition. If the appellants' interpretation is accepted then there is no condition to satisfy since every appeal pending before the IAD would be continued. Therefore, the automatic stay imposed with the filing of the appeal cannot be enough; more is needed to give meaning to s. 196 and the conditional phrase, "if the appellant has not been granted a stay."

[34] Second, the appellants' argument leads to the absurdity of concluding that Parliament intended to eliminate appeals for inadmissible people outside the country, while allowing appeals to proceed for inadmissible persons who are in the country. Section 49(1) applies only to removal orders, and hence only to people within the country. This leaves the unanswered question: why would Parliament create a broad exemption for persons in the country yet accord none to similar persons outside the country?

[35] Third, the appellants' interpretation appears to result in a redundancy inconsistent with the purpose of the Act. As just discussed, s. 49(1)(b) of the former Act imposes an automatic stay when an appeal is filed. Thus the simple act of filing an appeal would exempt the appeal from being discontinued by s. 196 of the *IRPA*. Thus there is little left for s. 196 to discontinue other than appeals that have been granted to s. 49(1.1) appellants. These people are a subset of serious criminals in the system. This raises the question of why Parliament would confine the provision to a subset, when its legislative purpose was concerned with serious criminals generally. As Evans JA stated, there is no cogent policy rationale for such a distinction (para. 43).

. . .

[38] In the end, the Minister's claim that the appellants' interpretation would render the transitional provisions largely redundant and meaningless is persuasive, and the appellants provide no viable counter argument.

3.5 Other Arguments

[39] To counter the apparent redundancy of s. 196 on their interpretation, the appellants raise a series of practical considerations that they submit should inform the interpretation of s. 196. These normative arguments may suggest an absurdity or legislative intention and inform the context of an enactment. As such, they may be properly considered in interpreting a disputed provision.

[40] The appellants' first practical argument is that had they known that their right to appeal would be retroactively removed, they would have proceeded differently in their criminal trials. The two appellants are in different positions in this regard, although Esteban adopts many of Medovarski's facts to support his case.

[41] Medovarski claims that had she known that she might be denied an appeal by s. 196 (and s. 64), she would have instructed her counsel to bring this fact to the attention of the sentencing judge, in support of a sentence of two years less a day, as opposed to two years. According to her, interpreting s. 196 in a manner which continues her appeal because of the automatic stay remedies this unjust situation. However, s. 64 has caught, or is likely to catch, any number of permanent residents who are or were in prison serving two-year terms at the time the *IRPA* was passed. They too might have sought two-year sentences less a day had they known that a two-year sentence would remove their right of appeal under the *IRPA*. Parliament chose not to account for this obvious situation.

[42] The appellants' second practical argument is that they are left in a worse position than had their cases been dealt with under either Act exclusively. Even though the *IRPA* removed a right of appeal, the appellants would have had other procedural protections, including an assessment report had they been dealt with entirely under the *IRPA*: *IRPA*, ss. 44(1) and 44(2). Under the former Act, procedures of equitable review were conducted at a later stage via the appeal. Parties were also given notice that the Minister intended to issue a "danger opinion" (which removed a right of appeal) (s. 70(5)) and an opportunity to make submissions. Under the transitional provisions as interpreted by the Minister, the appellants have lost recourse to both the former and the later mechanisms of appeal or review.

[43] The Minister raises factors which it submits balance the appellants' concerns. Medovarski will not be deported without an assessment of the risks she might face in her home country: *IRPA*, ss. 112(1), 113(d), 97 and 114(1)(b). Medovarski and Esteban can always appeal on humanitarian and compassionate grounds although they will have to do this outside the country: *IRPA*, s. 25(1). Finally, they retain their right to seek leave and judicial review of the removal order and other decisions leading to it: s. 72 of the *IRPA*. It remains true that the appellants were left with fewer options than had they proceeded exclusively under either Act. However, this alone does not suffice to negate the inference flowing from other considerations that Parliament intended this result.

[44] The appellants' third practical argument is that their appeals were discontinued after they had been filed. However, this argument is answered by the fact that the express

purpose of the *IRPA*'s transitional provisions is to deal with these pending appeals. Section 196 expressly provides that it operates despite s. 192, which is only engaged if a notice of appeal has been filed under the former Act. Thus any unfairness on this account is contemplated by the legislation.

. . .

[48] Esteban asserts that *Charter* values should inform the interpretation of s. 196. *Charter* values only inform statutory interpretation where "genuine ambiguity arises between two or more plausible readings, each equally in accordance with the intentions of the statute": *CanadianOxy Chemicals Ltd. v. Canada (Attorney General)*, [1999] 1 SCR 743, at para. 14. Both readings are not equally in accordance with the intention of the *IRPA*. Thus it is not necessary to consider *Charter* values in this case.

3.6 Conclusion on the Meaning of Section 196

[49] Despite the fairness arguments raised by the appellants, I conclude that the interpretation of s. 196 they suggest leads to a legislative redundancy and is inconsistent with the objectives of the *IRPA*. This conclusion finds further support in the text of s. 196 and principles of interpretation of bilingual statutes.

4. Conclusion

[50] Section 196 of the *IRPA*, properly interpreted, applies only to actively granted stays. The appellants were never the beneficiaries of actively granted stays. Therefore, s. 196 does not apply to them and their right to appeal their orders for removal were not preserved.

[51] I would dismiss the appeals with costs to the respondent.

———————————————

Under the Canadian Constitution, legislation must be enacted in both French and English by Parliament and by the legislatures of Manitoba, New Brunswick, and Quebec. In these jurisdictions the two language versions of an act or regulation are equally authentic—that is, both are official statements of the law and neither is paramount over the other. In Ontario, the legislature has enacted legislation providing for bilingual enactment and the equal authenticity of both language versions. The legislation of the territories follows the same model.

In principle, the French and English versions of bilingual legislation must say the same thing. In practice, there is occasionally a discrepancy between the versions, which must be resolved. In cases of a discrepancy, there is a range of possibilities:

- version A is ambiguous while version B lends itself to only one of the possible meanings of version A; version B is the shared meaning;
- both versions are ambiguous, but both lend themselves to a single, particular meaning; this is the shared meaning;
- both versions are clear but say different things; there is no shared meaning; or
- one version is broader in scope than the other; either the narrower version is the shared meaning or the two versions say different things so that there is no shared meaning.

In *R v. Daoust*, [2004] 1 SCR 217, the Supreme Court of Canada held that when one version of bilingual legislation is broader in scope than the other, the narrower version represents the shared meaning and should prevail unless there is evidence that the legislature intended the broader meaning. Most commentators find this analysis unduly mechanical and would urge the courts to take a more nuanced approach.

In *R v. Daoust*, the court acknowledged that the shared meaning is merely presumed and can be rebutted. In every case, the shared meaning must be tested against other indicators of legislative intent, both actual and presumed. Despite this acknowledgment, the court in *Daoust* disregarded strong evidence that the legislature intended to enact the rule embodied in the broader English version. Presumably, the court was influenced by the fact that this was penal legislation and, therefore, to be strictly construed.

In reaching its conclusion in *Medovarski*, what interpretation rules or techniques did the court rely on? In your view, what was the most compelling consideration? In your view, was the case rightly decided?

Canada (Attorney General) v. Mossop
[1993] 1 SCR 554

[The following account of the facts and judicial history of this case is taken from the judgment of Lamer CJ, who wrote the majority judgment. In the official report of the case, Lamer CJ's judgment appears first. However, in the version below, the dissenting judgment of L'Heureux-Dubé is set out after Lamer CJ's introduction. L'Heureux-Dubé fully canvasses the issues raised by the case and offers an accurate account of the principles governing the interpretation of human rights legislation.]

LAMER CJ:

I. Facts

In June 1985, the complainant Brian Mossop was employed in Toronto as a translator for the Department of the Secretary of State. On June 3, 1985, Mossop attended the funeral of the father of the man whom Mossop described as his lover. Mossop testified that the two men have known each other since 1974, and have resided together since 1976 in a jointly owned and maintained home. They share the day-to-day developments in their lives and maintain a sexual relationship. Each has made the other the beneficiary of his will. They are known to their friends and families as lovers.

At the time, Mossop's terms of employment were governed by a collective agreement between the Treasury Board and the Canadian Union of Professional and Technical Employees ("CUPTE"). Article 19.02 of this agreement contained a provision relating to bereavement leave calling for up to four days' leave upon the death of a member of an employee's "immediate family." This term was defined as:

> ... father, mother, brother, sister, spouse (including common-law spouse resident with the employee), child (including child of common-law spouse), or ward of the employee, father-in-law,

mother-in-law, and in addition a relative who permanently resides in the employee's household or with whom the employee permanently resides.

In the definition section of the agreement, at art. 2.01(s), it was provided that:

> (s) a "common-law spouse" relationship is said to exist when, for a continuous period of at least one year, an employee has lived with a person of the opposite sex, publicly represented that person to be his/her spouse, and lives and intends to continue to live with that person as if that person were his/her spouse.

The day after the funeral, Mossop applied for bereavement leave pursuant to art. 19.02 of the collective agreement. The application was turned down, and Mossop declined to accept the day of special leave he was offered in its stead.

When his grievance, filed with the approval of and pursued by his union, was rejected on the basis that the denial of his application was in accordance with the collective agreement, Mossop went to the appellant, the Canadian Human Rights Commission. There he laid complaints against his employer, the Department of the Secretary of State (to which was later added the Treasury Board), and his union, CUPTE. The complaints invoked ss. 7(b), 9(1)(c) and 10(b) of the *Canadian Human Rights Act*, RSC, 1985, c. H-6 (formerly SC 1976-77, c. 33, as amended) ("the CHRA").

. . .

II. *Relevant Statutory Provisions*

Canadian Human Rights Act, RSC, 1985, c. H-6

3(1) For all purposes of this Act, race, national or ethnic origin, colour, religion, age, sex, marital status, family status, disability and conviction for which a pardon has been granted are prohibited grounds of discrimination.

3(1) Pour l'application de la présente loi, les motifs de distinction illicite sont ceux qui sont fondés sur la race, l'origine nationale ou ethnique, la couleur, la religion, l'âge, le sexe, l'état matrimonial, la situation de famille, l'état de personne graciée ou la déficience.

7. It is a discriminatory practice, directly or indirectly,

. . .

(b) in the course of employment, to differentiate adversely in relation to an employee, on a prohibited ground of discrimination.

9(1) It is a discriminatory practice for an employee organization on a prohibited ground of discrimination

. . .

(c) to limit, segregate, classify or otherwise act in relation to an individual in a way that would deprive the individual of employment opportunities, or limit employment opportunities or otherwise adversely affect the status of the individual, where the individual is a member of the organization or where any of the obligations of the organization pursuant to a collective agreement relate to the individual.

10. It is a discriminatory practice for an employer, employee organization or organization of employers

. . .

(b) to enter into an agreement affecting recruitment, referral, hiring, promotion, training, apprenticeship, transfer or any other matter relating to employment or prospective
employment,

that deprives or tends to deprive an individual or class of individuals of any employment opportunities on a prohibited ground of discrimination.

III. Judgments

Canadian Human Rights Tribunal (1989), 10 CHRR D/6064

The Tribunal identified the fundamental question as being whether the denial of bereavement leave in accordance with the collective agreement was based on family status, the
prohibited ground of discrimination cited by Mossop. ...

. . .

[The tribunal concluded that the Treasury Board and CUPTE had infringed s. 10(b) by
entering into a collective agreement that reserved certain benefits to common law couples
of the opposite sex, thereby excluding same-sex couples. It wrote:]

> Having determined that persons of the same sex prima facie may have the status of a family
> under the Act, and having determined that the family of the complainant is treated differently
> under the Act than other families, including but not limited to families which are very similar
> in their characteristics to that of the complainant, this Tribunal therefore finds that the collec-
> tive agreement deprived the complainant of the employment opportunity of bereavement leave
> on a prohibited ground of discrimination, and that therefore each of the Treasury Board and
> CUPTE have committed a discriminatory practice under s. 10(b) of the Act.

. . .

Federal Court of Appeal, [1991] 1 FC 18

Marceau JA ... held that the Tribunal erred in interpreting the term "family status" in the
CHRA as including a homosexual relationship between two individuals. In so concluding,
Marceau JA examined the propositions on which the Tribunal based its reasoning and
noted that only a legal approach could lead to a proper understanding of the term "family
status." In this respect, he stated, at p. 35:

> To these serious difficulties I have with the propositions adopted by the Tribunal, I will add my
> concern with an approach that simply forgets that the word "family" is not used in isolation in
> the Act, but rather coupled with the word "status." A status, to me, is primarily a legal concept
> which refers to the particular position of a person with respect to his or her rights and limita-
> tions as a result of his or her being member of some legally recognized and regulated group. I
> fail to see how any approach other than a legal one could lead to a proper understanding of
> what is meant by the phrase "family status." Even if we were to accept that two homosexual
> lovers can constitute "sociologically speaking" a sort of family, it is certainly not one which is
> now recognized by law as giving its members special rights and obligations.

He added that the CHRA was amended in 1983, to express in English what the French version was already saying, "so that the English version must be taken to express the notion underlying the words used in French." He then concluded as follows, at p. 36:

> So, the reasoning of the Tribunal simply does not appear to me acceptable. The Tribunal had no authority to reject the generally understood meaning given to the word "family" and to adopt in its stead, through a consciously ad hoc approach, a meaning ill-adapted to the context in which the word appears and obviously not in conformity with what was intended when the word was introduced, as shown by the legislative history of the amendment.

In his analysis of the real issue underlying the complaint, Marceau noted that sexual orientation was the real ground of discrimination involved. ...

[Stone JA concurred in the result.]

L'HEUREUX-DUBÉ J (dissenting): I have had the opportunity of reading the reasons of Chief Justice Lamer and Justice La Forest, and with respect, I cannot agree with them nor with their disposition of this appeal. As the Chief Justice notes, this appeal concerns the interpretation of the term "family status," one of the enumerated grounds of discrimination in s. 3 of the *Canadian Human Rights Act*, RSC, 1985, c. H-6 (formerly SC 1976-77, c. 33 as amended) (the "Act").

· · ·

"Family Status" in s. 3 of the Act

1. *Interpretation of Human Rights Legislation*

It is well established in the jurisprudence of this Court that human rights legislation has a unique quasi-constitutional nature, and that it is to be given a large, purposive and liberal interpretation. In this regard, see *Insurance Corp. of British Columbia v. Heerspink*, [1982] 2 SCR 145; *Ontario Human Rights Commission v. Simpsons-Sears Ltd.*, [1985] 2 SCR 536; *Bhinder v. Canadian National Railway Co.*, [1985] 2 SCR 561; *Canadian National Railway Co. v. Canada (Canadian Human Rights Commission)*, [1987] 1 SCR 1114 ("Action Travail des Femmes"); *Robichaud v. Canada (Treasury Board)*, [1987] 2 SCR 84; *Zurich* ... (for a general review, see Alan L. W. D'Silva, "Giving Effect to Human Rights Legislation—A Purposive Approach" (1991), 3 *Windsor Rev. L. & S. Issues* 45). This long line of cases mandates that courts interpret human rights legislation in a manner consistent with its overarching goals, recognizing as did my colleague Sopinka J for the majority in *Zurich* ... , at p. 339, that such legislation is often "the final refuge of the disadvantaged and the disenfranchised." In interpreting a statute, Charter values must not be ignored. As McIntyre J observed in *RWDSU v. Dolphin Delivery Ltd.*, [1986] 2 SCR 573, at p. 602, referring to *Re Blainey and Ontario Hockey Association* (1986), 26 DLR (4th) 728:

> *Blainey* then affords an illustration of the manner in which Charter rights of private individuals may be enforced and protected by the courts, that is, by measuring legislation—government action—against the Charter.

In *Hills v. Canada (Attorney General)*, [1988] 1 SCR 513, at p. 558, for the majority, I stressed that "the values embodied in the Charter must be given preference over an interpretation which would run contrary to them." (See also *Slaight Communications Inc. v. Davidson*, [1989] 1 SCR 1038, at p. 1078.)

The respondent Attorney General of Canada argued that, although the Act should be interpreted as remedial legislation, the ordinary rules of interpretation should apply. Therefore, the Court of Appeal correctly examined the "plain meaning" and textual context of the term, as well as the intention of Parliament. As can be discerned from my opinion in *Thomson Newspapers Ltd. v. Canada (Director of Investigation and Research, Restrictive Trade Practices Commission)*, [1990] 1 SCR 425, at p. 570, I would agree that the rules of interpretation which have guided the courts to this day have not been set aside, and that they continue to play a role in the interpretation of legislation, including constitutional and quasi-constitutional documents. However, I also note Laskin CJ's words in *Miller v. The Queen*, [1977] 2 SCR 680, at p. 690, that the Court had a duty "not to whittle down the protections of the *Canadian Bill of Rights* by a narrow construction of what is a quasi-constitutional document." This observation applies *a fortiori* to human rights legislation, and has continued to be an important caution in the era of the Charter. In *Action Travail des Femmes* ... , Dickson CJ reviewed the jurisprudence on the interpretation of human rights legislation and, at p. 1134, stated the principle as follows:

> Human rights legislation is intended to give rise, amongst other things, to individual rights of vital importance, rights capable of enforcement, in the final analysis, in a court of law. I recognize that in the construction of such legislation the words of the Act must be given their plain meaning, but it is equally important that the rights enunciated be given their full recognition and effect. We should not search for ways and means to minimize those rights and to enfeeble their proper impact. Although it may seem commonplace, it may be wise to remind ourselves of the statutory guidance given by the federal Interpretation Act which asserts that statutes are deemed to be remedial and are thus to be given such fair, large and liberal interpretation as will best ensure that their objects are attained.

The Court has repeatedly warned of the dangers of strict or legalistic approaches which would restrict or defeat the purpose of quasi-constitutional documents. For example, in *Tremblay v. Daigle*, [1989] 2 SCR 530, at p. 553, this Court made it clear that the meaning of highly controversial terms "cannot be settled by linguistic fiat." (On avoiding narrow and technical interpretations of Charter rights, see also *Law Society of Upper Canada v. Skapinker*, [1984] 1 SCR 357, at pp. 365-67; *R v. Duarte*, [1990] 1 SCR 30; on avoiding inflexible categorizations, see *Re BC Motor Vehicle Act*, [1985] 2 SCR 486.)

The remarks of Wilson J in *Thomson Newspapers Ltd. v. Canada (Director of Investigation and Research, Restrictive Trade Practices Commission)*, *supra*, at p. 470, are apposite here:

> The principle of statutory construction, expressio unius, is ill-suited to meet the needs of Charter interpretation. It is inconsistent with the purposive approach to Charter interpretation which has been endorsed by the Court and which focuses on the broad purposes for which the rights were designed and not on mechanical rules which have traditionally been employed in interpreting detailed provisions of ordinary statutes in order to discern legislative intent.

Although made in the context of the Charter, and while it is clear that there are differences between constitutional and quasi-constitutional documents, these comments apply here since both types of documents require an interpretive approach that is broad and purposive, and identifies the values which the legislation was designed to protect. McIntyre J clearly was of this view when, speaking for a unanimous Court in *Ontario Human Rights Commission v. Simpsons-Sears, supra*, at pp. 546-47, he wrote:

> It is not, in my view, a sound approach to say that according to established rules of construction no broader meaning can be given to the Code than the narrowest interpretation of the words employed. The accepted rules of construction are flexible enough to enable the Court to recognize in the construction of a human rights code the special nature and purpose of the enactment (see Lamer J in *Insurance Corporation of British Columbia v. Heerspink*, [1982] 2 SCR 145, at pp. 157-58), and give to it an interpretation which will advance its broad purposes. Legislation of this type is of a special nature, not quite constitutional but certainly more than the ordinary—and it is for the courts to seek out its purpose and give it effect. The Code aims at the removal of discrimination. This is to state the obvious. Its main approach, however, is not to punish the discriminator, but rather to provide relief for the victims of discrimination.

In short, though traditional interpretational tools ought not be ignored, they must be applied in the context of a broad and purposive approach.

2. Purpose of the Act

The purpose of the Act, set out in s. 2 recited earlier, is to ensure that people have an equal opportunity to make for themselves the life that they are able and wish to have without being hindered by discriminatory practices. The social cost of discrimination is insupportably high, and these insidious practices are damaging not only to the individuals who suffer the discrimination, but also to the very fabric of our society. This Court decried the multiple harms caused by discrimination in the context of hate promotion in *R v. Keegstra*, [1990] 3 SCR 697. Dickson CJ remarked, at pp. 746-47, that the consequences of such discriminatory practices "bear heavily in a nation that prides itself on tolerance and the fostering of human dignity through, among other things, respect for the many racial, religious and cultural groups in our society." As McIntyre J confirmed in *Andrews v. Law Society of British Columbia*, [1989] 1 SCR 143, at p. 172, "[d]iscrimination is unacceptable in a democratic society because it epitomizes the worst effects of the denial of equality." The Act, in prohibiting certain forms of discrimination, has the express purpose of promoting the value of equality which lies at the centre of a free and democratic society. Our society is one of rich diversity, and the Act fosters the principle that all members of the community deserve to be treated with dignity, concern, respect and consideration, and are entitled to a community free from discrimination.

. . .

3. Textual Interpretation

It was argued that a correct interpretive approach would warrant that a textual interpretation be determinative, and that the coupling of the terms "family" and "status" in the English text of s. 3 of the Act required the Tribunal to construe "family status" as including only those families who have recognizable status at law. This is the way that the Court of Appeal approached the matter. Leaving aside for the moment the broad and purposive approach which, in my view, should guide the interpretation of human rights legislation, even if one were to take a textual approach to the interpretation of s. 3 of the Act, the result of such an interpretive exercise would not lead to the conclusions of the Court of Appeal, but rather would, in my view, support the Tribunal's findings.

First, the word "status" is capable of bearing several meanings. The *Concise Oxford Dictionary of Current English* (8th ed. 1990) provides the following definition:

> 1. social position, rank, relation to others, relative importance … . 2. (Law). person's relation to others as fixed by law … . 3. position of affairs … .

While the term "status" may be used to indicate status at law, it may indicate more factual matters of rank, social position, or relation to others. The use of the term "status" is not sufficient by itself to restrict the notion of "family status" to only those families that are recognized at law. Reference to the French version of the term, "situation de famille," is warranted here. *Le Petit Robert* (1990) provides the following definitions of the term "situation":

> 1. Le fait d'être en un lieu; manière dont une chose est disposée, située ou orientée … .
> 2. Ensemble des circonstances dans lesquelles une personne se trouve … . 3. Emploi, post rémunérateur régulier et stable … .

"Situation" is not a legal term, is broader than the English term "status," and encompasses a host of meanings. When the meaning of the French term is considered, it is apparent that the scope of "family status" has potential to be very broad. In French, the term "situation de famille" would not be used to express a legal notion. "État matrimonial" would.

As noted in the Court of Appeal reasons, until 1983, the French text of the Act prohibited discrimination on the basis of "situation de famille" while the English text of the Act prohibited discrimination on the basis of "marital status." In 1983 the Act was amended, the French text to include both "situation de famille" and "état matrimonial," the English text to include both "marital status" and "family status." The amendment did not simply modify the existing terms, but in fact expanded the Act. Had the intention been to narrow the scope of protection, it would have been simple to use one term or the other. In my view the purpose of the amendment could only have been to envelop the two notions. Furthermore, if both terms "situation de famille" and "état matrimonial," "marital status" and "family status," in the French or in the English texts, were similar, there would have been no need to juxtapose them. One such expression would have been sufficient as the legislator is not presumed to use meaningless words (P.-A. Côté, *The Interpretation of Legislation in Canada* (2nd ed. 1992), at p. 232).

In any event, I have difficulty with the Court of Appeal's proposition that the meaning of "family status" and its French equivalent can be determined through reference to what it found to be the more restrictive English term. First, as I have noted above, the English term is not necessarily more restrictive. Second, even if it could be said that "family status" encompassed only families with legal status, it would be highly inappropriate to interpret the term by relying on the more narrow meaning of the French and English texts. It is an established principle of interpretation in Canada that French and English texts of legislation are deemed to be equally authoritative (*R v. Turpin*, [1989] 1 SCR 1296), and where there is a discrepancy between the two, it is the meaning which furthers the purpose of the legislation which must prevail (*R v. Collins*, [1987] 1 SCR 265; see also P.-A. Côté, *supra*, at pp. 272-79). In this case, given that the purpose of the Act is to prevent discrimination and provide an equal opportunity to make the type of life one wishes, the broader of the two meanings should prevail.

A textual interpretation seems to me to support the conclusion of the Tribunal that "family status" should not be restricted to a narrow legal meaning. Nothing in the textual context indicates that the protection of the Act is to be extended only to certain types of legally validated families. On the contrary, the term "family status" suggests a broader protection that would prohibit discrimination against individuals on the basis of the internal structuring of their families. But, as I said above, a strict textual interpretation is not warranted here. That leaves then the argument concerning legislative intent.

4. Purpose and Intent

The intervener Focus on the Family asserted that the Tribunal should have considered the proceedings in Parliament in an attempt to more accurately discern the intention of Parliament at the time of the legislative enactment. They submitted that the extension of the term "family status" to include same-sex relationships would usurp the legislative function of Parliament, and give the term a meaning never intended by Parliament. This argument implies that the Tribunal exceeded its jurisdiction by interpreting the scope of "family status" as it did.

First, as regards the amendment itself and referring to the evidence before the Tribunal, this intervener argued that legislative debate supports their assertion that the members of the legislature intended the amendment simply to bring the French and English texts into conformity. As Lord Watson observed in *Salomon v. Salomon & Co.*, [1897] AC 22, at p. 38, the "Intention of the Legislature" is a common but very slippery phrase." Legislative intention can be difficult to ascertain, and it is dangerous to rely only on the legislative record in order to infer that intent. While such record may be of some assistance in certain types of cases (for example *Re Anti-Inflation Act*, [1976] 2 SCR 373), legislative intent is derived primarily from the legislation itself (*Hills v. Canada (Attorney General)*, *supra*, at p. 549; *Hunter v. Southam Inc.*, [1984] 2 SCR 145; *Re BC Motor Vehicle Act …*).

With this caveat, had Parliament intended that the protection for families be restricted to legally recognized families, the amendment to the Act could have made this clear. However, this was not done. Instead, the amendment increased the scope of protection by adding a new ground of discrimination to each text: both "marital status" and "family status" became prohibited grounds. As the terms are juxtaposed, it is reasonable to conclude that "family status" must be something other than "marital status," just as "situation de famille" must be something other than "état matrimonial." Since "état matrimonial" is closer to a legal notion, "situation de famille" or "family status" can only be broader. It was, of course, open to Parliament to define the concept of "family status" within the Act. It did not choose to do so, even in the face of debate about the meaning of the term. Instead, Parliament determined that the task of dealing with any ambiguity in any concepts in the Act should be left to the administrative board charged with the task of implementing the Act. I refer, in this regard, to the comments of the Minister of Justice as reported in the *Minutes of Proceed-*

ings and Evidence of the Standing Committee on Justice and Legal Affairs, Issue No. 114, December 20, 1982, at p. 17: "It will be up to the commission, the tribunals it appoints, and in the final cases, the courts, to ascertain in a given case the meaning to be given to these concepts." When asked why he was reluctant to define these terms within the Act itself, the Minister responded as follows:

> The reason for my reluctance to have such definitions included, Mr. Chairman, is that it is not in accord with the scheme of the bill. *These words are being interpreted by the Canadian Human Rights Commission. We trust them to interpret and issue regulations.*
>
> It is true, of course, that a court can always pronounce on the validity of this; but in most cases, the action of the commission is accepted. Generally speaking, we think that is a better way to proceed. [Emphasis added.]

(*Minutes of Proceedings and Evidence of the Standing Committee on Justice and Legal Affairs*, Issue No. 115, December 21, 1982, at p. 73.)

Though the members of Parliament may perhaps not at that precise moment have envisaged that "family status" would be interpreted by the Tribunal so as to extend to same-sex couples, the decision to leave the term undefined is evidence of clear legislative intent that the meaning of "family status," like the meaning of other undefined concepts in the Act, be left for the Commission and its tribunals to define. In my view, if the legislative record helps here in the search for legislative intent, it rather supports the Tribunal's wide and broad discretion in the interpretation of the provisions of its own Act.

An interpretation of a human rights document, or for that matter any legislation, that may not conform with Parliament's intention can be easily cured by Parliament itself. Because legislation can be amended more readily than a Constitution, legislatures which find the interpretations given by administrative tribunals inconsistent with legislative intent can always amend the legislation, or pass new legislation in order to modify that interpretation. ...

Even if Parliament had in mind a specific idea of the scope of "family status," in the absence of a definition in the Act which embodies this scope, concepts of equality and liberty which appear in human rights documents are not bounded by the precise understanding of those who drafted them. Human rights codes are documents that embody fundamental principles, but which permit the understanding and application of these principles to change over time. These codes leave ample scope for interpretation by those charged with that task. The "living-tree" doctrine, well understood and accepted as a principle of constitutional interpretation, is particularly well suited to human rights legislation. The enumerated grounds of discrimination must be examined in the context of contemporary values, and not in a vacuum. As with other such types of legislation, the meaning of the enumerated grounds in s. 3 of the Act is not "frozen in time" and the scope of each ground may evolve.

5. The Meaning of "Family Status"

Across the political spectrum, there is broad appreciation of the vital importance of strong, stable families. ...

In her article "'A Family Like Any Other Family': Alternative Methods of Defining Family in Law" (1990-1991), 18 *NYU Rev. L & Soc. Change* 1027, at p. 1029, Kris Franklin notes:

Families have long been viewed as among the most essential and universal units of society. This sense of the shared experience of family has led to an often unexamined consensus regarding what exactly constitutes a family. Thus, while "(w)e speak of families as though we all knew what family are," we see no need to define the concepts embedded within the term. [Footnotes omitted.]

This "unexamined consensus" leads many to feel that the term "family" in fact has a plain meaning. This belief is reflected in the decision of the Court of Appeal where Marceau JA asks the question, at p. 34, "Is it not to be acknowledged that the basic concept signified by the word has always been a group of individuals with common genes, common blood, common ancestors?" However, the unexamined consensus begins to fall apart when one is required to define the concepts which are embedded in the term "family" in the context of "family status." How are the boundaries of that status to be drawn? Is there a plain meaning for "family status"? Could it not be said that "family status" is an attribute of those who live as if they were a family, in a family relationship, caring for each other?

· · ·

The traditional conception of family is not the only conception. The American Home Economics Association (AHEA) defines a family as "two or more persons who share resources, share responsibility for decisions, share values and goals, and have commitments to one another over time" (adopted in 1973, see I. Diamond, *Families, Politics and Public Policy: A Feminist Dialogue on Women and the State* (1983), 1, at p. 8). K.G. Terkelsen in "Toward a Theory of the Family Life Cycle" in E. Carter and M. McGoldrick, eds., *The Family Life Cycle: A Framework for Family Therapy* (1980), 21, at p. 23, defines a family as a:

> small social system made up of individuals related to each other by reason of strong reciprocal affections and loyalties, and comprising a permanent household (or cluster of households) that persists over years and decades.

· · ·

In *Nurses and Families: A Guide to Family Assessment and Intervention* (2nd ed., forthcoming), Wright and Leahey comment as follows (at pp. 3-3 and 3-4):

> Designating a group of people with a term such as "couple," "nuclear family," "single-parent family," specifies attributes of membership but these distinctions of grouping are not more or less "families" by reason of labelling. It is the attributes of affection, strong emotional ties, a sense of belonging and durability of membership that determine family composition.

The multiplicity of definitions and approaches to the family illustrates clearly that there is no consensus as to the boundaries of family, and that "family status" may not have a sole meaning, but rather may have varied meanings depending on the context or purpose for which the definition is desired. This same diversity in definition can be seen in a review of Canadian legislation affecting the "family." The law has evolved and continues to evolve to recognize an increasingly broad range of relationships. Different pieces of legislation contain more or less restrictive definitions depending on the benefit or burden of the law to be imposed. These definitions of family vary with legislative purpose, and depend on the context of the legislation. By way of example, one may be part of a family for the purpose of receiving income assistance under welfare legislation, but not for the purpose of income tax legislation.

. . .

The evidence before the Tribunal was that the traditional family form is not the only family form, but co-exists with numerous others. Though there are Canadians whose experience of family does in fact accord with the traditional model, the way many people in Canada currently experience family does not necessarily fit with this model. For example, Harriet Michel, in "The Case for the Black Family" (1987), 4 *Harv. BlackLetter J* 21, gives a substantively different conception of family. She suggests that, in the US black community,

> [b]ecause slavery often denied us the right to live with our biological kin, our definition of family became any group of individuals who collectively come together in order to provide economic and emotional support to the members of the groups.

Similarly, Carol B. Stack, in *All Our Kin: Strategies for Survival in a Black Community* (1974), examined the family networks of the black urban poor. She describes networks of kinship among these groups that are quite different from the traditional understandings of family. These kinship groups include relations based on blood, but extend to include people who would not fit within the traditional model of family. Stack concludes that in studying these families, it is important to look at the way they live, without trying to fit the relationships into the traditional categories. …

. . .

The above discussion is not intended to provide an authoritative definition of what constitutes the family, but is rather to illustrate that a purposive approach to the term "family status" can result in an interpretation that can vary depending on the specific context. … The Tribunal did not conclude that there is one definition which will serve for all purposes, but rather determined that the task was to find a reasonable meaning which advanced the rights contained in the Act. Following this approach, it made this assertion, at p. D/6094:

> The Tribunal, giving the term "family status" a reasonable meaning which is neither the narrowest meaning of the term nor a minimizing of rights under the Act, holds that, prima facie, homosexuals in a relationship are not excluded from relying on that prohibited ground of discrimination.

. . .

6. *"Family Status" in Context*

The Tribunal did not ignore the difficulties involved in finding a practical and reasonable definition which could be applied to determine whether or not "family status" would apply in the matter before them. Given its interpretation of that term as set out in s. 3 of the Act, and accepting that there is no one definition which could serve for all purposes, the Tribunal adopted a functional approach which it describes at p. D/6094:

> As a practical matter, the Tribunal agrees with the complainant that terms should not be confined to their historical roots, but must be tested in today's world, against an understanding of how people are living and how language reflects reality. Dr. Eichler's evidence, as well as that of the complainant, was helpful in making these assessments.

Dr. Eichler's evidence was that it is possible to determine whether or not a family exists for a given purpose by using a functional approach. The functional approach involves an examination of a cluster of variables that may be commonly found in families. These variables might include the existence of a relationship of some standing in terms of time and with the expectation of continuance, self-identification as a family, holding out to the public of the unit as a family, an emotional positive involvement, sexual union, raising and nurturing of children, caregiving to children or adults, shared housework, internal division of life-maintenance tasks, co-residence, joint ownership or joint use of property or goods, joint bank accounts, and naming of other party as beneficiary of a life insurance policy. Dr. Eichler noted that the list is not exhaustive, nor is it determinative. Not all variables are present in any given family, and there is no one variable that is present in all families.

· · ·

Utilizing this functional approach, the Tribunal was required to determine whether or not Mr. Mossop and Mr. Popert could properly be considered to come within the scope of "family status." In reaching a determination, the Tribunal noted the importance of remaining focused on the purpose of the Act, and on an understanding of how people are living. It confirmed (at p. D/6094) that:

> Value judgments should play no part in this process, because they may operate to favour a view of the world as it might be preferred over the world as it is. The Tribunal notes the conclusion reached by Hugessen J in *Schaap* that the Act does not promote certain types of status over others and that the Act is intended to address group stereotypes.

· · ·

The Tribunal concluded that the specific relationship before it was one which, on the evidence, could come within the scope of "family status." ...

· · ·

The Collective Agreement

· · ·

[T]he evidence was that the relationship of these two men had functionally the same characteristics as other relationships for which bereavement leave was deemed appropriate. On the facts and in the context of a bereavement leave benefit, Mr. Mossop and Mr. Popert could clearly be called immediate family. However, as the Tribunal noted, the definition of "immediate family" in the collective agreement had the effect of excluding this couple. In fact, the exclusion rendered invisible the nature of the relationship between Mr. Mossop and Mr. Popert, and treated them as if it did not exist. The Tribunal could only find, as it did, that the collective agreement treats some types of familial relationships differently than others. It summarized its findings as follows, at p. D/6097:

> Having determined that persons of the same sex prima facie may have the status of a family under the Act, and having determined that the family of the complainant is treated differently [from] other families, including but not limited to families which are very similar in their characteristics to that of the complainant, this Tribunal therefore finds that the collective agreement deprived the complainant of the employment opportunity of bereavement leave on a prohibited ground of discrimination, and that therefore each of the Treasury Board and CUPTE have committed a discriminatory practice under s. 10(b) of the Act.

· · ·

The Attorney General also argued that the Tribunal erred in finding discrimination on the basis of "family status," rather than based on sexual orientation, a ground not found in s. 3 of the Act. ...

This argument is based on an underlying assumption that the grounds of "family status" and "sexual orientation" are mutually exclusive. However, categories of discrimination often overlap in significant measure. ...

· · ·

However, though multiple levels of discrimination may exist, multiple levels of protection may not. There are situations where a person suffers discrimination on more than one ground, but where only one form of discrimination is a prohibited ground. When faced with such situations, one should be cautious not to characterize the discrimination so as to deprive the person of any protection. This was the situation in *Bliss v. Attorney General of Canada*, [1979] 1 SCR 183, where discrimination on the basis of sex was characterized as discrimination on the basis of pregnancy, and therefore left outside the scope of protection. One should not lightly allow a characterization which excludes those from the scope of the Act who should legitimately be included. A narrow and exclusionary approach, in my view, is inconsistent with a broad and purposive interpretation of human rights legislation.

· · ·

The Tribunal, acting within its jurisdiction, identified Mr. Mossop's claim as one of discrimination on the basis of "family status." Based on the purpose of the Act, the purpose of the benefit, and all the evidence before it, it was perfectly reasonable for the Tribunal to conclude that the collective agreement violated s. 10(b) of the Act, a conclusion with which the Court has no reason to interfere.

· · ·

In the result, I would allow the appeal with costs throughout and reinstate the Tribunal's decision.

LAMER CJ (Sopinka and Iacobucci JJ concurring):

· · ·

IV. *Issues*

Did the Federal Court of Appeal err when it held that the term "family status" in the CHRA did not include a homosexual relationship between two individuals?

V. *Analysis*

The question before the Court in this case is one of statutory interpretation: it is therefore a question of law.

· · ·

Accordingly, the issue to be determined, on the facts of this case, is whether there was discrimination on the basis of Mr. Mossop's "family status" under the CHRA as it stood at the time the events occurred.

When Mr. Mossop was denied bereavement leave in June 1985, the CHRA did not prohibit discrimination on the basis of sexual orientation. In my opinion, this fact is a highly relevant part of the context in which the phrase "family status" in the Act must be interpreted. It is interesting to note in this regard that there was a recommendation by the Canadian Human Rights Commission that sexual orientation be made a prohibited ground of discrimination. Nevertheless, at the time of the 1983 amendments to the CHRA, no action was taken to implement this recommendation.

It is thus clear that when Parliament added the phrase "family status" to the English version of the CHRA in 1983, it refused at the same time to prohibit discrimination on the basis of sexual orientation in that Act. In my opinion, this fact is determinative. I find it hard to see how Parliament can be deemed to have intended to cover the situation now before the Court in the CHRA when we know that it specifically excluded sexual orientation from the list of prohibited grounds of discrimination contained in the Act. In the case at bar, Mr. Mossop's sexual orientation is so closely connected with the grounds which led to the refusal of the benefit that this denial could not be condemned as discrimination on the basis of "family status" without indirectly introducing into the CHRA the prohibition which Parliament specifically decided not to include in the Act, namely the prohibition of discrimination on the basis of sexual orientation.

. . .

While it may be argued that the discrimination here applies to homosexual couples through their familial relationship or in their "family status" and does not apply to the sexual orientation of Mr. Mossop as an individual as such, I am not persuaded by this distinction. I cannot conclude that by omitting sexual orientation from the list of prohibited grounds of discrimination contained in the CHRA, Parliament intended to exclude from the scope of that Act only discrimination on the basis of the sexual orientation of individuals. If such an interpretation were to be given to the CHRA, the result would be somewhat surprising: while homosexuals who are not couples would receive no protection under the Act, those who are would be protected.

Whatever may be my personal views in that regard, I find that Parliament's clear intent throughout the CHRA, before and at the time of the amendment of 1983, was to not extend to anyone protection from discrimination based on sexual orientation.

Absent a Charter challenge of its constitutionality, when Parliamentary intent is clear, courts and administrative tribunals are not empowered to do anything else but to apply the law. If there is some ambiguity as to its meaning or scope, then the courts should, using the usual rules of interpretation, seek out the purpose of the legislation and if more than one reasonable interpretation consistent with that purpose is available, that which is more in conformity with the Charter should prevail.

But, I repeat, absent a Charter challenge, the Charter cannot be used as an interpretative tool to defeat the purpose of the legislation or to give the legislation an effect Parliament clearly intended it not to have.

. . .

VI. *Conclusion*

For these reasons, I would dismiss the appeal.

LA FOREST J (Iacobucci J concurring): I have read the reasons of the Chief Justice and Justice L'Heureux-Dubé. I share the general approach of the Chief Justice and would dispose of the case in the manner he proposes. I think it advisable, however, to deal more directly with some of the issues raised by my colleague, L'Heureux-Dubé J. I shall, therefore, briefly set forth the main considerations that have led me to the conclusion I have reached.

. . .

2. Family Status

I turn, then, to the meaning to be attributed to the words "family status" under the ordinary rules of statutory interpretation. In determining the intent of Parliament, one must, of course, give to the words used in a statute their usual and ordinary sense having regard to their context and to the purpose of the statute. Here I shall focus particularly on the word "family" because the word "status" must inevitably attach to it. No one denies (and my colleague L'Heureux-Dubé J concedes this) that the dominant conception of family is the traditional family. That, to use the term L'Heureux-Dubé J uses, is the "unexamined consensus." That does not, of course, exhaust the meaning of the term, and we all know that in ordinary parlance it also comprises several derivative meanings that have a real connection with the dominant concept. I recognize, however, that particularly in recent years the word is loosely used to cover other relationships. The appellant here argues that "family status" should cover a relationship dependent on a same-sex living arrangement. While some may refer to such a relationship as a "family," I do not think it has yet reached that status in the ordinary use of language. Still less was it the case when the statute was enacted. In human terms, it is certainly arguable that bereavement leave should be granted to homosexual couples in a long-term relationship in the same way as it applies to heterosexual couples, but that is an issue for Parliament to address. It is not argued here that anything in the context supports the contention that this was the legislative purpose. The appellant's argument ultimately rests on the proposition that human rights statutes should be interpreted "purposefully" so as to favour all disadvantaged groups. I agree that the statute should be interpreted generously with a view to effect its purpose. But this brings us back to the question whether the addition of the words "family status" had as one of its legislative purposes the protection of persons living in the position of the appellant. As noted neither the language relied on nor the other grounds of discrimination listed support this. Nor is there any evidence in the surrounding context that this was the mischief Parliament intended to address, which could afford some credence to the argument that Parliament was using the words "family status" other than in their ordinary sense. As the Chief Justice observes, when one looks at extraneous evidence, there is nothing to show that Parliament intended to cover the situation of a same-sex couple. Indeed, so far as it goes—and I do not attach any significance to it except in the negative way I have just mentioned—this evidence would tend to support the opposite conclusion.

In sum, neither ordinary meaning, context, or purpose indicates a legislative intention to include same-sex couples within "family status." ...

[Cory and McLachlin JJ agreed with La Forest J on certain issues but agreed with L'Heureux-Dubé J on the statutory interpretation issue.]

In *Mossop* the problem before the court is the disputed meaning of certain language in s. 3 of the *Canadian Human Rights Act*. In your opinion, is the relevant language the word "family" alone or the expression "family status"? Do you think that "family status" in this context is a legal term of art?

Does the word "family" have a plain meaning? If so, should the court be bound by that meaning in interpreting s. 3 of the Act?

Notice the arguments relied on by L'Heureux-Dubé J in the following passage. Do you find them persuasive?

With this caveat, had Parliament intended that the protection for families be restricted to legally recognized families, the amendment to the Act could have made this clear. However, this was not done. Instead, the amendment increased the scope of protection by adding a new ground of discrimination to each text: both "marital status" and "family status" became prohibited grounds. As the terms are juxtaposed, it is reasonable to conclude that "family status" must be something other than "marital status," just as "situation de famille" must be something other than "état matrimonial." Since "état matrimonial" is closer to a legal notion, "situation de famille" or "family status" can only be broader. It was, of course, open to Parliament to define the concept of "family status" within the Act. It did not choose to do so, even in the face of debate about the meaning of the term. Instead, Parliament determined that the task of dealing with any ambiguity in any concepts in the Act should be left to the administrative board charged with the task of implementing the Act. I refer, in this regard, to the comments of the Minister of Justice as reported in the *Minutes of Proceedings and Evidence of the Standing Committee on Justice and Legal Affairs*, Issue No. 114, December 20, 1982, at p. 17: "It will be up to the commission, the tribunals it appoints, and in the final cases, the courts, to ascertain in a given case the meaning to be given to these concepts." When asked why he was reluctant to define these terms within the Act itself, the Minister responded as follows:

> The reason for my reluctance to have such definitions included, Mr. Chairman, is that it is not in accord with the scheme of the bill. *These words are being interpreted by the Canadian Human Rights Commission. We trust them to interpret and issue regulations.*
>
> It is true, of course, that a court can always pronounce on the validity of this; but in most cases, the action of the commission is accepted. Generally speaking, we think that is a better way to proceed. [Emphasis added.]

(*Minutes of Proceedings and Evidence of the Standing Committee on Justice and Legal Affairs*, Issue No. 115, December 21, 1982, at p. 73.)

Though the members of Parliament may perhaps not at that precise moment have envisaged that "family status" would be interpreted by the Tribunal so as to extend to same-sex couples, the decision to leave the term undefined is evidence of clear legislative intent that the meaning of "family status," like the meaning of other undefined concepts in the Act, be left for the Commission and its tribunals to define. In my view, if the legislative record helps here in the search for legislative intent, it rather supports the Tribunal's wide and broad discretion in the interpretation of the provisions of its own Act.

An interpretation of a human rights document, or for that matter any legislation, that may not conform with Parliament's intention can be easily cured by Parliament itself. Because legislation can be amended more readily than a Constitution, legislatures which find the interpretations

given by administrative tribunals inconsistent with legislative intent can always amend the legislation, or pass new legislation in order to modify that interpretation.

Both Lamer CJ and L'Heureux-Dubé J address the question of legislative intent. When
Parliament added the words "family status" to the English version of the Act in 1983, according to Lamer CJ it deliberately declined to extend the Act's protection to sexual orientation,
but according to L'Heureux-Dubé J it chose to confer discretion on the Human Rights Tribunal to define "family status" in any way that would advance the purposes of the Act. Which
version captures Parliament's intent? How do you know?

Suppose that Parliament declined to include same-sex couples within "family status" in
1983, and again in 1993 when the *Mossop* case was decided. Would it nonetheless be appropriate for the court to support the tribunal's interpretation of this expression?

CHAPTER EIGHT

Constraints on Legislative and Administrative Action

This chapter explores the role that the judiciary plays in constraining legislative and administrative or executive action, a theme discussed in less detail in chapters 3 and 5. In a democratic society, governmental actors face a wide range of constraints on their efforts to pursue their understanding of the public good. These constraints may include limits on the support available from political allies; the need to address criticism from political opponents; the scrutiny of the media and affected interest groups; the practical constraints imposed by limited financial resources, personnel, or information needed to pursue an initiative effectively; and sometimes the requirement of cooperation from other levels of government, either domestically or internationally.

For many types of policies or programs, the constraints imposed by the need to comply with the law will be the easiest ones for governmental actors to address. Nevertheless, the availability of law as a constraint on government is important, not only in principle but often as a practical matter. These legal limits are likely to be especially important for individuals and minority interest groups who are unable to achieve their aims in the political or bureaucratic arena.

In section I of this chapter, we consider the role that judicial review using the Constitution plays in a democratic society. The principle of constitutional supremacy implies a restriction on governmental action that is inconsistent with the Constitution. The Constitution, and particularly the *Canadian Charter of Rights and Freedoms*, is an important tool for controlling unlawful executive or administrative action. As a practical matter, the most common use of the Charter in the courts is to challenge law enforcement activities engaged in by the police. What makes the Constitution distinctive is that it can be used to challenge not only the validity of executive or administrative action, but the validity of legislation as well. One may wish to question how appropriate it is for unelected judges to use their power to interpret and apply the Constitution to thwart the will of the democratically elected representatives of the citizenry. Even if one accepts the legitimacy of judicial review as a general proposition, it is still necessary to explore the appropriate limits of this role, and to consider how judges might attempt to reconcile this aspect of their role with our legal system's general commitment to democratic government.

In section II, we consider judicial review of administrative decision making using the common law. In this part we focus on the institutional relationships between courts and different administrative bodies. Judicial review shapes administrative decision making in two ways— first by influencing the procedures used by governmental bodies in making decisions, and second by subjecting the substance of the decisions themselves to judicial oversight. A comprehensive treatment of the complex body of legal doctrines that makes up Canadian administrative law is beyond the scope of this introductory text. We will, however, explore the ways in which these two aspects of common law judicial review result in quite different types of institutional relationships between courts and administrative bodies.

I. THE ROLE OF CONSTITUTIONAL JUDICIAL REVIEW IN A DEMOCRATIC SOCIETY

A. The Justification for Constitutional Judicial Review

The passage excerpted below from Chief Justice Marshall's famous judgment in *Marbury v. Madison* offers a principled account of constitutional supremacy and the role the judiciary plays in ensuring that the written Constitution prevails over ordinary legislation. Chief Justice Marshall's argument in support of constitutional supremacy is simple but compelling.

Marbury v. Madison
5 US 137 (1803)

MARSHALL CJ: ... The question, whether an act, repugnant to the constitution, can become the law of the land, is a question deeply interesting to the United States; but, happily, not of an intricacy proportioned to its interest. It seems only necessary to recognize certain principles, supposed to have been long and well established, to decide it.

That the people have an original right to establish, for their future government, such principles as, in their opinion, shall most conduce to their own happiness, is the basis on which the whole American fabric has been erected. The exercise of this original right is a very great exertion; nor can it nor ought it to be frequently repeated. The principles, therefore, so established are deemed fundamental. And as the authority, from which they proceed, is supreme, and can seldom act, they are designed to be permanent.

This original and supreme will organizes the government, and assigns to different departments their respective powers. It may either stop here; or establish certain limits not to be transcended by those departments.

The government of the United States is of the latter description. The powers of the legislature are defined and limited; and that those limits may not be mistaken or forgotten, the constitution is written. To what purpose are powers limited, and to what purpose is that limitation committed to writing; if these limits may, at any time, be passed by those intended to be restrained? The distinction between a government with limited and unlimited powers is abolished, if those limits do not confine the persons on whom they are imposed, and if acts prohibited and acts allowed are of equal obligation. It is a proposition too plain to be contested, that the constitution controls any legislative act repugnant to it; or, that the legislature may alter the constitution by an ordinary act.

Between these alternatives there is no middle ground. The constitution is either a superior, paramount law, unchangeable by ordinary means, or it is on a level with ordinary legislative acts, and like other acts, is alterable when the legislature shall please to alter it.

If the former part of the alternative be true, then a legislative act contrary to the constitution is not law: if the latter part be true, then written constitutions are absurd attempts, on the part of the people, to limit a power in its own nature illimitable.

Certainly all those who have framed written constitutions contemplate them as forming the fundamental and paramount law of the nation, and consequently the theory of every such government must be, that an act of the legislature repugnant to the constitution is void.

This theory is essentially attached to a written constitution, and is consequently to be considered by this court as one of the fundamental principles of our society. It is not therefore to be lost sight of in the further consideration of this subject.

If an act of the legislature, repugnant to the constitution, is void, does it, notwithstanding its invalidity, bind the courts and oblige them to give it effect? Or, in other words, though it be not law, does it constitute a rule as operative as if it was a law? This would be to overthrow in fact what was established in theory; and would seem, at first view, an absurdity too gross to be insisted on. It shall, however, receive a more attentive consideration.

It is emphatically the province and duty of the judicial department to say what the law is. Those who apply the rule to particular cases, must of necessity expound and interpret that rule. If two laws conflict with each other, the courts must decide on the operation of each.

So if a law be in opposition to the constitution: if both the law and the constitution apply to a particular case, so that the court must either decide that case conformably to the law, disregarding the constitution; or conformably to the constitution, disregarding the law: the court must determine which of these conflicting rules governs the case. This is of the very essence of judicial duty.

If then the courts are to regard the constitution; and the constitution is superior to any ordinary act of the legislature; the constitution, and not such ordinary act, must govern the case to which they both apply.

Those then who controvert the principle that the constitution is to be considered, in court, as a paramount law, are reduced to the necessity of maintaining that courts must close their eyes on the constitution, and see only the law.

This doctrine would subvert the very foundation of all written constitutions.

It would declare that an act, which, according to the principles and theory of our government, is entirely void, is yet, in practice, completely obligatory.

It would declare, that if the legislature shall do what is expressly forbidden, such act, notwithstanding the express prohibition, is in reality effectual. It would be giving to the legislature a practical and real omnipotence with the same breath which professes to restrict their powers within narrow limits. It is prescribing limits, and declaring that those limits may be passed at pleasure.

That it thus reduces to nothing what we have deemed the greatest improvement on political institutions—a written constitution, would of itself be sufficient, in America where written constitutions have been viewed with so much reverence, for rejecting the construction. But the peculiar expressions of the constitution of the United States furnish additional arguments in favour of its rejection.

The judicial power of the United States is extended to all cases arising under the constitution.

Could it be the intention of those who gave this power, to say that, in using it, the constitution should not be looked into? That a case arising under the constitution should be decided without examining the instrument under which it arises?

This is too extravagant to be maintained.

In some cases then, the constitution must be looked into by the judges. And if they can open it at all, what part of it are they forbidden to read, or to obey?

The historical origins of the principle of constitutional supremacy are different in Canada than they are in the United States. As Madam Justice Wilson explained in her reasons for judgment concurring in the result in *Operation Dismantle v. The Queen*, [1985] 1 SCR 441, at 482-83, constitutional supremacy in Canada was originally grounded in s. 2 of the *Colonial Laws Validity Act, 1865* (UK, 28 & 29 Vic.), c. 63, which rendered void and inoperative any Act of a colonial legislature that was repugnant to an Act of the Imperial Parliament that extended to the colony. Because the *British North America Act* (now the *Constitution Act, 1867*) was an Act of the Imperial Parliament that was binding upon the colonial legislatures of Canada and its provinces, federal or provincial legislation that was found to be inconsistent with the *British North America Act* was therefore void for repugnancy with an Imperial statute. The *Statute of Westminster, 1931* made Canada and its provinces free from Imperial legislation, but s. 7 of the Act expressly exempted the *British North America Act* and its amendments from this freedom in order to preserve the principle of constitutional supremacy.

With the patriation of the Canadian Constitution in 1982, the principle of constitutional supremacy was expressly enshrined in s. 52(1) of the *Constitution Act, 1982*, which reads: "The Constitution of Canada is the supreme law of Canada, and any law that is inconsistent with the provisions of the Constitution is, to the extent of the inconsistency, of no force or effect."

B. The Limitations of Judicial Review

1. *The Issue of Justiciability*

Are all actions by the political branches of government "justiciable"—that is, amenable to oversight by the courts? In addition to providing the Supreme Court of Canada with an opportunity to explore the principle of constitutional supremacy, the *Operation Dismantle* case also tested the limits of the role that courts play in weighing governmental measures designed to protect national security against the standards imposed by the Constitution.

Operation Dismantle v. The Queen
[1985] 1 SCR 441

DICKSON J (Estey, McIntyre, Chouinard, and Lamer JJ concurring): This case arises out of the appellants' challenge under s. 7 of the *Canadian Charter of Rights and Freedoms* to the decision of the federal cabinet to permit the testing of the cruise missile by the United States of America in Canadian territory. The issue that must be addressed is whether the appellants' statement of claim should be struck out, before trial, as disclosing no reasonable cause of action. In their statement of claim, the appellants seek: (i) a declaration that the decision to permit the testing of the cruise missile is unconstitutional; (ii) injunctive relief to prohibit the testing; and (iii) damages. Cattanach J of the Federal Court, Trial Division, refused the respondents' motion to strike. The Federal Court of Appeal unanimously allowed the respondents' appeal, struck out the statement of claim and dismissed the appellants' action.

The facts and procedural history of this case are fully set out and discussed in the reasons for judgment of Madame Justice Wilson. I agree with Madame Justice Wilson that the appellants' statement of claim should be struck out and this appeal dismissed. I have reached this conclusion, however, on the basis of reasons which differ somewhat from those of Madame Justice Wilson.

In my opinion, if the appellants are to be entitled to proceed to trial, their statement of claim must disclose facts, which, if taken as true, would show that the action of the Canadian government could cause an infringement of their rights under s. 7 of the Charter. I have concluded that the causal link between the actions of the Canadian government, and the alleged violation of appellants' rights under the Charter is simply too uncertain, speculative and hypothetical to sustain a cause of action. Thus, although decisions of the federal cabinet are reviewable by the courts under the Charter, and the government bears a general duty to act in accordance with the Charter's dictates, no duty is imposed on the Canadian government by s. 7 of the Charter to refrain from permitting the testing of the cruise missile.

. . .

In the present case, the speculative nature of the allegation that the decision to test the cruise missile will lead to an increased threat of nuclear war makes it manifest that no duty is imposed on the Canadian government to refrain from permitting the testing. The government's action simply could not be proven to cause the alleged violation of s. 7 of the Charter and, thus, no duty can arise.

III. Justiciability

The approach which I have taken is not based on the concept of justiciability. I agree in substance with Madame Justice Wilson's discussion of justiciability and her conclusion that the doctrine is founded upon a concern with the appropriate role of the courts as the forum for the resolution of different types of disputes. I have no doubt that disputes of a political or foreign policy nature may be properly cognizable by the courts. My concerns in the present case focus on the impossibility of the Court finding, on the basis of evidence, the connection, alleged by the appellants, between the duty of the government to act in accordance with the *Charter of Rights and Freedoms* and the violation of their rights under s. 7. As stated above, I do not believe the alleged violation—namely, the increased threat of nuclear war—could ever be sufficiently linked as a factual matter to the acknowledged duty of the government to respect s. 7 of the Charter.

. . .

WILSON J (concurring in result only):

. . .

(1) Is the Government's Decision Reviewable?

. . .

(b) Non-justiciability

Le Dain and Ryan JJ in the Federal Court of Appeal were of the opinion that the issues involved in this case are inherently non-justiciable, either because the question whether testing the cruise missile increases the risk of nuclear war is not susceptible of proof and hence is not triable (per Ryan J) or because answering that question involves factors which are either inaccessible to a court or are of a nature which a court is incapable of evaluating (per Le Dain J). To the extent that this objection to the appellants' case rests on the inherent evidentiary difficulties which would obviously confront any attempt to prove the appellants' allegations of fact, I do not think it can be sustained. It might well be that, if the issue were allowed to go to trial, the appellants would lose simply by reason of their not having been able to establish the factual basis of their claim but that does not seem to me to be a reason for striking the case out at this preliminary stage. It is trite law that on a motion to strike out a statement of claim the plaintiff's allegations of fact are to be taken as having been proved. Accordingly, it is arguable that by dealing with the case as they have done Le Dain and Ryan JJ have, in effect, made a presumption against the appellants which they are not entitled, on a preliminary motion of this kind, to make.

I am not convinced, however, that Le Dain and Ryan JJ were restricting the concept of non-justiciability to difficulties of evidence and proof. Both rely on Lord Radcliffe's judgment in *Chandler v. D.P.P.*, [1964] AC 777, [1962] 3 All ER 142, 46 Cr. App. Rep. 347 (HL), and especially on the following passage at p. 151:

> The disposition and equipment of the forces and the facilities afforded to allied forces for defence purposes constitute a given fact and it cannot be a matter of proof or finding that the decisions of policy on which they rest are or are not in the country's best interests. I may add that I can think of few issues which present themselves in less triable form. It would be ingenuous to suppose that the kind of evidence that the appellants wanted to call could make more than a small contribution to its final solution. The facts which they wished to establish might well be admitted: even so, throughout history men have had to run great risk for themselves and others in the hope of attaining objectives which they prize for all. *The more one looks at it, the plainer it becomes, I think, that the question whether it is in the true interests of this country to acquire, retain or house nuclear armaments depends on an infinity of considerations, military and diplomatic, technical, psychological and moral, and of decisions, tentative or final, which are*

themselves part assessments of fact and part expectations and hopes. I do not think that there is anything amiss with a legal ruling that does not make this issue a matter for judge or jury. (Emphasis added)

In my opinion, this passage makes clear that in Lord Radcliffe's view these kinds of issues are to be treated as non-justiciable not simply because of evidentiary difficulties but because they involve moral and political considerations which it is not within the province of the courts to assess. Le Dain J maintains that the difficulty is one of judicial competence rather than anything resembling the American "political questions" doctrine. However, in response to that contention it can be pointed out that, however unsuited courts may be for the task, they are called upon all the time to decide questions of principle and policy. As Melville Weston points out in "Political Questions" (1925), 38 *Harv. L Rev.* 296 at 299:

> The word "justiciable" … is legitimately capable of denoting almost any question. That is to say, the questions are few which are intrinsically incapable of submission to a tribunal having an established procedure, with an orderly presentation of such evidence as is available, for the purpose of an adjudication from which practical consequences in human conduct are to follow. For example, when nations decline to submit to arbitration or to the compulsory jurisdiction of a proposed international tribunal those questions of honour or interest which they call "non-justiciable" they are really avoiding that broad sense of the word, but what they mean is a little less clear. Probably they mean only that they will not, or deem they ought not, endure the presentation of evidence on such questions, nor bind their conduct to conform to the proposed adjudications. So far as "non-justiciable" is for them more than an epithet, it expresses a sense of a lack of fitness, and not of any inherent impossibility, of submitting these questions to judicial or quasi-judicial determination.

In the 1950's and early 1960's there was considerable debate in Britain over the question whether restrictive trade practices legislation gave rise to questions which were subject to judicial determination: see Marshall, "Justiciability" in *Oxford Essays in Jurisprudence* (1961), ed. A.G. Guest; Summers, "Justiciability" (1963), 26 *MLR* 530; Stevens, "Justiciability: The Restrictive Practices Court Re-Examined," [1964] *Public Law* 221. I think it is fairly clear that the British restrictive trade practices legislation did not involve the courts in the resolution of issues more imponderable than those facing American courts administering the *Sherman Act*. Indeed, there is significantly less "policy" content in the decisions of the courts in those cases than there is in the decisions of administrative tribunals such as the Canadian Transport Commission or the CRTC. The real issue there, and perhaps also in the case at bar, is not the *ability* of judicial tribunals to make a decision on the questions presented, but the *appropriateness* of the use of the judicial techniques for such purposes.

I cannot accept the proposition that difficulties of evidence or proof absolve the Court from making a certain kind of decision if it can be established on other grounds that it has a duty to do so. I think we should focus our attention on whether the courts *should* or *must* rather than on whether they *can* deal with such matters. We should put difficulties of evidence and proof aside and consider whether as a constitutional matter it is appropriate or obligatory for the courts to decide the issue before us. I will return to this question later.

(c) The Political Questions Doctrine

It is a well established principle of American constitutional law that there are certain kinds of "political questions" that a court ought to refuse to decide. In *Baker v. Carr*, 369 US 186 (1962) at pp. 210-11, Brennan J discussed the nature of the doctrine in the following terms:

> We have said that "[i]n determining whether a question falls within (the political question) category, the appropriateness under our system of government of attributing finality to the action of the political departments and also the lack of satisfactory criteria for a judicial determination are dominant considerations." *Coleman v. Miller*, 307 US 433, 454-455. The non-justiciability of a political question is primarily a function of the separation of powers. Much confusion results from the capacity of the "political question" label to obscure the need for case-by-case inquiry. Deciding whether a matter has in any measure been committed by the Constitution to another branch of government, or whether the action of that branch exceeds whatever authority has been committed, is itself a delicate exercise in constitutional interpretation, and is a responsibility of this court as ultimate interpreter of a Constitution.

At p. 217 he said:

> It is apparent that several formulations which vary slightly according to the settings in which the questions arise may describe a political question, although each has one or more elements which identify it as essentially a function of the separation of powers. Prominent on the surface of any case held to involve a political question is found a textually demonstrable constitutional commitment of the issue to a coordinate political department; or a lack of judicially discoverable and manageable standards for resolving it; or the impossibility of deciding without an initial policy determination of a kind clearly for nonjudicial discretion; or the impossibility of a court's undertaking independent resolution without expressing lack of the respect due coordinate branches of government; or an unusual need for unquestioning adherence to a political decision already made; or the potentiality of embarrassment from multifarious pronouncements by various departments on one question.

While one or two of the categories of political question referred to by Brennan J raise the issue of judicial or institutional competence already referred to, the underlying theme is the separation of powers in the sense of the proper role of the courts vis-à-vis the other branches of government. In this regard it is perhaps noteworthy that a distinction is drawn in the American case law between matters internal to the United States on the one hand and foreign affairs on the other. In the area of foreign affairs the courts are especially deferential to the executive branch of government: see e.g. *Atlee v. Laird*, 347 F. Supp. 689 (1972) (US Dist. Ct.), at pp. 701 ff.

While Brennan J's statement, in my view, accurately sums up the reasoning American courts have used in deciding that specific cases did not present questions which were judicially cognizable, I do not think it is particularly helpful in determining when American courts will find that those factors come into play. In cases from *Marbury v. Madison*, 5 US (1 Cranch) 137 (1803) to *United States v. Nixon*, 418 US 683 (1974), the court has not allowed the "respect due coordinate branches of government" to prevent it from rendering decisions highly embarrassing to those holding executive or legislative office. In *Baker v. Carr* itself, *supra*, Frankfurter J, in dissent, expressed concern that the judiciary could not find manageable standards for the problems presented by the reapportionment of political districts. Indeed, some would say that the enforcement of the desegregation decision in *Brown v. Board of Education of Topeka*, 347 US 483 (1954), gave rise to similar problems of judicial unmanageability. Yet American courts have ventured into these areas undeterred.

· · ·

It might be timely at this point to remind ourselves of the question the court is being asked to decide. It is, of course, true that the federal Legislature has exclusive legislative jurisdiction in relation to defence under s. 91(7) of the *Constitution Act, 1867* and that the federal executive has the powers conferred upon it in ss. 9-15 of that Act. Accordingly, if the court were simply being asked to express its opinion on the wisdom of the executive's exercise of its defence powers in this case, the court would have to decline. It cannot substitute its opinion for that of the executive to whom the decision-making power is given by the Constitution. Because the *effect* of the appellants' action is to challenge the wisdom of the government's defence policy, it is tempting to say that the court should in the same way refuse to involve itself. However, I think this would be to miss the point, to fail to focus on the question which is before us. The question before us is not whether the government's defence policy is sound but whether or not it violates the appellants' rights under s. 7 of the *Charter of Rights and Freedoms*. This is a totally different question. I do not think there can be any doubt that this is a question for the courts. Indeed, s. 24(1) of the Charter, also part of the Constitution, makes it clear that the adjudication of that question is the responsibility of "a court of competent jurisdiction." While the court is entitled to grant such remedy as it "considers appropriate and just in the circumstances," I do not think it is open to it to relinquish its jurisdiction either on the basis that the issue is inherently non-justiciable or that it raises a so-called "political question": see Martin H. Redish, "Abstention, Separation of Powers, and the Limits of the Judicial Function" (1984), 94 *Yale LJ* 71.

I would conclude, therefore, that if we are to look at the Constitution for the answer to the question whether it is appropriate for the courts to "second guess" the executive on matters of defence, we would conclude that it is not appropriate. However, if what we are being asked to do is to decide whether any particular act of the executive violates the rights of the citizens, then it is not only appropriate that we answer the question; it is our obligation under the Charter to do so.

· · ·

(3) Could the Facts as Alleged Constitute a Violation of Section 7 of the Charter?

Section 7 of the *Canadian Charter of Rights and Freedoms* provides as follows:

> 7. Everyone has the right to life, liberty and security of the person and the right not to be deprived thereof except in accordance with the principles of fundamental justice.

Whether or not the facts that are alleged in the appellants' statement of claim could constitute a violation of s. 7 is, of course, the question that lies at the heart of this case. If they could not, then the appellants' statement of claim discloses no reasonable cause of action and the appeal must be dismissed. The appellants submit that on its proper construction s. 7 gives rise to two separate and presumably independent rights, namely the right to life, liberty and security of the person, and the right not to be deprived of such life, liberty and security of the person except in accordance with the principles of fundamental justice. In their submission, therefore, a violation of the principles of fundamental justice would only have to be alleged in relation to a claim based on a violation of the second right. As Marceau J points out in his reasons, the French text of s. 7 does not seem to admit of this two-rights interpretation since only one right is specifically mentioned. Moreover, as the respondents point out, the appellants' suggestion does not accord with the interpretation that the courts have placed on the similarly structured provision in s. 1(a) of the *Canadian Bill of Rights*: see e.g. *R v. Miller*, [1977] 2 SCR 680, *per* Ritchie J, at pp. 703-04.

The appellants' submission, however, touches upon a number of important issues regarding the proper interpretation of s. 7. Even if the section gives rise to a single unequivocal right not to be deprived of life, liberty or security of the person except in accordance with the principles of fundamental justice, there nonetheless remains the question whether fundamental justice is entirely procedural in nature or whether it has a substantive aspect as well. This, in turn, leads to the related question whether there might not be certain deprivations of life, liberty or personal security which could not be justified no matter what procedure was employed to effect them. These are among the most important and difficult questions of interpretation arising under the Charter but I do not think it is necessary to deal with them in this case. It can, in my opinion, be disposed of without reaching these issues.

In my view, even an independent, substantive right to life, liberty and security of the person cannot be absolute. For example, the right to liberty, which I take to be the right to pursue one's goals free of governmental constraint, must accommodate the corresponding rights of others. The concept of "right" as used in the Charter postulate the inter-relation of individuals in society all of whom have the same right. The aphorism that "A hermit has no need of rights" makes the point. The concept of "right" also premises the existence of someone or some group against whom the right may be asserted. As Mortimer J. Adler expressed it in *Six Great Ideas* (1981), at p. 144:

> Living in organized societies under effective government and enforceable laws, as they must in order to survive and prosper, human beings neither have autonomy nor are they entitled to unlimited liberty of action. Autonomy is incompatible with organized society. Unlimited liberty is destructive of it.

The concept of "right" used in the Charter must also, I believe, recognize and take account of the political reality of the modern state. Action by the state or, conversely, inaction by the state will frequently have the effect of decreasing or increasing the risk to the lives or security of its citizens. It may be argued, for example, that the failure of government to limit significantly the speed of traffic on the highways threatens our right to life and security in that it increases the risk of highway accidents. Such conduct, however, would not, in my view, fall within the scope of the right protected by s. 7 of the Charter.

In the same way, the concept of "right" as used in the Charter must take account of the fact that the self-contained political community which comprises the state is faced with at least the possibility, if not the reality, of external threats to both its collective well-being and to the individual well-being of its citizens. In order to protect the community against such threats it may well be necessary for the state to take steps which incidentally increase the risk to the lives or personal security of some or all of the state's citizens. Such steps, it seems to me, cannot have been contemplated by the draftsman of the Charter as giving rise to violations of s. 7. As John Rawls states in *A Theory of Justice* (1971), at p. 213:

> The government's right to maintain public order and security is ... a right which the government must have if it is to carry out its duty of impartially supporting the conditions necessary for everyone's pursuit of his interests and living up to his obligations as he understands them.

The rights under the Charter not being absolute, their content or scope must be discerned quite apart from any limitation sought to be imposed upon them by the government under s. 1. As was pointed out by the Ontario Court of Appeal in *Re Federal Republic of Germany and Rauca* (1983), 41 OR (2d) 225 at 244, 34 CR (3d) 97, 4 CCC (3d) 385, 4 CRR 42, 145 DLR (3d) 638:

> The Charter was not enacted in a vacuum and the rights set out therein must be interpreted rationally having regard to existing law ... .

There is no liberty without law and there is no law without some restriction of liberty: see Dworkin, *Taking Rights Seriously* (1977), p. 267. This paradox caused Roscoe Pound to conclude:

> There is no more ambiguous word in legal and juristic literature than the word right. In its most general sense it means a reasonable expectation involved in civilized life.

(See *Jurisprudence*, vol. 4 (1959), p. 56.)

It is not necessary to accept the restrictive interpretation advanced by Pratte J, which would limit s. 7 to protection against arbitrary arrest or detention, in order to agree that the central concern of the section is direct impingement by government upon the life, liberty and personal security of individual citizens. At the very least, it seems to me, there must be a strong presumption that governmental action which concerns the relations of the state with other states, and which is therefore not directed at any member of the immediate political community, was never intended to be caught by s. 7 even although such action may have the incidental effect of increasing the risk of death or injury that individuals generally have to face.

I agree with Le Dain J that the essence of the appellants' case is the claim that permitting the cruise missile to be tested in Canada will increase the risk of nuclear war. But even accepting this allegation of fact as true, which as I have already said I think we must do on a motion to strike, it is my opinion for the reasons given above that this state of affairs could not constitute a breach of s. 7. Moreover, I do not see how one can distinguish in a principled way between this particular risk and any other danger to which the government's action vis-à-vis other states might incidentally subject its citizens. A declaration of war, for example, almost certainly increases the risk to most citizens of death or injury. Acceptance of the appellants' submissions, it seems to me, would mean that any such declaration would also have to be regarded as a violation of s. 7. I cannot think that that could be a proper interpretation of the Charter.

This is not to say that every governmental action that is purportedly taken in furtherance of national defence would be beyond the reach of s. 7. If, for example, testing the cruise missile posed a direct threat to some specific segment of the populace—as, for example, if it were being tested with live warheads—I think that might well raise different considerations.

A court might find that that constituted a violation of s. 7 and it might then be up to the government to try to establish that testing the cruise with live warheads was justified under s. 1 of the Charter. Section 1, in my opinion, is the uniquely Canadian mechanism through which the courts are to determine the justiciability of particular issues that come before it. It embodies through its reference to a free and democratic society the essential features of our constitution including the separation of powers, responsible government and the rule of law. It obviates the need for a "political questions" doctrine and permits the court to deal with what might be termed "prudential" considerations in a principled way without renouncing its constitutional and mandated responsibility for judicial review. It is not, however, called into operation here since the facts alleged in the statement of claim, even if they could be shown to be true, could not in my opinion constitute a violation of s. 7.

2. The Issue of Enforcement

While Canadian judges accept the proposition that the Constitution is supreme and the corollary that it is their duty to interpret the Constitution and invalidate any legislation that is inconsistent with the Constitution, the practical reality is that courts normally have to rely on the executive and legislative branches of government for the enforcement of their decisions. Canadian courts are usually able to rely on the other branches of government for this support, but it is not inevitable that this will always be the case. In these circumstances, how aggressive may the courts be in usurping the executive or legislative function and imposing solutions?

Consider *Doucet-Boudreau v. Nova Scotia*. This case split the Supreme Court of Canada over the scope of the judicial power to grant a form of "structural injunction" as a remedy under s. 24(1) of the Charter for a breach by the executive branch of a positive Charter right. The trial judge had ordered the government of Nova Scotia to use its "best efforts" to build a French-language school or schools to comply with its duties under the minority language rights provision in s. 23 of the Charter. The judge had added to his order a requirement that the government provide him with periodic reports on its progress in this regard. A five-justice majority of the court concluded that this remedy came within a superior court's authority under s. 24. The minority argued that such an injunction usurped the role of the executive by placing the judiciary in the position of directing the implementation of law and government policy.

Doucet-Boudreau v. Nova Scotia (Minister of Education)
[2003] 3 SCR 3

IACOBUCCI and ARBOUR JJ (McLachlin CJ and Gonthier and Bastarache JJ concurring): [1] This appeal involves the nature of remedies available under s. 24(1) of the *Canadian Charter of Rights and Freedoms* for the realization of the minority language education rights protected by s. 23 of the Charter. The specific issue is whether a trial judge may, after ordering that a provincial government use its best efforts to build French-language school facilities by given dates, retain jurisdiction to hear reports on the progress of those efforts. The issue of broader and ongoing judicial involvement in the administration of public institutions is not before the Court in this case.

I. *Background and Judicial History*

[2] The appellants are Francophone parents living in five school districts in Nova Scotia (Kingston/Greenwood, Chéticamp, Île Madame-Arichat (Petit-de-Grat), Argyle, and Clare) and Fédération des parents acadiens de la Nouvelle-Écosse Inc., a non-profit organization that monitors the advancement of educational rights of the Acadian and Francophone minority in Nova Scotia. The Attorney General of Nova Scotia is the respondent, acting on behalf of the Department of Education of Nova Scotia.

[3] Apart from the specific facts of the case, it is most important to note the historical context on which this dispute is centred. As we will discuss below, French-language education in Nova Scotia has not had an enviable record of success. While the situation improved over the rather dismal record of the previous centuries, the twentieth century left much to be achieved. Section 23 of the Charter has been the hope of the French-speaking minority of Nova Scotia to redress the linguistic failings and inequality of history.

[4] It is conceded in this appeal that s. 23 of the Charter entitles the appellant parents to publicly funded French-language educational facilities for their children. For some time, Francophone parents in these five school districts of Nova Scotia had been urging their provincial government to provide homogeneous French-language schools at the secondary level in addition to the existing primary level facilities. The government of Nova Scotia, for its part, agreed: it did not dispute that the number of students warranted the facilities demanded. The government amended the *Education Act*, SNS 1995-96, c. 1, ss. 11-16, in 1996 to create the Conseil scolaire acadien provincial (the "Conseil"), a province-wide French-language school board, with a view to realizing the Charter's minority language education rights. However, while s. 11(1) empowered the Conseil to deliver and administer all French-language programs, only the Minister, with the approval of the Governor in Council, could construct, furnish and equip schools (see s. 88(1)). Although the government eventually announced the construction of the new French-language school facilities, construction of the promised schools never began. So in 1998, 16 years after the right was entrenched in the Constitution, the appellant parents applied to the Supreme Court of Nova Scotia for an order directing the Province and the Conseil to provide, out of public funds, homogeneous French-language facilities and programs at the secondary school level.

· · ·

II. *Issues*

· · ·

[12] The main issue in the appeal is simply this: having found a violation of s. 23 of the Charter and having ordered that the Province make its best efforts to provide homogeneous French-language facilities and programs by particular dates, did the Nova Scotia Supreme Court have the authority to retain jurisdiction to hear reports from the Province on the status of those efforts as part of its remedy under s. 24(1) of the Charter?

[13] Strictly speaking, only the retention of jurisdiction to hear reports, and not the "best efforts" order itself, is at issue in the present appeal. Nonetheless, the best efforts order

and the retention of jurisdiction were conceived by the trial judge as two complementary parts of a whole. A full appreciation of the balance and moderation of the trial judge's approach to crafting this remedy requires that the reports respecting the respondents' compliance with the order be viewed and evaluated in the context of the remedy as a whole.

· · ·

IV. Analysis

· · ·

B. The Retention of Jurisdiction

(1) The Importance of Context: Sections 23 and 24 of the Charter

[23] It is well accepted that the Charter should be given a generous and expansive interpretation and not a narrow, technical, or legalistic one ... . The need for a generous interpretation flows from the principle that the Charter ought to be interpreted purposively. While courts must be careful not to overshoot the actual purposes of the Charter's guarantees, they must avoid a narrow, technical approach to Charter interpretation which could subvert the goal of ensuring that right holders enjoy the full benefit and protection of the Charter. In our view, the approach taken by our colleagues LeBel and Deschamps JJ which appears to contemplate that special remedies might be available in some circumstances, but not in this case, severely undervalues the importance and the urgency of the language rights in the context facing LeBlanc J.

[24] The requirement of a generous and expansive interpretive approach holds equally true for Charter remedies as for Charter rights (*R v. Gamble*, [1988] 2 SCR 595; *R v. Sarson*, [1996] 2 SCR 223; *R v. 974649 Ontario Inc.*, [2001] 3 SCR 575, 2001 SCC 81 ("*Dunedin*")). ...

[25] Purposive interpretation means that remedies provisions must be interpreted in a way that provides "a full, effective and meaningful remedy for Charter violations" since "a right, no matter how expansive in theory, is only as meaningful as the remedy provided for its breach" (*Dunedin, supra*, at paras. 19-20). A purposive approach to remedies in a Charter context gives modern vitality to the ancient maxim *ubi jus, ibi remedium*: where there is a right, there must be a remedy. More specifically, a purposive approach to remedies requires at least two things. First, the purpose of the right being protected must be promoted: courts must craft *responsive* remedies. Second, the purpose of the remedies provision must be promoted: courts must craft *effective* remedies.

· · ·

[30] To put the matter of judicial remedies in greater context, it is useful to reflect briefly on the role of courts in the enforcement of our laws.

[31] Canada has evolved into a country that is noted and admired for its adherence to the rule of law as a major feature of its democracy. But the rule of law can be shallow without proper mechanisms for its enforcement. In this respect, courts play an essential role since they are the central institutions to deal with legal disputes through the rendering of judgments and decisions. But courts have no physical or economic means to enforce their judgments. Ultimately, courts depend on both the executive and the citizenry to recognize and abide by their judgments.

[32] Fortunately, Canada has had a remarkable history of compliance with court decisions by private parties and by all institutions of government. That history of compliance has become a fundamentally cherished value of our constitutional democracy; we must never take it for granted but always be careful to respect and protect its importance, otherwise the seeds of tyranny can take root.

[33] This tradition of compliance takes on a particular significance in the constitutional law context, where courts must ensure that government behaviour conforms with constitutional norms but in doing so must also be sensitive to the separation of function among the legislative, judicial and executive branches. While our Constitution does not expressly provide for the separation of powers (see *Re Residential Tenancies Act, 1979*, [1981] 1 SCR 714, at p. 728; *Douglas/Kwantlen Faculty Assn. v. Douglas College*, [1990] 3 SCR 570, at p. 601; *Reference re Secession of Quebec*, [1998] 2 SCR 217, at para. 15), the functional separation among the executive, legislative and judicial branches of governance has frequently been noted. (See, for example, *Fraser v. Public Service Staff Relations Board*, [1985] 2 SCR 455, at pp. 469-70.) In *New Brunswick Broadcasting Co. v. Nova Scotia (Speaker of the House of Assembly)*, [1993] 1 SCR 319, McLachlin J (as she then was) stated, at p. 389:

> Our democratic government consists of several branches: the Crown, as represented by the Governor General and the provincial counterparts of that office; the legislative body; the executive; and the courts. It is fundamental to the working of government as a whole that all these parts play their proper role. It is equally fundamental that no one of them overstep its bounds, that each show proper deference for the legitimate sphere of activity of the other.

[34] In other words, in the context of constitutional remedies, courts must be sensitive to their role as judicial arbiters and not fashion remedies which usurp the role of the other branches of governance by taking on tasks to which other persons or bodies are better suited. Concern for the limits of the judicial role is interwoven throughout the law. The development of the doctrines of justiciability, and to a great extent mootness, standing, and ripeness resulted from concerns about the courts overstepping the bounds of the judicial function and their role vis-à-vis other branches of government.

. . .

(b) The Reporting Order Respected the Framework of Our Constitutional Democracy

[70] Our colleagues LeBel and Deschamps JJ appear to consider that the issuance of an injunction against the government under s. 24(1) is constitutionally suspect and represents a departure from a consensus about Charter remedies (see para. 134 of the dissent). With respect, it is clear that a court may issue an injunction under s. 24(1) of the Charter. The power of courts to issue injunctions against the executive is central to s. 24(1) of the Charter which envisions more than declarations of rights. Courts do take actions to ensure that rights are enforced, and not merely declared. Contempt proceedings in the face of defiance of court orders, as well as coercive measures such as garnishments, writs of seizure and sale and the like are all known to courts. In this case, it was open to the trial judge in all the circumstances to choose the injunctive remedy on the terms and conditions that he prescribed.

(c) The Reporting Order Called on the Function and Powers of a Court

· · ·

[72] The difficulties of ongoing supervision of parties by the courts have sometimes been advanced as a reason that orders for specific performance and mandatory injunctions should not be awarded. Nonetheless, courts of equity have long accepted and overcome this difficulty of supervision where the situations demanded such remedies (see Sharpe ... , at paras. 1.260-1.380; *Attorney-General v. Birmingham, Tame, and Rea District Drainage Board*, [1910] 1 Ch. 48 (CA), aff'd [1912] AC 788 (HL); *Kennard v. Cory Brothers and Co.*, [1922] 1 Ch. 265, aff'd [1922] 2 Ch. 1 (CA)).

[73] As academic commentators have pointed out, the range of remedial orders available to courts in civil proceedings demonstrates that constitutional remedies involving some degree of ongoing supervision do not represent a radical break with the past practices of courts (see W.A. Bogart, "'Appropriate and Just': Section 24 of the Canadian Charter of Rights and Freedoms and the Question of Judicial Legitimacy" (1986), 10 *Dalhousie LJ* 81, at pp. 92-94; N. Gillespie, "Charter Remedies: The Structural Injunction" (1989-90), 11 *Advocates' Q* 190, at pp. 217-18; Roach, *Constitutional Remedies in Canada* ... , at paras. 13.50-13.80; Sharpe ... , at paras. 1.260-1.490). The change announced by s. 24 of the Charter is that the flexibility inherent in an equitable remedial jurisdiction may be applied to orders addressed to government to vindicate constitutionally entrenched rights.

[74] The order in this case was in no way inconsistent with the judicial function. There was never any suggestion in this case that the court would, for example, improperly take over the detailed management and co-ordination of the construction projects. Hearing evidence and supervising cross-examinations on progress reports about the construction of schools are not beyond the normal capacities of courts.

· · ·

(5) Conclusion

[87] Section 24(1) of the Charter requires that courts issue effective, responsive remedies that guarantee full and meaningful protection of Charter rights and freedoms. The meaningful protection of Charter rights, and in particular the enforcement of s. 23 rights, may in some cases require the introduction of novel remedies. A superior court may craft any remedy that it considers appropriate and just in the circumstances. In doing so, courts should be mindful of their roles as constitutional arbiters and the limits of their institutional capacities. Reviewing courts, for their part, must show considerable deference to trial judges' choice of remedy, and should refrain from using hindsight to perfect a remedy. A reviewing court should only interfere where the trial judge has committed an error of law or principle.

[88] The remedy crafted by LeBlanc J meaningfully vindicated the rights of the appellant parents by encouraging the Province's prompt construction of school facilities, without drawing the court outside its proper role. The Court of Appeal erred in wrongfully interfering with and striking down the portion of LeBlanc J's order in which he retained jurisdiction to hear progress reports on the status of the Province's efforts in providing school facilities by the required dates.

· · ·

LeBEL and DESCHAMPS JJ (dissenting) (Major and Binnie JJ concurring):

· · ·

II. The Nature of the Issues

· · ·

[94] At the outset, we wish to emphasize that we fully agree with our colleagues in their analysis of the nature and fundamental importance of language rights in the Canadian Constitution, as well as on the need for efficacy and imagination in the development of constitutional remedies. Indeed, we dissent because we believe that constitutional remedies should be designed keeping in mind the canons of good legal drafting, the fundamental importance of procedural fairness, and a proper awareness of the nature of the role of courts in our democratic political regime, a key principle of which remains the separation of powers. This principle protects the independence of courts. It also flexibly delineates the domain of court action, particularly in the relationship of courts not only with legislatures but also with the executive branch of government or public administration.

· · ·

IV. The Appropriate Role of the Judiciary

[105] While superior courts' powers to craft Charter remedies may not be constrained by statutory or common law limits, they are nonetheless bound by rules of fundamental justice, as we have shown above, and by constitutional boundaries, as we shall see below. In the context of constitutional remedies, courts fulfill their proper function by issuing orders precise enough for the parties to know what is expected of them, and by permitting the parties to execute those orders. Such orders are final. A court purporting to retain jurisdiction to oversee the implementation of a remedy, after a final order has been issued, will likely be acting inappropriately on two levels. First, by attempting to extend the court's jurisdiction beyond its proper role, it will breach the separation of powers principle. Second, by acting after exhausting its jurisdiction, it will breach the functus officio doctrine. We will look at each of these breaches in turn.

1. The Separation of Powers

[106] Courts are called upon to play a fundamental role in the Canadian constitutional regime. When needed, they must be assertive in enforcing constitutional rights. At times, they have to grant such relief as will be required to safeguard basic constitutional rights and the rule of law, despite the sensitivity of certain issues or circumstances and the reverberations of their decisions in their societal environment. Despite—or, perhaps, because of—the critical importance of their functions, courts should be wary of going beyond the proper scope of the role assigned to them in the public law of Canada. In essence, this role is to declare what the law is, contribute to its development and to give claimants such relief in the form of declarations, interpretation and orders as will be needed to remedy infringements of constitutional and legal rights by public authorities. Beyond these functions, an attitude of restraint remains all the more justified, given that, as the majority reasons acknowledge,

Canada has maintained a tradition of compliance by governments and public servants with judicial interpretations of the law and court orders.

· · ·

[111] More specifically, once they have rendered judgment, courts should resist the temptation to directly oversee or supervise the administration of their orders. They should generally operate under a presumption that judgments of courts will be executed with reasonable diligence and good faith. Once they have declared what the law is, issued their orders and granted such relief as they think is warranted by circumstances and relevant legal rules, courts should take care not to unnecessarily invade the province of public administration. To do otherwise could upset the balance that has been struck between our three branches of government.

[112] This is what occurred in the present case. When the trial judge attempted to oversee the implementation of his order, he not only assumed jurisdiction over a sphere traditionally outside the province of the judiciary, but also acted beyond the jurisdiction with which he was legitimately charged as a trial judge. In other words, he was functus officio and breached an important principle which reflects the nature and function of the judiciary in the Canadian constitutional order, as we shall see now.

2. *Functus Officio*

[115] If a court is permitted to continually revisit or reconsider final orders simply because it has changed its mind or wishes to continue exercising jurisdiction over a matter, there would never be finality to a proceeding, or, as G. Pépin and Y. Ouellette have perceptively termed it, the providing of [TRANSLATION] "legal security" for the parties (*Principes de contentieux administratif* (2nd ed. 1982), at p. 221) ... . The principle ensures that subject to an appeal, parties are secure in their reliance on the finality of superior court decisions.

· · ·

[117] In addition to this concern with finality, the question of whether a court is clothed with the requisite authority to act raises concerns related to the separation of powers, a principle that transcends procedural and common law rules. In our view, if a court intervenes, as here, in matters of administration properly entrusted to the executive, it exceeds its proper sphere and thereby breaches the separation of powers. By crossing the boundary between judicial acts and administrative oversight, it acts illegitimately and without jurisdiction. Such a crossing of the boundary cannot be characterized as relief that is "appropriate and just in the circumstances" within the meaning of s. 24(1) of the Charter.

V. *Application of the Relevant Principles to the Present Case*

[118] When the above principles are applied to the present facts, it is evident that McIntyre J's admonition in *Mills v. The Queen*, [1986] 1 SCR 863, that s. 24(1) "was not intended to turn the Canadian legal system upside down" is apropos (p. 953). In our view, the trial judge's remedy undermined the proper role of the judiciary within our constitutional order, and unnecessarily upset the balance between the three branches of government. As a result, the trial judge in the present circumstances acted inappropriately, and contrary to s. 24(1).

[119] As we noted above, the trial judge equivocated on the question of whether his purported retention of jurisdiction empowered him to make further orders. Regardless of which position is taken, the separation of powers was still breached. On the one hand, if he did purport to be able to make further orders, based on the evidence presented at the reporting hearings, he was *functus officio*. We find it difficult to imagine how any subsequent order would not have resulted in a change to the original final order. This necessarily falls outside the narrow exceptions provided by *functus officio*, and breaches that rule.

[120] Such a breach would also have resulted in a violation of the separation of powers principle. By purporting to be able to make subsequent orders, the trial judge would have assumed a supervisory role which included administrative functions that properly lie in the sphere of the executive. These functions are beyond the capacities of courts. The judiciary is ill equipped to make polycentric choices or to evaluate the wide-ranging consequences that flow from policy implementation. This Court has recognized that courts possess neither the expertise nor the resources to undertake public administration. In *Eldridge v. British Columbia (Attorney General)*, [1997] 3 SCR 624, at para. 96, it was held that in light of the "myriad options" available to the government to rectify the unconstitutionality of the impugned system, it was "not this Court's role to dictate how this is to be accomplished."

[121] In addition, if he purported to adopt a managerial role, the trial judge undermined the norm of co-operation and mutual respect that not only describes the relationship between the various actors in the constitutional order, but defines its particularly Canadian nature, and invests each branch with legitimacy. In *Vriend v. Alberta*, [1998] 1 SCR 493, Iacobucci J noted that "respect by the courts for the legislature and executive role is as important as ensuring that the other branches respect each others' role and the role of the courts" (para. 136). He discussed the wording of provisions of the Charter that expressed this norm of mutual respect (para. 137), and remarked that this norm has "the effect of enhancing the democratic process" (para. 139).

• • •

[127] The appellants argued that the trial judge retained jurisdiction only to hear reports, and that these hearings had purely "suasive" value. They also argued that the hearings were designed to hold "the Province's feet to the fire" (SCC hearing transcripts). They further suggested that the threat of having to report to the trial judge functioned as an incentive for the government to comply with the best efforts order. …

[128] If this characterization of the trial judge's activity is accurate, then the order for reporting sessions did not result in the exercise of adjudicative, or any other, functions that traditionally define the ambit of a court's proper sphere. Moreover, it resulted in activity that can be characterized as political. According to the appellants' characterization, a primary purpose of the hearings was to put public pressure on the government to act. This kind of pressure is paradigmatically associated with political actors. Indeed, the practice of publicly questioning a government on its performance, without having any legal power to compel it to alter its behaviour, is precisely that undertaken by an opposition party in the legislature during question period.

• • •

[133] We would reiterate, at this point, the importance of clarity and certainty in the provisions of a court order. If the trial judge had precisely defined the terms of the remedy, *in advance*, then the ensuing confusion surrounding his role may not have occurred.

Moreover, by complying with this essential element of fair procedure, he may have been able to avoid the constitutional breach of the separation of powers that followed.

Enforcement of the Constitution by the courts can present both practical problems and questions of principle. The following excerpt from the Supreme Court of Canada's decision in *Re Manitoba Language Rights* illustrates the difficulty Canadian courts have faced in finding a principled (and constitutionally sensible) way to address the consequences of a sweeping legislative disregard of constitutional rules.

Reference re Language Rights Under Section 23 of Manitoba Act, 1870 and Section 133 of Constitution Act, 1867
[1985] 1 SCR 721

THE COURT:

. . .

Manitoba's Language Legislation

[5] Section 23 of the *Manitoba Act, 1870* was the culmination of many years of co-existence and struggle between the English, the French, and the Metis in Red River Colony, the predecessor to the present day province of Manitoba. Though the region was originally claimed by the English Hudson's Bay Company in 1670 under its Royal Charter, for much of its pre-confederation history, Red River Colony was inhabited by anglophones and francophones in roughly equal proportions. On November 19, 1869 the Hudson's Bay Company issued a deed of surrender to transfer the North-West Territories, which included the Red River Colony, to Canada. The transfer of title took effect on July 15, 1870.

[6] Between November 19, 1869 and July 15, 1870, the provisional government of Red River Colony attempted to unite the various segments of the Red River Colony and drew up a "Bill of Rights" to be used in negotiations with Canada. A Convention of Delegates was elected in January 1870 to prepare the terms upon which Red River Colony would join the Confederation. The convention was made up of equal numbers of anglophones and franco-phones elected from the various French and English parishes.

[7] The final version of the Bill of Rights which was used by the convention delegates in their negotiations with Ottawa contained these provisions:

> That the English and French languages be common in the Legislature, and in the courts, and that all public documents, as well as all Acts of the Legislature, be published in both languages.
> That the judge of the Superior Court speak the English and French languages.

These clauses were re-drafted by the Crown lawyers in Ottawa and included in a Bill to be introduced in Parliament. The Bill passed through Parliament with no opposition from either side of the House, resulting in s. 23 of the *Manitoba Act, 1870*. In 1871 this Act was entrenched in the *British North America Act, 1871* (renamed *Constitution Act, 1871*, in the

Constitution Act, 1982, s. 53). The *Manitoba Act, 1870*, is now entrenched in the Constitution of Canada by virtue of s. 52(2)(b) of the *Constitution Act, 1982*.

[8] In 1890 *An Act to Provide that the English Language shall be the Official Language of the Province of Manitoba*, 1890 (Man.), c. 14 (hereafter "the *Official Language Act*") was enacted by the Manitoba Legislature. This Act provides:

> 1) Any statute or law to the contrary notwithstanding, the English language only shall be used in the records and journals of the House of Assembly for the Province of Manitoba, and in any pleadings or process in or issuing from any court in the Province of Manitoba. The Acts of the Legislature of the Province of Manitoba need only be printed and published in the English language.
>
> 2) This Act shall only apply so far as this Legislature has jurisdiction so to enact, and shall come into force on the day it is assented to.

[9] Upon enactment of the *Official Language Act, 1890*, the province of Manitoba ceased publication of the French version of legislative records, journals and Acts.

. . .

Legal Challenges to Manitoba's Language Legislation

[10] The *Official Language Act, 1890*, was challenged before the Manitoba courts soon after it was enacted. It was ruled *ultra vires* in 1892 by Judge Prud'homme of the County Court of St. Boniface, who stated: "Je suis donc d'opinion que le c. 14, 53 Vict. est ultra vires de la législature du Manitoba et que la clause 23, de l'Acte de Manitoba, ne peut pas être changée et encore moins abrogée par la législature de cette province": *Pellant v. Hebert*, first published in *Le Manitoba* (a French language newspaper), March 9, 1892, reported in (1981), 12 RGD 242. This ruling was not followed by the legislature or the government of Manitoba. The 1890 Act remained in successive revisions of the Statutes of Manitoba; the government did not resume bilingual publication of legislative records, journals or Acts.

[11] In 1909, the *Official Language Act, 1890* was again challenged in Manitoba courts and again ruled unconstitutional: *Bertrand v. Dussault*, January 30, 1909, Prud'homme Co. Ct. J, County Court of St. Boniface (unreported), reproduced in *Re Forest and Registrar of Court of Appeal of Manitoba* (1977), 77 DLR (3d) 445 at 458-62 (Man. CA). According to Monnin JA in *Re Forest*, supra, at p. 458: "This latter decision, not reported, appears to have been unknown or ignored."

[12] In 1976, a third attack was mounted against the *Official Language Act, 1890* and the Act was ruled unconstitutional: *R v. Forest* (1976), 74 DLR (3d) 704 (Man. Co. Ct.). Nonetheless, the *Official Language Act, 1890* remained on the Manitoba statute books; bilingual enactment, printing and publication of Acts of the Manitoba Legislature was not resumed.

[13] In 1979, the constitutionality of the *Official Language Act, 1890* was tested before this Court. On December 13, 1979, in *Attorney General of Manitoba v. Forest*, [1979] 2 SCR 1032, this Court, in unanimous reasons, held that the provisions of Manitoba's *Official Language Act, 1890* were in conflict with s. 23 of the *Manitoba Act, 1870*, and unconstitutional.

[14] On July 9, 1980, after the decision of this Court in *Forest*, the Legislature of Manitoba enacted *An Act Respecting the Operation of Section 23 of the Manitoba Act in Regard to*

Statutes, 1980 (Man.), c. 3 [also CCSM, c. S207]. The validity of this Act is the subject of question 4 of this Reference.

[15] In the fourth session (1980) and the fifth session (1980-1981) of the thirty-first legislature of Manitoba, the vast majority of the Acts of the legislature of Manitoba were enacted, printed and published in English only.

[16] Since the first session of the thirty-second legislature of Manitoba (1982), the Acts of the legislature of Manitoba have been enacted, printed and published in both English and French. However, those Acts that only amend Acts that were enacted, printed and published in English only and private Acts have in most instances been enacted in English only.

· · ·

[19] It might also be mentioned that on December 13, 1979, in *Attorney General of Quebec v. Blaikie*, [1979] 2 SCR 1016 (*Blaikie No. 1*), this Court held that the provisions of *Quebec's Charter of the French Language* (Bill 101), enacted in 1977, were in conflict with s. 133 of the *Constitution Act, 1867*. The Charter purported to provide for the introduction of Bills in the legislature in French only, and for the enactment of statutes in French only. The day after the decision of this court in *Blaikie No. 1*, the Legislature of Quebec re-enacted in both languages all those Quebec statutes that had been enacted in French only. See: *An Act respecting a judgment rendered in the Supreme Court of Canada on 13 December 1979 on the language of the legislature and the courts in Québec*, 1979 (Que.), c. 61.

[20] The implication of this court's holdings in *Blaikie No. 1*, and *Forest*, both *supra*, was that provincial Legislation passed in accordance with the *ultra vires* statutes, i.e., enacted in one language only, was itself in derogation of the constitutionally entrenched language provisions of the *Constitution Act, 1867*, and the *Manitoba Act, 1870*, and therefore invalid. In *Société Asbestos Ltée v. Société nationale de l'amiante*, [1979] CA 342, the Quebec Court of Appeal held, in a judgment also rendered December 13, 1979, that this was indeed the consequence of unilingual enactment and struck down two statutes that had not been enacted in English.

· · ·

B) *The Consequences of the Manitoba Legislature's Failure To Enact, Print and Publish in Both Languages*

[45] Section 23 of the *Manitoba Act, 1870*, entrenches a mandatory requirement to enact, print, and publish all Acts of the legislature in both official languages (see *Blaikie No. 1*, *supra*). It establishes a constitutional duty on the Manitoba Legislature with respect to the manner and form of enactment of its legislation. This duty protects the substantive rights of all Manitobans to equal access to the law in either the French or the English language.

[46] Section 23 of the *Manitoba Act, 1870*, is a specific manifestation of the general right of Franco-Manitobans to use their own language. The importance of language rights is grounded in the essential role that language plays in human existence, development and dignity. It is through language that we are able to form concepts; to structure and order the world around us. Language bridges the gap between isolation and community, allowing humans to delineate the rights and duties they hold in respect of one another, and thus to live in society.

[47] The constitutional entrenchment of a duty on the Manitoba legislature to enact, print and publish in both French and English in s. 23 of the *Manitoba Act, 1870*, confers upon the judiciary the responsibility of protecting the correlative language rights of all Manitobans including the Franco-Manitoban minority. The judiciary is the institution charged with the duty of ensuring that the government complies with the Constitution. We must protect those whose constitutional rights have been violated, whomever they may be, and whatever the reasons for the violation.

· · ·

[53] Canadian courts have been unanimous in finding that failure to respect mandatory requirements to enact, print and publish statutes and regulations in both official languages leads to inconsistency and thus invalidity: see, *Société Asbestos Ltée v. Société nationale de l'amiante, supra*; *Procureur général du Québec v. Collier*, [1983] CS 366; *Procureur général du Québec v. Brunet*, JE 83-510, reversed on other grounds, JE 84-62 (SC). These cases accord with the general principle that failure to comply with constitutional provisions dealing with the manner and form of the enactment of legislation will result in inconsistency and thus invalidity: see *Bribery Commissioner v. Ranasinghe* … .

[54] In the present case the unilingual enactments of the Manitoba legislature are inconsistent with s. 23 of the *Manitoba Act, 1870* since the constitutionally required manner and form for their enactment has not been followed. Thus they are invalid and of no force or effect.

C) *The Rule of Law*

1. *The Principle*

[55] The difficulty with the fact that the unilingual Acts of the legislature of Manitoba must be declared invalid and of no force or effect is that, without going further, a legal vacuum will be created with consequent legal chaos in the province of Manitoba. The Manitoba Legislature has, since 1890, enacted nearly all of its laws in English only. Thus, to find that the unilingual laws of Manitoba are invalid and of no force or effect would mean that only laws enacted in both French and English before 1890 would continue to be valid, and would still be in force even if the law had purportedly been repealed or amended by a post-1890 unilingual statute; matters that were not regulated by laws enacted before 1890 would now be unregulated by law, unless a pre-confederation law or the common law provided a rule.

[56] The situation of the various institutions of provincial government would be as follows: the courts, administrative tribunals, public officials, municipal corporations, school boards, professional governing bodies, and all other bodies created by law, to the extent that they derive their existence from or purport to exercise powers conferred by Manitoba laws enacted since 1890 in English only, would be acting without legal authority.

[57] Questions as to the validity of the present composition of the Manitoba legislature might also be raised. Under the *Manitoba Act, 1870*, the Legislative Assembly was to be composed of 24 members (s. 14), and voters were to be male and over 21 (s. 17). By laws enacted after 1890 in English only, the size of the Legislative Assembly was increased to 57 members, and all persons, both women and men, over 18 were granted the right to vote: see *Act to Amend "The Manitoba Election Act,"* 1916 (Man.), c. 36; *Act to Amend "The Election Act,"* 1969 (Man.), 2nd Sess., c. 7; *The Legislative Assembly Act*, RSM, c. L110, s. 4(1). If these

laws are invalid and of no force or effect, the present composition of the Manitoba Legislature might be invalid. The invalidity of the post-1890 laws would not touch the existence of
the Legislature or its powers since these are matters of federal constitutional law: *Constitution Act, 1867*, ss. 92, 92A, 93, 95; *Manitoba Act, 1870*, s. 2.

[58] Finally, all legal rights, obligations and other effects which have purportedly arisen
under all Acts of the Manitoba legislature since 1890 would be open to challenge to the
extent that their validity and enforceability depends upon a regime of unconstitutional
unilingual laws.

[59] In the present case, declaring the Acts of the legislature of Manitoba invalid and of
no force or effect would, without more, undermine the principle of the rule of law. The rule
of law, a fundamental principle of our Constitution, must mean at least two things. First,
that the law is supreme over officials of the government as well as private individuals, and
thereby preclusive of the influence of arbitrary power. Indeed, it is because of the supremacy
of law over the government, as established in s. 23 of the *Manitoba Act, 1870*, and s. 52 of
the *Constitution Act, 1982*, that this Court must find the unconstitutional laws of Manitoba
to be invalid and of no force and effect.

[60] Second, the rule of law requires the creation and maintenance of an actual order of
positive laws which preserves and embodies the more general principle of normative order.
Law and order are indispensable elements of civilized life. "The Rule of Law in this sense
implies … simply the existence of public order." (W.I. Jennings, *The Law and the Constitution* (5th ed. 1959), at p. 43.) As John Locke once said, "A government without laws is, I
suppose, a mystery in politics, inconceivable to human capacity and inconsistent with human society" (quoted by Lord Wilberforce in *Carl Zeiss-Stiftung v. Rayner & Keeler Ltd.
(No. 2)*, [1966] 2 All ER 536 (HL), at 577). According to Wade and Phillips, *Constitutional
and Administrative Law* (9th ed. 1977), at p. 89:

> … [T]he rule of law expresses a preference for law and order within a community rather than
> anarchy, warfare and constant strife. In this sense, the rule of law is a philosophical view of
> society which in the Western tradition is linked with basic democratic notions.

[61] It is this second aspect of the rule of law that is of concern in the present situation.
The conclusion that the Acts of the Legislature of Manitoba are invalid and of no force or
effect means that the positive legal order which has purportedly regulated the affairs of the
citizens of Manitoba since 1890 will be destroyed and the rights, obligations and other effects arising under these laws will be invalid and unenforceable. As for the future, since it is
reasonable to assume that it will be impossible for the legislature of Manitoba to rectify in-
stantaneously the constitutional defect, the Acts of the Manitoba Legislature will be invalid
and of no force or effect until they are translated, re-enacted, printed and published in both
languages.

[62] Such results would certainly offend the rule of law. …

• • •

2. Application of the Principle of the Rule of Law

[67] It is clear from the above that: (i) the law as stated in s. 23 of the *Manitoba Act,
1870*, and s. 52 of the *Constitution Act, 1982*, requires that the unilingual Acts of the Mani-

toba Legislature be declared to be invalid and of no force or effect, and (ii) without more, such a result would violate the rule of law. The task the court faces is to recognize the unconstitutionality of Manitoba's unilingual laws and the legislature's duty to comply with the "supreme law" of this country, while avoiding a legal vacuum in Manitoba and ensuring the continuity of the rule of law.

. . .

[73] There is no question that it would be impossible for all the Acts of the Manitoba legislature to be translated, re-enacted, printed and published overnight. There will necessarily be a period of time during which it would not be possible for the Manitoba Legislature to comply with its constitutional duty under s. 23 of the *Manitoba Act, 1870.*

[74] The vexing question, however, is what will be the legal situation in the Province of Manitoba for the duration of this period. The difficulties faced by the Province of Manitoba are two-fold: first, all of the rights, obligations and other effects which have arisen under the repealed, spent and current Acts of the Manitoba Legislature will be open to challenge, since the laws under which they purportedly arise are invalid and of no force or effect; and, second, the Province of Manitoba has an invalid and therefore ineffectual legal system until the Legislature is able to translate, re-enact, print and publish its current Acts.

. . .

[83] The only appropriate solution for preserving the rights, obligations and other effects which have arisen under invalid Acts of the Legislature of Manitoba and which are not saved by the *de facto* or other doctrines is to declare that, in order to uphold the rule of law, these rights, obligations and other effects have, and will continue to have, the same force and effect they would have had if they had arisen under valid enactments, for that period of time during which it would be impossible for Manitoba to comply with its constitutional duty under s. 23 of the *Manitoba Act, 1870.* The Province of Manitoba would be faced with chaos and anarchy if the legal rights, obligations and other effects which have been relied upon by the people of Manitoba since 1890 were suddenly open to challenge. The constitutional guarantee of rule of law will not tolerate such chaos and anarchy.

[84] Nor will the constitutional guarantee of rule of law tolerate the province of Manitoba being without a valid and effectual legal system for the present and future. Thus, it will be necessary to deem temporarily valid and effective the unilingual Acts of the Legislature of Manitoba which would be currently in force, were it not for their constitutional defect, for the period of time during which it would be impossible for the Manitoba Legislature to fulfil its constitutional duty. Since this temporary validation will include the legislation under which the Manitoba Legislature is presently constituted, it will be legally able to re-enact, print and publish its laws in conformity with the dictates of the Constitution once they have been translated.

[85] Analogous support for the measures proposed can be found in cases which have arisen under the doctrine of state necessity. Necessity in the context of governmental action provides a justification for otherwise illegal conduct of a government during a public emergency. In order to ensure rule of law, the courts will recognize as valid the constitutionally invalid Acts of the legislature. According to Professor Stavsky, "The Doctrine of State Necessity in Pakistan" (1983), 16 *Cornell Int. LJ* 341, at p. 344: "If narrowly and carefully applied, *the doctrine constitutes affirmation of the rule of law* (emphasis added)." The courts have applied the doctrine of necessity in a variety of circumstances. A number of cases have

involved challenges to the laws of an illegal and insurrectionary government. In the aftermath of the American Civil War, the question arose as to the validity of laws passed by the Confederate States. The courts in addressing this question were primarily concerned with ensuring that the rule of law be upheld. The principle which emerges from these cases can be summarized as follows: During a period of insurrection, when territory is under the control and dominance of an unlawful, hostile government and it is therefore impossible for the lawful authorities to legislate for the peace and good order of the area, the laws passed by the usurping government which are necessary to the maintenance of organized society and which are not in themselves unconstitutional will be given force and effect: see *Texas v. White*, 74 US 700 (1869); *Horn v. Lockhart*, 84 US 570 (1873); *United States v. Insurance Companies*, 89 US 99 (1875); *Baldy v. Hunter*, 171 US 388 (1898).

· · ·

[107] Turning back to the present case, because of the Manitoba legislature's persistent violation of the constitutional dictates of the *Manitoba Act, 1870*, the Province of Manitoba is in a state of emergency: all of the Acts of the Legislature of Manitoba, purportedly repealed, spent and current (with the exception of those recent laws which have been enacted, printed and published in both languages), are and always have been invalid and of no force or effect, and the legislature is unable to immediately re-enact these unilingual laws in both languages. The Constitution will not suffer a province without laws. Thus the Constitution requires that temporary validity and force and effect be given to the current Acts of the Manitoba Legislature from the date of this judgment, and that rights, obligations and other effects which have arisen under these laws and the repealed and spent laws of the province prior to the date of this judgment, which are not saved by the *de facto* or some other doctrine, are deemed temporarily to have been and continue to be effective and beyond challenge. It is only in this way that legal chaos can be avoided and the rule of law preserved.

3. The Issue of Legitimacy

The type of governmental intransigence described in *Re Manitoba Language Rights* is very much the exception in Canada's constitutional history. The more immediate concern for Canadian judges in exercising their mandate to uphold the Constitution is to identify principles that appropriately shape the exercise of this authority. Different aspects of the role played by the courts in reviewing the constitutional validity of legislation typically raise different issues concerning the relationship between democratically elected legislators and unelected judges. When judges are adjudicating constitutional challenges to the validity of legislation based on the division of powers provisions of ss. 91-95 of the *Constitution Act, 1867*, the issue is not whether some body of democratically elected legislators has the authority under the Constitution to pass the law that is in dispute, but whether the particular legislative body that has enacted the law has that authority within our federal system of government. The outcomes of particular cases, and even whole lines of authority, may provoke passionate debates between supporters of greater federal authority and those who prefer a more decentralized model of federalism. Nevertheless, it is hard to disagree with the idea that we need an impartial arbiter of federalism disputes, and in our system that role is played by the courts.

The advent of the *Canadian Charter of Rights and Freedoms* in 1982 has changed this aspect of the nature of the judicial role in constitutional adjudication. The Charter requires the courts to give constitutional effect to what Professor Noel Lyon has described as "vague but meaningful generalities"—ideas such as "freedom of thought, belief, opinion, and expression" in s. 2(b); "liberty," "security of the person," and "the principles of fundamental justice" in s. 7; "equality" in s. 15; and "such reasonable limits prescribed by law as can be demonstrably justified in a free and democratic society" in s. 1: see N. Lyon, "The Teleological Mandate of the Fundamental Freedoms: What To Do with Vague but Meaningful Generalities" (1982), 4 *Supreme Court Law Review* 57. The concern is that when judges give concrete shape to these and other ideas set out in the Charter and then invalidate laws that do not conform to their interpretation of these requirements, the rule of law may become subtly transformed into the rule of unelected judges.

It is true that on the whole, the Charter—and the courts' interpretation of it—has been largely popular. See, for instance, Joseph Fletcher and Paul Howe, "Public Opinion and the Courts," *Choices* (Institute for Research on Public Policy, May 2000). Yet because courts now regularly strike down (and reinterpret by "reading in") parliamentary statutes, they have sparked a wave of academic and political critiques that question, and sometimes denounce, their performance.

Most criticisms of constitutional judicial review can be reduced to two core complaints. The first is that under the banner of constitutional supremacy, courts have usurped power that is properly the domain of Parliament and the provincial legislatures. The argument is that the courts have expanded their proper role of interpreting the Constitution—and particularly the Charter—and have thereby unduly shrunk the zone of parliamentary supremacy. The second line of criticism is sparked by the substantive approach taken by the courts to particular rights, rights that may protect unpopular elements of society, such as people convicted of criminal offences, or prompt decisions, such as protection for gays and lesbians, disliked by those holding particular political, social, or religious views. A core question lies at the heart of both these complaints: in rendering their constitutional decisions, how much deference should courts show elected officials?

In the following passage from the Supreme Court of Canada's majority decision in *Vriend v. Alberta*, Mr. Justice Iacobucci uses the analogy of a dialogue to describe the relationship between courts and legislatures under the Charter. The Supreme Court in *Vriend* concluded that the Alberta legislature's failure to include sexual orientation as a prohibited ground of discrimination in the Alberta *Individual Rights Protection Act* violated the appellants' right to equality as protected by s. 15 of the Charter and that this action was not justified under s. 1. The majority also concluded that the appropriate remedy for this violation was to "read in" sexual orientation as a prohibited ground of discrimination for purposes of the Act.

Vriend v. Alberta
[1998] 1 SCR 493

CORY and IACOBUCCI JJ (Lamer CJC, Gonthier, McLachlin, and Bastarache JJ concurring): [1] In these joint reasons Cory J has dealt with the issues pertaining to standing, the application of the *Canadian Charter of Rights and Freedoms*, and the breach of s. 15(1) of the

Charter. Iacobucci J has discussed s. 1 of the Charter, the appropriate remedy, and the disposition.

. . .

IACOBUCCI J:

II. Remedy

A. Introduction: The Relationship Between the Legislatures and the Courts Under the Charter

[129] Having found the exclusion of sexual orientation from the *IRPA* to be an unjustifiable violation of the appellants' equality rights, I now turn to the question of remedy under s. 52 of the *Constitution Act, 1982*. Before discussing the jurisprudence on remedies, I believe it might be helpful to pause to reflect more broadly on the general issue of the relationship between legislatures and the courts in the age of the Charter.

[130] Much was made in argument before us about the inadvisability of the Court interfering with or otherwise meddling in what is regarded as the proper role of the legislature, which in this case was to decide whether or not sexual orientation would be added to Alberta's human rights legislation. Indeed, it seems that hardly a day goes by without some comment or criticism to the effect that under the Charter courts are wrongfully usurping the role of the legislatures. I believe this allegation misunderstands what took place and what was intended when our country adopted the Charter in 1981-82.

[131] When the Charter was introduced, Canada went, in the words of former Chief Justice Brian Dickson, from a system of Parliamentary supremacy to constitutional supremacy ("Keynote Address," in *The Cambridge Lectures 1985* (1985), at pp. 3-4). Simply put, each Canadian was given individual rights and freedoms which no government or legislature could take away. However, as rights and freedoms are not absolute, governments and legislatures could justify the qualification or infringement of these constitutional rights under s. 1 as I previously discussed. Inevitably disputes over the meaning of the rights and their justification would have to be settled and here the role of the judiciary enters to resolve these disputes. Many countries have assigned the important role of judicial review to their supreme or constitutional courts (for an excellent analysis on these developments see D.M. Beatty, ed., *Human Rights and Judicial Review: A Comparative Perspective* (1994); B. Ackerman, "The Rise of World Constitutionalism" (1997), 83 *Virginia L Rev.* 771).

[132] We should recall that it was the deliberate choice of our provincial and federal legislatures in adopting the Charter to assign an interpretive role to the courts and to command them under s. 52 to declare unconstitutional legislation invalid.

[133] However, giving courts the power and commandment to invalidate legislation where necessary has not eliminated the debate over the "legitimacy" of courts taking such action. As eloquently put by A.M. Bickel in his outstanding work *The Least Dangerous Branch: The Supreme Court at the Bar of Politics* (2nd ed. l986), "it thwarts the will of representatives of the ... people" (p. 17). So judicial review, it is alleged, is illegitimate because it is anti-democratic in that unelected officials (judges) are overruling elected representatives (legislators) (see e.g. A.A. Peacock, ed., *Rethinking the Constitution: Perspectives on Canadian Constitutional Reform, Interpretation, and Theory* (1996); R. Knopff and F.L. Morton,

Charter Politics (1992); M. Mandel, *The Charter of Rights and the Legalization of Politics in Canada* (1994), c. 2).

[134] To respond, it should be emphasized again that our Charter's introduction and the consequential remedial role of the courts were choices of the Canadian people through their elected representatives as part of a redefinition of our democracy. Our constitutional design was refashioned to state that henceforth the legislatures and executive must perform their roles in conformity with the newly conferred constitutional rights and freedoms. That the courts were the trustees of these rights insofar as disputes arose concerning their interpretation was a necessary part of this new design.

[135] So courts in their trustee or arbiter role must perforce scrutinize the work of the legislature and executive not in the name of the courts, but in the interests of the new social contract that was democratically chosen. All of this is implied in the power given to the courts under s. 24 of the Charter and s. 52 of the *Constitution Act, 1982*.

[136] Because the courts are independent from the executive and legislature, litigants and citizens generally can rely on the courts to make reasoned and principled decisions according to the dictates of the constitution even though specific decisions may not be universally acclaimed. In carrying out their duties, courts are not to second-guess legislatures and the executives; they are not to make value judgments on what they regard as the proper policy choice; this is for the other branches. Rather, the courts are to uphold the Constitution and have been expressly invited to perform that role by the Constitution itself. But respect by the courts for the legislature and executive role is as important as ensuring that the other branches respect each others' role and the role of the courts.

[137] This mutual respect is in some ways expressed in the provisions of our constitution as shown by the wording of certain of the constitutional rights themselves. For example, s. 7 of the Charter speaks of no denial of the rights therein except in accordance with the principles of fundamental justice, which include the process of law and legislative action. Section 1 and the jurisprudence under it are also important to ensure respect for legislative action and the collective or societal interests represented by legislation. In addition, as will be discussed below, in fashioning a remedy with regard to a Charter violation, a court must be mindful of the role of the legislature. Moreover, s. 33, the notwithstanding clause, establishes that the final word in our constitutional structure is in fact left to the legislature and not the courts (see P. Hogg and A. Bushell, "The Charter Dialogue Between Courts and Legislatures" (1997), 35 *Osgoode Hall LJ* 75).

[138] As I view the matter, the Charter has given rise to a more dynamic interaction among the branches of governance. This interaction has been aptly described as a "dialogue" by some (see e.g. Hogg and Bushell, *supra*). In reviewing legislative enactments and executive decisions to ensure constitutional validity, the courts speak to the legislative and executive branches. As has been pointed out, most of the legislation held not to pass constitutional muster has been followed by new legislation designed to accomplish similar objectives (see Hogg and Bushell, *supra*, at p. 82). By doing this, the legislature responds to the courts; hence the dialogue among the branches.

[139] To my mind, a great value of judicial review and this dialogue among the branches is that each of the branches is made somewhat accountable to the other. The work of the legislature is reviewed by the courts and the work of the court in its decisions can be reacted to by the legislature in the passing of new legislation (or even overarching laws under s. 33

of the Charter). This dialogue between and accountability of each of the branches have the effect of enhancing the democratic process, not denying it.

[140] There is also another aspect of judicial review that promotes democratic values. Although a court's invalidation of legislation usually involves negating the will of the majority, we must remember that the concept of democracy is broader than the notion of majority rule, fundamental as that may be. In this respect, we would do well to heed the words of Dickson CJ in *Oakes* ... , at p. 136:

> The Court must be guided by the values and principles essential to a free and democratic society which I believe to embody, to name but a few, respect for the inherent dignity of the human person, commitment to social justice and equality, accommodation of a wide variety of beliefs, respect for cultural and group identity, and faith in social and political institutions which enhance the participation of individuals and groups in society.

[141] So, for example, when a court interprets legislation alleged to be a reasonable limitation in a free and democratic society as stated in s. 1 of the Charter, the court must inevitably delineate some of the attributes of a democratic society. Although it is not necessary to articulate the complete list of democratic attributes in these remarks, Dickson CJ's comments remain instructive (see also: *R v. Keegstra*, [1990] 3 SCR 697 (SCC), *per* Dickson CJ; *B. (R.) v. Children's Aid Society of Metropolitan Toronto* (1994), [1995] 1 SCR 315 (SCC), *per* La Forest J).

[142] Democratic values and principles under the Charter demand that legislators and the executive take these into account; and if they fail to do so, courts should stand ready to intervene to protect these democratic values as appropriate. As others have so forcefully stated, judges are not acting undemocratically by intervening when there are indications that a legislative or executive decision was not reached in accordance with the democratic principles mandated by the Charter (see W. Black, "*Vriend*, Rights and Democracy" (1996), 7 *Constitutional Forum* 126; D.M. Beatty, "Law and Politics" (1996), 44 *Am. J Comp. L* 131, at p. 149; M. Jackman, "Protecting Rights and Promoting Democracy: Judicial Review Under Section 1 of the Charter" (1997), 34 *Osgoode Hall LJ* 661).

These comments deserve further elaboration on two points: (1) built-in deference, and (2) the "dialogue" model.

Built-in deference. First, as we have suggested elsewhere, the Canadian Constitution does preserve a huge swath of parliamentary sovereignty. As Iacobucci J puts it in *Vriend*, the "parliamentary safeguards" remain, despite the court's "reading-in" approach: "Governments are free to modify the amended legislation by passing exceptions and defences which they feel can be justified under s. 1 of the Charter. ... Moreover, the legislators can always turn to s. 33 of the Charter, the override provision, which in my view is the ultimate 'parliamentary safeguard'": see [1998] 1 SCR 493, at para. 178.

Section 1 of the Charter provides that the rights contained within it are guaranteed, but then subject "to such reasonable limits prescribed by law as can be demonstrably justified in a free and democratic society." Drawing from this language, the court has articulated a complex justification test that may excuse a violation of a substantive Charter right, should its conditions be met. See, for example, *R v. Oakes*, [1986] 1 SCR 103 and its progeny. In other words, rights in the Charter are not absolute.

Moreover, many of the rights in the Charter (those enshrined in ss. 2 and 7-15) may be overridden by the exercise of democratic will. Section 33—the "notwithstanding" provision—allows Parliament to "expressly declare in an Act of Parliament … that the Act or a provision thereof shall operate notwithstanding" these Charter rights. Section 33 does not require a "super-majority." It may be invoked through the regular enactment process, albeit subject to periodical renewal. It is, in other words, abundantly available to any Parliament or provincial legislature. Thus, s. 33 preserves a large measure of parliamentary supremacy, though the political price exacted for explicitly overriding constitutionally protected rights has been sufficiently high that, to date at least, Canadian political leaders rarely have been willing to pay it.

The "dialogue" model. Second, the *Vriend* decision invokes a sort of "dialogue" between courts and legislatures. This "dialogue" was described by retired Supreme Court justice Bertha Wilson in an article entitled "We Didn't Volunteer":

> [T]he central feature of the Charter is that all branches of government—the legislatures, the executive and the judiciary—have an equal responsibility to carry out the Charter's mandate, and we should concentrate on their reciprocal roles. If we do this, we see that a sort of "dialogue" is going on. First, the legislatures have to examine any legislation they are contemplating passing in order to ensure that they have discharged their responsibility of Charter compliance. Then, if that legislation, once passed, is called into question, the courts must ask themselves: Did the legislature discharge its responsibility to comply with the Charter when it passed this legislation? If the answer is yes, there is no problem. If the answer is no, then the courts are obliged to strike down the legislation, though in so doing they must identify its vitiating aspects as clearly as possible so that the legislature will be in a position to correct them. The matter then goes back to the legislature for the appropriate remedial action. The courts' assessment of the legislation's constitutionality is not the last word; it is merely one step in the process.

(Bertha Wilson, "We Didn't Volunteer" (April 1999), *Policy Options* 8, at 10. See also Peter W. Hogg and Allison A. Bushell, "The Charter Dialogue Between Courts and Legislatures" (1997), 35 *Osgoode Hall LJ* 75, at 82.)

Other observers dismiss this concept of "dialogue." In an article entitled "Dialogue or Monologue?" Professor Morton argues that the putative dialogue

> is usually a monologue, with judges doing most of the talking and legislatures most of the listening. They suggest that the failure of a government to respond effectively to judicial activism is a matter of personal courage, or the lack thereof, on the part of government leaders. The fault, if there is any, rests with individuals. By contrast, I believe that legislative paralysis is institutional in character—that, in certain circumstances, legislative non-response in the face of judicial activism is the "normal" response. When the issue in play is cross-cutting and divides a government caucus, the political incentive structure invites government leaders to abdicate responsibility to the courts—and this may be even more true in a parliamentary as opposed to a presidential system. If I am correct, the Canadian tradition of responsible government is in for a rough ride in our brave new world of Charter democracy.

(F.L. Morton, "Dialogue or Monologue?" (April 1999), *Policy Options* 23, at 26, online: http://irpp.org/po/archive/apr99/morton.pdf.)

Views such as those expressed by Professor Morton have sparked a spirited defence from some academic writers, and from judges themselves. At the 2004 Conference on the Law and Parliament, Supreme Court Chief Justice Beverley McLachlin had this to say.

Remarks of the Right Honourable Beverley McLachlin, P.C.
Respecting Democratic Roles
(Ottawa: Supreme Court of Canada, November 22, 2004), online:
http://www.scc-csc.gc.ca/court-cour/ju/spe-dis/bm04-11-12-eng.asp

What is the role of the Courts? At its most basic, it is to decide legal disputes that citizens and the government ask them to decide. In deciding these disputes, the Courts discharge a number of functions essential to democratic governance. First, they define the precise contours of the division of legislative powers between the federal and provincial governments. Second, they rule on legislation alleged to be unconstitutional for violation of the Charter, and in doing so define the scope of constitutional rights and freedoms. Third, the courts exercise *de facto* supervision over the hosts of administrative tribunals created by Parliament and the Legislatures.

The development of the modern regulatory state and the adoption of a constitutional bill of rights in the form of the Charter have increased the importance of these functions. The judicial branch of governance in modern democracies is now more significant and more visible than it was in 19th century British parliamentary democracy. That cannot be denied. But is this unconstitutional? Not, I would suggest, in any meaningful sense of the word. Parliament and the legislatures, in response to the perceived needs of the modern democracy we claim as ours, have created administrative tribunals and entrenched fundamental rights. This has increased the scope of matters on which the courts must adjudicate in discharging their traditional role. But the role remains essentially the same—to answer the legal questions that individuals and governments bring before it.

What then of the accusation that courts have gone beyond their proper role? The charge is made that activist judges—politicians cloaked in judicial robes—have gone beyond impartial judging to advocate for special causes and achieve particular political goals, and that this is undemocratic.

If it is true that judges are acting in this way, then they are indeed going beyond the role allotted to them by the Constitution. The judicial role is to resolve disputes and decide legal questions which others bring before the courts. It is not for judges to set the agendas for social change, or to impose their personal views on society. The role of judges is to support the rule of law, not the rule of judicial whim. Judges are human beings; but they must strive to judge impartially after considering the facts, the law and the submissions of parties on all sides of the question. In our constitutional framework, the role of the politician and the role of the judge are very different. The political role is to initiate the debate and to vote according to judgment on what is best for the country. The judicial role, by contrast is to resolve legal disputes formulated by others, impartially on the basis of the facts and the law.

But is the charge true? Have judges become political actors? Are they encroaching on terrain that is not theirs under our Constitution? In my opinion, the answer is no.

When we deconstruct the charge that the courts are overstepping their boundaries, we find that the claim can be understood in four different ways. First, the claim may be understood as saying that judges should never go against the will of elected representatives. This suggests that the choices of Parliament and legislative assemblies should never be undone by unelected judges. But that, as I have argued, is plainly false under our Constitution. The Legislative and the Executive strive in good faith to discharge their role in a manner that is consistent with our Constitution. They seek to bring forward laws which do not impinge on the Charter, and to implement those laws without infringing fundamental rights. But every now and then, these efforts are called into question, and someone must arbitrate the dispute. Under our Constitution, that "someone" is the judicial branch. As I said earlier, the terms of our *Constitution Acts* call on judges to be the arbiters of constitutional validity, both in terms of division of powers, and in terms of respect for fundamental rights. In performing that duty, judges must inevitably strike down legislation, and go against the will of elected representatives, whenever it fails to meet our constitutional standards.

Second, the charge of judicial activism may be understood as saying that judges are pursuing a particular political agenda, that they are allowing their political views to determine the outcome of cases before them. Very often, on this version, judges are seen as activist when one disagrees with their conclusions. Behind this criticism lies the assumption that the parameters of constitutional adjudication are so indeterminate that judges can bend them at will in the service of their own political objectives.

This version of the charge is also problematic, in my view. It is a serious matter to suggest that any branch of government is deliberately acting in a manner that is inconsistent with its constitutional role. Such a suggestion inevitably breeds cynicism, and undermines public confidence in all of our institutions of governance. It should not be made without convincing evidence of its truth. The evidence that judges in Canada pursue private political agendas is lacking. Judges are conscious of their special but limited role. Their judgments are replete with the need to defer to Parliament and the legislation on complex social issues. Should judges err and impose their personal views instead of the law, they are likely to be overturned on appeal. They may also be subject to internal censure. A visit to any of the thousands of courtrooms in this country—from the local magistrate courts to the Supreme Court of Canada—is unlikely to discover judges acting like politicians. Rather, it will find them discussing the facts of the case and how the law applies to them. This is not some form of role play. It is the morality of their role. An objective review of the thousands of judicial decisions reported each year reveals that judicial concern is focussed not on plans to change society, but on interpreting and applying the law in a way that reflects legislative purpose.

The idea that judges are implementing their own political agenda may emerge from the fact that judges sometimes make decisions that have political implications. But it is wrong to jump from this indisputable fact to the conclusion that judges are therefore assuming the political role. The law is the mechanism by which our society regulates itself. That is the business of politicians. But when the validity and interpretation of the laws is brought before the courts, that is the business of judges. The role of judges may take them into subject matter claimed by politicians. But it does not follow that the judges are acting as politicians; the judicial role remains distinct from the political.

In short, I suggest that the second version of the charge of judicial activism is false. The evidence suggests that constitutional adjudication is not a radically indeterminate activity, and that judges are not hiding behind it to pursue political agendas.

The third version of the charge of judicial activism begins from the opposite assumption. It assumes that law is a totally determinate black and white activity. From there, it proceeds to say that judges should apply the law, not make the law, or rewrite the law. This version of the charge of judicial activism rests on a mistaken perception of the nature of legal decision-making. The law does not apply itself, and the answers to constitutional questions are not obvious or pre-ordained. If they were, we would not need judges. It follows that there is no clear demarcation between applying the law, interpreting the law, and making the law. The Charter is an abstract document, made up of general propositions which must be given concrete application. To give it meaning, and to make it relevant to the lives of Canadians, judges must make choices among competing readings of our constitutional text, choices which can have long term normative consequences. All of this is perfectly consistent with the traditional role of judges in our country.

Let me turn, finally, to the fourth version of the charge of judicial activism. This version suggests that judges are making decisions that should be made by elected representatives, who alone possess the necessary legitimacy for law-making and the institutional competence to weigh all the factors that must be considered in making difficult choices of public policy for Canadians. This is a more subtle claim. Let me simply say that judges are sensitive to this concern, but have little choice in the matter.

Where a legal issue is properly before a court, not deciding is not an option. When a citizen claims that the state has violated his or her constitutional rights, the Courts must referee the dispute. They do so with all necessary deference to legislative and executive expertise in weighing competing demands on the public purse, and competing perspectives on public policy. In deciding difficult social issues, the courts act with deference to the decisions of the legislative branch. Judges recognize that:

> ... in certain types of decisions there may be no obviously correct or obviously wrong solution, but a range of options each with its advantages and disadvantages. Governments act as they think proper within a range of reasonable alternatives, and the [Supreme] Court acknowledged in *M. v. H.* ... that "the role of the legislature demands deference from the courts to those types of policy decisions that the legislature is best placed to make." [*Newfoundland and Labrador Association of Public and Private Employees v. Her Majesty The Queen in Right of Newfoundland*, 2004 SCC 66, at para. 83.]

There are, however, limits. Deference does not mean simply rubber stamping laws. If a law is unconstitutional, it is the duty of the courts to say so. In the words of my colleague Ian Binnie, in the recent decision of *Newfoundland v. NAPE*:

> ... Whenever there are boundaries to the legal exercise of state power such boundaries have to be refereed. Canadian courts have undertaken this role in relation to the division of powers between Parliament and the provincial legislatures since Confederation. The boundary between an individual's protected right or freedom and state power must also be refereed. The framers of the Charter identified the courts as the referee. While I recognize that the separation of powers is an important constitutional principle, I believe that the s. 1 test set out in *Oakes* and the

rest of our voluminous s. 1 jurisprudence already provides the proper framework in which to consider what the doctrine of separation of powers requires in particular situations, as indeed was the case here. To the extent [that some would] invite a greater level of deference to the will of the legislature, I believe acceptance of such an invitation would simply be inconsistent with the clear words of s. 1 and undermine the delicate balance the Charter was intended to achieve. [2004 SCC 66, at para. 116.]

In the end, when we examine what is really being said, the claim fails that judges are overstepping the proper constitutional boundaries of their role.

Let me return to where I began. In our constitutional democracy, each branch of government—legislative, executive and judicial—has an important role to play in Canadian democracy. The role of each branch is different and complementary. The essence of each remains the same through the centuries. The legislative branch's role is to make laws. The executive branch's role is to enforce the law. And the judicial branch's role is to interpret the law and resolve disputes arising from the law. Each branch is a vital part of our democracy. Each branch must discharge its role with integrity and respect for the proper constitutional roles of the other branches. To do less is to diminish our democracy and imperil our future.

The existence of unwritten, but legally enforceable, constitutional principles creates an additional layer of complexity in the debate concerning the appropriate role of the courts in constitutional adjudication. When a court strikes down a law because the court believes that the law unjustifiably infringes rights protected by the Charter, it is fulfilling an obligation that was explicitly assigned to it by the Constitution. As Mr. Justice Iacobucci observed at para. 137 of his reasons for judgment in the *Vriend* case, "it was the deliberate choice of our provincial and federal legislatures in adopting the Charter to assign an interpretive role to the courts and to command them under s. 52 to declare unconstitutional legislation invalid." When a court invalidates a law because it is inconsistent with an unwritten constitutional principle, it can appear to some observers that the court is unjustifiably creating for itself a mandate to interfere with the democratic process. As the Supreme Court of Canada's decisions in *Reference re Secession of Quebec* and *Re Manitoba Language Rights* illustrate, recourse to unwritten constitutional principles has sometimes enabled Canadian courts to achieve creative solutions to constitutional dilemmas that are not easily resolved with reference to the text of the Constitution alone. On the other hand, it should be noted that even some members of the Supreme Court of Canada have occasionally expressed the concern that the courts may be exceeding the proper boundaries of their role in constitutional adjudication by making use of unwritten constitutional principles. Consider the following passage from Mr. Justice La Forest's partial dissent in *Reference re Remuneration of Judges of the Provincial Court of Prince Edward Island*.

Reference re Remuneration of Judges of the Provincial
Court of Prince Edward Island
[1997] 3 SCR 3

LA FOREST J (dissenting): ... [300] My concern arises out of the nature of judicial power. As I see it, the judiciary derives its public acceptance and its strength from the fact that judges do not initiate recourse to the law. Rather, they respond to grievances raised by those who come before them seeking to have the law applied, listening fairly to the representations of all parties, always subject to the discipline provided by the facts of the case. This sustains their impartiality and limits their powers. Unlike the other branches of the government, the judicial branch does not initiate matters and has no agenda of its own. Its sole duty is to hear and decide cases on the issues presented to it in accordance with the law and the Constitution. And so it was that Alexander Hamilton referred to the courts as "the least dangerous" branch of government: *The Federalist, No. 78.*

[301] Indeed courts are generally reluctant to comment on matters that are not necessary to decide in order to dispose of the case at hand. This policy is especially apposite in constitutional cases, where the implications of abstract legal conclusions are often unpredictable and can, in retrospect, turn out to be undesirable. After adverting to a number of decisions of this Court endorsing this principle, Sopinka J stated the following for the majority in *Phillips v. Nova Scotia (Commission of Inquiry into the Westray Mine Tragedy),* [1995] 2 SCR 97, at para. 9:

> The policy which dictates restraint in constitutional cases is sound. It is based on the realization that unnecessary constitutional pronouncements may prejudice future cases, the implications of which have not been foreseen. Early in this century, Viscount Haldane in *John Deere Plow Co. v. Wharton*, [1915] AC 330, at p. 339, stated that the abstract logical definition of the scope of constitutional provisions is not only "impracticable, but is certain, if attempted, to cause embarrassment and possible injustice in future cases."

... Notably, Sopinka J uttered this admonition in a case in which the relevant legal issue was fully argued in both this Court and in the court below. The policy of forbearance with respect to extraneous legal issues applies, *a fortiori*, in a case where only the briefest of allusion to the issue was made by counsel.

[302] I am, therefore, deeply concerned that the Court is entering into a debate on this issue without the benefit of substantial argument. I am all the more troubled since the question involves the proper relationship between the political branches of government and the judicial branch, an issue on which judges can hardly be seen to be indifferent, especially as it concerns their own remuneration. In such circumstances, it is absolutely critical for the Court to tread carefully and avoid making far-reaching conclusions that are not necessary to decide the case before it. If the Chief Justice's discussion was of a merely marginal character—a side-wind so to speak—I would abstain from commenting on it. After all, it is technically only *obiter dicta*. Nevertheless, in light of the importance that will necessarily be attached to his lengthy and sustained exegesis, I feel compelled to express my view.

II. The Effect of the Preamble to the Constitution Act, 1867

[303] I emphasize at the outset that it is not my position that s. 11(d) of the Charter and ss. 96-100 of the *Constitution Act, 1867* comprise an exhaustive code of judicial independence. As I discuss briefly later, additional protection for judicial independence may inhere in other provisions of the Constitution. Nor do I deny that the Constitution embraces unwritten rules, including rules that find expression in the preamble of the *Constitution Act, 1867*; see *New Brunswick Broadcasting Co. v. Nova Scotia (Speaker of the House of Assembly)*, [1993] 1 SCR 319. I hasten to add that these rules really find their origin in specific provisions of the Constitution viewed in light of our constitutional heritage. In other words, what we are concerned with is the meaning to be attached to an expression used in a constitutional provision.

[304] I take issue, however, with the Chief Justice's view that the preamble to the *Constitution Act, 1867* is a source of constitutional limitations on the power of legislatures to interfere with judicial independence. In *New Brunswick Broadcasting, supra*, this Court held that the privileges of the Nova Scotia legislature had constitutional status by virtue of the statement in the preamble expressing the desire to have "a Constitution similar in Principle to that of the United Kingdom." In reaching this conclusion, the Court examined the historical basis for the privileges of the British Parliament. That analysis established that the power of Parliament to exclude strangers was absolute, constitutional and immune from regulation by the courts. The effect of the preamble, the Court held, is to recognize and confirm that this long-standing principle of British constitutional law was continued or established in post-Confederation Canada.

[305] There is no similar historical basis, in contrast, for the idea that Parliament cannot interfere with judicial independence. At the time of Confederation (and indeed to this day), the British Constitution did not contemplate the notion that Parliament was limited in its ability to deal with judges.

. . .

[311] … By expressing a desire to have a Constitution "similar in Principle to that of the United Kingdom," the framers of the *Constitution Act, 1867* did not give courts the power to strike down legislation violating the principle of judicial independence. The framers did, however, entrench the fundamental components of judicial independence set out in the *Act of Settlement* such that violations could be struck down by the courts. This was accomplished, however, by ss. 99-100 of the *Constitution Act, 1867*, not the preamble.

[312] It might be asserted that the argument presented above is merely a technical quibble. After all, in Canada the Constitution is supreme, not the legislatures. Courts have had the power to invalidate unconstitutional legislation in this country since 1867. If judicial independence was a "constitutional" principle in the broad sense in nineteenth-century Britain, and that principle was continued or established in Canada as a result of the preamble to the *Constitution Act, 1867*, why should Canadian courts resile from enforcing this principle by striking down incompatible legislation?

[313] One answer to this question is the ambit of the *Act of Settlement*. The protection it accorded was limited to superior courts, specifically the central courts of common law; see Lederman, *supra*, at p. 782. It did not apply to inferior courts. While subsequent legislation did provide limited protection for the independence of the judges of certain statutory

courts, such as the county courts, the courts there were not regarded as within the ambit of the "constitutional" protection in the British sense. Generally the independence and impartiality of these courts were ensured to litigants through the superintendence exercised over them by the superior courts by way of prerogative writs and other extraordinary remedies. The overall task of protection sought to be created for inferior courts in the present appeals seems to me to be made of insubstantial cloth, and certainly in no way similar to anything to be found in the United Kingdom.

[314] A more general answer to the question lies in the nature of the power of judicial review. The ability to nullify the laws of democratically elected representatives derives its legitimacy from a super-legislative source: the text of the Constitution. This foundational document (in Canada, a series of documents) expresses the desire of the people to limit the power of legislatures in certain specified ways. Because our Constitution is entrenched, those limitations cannot be changed by recourse to the usual democratic process. They are not cast in stone, however, and can be modified in accordance with a further expression of democratic will: constitutional amendment.

[315] Judicial review, therefore, is politically legitimate only insofar as it involves the interpretation of an authoritative constitutional instrument. In this sense, it is akin to statutory interpretation. In each case, the court's role is to divine the intent or purpose of the text as it has been expressed by the people through the mechanism of the democratic process. Of course, many (but not all) constitutional provisions are cast in broad and abstract language. Courts have the often arduous task of explicating the effect of this language in a myriad of factual circumstances, many of which may not have been contemplated by the framers of the Constitution. While there are inevitable disputes about the manner in which courts should perform this duty, for example by according more or less deference to legislative decisions, there is general agreement that the task itself is legitimate.

[316] This legitimacy is imperiled, however, when courts attempt to limit the power of legislatures without recourse to express textual authority. From time to time, members of this Court have suggested that our Constitution comprehends implied rights that circumscribe legislative competence. On the theory that the efficacy of parliamentary democracy requires free political expression, it has been asserted that the curtailment of such expression is *ultra vires* both provincial legislatures and the federal Parliament: *Switzman v. Elbling*, [1957] SCR 285, at p. 328 (per Abbott J); *OPSEU v. Ontario (Attorney General)*, [1987] 2 SCR 2, at p. 57 (per Beetz J); see also: *Reference re Alberta Statutes*, [1938] SCR 100, at pp. 132-35 (per Duff CJ), and at pp. 145-46 (per Cannon J); *Switzman, supra*, at pp. 306-7 (per Rand J); *OPSEU, supra*, at p. 25 (per Dickson CJ); *Fraser v. Public Service Staff Relations Board*, [1985] 2 SCR 455, at pp. 462-63 (per Dickson CJ); *RWDSU v. Dolphin Delivery Ltd.*, [1986] 2 SCR 573, at p. 584 (per McIntyre J).

[317] This theory, which is not so much an "implied bill of rights," as it has so often been called, but rather a more limited guarantee of those communicative freedoms necessary for the existence of parliamentary democracy, is not without appeal. An argument can be made that, even under a constitutional structure that deems Parliament to be supreme, certain rights, including freedom of political speech, should be enforced by the courts in order to safeguard the democratic accountability of Parliament. Without this limitation of its powers, the argument runs, Parliament could subvert the very process by which it acquired its legitimacy as a representative, democratic institution ... . It should be noted, however, that

the idea that the Constitution contemplates implied protection for democratic rights has been rejected by a number of eminent jurists as being incompatible with the structure and history of the Constitution; see *Attorney General for Canada and Dupond v. Montreal*, [1978] 2 SCR 770, at p. 796 (per Beetz J); Bora Laskin, "An Inquiry into the Diefenbaker Bill of Rights" (1959), 37 *Can. Bar Rev.* 77, at pp. 100-103; Paul C. Weiler, "The Supreme Court and the Law of Canadian Federalism" (1973), 23 *UTLJ* 307, at p. 344; Peter W. Hogg, *Constitutional Law of Canada* (3rd ed. 1992 (loose-leaf)), vol. 2, at pp. 31-12 and 31-13.

[318] Whatever attraction this theory may hold, and I do not wish to be understood as either endorsing or rejecting it, it is clear in my view that it may not be used to justify the notion that the preamble to the *Constitution Act, 1867* contains implicit protection for judicial independence. Although it has been suggested that guarantees of political freedom flow from the preamble, as I have discussed in relation to judicial independence, this position is untenable. The better view is that if these guarantees exist, they are implicit in s. 17 of the *Constitution Act, 1867*, which provides for the establishment of Parliament; see Gibson ... , at p. 498. More important, the justification for implied political freedoms is that they are supportive, and not subversive, of legislative supremacy. That doctrine holds that democratically constituted legislatures, and not the courts, are the ultimate guarantors of civil liberties, including the right to an independent judiciary. Implying protection for judicial independence from the preambular commitment to a British-style constitution, therefore, entirely misapprehends the fundamental nature of that constitution.

[319] This brings us back to the central point: to the extent that courts in Canada have the power to enforce the principle of judicial independence, this power derives from the structure of Canadian, and not British, constitutionalism. Our Constitution expressly contemplates both the power of judicial review (in s. 52 of the *Constitution Act, 1982*) and guarantees of judicial independence (in ss. 96-100 of the *Constitution Act, 1867* and s. 11(d) of the Charter). While these provisions have been interpreted to provide guarantees of independence that are not immediately manifest in their language, this has been accomplished through the usual mechanisms of constitutional interpretation, not through recourse to the preamble. The legitimacy of this interpretive exercise stems from its grounding in an expression of democratic will, not from a dubious theory of an implicit constitutional structure. The express provisions of the Constitution are not, as the Chief Justice contends, "elaborations of the underlying, unwritten, and organizing principles found in the preamble to the *Constitution Act, 1867*" (para. 107). On the contrary, they are the Constitution. To assert otherwise is to subvert the democratic foundation of judicial review.

II. JUDICIAL REVIEW OF ADMINISTRATIVE ACTION

Judicial review of executive or administrative action raises somewhat different questions about institutional relationships than does judicial review of legislative action. To be sure, there is some overlap between these questions, at least to the extent that judges will normally want to respect the choice of democratically elected legislatures to allocate decision-making authority to institutions other than courts. On the other hand, the judicial invalidation of particular administrative acts on non-constitutional grounds often does not preclude the decision-maker from repeating his or her actions, this time in compliance with standards set out in the statute delegating power (as now assessed by the court) or common law proced-ural fairness (again, as assessed by the court). And, even if the court concludes that there is no fashion in which the actions of the administrative decision-maker could comply with existing statutory authority, it remains open to the legislature to modify the law in ways that validate the same action, if taken subsequent to the change in the law.

For these reasons, constitutional review of legislative action constrains democratically elected legislatures in a way that judicial review of administrative action using ordinary legal principles does not. As a result, non-constitutional review by judges of the actions of admin-istrative officials does not tend to raise the same kinds of questions about the democratic legitimacy of judicial review that arise when judges engage in the constitutional review of legislation.

This does not mean, however, that it is irrelevant to consider the proper institutional rela-tionship between courts and administrative decision-makers. At a superficial level, these re-lationships can be said to be established by the legal rules (typically found in statutes) that define the scope of authority of the administrative decision-maker whose actions are under review. In practice, however, these relationships are influenced significantly by two bodies of common law rules, one of which deals with fair administrative procedure and the other of which concerns judicial review of the substance of administrative decisions. There are some statutes that set out rules governing administrative procedure, such as the Ontario *Statutory Powers Procedure Act*, RSO 1990, c. S.22 and the British Columbia *Administrative Tribunals Act*, SBC 2004, c. 45, and other statutory provisions that affect the rules governing judicial review, such as s. 18.1 of the *Federal Courts Act*, RSC 1985, c. F-7 and ss. 58-59 of the British Columbia *Administrative Tribunals Act*. Even where the common law has been modified by statute, how-ever, it establishes the background legal expectations for fair administrative procedure and judicial supervision of the legal validity of administrative decisions, and thus is worthy of our consideration.

A. Controlling Procedures: The Duty To Be Fair

Administrative decision-makers are generally required by the common law to act fairly to-ward those persons affected by their decisions. In this context, the duty to be fair refers to the *procedures* adopted by the decision-maker, as opposed to imposing a substantive obligation of a *fair outcome*. Historically, the requirements of procedural fairness, at that time referred to as the "rules of natural justice," were found to apply only to decision-makers carrying out a "judicial or quasi-judicial function," a narrowly defined class of administrative decisions that was confined to cases where the decision-maker was determining the legal rights of a per-son, but excluded cases where decision-makers were determining matters of policy, regard-less of their affect on individuals.

The difficulty with the traditional rules of natural justice from a policy perspective was that they failed to afford any procedural protections to those affected by decisions found to be of a legislative or administrative nature, although it was becoming clearer that these deci-sions could have significant impacts on individuals. From a legal perspective, the distinction between judicial and quasi-judicial decisions, on the one hand, and legislative and adminis-trative decisions, on the other, was hard to maintain because judicial functions could be carried out by administrative actors whose principal function was legislative or administrative. Moreover, some decision-making processes engaged both adjudicatory and policy de-termination functions. As a consequence of these difficulties, common law courts developed a more flexible approach to the procedural obligations of decision-makers under the rubric of the duty to be fair. In England, the move toward a more flexible approach was firmly adopted in *Ridge v. Baldwin*, [1964] AC 40 (HL) and in Canada in *Nicholson v. Haldimand-Norfolk (Regional) Police Commissioners*, [1979] 1 SCR 311.

The essence of the content of the rules of natural justice was captured by these two max-ims: *audi alteram partem*—the right of a person to know and answer the case against him or her—and *nemo judex in sua causa*—requiring that a person not be the judge in his or her own cause (that is, that an administrative decision-maker not be biased). The extent of their application depended on the particular context. The contours of the duty to be fair are con-sidered in the excerpts that follow.

Baker v. Canada (Minister of Citizenship & Immigration)
[1999] 2 SCR 817

[The appellant, who was a citizen of Jamaica, was the subject of a deportation order. Prior to the order being issued, the appellant had lived in Canada for 11 years, but never became a permanent resident. During the time she lived in Canada, she had four children. She also suffered from mental illness, for which she received treatment. The appellant sought an exemption to applying for permanent residency status from outside of Canada on "humani-tarian and compassionate" (H & C) considerations, on the grounds that her deportation was not in the best interests of her children, who would suffer in her absence, and that her de-portation would negatively affect her mental health. Her application was denied by immi-gration officials. She was not given official reasons for the denial of her application, but she did receive a copy of notes taken by one of the reviewing immigration officers (Lorenz, whose notes were used by a more senior immigration officer, Caden, who was the decision-maker). These notes disclosed a lack of concern regarding the interests of her children and were insensitive to her mental health issues. The appellant sought to have the H & C deci-sion reviewed by the Court on the grounds that she was denied procedural fairness, includ-ing bias, and that the decision itself was unreasonable in that it failed to account for the best interests of her children. On this last point, the appellant argued that the best interests of children were to be a primary consideration under the *Convention on the Rights of the Child*, an international treaty to which Canada was a party (but had not implemented in Canadian domestic law).]

L'HEUREUX-DUBÉ J: …

C. Procedural Fairness

[18] The first ground upon which the appellant challenges the decision made by Officer Caden is the allegation that she was not accorded procedural fairness. She suggests that the following procedures are required by the duty of fairness when parents have Canadian chil-dren and they make an H & C application: an oral interview before the decision-maker,

notice to her children and the other parent of that interview, a right for the children and the other parent to make submissions at that interview, and notice to the other parent of the interview and of that person's right to have counsel present. She also alleges that procedural fairness requires the provision of reasons by the decision-maker, Officer Caden, and that the notes of Officer Lorenz give rise to a reasonable apprehension of bias.

[19]   In addressing the fairness issues, I will consider first the principles relevant to the determination of the content of the duty of procedural fairness, and then address Ms. Baker's arguments that she was accorded insufficient participatory rights, that a duty to give reasons existed, and that there was a reasonable apprehension of bias.

[20]   Both parties agree that a duty of procedural fairness applies to H & C decisions. The fact that a decision is administrative and affects "the rights, privileges or interests of an individual" is sufficient to trigger the application of the duty of fairness: *Cardinal v. Kent Institution*, [1985] 2 SCR 643 (SCC) at p. 653. Clearly, the determination of whether an applicant will be exempted from the requirements of the Act falls within this category, and it has been long recognized that the duty of fairness applies to H & C decisions: *Sobrie v. Canada (Minister of Employment & Immigration)* (1987), 3 Imm. LR (2d) 81 (Fed. TD) at p. 88; *Said v. Canada (Minister of Employment & Immigration)* (1992), 6 Admin. LR (2d) 23 (Fed. TD); *Shah v. Canada (Minister of Employment & Immigration)* (1994), 170 NR 238 (Fed. CA).

(1) Factors Affecting the Content of the Duty of Fairness

[21]   The existence of a duty of fairness, however, does not determine what requirements will be applicable in a given set of circumstances. As I wrote in *Knight v. Indian Head School Division No. 19*, [1990] 1 SCR 653 (SCC) at p. 682, "the concept of procedural fairness is eminently variable, and its content is to be decided in the specific context of each case." All of the circumstances must be considered in order to determine the content of the duty of procedural fairness: *Knight* at pp. 682-83; *Cardinal, supra*, at p. 654; *Old St. Boniface Residents Assn. Inc. v. Winnipeg (City)*, [1990] 3 SCR 1170 (SCC), *per* Sopinka J.

[22]   Although the duty of fairness is flexible and variable, and depends on an appreciation of the context of the particular statute and the rights affected, it is helpful to review the criteria that should be used in determining what procedural rights the duty of fairness requires in a given set of circumstances. I emphasize that underlying all these factors is the notion that the purpose of the participatory rights contained within the duty of procedural fairness is to ensure that administrative decisions are made using a fair and open procedure, appropriate to the decision being made and its statutory, institutional, and social context, with an opportunity for those affected by the decision to put forward their views and evidence fully and have them considered by the decision-maker.

[23]   Several factors have been recognized in the jurisprudence as relevant to determining what is required by the common law duty of procedural fairness in a given set of circumstances. One important consideration is the nature of the decision being made and the process followed in making it. In *Knight, supra*, at p. 683, it was held that "the closeness of the administrative process to the judicial process should indicate how much of those governing principles should be imported into the realm of administrative decision making." The more the process provided for, the function of the tribunal, the nature of the decision-

making body, and the determinations that must be made to reach a decision resemble judicial decision making, the more likely it is that procedural protections closer to the trial model will be required by the duty of fairness. See also *Old St. Boniface, supra*, at p. 1191; *Russell v. Duke of Norfolk*, [1949] 1 All ER 109 (Eng. CA) at p. 118; *Syndicat des employés de production du Québec & de l'Acadie v. Canada (Human Rights Commission)*, [1989] 2 SCR 879 (SCC) at p. 896, *per* Sopinka J.

[24] A second factor is the nature of the statutory scheme and the "terms of the statute pursuant to which the body operates": *Old St. Boniface, supra*, at p. 1191. The role of the particular decision within the statutory scheme and other surrounding indications in the statute help determine the content of the duty of fairness owed when a particular administrative decision is made. Greater procedural protections, for example, will be required when no appeal procedure is provided within the statute, or when the decision is determinative of the issue and further requests cannot be submitted: see D.J.M. Brown and J.M. Evans, *Judicial Review of Administrative Action in Canada* (loose-leaf), at pp. 7-66 to 7-67.

[25] A third factor in determining the nature and extent of the duty of fairness owed is the importance of the decision to the individual or individuals affected. The more important the decision is to the lives of those affected and the greater its impact on that person or those persons, the more stringent the procedural protections that will be mandated. This was expressed, for example, by Dickson J (as he then was) in *Kane v. University of British Columbia*, [1980] 1 SCR 1105 (SCC) at p. 1113:

> A high standard of justice is required when the right to continue in one's profession or employment is at stake. … A disciplinary suspension can have grave and permanent consequences upon a professional career.

As Sedley J (now Sedley LJ) stated in *R v. Higher Education Funding Council* (1993), [1994] 1 All ER 651 (Eng. QB), at p. 667:

> In the modern state the decisions of administrative bodies can have a more immediate and profound impact on people's lives than the decisions of courts, and public law has since *Ridge v. Baldwin*, [1963] 2 All ER 66, [1964] AC 40 been alive to that fact. While the judicial character of a function may elevate the practical requirements of fairness above what they would otherwise be, for example by requiring contentious evidence to be given and tested orally, what makes it "judicial" in this sense is principally the nature of the issue it has to determine, not the formal status of the deciding body.

The importance of a decision to the individuals affected, therefore, constitutes a significant factor affecting the content of the duty of procedural fairness.

[26] Fourth, the legitimate expectations of the person challenging the decision may also determine what procedures the duty of fairness requires in given circumstances. Our Court has held that, in Canada, this doctrine is part of the doctrine of fairness or natural justice, and that it does not create substantive rights: *Old St. Boniface, supra*, at p. 1204; *Reference re Canada Assistance Plan (Canada)*, [1991] 2 SCR 525 (SCC) at p. 557. As applied in Canada, if a legitimate expectation is found to exist, this will affect the content of the duty of fairness owed to the individual or individuals affected by the decision. If the claimant has a legitimate expectation that a certain procedure will be followed, this procedure will be required by the duty of fairness: *Qi v. Canada (Minister of Citizenship & Immigration)* (1995), 33 Imm.

LR (2d) 57 (Fed. TD); *Mercier-Néron v. Canada (Minister of National Health & Welfare)* (1995), 98 FTR 36 (Fed. TD); *Bendahmane v. Canada (Minister of Employment & Immigration)*, [1989] 3 FC 16 (Fed. CA). Similarly, if a claimant has a legitimate expectation that a certain result will be reached in his or her case, fairness may require more extensive procedural rights than would otherwise be accorded: D.J. Mullan, *Administrative Law* (3rd ed. 1996), at pp. 214-15; D. Shapiro, "Legitimate Expectation and Its Application to Canadian Immigration Law" (1992), 8 *JL & Soc. Pol'y* 282, at p. 297; *Canada (Attorney General) v. Canada (Human Rights Tribunal)* (1994), 76 FTR 1 (Fed. TD). Nevertheless, the doctrine of legitimate expectations cannot lead to substantive rights outside the procedural domain. This doctrine, as applied in Canada, is based on the principle that the "circumstances" affecting procedural fairness take into account the promises or regular practices of administrative decision-makers, and that it will generally be unfair for them to act in contravention of representations as to procedure, or to backtrack on substantive promises without according significant procedural rights.

[27] Fifth, the analysis of what procedures the duty of fairness requires should also take into account and respect the choices of procedure made by the agency itself, particularly when the statute leaves to the decision-maker the ability to choose its own procedures, or when the agency has an expertise in determining what procedures are appropriate in the circumstances: Brown and Evans, *supra*, at pp. 7-66 to 7-70. While this, of course, is not determinative, important weight must be given to the choice of procedures made by the agency itself and its institutional constraints: *I.W.A. Local 2-69 v. Consolidated Bathurst Packaging Ltd.*, [1990] 1 SCR 282 (SCC), *per* Gonthier J.

[28] I should note that this list of factors is not exhaustive. These principles all help a court determine whether the procedures that were followed respected the duty of fairness. Other factors may also be important, particularly when considering aspects of the duty of fairness unrelated to participatory rights. The values underlying the duty of procedural fairness relate to the principle that the individual or individuals affected should have the opportunity to present their case fully and fairly, and have decisions affecting their rights, interests, or privileges made using a fair, impartial, and open process, appropriate to the statutory, institutional, and social context of the decision.

(2) Legitimate Expectations

[29] I turn now to an application of these principles to the circumstances of this case, to determine whether the procedures followed respected the duty of procedural fairness. I will first determine whether the duty of procedural fairness that would otherwise be applicable is affected, as the appellant argues, by the existence of a legitimate expectation based upon the text of the articles of the Convention [on the Rights of the Child] and the fact that Canada has ratified it. In my view, however, the articles of the Convention and their wording did not give rise to a legitimate expectation on the part of Ms. Baker that when the decision on her H & C application was made, specific procedural rights above what would normally be required under the duty of fairness would be accorded, a positive finding would be made, or particular criteria would be applied. This Convention is not, in my view, the equivalent of a government representation about how H & C applications will be decided, nor does it suggest that any rights beyond the participatory rights discussed below will be accorded.

Therefore, in this case there is no legitimate expectation affecting the content of the duty of fairness, and the fourth factor outlined above therefore does not affect the analysis. It is unnecessary to decide whether an international instrument ratified by Canada could, in other circumstances, give rise to a legitimate expectation.

(3) Participatory Rights

[30] The next issue is whether, taking into account the other factors related to the determination of the content of the duty of fairness, the failure to accord an oral hearing and give notice to Ms. Baker or her children was inconsistent with the participatory rights required by the duty of fairness in these circumstances. At the heart of this analysis is whether, considering all the circumstances, those whose interests were affected had a meaningful opportunity to present their case fully and fairly. The procedure in this case consisted of a written application with supporting documentation, which was summarized by the junior officer (Lorenz), with a recommendation being made by that officer. The summary, recommendation, and material was then considered by the senior officer (Caden), who made the decision.

[31] Several of the factors described above enter into the determination of the type of participatory rights the duty of procedural fairness requires in the circumstances. First, an H & C decision is very different from a judicial decision, since it involves the exercise of considerable discretion and requires the consideration of multiple factors. Second, its role is also, within the statutory scheme, as an exception to the general principles of Canadian immigration law. These factors militate in favour of more relaxed requirements under the duty of fairness. On the other hand, there is no appeal procedure, although judicial review may be applied for with leave of the Federal Court—Trial Division. In addition, considering the third factor, this is a decision that in practice has exceptional importance to the lives of those with an interest in its result—the claimant and his or her close family members—and this leads to the content of the duty of fairness being more extensive. Finally, applying the fifth factor described above, the statute accords considerable flexibility to the Minister to decide on the proper procedure, and immigration officers, as a matter of practice, do not conduct interviews in all cases. The institutional practices and choices made by the Minister are significant, though of course not determinative factors to be considered in the analysis. Thus, it can be seen that although some of the factors suggest stricter requirements under the duty of fairness, others suggest more relaxed requirements further from the judicial model.

[32] Balancing these factors, I disagree with the holding of the Federal Court of Appeal in *Shah, supra,* at p. 239, that the duty of fairness owed in these circumstances is simply "minimal." Rather, the circumstances require a full and fair consideration of the issues, and the claimant and others whose important interests are affected by the decision in a fundamental way must have a meaningful opportunity to present the various types of evidence relevant to their case and have it fully and fairly considered.

[33] However, it also cannot be said that an oral hearing is always necessary to ensure a fair hearing and consideration of the issues involved. The flexible nature of the duty of fairness recognizes that meaningful participation can occur in different ways in different situations. The Federal Court has held that procedural fairness does not require an oral hearing in these circumstances: see, for example, *Said, supra,* at p. 30.

[34] I agree that an oral hearing is not a general requirement for H & C decisions. An interview is not essential for the information relevant to an H & C application to be put before an immigration officer, so that the humanitarian and compassionate considerations presented may be considered in their entirety and in a fair manner. In this case, the appellant had the opportunity to put forward, in written form through her lawyer, information about her situation, her children and their emotional dependence on her, and documentation in support of her application from a social worker at the Children's Aid Society and from her psychiatrist. These documents were before the decision-makers, and they contained the information relevant to making this decision. Taking all the factors relevant to determining the content of the duty of fairness into account, the lack of an oral hearing or notice of such a hearing did not, in my opinion, constitute a violation of the requirements of procedural fairness to which Ms. Baker was entitled in the circumstances, particularly given the fact that several of the factors point toward a more relaxed standard. The opportunity, which was accorded, for the appellant or her children to produce full and complete written documentation in relation to all aspects of her application satisfied the requirements of the participatory rights required by the duty of fairness in this case.

(4) The Provision of Reasons

[35] The appellant also submits that the duty of fairness, in these circumstances, requires that reasons be given by the decision-maker. She argues either that the notes of Officer Lorenz should be considered the reasons for the decision, or that it should be held that the failure of Officer Caden to give written reasons for his decision or a subsequent affidavit explaining them should be taken to be a breach of the principles of fairness.

[36] This issue has been addressed in several cases of judicial review of humanitarian and compassionate applications. The Federal Court of Appeal has held that reasons are unnecessary: *Shah, supra*, at pp. 239-40. It has also been held that the case history notes prepared by a subordinate officer are not to be considered the decision-maker's reasons: see *Tylo v. Canada (Minister of Employment & Immigration)* (1995), 90 FTR 157 (Fed. TD) at pp. 159-60. In *Gheorlan v. Canada (Secretary of State)* (1995), 26 Imm. LR (2d) 170 (Fed. TD), and *Chan v. Canada (Minister of Citizenship & Immigration)* (1994), 87 FTR 62 (Fed. TD), it was held that the notes of the reviewing officer should not be taken to be the reasons for decision, but may help in determining whether a reviewable error exists. In *Marques v. Canada (Minister of Citizenship & Immigration)* (1995), 116 FTR 241 (Fed. TD), an H & C decision was set aside because the decision making officer failed to provide reasons or an affidavit explaining the reasons for his decision.

[37] More generally, the traditional position at common law has been that the duty of fairness does not require, as a general rule, that reasons be provided for administrative decisions: *Northwestern Utilities Ltd. v. Edmonton (City)* (1978), [1979] 1 SCR 684 (SCC); *Supermarchés Jean Labrecque Inc. v. Québec (Tribunal du travail)*, [1987] 2 SCR 219 (SCC) at p. 233; *Public Service Board of New South Wales v. Osmond* (1986), 159 CLR 656 (Australia HC) at pp. 665-66.

[38] Courts and commentators have, however, often emphasized the usefulness of reasons in ensuring fair and transparent decision-making. Though *Northwestern Utilities* dealt with a statutory obligation to give reasons, Estey J held as follows, at p. 706, referring to the desirability of a common law reasons requirement:

This obligation is a salutary one. It reduces to a considerable degree the chances of arbitrary or capricious decisions, reinforces public confidence in the judgment and fairness of administrative tribunals, and affords parties to administrative proceedings an opportunity to assess the question of appeal. …

The importance of reasons was recently reemphasized by this Court in *R v. Campbell*, [1997] 3 SCR 3 (SCC) at pp. 109-10.

[39] Reasons, it has been argued, foster better decision making by ensuring that issues and reasoning are well articulated and, therefore, more carefully thought out. The process of writing reasons for decision by itself may be a guarantee of a better decision. Reasons also allow parties to see that the applicable issues have been carefully considered, and are invaluable if a decision is to be appealed, questioned, or considered on judicial review: R.A. Macdonald and D. Lametti, "Reasons for Decision in Administrative Law" (1990), 3 *CJALP* 123, at p. 146; *Williams v. Canada (Minister of Citizenship & Immigration)*, [1997] 2 FC 646 (Fed. CA) at para. 38. Those affected may be more likely to feel they were treated fairly and appropriately if reasons are given: de Smith, Woolf, & Jowell, *Judicial Review of Administrative Action* (5th ed. 1995), at pp. 459-60. I agree that these are significant benefits of written reasons.

[40] Others have expressed concerns about the desirability of a written reasons requirement at common law. In *Osmond, supra*, Gibbs CJ articulated, at p. 668, the concern that a reasons requirement may lead to an inappropriate burden being imposed on administrative decision-makers, that it may lead to increased cost and delay, and that it "might in some cases induce a lack of candour on the part of the administrative officers concerned." Macdonald and Lametti, *supra*, though they agree that fairness should require the provision of reasons in certain circumstances, caution against a requirement of "archival" reasons associated with court judgments, and note that the special nature of agency decision-making in different contexts should be considered in evaluating reasons requirements. In my view, however, these concerns can be accommodated by ensuring that any reasons requirement under the duty of fairness leaves sufficient flexibility to decision-makers by accepting various types of written explanations for the decision as sufficient.

· · ·

[43] In my opinion, it is now appropriate to recognize that, in certain circumstances, the duty of procedural fairness will require the provision of a written explanation for a decision. The strong arguments demonstrating the advantages of written reasons suggest that, in cases such as this where the decision has important significance for the individual, when there is a statutory right of appeal, or in other circumstances, some form of reasons should be required. This requirement has been developing in the common law elsewhere. The circumstances of the case at bar, in my opinion, constitute one of the situations where reasons are necessary. The profound importance of an H & C decision to those affected, as with those at issue in *Orlowski*, *R v. Civil Service Appeal Board*, and *R v. Secretary of State for the Home Department*, militates in favour of a requirement that reasons be provided. It would be unfair for a person subject to a decision such as this one which is so critical to their future not to be told why the result was reached.

[44] In my view, however, the reasons requirement was fulfilled in this case, since the appellant was provided with the notes of Officer Lorenz. The notes were given to Ms. Baker when her counsel asked for reasons. Because of this, and because there is no other record of

the reasons for making the decision, the notes of the subordinate reviewing officer should be taken, by inference, to be the reasons for decision. Accepting documents such as these notes as sufficient reasons is part of the flexibility that is necessary, as emphasized by Macdonald and Lametti, *supra*, when courts evaluate the requirements of the duty of fairness with recognition of the day-to-day realities of administrative agencies and the many ways in which the values underlying the principles of procedural fairness can be assured. It upholds the principle that individuals are entitled to fair procedures and open decision-making, but recognizes that in the administrative context, this transparency may take place in various ways. I conclude that the notes of Officer Lorenz satisfy the requirement for reasons under the duty of procedural fairness in this case, and they will be taken to be the reasons for decision.

(5) Reasonable Apprehension of Bias

[45] Procedural fairness also requires that decisions be made free from a reasonable apprehension of bias, by an impartial decision-maker. The respondent argues that Simpson J was correct to find that the notes of Officer Lorenz cannot be considered to give rise to a reasonable apprehension of bias because it was Officer Caden who was the actual decision-maker, who was simply reviewing the recommendation prepared by his subordinate. In my opinion, the duty to act fairly and therefore in a manner that does not give rise to a reasonable apprehension of bias applies to all immigration officers who play a significant role in the making of decisions, whether they are subordinate reviewing officers, or those who make the final decision. The subordinate officer plays an important part in the process, and if a person with such a central role does not act impartially, the decision itself cannot be said to have been made in an impartial manner. In addition, as discussed in the previous section, the notes of Officer Lorenz constitute the reasons for the decision, and if they give rise to a reasonable apprehension of bias, this taints the decision itself.

[46] The test for reasonable apprehension of bias was set out by de Grandpré J, writing in dissent, in *Committee for Justice & Liberty v. Canada (National Energy Board)* (1976), [1978] 1 SCR 369 (SCC) at p. 394:

> ... the apprehension of bias must be a reasonable one, held by reasonable and right minded persons, applying themselves to the question and obtaining thereon the required information. ... [T]hat test is "what would an informed person, viewing the matter realistically and practically—and having thought the matter through—conclude. Would he think that it is more likely than not that [the decision-maker], whether consciously or unconsciously, would not decide fairly."

This expression of the test has often been endorsed by this Court, most recently in *R v. S. (R.D.)*, [1997] 3 SCR 484 (SCC) at para. 11, *per* Major J; at para. 31, *per* L'Heureux-Dubé and McLachlin JJ; and at para. 111, *per* Cory J.

[47] It has been held that the standards for reasonable apprehension of bias may vary, like other aspects of procedural fairness, depending on the context and the type of function performed by the administrative decision-maker involved: *Newfoundland Telephone Co. v. Newfoundland (Board of Commissioners of Public Utilities)*, [1992] 1 SCR 623 (SCC); *Old St. Boniface, supra*, at p. 1192. The context here is one where immigration officers must regu-

larly make decisions that have great importance to the individuals affected by them, but are also often critical to the interests of Canada as a country. They are individualized, rather than decisions of a general nature. They also require special sensitivity. Canada is a nation made up largely of people whose families migrated here in recent centuries. Our history is one that shows the importance of immigration, and our society shows the benefits of having a diversity of people whose origins are in a multitude of places around the world. Because they necessarily relate to people of diverse backgrounds, from different cultures, races, and continents, immigration decisions demand sensitivity and understanding by those making them. They require a recognition of diversity, an understanding of others, and an openness to difference.

[48] In my opinion, the well-informed member of the community would perceive bias when reading Officer Lorenz's comments. His notes, and the manner in which they are written, do not disclose the existence of an open mind or a weighing of the particular circumstances of the case free from stereotypes. Most unfortunate is the fact that they seem to make a link between Ms. Baker's mental illness, her training as a domestic worker, the fact that she has several children, and the conclusion that she would therefore be a strain on our social welfare system for the rest of her life. In addition, the conclusion drawn was contrary to the psychiatrist's letter, which stated that, with treatment, Ms. Baker could remain well and return to being a productive member of society. Whether they were intended in this manner or not, these statements give the impression that Officer Lorenz may have been drawing conclusions based not on the evidence before him, but on the fact that Ms. Baker was a single mother with several children, and had been diagnosed with a psychiatric illness. His use of capitals to highlight the number of Ms. Baker's children may also suggest to a reader that this was a reason to deny her status. Reading his comments, I do not believe that a reasonable and well-informed member of the community would conclude that he had approached this case with the impartiality appropriate to a decision made by an immigration officer. It would appear to a reasonable observer that his own frustration with the "system" interfered with his duty to consider impartially whether the appellant's admission should be facilitated owing to humanitarian or compassionate considerations. I conclude that the notes of Officer Lorenz demonstrate a reasonable apprehension of bias.

Note that in para. 27 of her reasons for decision in *Baker*, Madam Justice L'Heureux-Dubé stated that one of the factors to be considered in determining what procedures are required in any particular instance are the procedures chosen by the agency itself. The model for fair administrative procedure is based on the key elements of procedure in the courts: the right to a hearing and the right to an impartial decision-maker. Nevertheless, as the *Baker* case itself illustrates, the model is sufficiently flexible that it can be applied in bureaucratic decision-making settings that bear little resemblance to a civil or criminal trial. One way of thinking about the role that agency choices of procedure play in determining the content of fair administrative procedure is to suggest that courts will, within limits, defer to these procedural choices. The extent to which courts extend deference to procedural choices made by agencies is clearly limited. Not only is the model of fair procedure based on the functioning of courts, but the courts themselves are the ultimate arbiters of fair procedure. Moreover, they make these decisions taking into account a variety of factors, only one of which is the procedural choice made by the agency itself. The idea of deference takes on greater prominence in the next area we will examine, which is judicial review of the substance of administrative decisions.

B. Substantive Judicial Review

The Supreme Court of Canada's 2008 decision in *Dunsmuir v. New Brunswick*, [2008] 1 SCR 190 ushered in a new and, at least in comparison with the earlier jurisprudence, simplified body of law governing common law judicial review of the substance of administrative decisions. At the heart of this body of law is the idea that all administrative decisions should be subject to review using one of two "standards of review." The stricter standard of review is called "correctness" and the more deferential standard of review is called "reasonableness." The court sets out a multifactorial analysis to determine which standard should be employed with respect to any particular aspect of administrative decision. Before we consider how this analysis is carried out, however, it is worthwhile to think about the purpose of having different standards of review in the first place.

When we establish systems that enable parties that are unhappy with particular decisions to seek review of them, we have a natural tendency to differentiate the role of the review body from that of the original decision-maker. It is, of course, possible to establish a system of *de novo* review in which the reviewing body essentially duplicates the process employed by the original decision-maker. Generally we are reluctant to do this because it seems inefficient and encourages people who are disappointed with a decision to seek review even if there is no reason to believe that the original decision was erroneous. Within the judicial system, for example, appeal courts use different procedures from trial courts (they do not normally hear oral testimony, for example, whereas it is common for trial courts to do so) and, as Madam Justice Deschamps points out at paras. 161-162 of her concurring reasons in *Dunsmuir*, appellate judges use a different standard of review in assessing the findings of trial judges on questions of fact and mixed fact and law than they do in reviewing their decisions on questions of law. Trial judges are considered to be in a better position than appellate judges to make factual determinations and apply the law to the facts because they have first-hand knowledge of the testimony before them, whereas the judges on appeal must rely on the paper record of the proceedings. This does not mean that the trial judge's findings on questions of fact and mixed fact and law are immune from appellate review, but appeal courts are more reluctant to interfere with the trial judge's conclusions on these types of issues than they are in reviewing the trial judge's decisions concerning questions of law.

As you read the reasons for judgment offered by different members of the Supreme Court of Canada in *Dunsmuir*, consider the extent to which the structure of review of administrative decisions they describe differs from appellate review in the courts. Pay particular attention to the reasons offered for giving at least some administrative decision-makers greater deference with respect to decisions on questions of law than would be accorded to trial judges on appellate review. How successful are the judgments in creating a structure for review that accommodates all of the different types of administrative decision-makers that we studied in chapter 5? Note as well that although the entire court agrees that the law governing the standards of review of administrative decisions requires simplification, Mr. Justice Binnie and Madam Justice Deschamps (writing for herself and Justices Charron and Rothstein) propose quite different ways of achieving that simplification than do Justices Bastarache and LeBel writing for the majority. To what extent do these differences reflect different approaches to the relationship between courts and administrative decision-makers?

The *Dunsmuir* case concerned a court clerk whose "at pleasure" appointment was terminated by the Department of Justice. Although there had been concerns about Dunsmuir's job performance, the department did not allege that it had cause for terminating his appointment. Dunsmuir exercised his statutory right to grieve his dismissal, and an adjudicator found that the termination of his employment had been improper and ordered his reinstatement. The department successfully sought judicial review from the New Brunswick Court of Queen's Bench, and Dunsmuir's appeal was dismissed by the New Brunswick Court of Appeal. The entire Supreme Court of Canada agreed that the appeal from this decision should be dismissed, but offered three different sets of reasons for coming to this conclusion.

Dunsmuir v. New Brunswick
[2008] 1 SCR 190

BASTARACHE and LeBEL JJ (McLachlin CJ and Fish and Abella JJ concurring):

I. Introduction

[1] This appeal calls on the Court to consider, once again, the troubling question of the approach to be taken in judicial review of decisions of administrative tribunals. The recent history of judicial review in Canada has been marked by ebbs and flows of deference, confounding tests and new words for old problems, but no solutions that provide real guidance for litigants, counsel, administrative decision makers or judicial review judges. The time has arrived for a reassessment of the question.

. . .

III. Issue 1: Review of the Adjudicator's Statutory Interpretation Determination

A. Judicial Review

[27] As a matter of constitutional law, judicial review is intimately connected with the preservation of the rule of law. It is essentially that constitutional foundation which explains the purpose of judicial review and guides its function and operation. Judicial review seeks to address an underlying tension between the rule of law and the foundational democratic principle, which finds an expression in the initiatives of Parliament and legislatures to create various administrative bodies and endow them with broad powers. Courts, while exercising their constitutional functions of judicial review, must be sensitive not only to the need to uphold the rule of law, but also to the necessity of avoiding undue interference with the discharge of administrative functions in respect of the matters delegated to administrative bodies by Parliament and legislatures.

. . .

[30] In addition to the role judicial review plays in upholding the rule of law, it also performs an important constitutional function in maintaining legislative supremacy. As

noted by Justice Thomas Cromwell, "the rule of law is affirmed by assuring that the courts have the final say on the jurisdictional limits of a tribunal's authority; second, legislative supremacy is affirmed by adopting the principle that the concept of jurisdiction should be narrowly circumscribed and defined according to the intent of the legislature in a contextual and purposeful way; third, legislative supremacy is affirmed and the court-centric conception of the rule of law is reined in by acknowledging that the courts do not have a monopoly on deciding all questions of law" ("Appellate Review: Policy and Pragmatism," in *2006 Isaac Pitblado Lectures, Appellate Courts: Policy, Law and Practice*, V-1, at p. V-12). In essence, the rule of law is maintained because the courts have the last word on jurisdiction, and legislative supremacy is assured because determining the applicable standard of review is accomplished by establishing legislative intent.

. . .

B. Reconsidering the Standards of Judicial Review

[34] The current approach to judicial review involves three standards of review, which range from correctness, where no deference is shown, to patent unreasonableness, which is most deferential to the decision maker, the standard of reasonableness *simpliciter* lying, theoretically, in the middle. In our view, it is necessary to reconsider both the number and definitions of the various standards of review, and the analytical process employed to determine which standard applies in a given situation. We conclude that there ought to be two standards of review—correctness and reasonableness.

[35] The existing system of judicial review has its roots in several landmark decisions beginning in the late 1970s in which this Court developed the theory of substantive review to be applied to determinations of law, and determinations of fact and of mixed law and fact made by administrative tribunals. In *Canadian Union of Public Employees, Local 963 v. New Brunswick Liquor Corp.*, [1979] 2 SCR 227 ("*CUPE*"), Dickson J introduced the idea that, depending on the legal and administrative contexts, a specialized administrative tribunal with particular expertise, which has been given the protection of a privative clause, if acting within its jurisdiction, could provide an interpretation of its enabling legislation that would be allowed to stand unless "so patently unreasonable that its construction cannot be rationally supported by the relevant legislation and demands intervention by the court upon review" (p. 237). Prior to *CUPE*, judicial review followed the "preliminary question doctrine," which inquired into whether a tribunal had erred in determining the scope of its jurisdiction. By simply branding an issue as "jurisdictional," courts could replace a decision of the tribunal with one they preferred, often at the expense of a legislative intention that the matter lie in the hands of the administrative tribunal. *CUPE* marked a significant turning point in the approach of courts to judicial review, most notably in Dickson J's warning that courts "should not be alert to brand as jurisdictional, and therefore subject to broader curial review, that which may be doubtfully so" (p. 233). Dickson J's policy of judicial respect for administrative decision making marked the beginning of the modern era of Canadian administrative law.

[36] *CUPE* did not do away with correctness review altogether and in *Bibeault*, the Court affirmed that there are still questions on which a tribunal must be correct. As Beetz J explained, "the jurisdiction conferred on administrative tribunals and other bodies created by statute is limited, and ... such a tribunal cannot by a misinterpretation of an enactment

assume a power not given to it by the legislator" (p. 1086). *Bibeault* introduced the concept of a "pragmatic and functional analysis" to determine the jurisdiction of a tribunal, abandoning the "preliminary question" theory. In arriving at the appropriate standard of review, courts were to consider a number of factors including the wording of the provision conferring jurisdiction on the tribunal, the purpose of the enabling statute, the reason for the existence of the tribunal, the expertise of its members, and the nature of the problem (p. 1088). The new approach would put "renewed emphasis on the superintending and reforming function of the superior courts" (p. 1090). The "pragmatic and functional analysis," as it came to be known, was later expanded to determine the appropriate degree of deference in respect of various forms of administrative decision making.

[37] In *Canada (Director of Investigation and Research) v. Southam Inc.*, [1997] 1 SCR 748, a third standard of review was introduced into Canadian administrative law. The legislative context of that case, which provided a statutory right of appeal from the decision of a specialized tribunal, suggested that none of the existing standards was entirely satisfactory. As a result, the reasonableness *simpliciter* standard was introduced. It asks whether the tribunal's decision was reasonable. If so, the decision should stand; if not, it must fall. In *Southam*, Iacobucci J described an unreasonable decision as one that "is not supported by any reasons that can stand up to a somewhat probing examination" (para. 56) and explained that the difference between patent unreasonableness and reasonableness *simpliciter* is the "immediacy" or "obviousness" of the defect in the tribunal's decision (para. 57). The defect will appear on the face of a patently unreasonable decision, but where the decision is merely unreasonable, it will take a searching review to find the defect.

[38] The three standards of review have since remained in Canadian administrative law, the approach to determining the appropriate standard of review having been refined in *Pushpanathan v. Canada (Minister of Citizenship and Immigration)*, [1998] 1 SCR 982.

[39] The operation of three standards of review has not been without practical and theoretical difficulties, neither has it been free of criticism. One major problem lies in distinguishing between the patent unreasonableness standard and the reasonableness *simpliciter* standard. The difficulty in distinguishing between those standards contributes to the problem of choosing the right standard of review. An even greater problem lies in the application of the patent unreasonableness standard, which at times seems to require parties to accept an unreasonable decision.

. . .

C. *Two Standards of Review*

[43] The Court has moved from a highly formalistic, artificial "jurisdiction" test that could easily be manipulated, to a highly contextual "functional" test that provides great flexibility but little real on-the-ground guidance, and offers too many standards of review. What is needed is a test that offers guidance, is not formalistic or artificial, and permits review where justice requires it, but not otherwise. A simpler test is needed.

(1) *Defining the Concepts of Reasonableness and Correctness*

[44] As explained above, the patent unreasonableness standard was developed many years prior to the introduction of the reasonableness *simpliciter* standard in *Southam*. The intermediate standard was developed to respond to what the Court viewed as problems in

the operation of judicial review in Canada, particularly the perceived all-or-nothing approach to deference, and in order to create a more finely calibrated system of judicial review
(see also L. Sossin and C.M. Flood, "The Contextual Turn: Iacobucci's Legacy and the Standard of Review in Administrative Law" (2007), 57 *UTLJ* 581). However, the analytical problems that arise in trying to apply the different standards undercut any conceptual usefulness
created by the inherently greater flexibility of having multiple standards of review. Though
we are of the view that the three-standard model is too difficult to apply to justify its retention, now, several years after *Southam*, we believe that it would be a step backwards to simply remove the reasonableness *simpliciter* standard and revert to pre-*Southam* law. As we see
it, the problems that *Southam* attempted to remedy with the introduction of the intermediate standard are best addressed not by three standards of review, but by two standards, defined appropriately.

[45] We therefore conclude that the two variants of reasonableness review should be
collapsed into a single form of "reasonableness" review. The result is a system of judicial
review comprising two standards—correctness and reasonableness. But the revised system
cannot be expected to be simpler and more workable unless the concepts it employs are
clearly defined.

[46] What does this revised reasonableness standard mean? Reasonableness is one of the
most widely used and yet most complex legal concepts. In any area of the law we turn our
attention to, we find ourselves dealing with the reasonable, reasonableness or rationality. But
what is a reasonable decision? How are reviewing courts to identify an unreasonable decision in the context of administrative law and, especially, of judicial review?

[47] Reasonableness is a deferential standard animated by the principle that underlies
the development of the two previous standards of reasonableness: certain questions that
come before administrative tribunals do not lend themselves to one specific, particular
result. Instead, they may give rise to a number of possible, reasonable conclusions. Tribunals have a margin of appreciation within the range of acceptable and rational solutions. A
court conducting a review for reasonableness inquires into the qualities that make a decision reasonable, referring both to the process of articulating the reasons and to outcomes.
In judicial review, reasonableness is concerned mostly with the existence of justification,
transparency and intelligibility within the decision-making process. But it is also concerned
with whether the decision falls within a range of possible, acceptable outcomes which are
defensible in respect of the facts and law.

[48] The move towards a single reasonableness standard does not pave the way for a
more intrusive review by courts and does not represent a return to pre-*Southam* formalism.
In this respect, the concept of deference, so central to judicial review in administrative law,
has perhaps been insufficiently explored in the case law. What does deference mean in this
context? Deference is both an attitude of the court and a requirement of the law of judicial
review. It does not mean that courts are subservient to the determinations of decision makers, or that courts must show blind reverence to their interpretations, or that they may be
content to pay lip service to the concept of reasonableness review while in fact imposing
their own view. Rather, deference imports respect for the decision-making process of adjudicative bodies with regard to both the facts and the law. The notion of deference "is
rooted in part in a respect for governmental decisions to create administrative bodies with
delegated powers" (*Canada (Attorney General) v. Mossop*, [1993] 1 SCR 554, at p. 596, *per*

L'Heureux-Dubé J, dissenting). We agree with David Dyzenhaus where he states that the concept of "deference as respect" requires of the courts "not submission but a respectful attention to the reasons offered or which could be offered in support of a decision": "The Politics of Deference: Judicial Review and Democracy," in M. Taggart, ed., *The Province of Administrative Law* (1997), 279, at p. 286 (quoted with approval in *Baker*, at para. 65, *per* L'Heureux-Dubé J; *Ryan*, at para. 49).

[49] Deference in the context of the reasonableness standard therefore implies that courts will give due consideration to the determinations of decision makers. As Mullan explains, a policy of deference "recognizes the reality that, in many instances, those working day to day in the implementation of frequently complex administrative schemes have or will develop a considerable degree of expertise or field sensitivity to the imperatives and nuances of the legislative regime": D.J. Mullan, "Establishing the Standard of Review: The Struggle for Complexity?" (2004), 17 *CJALP* 59, at p. 93. In short, deference requires respect for the legislative choices to leave some matters in the hands of administrative decision makers, for the processes and determinations that draw on particular expertise and experiences, and for the different roles of the courts and administrative bodies within the Canadian constitutional system.

[50] As important as it is that courts have a proper understanding of reasonableness review as a deferential standard, it is also without question that the standard of correctness must be maintained in respect of jurisdictional and some other questions of law. This promotes just decisions and avoids inconsistent and unauthorized application of law. When applying the correctness standard, a reviewing court will not show deference to the decision maker's reasoning process; it will rather undertake its own analysis of the question. The analysis will bring the court to decide whether it agrees with the determination of the decision maker; if not, the court will substitute its own view and provide the correct answer. From the outset, the court must ask whether the tribunal's decision was correct.

(2) Determining the Appropriate Standard of Review

[51] Having dealt with the nature of the standards of review, we now turn our attention to the method for selecting the appropriate standard in individual cases. As we will now demonstrate, questions of fact, discretion and policy as well as questions where the legal issues cannot be easily separated from the factual issues generally attract a standard of reasonableness while many legal issues attract a standard of correctness. Some legal issues, however, attract the more deferential standard of reasonableness.

[52] The existence of a privative or preclusive clause gives rise to a strong indication of review pursuant to the reasonableness standard. This conclusion is appropriate because a privative clause is evidence of Parliament or a legislature's intent that an administrative decision maker be given greater deference and that interference by reviewing courts be minimized. This does not mean, however, that the presence of a privative clause is determinative. The rule of law requires that the constitutional role of superior courts be preserved and, as indicated above, neither Parliament nor any legislature can completely remove the courts' power to review the actions and decisions of administrative bodies. This power is constitutionally protected. Judicial review is necessary to ensure that the privative clause is read in its appropriate statutory context and that administrative bodies do not exceed their jurisdiction.

[53] Where the question is one of fact, discretion or policy, deference will usually apply automatically (*Mossop*, at pp. 599-600; *Dr. Q*, at para. 29; *Suresh*, at paras. 29-30). We believe that the same standard must apply to the review of questions where the legal and factual issues are intertwined with and cannot be readily separated.

[54] Guidance with regard to the questions that will be reviewed on a reasonableness standard can be found in the existing case law. Deference will usually result where a tribunal is interpreting its own statute or statutes closely connected to its function, with which it will have particular familiarity: *Canadian Broadcasting Corp. v. Canada (Labour Relations Board)*, [1995] 1 SCR 157, at para. 48; *Toronto (City) Board of Education v. OSSTF, District 15*, [1997] 1 SCR 487, at para. 39. Deference may also be warranted where an administrative tribunal has developed particular expertise in the application of a general common law or civil law rule in relation to a specific statutory context: *Toronto (City) v. CUPE*, at para. 72. Adjudication in labour law remains a good example of the relevance of this approach. The case law has moved away considerably from the strict position evidenced in *McLeod v. Egan*, [1975] 1 SCR 517, where it was held that an administrative decision maker will always risk having its interpretation of an external statute set aside upon judicial review.

[55] A consideration of the following factors will lead to the conclusion that the decision maker should be given deference and a reasonableness test applied:

- A privative clause: this is a statutory direction from Parliament or a legislature indicating the need for deference.
- A discrete and special administrative regime in which the decision maker has special expertise (labour relations for instance).
- The nature of the question of law. A question of law that is of "central importance to the legal system … and outside the … specialized area of expertise" of the administrative decision maker will always attract a correctness standard (*Toronto (City) v. CUPE*, at para. 62). On the other hand, a question of law that does not rise to this level may be compatible with a reasonableness standard where the two above factors so indicate.

[56] If these factors, considered together, point to a standard of reasonableness, the decision maker's decision must be approached with deference in the sense of respect discussed earlier in these reasons. There is nothing unprincipled in the fact that some questions of law will be decided on the basis of reasonableness. It simply means giving the adjudicator's decision appropriate deference in deciding whether a decision should be upheld, bearing in mind the factors indicated.

[57] An exhaustive review is not required in every case to determine the proper standard of review. Here again, existing jurisprudence may be helpful in identifying some of the questions that generally fall to be determined according to the correctness standard (*Cartaway Resources Corp. (Re)*, [2004] 1 SCR 672, 2004 SCC 26). This simply means that the analysis required is already deemed to have been performed and need not be repeated.

[58] For example, correctness review has been found to apply to constitutional questions regarding the division of powers between Parliament and the provinces in the *Constitution Act, 1867*: *Westcoast Energy Inc. v. Canada (National Energy Board)*, [1998] 1 SCR 322. Such questions, as well as other constitutional issues, are necessarily subject to correctness review because of the unique role of s. 96 courts as interpreters of the Constitution:

Nova Scotia (Workers' Compensation Board) v. Martin, [2003] 2 SCR 504, 2003 SCC 54; Mullan, *Administrative Law*, at p. 60.

[59] Administrative bodies must also be correct in their determinations of true questions of jurisdiction or *vires*. We mention true questions of *vires* to distance ourselves from the extended definitions adopted before *CUPE*. It is important here to take a robust view of jurisdiction. We neither wish nor intend to return to the jurisdiction/preliminary question doctrine that plagued the jurisprudence in this area for many years. "Jurisdiction" is intended in the narrow sense of whether or not the tribunal had the authority to make the inquiry. In other words, true jurisdiction questions arise where the tribunal must explicitly determine whether its statutory grant of power gives it the authority to decide a particular matter. The tribunal must interpret the grant of authority correctly or its action will be found to be *ultra vires* or to constitute a wrongful decline of jurisdiction: D.J.M. Brown and J.M. Evans, *Judicial Review of Administrative Action in Canada* (loose-leaf), at pp. 14-3 to 14-6. An example may be found in *United Taxi Drivers' Fellowship of Southern Alberta v. Calgary (City)*, [2004] 1 SCR 485, 2004 SCC 19. In that case, the issue was whether the City of Calgary was authorized under the relevant municipal acts to enact bylaws limiting the number of taxi plate licences (para. 5, *per* Bastarache J). That case involved the decision-making powers of a municipality and exemplifies a true question of jurisdiction or *vires*. These questions will be narrow. We reiterate the caution of Dickson J in *CUPE* that reviewing judges must not brand as jurisdictional issues that are doubtfully so.

[60] As mentioned earlier, courts must also continue to substitute their own view of the correct answer where the question at issue is one of general law "that is both of central importance to the legal system as a whole and outside the adjudicator's specialized area of expertise" (*Toronto (City) v. CUPE*, at para. 62, *per* LeBel J). Because of their impact on the administration of justice as a whole, such questions require uniform and consistent answers. Such was the case in *Toronto (City) v. CUPE*, which dealt with complex common law rules and conflicting jurisprudence on the doctrines of *res judicata* and abuse of process—issues that are at the heart of the administration of justice (see para. 15, *per* Arbour J).

[61] Questions regarding the jurisdictional lines between two or more competing specialized tribunals have also been subject to review on a correctness basis: *Regina Police Assn. Inc. v. Regina (City) Board of Police Commissioners*, [2000] 1 SCR 360, 2000 SCC 14; *Quebec (Commission des droits de la personne et des droits de la jeunesse) v. Quebec (Attorney General)*, [2004] 2 SCR 185, 2004 SCC 39.

[62] In summary, the process of judicial review involves two steps. First, courts ascertain whether the jurisprudence has already determined in a satisfactory manner the degree of deference to be accorded with regard to a particular category of question. Second, where the first inquiry proves unfruitful, courts must proceed to an analysis of the factors making it possible to identify the proper standard of review.

[63] The existing approach to determining the appropriate standard of review has commonly been referred to as "pragmatic and functional." That name is unimportant. Reviewing courts must not get fixated on the label at the expense of a proper understanding of what the inquiry actually entails. Because the phrase "pragmatic and functional approach" may have misguided courts in the past, we prefer to refer simply to the "standard of review analysis" in the future.

[64] The analysis must be contextual. As mentioned above, it is dependent on the application of a number of relevant factors, including: (1) the presence or absence of a privative clause; (2) the purpose of the tribunal as determined by interpretation of enabling legislation; (3) the nature of the question at issue, and; (4) the expertise of the tribunal. In many cases, it will not be necessary to consider all of the factors, as some of them may be determinative in the application of the reasonableness standard in a specific case.

D. Application

[65] Returning to the instant appeal and bearing in mind the foregoing discussion, we must determine the standard of review applicable to the adjudicator's interpretation of the *PSLRA*, in particular ss. 97(2.1) and 100.1, and s. 20 of the *Civil Service Act*. That standard of review must then be applied to the adjudicator's decision. In order to determine the applicable standard, we will now examine the factors relevant to the standard of review analysis.

(1) Proper Standard of Review on the Statutory Interpretation Issue

[66] The specific question on this front is whether the combined effect of s. 97(2.1) and s. 100.1 of the *PSLRA* permits the adjudicator to inquire into the employer's reason for dismissing an employee with notice or pay in lieu of notice. This is a question of law. The question to be answered is therefore whether in light of the privative clause, the regime under which the adjudicator acted, and the nature of the question of law involved, a standard of correctness should apply.

[67] The adjudicator was appointed and empowered under the *PSLRA*; s. 101(1) of that statute contains a full privative clause, stating in no uncertain terms that "every order, award, direction, decision, declaration or ruling of … an adjudicator is final and shall not be questioned or reviewed in any court." Section 101(2) adds that "[n]o order shall be made or process entered, and no proceedings shall be taken in any court, whether by way of injunction, judicial review, or otherwise, to question, review, prohibit or restrain … an adjudicator in any of its or his proceedings." The inclusion of a full privative clause in the *PSLRA* gives rise to a strong indication that the reasonableness standard of review will apply.

[68] The nature of the regime also favours the standard of reasonableness. This Court has often recognized the relative expertise of labour arbitrators in the interpretation of collective agreements, and counselled that the review of their decisions should be approached with deference: *CUPE*, at pp. 235-36; *Canada Safeway Ltd. v. RWDSU, Local 454*, [1998] 1 SCR 1079, at para. 58; *Voice Construction*, at para. 22. The adjudicator in this case was, in fact, interpreting his enabling statute. Although the adjudicator was appointed on an *ad hoc* basis, he was selected by the mutual agreement of the parties and, at an institutional level, adjudicators acting under the *PSLRA* can be presumed to hold relative expertise in the interpretation of the legislation that gives them their mandate, as well as related legislation that they might often encounter in the course of their functions. See *Alberta Union of Provincial Employees v. Lethbridge Community College*. This factor also suggests a reasonableness standard of review.

[69] The legislative purpose confirms this view of the regime. The *PSLRA* establishes a time- and cost-effective method of resolving employment disputes. It provides an alternative to judicial determination. Section 100.1 of the *PSLRA* defines the adjudicator's powers in deciding a dispute, but it also provides remedial protection for employees who are not unionized. The remedial nature of s. 100.1 and its provision for timely and binding settlements of disputes also imply that a reasonableness review is appropriate.

[70] Finally, the nature of the legal question at issue is not one that is of central importance to the legal system and outside the specialized expertise of the adjudicator. This also suggests that the standard of reasonableness should apply.

[71] Considering the privative clause, the nature of the regime, and the nature of the question of law here at issue, we conclude that the appropriate standard is reasonableness. We must now apply that standard to the issue considered by the adjudicator in his preliminary ruling.

(2) Was the Adjudicator's Interpretation Unreasonable?

[72] While we are required to give deference to the determination of the adjudicator, considering the decision in the preliminary ruling as a whole, we are unable to accept that it reaches the standard of reasonableness. The reasoning process of the adjudicator was deeply flawed. It relied on and led to a construction of the statute that fell outside the range of admissible statutory interpretations.

[73] The adjudicator considered the New Brunswick Court of Appeal decision in *Chalmers (Dr. Everett) Hospital v. Mills* as well as amendments made to the *PSLRA* in 1990 (SNB 1990, c. 30). Under the former version of the Act, an employee could grieve "with respect to … disciplinary action resulting in discharge, suspension or a financial penalty" (s. 92(1)). The amended legislation grants the right to grieve "with respect to discharge, suspension or a financial penalty" (*PSLRA*, s. 100.1(2)). The adjudicator reasoned that the referential incorporation of s. 97(2.1) in s. 100.1(5) "necessarily means that an adjudicator has jurisdiction to make the determination described in subsection 97(2.1), i.e. that an employee has been discharged or otherwise disciplined for cause" (p. 5). He further stated that an employer "cannot avoid an inquiry into its real reasons for a discharge, or exclude resort to subsection 97(2.1), *by simply stating that cause is not alleged*" (*ibid.* (emphasis added)). The adjudicator concluded that he could determine whether a discharge purportedly with notice or pay in lieu of notice was in reality for cause.

[74] The interpretation of the law is always contextual. The law does not operate in a vacuum. The adjudicator was required to take into account the legal context in which he was to apply the law. The employment relationship between the parties in this case was governed by private law. The contractual terms of employment could not reasonably be ignored. That is made clear by s. 20 of the *Civil Service Act*. Under the ordinary rules of contract, the employer is entitled to discharge an employee for cause, with notice or with pay in lieu of notice. Where the employer chooses to exercise its right to discharge with reasonable notice or pay in lieu thereof, the employer is not required to assert cause for discharge. The grievance process cannot have the effect of changing the terms of the contract of employment. The respondent chose to exercise its right to terminate without alleging cause in this case. By

giving the *PSLRA* an interpretation that allowed him to inquire into the reasons for discharge where the employer had the right not to provide—or even have—such reasons, the
adjudicator adopted a reasoning process that was fundamentally inconsistent with the
employment contract and, thus, fatally flawed. For this reason, the decision does not fall
within the range of acceptable outcomes that are defensible in respect of the facts and the
law.

[75] The decision of the adjudicator treated the appellant, a non-unionized employee, as
a unionized employee. His interpretation of the *PSLRA*, which permits an adjudicator to
inquire into the reasons for discharge where notice is given and, under s. 97(2.1), substitute
a penalty that he or she determines just and reasonable in the circumstances, creates a requirement that the employer show cause before dismissal. There can be no justification for
this; no reasonable interpretation can lead to that result. Section 100.1(5) incorporates
s. 97(2.1) by reference into the determination of grievances brought by non-unionized employees. The employees subject to the *PSLRA* are usually unionized and the terms of their
employment are determined by collective agreement; s. 97(2.1) explicitly refers to the collective agreement context. Section 100.1(5) referentially incorporates s. 97(2.1) *mutatis
mutandis* into the non-collective agreement context so that non-unionized employees who
are discharged *for cause and without notice* have the right to grieve the discharge and have
the adjudicator substitute another penalty as seems just and reasonable in the circumstances. Therefore, the combined effect of s. 97(2.1) and s. 100.1 cannot, on any reasonable
interpretation, remove the employer's right under contract law to discharge an employee
with reasonable notice or pay in lieu of notice.

· · ·

The following are the reasons delivered by

BINNIE J: [119] I agree with my colleagues that the appellant's former employment relationship with the respondent is governed by contract. The respondent chose to exercise its
right to terminate the employment without alleging cause. The adjudicator adopted an unreasonable interpretation of s. 20 of the *Civil Service Act*, SNB 1984, c. C-5.1, and of
ss. 97(2.1) and 100.1 of the *Public Service Labour Relations Act*, RSNB 1973, c. P-25. The
appellant was a non-unionized employee whose job was terminated in accordance with
contract law. Public law principles of procedural fairness were not applicable in the circumstances. These conclusions are enough to dispose of the appeal.

[120] However, my colleagues Bastarache and LeBel JJ are embarked on a more ambi-
tious mission, stating that:

> Although the instant appeal deals with the particular problem of judicial review of the deci-
> sions of an adjudicative tribunal, these reasons will address first and foremost *the structure and
> characteristics of the system of judicial review as a whole.*

· · ·

> … The time has arrived to re-examine the Canadian approach to judicial review of admin-
> istrative decisions and *develop a principled framework that is more coherent and workable.*
> [Emphasis added; paras. 33 and 32.]

[121] The need for such a re-examination is widely recognized, but in the end my colleagues' reasons for judgment do not deal with the "system as a whole." They focus on administrative tribunals. In that context, they reduce the applicable standards of review from three to two ("correctness" and "reasonableness"), but retain the pragmatic and functional analysis, although now it is to be called the "standard of review analysis" (para. 63). A broader reappraisal is called for. Changing the name of the old pragmatic and functional test represents a limited advance, but as the poet says:

> What's in a name? that which we call a rose
> By any other name would smell as sweet;

(*Romeo and Juliet*, Act II, Scene ii)

[122] I am emboldened by my colleagues' insistence that "a holistic approach is needed when considering fundamental principles" (para. 26) to express the following views. Judicial review is an idea that has lately become unduly burdened with law office metaphysics. We are concerned with substance not nomenclature. The words themselves are unobjectionable. The dreaded reference to "functional" can simply be taken to mean that generally speaking courts have the last word on what *they* consider the correct decision on legal matters (because deciding legal issues is their "function"), while administrators should generally have the last word within *their* function, which is to decide administrative matters. The word "pragmatic" not only signals a distaste for formalism but recognizes that a conceptually tidy division of functions has to be tempered by practical considerations: for example, a labour board is better placed than the courts to interpret the intricacies of provisions in a labour statute governing replacement of union workers; see e.g. *Canadian Union of Public Employees, Local 963 v. New Brunswick Liquor Corp.*, [1979] 2 SCR 227.

[123] Parliament or a provincial legislature is often well advised to allocate an administrative decision to someone other than a judge. The judge is on the outside of the administration looking in. The legislators are entitled to put their trust in the viewpoint of the designated decision maker (particularly as to what constitutes a reasonable outcome), not only in the case of the administrative tribunals of principal concern to my colleagues but (taking a "holistic approach") also in the case of a minister, a board, a public servant, a commission, an elected council or other administrative bodies and statutory decision makers. In the absence of a full statutory right of appeal, the court ought generally to respect the exercise of the administrative discretion, particularly in the face of a privative clause.

[124] On the other hand, a court is right to insist that *its* view of the correct opinion (i.e. the "correctness" standard of review) is accepted on questions concerning the Constitution, the common law, and the interpretation of a statute other than the administrator's enabling statute (the "home statute") or a rule or statute closely connected with it; see generally D.J.M. Brown and J.M. Evans, *Judicial Review of Administrative Action in Canada* (looseleaf), at para. 14:2210.

[125] Thus the law (or, more grandly, the "rule of law") sets the boundaries of potential administrative action. It is sometimes said by judges that an administrator acting within his or her discretion "has the right to be wrong." This reflects an unduly court-centred view of the universe. A disagreement between the court and an administrator does not necessarily mean that the administrator is wrong.

· · ·

C. *The Need To Reappraise the Approach to Judicial Review*

[132] The present difficulty, it seems, does not lie in the component parts of judicial review, most of which are well entrenched in decades of case law, but in the current methodology for putting those component parts into action. There is afoot in the legal profession a desire for clearer guidance than is provided by lists of principles, factors and spectrums. It must be recognized, of course, that complexity is inherent in all legal principles that must address the vast range of administrative decision making. The objection is that our present "pragmatic and functional" approach is more complicated than is required by the subject matter.

[133] People who feel victimized or unjustly dealt with by the apparatus of government, and who have no recourse to an administrative appeal, should have access to an independent judge through a procedure that is quick and relatively inexpensive. Like much litigation these days, however, judicial review is burdened with undue cost and delay. Litigants understandably hesitate to go to court to seek redress for a perceived administrative injustice if their lawyers cannot predict with confidence even what standard of review will be applied. The disposition of the case may well *turn* on the choice of standard of review. If litigants do take the plunge, they may find the court's attention focussed not on their complaints, or the government's response, but on lengthy and arcane discussions of something they are told is the pragmatic and functional test. Every hour of a lawyer's preparation and court time devoted to unproductive "lawyer's talk" poses a significant cost to the applicant. If the challenge is unsuccessful, the unhappy applicant may also face a substantial bill of costs from the successful government agency. A victory before the reviewing court may be overturned on appeal because the wrong "standard of review" was selected. A small business denied a licence or a professional person who wants to challenge disciplinary action should be able to seek judicial review without betting the store or the house on the outcome. Thus, in my view, the law of judicial review should be pruned of some of its unduly subtle, unproductive, or esoteric features.

· · ·

H. *A Broader Reappraisal*

[144] "Reasonableness" is a big tent that will have to accommodate a lot of variables that inform and limit a court's review of the outcome of administrative decision making.

[145] The theory of our recent case law has been that once the appropriate standard of review is selected, it is a fairly straightforward matter to apply it. In practice, the criteria for selection among "reasonableness" standards of review proved to be undefinable and their application unpredictable. The present incarnation of the "standard of review" analysis requires a threshold debate about the four factors (non-exhaustive) which critics say too often leads to unnecessary delay, uncertainty and costs as arguments rage before the court about balancing expertise against the "real" nature of the question before the administrator, or whether the existence of a privative clause trumps the larger statutory purpose, and so on.

And this is all mere *preparation* for the argument about the actual substance of the case. While a measure of uncertainty is inherent in the subject matter and unavoidable in litigation (otherwise there wouldn't be any), we should at least (i) establish some presumptive rules and (ii) get the parties away from arguing about the tests and back to arguing about the substantive merits of their case.

[146] The going-in presumption should be that the standard of review of any administrative outcome on grounds of substance is not correctness but reasonableness ("contextually" applied). The fact that the legislature designated someone other than the court as the decision maker calls for deference to (or judicial respect for) the outcome, absent a broad statutory right of appeal. Administrative decisions generally call for the exercise of discretion. Everybody recognizes in such cases that there is *no* single "correct" outcome. It should also be presumed, in accordance with the ordinary rules of litigation, that the decision under review *is* reasonable until the applicant shows otherwise.

[147] An applicant urging the non-deferential "correctness" standard should be required to demonstrate that the decision under review rests on an error in the determination of a *legal* issue not confided (or which constitutionally *could* not be confided) to the administrative decision maker to decide, whether in relation to jurisdiction or the general law. Labour arbitrators, as in this case, command deference on legal matters within their enabling statute or on legal matters intimately connected thereto.

[148] When, then, should a decision be deemed "unreasonable"? My colleagues suggest a test of *irrationality* (para. 46), but the editors of de Smith point out that "many decisions which fall foul of [unreasonableness] have been coldly rational" (de Smith, Woolf & Jowell, *Judicial Review of Administrative Action* (5th ed. 1995), at para. 13-003). A decision meeting this description by this Court is *CUPE v. Ontario (Minister of Labour)*, [2003] 1 SCR 539, 2003 SCC 29, where the Minister's appointment of retired judges with little experience in labour matters to chair "interest" arbitrations (as opposed to "grievance" arbitrations) between hospitals and hospital workers was "coldly rational" in terms of the Minister's own agenda, but was held by a majority of this Court to be patently unreasonable in terms of the history, object and purpose of the authorizing legislation. He had not used the appointment power for the purposes for which the legislature had conferred it.

[149] Reasonableness rather than rationality has been the traditional standard and, properly interpreted, it works. That said, a single "reasonableness" standard will now necessarily incorporate *both* the degree of deference formerly reflected in the distinction between patent unreasonableness and reasonableness *simpliciter, and* an assessment of the range of options reasonably open to the decision maker in the circumstances, in light of the reasons given for the decision. Any reappraisal of our approach to judicial review should, I think, explicitly recognize these different dimensions to the "reasonableness" standard.

• • •

DESCHAMPS J (Charron and Rothstein JJ concurring): [158] The law of judicial review of administrative action not only requires repairs, it needs to be cleared of superfluous discussions and processes. This area of the law can be simplified by examining the *substance* of the work courts are called upon to do when reviewing any case, whether it be in the context of administrative or of appellate review. Any review starts with the identification of the questions at issue as questions of law, questions of fact or questions of mixed fact and law. Very little else needs to be done in order to determine whether deference needs to be shown to an administrative body.

[159] By virtue of the Constitution, superior courts are the only courts that possess inherent jurisdiction. They are responsible both for applying the laws enacted by Parliament and the legislatures and for insuring that statutory bodies respect their legal boundaries. Parliament and the legislatures cannot totally exclude judicial oversight without overstepping the division between legislative or executive powers and judicial powers. Superior courts are, in the end, the protectors of the integrity of the rule of law and the justice system. Judicial review of administrative action is rooted in these fundamental principles and its boundaries are largely informed by the roles of the respective branches of government.

[160] The judicial review of administrative action has, over the past 20 years, been viewed as involving a preliminary analysis of whether deference is owed to an administrative body based on four factors: (1) the nature of the question, (2) the presence or absence of a privative clause, (3) the expertise of the administrative decision maker and (4) the object of the statute. The process of answering this preliminary question has become more complex than the determination of the substantive questions the court is called upon to resolve. In my view, the analysis can be made plainer if the focus is placed on the issues the parties need to have adjudicated rather than on the nature of the judicial review process itself. By focusing first on "the nature of the question," to use what has become familiar parlance, it will become apparent that all four factors need not be considered in every case and that the judicial review of administrative action is often not distinguishable from the appellate review of court decisions.

[161] Questions before the courts have consistently been identified as either questions of fact, questions of law or questions of mixed fact and law. Whether undergoing appellate review or administrative law review, decisions on questions of fact always attract deference. The use of different terminology—"palpable and overriding error" versus "unreasonable decision"—does not change the substance of the review. Indeed, in the context of appellate review of court decisions, this Court has recognized that these expressions as well as others all encapsulate the same principle of deference with respect to a trial judge's findings of fact: *H.L. v. Canada (Attorney General)*, [2005] 1 SCR 401, 2005 SCC 25, at paras. 55-56. Therefore, when the issue is limited to questions of fact, there is no need to enquire into any other factor in order to determine that deference is owed to an administrative decision maker.

[162] Questions of law, by contrast, require more thorough scrutiny when deference is evaluated, and the particular context of administrative decision making can make judicial review different than appellate review. Although superior courts have a core expertise to interpret questions of law, Parliament or a legislature may have provided that the decision of an administrative body is protected from judicial review by a privative clause. When an administrative body is created to interpret and apply certain legal rules, it develops specific expertise in exercising its jurisdiction and has a more comprehensive view of those rules. Where there is a privative clause, Parliament or a legislature's intent to leave the final decision to that body cannot be doubted and deference is usually owed to the body.

[163] However, privative clauses cannot totally shield an administrative body from review. Parliament, or a legislature, cannot have intended that the body would be protected

were it to overstep its delegated powers. Moreover, if such a body is asked to interpret laws in respect of which it does not have expertise, the constitutional responsibility of the superior courts as guardians of the rule of law compels them to insure that laws falling outside an administrative body's core expertise are interpreted correctly. This reduced deference insures that laws of general application, such as the Constitution, the common law and the *Civil Code*, are interpreted correctly and consistently. Consistency of the law is of prime societal importance. Finally, deference is not owed on questions of law where Parliament or a legislature has provided for a statutory right of review on such questions.

[164] The category of questions of mixed fact and law should be limited to cases in which the determination of a legal issue is inextricably intertwined with the determination of facts. Often, an administrative body will first identify the rule and then apply it. Identifying the contours and the content of a legal rule are questions of law. Applying the rule, however, is a question of mixed fact and law. When considering a question of mixed fact and law, a reviewing court should show an adjudicator the same deference as an appeal court would show a lower court.

[165] In addition, Parliament or a legislature may confer a discretionary power on an administrative body. Since the case at bar does not concern a discretionary power, it will suffice for the purposes of these reasons to note that, in any analysis, deference is owed to an exercise of discretion unless the body has exceeded its mandate.

[166] In summary, in the adjudicative context, the same deference is owed in respect of questions of fact and questions of mixed fact and law on administrative review as on an appeal from a court decision. A decision on a question of law will also attract deference, provided it concerns the interpretation of the enabling statute and provided there is no right of review.

[167] I would be remiss were I to disregard the difficulty inherent in any exercise of deference. In *Toronto (City) v. CUPE, Local 79*, [2003] 3 SCR 77, 2003 SCC 63, LeBel J explained why a distinction between the standards of patent unreasonableness and unreasonableness *simpliciter* is untenable. I agree. The problem with the definitions resides in attempts by the courts to enclose the concept of reasonableness in a formula fitting all cases. No matter how this Court defines this concept, any context considered by a reviewing court will, more often than not, look more like a rainbow than a black and white situation. One cannot change this reality. I use the word "deference" to define the contours of reasonableness because it describes the attitude adopted towards the decision maker. The word "reasonableness" concerns the decision. However, neither the concept of reasonableness nor that of deference is particular to the field of administrative law. These concepts are also found in the context of criminal and civil appellate review of court decisions. Yet, the exercise of the judicial supervisory role in those fields has not given rise to the complexities encountered in administrative law. The process of stepping back and taking an *ex post facto* look at the decision to determine whether there is an error justifying intervention should not be more complex in the administrative law context than in the criminal and civil law contexts.

[168] In the case at bar, the adjudicator was asked to adjudicate the grievance of a nonunionized employee. This meant that he had to identify the rules governing the contract. Identifying those rules is a question of law. Section 20 of the *Civil Service Act*, SNB 1984,

c. C-5.1, incorporates the rules of the common law, which accordingly become the starting point of the analysis. The adjudicator had to decide whether those rules had been ousted by the *Public Service Labour Relations Act*, RSNB 1973, c. P-25 ("*PSLRA*"), as applied, *mutatis mutandis*, to the case of a non-unionized employee (ss. 97(2.1), 100.1(2) and 100.1(5)). The common law rules relating to the dismissal of an employee differ completely from the ones provided for in the *PSLRA* that the adjudicator is regularly required to interpret. Since the common law, not the adjudicator's enabling statute, is the starting point of the analysis, and since the adjudicator does not have specific expertise in interpreting the common law, the reviewing court does not have to defer to his decision on the basis of expertise. This leads me to conclude that the reviewing court can proceed to its own interpretation of the rules applicable to the non-unionized employee's contract of employment and determine whether the adjudicator could enquire into the cause of the dismissal. The applicable standard of review is correctness.

Although the *Dunsmuir* decision simplified the task of determining what standard of review should be applied to different types of decisions, the result of that analysis is not always obvious. In the *Mowat* decision, set out below, the Federal Court of Appeal considered the appropriate standard for reviewing a decision of the Canadian Human Rights Tribunal that concluded that the tribunal had the power to make an award of costs to a successful human rights complainant. The Supreme Court of Canada granted leave to appeal this decision on April 22, 2010 (2010 CarswellNat 934, 407 NR 387(n) (SCC)). Consider the arguments for and against upholding the Federal Court of Appeal's decision with respect to the appropriate standard of review.

Canada (Attorney General) v. Mowat
2009 FCA 309

LAYDEN-STEVENSON JA (Létourneau and Sexton JJA concurring): [1] The issue for determination on this appeal has not been previously considered by this Court. The primary question is whether the Canadian Human Rights Tribunal (the Tribunal) has the authority to grant legal costs to a successful complainant under the provisions of the *Canadian Human Rights Act*, RS 1985, c. H-6 (the Act).

[2] A judge of the Federal Court (the application judge) reviewed the Tribunal's decision on a standard of review of reasonableness and concluded that the Tribunal's determination that it had the authority to award costs was reasonable.

[3] The appellant Attorney General of Canada (AG) asserts that the application judge erred in choosing the applicable standard of review. Further, he erred in concluding that the Tribunal has the power to award costs. The AG maintains that no such authority exists, on any standard of review. The intervener, the Canadian Human Rights Commission (the Commission), says otherwise.

[4] Resolution of these issues requires a determination of the appropriate standard of review to be applied to the Tribunal's decision and an examination of the application judge's

analysis. The application judge was required to choose the proper standard of review and to apply it correctly.

[5] For the reasons that follow, I conclude that the applicable standard of review is correctness. I also find that Parliament did not grant the Tribunal the authority to award legal costs to a successful complainant. Consequently, I would allow the appeal.

. . .

The Legislative Context

[21] Human rights legislation is fundamental law and quasi-constitutional in nature. The purpose of the Act, set out in section 2, is to ensure people have an equal opportunity to make for themselves the life that they are able and wish to have without being hindered by discriminatory practices.

[22] In order to promote the goal of equal opportunity for each individual, the Act seeks to prevent discriminatory practices. Its purpose is not to punish wrongdoing but to prevent discrimination: *CNR* [*CNR v. Canada (Human Rights Commission)*, 1987 CanLII 109 (SCC), [1987] 1 SCR 1114]. Specific prohibited grounds of discrimination and discriminatory practices are set out in the Act.

[23] The Commission and the Tribunal are established pursuant to the Act. Among other things, the Commission is charged with responsibility for human rights research and public education, the investigation and processing of complaints up to the point of adjudication, maintaining close liaisons with similar bodies in the provinces and considering recommendations from public interest groups. On its appearances before the Tribunal, the Commission represents the public interest (section 51 of the Act).

[24] The Tribunal functions as an adjudicative body. Its responsibilities were described in *Bell Canada v. CTEA*, [2003] 1 SCR 884 (SCC) (Bell Canada), at paragraph 23, as follows:

> It conducts formal hearings into complaints that have been referred to it by the Commission. It has many of the powers of a court. It is empowered to find facts, to interpret and apply the law to the facts before it, and to award appropriate remedies. Moreover, its hearings have much the same structure as a formal trial before a court. The parties before the Tribunal lead evidence, call and cross-examine witnesses, and make submissions on how the law should be applied to the facts. The Tribunal is not involved in crafting policy, nor does it undertake its own independent investigations of complaints; the investigative and policy-making functions have deliberately been assigned by the legislature to a different body, the Commission.

[25] This case is concerned with subsection 53(2) of the Act which furnishes the Tribunal with broad remedial powers where, at the conclusion of the inquiry, the Tribunal finds that the complaint is substantiated. Specifically in issue is paragraph 53(2)(c). It provides:

<table>
<tr><td>

Canadian Human Rights Act,
RS 1985, c. H-6

53(2) If at the conclusion of the in-
quiry the member or panel finds that
the complaint is substantiated, the
member or panel may, subject to sec-
tion 54, make an order against the per-
son found to be engaging or to have
engaged in the discriminatory practice
and include in the order any of the fol-
lowing terms that the member or panel
considers appropriate:

· · ·

    (c) that the person compensate
the victim for any or all of the wages
that the victim was deprived of and
for any expenses incurred by the
victim as a result of the discrimina-
tory practice;

</td><td>

*Loi canadienne sur les droits de la
personne* (LR, 1985, ch. H-6)

53(2) À l'issue de l'instruction, le
membre instructeur qui juge la plainte
fondée, peut, sous réserve de l'article
54, ordonner, selon les circonstances, à
la personne trouvée coupable d'un acte
discriminatoire:

· · ·

    c) d'indemniser la victime de la
totalité, ou de la fraction des pertes
de salaire et des dépenses entraînées
par l'acte;

</td></tr>
</table>

· · ·

The Standard of Review

· · ·

[28] *Dunsmuir v. New Brunswick*, [2008] 1 SCR 190 (SCC) (*Dunsmuir*) established a
two-step process for determining the applicable standard of review. The first step requires
the court to "ascertain whether the jurisprudence has already determined in a satisfactory
manner the degree of deference to be accorded with regard to a particular category of question" (para. 62).

[29] Historically, the Supreme Court of Canada, in addressing human rights tribunals,
has nearly unanimously held that where the general question is one of statutory interpretation, it constitutes a question of law and is to be reviewed on a standard of correctness. The
superior expertise of human rights tribunals relates to fact-finding and adjudication in a
human rights context and does not extend to general questions of law: *Canada (Attorney
General) v. Mossop*, [1993] 1 SCR 554 (SCC) (*Mossop*); *University of British Columbia v.
Berg*, [1993] 2 SCR 353 (SCC) (*Berg*); *Pezim v. British Columbia (Superintendent of Brokers)*,
[1994] 2 SCR 557 (SCC) (*Pezim*); *Gould v. Yukon Order of Pioneers*, [1996] 1 SCR 571 (SCC)
(*Gould*); *Ross v. New Brunswick School District No. 15*, 1996 CanLII 237 (SCC), [1996] 1
SCR 825 (*Ross*).

[30] *Dunsmuir*, and more recently *Khosa v. Canada (Minister of Citizenship & Immigration)*, 2009 SCC 12 (SCC) (*Khosa*) cautioned that "with or without a privative clause, a
measure of deference has come to be accepted as appropriate where a particular decision
had been allocated to an administrative decision maker rather than to the courts. This defer-

ence extended not only to facts and policy but to a tribunal's interpretation of its constitutive statute and related enactments…"(*Khosa* (para. 25)). This proposition has been characterized as a presumption that tribunals' interpretation of their enabling legislation is normally reviewable on a standard of reasonableness: *Dunsmuir* at paragraph 146; *Public Service Alliance of Canada v. Canadian Federal Pilots Association and Attorney General of Canada*, 2009 FCA 223 (CanLII), 2009 FCA 223 (*PSAC*) (para. 36). Given the teachings of *Dunsmuir* and *Khosa*, prudence dictates that a standard of review analysis is advisable.

. . .

Analysis

[34] The questions before the Tribunal and the Federal Court were whether the Tribunal had the authority to award costs to the complainant and whether the authority could be found in paragraph 53(2)(c) of the Act which authorizes the Tribunal to compensate a complainant for any expenses incurred as a result of the discriminatory practice.

[35] It is not disputed that the Tribunal had the authority to determine these questions. What is in issue is whether the Tribunal's decision had to be correct or whether it sufficed that it be reasonable. In other words, what is the standard of review applicable to the decision of the Tribunal and did the Federal Court apply the correct standard to the determination of the issue?

[36] Determining the standard of review requires "an analysis of the factors making it possible to identify the proper standard of review" *Dunsmuir* (para. 62). The analysis is contextual (para. 64).

[37] Before addressing the factors of the standard of review analysis, it bears repeating that the applicable standard of review will normally be that of reasonableness: *Dunsmuir*; *Khosa*. The Tribunal is accorded deference because of its experience and expertise, provided that the process it used is justified, transparent and intelligible and that its decision "falls within a range of possible, acceptable outcomes which are defensible in respect of the facts and law": *Dunsmuir* (para. 47). However, if the standard of review analysis yields a standard of review of correctness, no deference is owing.

[38] *Dunsmuir* identified three situations where the correctness standard of review is appropriate. A true question of jurisdiction "where the tribunal must explicitly determine whether its statutory grant of power gives it the authority to decide a particular matter" is the first situation (para. 59). The second is where there is a question of general law "that is both of central importance to the legal system as a whole and outside the adjudicator's specialized area of expertise" (para. 60). The third situation is where a determination of jurisdiction between two competing tribunals is required (para. 61).

[39] I turn now to the factors of the standard of review analysis. The Act does not contain a privative clause. There is no statutory right of appeal. The application judge determined that this factor tends toward a lesser degree of deference. While I do not disagree, the absence of a privative clause is by no means determinative and may be regarded as neutral.

[40] The legislative context has been discussed earlier in these reasons. The purpose of the Act is remedial and it seeks to prevent discriminatory practices. It serves the public interest and also engages a private interest in that it seeks to remedy specific violations of the

Act. The particular provision in issue deals with the Tribunal's power to compensate a victim for "wages the victim was deprived of and for any expenses incurred by the victim as a result of the discriminatory practice."

[41] The Tribunal functions as an adjudicative body, conducts formal hearings into complaints that have been referred to it by the Commission and awards appropriate remedies pursuant to the powers accorded it by subsection 53(2) of the Act. Subsection 48.1(2) requires that members of the Tribunal have "experience, expertise and interest in, and sensitivity to, human rights." Subsection 50(2) empowers the Tribunal to decide "all questions of law or fact necessary to determining the matter." This has been described as "a general power to consider questions of law, including questions pertaining to the *Charter* and the *Canadian Bill of Rights*": *Bell Canada* (para. 47) citing *Cooper v. Canada (Human Rights Commission)*, [1996] 3 SCR 854 (SCC); see also *Mossop* (para. 44) and *Ross* [*v. New Brunswick School District No. 15*, [1996] 1 SCR 825] at p. 849. This factor, on its own, tends to favour deference.

[42] The nature of the question is narrow and discrete. Does compensation for "any expenses incurred by the victim as a result of the discriminatory practice" include payment of the victim's legal costs in relation to the hearing before the Tribunal? The interpretation of the provision is critical because the Tribunal's jurisdiction to award legal costs will ultimately turn on it. For the reasons that follow, I conclude that it is both a question of general law of central importance to the legal system as a whole and one that is outside the specialized expertise of the Tribunal.

[43] There is no debate that the Tribunal is a specialized one in relation to matters of human rights. However, the concern is not with either general or specialized expertise. Rather, it is with the Tribunal's expertise in relation to the specific issue before it. I do not believe that the nature of the question at hand engages the human rights subject matter in which the Tribunal has expertise.

[44] This is not a context-specific setting. There is no factual component entailed in the analysis. Expertise in human rights is not required and does not assist in the interpretation of the narrow question arising from the provision. The Tribunal's authority to award costs of a proceeding to a successful complainant has nothing to do with the substance of human rights. Rather, the Tribunal must determine a pure question of law, specifically, one that determines the bounds of its authority. The Tribunal has no institutional or experiential advantage over the court and is no better-positioned than the court in this respect.

[45] The question has not been answered consistently by the Tribunal and is the subject of diverse opinions in the Federal Court. It comes before this Court for the first time. It is difficult, if not impossible, to conclude that the answer (either yes or no) can be said to fall within a range of possible acceptable outcomes. There is much to be said for the argument that where there are two conflicting lines of authority interpreting the same statutory provision, even if each on its own could be found to be reasonable, it would not be reasonable for a court to uphold both: *Taub v. Investment Dealers Assn. of Canada*, 2009 ONCA 628 (CanLII), 2009 ONCA 628 (*Taub*) (para. 65). I endorse and adopt the comments in *Abdoulrab v. Ontario (Labour Relations Board)*, 2009 ONCA 491 (*Abdoulrab*) (para. 48) where Juriansz JA stated:

From a common sense perspective, it is difficult to accept that two truly contradictory interpretations of the same statutory provision can both be upheld as reasonable. If two interpretations of the same statutory provision are truly contradictory, it is difficult to envisage that both
would fall within the range of acceptable outcomes. More importantly, it seems incompatible
with the rule of law that two contradictory interpretations of the same provision of a public
statute, by which citizens order their lives, could both be accepted as reasonable.

[46] As Feldman JA commented in *Taub*, "it accords with the rule of law that a public
statute that applies equally to all affected citizens should have a universally accepted interpretation" (para. 67).

[47] Further, in my view, alleged victims of discriminatory practices are entitled to
know, in circumstances where they retain counsel to represent them at the hearing before
the Tribunal, whether, if successful, they may be entitled to legal costs in relation to the
proceeding. Alleged discriminators are similarly entitled to know, if the claim is substantiated, whether significant cost consequences may follow. Further, because of the public interest mandate of the Tribunal and the public interest nature of the legislation, the issue has an
influence on society at large. The question is one that calls for certainty and consistency.
Consequently, I regard the question as both a general question of law of central importance
to the legal system as a whole and one that is outside the specialized area of the Tribunal's
expertise. In accordance with the teaching of *Dunsmuir*, the standard of review is correctness (para. 55).

. . .

Interpretation of the Provision

. . .

Analysis

[75] The proper approach to statutory interpretation has been articulated repeatedly by
the Supreme Court of Canada and is so entrenched that reference to specific authority is not
necessary. The goal is to seek the intent of Parliament by reading the words of the provision
in context and according to their grammatical and ordinary sense, harmoniously with the
scheme and the object of the statute. In accordance with this fundamental principle, the
search for parliamentary intent constitutes an exercise in ascertaining what Parliament set
out to accomplish. In this case, the quest is to determine whether Parliament intended to
endow the Tribunal with the authority to award costs to a successful complainant. For the
reasons that follow, I conclude that Parliament did not intend to grant, and did not grant, to
the Tribunal the power to award costs.

[76] The exercise requires an examination of the words "expenses" ("dépenses" in
French) and "costs" ("dépens"). The Act does not define "expenses" and is silent with respect
to "costs." The provision in issue is a compensatory one: *CNR* (para. 39). In paragraph
53(2)(c), the word "expenses" is broad and non-specific. It takes its colour from the word
"compensate," for only those expenses incurred as a result of the discriminatory practice
qualify for compensation. The word "costs," however, is another matter. I agree with the appellant that the word "costs" is a legal term of art.

[77] A legal term of art is a word or expression that, through usage by legal profession-als, has acquired a distinct legal meaning. It has a technical meaning because of its conven-tional use by lawyers and judges: Ruth Sullivan, *Sullivan on the Construction of Statutes*, 5th ed. (Markham, Ont.: LexisNexis Canada, 2008) at 57 and 61. That is, it has a settled legal definition.

[78] In *Reference re National Energy Board Act*, [1986] 3 FC 275 (Fed. CA), leave to ap-peal dismissed, (1986), 23 Admin. LR xxi (note) (SCC) (*NEB Reference*), the Federal Court of Appeal referred to the "accurate and useful discussion as to the normal legal meaning of 'costs'" of the Ontario Divisional Court in *Regional Municipality of Hamilton-Wentworth and Hamilton-Wentworth Save the Valley Committee, Inc. et al.* (1985), 51 OR (2d) 23 (Div. Ct.) (*Hamilton-Wentworth*), where it was determined that the word "costs" as used in the legal sense is a word having a well-defined meaning. In *Hamilton-Wentworth*, the court stated "[f]rom the earliest times, it has been recognized that the power to award 'costs' must be found in a statute." Describing the nature of costs, it said:

> The characteristics of costs, developed over many years are:
> (1) They are an award to be made in favour of a successful or deserving litigant, payable by the loser.
> (2) Of necessity, the award must await the conclusion of the proceeding, as success or entitlement cannot be determined before that time.
> (3) They are payable by way of indemnity for allowable expenses and services incurred relevant to the case or proceeding.
> (4) They are not payable for the purpose of assuring participation in the proceedings.

[79] The concept of costs in the context of administrative tribunals carries the same general connotation as legal costs: *Bell Canada v. Consumers' Association of Canada*, 1986 CanLII 49 (SCC), [1986] 1 SCR 190; see also *Re. Bell Canada and Telecom. Decision CRTC 79-5*, [1982] 2 FC 681 (CA), leave to appeal dismissed, [1982] SCCA No. 299.

[80] In the specific context of human rights legislation, the matter of costs was discussed in *Ontario (Liquor Control Board) v. Ontario (Ontario Human Rights Commission)* (1988), 25 OAC 161, 27 OAC 246 (addendum) (Div. Ct.). The court concluded as follows:

> There is no inherent jurisdiction in a court, nor in any other statutory body, to award costs ... The Board of Inquiry is created by the Ontario Human Rights Code [citation omitted]. As a statutory body it can only have jurisdiction to award costs if such jurisdiction is expressly given to it either by the Code or some other act ... The power of the Board of Inquiry under s. 40(1) to make "restitution including monetary compensation" is not an express provision for the award of costs to complainants under the Code. The rule of liberal interpretation to carry out the objects of the Code to, as far as possible, remedy the effects of and prevent discrimination do not apply to procedural matters or the question of costs.

[81] Similarly, in *Moncton v. Buggie and NB Human Rights Commission* (1985), 21 DLR (4th) 266, 65 NBR (2d) 210 (CA) (*Buggie*), leave to appeal dismissed, (SCC), the New Brunswick Court of Appeal concluded that although paragraph 21(1)(c) of the New Bruns-wick Act provided the Commission the power to "issue whatever order it deems necessary to carry into effect the recommendation of the Board," such power did not carry with it the power to award costs against a party.

[82] In *Halifax (Regional Municipality) v. Nova Scotia (Human Rights Commission)*, 2005 NSCA 70, 253 DLR (4th) 506, 232 NSR (2d) 161 (NS CA) (*Halifax*), MacDonald CJ examined the provision in the Nova Scotia legislation empowering a board of inquiry to order any party who has contravened the Act to "do any act or thing that constitutes full compliance with the Act and to rectify any injury caused to any person or class of person or to make compensation therefore." In comprehensive and thoughtful reasons, the Chief Justice reviewed the history of costs and the relevant jurisprudence. He arrived at the following conclusions:

- a compensation award is separate and distinct from an award for costs. The former relates to the victim's injury, the latter relates to the process;
- legal fees flowing from, but unrelated to prosecuting the claim can be compensable, but legal fees incidental to prosecuting the claim are not compensable;
- it is one thing to give the legislation a broad and liberal interpretation so as to ensure its objects are met. It is quite another to cloak the Board with jurisdiction that the legislature did not give to it;
- the Board had no power to award the complainant legal costs.

                                        . . .

[91] I have not overlooked the issue of implied jurisdiction although I have some difficulty with the notion that a power to award costs could exist because of implied authority when it appears to be settled law that nothing less than express authority will suffice. However, if the power in issue is susceptible to a grant by way of implication, the prerequisite to found it is not present.

[92] The concept of implied jurisdiction is summarized in *ATCO Gas & Pipelines Ltd. v. Alberta (Energy & Utilities Board)*, [2006] 1 SCR 140 (SCC) (*ATCO*) at paragraph 51 as follows:

> ... [T]he powers conferred by an enabling statute are construed to include not only those expressly granted but also, by implication, all powers which are practically necessary for the accomplishment of the object intended to be secured by the statutory regime created by the legislature [citation omitted]. Canadian courts have in the past applied the doctrine to ensure that administrative bodies have the necessary jurisdiction to accomplish their statutory mandate.

[93] There is no evidence of practical necessity for the exercise of the power to award costs to enable the Tribunal to attain the objects expressly prescribed by Parliament. In Halifax, MacDonald CJ concluded that "this authority [to award costs] is not necessary to achieve the stated legislative objectives." In coming to that conclusion, he referred to the comments of the Supreme Court in *Canada (Human Rights Commission) v. Canadian Liberty Net*, [1998] 1 SCR 626 (SCC) (*Canadian Liberty Net*) (para. 16) to the effect that a power can only be implied where "that power is actually necessary for the administration of the terms of the legislation; coherence, logicality, or desirability are not sufficient."

[94] I also agree with the observation of Heald J in *NEB Reference* that there is an additional reason for not invoking the doctrine of necessary implication. At paragraph 14, he opined that the Parliament of Canada and the provincial legislatures have demonstrated their ability in various pieces of legislation to explicitly confer on tribunals a general power

to award costs. "From this I think it possible to infer that in the absence of an express statutory provision conferring the power to award costs, such power should not be implied." Notably, express provision is made for witness fees (s. 50(6)) and the awarding of interest (s. 53(4)).

[95] I return to where I began. The quest is to determine whether Parliament intended to endow the Tribunal with the authority to award costs to a successful complainant. For the reasons given, I conclude that Parliament did not intend to grant, and did not grant, to the Tribunal the power to award costs. To conclude that the Tribunal may award legal costs under the guise of "expenses incurred by the victim as a result of the discriminatory practice" would be to introduce indirectly into the Act a power which Parliament did not intend it to have.